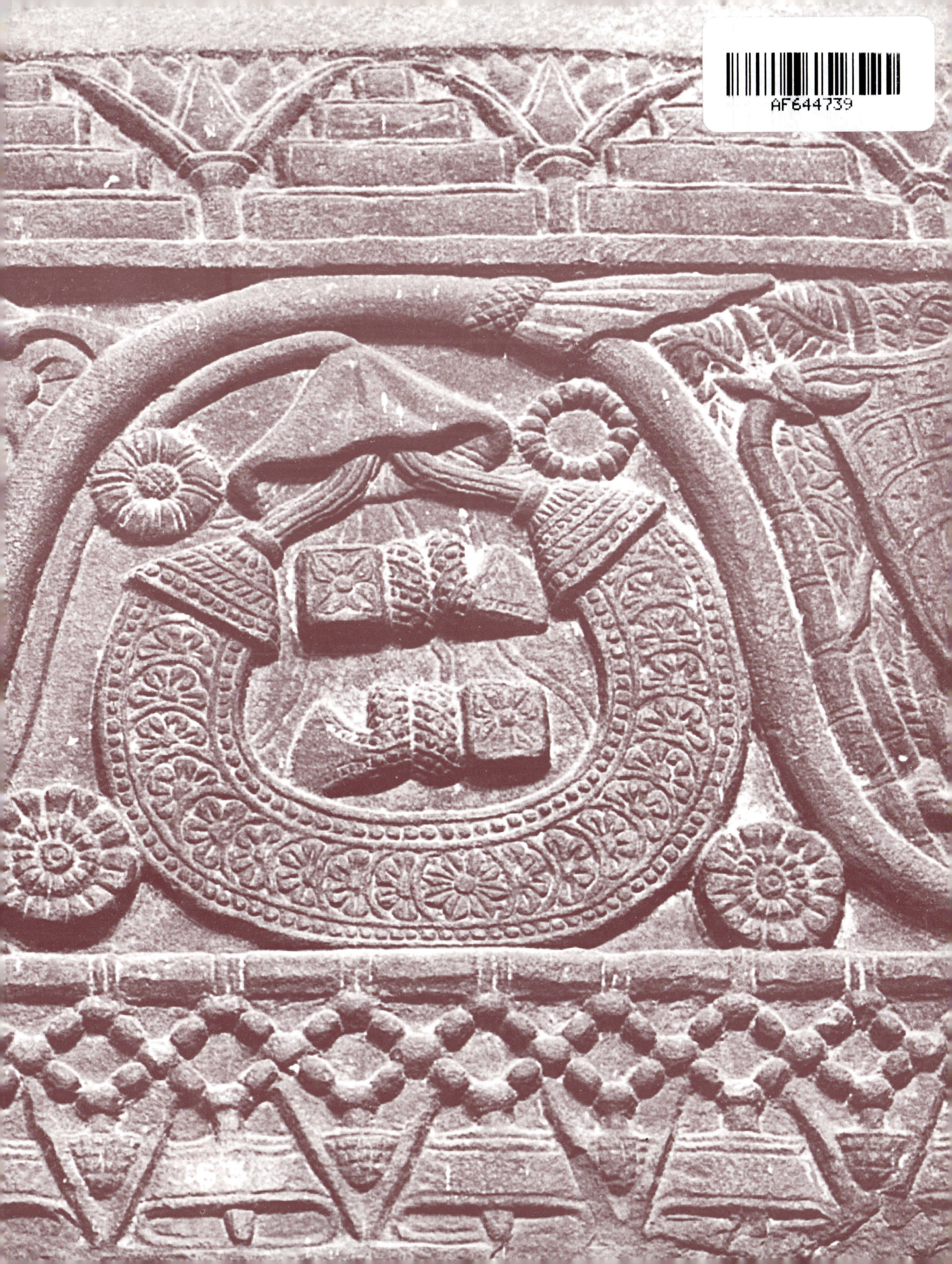

AF644739

# Gods, Men and Women

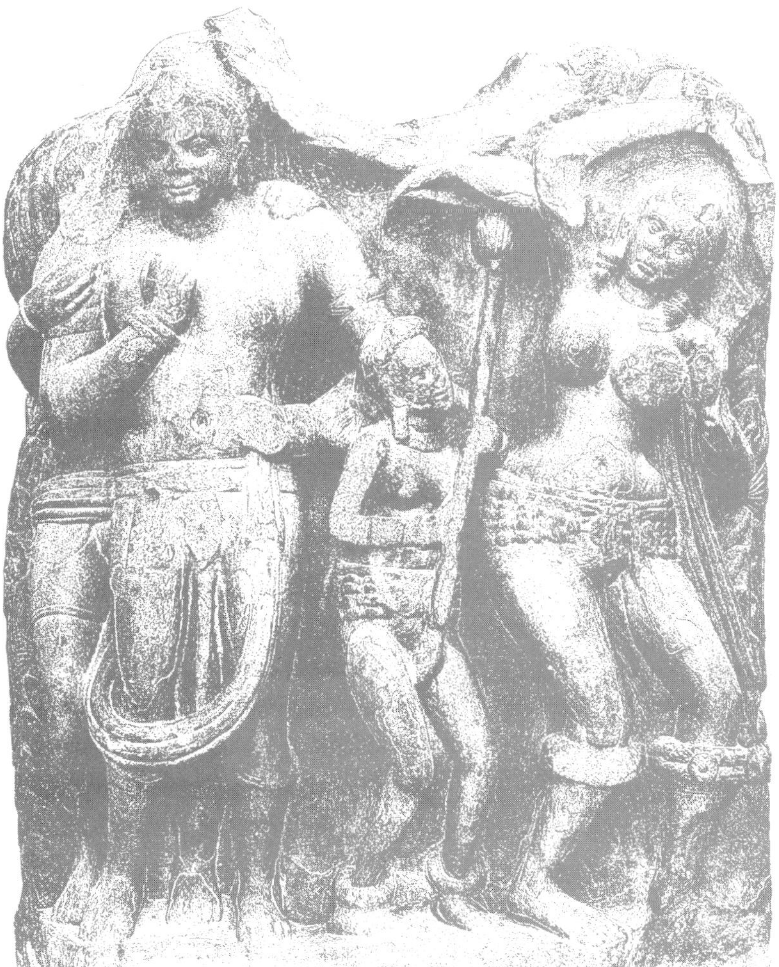

*For*

Ashish Abrol

and

Kaveri

Perspectives in Indian Art & Archaeology, no. 12

# Gods, Men and Women

## Gender and Sexuality in Early Indian Art

by

Seema Bawa

DK PRINTWORLD

Publishers of Indian Traditions

**Cataloging in Publication Data — DK**
[Courtesy: D.K. Agencies (P) Ltd. <docinfo@dkagencies.com>]

**Bawa, Seema.**

Gods, men and women : gender and sexuality in early Indian art / by Seema Bawa.

p. cm.

(Perspectives in Indian art & archaeology, no. 12).
Includes bibliographical references (p. ) and index.
ISBN 13: 9788124606643

1. Sex role in art. 2. Sex in art. 3. Gender identity in art. 4. Women in art. 5. Hindu goddesses in art. 6. Hindu art. 7. Art, Ancient — India. I. Title. II. Series : Perspectives in Indian art & archaeology, no. 12.

DDC 704.94280954 22

© Seema Bawa, 1968-
*First published in 2013*
ISBN 13: 978-81-246-0664-3 (HB)

All rights reserved. No part of this publication may be reproduced or transmitted, except brief quotations, in any form or by any means, electronic or mechanical, including photocopying, recording, or any information storage or retrieval system, without prior written permission of the copyright holder, indicated above, and the publishers.

*Printed and published by:*
D.K. Printworld (P) Ltd.
*Regd. Office: 'Vedaśrī'*, F-395, Sudarshan Park
(Metro Station: Ramesh Nagar)
New Delhi - 110 015
*Phones:* (011) 2545 3975, 2546 6019; *Fax*: (011) 2546 5926
*e-mail:* indology@dkprintworld.com
*Website*: www.dkprintworld.com

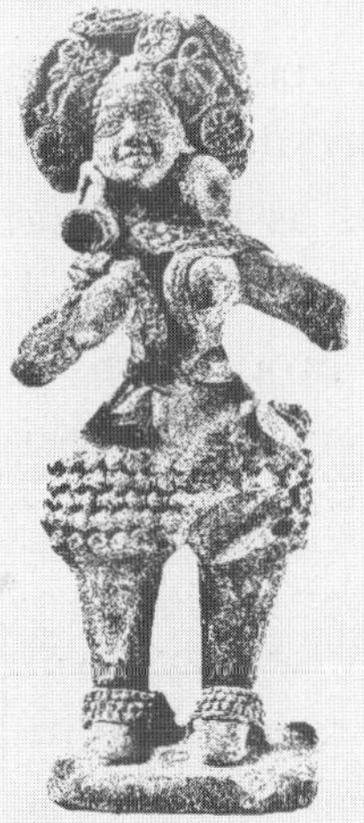

# Preface

This book attempts to locate gender and image representation at the centre of both history and art. As such it is a socio-cultural study of histories of power, of patriarchal dominance inscribed on monuments and sculptures through spatial relationships and modes of representation, a subject that has seldom been studied till now. The work focuses on a gendered study of early art because the visual discourse of this period is so rich in material pertaining precisely to this subject. By early Indian Art, I seek to refer largely to the art of the period from 181 BCE to CE 320. The art, as produced and consumed during the period, when examined from a gendered perspective reveals significant depth and meaning.

The period that has been selected for study (181 BCE to CE 320) is significant in that it was from this time onwards that we find a systematic and large body of art. It was a period of great turmoil and flux in the socio-cultural, politico-economic and religious spheres, giving rise to a number of contesting ideologies and gender complexities.

The early Indian period that has been elucidated in this work is that of development of engendered representation in art, with the creation of both aesthetic and sexual archetypes and stereotypes — of various categories of women recovered from art and texts of females, of mothers, wives, nuns and prostitutes, semi-divine *yakṣīs* and ogresses and temptresses. Stereotypes and archetypes were constructed on the basis of gender roles, rather than on sex. The feminine is essentialised as beautiful and graceful but also as physically uncontrolled or uncontrollable, while the masculine is seen as mentally restrained, competent and physically brave, and this perception is mirrored in artistic production. While there is an effort at creating aesthetically pleasing male and female forms, masculinity is projected through strong, solid, straight-standing and frontally-gazing figures taking the forms of semi-divine beings such as *yakṣa*s or human men.

The process of engendering is reflected by various attributes of the representations: nudity or its absence, ornamentation, gesture, direction of gaze, or context. For example, it may be concluded that nudity, especially with regard to female figures, is not universal in post-Mauryan art, and its depiction is predicated on the sex/gender representation sought to be projected through the art.

The female body is essential in engendering the art of early India, especially given that the female and feminine were defined by their physical attributes. The majority of female figures in the art of the post-Mauryan period display prominently marked genitalia (explicitly or through transparent drapery) and prominent, round, full breasts, especially in the Kuṣāṇa artistic tradition. Ideologically women as sexual-reproductive beings are defined by their reproductive body. This is effectively elucidated through aesthetic representations.

The relative silence of the mainstream patriarchal religious discourse with regard to the identity and characteristics of certain female deities such as Lajjā Gaurī, Ṣaṣṭhī, and goat-headed goddess is significant. Our research reveals an attempt to make invisible and marginalise powerful and revered feminine images which were not, or could not be, assimilated into major pantheons as wives and consorts. The ignoring of the presence of such goddesses does not stop the production of mother-goddess figures. In an economy based on expanding agriculture, women play an important role both because their work is valuable in the fields and also because they have a control over nature's ritual and reproductivity. The explanation for such a phenomenon may lie in various local cultic beliefs based on the relationship of women with life-giving sexuality, and on feminine socio-ritual practices related to pregnancy and childbirth.

This book views the engendering process not as a linear, monolithic development. Certain representations, both cultic and artistic, are representative only in this period and offer insights into the creation of gender roles both in art and society. The degree of patriarchal dominance is neither uniform over time, nor evenly spread over all religious ideologies. A multiplicity of voices have been discovered within rampant misogynisms that fracture, challenge or even invert this discourse.

The increased patriarchalisation of the organised religions leads to the disappearance of some female-dominated cults and figures, and of the *bhikkhuṇī saṁgha*. This is predicated upon the decreasing agency of women in the patronage of artistic production. This book is an attempt to recover the crystallisation of gender, and the setting forth of gender archetypes in the pre-Gupta period thus gives interesting insights into the intention, agency and patronage patterns in early Indian art.

It is a matter of pleasure for me that the book is being published by D.K. Printworld, a leading publisher of art and Indological books.

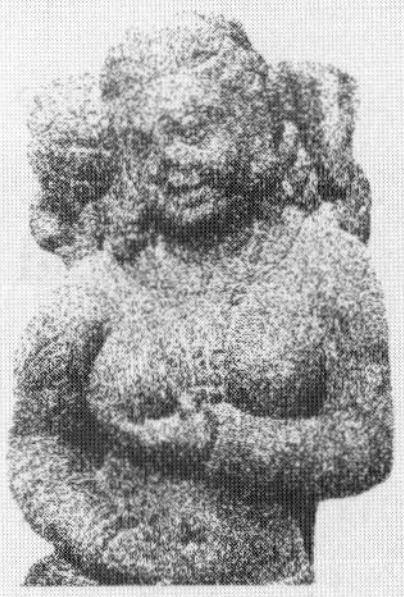

# Acknowledgements

The multitude of feminine figures in the sculptures of early Indian art inspired me to enquire into their intentionality and significance. This resulted in an extended period of study during which the thesis was researched and written, and subsequently took the form of this book. In accomplishing this task, I had received immense encouragement and support from various quarters that I seek to humbly acknowledge.

I am profusely grateful to my supervisor Prof. T.S. Maxwell, without whose help this work would not have been possible. His invaluable insights, perceptive criticism and rigorous supervision were a source of inspiration and guidance. He is truly a modern epitome of a traditional Indian seer or *guru* in the tradition of the Upaniṣads.

I am grateful to the University Grants Commission (UGC) for Minor Research Grant which assisted me to undertake extensive fieldwork. I am also indebted to the UGC and Deutscher Akademisher Auslandaustausch Dienst (DAAD) for awarding me the Sandwich grant to study at the University of Bonn, Germany. I am thankful to Seminar für Orientalische Kunstgeschichte for hosting me and also to Insitut für Indology, Universität Bonn, Germany, for making available the rare and rich collection of their books. At DAAD, I would like to reserve my special gratitude for Ms. Pratibha Jhalani.

I would like to give a special acknowledge-ment to Sh. Sarabjeet

Singh Babra, who, along with Sh. Paramjeet Singh, photographed precious museum collections in high resolution, especially for this book. Dr. Donald Statdner generously shared his images for the section on *gaṇikā*s and for showing an interest in the publication. Prof. S. Settar commented on the thesis, sharing insights which have been included and acknowledged in this book. Dr. Gautam Sengupta also read and commented on the research which have added value to the subsequent publication.

I also thank Dr. ArputhaRani Sengupta, my internal supervisor. Dr. Hari Om, the Principal, and the authorities of Sri Aurobindo College, Delhi University, also deserve gratitude for granting me leave and extending other facilities. Sh. Susheel Mittal, Rajendra Agarwal and all other members of the production team at D.K. Printworld have been extremely courteous and co-operative in all matters related to the publication, sharing great interest and knowledge to make this book a creditable contribution to works on ancient Indian arts.

I would like to acknowledge the support of Sh. J.S. Yadav and other staff members of the American Institute of Indian Studies, Gurgaon, for assisting me in locating the required illustration materials. I would be failing in my duty if I do not mention the co-operation received from National Museum and National Museum Institute, and Vishveshvaranand Vedic Research Institute, Hoshiarpur, in making the study materials available to me. I am further indebted to the American Institute of Indian Studies and to the National Museum which provided photo prints of varied monuments and antiquities.

During my fieldwork, numerous people had helped me without whom it would have been difficult to complete my task: at Saṅghol, Sh. Tek Chand and Sh. Sharma; ASI staff at various sites such as Karle, Bhaj, Kanherī, Sāñcī, Andher, Udaigiri, Pītalkhorā, and Sārnāth; directors and staff of various museums who allowed me to access their collections especially Indian Museum, Kolkata, Site Museum at Saṅghol, archaeological museums at Ropar and Hoshiarpur (Punjab), State Museum, Lucknow, Allahabad Museum, Mathura Museum, Site Museum at Soṅkh, Sārnāth Museum (Uttar Pradesh), Patna Museum and Vaiśālī Museum (Bihar), and Vidiśā, Sāñcī and Bhopal Museums (Madhya Pradesh).

I would also like to thank Sh. Y.V.S.T. Sai and Sh. Ishwar Singh for their timely help. Sh. Rajat Sodhi was a pillar of strength during the preparation of the thesis. My parents Manmohan and Sunandi Bawa were always by my side and were extremely tolerant and understanding to my involvement and dedication to my work. Other family members have shown similar forbearance and I thank them all; Anu, Arun, Sanjana, Poonam along with Vijay and S.K. Abrol.

I would like to thank my husband Ashish Abrol and my close friend Meena Chakravorty for reading and commenting on the book. Their suggestions have added value to it. I also thank Ashish, for indulging, supporting and encouraging me whenever the spirits were low. In the vein of P.G. Wodehouse, I would also like to acknowledge the contribution of my daughter Kaveri without whom this book would have been completed in half the time. Her presence in my world has certainly helped me in understanding some gender roles and biological impulses such as maternality, better.

While efforts have been made to place photographs near the relevant text, design consideration have sometimes made this difficult. For this and any other mistakes or oversights, I request the reader's indulgence. I would like to re-iterate that this is but one way of looking at the visual and textual material available to us from the early period, among the very many perspectives.

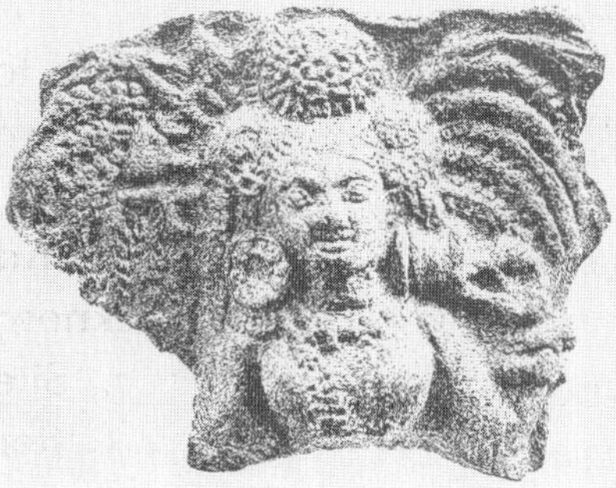

# Contents

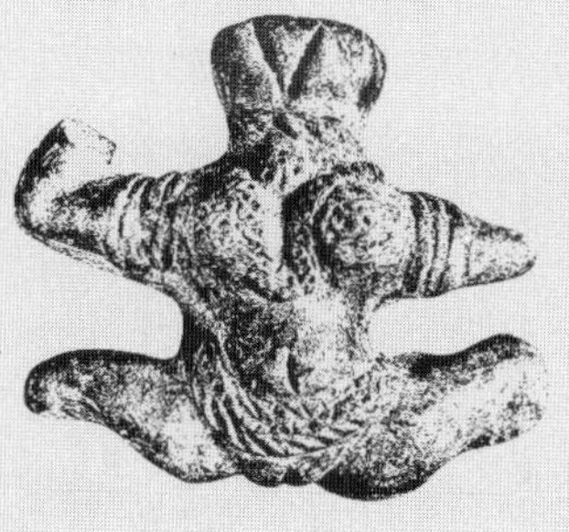

# Key to Transliteration

### Vowels

| | | | | | | | |
|---|---|---|---|---|---|---|---|
| अ *a* (Roman) | आ *ā* (palm) | इ *i* (it) | ई *ī* (police) | उ *u* (put) | ऊ *ū* (rule) | ऋ *ṛ* (rig) | ॠ *ṝ*[1] |
| ऌ *ḷ* (able) | ॡ *ḹ*[1] | ए *e* (there) | ऐ *ai* (aisle) | ओ *o* (no) | औ *au* (loud) | | |

### Consonants

| | | | | | |
|---|---|---|---|---|---|
| **Guttural** | क *ka* (skate) | ख *kha*[2] (blockhead) | ग *ga* (gate) | घ *gha*[2] (ghost) | ङ *ṅa* (sing) |
| **Palatal** | च *ca* (chunk) | छ *cha*[2] (catch him) | ज *ja* (john) | झ *jha*[2] (hedgehog) | ञ *ña* (bunch) |
| **Cerebral** | ट *ṭa* (start) | ठ *ṭha*[2] (anthill) | ड *ḍa* (dart) | ढ *ḍha*[2] (godhead) | ण *ṇa* (under) |
| **Dental** | त *ta* (path) | थ *tha*[2] (thunder) | द *da* (that) | ध *dha*[2] (this) | न *na* (numb) |
| **Labial** | प *pa* (spin) | फ *pha*[2] (philosophy) | ब *ba* (bin) | भ *bha*[2] (abhor) | म *ma* (much) |
| **Semi-vowels** | य *ya* (young) | र *ra* (drama) | ल *la*[3] (luck) | व *va*[4] (vile) | |
| **Sibilants** | श *śa*[5] (shove) | ष *ṣa*[5] (bushel) | स *sa* (so) | ह *ha* (hum) | |
| **Others** | क्ष *kṣa* (*kṣatriya*) | त्र *tra* (*triśūla*) | ज्ञ *jña* (*jñānī*) | | |

अं (ं) *ṁ anusvāra* is a nasal off-glide that immediately follows the pronunciation of a vowel as in *saṁskṛti*.

अः *visarga* = *ḥ* consists in abrupt release of breath after a vowel as in *prātaḥ*.

ऽ *avagraha* shows non-pronunciation, that is, deletion of "a" after "e" or "o" as in *ime 'vasthitāḥ*. In Vedic Sanskrit, it can also show word division.

### Hindi letters (extras)

| | | | |
|---|---|---|---|
| ँ = *m̐* (*candrabindu*) | ं = ṅ (*anusvāra*) | ड़ = *ṛa* | ढ़ = *ṛha* |

[1] Longer form of the preceding vowel.

[2] Aspirated forms of the preceding consonants. The compound words given as examples should be pronounced without a syllabic break at the underlined places. "tha" and "pha" should not be pronounced as fricatives.

[3] retroflexed and written "L" as "*la*" in certain phonetic contexts.

[4] Pronounced like "w", without aspiration.

[5] "śa" is palatal; "ṣa" cerebral or retroflex.

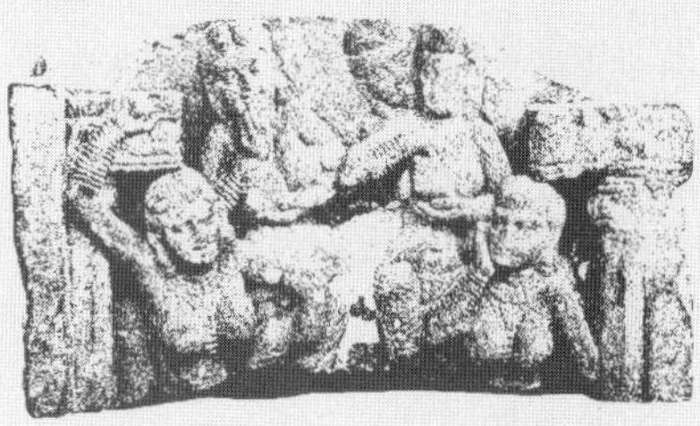

# Abbreviations

| | |
|---|---|
| AIIS | American Institute of Indian Studies |
| AM | Allahabad Museum |
| *ARASI* | *Annual Report of the Archaeological Survey of India* |
| *AŚ* | *Arthaśāstra* |
| *ASIAR* | *Archaeological Survey of India Annual Report* |
| *AV* | *Atharvaveda* |
| Barua, *Bharhut* | B.M. Barua, *Bharhut,* 3 pts., Patna: Indological Books Corporation, 1979 (Reprint) |
| *BMAUP* | *Bulletin of Museums and Archaeology of Uttar Pradesh* |
| *BPWM* | *Bulletin of Prince of Wales Museum*, Bombay |
| *CII* | *Corpus Inscriptionum Indicarum* |
| Cowell, *Jātaka* | E.D. Cowell, ed., *The Jātaka or Stories of the Buddha's Former Births*, translated from the Pāli by various hands, 6 vols., Delhi: Motilal Banarsidass, 1990. |
| *EI* | *Epigraphia Indica* |
| *EPW* | *Economic and Political Weekly* |
| ERS | Elizabeth Rosen Stone, *The Buddhist Art of Nāgārjunakoṇḍa*, Delhi: Motilal Banarsidass, 1994 |
| *EW* | *East and West* |

| | |
|---|---|
| GMAG | Government Museum and Art Gallery, Chandigarh |
| GMM | Government Museum, Mathura |
| *IA-AR* | *Indian Archaeology — A Review* |
| *IESHR* | *Indian Economic and Social History Review* |
| *IHQ* | *Indian Historical Quarterly* |
| IM | Indian Museum, Kolkata |
| *JAS* | *Journal of Asiatic Society* |
| *JISOA* | *Journal of Indian Society of Oriental Art* |
| *JNSI* | *Journal of Numismatic Society of India* |
| *JRAS* | *Journal of Royal Asiatic Society* |
| *JRASB* | *Journal of Royal Asiatic Society, Bengal* |
| *JUPHS* | *Journal of Uttar Pradesh Historical Society* |
| LL | Lüders List, *Epigraphia Indica X* |
| *Manu* | *Manusmṛti* |
| *MASI* | *Memoirs of Archaeological Survey of India* |
| *Mbh.* | *Mahābhārata* |
| *Mṛcch.* | Śūdraka's *Mṛcchakaṭika* |
| *MWSE* | Monier-Williams *Sanskrit English Dictionary* |
| NM | National Museum, New Delhi |
| *NŚ* | *Nāṭyaśāstra* of Bharata |
| PTS | Pali Text Society |
| *ṚV* | *Ṛgveda* |
| RK | Robert Knox, *Amarāvatī Buddhist Sculpture from the Great Stūpa,* London: British Museum, 1992 |
| SML | State Museum , Lucknow |
| *Śat Br.* | *Śatapatha Brāhmaṇa* |
| *Tat Br.* | *Taittirīya Brāhmaṇa* |
| *TS* | *Taittirīya Saṁhita* |

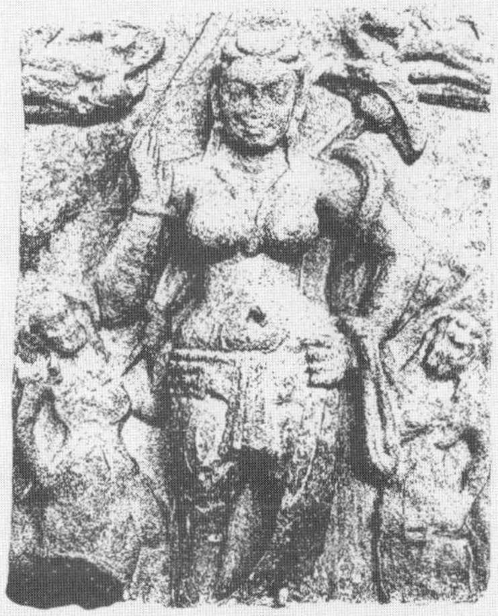

# List of Plates

# Introduction

A paradox that any study of traditional Indian art has to grapple with is the one between the profusion of representations of female figures such as goddesses and the submissive status of women in contemporary society. The inspiration for this work arose through a desire to examine not just why such a paradox exists but how it emerges philosophically and in the visual arts. Are goddesses not women/female/feminine? Art gives a vantage point through aspects such as clothing/jewellery/posture and gaze to examine these concerns.

This book attempts to locate gender and image representation at the centre of both history and art. As such it is a socio-cultural study of histories of power, of patriarchal dominance inscribed on monuments and sculptures through spatial relationships and modes of representation. This work focuses on a gendered study of that art because the visual discourse of this period is so rich in material pertaining precisely to this subject.[1] By early Indian Art, I seek to refer largely to the art of the period from 181 BCE to CE 320. The art, as produced and consumed during the period, when examined from a gendered perspective reveals significant depth and meaning.

The period that has been selected for study (181 BCE to CE 320) is significant in that it was from this time onwards that we find a systematic and large body of art. It was a period of great turmoil and flux in the socio-cultural, politico-economic and religious spheres, giving rise to a number of contesting ideologies and gender complexities. In the field of art, it was a period when a number of archetypes (and stereotyping) related to religious iconography, body and gender roles were constructed and fixed. An exploration of these will reveal embedded or ideologically inherent notions related to form, femininity and masculinity.

Gendered readings provide one valid vantage point from which to view art. It is an approach that in conjunction with the art-historical processing of style, chronology and technique, opens up many layers of interpretation and analysis. The gendering of early art also makes available material that is helpful in viewing the art of subsequent periods, providing models that either continue or are transformed or get discontinued in Gupta and post-Gupta art, thus providing vital information about socio-religious processes that shape both the earlier and later periods.

Patriarchy informs all contemporary socio-religious ideologies, whether Buddhist or Hindu, and it becomes clear upon investigation that patriarchy is a dominant factor in determining both the course and the content of art production. In this work I have attempted to investigate and interpret representations — visual and to a limited extent textual — that are available from the period under consideration, with a view to discovering what they may reveal concerning the specific art objects, but also concerning the male and female figures represented by them.

### Historiography of Gender and Art in Ancient India

The literature on ancient India in general and ancient Indian art in particular has been gender-neutral if not gender-blind in the past. Richard Goldsmith has noted that there is an inadequate understanding of the profound role that social construction of gender has played in the formation of Indian social and religious life.[2] This paucity of adequate understanding has been accompanied by an inadequate analysis of gender and power relations in the social history of India, and the lack of it is still more noticeable in the field of art and architecture.

Cultural artefacts such as texts, buildings, images or figures are in the first place only *re-presentations*. No rendering or description of artefacts can be politically neutral; each such system is inflected by ideology. Before being re-read and scrutinised in the early twenty-first century they were viewed selectively to correspond to certain notions of ancient culture through the process of editing and photographing and written into histories that are modern reconstructions of the ancient past. One such perspective on art is exemplified in Western writers such as Fergusson, Cousens, Cunningham and later Vogel and Foucher. To varying degrees their critique is inflected by an imperialist agenda or a bias towards the superiority of Western models.[3] Fergusson, convinced of the moral superiority of the Western Anglo-Saxon civilisation saw the Indian works as deficient, "effete" but not insane; Cousens too echoed a similar perspective but with lesser virulence. Kumkum Roy opines that "The colonisers attempted to term the entire colonised civilisation as feminine."[4] Cunningham saw in the plenitude or amorphousness of Indian art a certain feminine decadence or "lack" of robust rationality as against a rational masculine Western discourse. V.A. Smith, too, epitomises the Western approach towards ancient Indian Art. He wrote about the Mathurā *yakṣīs*, and I quote, "They exhibit lasciviousness combined with grossness. While Chandra and Culakoka and their sisters have the appearance of heavenly nymphs, their unworthy descendants are mere courtesans, exhibiting their opulent charms and gaudy jewellery."[5]

In direct contradistinction, Indian historians such as V.S. Agrawala or A.K. Coomaraswamy chose to publish and comment on specific art styles such as Gandhāra and Mathurā partly in order to prove certain nationalist agendas-related indigenous origins and inspirations for the Indian artistic genius and also in order to valorise depending on their ideological positions. Coomaraswamy articulated the argument that the "sheer physicality of the earliest male images from Mathurā . . . was directly related to and emanated from pre-existing notions of male energy."[6] These histories were inflected by imperialism, nationalism and ideology, including the ideology of art history as a discourse of rationality.

Although much has been written on the position and status of women in ancient society, this exercise has largely been conducted within the larger discourse of imperialist and nationalist historiography. Imperialist historians stressed the ignoble position of women and the increasing dis-privileging of the sex. Colonial writing on Indian art tended to focus on nakedness and what was seen as "immorality" in secular portrayals, and viewed all depictions, including and especially its male representations, as feminine and effeminate.[7] This was a strategy through which the colonised people and their culture were ideologically denigrated and perceived as powerless through the use of gendered categories.[8] Another approach was to visualise the powerless and lowly "position of women" in text and art and to use this to designate a civilisation as barbarous and backward-looking. Position of women became an index of civilisation. "Women made an irreversible entry into the political discourse as symbolic pawn in a complex ideological battle."[9]

Nationalist historians like Altekar[10] responded to an imperialist denigration of the Indian people through the use of history and art history by trying to establish the relative freedom and empowered status of women, especially in the relatively pure ancient period, untouched as it was by corrupting foreign influences where there was no seclusion of women or *satī* and there was late marriage and access to education. In order to achieve this aim they highlight individual instances of "visible" women such as Gārgī and women seers in the *Ṛgveda*.[11] Altekar, in particular, sees a decline in women's familial status, religious rights, and in their participation in public life as against a marginal improvement in their proprietary status. He views women's agency as problematic; he regards non-Aryan women as being partially responsible for the decline in caste women's status.[12] Alternatively, authors such as R.C. Dutt and R.G. Bhandarkar exalt the empowerment of women within the household, where they rule the domestic/private domain. However, they subscribe to the idea that the depiction of female images in Hindu art was obscene, immoral and therefore embarrassing. Thus they marginalised Indian art in general.

Early twentieth century nationalist art historians such as Coomaraswamy recovered the female figures and the feminine highlighting the visibility of goddesses within both the textual and the artistic traditions.[13] Coomaraswamy located the feminine within the philosophical domain, which according to him could not be, and was not, understood by the Western writers. By linking art production to *māyā* and *śakti*, feminine and feminised abstractions, he gendered art production and located it within the discourse of plentitude and prosperity.[14] Thus there is an engenderment of the feminine and it is seen as a positive as against the Orientalist denigration of the amorphousness as a "lack" but as a "presence," a philosophical "is-ness" of *māyā* and *śakti*. Coomaraswamy however abstracts these representations from the socio-religious milieu of the producers and consumers of the art.

Isabel Horner is an exception in so far as hers was the first sustained effort to locate women outside the stereotypical notions of women in early Indian societies. She not only viewed women in their social roles but also noted their economic roles. She also perceived the monastic order for women as providing an alternative women-based community, which provided them with specific forms of self-expression and articulation of religious experience. This analysis of women valorises them and takes them beyond the realm of dress, ornaments and aesthetics that "trivialise women." She looks at issues such as female sexuality and not simply the decorative attributes of women.[15] This analysis, though very significant for the gendering of women, does not relate to the realm of art. My study, on the other hand, does attempt a gendered reading through analysing aspects such as dress, ornaments, posture, gaze and aesthetics within Buddhist and other religious ideologies.

In feminist historiography of the ancient period, art and archaeology of gender are relatively new concerns. The emphasis of the feminist historiographer has largely been on studying prehistoric cultures of the Americas and Australia. Recent forays, however, have been made into reinterpreting classical archaeology from a gender perspective. The main area of focus of these efforts has been the relationship between women, space and archaeology. While in most of these studies art has been used as a kind of secondary tool to reinforce theories related to power structures within gender, interest in art as a valid category for the reconstruction of gender issues has been growing. In India, however, this interest has been very limited, especially with reference to ancient art.

However, recent historians of gender argue that in order to understand the roots of patriarchy and gender formation, and through this understanding create gender equality in society, it is not enough to investigate the position and status of women in ancient India. Instead they advocate an inquiry into the processes of creation and of institutionalisation of gender differences and oppression; that is the warp and woof of power and ideology of patriarchy. Such efforts open up "the possibility of situating women's history within the broad perspective of social history, which in turn permits the raising of a range of questions."[16]

The first systematic attempt at gender analysis of Indian art is Vidya Dehejia's edited work, *Representing the Body*. Not only does it raise issues of spectatorship and agency, it is also the first to deal with the male sexual body as a gendered entity. It also looks at colonial and nationalist approaches to the female and the feminine in Indian art from the vantage point of agency. Vidya Dehejia uses the term "engendering Indian art" to explain how gender issues and differences can be used to offer an alternate perspective into various source materials. Such a perspective goes into the *arche* (archives) of the times to attempt to recover as to how the production and consumption of such sources were related to gender roles that existed or were being developed. Accordingly, Dehejia and other feminist critiques see these gender issues as "embedded" or inextricably entrenched in the sources in the form of notions relating to the feminine, femininity, masculinity, and gender stereotypes as well as archetypes (arche-type).

Some research has been done on the patronage pattern of male and female donors, especially in connection with Buddhist buildings. Upinder Singh and Kumkum Roy[17] have analysed the donative inscriptions from Sāñcī, and Barbara Stoler Miller's edited work[18] also reveals patronage patterns in art with special reference to women.

The writings on representation of women are deeply gendered and informed by the ideological framework within which the art was viewed. The imperialists, as seen above, used the irrationality and purported unnatural and immoral elements found in it to condemn the civilisation and culture of the subject people and thus glorify the Western artistic tradition. The nationalists marginalised the sensual and the secular aspects and highlighted the power of feminine force to justify female imagery. Later spiritualist-nationalist art historians propounded a very influential and effective theory, which located the feminine within the discourse of the mysterious, fertile and creative forces, thus valorising the feminine without necessarily examining or privileging femininity, masculinity or difference in gendering of these images. Recent intellectual exercises attempt to engender Indian art by seeing women as socio-sexual beings on one hand and by locating the female figures within the philosophic and spiritual domain on the other. These readings seek a balance between the metaphysical and material aspects of the artefacts and my project uses a similar methodological framework.

The historiography of early Indian art has been largely bifurcated into two approaches. The first approach is entirely art historical, and its emphasis has been on identifying and classifying sculptures into two schools of art, archaic, Gandhāra, Mathurā and Amarāvatī. Prodigious scholarship has been devoted to this task with pioneering work having been done in this direction by A. Foucher, J. Ph. Vogel and A.K. Coomaraswamy. Recently the contributions of Lolita Nehru, Allchins et al., and R.C. Sharma have shed light on influences that go into making of post-Mauryan art styles. Some work has also been done on terracotta art of the period, significantly that of Amy Poster and Stephen Huyler, whose monographs on the subject have added immensely to the knowledge of this "minor art" of the period.

Under the second approach, research has focused on the process of urbanisation during the time, basing itself on archaeological and textual sources. The works of K.T.S. Sarao, G. Erdosy, Sjoberg, and F.R. Allchins are notable. Other approaches to urbanisation include that of Makkan Lal whose monograph reveals settlement archaeology of early India while Sunder Rajan explains the dynamics of the relationship between the town and the village. Renu Thakur identifies the typology of settlements. V.K. Thakur, A. Ghosh, F.R. Allchins and D.K. Chakrabarti have analysed post-Mauryan urbanisation in its geo-political context and looked at material determinants that provided a boost to the urban process. Within this, production of art is taken up but an analysis of the urban character of this art is inadequate.

Amita Ray has looked at the representation of cities, villages and urban settlements in contemporary art and text. In most other works, urban art is usually treated as an adjunct of a larger process of urbanisation, an indicator of an expanding urban economy. Most theories of urbanisation such as that of G. Childe and R. McAdams take monumental architecture as an important symbol — a symbol that not only proves the existence of a large surplus, capable of supporting such extensive construction activity but also of an ideological system that demands such symbols of religious or political power. Some research such as that of Kumkum Roy has tried to locate differences in patronage patterns available during the time, especially in connection with Buddhist buildings.

Archaeological excavations have revealed the existence of monuments, mainly Buddhist and Jaina, belonging to the period. Scholarships on sites like Sāñcī, Bharhut, Amarāvatī are extensive.

**Contextualising Engendered Readings**

The changing milieu also led to changes in imagery. Aspects such as the relative absence of nuns, a prolific presence of *mithuna*, the transformation of *yakṣī*, and the discontinuation of certain representations such as Śaṣṭhī and Naigameṣī exemplify some of these changes. An investigation into the processes of these transformations is significant for "engendering" Indian art.

Apparently, there is an increasing sensualisation of certain representational types with an increase in patriarchal dominance (as can be gleaned from the textual tradition) in society leading to a dilution in original cultic functions related to fertility and fecundity.[19]

This leads one to reconsider the matter of classification of women, in traditional and modern writing, into women, goddesses, celestial beings, and ogresses. Juxtaposed to these are their male counterparts — men, gods, ogres — as any gendered analysis is incomplete without a comparative study of the manner in which both the genders/sexes were represented within the artistic discourse. I feel that early Indian art did naturalise (by making certain notions appear normative) sex/gender roles by perceiving certain categories of women as inherently evil and sexually aggressive in the vein of the dominant textual tradition, as explicated in the next chapter. The man is the normative and the woman is seen as the "aberration." Gender roles of the wife, mother and prostitute seem to be graphically illustrated in both the religious and secular sculptures from the post-Mauryan layers as has been attempted in this research.

A major device for perpetuating patriarchy was control over female sexuality. Unrestrained sexuality was viewed as dangerous in all religious ideologies and attempts were made to restrain it, though the strategies were different. One of the ways in which Buddhism and Jainism sought to do this was through exalting asceticism as an ideal for both men and women.[20] Brāhmanism achieved it in painting graphic pictures of women's sexual proclivity towards unrestrained and promiscuous behaviour. Thus any woman outside the household, which contained her sexuality within expected societal norms, or the *saṁgha,* which denied her sexuality, could be seen as an ogress or a siren.

One of the feminist stereotypes that I re-examine is, that of men=public and women=private. Donative inscriptions of the period reveal the presence of a number of women in the religio-social field, and their presence in the public domain is also felt in narrative friezes and reliefs, where they are shown in physical spaces that may be termed public, such as balconies. Women also negotiate the public sphere as nuns and prostitutes, and their presence is visualised through art.

Further, patriarchal oppression is never monolithic; it differed across race, caste and class, and there were pluralities of discourses and practices. I am aware that such an approach is anachronistic in that it invokes and uses theories and notions about male-female power relationships that are a product of a modern society on a culturally distant subject, thus imposing categories and classifications that are alien to it. This, however, is the method of all scholarship investigating the past, not only that of women's studies.

### Methodology

Feminist approaches to the body, sexuality, agency and sex/gender roles can prove helpful for such an analysis. Here it will be in order to clarify the difference between gender studies and feminist approaches. While gender studies like this research uses feminist approaches, tools and terminology; the *telos* or objective is distinct as these tools, which are not part of a prescriptive design but merely diagnostic tools, which in conjunction with other tools of an interdisciplinary approach, reveal layers of "embedded" ideology and meaning.

Feminist historians like Lerner have stressed that while men composed most of the literature in the pre-modern period, the only way to recover women is through reading silences and absences.[21] This is not necessarily true of art in our period and context because women are present in the form of divine, semi-divine and secular entities, even if the intention of putting them there was imprecatory. It is therefore important to view them in their context, which is generally religious that is inspired by religion and found in religious contexts (Hindu or Buddhist holy places).

### Women and Agency

Another way in which one can study the construction of gender identities through art is by examining the agency of women. That women did patronise monuments is evident from the donative inscriptions, but whether they had substantial power over what was being represented is doubtful. The imagery that was sponsored by individual donors, both men and women, was probably not created or planned by them, but part of a preconceived design; in the Buddhist context, it is monks who are mentioned in inscriptions as the supervisors of building projects, and nuns have far less power in general than monks. However art production may have been relatively less regulated by normative patriarchal discourse than the textual tradition, perhaps because it catered to a wider and more diverse audience.

The agency of women was limited to the right to contribute materially to art production and to be able to visit and view the fruit of their donation. Unfortunately one cannot recover the way art was consumed, that is, whether women viewed it differently from men. The only thing that can be stated with relative certainty is that they did form part of the audience.

Donations and patronage link art with the contemporary socio-economic context and therefore it is important to see the way in which men and women contributed towards the production of art. It is important to bear in mind, of course, that they were not patronising art *per se*, or in the modern sense, but acquiring religious or spiritual merit through the act of donation.

Women are associated almost exclusively with the religious inscriptions and donations, while men are associated with the political field as well. Amongst the many aspects of patronage that may be subjected to intellectual scrutiny, elements related to differentiated mobility and linkages with resource networks reveal variations in gendered donation patronage. Women as a category are identified by their familial identity while men also mention their *śreṇī*, *varṇa* or *jāti* identity in their donative inscriptions. This pattern is also applicable to nuns. This suggests that the economic and social status of women depended on their familial base.[22] Thus with the increasing disprivileging of women in terms of property and inheritance their agency in terms of donation and patronage also declined.

It is not enough to study female/femininity in isolation; rather one should view these in comparison to the male/masculinity, because gender identities are relational. Nor is it enough to study them in a synchronic manner. What merits examination are the transformations in such depictions. In fact, one of the ways that we can see the evolution or transformation in the nature of patriarchy is to see whether the agency and representation of women evolves during this period. This may be linked to the increased acculturation and Brāhmanisation, leading to entrenchment of patriarchy. This can be seen in a progressive decline in the percentage of women donors from approximately three fourth at Bharhut to half being female donors at Sāñcī, and even less at Mathurā and Sārnāth according to the surviving records.

The choice of subject is a significant factor in engendering art. This is based on an assumption that the audience as well as the producer of the art piece perceived much more in the depiction than just a random arrangement of figures or motifs. It is essential, in studying gender in art, to focus on which aspects of male and female are emphasised and how men and women are depicted on the bas-reliefs and statues of the period. Examining the physical space within the monument as well as the placement of the artwork and its size in relation to other figures enables us to read and interpret images in a gendered perspective.

The methodology with regard to gaze, dress and posture needs some explication. The term "gaze" relates to the concept of reification or objectification of the viewed by the viewer in terms of the intentionality of the gaze. Gaze, viewing or "the eye of the Other," is thus not an innocent act; as John Berger states, "men act and women appear. Men look at women and women watch themselves being looked at."[23] While the gaze of the spectator and how they perceive the figures cannot be recovered; some aspects can be gleaned from contemporary textual sources such as the *Nāṭyaśāstra*. The gaze further refers to the "internal gaze" of the artefact; as to whether the figure is looking at itself, its male counterpart (in a *mithuna*) or looking at the viewer (like the divine figures). The "external gaze" refers to how the viewer may perceive art, and where his/her attention is focused. Posture too, reveals aspects relating to gender roles; whether the figure is solid, static or in motion, maternal, sensual or provocative, whether the view is frontal or the rear view; all reveal aspects about the social gender roles. Dress reveals a lot; nudity, scanty clothes on certain kind of figures have certain specific signification. Ornaments such as necklaces may have symbolic functions as also garments such as the *mekhalā* may symbolise *āyuṣ* or long life.

This work first identifies a category of the artefact that lends itself to gendered study. This category can be a cultic figure such as Lajjā-Gaurī, or a social type such as a maternal figure or a semi-divine category like the *yakṣī-śālabhañjikā*. The category is then subjected to an examination in the following pattern:

1. On typological basis, figures are segregated, classified and studied.

2. This is followed by a description of either all available representations or significant chosen representations. This is further followed by a description and analysis of analogous representations of similar kind or of male/female figures.

3. Then an identification of these figures is attempted on the basis of secondary sources with a clear spelling out of why the research agrees or disagrees with the stated opinions. In certain other cases, such as the breast offering posture, I have made the identification myself. Collating and describing available opinions has been done, as it is significant for both engendering and identification of the image.

4. Sources like contemporary textual such as the Vedic literature, Buddhist/Jain texts, Śāstric literature such as the *Nāṭyaśāstra*, the Gṛhyasūtras, medical literature, and classical dramas are examined. Details of textual sources are referred to in a subsequent section. Epigraphic evidences are examined either for the identification of the image/representation, the societal context, or of the donor if significant to the engendering of the representation.

5. Finally the works are "engendered" or examined from a gender perspective in relation to their socio-cultural, socio-religious, socio-sexual or metaphysical contexts. Aberrations, discontinuities, silences and gaps have also been examined as artistic representations or the process of engendering them can never be contained within a monolithic critique.

**Text-Image Study**

Any effort at studying gender in art must take texts into account. One must however keep in mind that the textual tradition codified by the political and religious elite often ignores the lower orders or defines them in terms of its own elaborate and divinely ordained paradigms. Thus those groups outside the pale of ritual purity of *varṇāśramadharma,* that is, women, could not create, disseminate and preserve similar texts and images.[24]

The *Therīgāthā* is an exception to this rule, as it records the voice of senior nuns, the *therī*s. Women may have had some agency in deciding the visual discourse as seen above and this may have led to a divergence between the gendered representations in the two traditions. It is also possible that the audiences for texts and for visual representations were not composed of the same people, and that similar episodes lend themselves to varied gendered interpretations.

This is demonstrated by the difference in popular narrative as codified by monk-editors in the Jātaka stories and their illustration in narrative reliefs in early Buddhist art. In the latter, since the whole story could not be narrated, only one or certain episodes were chosen for depiction and these are the very moments that are significant in revealing the difference in gendering of text and image.

Any attempt at engendering ancient art, such as mine, has to be multidisciplinary in scope and draws on a number of resources including history, women's study, anthropology, sociology and, to a limited extent, psychology. The multidisciplinary approach indicates efforts to come to terms with differences of sex/gender arrangements, caste and heterodoxy.

The nomenclature used to denote the time period through this work is that which is commonly accepted, namely the usage of dynastic eras to designate a particular span of time. However, the phrase "Śuṅga art," for example, does not necessarily refer to art produced within territories occupied by the Śuṅgas directly, or to art patronised by the Śuṅgas themselves; rather, it refers to art produced in the span of time roughly coinciding with Śuṅga rule in central and north India. Similarly, the term "Kuṣāṇa art" refers to art produced broadly within the Kuṣāṇas' dominions during the first two and a half centuries of the Common Era, which may be identified by some characteristics that art historians call Kuṣāṇa.

This work does not discuss the whole of the large body of Brāhmanical, Buddhist and Jaina sacred imagery produced in the early period. The forms of Viṣṇu, Śiva, the Buddha, *bodhisattvas*, and Durgā do not fall within the purview of my research. Nor does my work take into account issues related to alternative sexualities such as trans-sexuality or androgyny, which can largely be seen within philosophical and theological discourse rather than being based on socio-sexual constructs.

I also do not put forth an independent alternative chronological or stylistic analysis, but rely on commonly accepted theories on this subject. However, I have commented on the change in representation and its significance for the construction or transformation of gender whenever applicable.

### Sources

One of the major sources are the research archaeological data available in reports on excavation published by ASI and allied institutions such as museums.[25] Appropriate textual studies that corroborate and qualify data found from excavations and antiquities have been examined in so far as they provide us with information about the social, economical and religious context of the age while providing a mental world view of the age and the area.

Epigraphic sources published in the *Epigraphia Indica* and *The Corpus Inscriptionum Indicarum* provide vital information on patronage, pilgrimage, dates, narrative, religious affiliations, and artistic traditions of the people of the age. Sculptural remains, be it in any material, free standing or part of an architectural edifice are the most important source of information. Terracotta plaques and figures that were widely prevalent are vital source of study.

### Textual Sources

Since a significant majority of the surviving archives of art from this period are Buddhist, I have drawn heavily from Buddhist texts. Of these, the *Therīgāthā* (BCE second-first century),[26] a collection of verses ascribed to senior nuns, is one of the most significant and singular sources for recovering the voice of women. Its counterpart, the *Theragāthā*, a collection of psalms of senior monks, provides an important counterview of personal and collective perceptions of experiences and achievements of monks and nuns. The two *kāvyas* by Aśvaghoṣa, the *Buddhacarita*[27] and *Saundarānanda*[28] (50 BCE to CE 100), are useful not only for studying the narrative related to the Buddha's life, but for their revealing of the gender stereotypes that informed the poetic conventions of the period. Similarly, Jātakas,[29] Avadānakathās such as the *Divyāvadāna* (*c.* second century CE) and other popular stories related to the life of Buddha, which are also illustrated on the monuments, are used in this research. The former were probably compiled by the fifth century of the Christian Era, though inscriptional and sculptural evidence suggests that some of the stories were known as early as the third century BCE. These *gāthās* come closest to we can come to reconstructing the "popular" perceptions in early Indian context. I have also used Vinaya texts for examining attitudes towards renunciation which informed the production of, and the omission of, certain gender categories in art.

Of the early Jaina Sūtras, the *Rājapraśeniya-sūtra* and the *Jīvājīvābhigama Sūtra* (*c*. second-third century) provide us with valuable information about the organisation and *alaṁkāra* (ornamentation) of monuments such as the *stūpa*. Other texts, such as the *Kalpasūtra* and the *Bhagavatī-Sūtra*, not only give the religious backdrop but also reveal a rich narrative tradition which helps in identifying certain images and representations.

Brāhmanical texts, especially the *Ṛgveda*, *Atharvaveda*, *Śatapatha Brāhmaṇa*, *Taittirīya Brāhmaṇa*, *Mānava-Gṛhyasūtra*, *Kauṣītakī Gṛhyasūtra* and other Śrauta- and Gṛhyasūtras provide us with a philosophic and ritual background for many images. The *Manusmṛti*[30] (*c*. second-first century BCE), the *Mahābhārata* and stray references to the *Rāmāyaṇa* have also been used to illustrate contemporary perceptions regarding gender relations.

Gendered readings are more accessible in the secular literary tradition. Works on drama and dramaturgy such as Bharata's *Nāṭyaśāstra* (second century BCE to third century CE),[31] and actual plays such as Śūdraka's *Mṛcchakaṭika*[32] (second-third century CE ?), Bhāsa's *Daridra Cārudatta* (first century BCE-first century CE) and later plays such as Kālidāsa's *Mālavikāgnimitram* (*c*. early fifth century), are sources of information concerning non-religious representations. They also help us decode the embedded gender signifiers in imagery. The milieu in Śūdraka's *Mṛcchakaṭika* suggests a thriving Buddhist tradition and an urban sensibility of *nāgarakas*. It is set in Ujjayinī which was one of the important urban centres in early India.

Medical literature such as the *Suśruta Saṁhitā*, *Caraka Saṁhitā* and *Kaśyapa Saṁhitā* incorporates information about deities such as the *bālagrahas*, which are absent in the mainstream religious traditions.

Prescriptive Śāstric texts such as Vātsyāyana's *Kāmasūtra*[33] and Kauṭilya's *Arthaśāstra*[34] reveal the socio-sexual behavioural codes of the time. The *Kāmasūtra* has been ascribed to north India, datable between the first-fourth century CE and falls within our period. While the major portion of the *Arthaśāstra* was composed during the Mauryan period, certain sections are considered to be later interpolations added during the first two centuries of the Christian Era.

As far as possible I have tried to cite the text in the original language, together with a translation, which at least approximates the original meaning. Where a cited translation is itself gendered, this is indicated, at least in the footnotes, bearing in mind that language in itself is a signifier of gendering.

### Context

The period of this work (181 BCE to CE 320) is marked by an expanding economy and socio-religious transformations. It is obvious that over a period of more than three centuries art and architecture evolved considerably. The changes and continuities in themes, styles and representations, both qualitatively and quantitatively, serve as barometers of the changing fortunes of urban centres, which in turn led to changes in gendered representations. A detailed note on the historical context is given in the Appendix to this work.

R.S. Sharma has also commented on the essential socio-cultural connection between Buddhism and urbanisation, in which he has pointed out that Buddhism encouraged or accepted many urban practices, such as prostitution, usury and eating houses, which had hitherto been frowned upon by Brāhmanism.[35] It is therefore not surprising that the Buddhist *saṁgha* was patronised by urban communities such as guilds, merchants and artisans. We have numerous inscriptions that give us information about the patrons. From Sāñcī itself, we can see the majority is from urban centres, many from nearby Vidiśā. Further in Bharhut, near Satanā, donors from Vidiśā and Ujjain abound.

This was an age in which non-royal gifts and donations by women abounded. The relevant epigraphs can provide vital clues concerning the audience for whom art was produced and the ways in which it was consumed by the people who visited the *stūpa*s, *caitya*s and *vihāra*s, and probably also *devālaya*s, on which this art was displayed. How this informed and influenced thematic and stylistic choices in art is one of the questions I ask of our sources.

The artistic evolution of subjects and styles is no less significant. Under the impetus of ideological and religious changes, along with foreign influences brought into north India by Roman and Greek traders and craftspeople, images of deities, especially of the Buddha, started to be made. The visual exaltation of kingship is a key ingredient of the sculptural tradition. Schools and styles of art evolved.

The connection between space that can be considered sacred (the precincts of a *stūpa* or *devālaya*) and the city seems a complex one in the post-Maurya era. Though demarcated and often located physically outside the city, these sacred complexes were integral parts of the urban landscape.

All over the northern India in the post-Mauryan period we come across *stūpa-vihāra* complexes that lie outside the city. At Soṅkh we have a *nāga* temple on the outskirts, and at Nāgārjunakoṇḍa a temple of Hārītī is found a little distance from the main complex. We also hear of numerous *yakṣa* shrines or tree shrines outside the town. From early times, Buddhists preferred sites on the outskirts of the city, where the monks could meditate in peace and hold discussions as well as be close enough to the urban centre to beg for alms. Patronage for the Buddhist *saṁgha* was largely dependent on the cities and towns where there was a concentration of wealth, resources and laity. The villages, by comparison, would have been scattered over a large area and the distances would also make them less accessible. We should also bear in mind that the resources of the village population would be limited in comparison with those of urban communities such as merchants and artisans. Thus for economic reasons alone it would have made more sense for the monastic complex to be situated near the city. This is not a universal practice, however, since at Taxila and Soṅkh we have apsidal temples and *stūpa*s within the precinct of the town itself.

The *bhikkhus*/*bhikkhuṇī*s also mediate between the country and the city. Peter Burke has referred to the medieval friars in Europe as the men of the market as well as the men of the university.[36] This is also true of the *bhikkhu*s and *bhikkhuṇī*s of the Buddhist *saṁgha*, in the sense that they belonged both to the *vihāra* and the city. They are the ones who dealt on a daily basis with the common people, and took the little tradition upwards leading to its incorporation and institutionalisation by mainstream religions, and this is seen in the Jātakas. According to Uma Chakravarti, folk narratives retained some autonomy from the homogenised master-narrative.[37] This was the contribution of the *bhikkhu* who used the folk tales to popularise the Buddhist doctrine, with its inherent gendered misogynist ideology, and make it more accessible. Similarly, it is possible that art and architectural practices travelled with these monks and nuns.

**Notes and References**

1. The civilisation reflected in the pre-Mauryan period may be termed the *āraṇyaka-grāma*, a forest-polis civilisation. The creative centre of this civilisation is not seen as the *grāma* or later the *nagara* but the *āraṇyaka* the forest. In the post-Mauryan period, especially in the Buddhist context the civilisation can be viewed as *vihāra-nagara* or monastery-polis civilisation. Ideologically, the city is the centre of the Buddhist universe, while the countryside/forest is exalted in the Brahmanical literary sources. The *vihāra* and the *nagara* cross-fertilise each other and were complementary to each other to create the matrix of the post-Mauryan counterpart of the City of Gods. There were notions or idealised constructs of Cities of Gods such as Alakā, the city of Kubera or Indrapura, the city of Indra. In the Buddhist texts, the ideal city is ruled by manifestation of the Buddha, who as *vijigiṣu*, the universal *cakravartin* monarch rules from a city at whose centre is Mount Meru.
2. See Padmanabhan Jaini, *Gender and Salvation: Jaina Debates on the Spiritual Liberation of Women*, New Delhi: Munshiram Manoharlal, 1992, p. xii.
3. See Catherine B. Asher and Thomas R, Metcalf, eds., *Perceptions of South Asia's Visual Past*, New Delhi: AIIS and OUP, 1994 especially Gary Michael Tartakov, "Changing Views of India's Art Hsitory", pp. 15-36.
4. Kumkum Roy, ed., *Women in Early Indian Society*, New Delhi: Manohar, 1999, p. 2.
5. Cited in Gustav Roth, "The Women and Tree Motif", *Journal of the Asiatic Society, Letters and Science*, vol. XXIII, no. 1, 1957, p. 100.
6. Vidya Dehejia, ed., *Representing the Body*, Kali for Women, New Delhi, 1997, p. 48.
7. Kumkum Roy, op. cit., p. 2.
8. For the historiography of gendering of art see Annapurna Garimella, "Engendering Indian Art", in Vidya Dehejia, op. cit., pp. 22-41.
9. Kumkum Roy, op. cit., p. 2 citing Deniz Kandiyoti, "From Empire to Nation State: Transformations of the Woman Question in Turkey", in S. Jay Klienberg, ed., *Retrieving Women's History: Changing Perception of the Role of Women in Politics and Society*, Oxford: Berg Publishers Ltd., pp 219-40.
10. A.S. Altekar, *The Position of Women in Hindu Civilisation from Prehistoric Times to the Present Day*, New Delhi: Motilal Banarsidass , 1995 (rpt., 2nd edn., 1959).
11. Uma Chakravarti, "Beyond The Altekarian Paradigm: Towards a New Understanding of Gender Relations in Early Indian History", in Kumkum Roy, ed., *Women in Early Indian Societies*, New Delhi: Manohar, 1999, p. 76.
12. A.S. Altekar op. cit., pp. 345-46.
13. A. Garimella, op. cit, pp 34-36; Uma Chakravarti and K. Roy in "Breaking out of Invisibility: Rewriting the History of Women in Ancient India", in S. Jay Klienberg ed., *Retrieving Women's History: Changing Perspectives on the Role of Women in Politics and Society*, p. 319.
14. A. Garimella, op. cit., p. 35.
15. Kumkum Roy, op. cit., p. 7.
16. Ibid.
17. Kumkum Roy, "Women and Men Donors At Sāñcī: A Study of The Inscriptional Evidence", in L.K. Bajpai, ed., *Position and Status of Women in Ancient India*, vol. I, Varanasi, 1988, pp. 209-23; Upinder Singh, "Sāñcī: The History of Patronage of Ancient Buddhist Establishment", *IESHR*, vol. XXXIII, no. 1, 1996, pp. 1-37.
18. Barbara Stoler Miller, ed., *The Powers of Art: Patronage in Indian Culture*, New Delhi: Oxford University Press, 1992.

19. Devangana Desai, *Erotic Sculpture of India: A Socio-Cultural Study*, New Delhi: Tata McGraw Hill, 1985, pp. 16, 26.

20. While the world of the householder or the social domain was distinct from the monastic, the latter was an ideal to be aspired to. Some commentators seek to emphasise that asceticism was an ideal only in the spiritual philosophic sphere and not necessarily in the domestic social sphere. While this may have been true, the ascetic ideal was certainly viewed as being on a higher moral plane.

21. Gerda Lerner, *The Creation of Patriarchy*, Oxford University Press, New York, 1986, p. 5.

22. Kumkum Roy, op. cit., p. 212.

23. John Berger, *Ways of Seeing*, New Delhi: Penguin Press, 1975, p. 125.

24. P. Jaini, op. cit., p. x; Kumkum Roy, *Women in Early Indian Society*, p. 8, says women had no voice in the composition, compilation, preservation and transmission of such texts.

25. I have made field trips to various excavation sites such as Sanghol, Sunet, Vidiśā, Bhīta, Ujjain, Mathurā, Jhusi, Kauśāmbī, Kāśī, Kārle, Bhaja, Bhedsā, Pītalkhorā, Ajantā Kānheri, among others. Site museums and regional museums too have figured prominently in the field trips.

26. *Theragāthā*, tr. K.R. Norman, London: Pali Text Society, 1969; *Therīgāthā*, ed. Mrs. Rhys Davids, London: Oxford University Press, 1909; *Therīgāthā: The Elders' Verses, II*, tr. K.R. Norman, London: Pali Text Society, 1971. These are Psalms of the Elders, Monks and Nuns. The *Therīgāthā* is a rare text in which women's voices are recorded, however, formalised may be the format. Nuns formed a significant portion of patrons of art in the period and their attitudes towards religion, society and piety are significant.

27. *The Buddhacarita or Acts of The Buddha*, tr. E.H. Johnston, New Delhi: Motilal Banarsidass, 1972.

28. *Saundarānanda of Aśvaghoṣa*, ed. E.H. Johnston, New Delhi: Motilal Banarsidass, 1975.

29. *The Jataka or Stories of the Buddha's Former Births, Translated From the Pali By Various Hands*, 6 vols., ed. E.D. Cowell, New Delhi: Motilal Banarsidass, 1990 (rpt.).

30. *The Laws of Manu*, tr. Wendy Doniger with Brian K. Smith, New Delhi: Penguin Books, 1992 (rpt.); *The Laws of Manu*, tr. George Bühler, SBE, vol. 25, Oxford: Clarendon Press, 1886; rpt., New Delhi: Low Price Publications, 2002.

31. *Nāṭyaśāstra Ascribed to Bharata Muni*, 2 vols., ed. and tr. Manmohan Ghosh, Calcutta: Granthalaya Pvt. Ltd., 1967. The text has been dated between second century BCE to third century CE. This treatise lays down the rules and character of drama and dance. It refers to proscenium structures, performances, festivals, players and audience, especially in the urban context.

32. *The Mṛchhakaṭika of Śūdraka*, ed. M.R. Kale, New Delhi: Motilal Banarsidass, (3rd rev. edn.), 1972. The date of this text is debatable. Some scholars place it between the second-third century CE and others in the Gupta period. The play is very significant indicator of the life, attitudes and sensibilities found in north India towns. Especially revealing for understanding gender relations. It has been interpreted as having inspired the Bacchanalian scenes found at Mathurā.

33. *Kāmasūtra of Vātsyāyana*, Mulk Raj Anand and Lance Dane, New Delhi: Arnold Heinemann, 1982; *Kāmasūtra*, ed. and tr. Richard F. Burton, New Delhi: Penguin, rpt. 1987.

34. *Arthaśāstra of Kauṭilya*, ed. and tr. R. Shamasastry, Mysore (8th edn.) 1967: Date is debatable though the core is probably Mauryan, though additions were made up to the third century CE.

35. R.S. Sharma, *Material Culture and Social Formations in Ancient India*, Delhi: Macmillan Publishers, 1983, pp. 124-28.

36. Peter Burke, *Popular Culture in Early Modern Europe*, ACLS, POD, 2008, pp. 70-71.

37. Uma Chakravarti, *Men, Women and Beasts: The Interface Between High Tradition and Popular Tradition in Cultural Production*, New Delhi: Nehru Memorial Museum and Library, 1992.

# 1

# Gender and Art
## Paradigms and Problematics

Concepts such as nudity, fertility, *prakṛti*, have become part of the vocabulary of the history of early Indian art, and are accepted as universal and as given. Their gendered nature and multiple meanings embedded therein have thus been largely ignored. This gender blindness is evident in the classification of images such as Śrī-Lakṣmī, Mother and Child, *yakṣī* into "categories" that seek universal explanations for otherwise inexplicable representations. An alternate method of seeking the engendered meanings of such representations throws up a more gender sensitive picture of the society of early India; a picture gleaned through a study of representations, their transformation and evolution over a period of five centuries (200 BCE to 300 CE).

The art of this period is certainly not the earliest art produced in India. It is, however, the first body of art that survives in significant quantities and encompasses within its ambit considerable regional variations.[1] This art forms a basis for subsequent art forms, and many gender identities find representation. Thus it lends itself to an analysis from a gender perspective. The period is also critical for gender formation and setting forth of gender archetypes and stereotypes. Gender formation, in turn, has a far-reaching effect on art production. A recovery of the archives of the times leading to crystallisation of gender, and the setting forth of gender archetypes, is therefore useful for an understanding of intention, agency and patronage patterns in early Indian art.

The section below seeks to outline the manner in which gender is constructed within the largely patriarchal ideologies of Brāhmanism-Hinduism, Buddhism and Jainism. The analysis takes cognisance of the fact that the patriarchal dominance is neither uniform over time, nor evenly spread over all religious ideologies. Within the above framework, a study of the concomitant influence of this dominance over art production and consumption is also attempted. While Buddhism and Jainism are opposed to the rigid and hierarchical Brāhmanical ritual and social structure, they rarely critique the powerful patriarchy inherent in Brāhmanism. Buddhism and Jainism, instead privilege renunciation, withdrawal from the secular social world and an avoidance of the sensual/sexual. Thus canonical Buddhists and Jaina texts often propagate a vehemently negative perception of women, particularly in relation to female anatomy.[2]

Certain attitudes towards masculinity and femininity crystallise during this period, leading to the construction of archetypes and stereotypes. Most of the texts composed during the period reflect and reinforce them. The *Manusmṛti*, one of the most influential socio-legal treatises of the period, is a prime example. Art production is an integral part of such a process and art in turn may have influenced the manner in which these religious systems perceived men and women in their own society or societies.

While the dominant discourse intrinsic in all the above ideologies is largely misogynist; a multiplicity of voices[3] exists within these rampant misogynisms that fracture, challenge or even invert the dominant. For example, the Jātaka tradition, in its origin, is relatively autonomous of monk-male-canonical control, and records resistances to dominant patriarchal ideas.[4] Women, along with the marginalised poor and low castes,[5] do attempt to invert the dominant paradigm, though with limited success. In art too, there is a certain strain or discourse that is not completely subsumed by the seemingly all-encompassing patriarchy; this allows a space for women that may not have been envisaged for them in texts. This divergence between text and visual representation, studied in this work, significantly reveals the multiplicity of voices within gender formation.

It may however be mentioned that gender identities, as constructed in text and image, are not monolithic. Men and women are depicted in accordance with the roles that they were ascribed or that they assumed (in the art production of the period) such as those of prince/princess, monk, nun, *yakṣa, yakṣī*. Each ideology, in order to understand and organise its reality, creates well-defined conceptual categories.

Over a period of time categorisations based on gender and sex have been attempted. The Jaina text *Jīvājīvābhigama Sūtra*, while dealing with the entire created world, divides females into *tiyañcayonikastrī*s, *manuṣyastrī*s and *devastrī*s, i.e female animals, humans and divinities.[6] Classical Sanskrit texts such as the *Nāṭyaśāstra* classify women into three categories, viz. *devī*, *nāyikā* and *gaṇikā* corresponding to goddess, heroine (human) and prostitute.[7] Such a classification, on the one hand, is based on the gender roles expected of women, and on the other on their status in the eye of the beholder; the highest being the *devī* and the lowest the *gaṇikā*.

Without assigning value to any group, one classification of women this work makes is under four groups: wives, mothers, non-wives and semi-divine feminine representations (which are outside conventional societal groupings).[8] The most important category of women, in both the

Brāhmanic and the heterodox textual tradition, is that of the **wife**, the basis of the legitimate family. From her wifehood emerges the class of **mothers**, since legitimate wives alone are allowed to be conferred legitimate motherhood (there were mothers outside marriage but such women were not considered part of the social ordering). Closely connected with motherhood are the care and/or protection of children. In the third category lie women who did not perform functions that were considered socially productive, and are marginalised as women in society, i.e as **non-wives** — prostitutes and nuns. A majority of divine and human women are subsumed within the above categories. The group of the **semi-divine beings** — *yakṣīs*, *Apsaras*es, demonesses and ogresses — seem to be only partially governed by patriarchal order and are therefore more apt to transgress prescribed gender ideals.

There are some concepts that cut across the division of women described above. These include women's relationship to salvation, to creation, conceptualising of the female body as nude and fertile and the construction of other gender stereotypes. These concepts apply in varying degrees to different groupings of women — as wife, mother, non-wife or semi-divine *yakṣī*/ogress.

The above exercise may prove to be more meaningful for art historical research in the framework envisaged by Judith Butler. She opines that gender is not just a social construct, but a kind of performance, a show we put on, a set of signs we wear, as costume or design — hence as far from essence as can be.[9] Given this, gender can be recognised through certain outward manifestations. These include postures, clothes, and jewellery (visible in sculptures and paintings) that are used only by a single gender or may be shared by two or more genders.[10] In the latter case, the question as to whether similar devices and emblems may connote the same thing, or differ in implications from gender to gender, is beneficial.

This work recognises that the production of representational images is a cultural means of responding to and shaping the conditions of social existence. The selection of features to be incorporated in human images promulgates stereotypes of natural and essential human behaviour.[11] Attitudes, stereotypes and choices inherent in text and image are critical to engendering the art of early India.

### 1.1 Sex-Gender

Women as a sex are perceived as a separate group due to their biological distinctiveness. Gerda Lerner states that this term defines women, not as sub-group or a minority group, but as half of the whole. Men are the only other sex. Sex is based on biology.[12]

Gender is the cultural definition of behaviour defined as appropriate to the sexes in a given society at a given time. In so far as gender is a construct, it has a form and a manifestation that has been encoded into stereotypes and notions of what constitutes masculinity and femininity, along with an idealisation of the same. Thus, gender is defined by a set of cultural roles. It is a costume, a mask in which men and women act out their unequal relationships. This inequality is reflected in the art of a particular society. In certain societies, making women invisible in art and through absence in the dominant discourses of the time manifests this. In case of ancient India women are very visible both in history[13] and in the visual world.[14] However, this visibility in the early Indian art does not signify either equality of status or equivalence of power in the socio-legal sphere.

The complex interaction between Sex and Gender can be understood through what has been termed the sex-gender system, referring to the institutionalised system which allots resources, property and privileges to persons according to culturally defined gender roles.[15] Thus it is sex that determines that women are child-bearers and it is the sex-gender system which assumes that they should be child-rearers. Gender is a set of culturally constructed social relationships to which we can give the same label cross-linguistically or cross-culturally, because they are connected to sex differences in which the connections are conventional and arbitrary in so far as they are not reducible to, or directly derivative of, natural biological facts.[16]

Men, too, like women, do not constitute a monolithic group. Their access to power, resources and positions, however, are based on factors such as class, caste and the like. The essential difference between the genders in early India is that the primary identity of men is linked to their social and economic status, but for women their primary identity is located in the fact that they are women (or female) as a sex. Their secondary identity is linked to the gender role they fulfil, be it as a wife, mother or prostitute. It is only subsequent to the establishment of these identities that women are classified according to the caste and class to which they belong.[17]

The endeavour in this work is to recover the forms and contexts in which patriarchal dominance over women appears. Art is one way in which unequal gender relationships are fixed and legitimised. Art and architecture represent, from the vast infinity of human experience, certain select moments in monumental images and rituals. They thus reveal the thematic and material choices that the patron, sculptor or the institution make. Such "moments" represent those aspects of action that reinforce the formation of an elite class, stereotyping all women (and men) in extremely limited ways.

This work seeks to recover gender dichotomy created through gender stereotyping and the increasing sexualisation of representations in texts, images, and monuments of the period. This includes a historiography of how gender imagery has been understood, and how the dominant approaches have led to the reinforcement of gender stereotypes in the modern perception of ancient Indian art.

History of ancient Indian art has had limited engenderment, with most authors providing gender neutral, if not gender blind, explanations for the overtly sexualised images of men and women in the period.[18] Some effort has been made to rectify this in recent years by scholars such as Vidya Dehejia who feel that in art we see a positive engenderment through the affiliation of woman with nature and fertility.[19] This positive engenderment is, however, neither uniform nor the only engendered factor within the artistic discourse. The study of the issue of engenderment in terms of the ideal models of femininity and masculinity constructed in contemporary texts can be salutary. They reveal connections that reinforced notions about idealised behaviour expected of the two genders and the mechanisms employed to enforce such behavioural patterns. Patriarchy is a system of dominance that uses both state control as well as ideology to perpetuate itself.[20] Ideological conditioning seems to have been the more pervasive means of achieving this dominance. This is manifested in the texts as well as in the arts by creating categories and stereotypes that became accepted and socialised and internalised.

Gender polarity, however, is not seminal in structuring the study of women. Art historians do not dichotomise objects into "art" (as opposed to non-art) or "history" (as opposed to criticism). The perceived separation between architecture and the "minor," "decorative," or pictorial arts, too, is not material to such an analysis. Historians need not sever the sacred from the secular, Sanskrit or classical sources from vernacular texts, or literature from other writings. Current scholarship finds choices between the historically contingent and absolute universal "causes" less problematic. Sex/gender systems, as has been pointed out, are not a-historical emanations of the human mind; they are products of historical human activity. The given stereotypes or truths in art history relating to gender portrayal should thus be displaced from their privileged positions. This book re-examines some such "truths," to reveal yet another layer in the artistic record that contributes to the ideological work of gender formation. The multiplicity of meanings that artworks contain and their role in the ideological formation of gender identities are also examined.

## 1.2 Strīsvabhāva-Strīdharma

Apart from a process of dis-privileging of women as a category that took place, a more effective de-valorisation of women was being effected as well. This is mirrored in the textual tradition of this period. Women are defined as an inferior and evil set of beings. They are depicted as culturally and biologically — and therefore inherently — inferior and evil. This intrinsic evilness is referred to as *strīsvabhāva*, the inherent *svabhāva* or *prakṛti* (nature or character) of women. It is thus a taint that can never be removed, but only socialised and controlled within the framework of the *varṇāśramadharma*, rendering it less dangerous. Such socialisation can be successful if women follow their *strīdharma*, that is, the right conduct prescribed for women.

Julia Leslie first studies the *strīsvabhāva* and *strīdharma* dichotomy in the context of an early modern text called the *Strīdharmapaddhati*,[21] which is further applied by Uma Chakravarti to a larger context of impulse control in women through instruments of state and ideology.[22] The *strīsvabhāva-strīdharma* model helps us understand the contemporary perception of both genders, though it specifically refers to women. The concepts can be usefully applied to the cultural sphere, especially to investigate whether and to what extent these concepts influenced the production and consumption of arts.

Women of all *varṇa*s as a category are often grouped with the śūdras who as a *varṇa* occupy an inferior social position. In the *Nāṭyaśāstra* the secondary position of women is clearly articulated in the statement, "Fear relates to women and persons of the inferior type."[23] Being born a woman or a śūdra is seen to be the result of sins committed in a previous birth.[24] This inferiority is reinforced through rituals. It is prescribed that a twice-born (*dvija*) should perform the bathing ritual with *mantra*s but women and śūdras without *mantras*.[25] Women are deprived the right of Vedic education and *upanayana*[26] and were increasingly relegated to the status of śūdras. Like the latter, they had to sip water only once rather than twice to purify themselves.[27]

As early as the later Vedic period, women are linked with other "impure" creatures. In the *Śatapatha Brāhmaṇa*, it is articulated that a woman, a śūdra, a dog and a crow are all embodiments of untruth, sin and darkness.[28] This impurity has been regarded as the source of evil in all women. On the one hand they were often equated to impure beings like śūdras, dogs, and so forth, while on the other there was the impurity of menstruation, a biological phenomenon. Blood, especially menstrual blood, is considered to be one of the twelve impurities of the body.[29] It is also a reminder of the sin of brāhmaṇa-murder, *brāhmaṇa-hatyā* that women as a category accepted on behalf of Indra. This story is first mentioned in *Taittirīya-Saṁhitā*[30] and is repeated with some changes in the *Mahābhārata*.[31] In order to escape the consequence of the sin of brāhmanicide, Indra transferred it to the earth, trees and women. Each was granted a boon to compensate for their taking on the guilt of brāhminicide; women received the boon that, unlike other animals, they will be able to enjoy sexual pleasure at any time. But as punishment for assuming one-third of the guilt women have to menstruate.[32] Menstruation is thus simultaneously a sign of women's sexuality and impurity. It also marks the woman permanently as a scapegoat for male transgressions against their own patriarchal law. By means of this myth, the scapegoat-identity becomes an inescapable part of woman's "nature" (*strīsvabhāva*). The patriarchal system can only survive on the basis of this perception.

The idea that sexuality constitutes women's essential nature is stressed in these texts. Through this ideational construct, it is apparent that the physical and biological composition of women becomes integral to gender formation in the period. This is mirrored to an extent in contemporary art. The emphasis on sexuality, which seems to be built into early sculptures, especially of women, has often been commented upon.[33] What is uncertain is whether this sexuality in art has only negative connotations or whether it contains multiple meanings that are not confined to the idea of degrading and uncontrolled feminine sexuality.

The texts, be they Brāhmanical, Buddhist or Jaina, are however almost unequivocal on the issue of women's evilness and sexual inconstancy. Misogyny seems like a common thread that connects texts of various religious systems. As early as the *Śatapatha Brāhmaṇa*, the need to control the sexuality of women and its dangerous inconstant nature is expressed. It is feared that the wife may go to other men.[34] The *Āpastamba Dharmasūtra* states that husbands should not allow other men to go near the wife lest their seed fall into her.[35] The central notion here is that the wife would either welcome the advances of another man if he came within her orbit or would be too weak to resist these advances and also that such an act would result in endangering the purity of the offspring.

The cause of such unfaithfulness is seen to be the inherent character of women, which is considered sinful by nature. In the *Mahābhārata* women were considered evil right from the beginning of creation.[36] At the time of creation the original Manu gave to women the habit of lying, sitting around, an indiscriminate love of ornaments, anger, meanness and bad conduct.[37]

Similar misogynist references to the inherent nature of women are also found in Buddhist literature of the time. Women are a sex composed of wickedness and guile; womankind holds truth for falsehood and falsehood for truth.[38] Also they are as unstable as sand and as cruel as snakes.[39]

The Jātaka stories abound with references to fickle women.[40] For example, in one of the stories[41] it is contended, "As greedily as cows seek pastures anew, women never satiated, yearn for mate upon mate." Even an old woman is considered a sexual hazard in the *Asatamantra Jātaka*.[42] In another case, in the *Bandhanamokkha Jātaka*, the inconstancy of the queen is explained by the chaplain, "she is not to blame for the passions of women are insatiate and she does but act according to her inborn nature."[43]

The *Saundarānanda* by Aśvaghoṣa gives a poetic account of the life of Sundarī and Nanda, the latter being the recalcitrant cousin of Gautama whom the Buddha eventually persuades to leave his wife and join the *bhikkhu saṁgha*, the monk community. A benevolent disciple of the Buddha (in Canto VIII) explains the evil influence of women on men:

> The blazing fire can be held, the bodiless wind can be held, the furious can be held but the minds of women cannot be held. Women take no account of beauty, sovereignty, intelligence, race and valour. They strike indiscriminately like rivers infested with crowds of crocodiles. A woman never heeds soft words or coaxing or affection. Even a well-tested woman is fickle, therefore place no more trust in them than in enemies.[44]

Here, on the one hand, the idea of women as evil, unfaithful and untrustworthy is elaborated and, on the other, the concept of women as the "Other," the enemy, is articulated. Thus, all women-evil-sexual are seen to be enemies of the faith and principal factors that would lead to the downfall of men-virtuous-ascetics. In such a discourse the gender dichotomy is so constructed that the male is normative while the female is an aberration and therefore requires to be restrained as well as to be resisted.

The difficulty women have in maintaining prescribed gender roles is elucidated through transgressions. "They are (as masterful) as husbands and (as submissive) as sons to the vicious. They behave greedily with the rich and treat the poor with contempt."[45] Such "contrary" behaviour — contrary to male ideals of femininity — on the part of women arises from a perceived impurity of mind, which in turn is associated with the biological construction of the sex itself. The monk trying to convince Nanda comments, "Such is the mind of woman, ungrateful, ignoble, unsteady; how can the wise man set his heart on such capricious creatures."[46] He goes on to ask, "but if you do not see how their hearts are flighty, subtle in intention and working mischief by deceit, do you not see how their bodies are impure, verily oozing abodes of evil."[47] "The purity you see in nails, teeth, skin and hair which are impure is nothing but imagination on your part. Do you not see, you simpleton, the real *nature and origin* (emphasis mine) of women?"[48]

First, the physical characteristics that constitute feminine attractiveness such as hair and skin are linked to sexuality (or at least sexual temptation for men). Secondly, the danger and evilness of women is embedded in contemporary notions of female sexuality. Such is the danger that woman's sexuality presents that lawgivers have to make special provisions for guarding against it so that women themselves do not transgress sexual and social norms. Similar rules are naturally not applicable to the guardians of women, viz. men. Manu states that women need to be guarded all the time. The reason given for caution is that the essential nature of women is insatiable. "Women do not care for beauty, nor is their attention fixed on age, (thinking), '(it is enough that) he is a man,' they give themselves to the handsome and to the ugly. Through their passion for men, through their mutable temper, through their natural heartlessness, they become disloyal towards their husbands, however, carefully they may be guarded in this (world)."[49] It goes on to say that "knowing their disposition, which the Lord of Creatures laid in them at the creation to be such, every man should exert to guard them."[50]

The basis of the idea that it is imperative to stringently guard female sexuality lies in the responsibility of women to produce legitimate children.

> The production of children, the nurture of those born and the daily life of men, (in these matters) the wife is visibly the cause. Offspring, (the due performance of) religious rites, faithful service, highest conjugal happiness and heavenly bliss for the ancestors and oneself, depend on one's wife alone.[51]

Thus, so far we have seen that in the majority of narrative and normative texts of the period *strīsvabhāva* or *strīprakṛti* is considered to be evil, sexually uncontrolled and inherent. On the other hand, we have another idea emerging: that of the good wife, performing her *strīdharma* by serving her husband. Broadly, the *strīdharma* doctrine dictates that women should be faithful and subservient to their husband and through such behaviour fulfil their *dharma*. This is their primary and singular *svadharma* or own *dharma* (righteous duty). In contradistinction to this, men had many layers of *dharma* that they could and ought to perform such as *jāti, varṇa, śreṇī dharma*s based on caste, class and guild affiliations. The prescription of *strīdharma* or *pativratādharma* (duty of the vows to one's husband) serves to control and organise the maternal reproductive power of women within a patriarchal system. This model is a significant ideological construct that is ideally internalised by women and which sought to ensure the voluntary subordination of women. Its endurance and influence over societal patterns till present times testifies to the effectiveness of the "ideal."[52] The impact and implications of the *strīdharma* concept on the representation of the wife and the couple in art will be dealt in detail later in this study.[53]

In this conflict between nature and duty one can view *strīsvabhāva* as the biological given or a natural state, while *strīdharma* is an ideal gender role that women are supposed to inculcate. This is further clarified in a brief survey of social behaviour prescribed for women in contemporary normative literature. Manu says that no woman can be guarded by force alone and it is a woman who guards herself who is well guarded.[54] Manu says that a woman controlling her thoughts, speech, and acts, who does not violate her duty towards her lord, dwells with him after death in heaven, and is called *sādhvī* (the faithful wife) by the virtuous.[55] This ideal of self-sacrificing service is reflected in the Buddhist literature also such as the *Sambula Jātaka*[56] where the virtuous wife is able to cure her husband of leprosy through the power of her virtue.

The desire to convert the *strīsvabhāva* into *strīdharma* reflected in stories such as the *Sambulā Jātaka* demonstrates one manner in which ideological conditioning is achieved. Similar strategies of socialisation are witnessed in art also where certain gender roles are glorified, and others vilified. Vilification occurs when the *strīdharma* ideal is disregarded and sexuality is not controlled within the legitimate institution of the patriarchal family. It then takes on demonic proportions as in the case of the Assamukhi *yakkhi*[57] (*Pls*. 7.24, 7.25, 7.26, 7.27) who devours her lovers, or the sirens who entice sailors and then kill them.[58] In the oft-depicted *Chaddanta Jātaka*[59] (*Pls*. 4.42, 4.43), Culā, the junior wife and chief queen in a later birth, is jealous and evil and is contrasted to the good and benevolent *bodhisattva*. Sexual freedom is depicted as simultaneously dangerous and enticing in the narrative art of the period, as further discussed in the Chapter 7 on "Strategies of Evil."

The role of wife as tame and accepting is

similarly repeated in representational types such as the *dampati* and also in narrative art. In the latter category one can place famous parables like the *Vessantara Jātaka* where the wife of Prince Vessantara (along with the children) is given away in charity by the prince himself. Women and children are deprived of any agency in this story, devoted as it is to extolling the virtues of the prince.

In fact, women and children are often constructed in similar fashion, perhaps to emphasise their dependent status. This is done in art either using the device of diminution (though this is not confined to depiction of women alone; it is applied to all subordinate beings) or/and by placing the child on the left, which is traditionally regarded as the feminine side. This is also the position occupied by the woman in the *dampati* portrayals, which depict legitimate man-wife relationships. In case of *mithuna* (erotic couples) the opposite placement is applied as if to emphasise the purely sexual but non-productive or at least non-socialised nature of the relationship.

In the entire textual discourse one finds very few voices contesting the dominant discourse on inherent nature of women. One such voice is that of Somā, a *therī* or nun, recorded in the *Therīgāthā* and also in the *Saṁyutta Nikāya*. In response to the challenge posed by Māra, the Evil One, on the futility of women trying to reach *nirvāṇa*, she replies:

> What should a woman's nature signify
> When consciousness is tense and firmly set,
> When knowledge rolleth ever on, when she
> By insight rightly comprehends the Norm?
> To one for whom the question doth arise:
> Am I a woman [in these] matters, or
> Am I a man, or what not am I then?
> To such a one is Māra fit to talk.[60]

In the other version the ability to overcome women's nature is even more strongly stated:

> How should a woman's nature hinder us/
> Whose hearts are firmly set, who ever move
> How should a woman's nature hinder us . . .
> With growing knowledge onward in the path?
> What can that signify to one in whom
> Insight doth truly comprehend the norm?
> On every hand the love of pleasure fields,
> And the thick gloom of ignorance is rent
> In twain. Know this, O Evil One, avaunt!
> Here, O Destroyer! Shalt thou not prevail.[61]
>
> — tr. Mrs. Rhys Davids

### 1.3 Beautiful Women and Self-Controlled Men

A text-image study of men and women is significant in so far as it indicates how gender is perceived and constructed by a particular society, the manner in which behaviour and ideals are socialised. The feminine is essentialised as beautiful and graceful but also physically uncontrolled or uncontrollable and the masculine as mentally restrained, competent and physically brave.[62]

In this context I would like to put forward that feminisation is usually accompanied by eroticisation of the female; men construct the discourse of pleasure and beauty (see *Pls.* 1.5, 1.6). In art, such a discourse may have been used for didactic purposes or to attract divine and human pleasure, but it is the hegemonic patriarchal ideology, which decides what and how it was to be displayed. (Both masculinity and femininity are constructed by men, creating a gendered imagery.) This is evident in the manner in which the ideal of femininity is projected throughout the art of the early period. The majority of reliefs, sculptures, and terracottas depict women with large breasts, small waists and wide hips. I would like to add that in the art of the period and also of subsequent periods, women themselves (*Pls.* 4.35, 4.36) or male paramours (*Pls.* 4.30, 4.31, 4.33) assisting women are shown as enhancing their physical beauty through the application of make-up, combing of hair, bathing (*Pl.* 6.19), and looking at themselves in the mirror (*Pl.* 6.18), as seen in the *yakṣī-śālabhañjikā* depictions as well as in the *Saundarānanda* episodes. *Śṛṅgāra* or decorating the self seems to be a feminine domain. *Śṛṅgāra* is also a *rasa-bhāva* that evokes erotic love and is considered incomplete without women; women are considered essential for its evocation in performance.[63] I have as yet not encountered any parallel representation of a man engaged in *śṛṅgāra* in early Indian art.

Physical beauty is to a large extent associated with sexuality. It follows that women, being defined by their sexuality should be beautiful (one may extend this argument to say that this emphasis on charming physical form is to compensate for the lack of ideal "masculine" traits like behavioural and mental self-restraint and asceticism). Women are classified according to the stages of youth: through dresses, posture, and their limbs as well as (inner) qualities.[64] It is clear from the description of these four stages that the body and its ornamentation are of primary importance when it comes to imagining the female as a woman, especially as a public, *bāhya* (outside) woman. A woman in her primary youth has an enthusiasm for sexual acts, is characterised by plump thighs, cheeks, hips and breasts which are firm and conducive to (lit. charming in) love's pleasures.[65] Similarly, the other stages are characterised by full and round limbs, plump breasts and a slender waist or the lack of all these. It is said that a woman has her female charms reduced if she has slightly pale cheeks, or less fleshy hips, lips, and breasts; and also reduced enthusiasm for sexual acts.[66] In the *Arthaśāstra*, a prostitute is to be classified as belonging to the first, middle and highest rank according to her beauty and splendid jewellery. If she were to lose the first then she could become a nurse (*mātṛkā*), but if she lost the second, or if it were stolen, she or the thief is to be fined.[67] It is therefore required that *veśyā*s and *gaṇikā*s (prostitutes and courtesans) be beautiful. In contradistinction, nuns are to be deliberately made unattractive and marked off as sexually unavailable by depriving them of attributes that constitute beauty, for example by shaving off their hair. Prostitutes and nuns represent the two ends of female sexuality. The former is used and celebrated for sexuality while the sexuality is denied to the latter.[68]

This physical, mental and social gender bipolarity[69] between men and women, constructed through cultural instruments such as literature and art, reflects societal concerns and stereotypes. Direct connections between Śāstric texts on cultural production, and the actual visual product, are difficult to establish; nevertheless one can posit that they were products of common cultural milieu. It has been asserted in early Vāstuśāstra and Śilpaśāstra texts, such as the *Viṣṇudharmottara Purāṇa*, that the canons of painting are difficult to understand without an acquaintance with dancing.[70] Classical Indian drama too depends a great deal on dance. Visual and performing arts are considered to be interdependent in the *Nāṭyaśāstra*.[71]

The *Nāṭyaśāstra* is a useful text for a study such as ours because it talks about representation and the response that such portrayal should invoke in the audience. The *rasa-bhāva* theory expounded in the *Nāṭyaśāstra* and elaborated upon by commentators like Abhinavagupta[72] reveals the manner in which men and women are articulated on stage.

While the date of the *Nāṭyaśāstra* has been disputed, the estimates ranging from the fifth century BCE to the first century CE, it can be said with a degree of certainty that it was in existence in the post-Mauryan, pre-Gupta period and is possibly anterior to Bhāsa.[73] It has been ascribed to Bharata Muni who himself acknowledges that it was based on pre-existing traditions and texts of anterior dramatologists.[74]

The *Nāṭyaśāstra* too has references to an ideal man and an ideal woman. It also takes cognisance of various differences in human kind and classifies men and women on the basis of their physical and mental characteristics. Such descriptions help us analyse the manner in which a woman's body is constituted in the literary tradition. This is also reflected in visual terms in the art of the period. A further investigation as to how feminine identities are envisaged and constructed differently from masculine identities may help us recover gender biases embedded in such representations.

The *rasa-bhāva* theory is the foundation upon which the entire theory of performance is based. *Bhāva* is the feeling, emotion, sentiment that an actor portrays on stage, and *rasa* is the response that *bhāva* invokes in the audience. The circumstances or reasons that cause this *bhāva* to be evoked are called *vibhāva* while the changes that an actor causes in himself/herself and the tools that s/he uses to portray a particular *bhāva* are called *anubhāva*. For example, if s/he wants to portray the *krodha-bhāva*, the *vibhāva* will be humiliation by someone, which will subsequently lead to anger, and *anubhāva* would be knitted eyebrows, bitten lips, heavy breathing, and big, strong steps on stage.[75]

It is explained in the *Nāṭyaśāstra* that *bhāva* arises from *sattva* (essence) and *sattva*[76] partakes in the nature of the body. It goes on to say that *sattva* with excessive feeling manifests itself in relation to persons of the female sex,[77] implying that women as a gender have an essentially uncontrolled nature.

It explains that the ten natural graces of women, *strīnāṁ svabhāva*, are sportive mimicry, amorous gesture, dishabille, confusion, hysterical mood, and manifestation of affection, pretended anger, affected coldness, lolling and want of response.[78] The *Nāṭyaśāstra* goes on to describe the involuntary graces of women and then gives the eight aspects of *sattva* of the male gender.

I describe these female graces and male *sattva* (essence) in detail because, though some of the terms used for both masculine and feminine *sattva* and *alaṁkāra* are the same, the terms connote different qualities for each gender. The *Nāṭyaśāstra* itself is cognisant of these differences, stating that in theatrical production the psychological states (*bhāva*) of women are all to be made graceful and those of men are to be endowed with self-control and equanimity.[79]

Such differentiation within the original text may be recognised as a gendered understanding of constituent characteristics of the sexes as attributes of idealised behaviour, and characteristics are cultural constructs, not biologically predetermined.[80]

For women the word *śobhā*[81] is explained as

*rūpa-yauvana-lāvaṇya*
*rūpabhogopabṛnhitaiḥ* ।
*alaṅkāraṇamaṅgānāṁ yat*
*sā śobheti bhaṇyate* ॥

This has been translated by Manmohan Ghosh as the decoration of limbs on account of good physical form, youth and loveliness being rendered manifest after the enjoyment of love is called *śobhā* (beauty).[82]

Compare this to the description of *śobhā* as it is used for men.

*Dākṣyaṁ śauryamathotsāho*
*nīcārtheṣu jugupsanaṁ* ।
*uttamaiśca gunaiḥ spardhā*
*yatra śobheti sā smṛtā* ॥[83]

*Śobhā* here has been translated as: "skill (in various things), heroism and energy, aversion to mean acts and emulation of the best virtues constitute Brilliant Character — *śobhā*."

Another characteristic attributed both to men and women is *mādhurya*[84] that for women is *sarvāvasthāviśeśeṣu dīpteṣu laliteṣu ca, anulbaṇatvaṁ ceṣṭāyā mādhuryamiti kīrtitaṁ.*[85] This has been translated as "moderation of the movement (of limbs) in all conditions, especially in radiance (*dīpti*) and in lolling (*lalita*) is called Delicacy, *mādhurya*."[86] For men the same term has been characterised as

*abhyasāt karaṇānāṁ tu*
*śliṣṭatvaṁ yatra jāyate* ।
*mahatsvapi vikāreṣu*
*tanmādhuryamiti smṛtaṁ* ॥[87]

According to Ghosh this may be rendered as "If due to (long) practice (in this direction) one's sense organs retain their firmness even when great changes in the natural state have occurred, it is called Self-possession, *mādhurya*."

Another term shared by men and women is *audārya* though it connotes different qualities for both. For women it has been described as *audāryaṁ praśrayaḥ proktaḥ sarvāvasthānugo budhaiḥ*[88] (courteous bearing in all situations is called *audārya* by the wise). While for men it signifies

*dānam-abhyupapattiśca*
*tathā ca priyabhāṣaṇaṁ* ।
*svajane vā pare vāpi*
*tad-audāryam-iti smṛtaṁ* ॥[89]

Making gifts, bestowing favours and speaking sweet words to others as well as to one's own men is called Nobility (*audārya*).

The other qualities prescribed for men and women in the *Nāṭyaśāstra* are indicative of the stereotypical gender behaviour/qualities expected of the two. Traits considered attractive for women are *kānti — vijṇeyā ca tathā kāntiḥ śobhā eva pūrṇamanmatha,* along with *dīpti — kānti revati vistīrṇa dīpti ṛtyabhidhīyate.* "Beauty which is full of a lover's passion is called charm — *kānti.* A high degree of charm is called radiance — *dīpti.*"[90]

In contrast, it is advocated for men that they should inculcate *cāpale nānupahatā sarvārtheṣvivikatthanā, svabhāṅkī citta vṛtti-dhaviya mitya bhi dhīyate* — a natural bent of mind that is in all matters free from rashness and boasting which is called *dhairya* (self control).[91] The quality of not becoming agitated in speaking or acting anything (lit. in practice) is called courage — *prāgalbhya*[92]*-prayoganiḥ sādhvasatā prāgalbhyaṁ samudāhūtaṁ.* Other virtues prescribed for men are *vilāsa*[93] and *sthira sañcāriṇī*; the latter has been translated as Graceful Bearing constituted by "eyes moving straight, gait as graceful as that of a bull, and smiling words."

Even the *rasas* recommended for the consumption of men and women are different. While men are able to enjoy the more serious *rasas*, women can enjoy the *hāsya-rasa*.

Young people are pleased to see (the presentation of) love, the learned a reference to some (religious and philosophical) doctrine, the seekers after money to the topics of wealth, and the passionless the topics of liberation. Heroic persons are always pleased in the Odious and the Terrible Sentiments, personal combats and battles, and the old people in Purāṇic legends, and tales of virtue. And common women, children and uncultured persons are always delighted with the Comic Sentiment and remarkable costumes and make-up.[94]

Women and children are perceived as a gender that is uncultured.

The above-cited excerpts from the *Nāṭyaśāstra* make it clear that delineating distinct and separate gender identities is sought through performance. This is achieved through the differing qualities that women and men are supposed to portray. Even terms used in the text suggest a gender-differentiated manner. The same words connote different characteristics to describe men and women. While those words related to women tend to describe their physical characteristics and charm of manner — qualities for the gratification of males and useful for the private or domestic sphere — those related to men illustrate their ability, self-control and generosity, attributes important for public activity. Gender archetypes thus constructed for representation make women the lesser being — less evolved and sophisticated and therefore not fit for "higher activities and understanding."

Faced with a lack of evidence, one cannot ascribe an exact approximation between the *Nāṭyaśāstra* (*NŚ*) and sculpture. Certain similarities between the *NŚ* and sculptural production are noticeable which may indeed derive from a common cultural matrix from which the two traditions drew inspiration. One

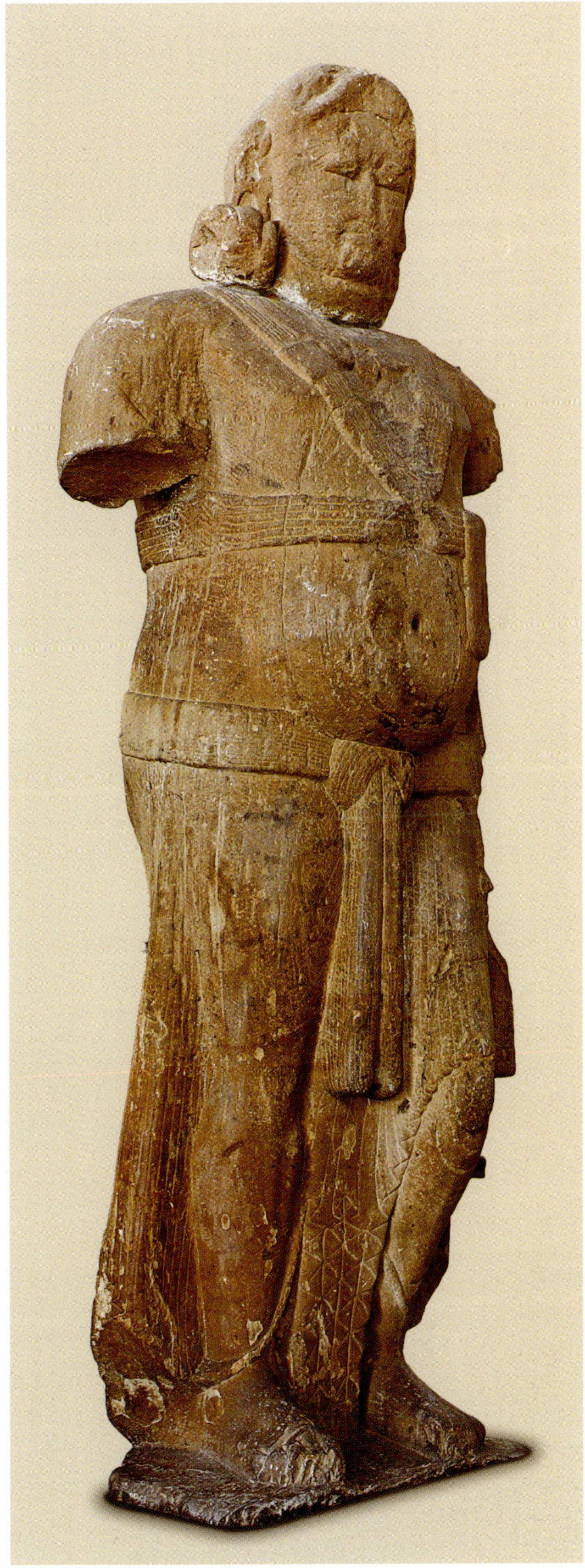

1.1 *Yakṣa*, inscribed, made by Gomitaka, the pupil of Kuṇika, standing, Buff sandstone, second century BCE, Parkham, Mathurā district, UP. GMM.

striking element shared by the two is that the feminine is represented through physical traits, which emphasise sexuality and beauty (*Pls.* 1.2, 1.3), while the masculine is represented so as to highlight strength and nobility (*Pls.* 1.1, 6.5). It may be surmised from the above exposition that similar archetypes may have been utilised while making sculptural images. The *Nāṭyaśāstra* exposition may help us read the gender codes embedded in sculptural representation.

The emphasis on physicality in constituting the feminine has been noticed within the Buddhist and Jaina discourse. In the *Therīgāthā*, the names of nuns such as Abhirūpa Nanda and Sundarī Nandā are descriptive of their beautiful forms. In fact, the beauty of *therī*s (nuns) is commented upon and condemned on account of its presumed transience/superficiality.[95] This is especially true of former courtesans whose feminine body is indeed beautiful, but this beauty is illusory and temporary.

### 1.4 The Body: Spiritual and Physical

Physicality is therefore significant in gendering the female image. The locus of this physicality — the body, which is a deeply gendered entity — thus merits deeper scrutiny. Given the above discussion on the inherent nature of women and on engendered performance, it is possible to say that gender differences are perceived and articulated in representations through the bodies of the two genders. Gender is to be accepted as contingent role-playing, projected through performance made of feminine and masculine qualities, rather than a given based on characteristics inherent in male and female physiology. Once this premise is accepted, we can

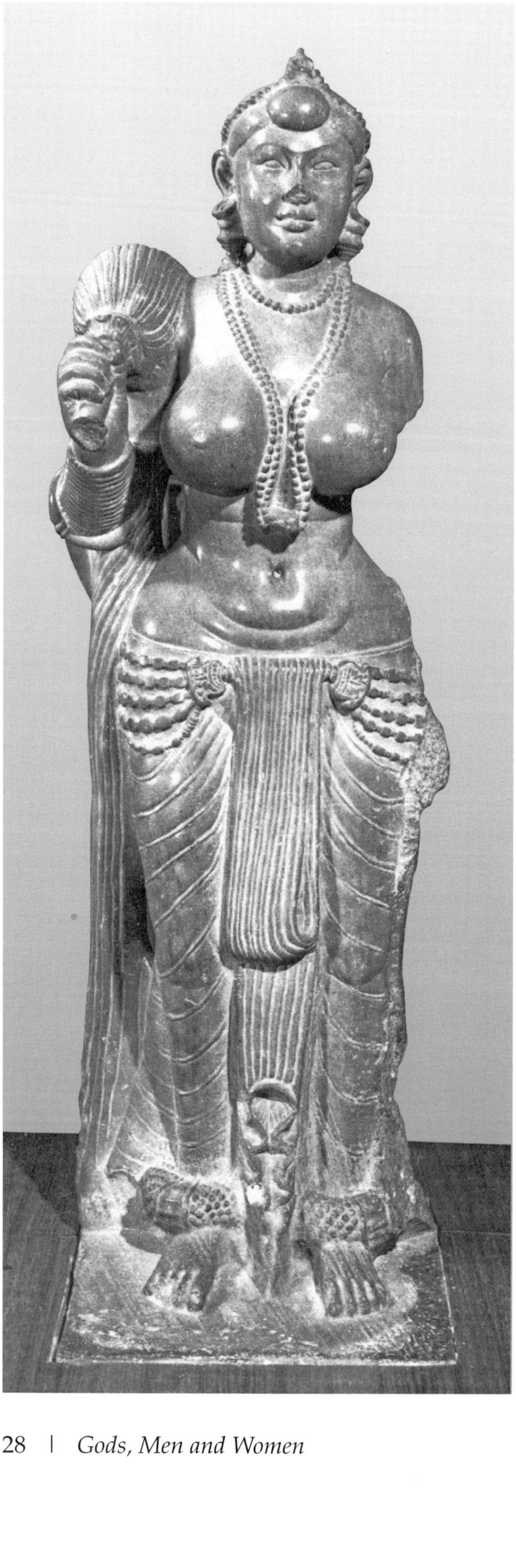

1.2 *Yakṣī*, Chunar sandstone, third century BCE, Didarganj, Patna Museum.

try to look for essentialising attributes in bodies constructed in sculpture and other cultural products. To achieve this requires an investigation of stereotypes located in the bodies of men and women as delineated in art.

The study of the body in the context of ancient Indian art takes into account the role of art, eroticism and visuality — the gendered nature of seeing and power relations. It requires a search for polarities such as viewer/viewed = subject/object = active/passive = male/female = sexually empowered/sexually disempowered.[96] Whether such semantic and conceptual distinctions exist as neat categories during the early period is doubtful, though we have seen that in contemporary texts such as the *Nāṭyaśāstra*, certain dichotomies between genders are articulated, such as active/passive = mental/physical = male/female.

At the same time, for all the patriarchal control inherent in Indian culture, viewing is not just considered a male prerogative, nor is the arousal of homoerotic desire the prime issue in the reception and function of Indian art. Women too are presented as viewing males with desiring, eroticised glances or gazes, which frequently involve seeing the male as an artwork of sorts. In sum, what people see — whether real or artistic, male or female — is often presented in ancient Indian literature as inflicting a wide range of emotional and cognitive states on the viewer, whether male or female. However, if we take the testimony of the *Nāṭyaśāstra*, men are less likely to participate in "effeminate" behaviour or roles, such as the *śṛṅgāra-bhāva* that is more or less the exclusive domain of women.

In the surviving evidence, most visual representations have been located within a religious context. By association the body may be viewed as both spiritual and physical. In the case of representation of deities, the body can be, and often is, spiritual with metaphysical meanings embedded into it. With the human and semi-divine figures we can view the body and its engendering at both spiritual and physical levels.

### 1.5 The Body and Salvation

As a biological entity the female body is a significant factor in soteriological issues, especially in Jainism. Whether or not women could achieve *nirvāṇa*, and if not whether this was because of the biological inferiority of the female body as an issue evoked considerable debate amongst religious ideologues, with differing positions being argued by rival schools of the same religion.

Despite the supposed orthodoxy within Brāhmanism and its rigid patriarchal norms, one can discern contradictory positions *vis-à-vis* women.[97] On the one hand, goddesses are considered powerful, influential and effective;[98] on the other hand, we have the systemic and consistent disprivileging of women in historical texts.[99]

Despite the presence of various goddesses perceived to be special divine beings and not ordinary women within the Brāhmanic pantheon, Brāhmanism by arguing that by birth women are incapable of the right conduct and knowledge that can lead to *mokṣa*, almost unequivocally denies them salvation. The only way women can ordinarily hope to achieve *mokṣa* is to observe their *strīdharma*, to be good wives and mothers and eventually be reborn as a twice-born man, *dvija*, and it is only as a man can they succeed in achieving *mokṣa*.

Though patriarchal restrictions are more loosely prescribed in heterodox religious traditions, there is a tension within them on the issue of the ability of women playing a religiously active role, and especially regarding their capability to achieve *nirvāṇa* and *arhatship*. With their concern with renunciation of the world of sensual desire, the dominant ideological positions within Buddhism and Jainism reflect extreme misogynism focusing particularly on the female anatomy.[100]

In early Buddhism, there are no female *bodhisattvas*, though they could take on an animal form. Even the most religiously diligent women, in the view of Sāriputra, cannot acquire Buddhahood because women as a category cannot realise the status of Brahmā, Śakra, Great King, Emperor or an irreversible *bodhisattva*.[101] One of the most potent reasons given for this inability is that women do not have a penis, which could be sheathed as a sign of asexuality.[102]

Within Buddhism multi-vocal attitudes exist ranging from positive attitudes towards the female and the feminine to the completely derogatory and negative. Alan Sponberg is of the opinion that, in early Buddhism, we do not see "ambivalence of a single, uncertain voice" but "a multiplicity of voices," each expressing a different set of concerns among the members of the early Buddhist community. These ranged from soteriological inclusiveness, institutional inclusiveness and ascetic misogyny of the Theravādins to the soteriological androgyny of the Mahāyānists.[103] While salvation is available for women, there is a lot of scepticism within Buddhism about women's nature and their ability to achieve it.

In the *Therīgāthā* there are few instances of *therīs* achieving *nibbāna* or *nirvāṇa*. The monks reach *nibbāna* with greater ease because they follow the path of *brahmacarya* that combines celibacy with renunciation.[104] This path was not easily available for women, whose body is perceived to be the greatest obstacle to the attainment of *nibbāna*. The body is envisaged as foul smelling and dripping with death, a veritable noose of death with its skin-deep attractiveness enhanced by jewellery, unguents and clothes. This female body is the house of desire, and to overcome this desire the nun or the monk has to view it as ageing and decaying.

Padmanābha Jaini has recovered a lively debate between the Digambaras and the Śvetāmbaras (and later the Yāpanīyas)[105] on whether or not women can achieve salvation. The Digamabaras in CE 150 argue that a woman is unable to attain *mokṣa* due to her female body.[106] This follows from the fundamental idea that the female body is inferior to the male body. In Jaina texts, one of the main obstacles to women obtaining salvation is the biophysical argument that since women menstruate they cannot wander naked. Menstruation is also seen to encourage the growth of organisms, which leads to involuntary pain and harm to them through the agency of women; therefore women cannot achieve non-attachment, and neither can they therefore attain *arhatship*. The Śvetāmbaras who were active in the early centuries of the Christian Era, and later the Yāpanīyas, counter this with the statement that women are capable of attaining *nirvāṇa*. To prove their point, they argued that though women cannot achieve the ultimate low extremes of hell based on extreme demerit, they can still gain knowledge leading to salvation. This event would be an *āścariya*, or an extraordinary event like the fact that the nineteenth *tīrthaṁkara*, Mallinātha was a woman. Moreover, given that a male or a female can possess either of the three libidos — male, female

1.3 Two women under *aśoka* tree, Mathurā sandstone, first century CE, Kota, Mathurā district. GMM No. 00F.11. (facing page)

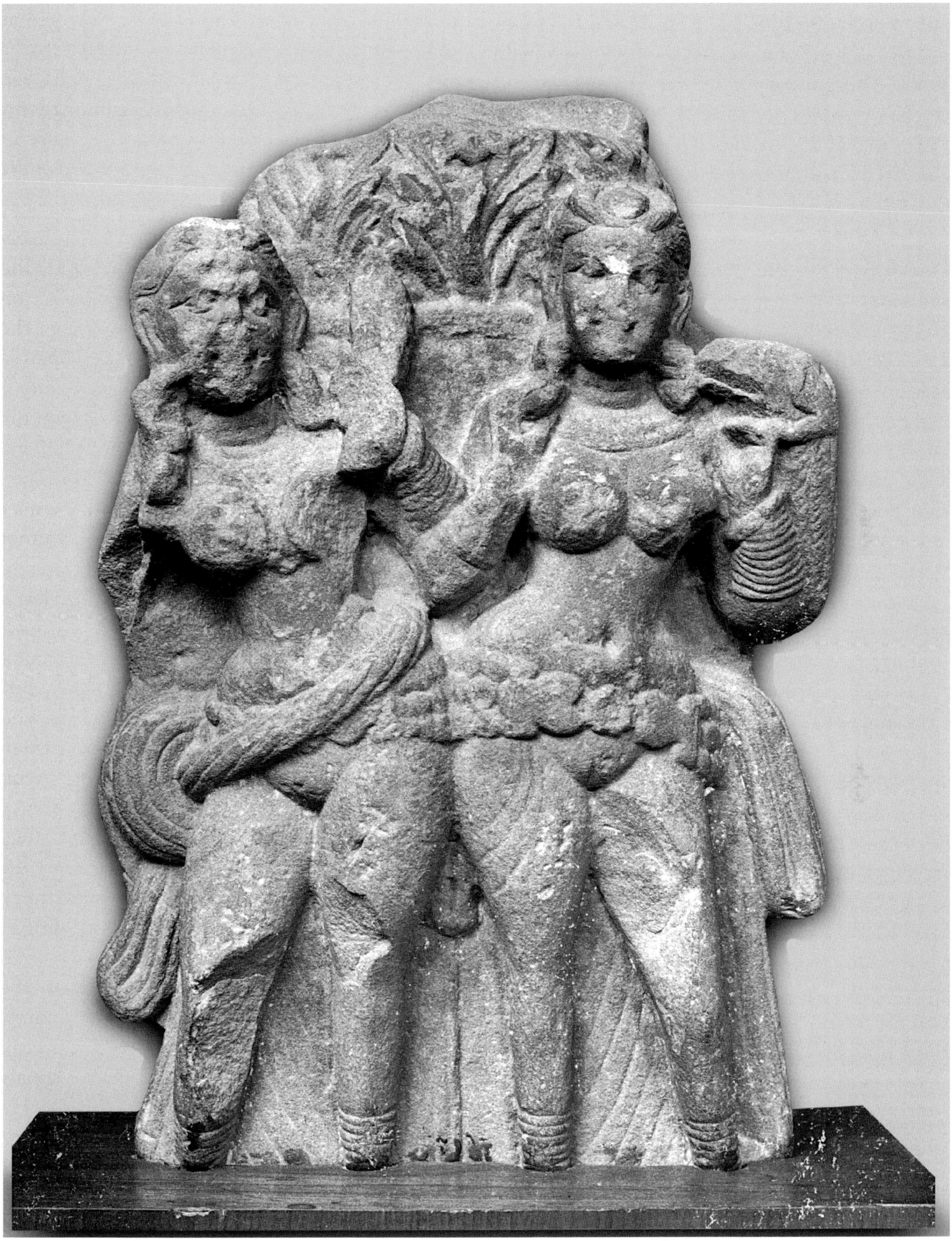

and hermaphrodite — a male can achieve salvation even if he possesses *strīveda* or female libido. Thus, a woman can also achieve *mokṣa* if she has *strīveda* or *puṁsaveda*. Moreover, while it is true that women cannot go naked, this does not prevent them from attaining *mokṣa*.

### 1.6 Nakedness

One of the noticeable features of ancient Indian sculpture is the exposure of naked and semi-naked bodies to the gaze of the viewer. Nudity in art has often been commented upon with various reasons given for the apparent nakedness of the figures.[107] Two major explanatory frameworks have traditionally been built around these nudes, especially nude female figures. One school posits that nudity has no pejorative connotations in ancient Indian art since it is derived from the hot tropical climate and the prevalent social mores that accept nudity as natural.[108] The other opinion seems to favour the fertility implications of naked female body linked to the exposure of reproductive sexual organs. Thus, according to Coomaraswamy, as in the Aegean, so in India, feminine divinities may or may not be represented with clothing other than jewellery. When without clothing, perhaps the magical efficacy of the divine body is felt to act more freely, and perhaps the clothing may have been thought to conserve it. But even when clothing is present (he does not believe that many, if any, of the Mathurā railing pillar figures are really nude) the sexual parts are clearly shown as if to emphasise the source of fruitfulness.[109] A recent third intervention problematising the issue of female nudity has looked at the manner in which Indian and Western art historians perceive and comment upon the Indian female nude, with special reference to Khajurāho sculptures and paintings of M.F. Hussain.[110]

The above explanations are plausible separately or simultaneously. The attempt in this analysis, however, is not to give reasons for the existence of naked figures; rather I want to engender these figures through reading gender identities inherent in the portrayal of a nude body.

Art makes the body visible and valorises it. Naked bodies, male and female, unequivocally expose sex signifiers; therefore they are of the utmost importance in establishing the primary sexual identity of the figures depicted and their secondary gender identity as male/female and men/women. One can also attempt to retrieve the connotations of the depiction by placing these images in their textual context, if any.[111] However, while discussing the issue of unclothed female and male figures, one must keep in mind that the textual tradition may reflect criteria that are not directly applicable to art. Textual references may only mirror the attitude of contemporary society towards nudity in the mundane world, rather than in the religious and artistic spheres. For example, in the *Atharvaveda* there is a hymn devoted to a ritual involving the Mahā Nagna and Mahā Nagnī, the Great Male Nude and the Great Female Nude,[112] which clearly has cultic significance, and such cultic practices may not be actuated in social activity. The attitudes reflected in contemporary texts may in fact be applicable only to mortal women rather than to goddesses who are not perceived of in lay social terms. Nevertheless, the fact that norms regarding clothing and nudity, referred to below[113] exist, is significant. The naked body in art then may take on extended significance including those of transcending norms set by patriarchal society.

1.4 Three Rail Posts with *yakṣīs*, red sandstone, second century CE, Bhūteśvara, Mathurā. IM A 24845/ M 15 a, b. (facing page)

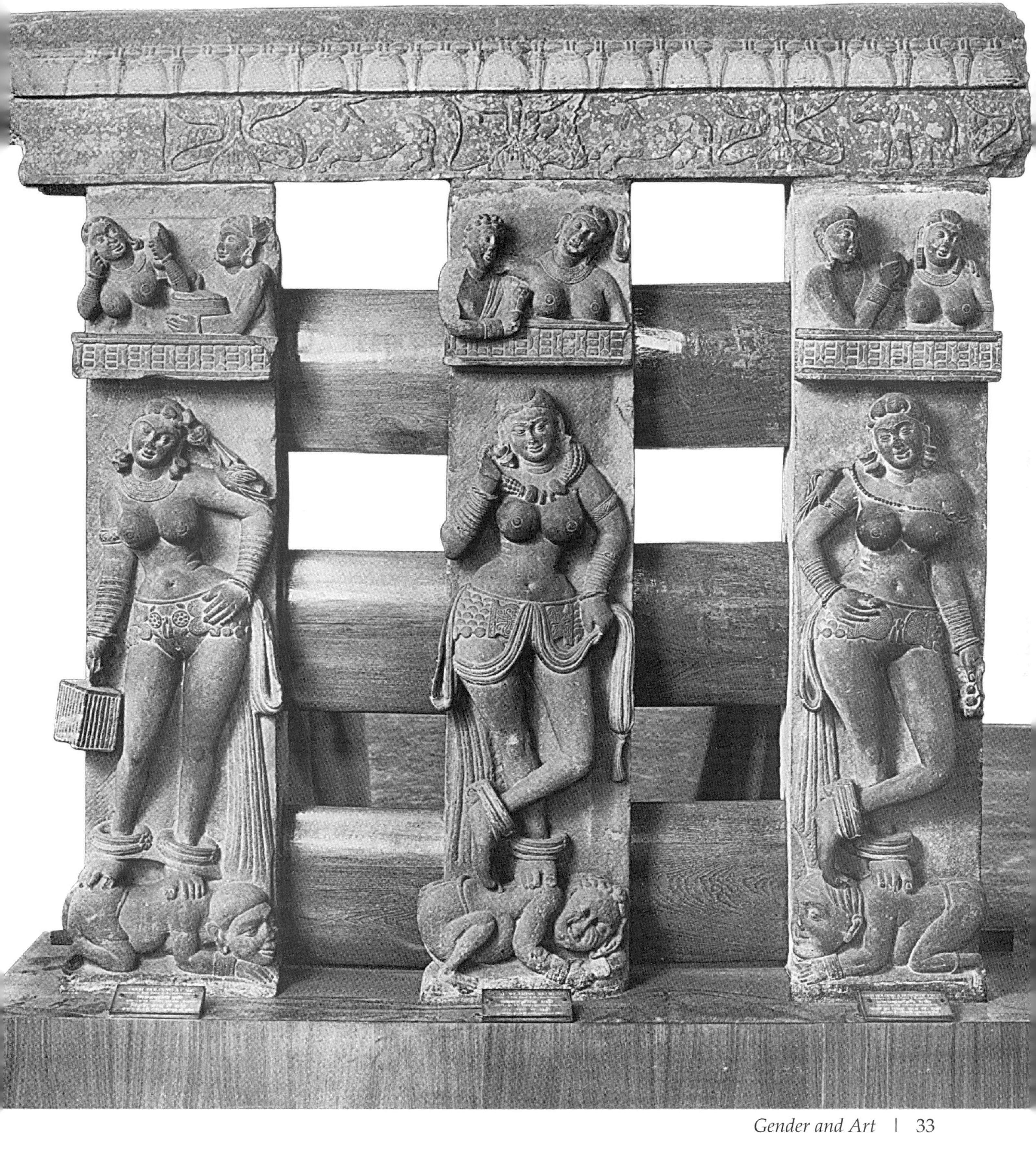

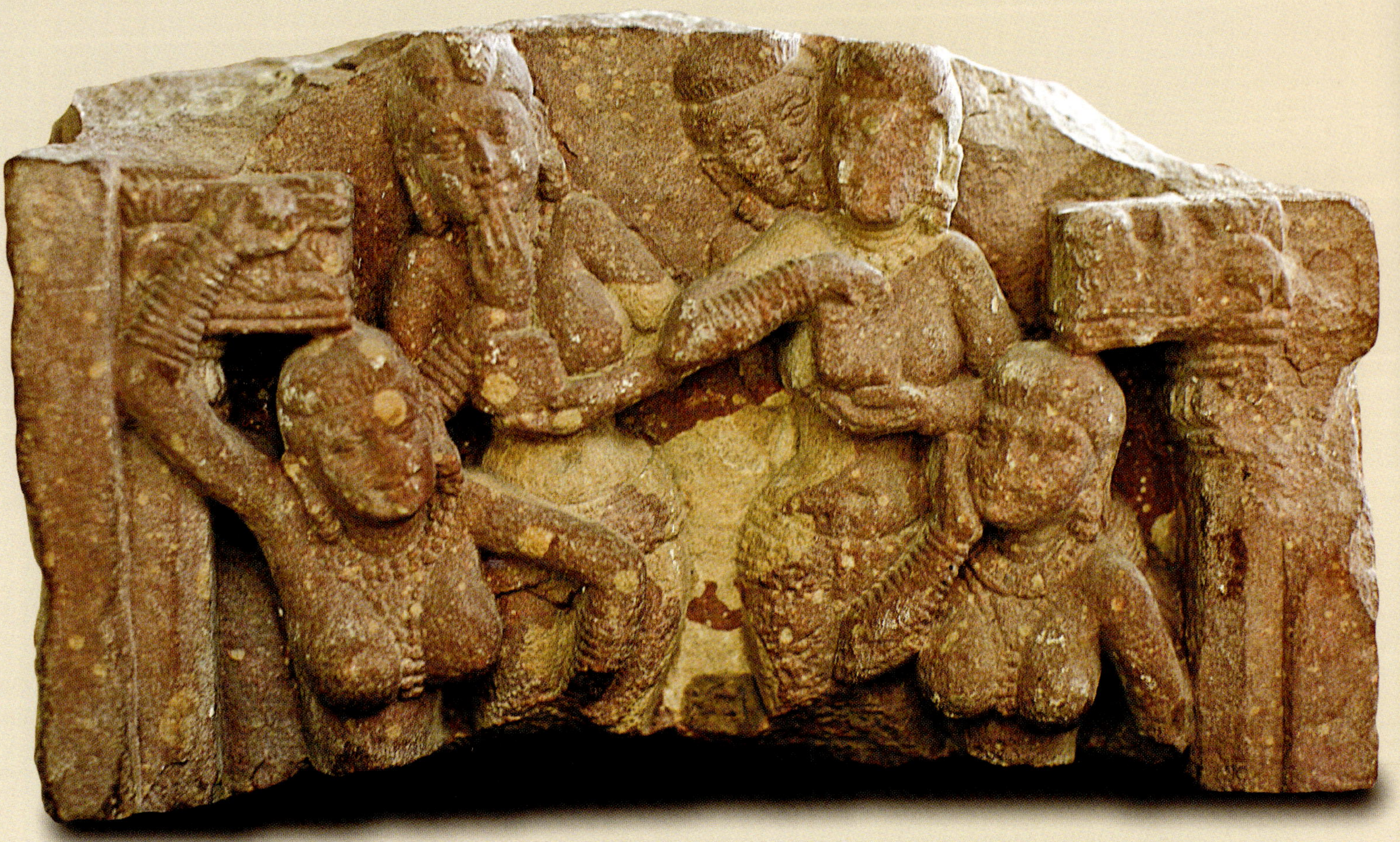

1.5 Panel below two Indo Persepolitan pilasters showing five women engaged in feasting and dance, Mathurā sandstone, second century CE, Kaṭhautī kā kuāṅ, Mathurā district, UP. GMM No. 14.405.

Early Indian art is marked by a progressively increasing sexuality.[114] This includes the sexualisation of the male (and female) body, with a plethora of naked or more often transparently clad male and female figures. However, it is noteworthy that male nudity, unlike female nudity is rarely mentioned in texts, pejoratively or otherwise. Visually though, male nakedness in depictions of the Buddha (*Pl.* 6.11), *bodhisattvas* (*Pl.* 6.12), Jaina *tīrthaṁkara*s and ascetics is encountered, and it seems to carry no inherent negative connotations. By the time we come to the Kuṣāṇa period most of the *bodhisattva* and *yakṣa* figures have prominently delineated genitalia under the folds of their transparent drapery.[115] It has been suggested that this phenomenon is related to the idealisation of the Buddha and the *boddhisattva* as a *cakravartin mahāpuruṣa* with the 32 *lakṣaṇa*s of the *cakravartin*. One of the *lakṣaṇa*s, according to the *Citralakṣaṇa*

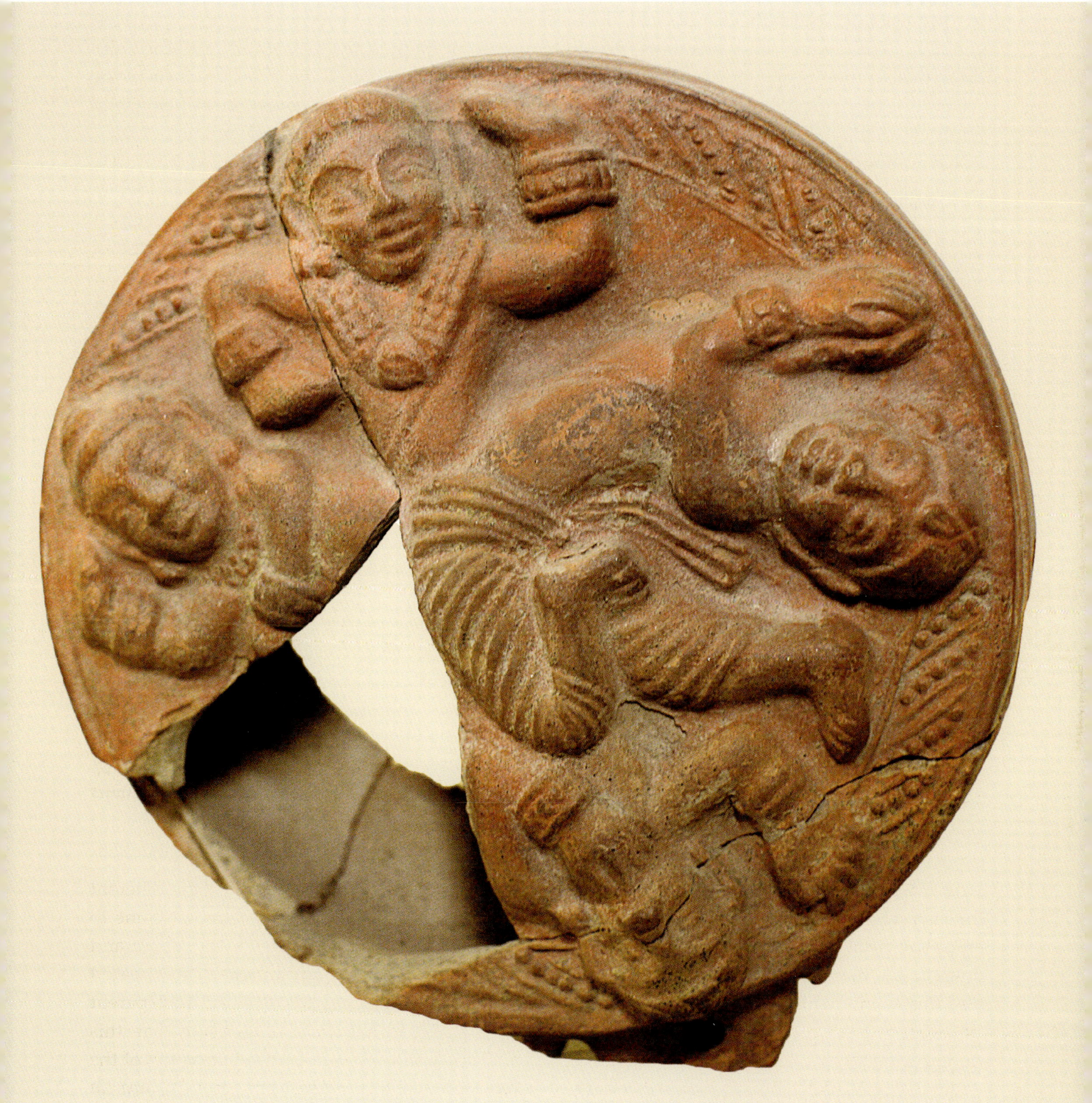

1.6 Men dancing in a circle, Terracotta, second century CE, Mathurā, GMM.

of Nagnajita (*c.* eleventh century CE), is the genitalia, with exact measurements given.[116] Nevertheless not every male figure has its sexuality emphasised, nor does male nudity imply sexual availability, homoeroticism or visual gratification for women.[117]

Female nudity is far more widespread in art;[118] it does carry negative implications — sexual as well as spiritual. The female body was sexually delineated over a period of 500 years studied here from the early art of Bharhut up to the Mathurā period. The female body is often articulated as naked or semi-naked with nude fleshy breasts, scarcely concealed pudenda, and profuse ornamentation (*Pls.* 1.3, 1.4).[119] In the following chapters it will be demonstrated how such nudity is used to construct various female bodies — of *apsaras-śālabhañjikā*, mothers, prostitutes and wives — and the degree to which nudity is significant in constituting each category.

It is difficult to reconstruct what this nudity would connote for the contemporary viewer, though it is possible to say that in the textual tradition there is an opprobrious element attached to exposure in public. The Buddhists enacted certain codes to ensure that naked bodies did not violate societal order. The Vinaya rules enacted by the Buddha for nuns prescribed that they should wear a bodice at all times because exposure invited ridicule and bawdiness from others.[120] The locus of sensuality is also placed by the Vinaya in the body above the knee — the same area that is usually left uncovered or scarcely draped in the female figures sculpted on Buddhist monuments.

There is an interesting reference to a naked *yakṣiṇī* in the *Manorathapūraṇī* of Buddhaghoṣa. Commenting on the *Aṅguttara Nikāya*,[121] where the Buddha speaks of the five disadvantages of Modhur (modern Mathurā), including its fierce *yakṣa*s, Buddhaghoṣa recounts a story. Describing a visit of the Buddha to Mathurā, the story says that just as he entered the outer precincts of the town, a naked *yakṣiṇī* stationed herself before him with her hands outstretched and her tongue sticking out.[122] The Buddha, apparently disgusted, turned back from the town and set up residence in a monastery outside the city.[123] Perhaps this disgust was rooted in the aggressive nudity of the *yakṣiṇī*. The profusion of the apparently semi-clad *yakṣī-śālabhañjikā*s on Buddhist structures, however seems to be in contradiction to this antipathy towards naked female form.

Additional references to Buddhist attitudes towards nudity are also to be found in Aśvaghoṣa's *Buddhacarita*. Perturbed by Gautama's resolve to renounce the world, his father Śuddhodana encourages women of the harem to distract Gautama from his resolve by entrancing his senses with worldly pleasures. These women pretended to be intoxicated with liquor (*madaneniya varijitaḥ*) and touched him with their firm, rounded (*pinaiḥ*), close-set (*saṁhataiḥ*) and charming breasts (*stanaiḥ*) they repeatedly allowed their blue lower garment to fall (*strasta-nīlāṁśukaiḥ*), leaving the jewelled girdle exposed to the gaze. Wet with ointment (*ardhānulepana*) . . . and smelling of spirituous liquor, they displayed their bosoms like golden jars.[124] This display of "shamelessness" has the opposite to the expected effect on Gautama, instead of being attracted he is disgusted.[125] Exposure of the breasts and genitalia in this context is not a positive indicator of fertility, nor is it considered to be a natural state for women.

That nakedness is not looked upon as natural and acceptable is also clear from invective address for women. For example, in the *Arthaśāstra* it is said that "women of refractive nature shall be taught manners by using not even such expressions such as "Thou, half naked; thou, fully naked; thou, cripple; thou, fatherless; thou, motherless."[126]

In the Karṇa-Parva of the *Mahābhārata*[127] there is a reference to a prevalent belief regarding the Bāhlika country whose women were considered a blemish on mankind, as in their case it was not possible to determine the legitimacy of children and hence sisters and not sons are the heirs. It further states that women of Sakala (Sialkot) in the country of Madra dance and laugh naked. These women are licentious and self-willed and indulge in sexual intercourse in the open. In the Ādi-Parva,[128] in the "Śvetaketu and Uddālaka" episode, Uddālaka tells Śvetaketu that all women in the world were uncovered and self-willed and that this had been the practice from time immemorial, thus committing all of primitive womankind to a state of shameless licentiousness. Similar references are found in the Śānti-Parva of the *Mahābhārata*,[129] and also later texts such as the *Bṛhatsaṁhitā*[130] and *Rājataraṅgiṇī*.[131]

Hala's *Saptaśatī* also seems to indicate that covering the upper part of the body is an accepted convention.[132] Women wore a bodice called *kañcukī*, the ends of which were tied together under the breasts, and it was not entirely removed even in private.[133] By the time the major

1.7 Large back piece of a royal throne, ornamented with 13 plaques with carving of women in various modes: Note part of this specimen is reconstructed. Ivory, late first to early third centuries CE, Begram, Kabul Museum.

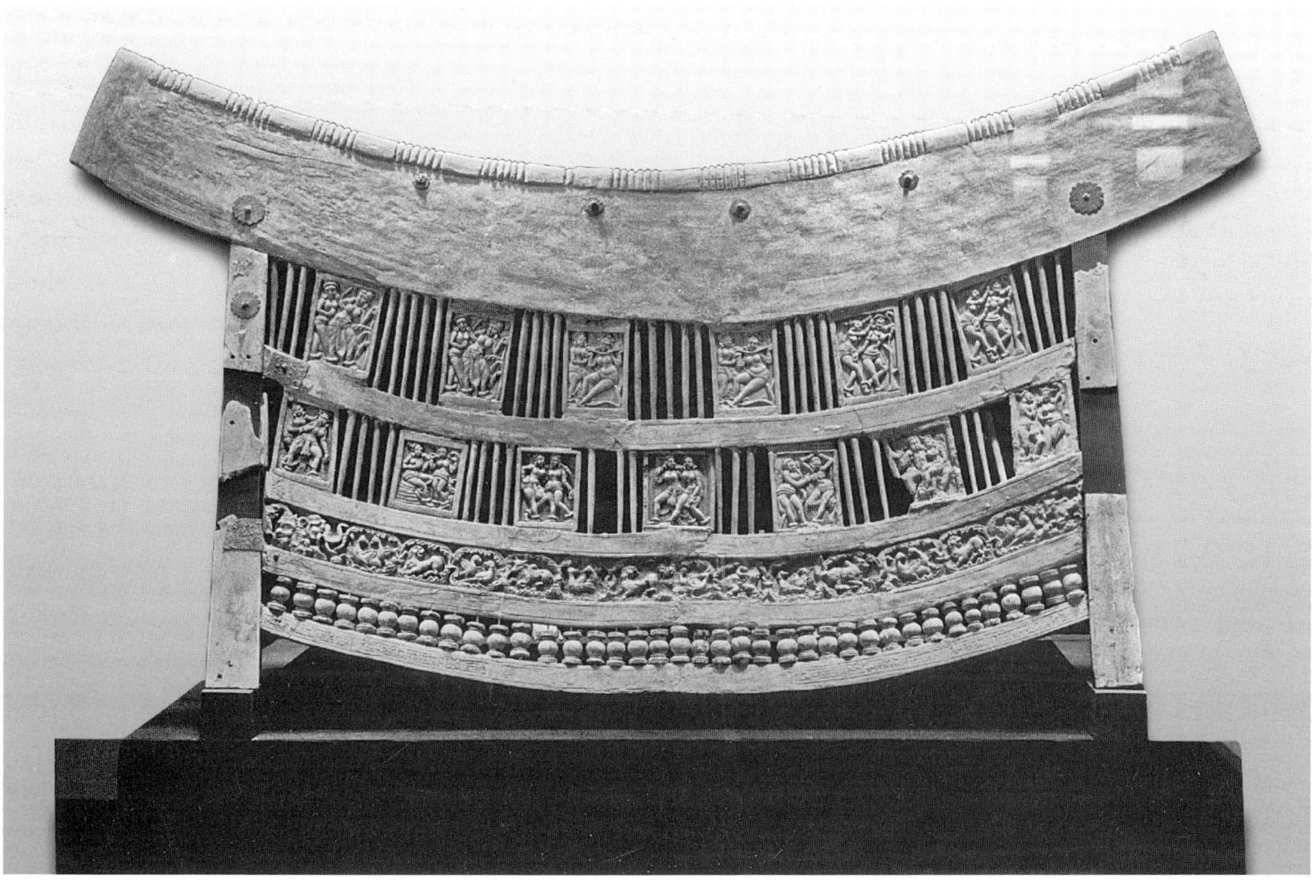

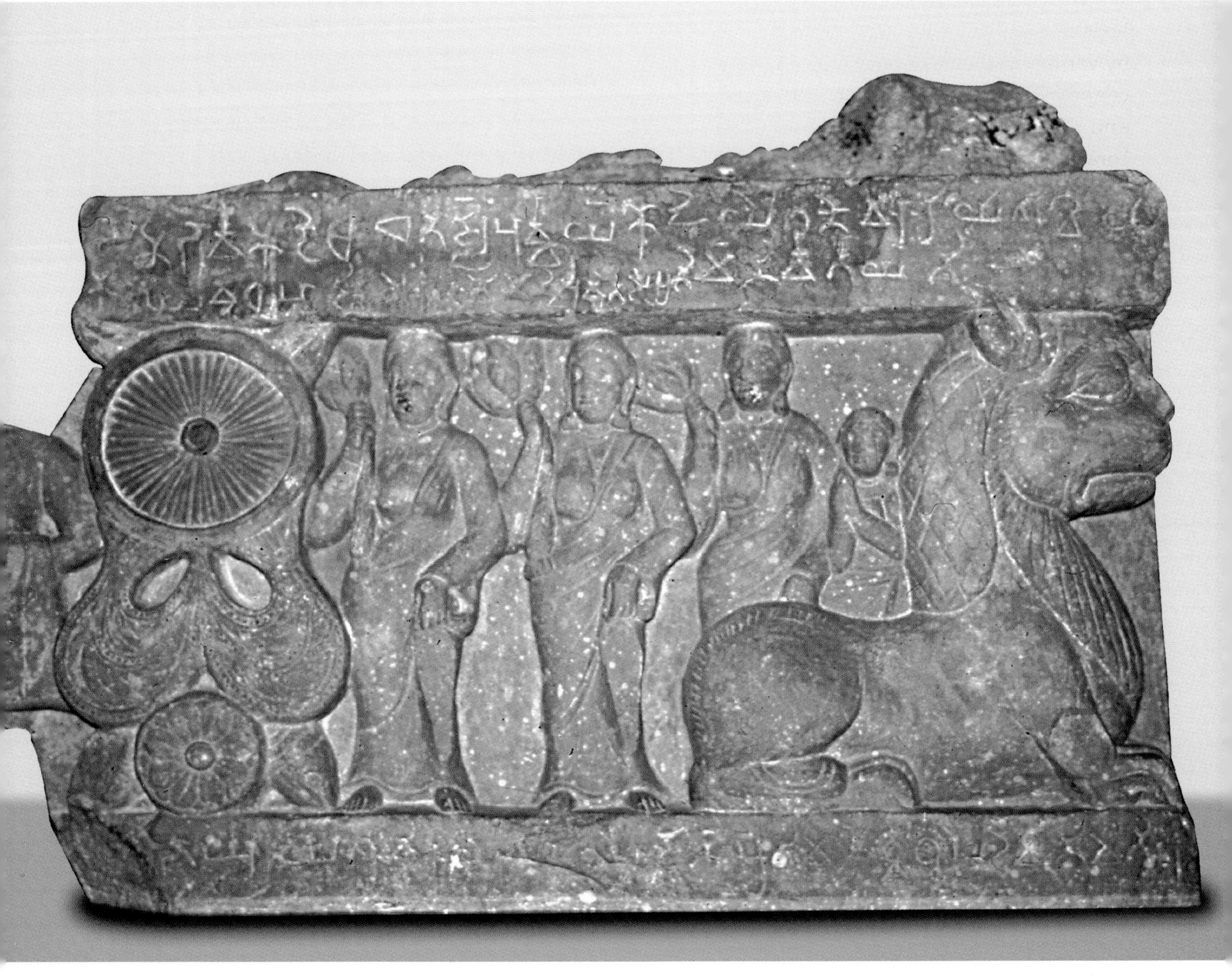

1.8 Women bearing offering of flowers, fully clothed, fragment of an *āyāgapaṭṭa*, red sandstone, second century CE, Kaṅkālī Ṭīlā, Mathurā. SML.

body of the Dharmaśāstra literature was composed between *c.* 200 BCE to CE 400, it is clearly laid down that a woman's navel should never be exposed and her legs should be covered down to the ankles.[134]

The references from Buddhist and Brāhmanic texts cited above contradict the notion, advocated by various authors,[135] that there were no negative connotations attached to nudity in ancient India, and therefore that it was an acceptable convention to portray male and female figures naked.

A connection with nudity and motherhood has also been made, claiming that naked bodies expose the reproductive organs, which implies indirect and inherent reference to fertility. Certain rituals from central India recorded in the nineteenth century do reinforce the essential connection between the female nudity and fertility. It was believed that in the case of a drought, women of the village went to the fields at night, stripped naked and lay on the ground or yoked themselves to the plough and pulled it, to encourage the earth mother to produce food.[136] How far such a sympathetic connection between female nudity and fertility of soil informs the sculptural tradition in the past is difficult to determine.

### 1.7 The Provocative Body

The textual tradition thus does not necessarily valorise naked bodies. Visually also the purpose of nudity in art is neither universally voyeuristic nor provocative, though an element of pleasure is intrinsic in the act of viewing such an art object.

In order to determine whether or not a relief or a statue is provocatively delineated, one has to examine both the internal and external factors related to it. In the former category, the internal factors, I propose to look at the posture and gaze of the sculptural piece. The external factors are constituted by the context within which the art object is placed — for example, whether the art object is part of a larger frieze or a group (*pl.* 1.8), or carved as an independent piece. Another element that would influence the reading of a particular piece as provocatively delineated (or otherwise) would be its architectural placement: for example, whether it is part of a *stūpa* or railing, or a cult object. The third concern is that of intention, the interpretation of which will inevitably contain elements of subjectivity, since we have few epigraphic or even textual references to specific representations in and around monuments from the art of the early period.

In terms of posture, one observes differences in representations of male and female figures. Men may be depicted standing in a *tribhaṅga* posture, though this is a posture commonly adopted by feminine figures. However, variations do occur in feminine imagery, sometimes at the same site. For example, at Sāñcī, the *śālabhañjikā* figures placed on the *toraṇa* brackets are voluptuous, sensuous and in *tribhaṅga* (*Pl.* 6.34). On the same *toraṇa* architrave are Gaja-lakṣmī figures, seated or standing on lotus seats, in *samabhaṅga* posture (*Pls.* 2.2.6, 2.2.7). Both the *śālabhañjikā*s and the goddesses are semi-naked in so far as the *dhotī* covering the lower limbs is transparent; yet the former are provocatively depicted while the latter invokes elements of divinity. Similarly, in the art at Mathurā, the massive, solid and *samabhaṅga* sculptures of goddesses such as Ṣaṣṭhī (*Pls.* 3.4.1, 3.4.2, 3.4.3, 3.4.4, 3.4.5), Hāritī (*Pls.* 3.2.1, 3.2.2, 3.2.3, 3.2.4, 3.2.5), and Vasudharā (*Pl.* 3.3.1) may be contrasted with the provocatively and sensuously delineated *yakṣī-śālabhañjikā* figures found on the *stambha*s of railings and *vedikā*s. Broadly, I would suggest that the *yakṣī-śālabhañjikā* figures are usually shown actively in movement (*Pls*. 6.16 to 6.26) while the goddesses are shown static (*Pls*. 1.10, 1.11), giving the impression of immortality and immovability. The goddesses look straight at the viewer, while the gaze of the *yakṣīs* is fixed on their own bodies.

Both the goddesses and certain *yakṣī-śālabhañjikā* depictions share a common characteristic, which is that the figure is shown holding either her own *mekhalā* (girdle) (*Pl*. 1.4) or cloth sash tied around the waist or that of her male companion (*Pl*. 4.30). The opposite combination is also to be found, though the male partner is generally shown as pulling at the girdle of the female (*Pl*. 4.14). Such action is seen in the *mithuna* depictions and narrative friezes. There are indications that such acts were considered provocative or improper and therefore frowned upon. However, it is not specified whether these acts were proscribed in public or in private. The *Arthaśāstra*, in the context of transgressions of rules concerning the loosening of the tie of the *mekhalā* or waistband, says that "if a woman engages herself in amorous sports, or drinking in the face of an order to the contrary, she shall be fined three *paṇas*; a woman, holding out her hair, the *tie of her dress around her loins* (emphasis is mine), her teeth or nails, shall pay the first amercement; and a man, doing the same, twice the first amercement."[137] The reference from Aśvaghoṣa's *Buddhacarita* cited earlier reinforces the position held by the *Arthaśāstra* that exposure of the lower body and loosening the jewelled girdle were considered amorous activities, and tantamount to seductive behaviour. Given the textual position, the frequent occurrence of such acts on sculptures may not be without significance. The sculptor/visualiser must have been aware of this convention and yet depicts a certain improper relationship between genders on public religious structures.

*Śālabhañjikā* figures as architectural motifs carved on *toraṇas* and *vedikā* pillars, for example, are described in a Jaina text, the *Rājapraśnīya Sūtra*, as "standing in various graceful poses, well supported (on couchant figures), beautifully ornamented, wearing garments painted in various colours, and necklaces of various designs, slender waisted, having round prominent breasts, eyes with red corners and black curly hair, standing under *aśoka* trees and holding their distended boughs, *stealing the hearts of gods as it were with their rolling glances and teasing as it were with the play of their eyes* (emphasis mine)."[138] This passage suggests that these figures were provocatively carved in order to entice male gods. No doubt the gaze of mortal men too found pleasure in regarding these figures.

In general, male figures are rarely provocatively delineated. Even in scenes such as the *Saundarānanda*, the sensual aspect is centred on the woman at whom the male gazes or on the man who makes amorous advances towards the woman (*Pls*. 4.30 to 4.34 and *Pl*. 4.38). The male is the agency in the provocative gestures while the females are the recipients, especially in narrative reliefs where movement or activity is indicated.

### 1.8 Fertility

The use of the term "fertility" in describing an art object indicates that the art-historian using it thinks that the society, which produced the object, believed in its ability to induce/increase the reproductive powers of animal/human/plant species. In India in particular, women, through their association with *prakṛti*[139] (nature), have been assigned the special role of assisting fertility. The male counterpart of *prakṛti* is *puruṣa*,[140] a word primarily meaning male. The endeavour here is not to trace this complicated issue of female = *prakṛti* = fertility but to discover

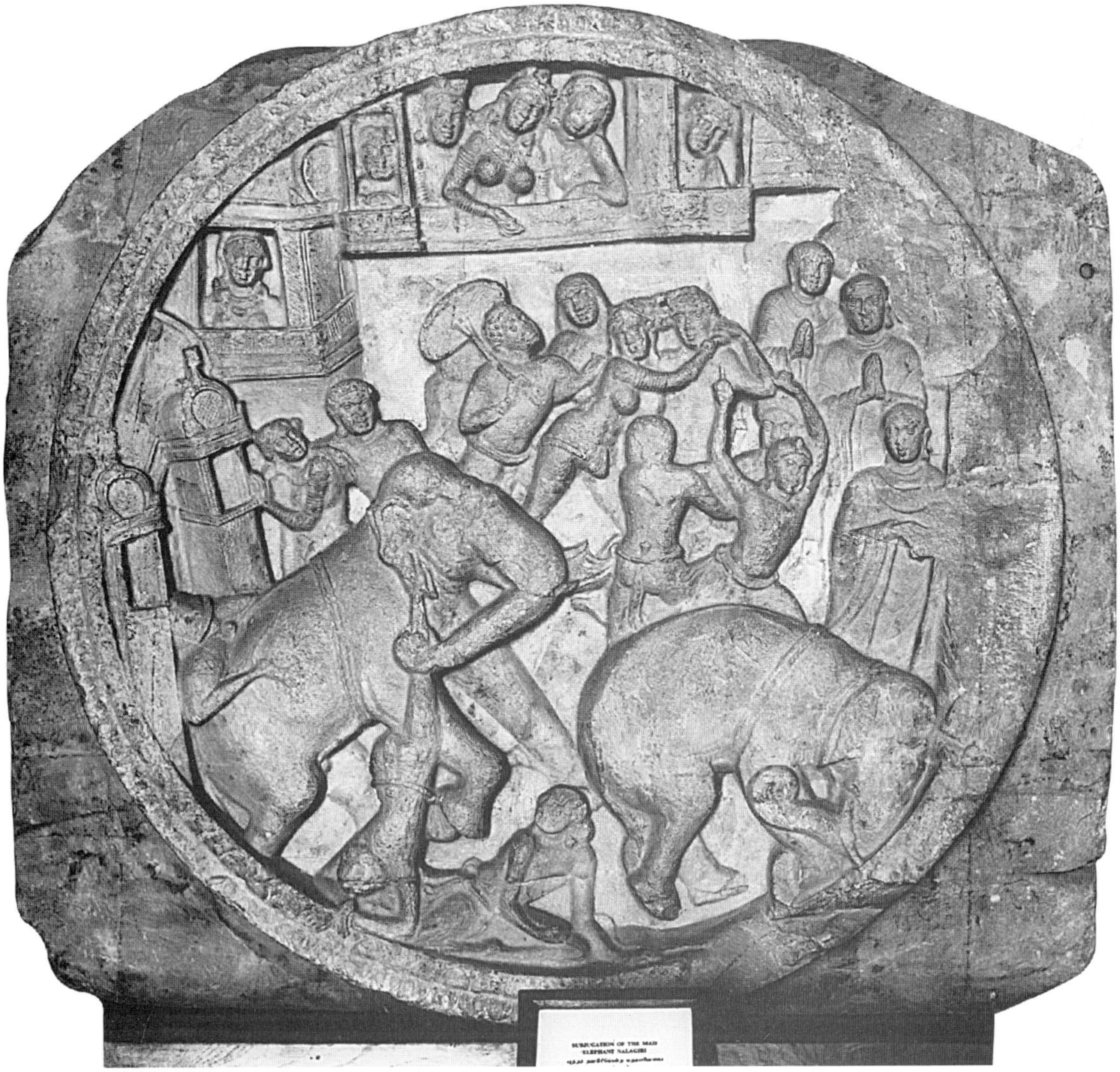

1.9 Nalagiri episode, rail pillar, marble, second century CE, Amarāvatī. Madras Museum.

whether Indian texts refer to particular representational types as having the ability to increase reproductive power through the process of sympathetic magic, symbiosis or osmosis.

Early writers on ancient Indian art, especially nationalist historiographers, tended to emphasise the fertility aspect of female figures. This was partly due to a desire to valorise ancient culture and partly to defend Indian art against European accusations of excessive eroticism.[141] Their interpretations were largely accepted and enlarged upon by almost all twentieth century writers.

Ananda Coomaraswamy, an influential proponent of the fertility element in Indian art, observes that "a comparison of the nude goddess with Sirimā Devatā or Sudhātā from Bharhut serves to emphasise that none of the examples at Bharhut nor any of the later voluptuous types of Indian religious art, are to be regarded as erotic works in the modern or European sense. The consciousness of the identity of beauty and

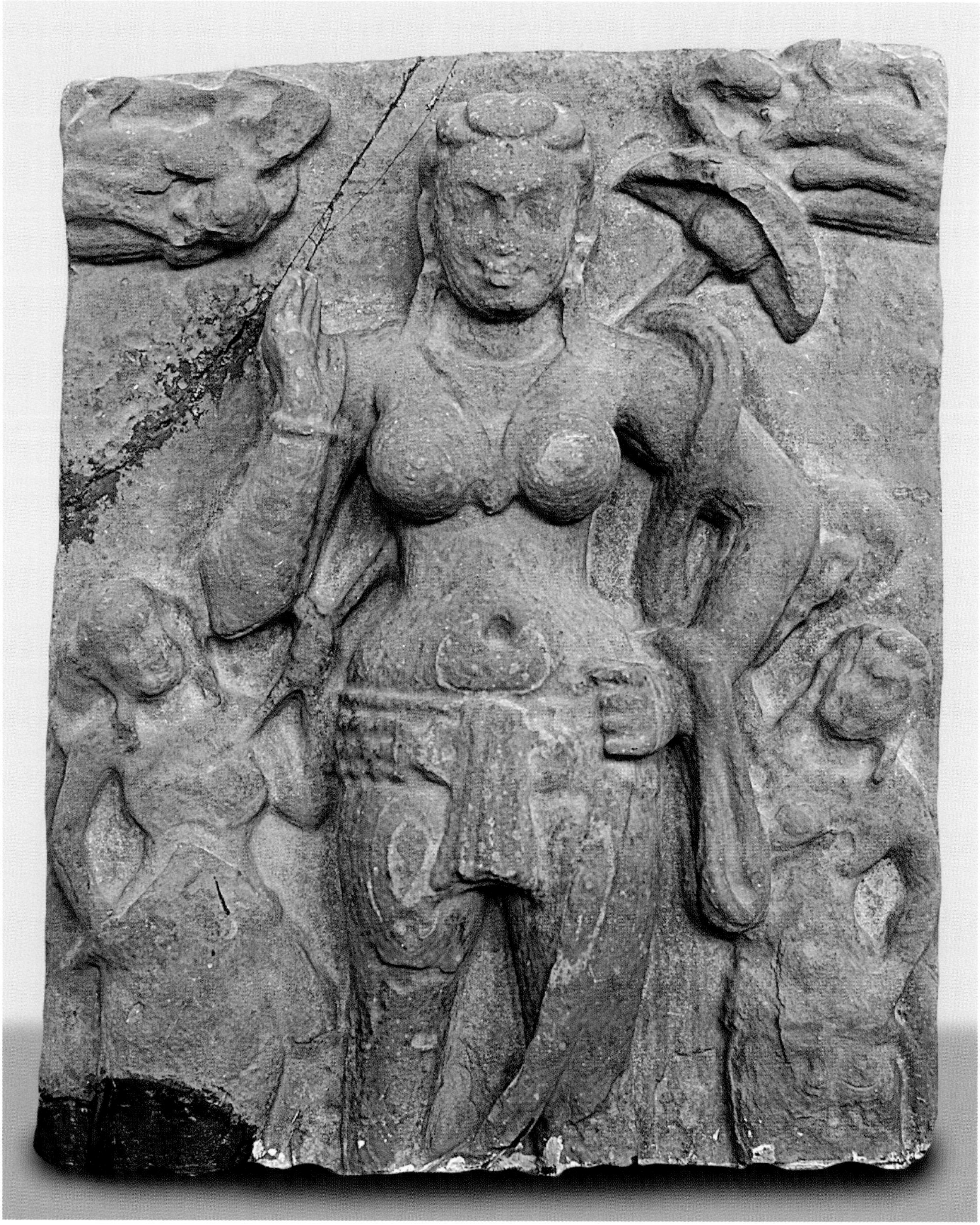

1.10 Goddess with *chatra*, female attendants, red sandstone, second century CE, Mathurā Museum, GMM.

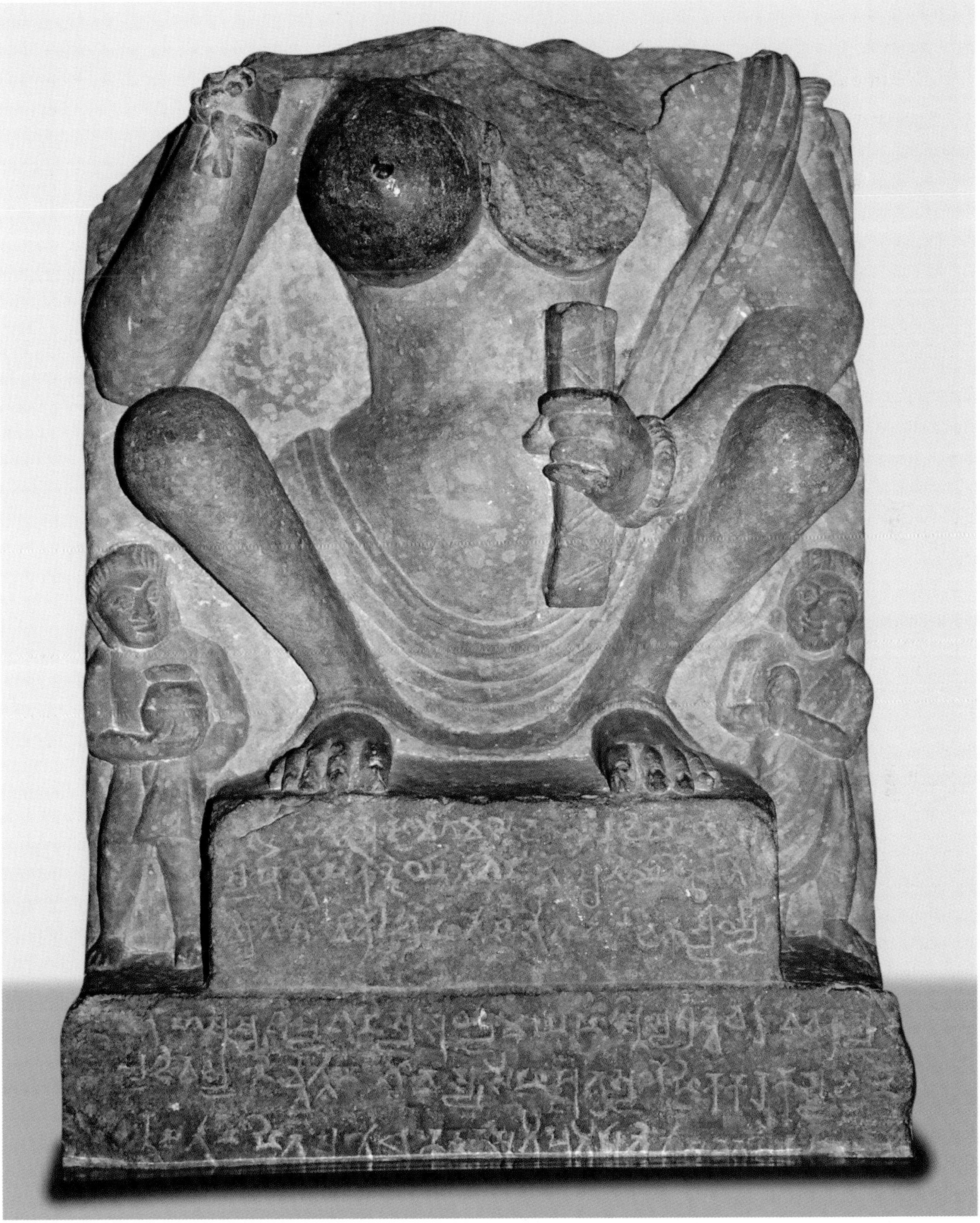

1.11 An inscribed sculpture of Goddess Sarasvatī, Kaṅkālī Ṭīlā, Mathurā, red sandstone, second century CE, 132 CE. SML J. 84.

fruitfulness has never been lost in India, and this is why even the most spiritual types preserved their volume and vitality for so long."[142]

Similarly, Stella Kramrisch links feminine beauty with fertility:

> There is no better counterpart in the world to the ideal of female beauty in Indian art with its extremely pronounced forms than that of the Palaeolithic Venus from Willendorf. . . . No doubt it is a pre-Āryan ideal of physical perfection resulting in beauty becoming synonymous with fertility.[143]

The basis of this thesis is the idea that one should not regard these ideals to be of a purely material and physical significance; as remarked by Zimmer, "To the Indian, the outer appearance is the truthful mirror of the inner structure of the soul."[144]

I find it somewhat inexplicable that fertility as a concept is used to explain the presence of variegated categories of motifs, ranging from inanimate objects to animate beings,[145] be it a lotus, an elephant,[146] a *yakṣa*,[147] a *nāga*,[148] a *śālabhañjikā*,[149] or the couple (*mithuna*), either directly or through a process of association.

The element of fertility *vis-à-vis* Indian art deserves closer scrutiny in so far as it has profound implications for the construction of gender hierarchies in ancient India. If we are able to attribute a specific purpose and intention to the kind of sculptures under consideration, namely that of encouraging fruitfulness, then it follows that we can also ascribe agency to the figures and motifs such as *yakṣīs*, *śālabhañjikā* and the like. This would imply that the gender role imputed to women in these was positive and understood as such by the audience for whom it was intended. Thus, the primary gender identity of women is linked to their roles as reproducers and therefore perceived as useful and positive. Reproductivity is an intrinsic part of feminine sexuality, which, as the discussion on *strīsvabhāva* shows, has often been perceived in negative terms. In this context a monolithic reading of sculptures as denoting fertility becomes problematic, especially in those reliefs where there are no direct references to motherhood.

The purpose behind the carving of a sculpture and its placement is rarely provided either in textual sources or in epigraphic records. One has to assume that there were no negative intentions in putting up a sculpture *per se*, that is, that the theme depicted is not inauspicious for the monument. It may have had apotropaic or didactic purposes. However, the gender signifiers may not necessarily connote the same intention. For example, while the putting up of a *śālabhañjikā* may have been designed to make the monument complete and auspicious; the *śālabhañjikā* may not have been construed as an ideal model for gender behaviour expected of women. The same may hold true for representations of *mithuna* couples.[150]

This can be detected to some extent in the discussion on provocative imagery (see above). As we have seen, the *Rājapraśnīya Sūtra* of the Jainas claims that the *śālabhañjikās* carved on the railing of the *stūpa* are charming enough to attract the (sexual?) attention of the gods. This does not suggest any direct link between the monument and fertility; neither does it preclude the possibility that the sexuality inherent in the figure may lead to reproductive consequences, but any such implications would be secondary and derivative.

In any case, we have very few references in the texts to the *alaṁkāra* or decoration of either secular or religious buildings. In the *Nāṭyaśāstra*, while discussing the raising of a stage of the oblong type, the author recommends that

> The construction of the walls being finished, they should be plastered and carefully whitewashed. After they have been smeared [with plaster and lime] and made perfectly clean and beautifully plain, paintings should be executed on them. In these paintings should be depicted creepers, men, women and their amorous exploits, *ātmabhogajam* (lit. due to self-indulgence or enjoyment of self).[151]

In the description of a square playhouse it says that after raising (for the stage of *raṅgapīṭha*) a plinth of eight cubit (square, more) pillars should be raised to support the roof of the playhouse. "These pillars should be decorated with figurines of 'woman-with-a-tree (*śālastrī*).'"[152] The text does not specify as to why these devices should be painted or carved on the stage, nor does it discuss their efficacy as instruments of fertility.

Some symbols, devices or figures that may originally have been regarded as imparting fertility seem to have lost this specific meaning over a period of time; they were transformed or replaced by other more potent or explicit symbols.[153]

### 1.9 Time, Transformation and the Image

As a process, gender formation involves transformations that are sensitive to social, economic, religious and theological changes. Images adapt to these changes too, as is evident from the art created between the "Śuṅga-Sātavāhana" and the Kuṣāṇa eras.[154] To take an example, the depiction of the demonic aspects of female sexuality as reflected in the Jātaka stories (*Pls.* 7.18 to 7.30) is noticeable in Śuṅga-Sātavāhana art (first century BCE – CE first century). The Jātakas, mainly depicted at Bharhut, Bodh-Gayā and to a lesser extent at Sāñcī, demonstrate this dangerous aspect of womanhood. The other image-type for women represented at these sites is the goddess/*yakṣī* figure. The advent of the Kuṣāṇas marks a change in terms of treatment and thematic choices. The art produced under the Kuṣāṇas at the emerging centres of art such as Mathurā and associated regions is very different in the representational choices. The popularity of Jātaka legends wanes with the increase in the number and variations of the *yakṣī-śālabhañjikā* figures. Even narrative art takes on a more secular character (*pl.*      ) with the inclusion of the Sundarī and Nanda episode and *Mṛcchakaṭikam-Daridra Cārudatta* story. The divine and semi-divine figures continue to be made; though in these too there is a distinct evolution, with a clearer distinction being envisaged between the two categories.

This transformation may be attributed partly to a shift of the foci of art activity from areas adjacent to cities, meant to be pilgrimage centres, to the city itself. There is a movement of sites from pilgrim centres such as Bharhut and Bodh-Gayā to secular towns such as Mathura and Taxila. The geographical shift implies a concomitant alteration in spectatorship pattern. Viewers are no longer pilgrims who have travelled great distances to partake in the religious sanctity attached to the *stūpa*.[155] Instead, the audience now comprises the ordinary inhabitants of towns who would be able to view the embellishments on the façade of the *stūpa* as they went about their daily business. (See the Sirkap (Taxila) site plan and also that of Mathurā for the location of the *stūpa*s *vis-à-vis* the town.) The *bhikkhu* and *bhikkhuṇī saṁgha* of the Buddhists concurrently experienced changes with a relaxation in Vinaya rules and changes in the relationship between the laity and the *saṁgha* through mercantile donations and land grants.[156] This implies an increased interaction between the *saṁgha* and lay society.

Another factor discussed before is the

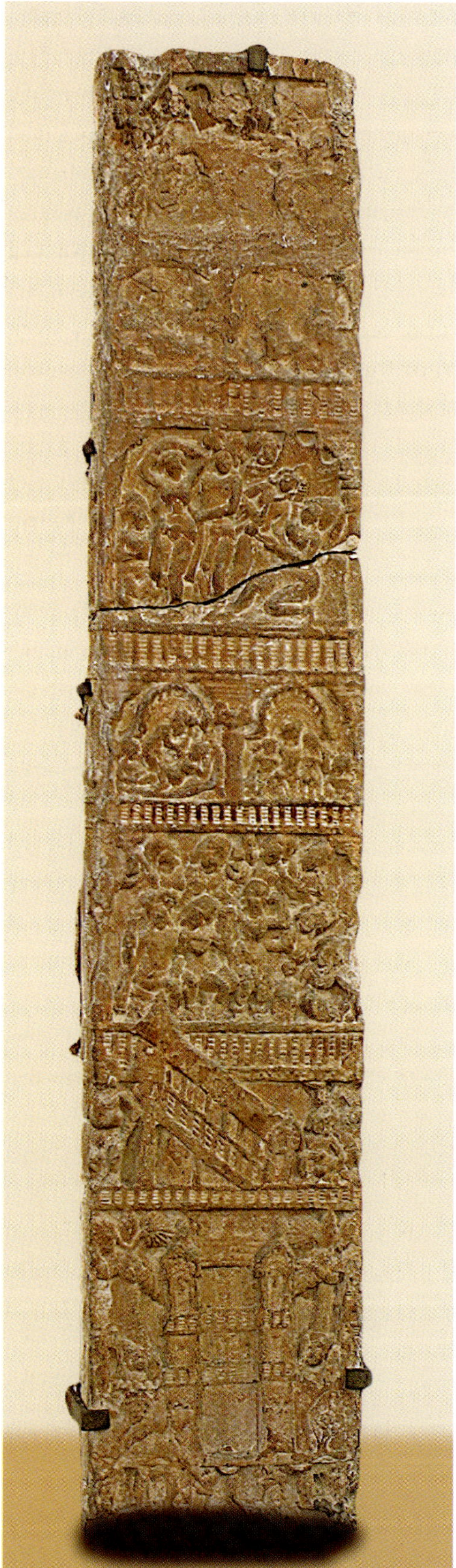

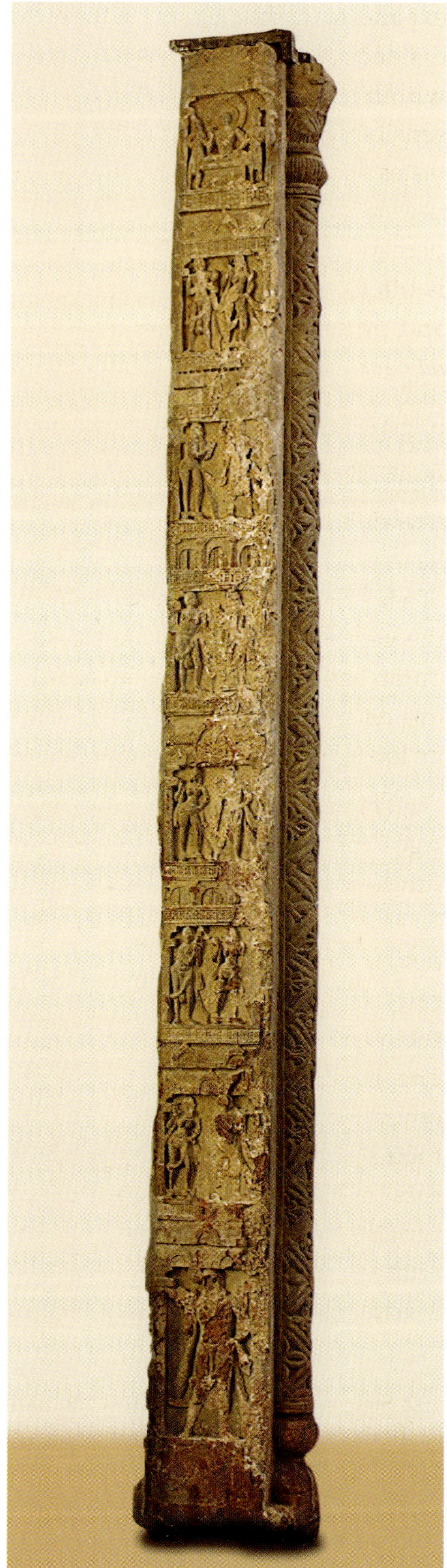

expanding urbanisation and the rise of long-distance trade along with increased contact within larger areas of the Empire. An urbanised sensibility accompanies this development as the tastes and desires of the laity transform. The *nāgaraka* became the ideal man as can be perceived in the literature. A man about town, he is often depicted in the company of courtesans and prostitutes and cultivates the arts.[157] Such a *nāgaraka* is seen in the person of Cārudatta in the play *Mṛcchakaṭikam*, whose interest in religion and politics is tepid. Śarvilaka, the brāhmaṇa thief, also seems to mirror this indifference, if not irreverence, which is evident in the scene where he uses his *yajñopavīta* to measure a hole in a wall of a house he plans to rob.[158] Given such a context, the gendered messages carved on the surviving outer railings of religious edifices were also influenced. The danger that women represent is no longer just inherent and evil, but also enticing.

This is paralleled in the concept of the Kali Age Crisis, a distopian concept which envisages a future era of Kaliyuga where world order would be inverted and the norms transgressed in all fields. The first such crisis has been dated in the early centuries of the Christian Era when the socio-economic situation was in a state of flux.[159] The indications of this crisis are that, among other things, women would stop performing their *strīdharma* and become lazy. It is stated that this would lead to the downfall of the *varṇāśramadharma*. There would be *varṇasaṁkara* with women indulging in *pratiloma* and *anuloma* marriages (marrying above and below their *varṇa* status), leading to the intermixture of *varṇa*s and the creation of new castes.[160]

1.12 Stele with *kāmāloka* scenes, red sandstone, first century BCE, Maholi Paur, UP, GMM No. P. 79. (facing page left)

1.13 Rail post with *kāmāloka* scenes, red sandstone, first century BCE, Mathurā district, UP. GMM No. I. 11. (facing page right)

Part of this change is also reflected in the concluding verses of the *Saundarānanda*. This composition by Aśvaghoṣa contains many references to, and descriptions of, the beauty of Sundarī and an ideal relationship between her and Nanda. Yet it is meant to propagate the message of non-attachment and dissuade Nanda and other backsliders from attaching themselves to women. Aśvaghoṣa's defense of the beauty of his poem is worth quoting in its entirety since it is one of the rare occasions where the cultural producer comments on the intent of his own product. He says,

> This poem, dealing thus with the subject of salvation, has been written in the *kāvya* style, not to give pleasure, but to further the attainment of tranquillity and with the intention of capturing the hearers devoted to other things. For, that I have handled other subjects in it besides salvation, is in accordance with the laws of *kāvya* (poetry) to make it palatable, as sweet is put into a bitter medicine to make it drinkable. Since I saw mankind given over to the pleasures of the objects of the senses and averse from salvation, I have here told of the final truth under the guise of a *kāvya*, considering salvation to be supreme. Let the reader understand this and study attentively in it that which leads to tranquillity and not that which is merely pleasurable as only the residue of gold is taken after it has been separated from the metal dust.[161]

These two verses bear eloquent testimony to two facts. First, that there was a decline in ascetic qualities or at the very least a decline in interest in the message of non-attachment given by the Buddha. Secondly, beautiful creations can be used to entice people to receive the message of salvation through non-attachment. This perception of contemporary society in the first two centuries of the Christian Era is in agreement with the urbanised discourse referred to above.

Transposing the argument to the visual sphere, one may posit that certain devices, in the form of beautiful and voluptuous women, were used on religious monuments such as *stūpa*s and *caitya*s with similar intentions. In a patriarchal set-up this strategy may have attracted the relatively more empowered males. It may be stated that most of the images depicted, that is *yakṣī-śālabhañjikā*s and other semi-divine creatures, were considered to be outside the parameters of society and of the norms that dictated feminine conduct in it. Therefore, these images could be made aesthetically pleasing and sexually attractive without overtly transgressing patriarchal restrictions.

The post-Mauryan period was one in which society remained in flux, as can be gleaned from the emphasis on impending *varṇasaṁskaraṇa*. Clearly, gender and its crystallisation is one of the hegemonies that develop over this period. This process and its relation to art objects can be seen through textual and other extant sources. Art, unlike canonical literature, often has multiple intentionality: theological, embellishing, didactic, attracting and edifying, in addition to the actual *techne* or process of creating the art form. The analysis of art objects thus jostles with ideological forms and power structures in a complex fashion and speaks in multiple voices.

### Notes and References

1. N. Ray, *Mauryan and Post-Mauryan Art*, New Delhi: ICHR, 1975, p. 52.
2. Padmanabhan Jaini, *Gender and Salvation: Jaina Debates on Spiritual Liberation of Women*, New Delhi: Munshiram Manoharlal., 1991, p. xi.
3. For Buddhism see J. I. Cobezon, ed., *Buddhism, Sexuality and Gender*, Albany: SUNY Press, 1995.
4. Uma Chakravarti, *Men, Women and Beasts: The Interface between High Tradition and Popular Tradition in Cultural Production*, Nehru Memorial Museum & Library, New Series 2, LXV, 1992, pp. 27-31.
5. Richard Goldman says that women and lower castes are praised when they conform to the social roles allotted to them or are reviled when they do not. In P. Jaini, op. cit., p. x.
6. *Jīvājīvābhigama Sūtra*, ed. Rajendra Muni, Sri Agam Prakashan Samiti, Beawar 1989, p. 118, 2.45. These are further classified into types based on physiology or the region they occupied.
7. *Nāṭyaśāstra*, XXXIV.39, XXIV.99-100. This is but one categorisation envisaged by the *Nāṭyaśāstra*: the other classifications are based on the divinity or otherwise of women (and men) that would make them *yakṣī*s, *Apsaras*es, etc. Another division that is seen both in the *Nāṭyaśāstra* XXIV.120-142 and the *Kāmasūtra*, II, Ch I is based on the animal that a particular group of women may resemble such as cow, elephant, etc.
8. The classification of women into categories highlights the non-homogeneous nature of women on one hand, and on the other it qualifies the gender roles they perform. Simone de Beauvoir, *The Second Sex*, Middlesex: Penguin Books, rpt. 1987, Section V, has grouped women as The Married Woman, The Mother, Prostitutes and Hetaerae, viewed within societal order and life cycles, terming these as situations in which groups of women are placed by modern patriarchal order.
9. http://www.colorado.edu/English/ENG2021 klages/butler.html. 08-01-02, 18.43. Also Judith Butler, *Gender Trouble: Feminism and the Subversion of Identity*, New York: Routledge, 1990, p. 176.

10. The Jainas refer to three biological genders based on sexuality — male (*puṁliṅga*), female (*strīliṅga*) and intermediate (*napuṁsakaliṅga*) which roughly corresponds to hermaphrodite in that its gender signs are not strictly male or female. These also correspond to libidos or *veda* — male, female and intermediate: Cf. P. Jaini, op. cit., p. 11. It may be remembered that children often form a separate gender in anthropological and sociological studies.

11. These may be incorporated in any representations be it divine, semi-divine, human. Also see Judith Butler, op. cit.

12. G. Lerner, *Creation of Patriarchy*, New York: Oxford University Press, 1986, p. 238.

13. Uma Chakravarti, "Conceptualising Brāhmanical Patriarchy in Early India: Gender, Caste, Class and State", *EPW*, April, 1993, p. 579.

14. Seema Bawa, *Religion and Art of the Chamba Valley*, New Delhi: Agam Kala Prakashan, 1998, p. 153.

15. G. Lerner, op. cit., p. 238.

16. Judith Butler, op. cit., pp. 9-11, 30-31.

17. Women in ancient India therefore faced a double subordination, first due to their sex/gender and secondly due to their caste/class position; a subordination that has been carried through the centuries into present society. Women and the lower castes have been subjected to humiliating conditions in Hindu society. Caste hierarchy and gender hierarchy are the organising principles of the Brāhmanical social order with close interconnections, Uma Chakravarti, op. cit., p. 579. One way this is manifested is in the access of both genders to sexual choice. This is reflected in prescriptions on legal marriages given in the Dharmaśāstras, where it is decreed that men can marry women of their own and lower *varṇas*, while women are allowed to marry men only of their own *varṇa* or higher *varṇas* (*pratiloma* and *anuloma* marriages) though the latter practice is also frowned upon. See *Manu*. IX.85-87; also P.V. Kane, *History of Dharmaśāstras*, vol. 2, part 2. Men also had greater access to sexual intercourse than women; infidelity and bigamy are accepted social conduct for men but is condemned as socially and sexually deviant behaviour when indulged in by women.

18. Infra, Introduction section on historiography of gender.

19. Vidya Dehejia, *Representing the Body: Gender Issues in Indian Art*, New Delhi: Kali for Women, 1997, p. 2.

20. See Uma Chakravarti, op. cit., pp. 127-44.

21. I.J. Leslie, "Strīsvabhāva: The Inherent Nature of Women", in *Oxford University Papers on India*, vol. 1, part 1, Delhi, 1986, pp. 28-58, Also, I. Julia Leslie, ed. & tr., *Tryambakayajvan's The Perfect Wife: Strīdharmapaddhati*, New Delhi: Penguin Books, 1995.

22. Uma Chakravarti, "Preliminary Observations on the Impulse Control of Women in Early India: Ideology, Kinship and The State As Mechanisms of Control", in K.D. Bajpai, ed., *Position and Status of Women in Ancient India*, Banaras Hindu University, Varanasi, 1992, pp. 127-44.

23. *NŚ*, VII.21: *bhayaś naś strīṇacaprakṛttikam* . . .

24. *Mbh*. XIII.120.9: *śubhakṛcchubayoniṣu pāpakṛtapāpayoniṣu, upapadyati dharmajña yathādharmaṁ yathāgamam*. Also *Manu*, XII.4, 9.

25. *Manu*, II.66-7, *Yājñavalkaya Smṛti*, 1.13.

26. *Manu*, IX.18 *nāsti strīṇām kriyā mantrairiti dharme vyavasthitaḥ, nirindrayā hyamantrāśca strīyo anṛtamiti sthitiḥ*.

27. Ibid., V.139.

28. *Śat. Br.*, XIV.1.1.31: *anūtaś strī śūdraḥ sva kṛṣṇaḥ sakunis*. For further references see R.S. Sharma, *Perspectives on Social and Economic History*, New Delhi: Munshiram Manoharlal, 1983, Chapter: Co-references to Woman and Sudras in Early Literature, pp. 45-48.

29. *Manu*, V.135.

30. *Taittirīya Saṁhitā*, II.5.1.

31. *Mbh*., XII.329.28-41.

32. Cf. Wendy O'Flaherty, *The Origins of Evil in Hindu Mythology*, New Delhi: Motilal Banarsidass, 1988, pp. 144-54. Here she discusses the story of the sin attached to Indra for killing the brāhmaṇa Vūtta or Viśvarūpa.

33. Ananda Coomaraswamy, *History of Indian and Indonesian Art*, New York: Dover Publications, 2[nd] edn., 1965, p. 64; Benjamin Rowland Jr., *Art in East and West*, Beacon Press, Boston, 1954, p. 19; Stanislaw J. Czuma, *Sculpture: Images from Early India*, Cleveland: The Cleveland Museum of Art, 1985, p. 102.

34. *Śat.Br.*, 13.1.21.

35. *Āpastamba Dharmasūtra*, II.6.13.7.

36. *Mbh.* II.6.13.7.

37. *Manu*, IX.17: *śayyāsanamalamkāraṁ kāmaṁ krodhamanāryatāṁ; drogdhṛbhāvam kucaryāṁ ca strībhyo manurakalpayat.*

38. Cowell, *Jātaka*, I.155.

39. Ibid., I.156.

40. It may be noted at this point that the Jātakas as they exist today are internally stratified. They have three parts first being an introduction to the tale proper, usually by the Buddha, citing the tale as an exemplum. The tale itself is derived from the popular tradition adapted to the didactic project. The third, a short conclusion is usually the Buddha identifying the protoganist as himself, Ānanda, Māra, etc. in their previous births. The first and the last parts are clearly interpolations made by the Monk editors and are far more orthodox, patriarchal and misogynist in tenor than the popular tradition.

41. Ibid., no. 267.

42. Ibid., no. 152.

43. Ibid., nos. 264-66.

44. *Saundarānanda*, VIII.36-8; also *na vapurvimṛśanti na sriyaṁ na matiṁ nāpi kulaṁ na vikramaṁ; praharṇtyaviśeṣataḥ striyaḥ sarito yahākulākulā iva na vāco madhuraṁ na lālanaṁ smarati strī na ca sauhṛdaṁ kvacit kalitā vanitaeva cañcalā tadihariṣivava nāvalambyate*, [VIII.37-39].

45. Ibid., IX.39.

46. Ibid., VIII.46.

47. Ibid., VIII.47: *atha sūkṣmamati dvayāśivaṁ laghu tāsāṁ hṛdayaṁ na paśyasi; kimu kāyamasadgṛhaṁ śravadvanitānāmuśuciṁ na paśyasi.*

48. Ibid., VIII.54: *śubhatāmaśubheṣu kalpayannakhadantatvacakeśaromasu; avicakṣaṇa kim na paśyasi prakṛtim ca prabhavam ca yoṣitāṁ.*

49. *Manu*, IX.14-15: *naita rūpam parīkṣante nāsām vayasi saṅsthitiḥ, rūpam vā virūpam vā pumānityeva bhuñjate*। *pauṅścalyācclacit tatācacanaih snehyācca svabhāvataḥ, rakṣita yatnato apiḥ bhirtṛśveta vikurvate.*

50. Ibid. IX.16: *evam svabhāvam jñātvāsām prajāpatinisargajam, paramam yatramātiṣṭetpuruṣo rakṣaṇam prati.*

51. Ibid. IX.27-8: *utpādenampatyasya jātsya paripālanam, pratyarthaṁ lokayātrāyāḥ pratyakṣam strī nibandhanaṁ.*

52. In cultural productions, especially modern Indian "Bollywood" cinema, this concept has been seminal in moulding and reflecting popular perceptions of the good woman-good wife, who is perpetually submissive.

53. Infra, Chapter 4 and Chapter 7.

54. *Manu*, IX.12: *arakṣitā gṛhe rudhdāḥ puruṣa-irāptakāribhiḥ, ātmānamātmanā yāstu rakṣeyuṣṭāḥ surakṣitāḥ.*

55. Ibid. IX.29.

56. Cowell, *Jātaka*, no. 519.

57. Ibid, no. 432, *Padukuśalamānava Jātaka.*

58. Ibid, no. 536, *Valahassa Jātaka.*

59. Ibid, no. 514.

60. *Saṁyutta Nikāya*, V.2., Also see *Therigāthā*, PTS, (1964), p. 181-82.

61 *Therīgāthā*, XXXVI. p. 45.

62. Daud Ali, *Courtly Culture and the Political Life in Early Medieval India*, Cambridge: Cambridge University Press, 2006, p. 147.

63. *Nāṭyaśāstra*, VI.45-48.

64 Ibid., XXV.43: *sarvāsāṁ nāriṇāṁ yauvanalīlā-scatasraḥ syuḥ* । *nepathyarūpaceṣṭāguṇaistu śṛngāramāsādhya* ॥

65. Ibid., XXV.44: *pīnoruganḍa jaghanādhana-ghrastanaṁ karkaśaṁ ratimanojñyaṁ* । *surataṁ prati sotsāhaṁ prathamaṁ tadhyovanaṁ jñyeyaṁ* ॥

66. Ibid., XXV, pp. 45-48.

67. *Arthaśāstra*, 2.XXVII.123, p. 136.

68. Infra, Chapter V: The Non-Wives: Nuns and Prostitutes.

69. Stewart, "Art, Desire and the Body in Ancient Greece," *BMCR* 99.10.9 http://omega.cohums.ohio-state.edu/hyper-lists/bmcr-1/1999/0.216.html. 1.2.2002, 17.07 p.m.

70. *Viṣṇudharmottara Purāṇa* II.2.4.

71. It describes various male postures, and female postures that help study postures and gestures in ancient sculptures and painting. For example, Bhoja's *Samarāṅgaṇa-Sūtradhāra*, a medieval encyclopaedic work while describing the rules of making images, also describes the hand gestures almost in the language of the *Nāṭyaśāstra*.

72. M.L. Varadpande, *History of Indian Theatre*, New Delhi: Publications Division, 1987.

73. For the date of *Nāṭyaśāstra*, Manmohan Ghosh has placed the *NŚ* in 500 BCE, Regnaud prefers to place it in the fourth century, Hariprasada Sastri in the second century BCE, Sylvan Levi around CE 300, a date that P.V. Kane also ascribes to the *NŚ*, while A.B. Keith holds that the lower limit is third century CE and S.K. De says that it could be dated only to fourth-sixth century, Kapila Vatsyayana places it between the second and fourth centuries CE.

74. *Nāṭyaśāstra*, Introduction, lxii.

75. Ibid., VII.15-20.

76. Monier-Williams, *Sanskrit-English Dictionary*, p. 1135 explains *sattva* as the true essence, spirit, mind, character, being, existence, reality.

77. *Nāṭyaśāstra*, XXIV.9.

78. Ibid., XXIV.12-3: *līlā vilāso vicchittirvibhramaḥ kilikiñcitaṁ* । *moṭṭāyitaṁ kuṭṭamitaṁ bibboko lalitaṁ tathā* ॥ *vihṛtaṁ ceti vijñeyā daśa strīṇāṁ svabhāvajāḥ* ॥

79. Ibid., XXXVI.64: *sarve tu lalitā bhāvāḥ strīṇāṁ kāryāḥ prayogataḥ* । *dhairyamādhuryasampannā bhāvāḥ kāryāśca pauruṣāḥ* ॥

80. The translator, Manmohan Ghosh, has built upon these by adding diverse adjectival phrases for men and women that emphasise the differences. What is revealed in this translation of the *Nāṭyaśāstra* (as in most translations) is a double gendering of the language, both by the original author and by the translator, who create their idealised images of femininity and masculinity.

81. *MWSE*, p. 1052 *śobhā*: beauty, lustre, brilliance, grace, loveliness.

82. *NŚ*, XXIV.25.

83. *NŚ*, XXIV.32.

84. *MSWE*, p. 809, *mādhurya*, lit. sweetness.

85. *NŚ*, XXIV. 27.

86. *MWSE*., p. 897. *lalita:* sported, played, wanton, amorous, voluptuous, artless, innocent, soft, gentle, charming. Also wished for, desired.

87. *NŚ*, XXIV.34.

88. Ibid., XXIV.29.

89. Ibid., XXIV.38.

90. Ibid., XXIV.26.

91. Ibid., XXIV.28.

92. *MWSE*., p. 659, *pragulbhya*: to be bold or confident, behave resolutely, brave, strong, able. *NŚ*, XXIV.29.

93. *Vilāsa* is usually associated with revelling, generally in public sphere.

94. *NŚ*, XXVII.60-61.

95. Kumkum Roy, "Of Theras and Therīs: Visions of Liberation in the Early Buddhist Tradition", in Vijaya Ramaswamy ed., *Re-searching Indian Women*, New Delhi: Manohar, 2003, p. 80. She also notes that when *bhikkhus* are named after their physical attributes the focus is on external deformities combined with less tangible skills.

96. Stewart, "Art, Desire and the Body in Ancient Greece," *BMCR* 99.10.9 http://omega.cohums.ohio-state.edu/hyper-lists/bmcr-1/1999/0.216.html. 1.2.2002, 17.07 p.m.

97. Uma Chakravarti and Kumkum Roy, "Breaking Out of Invisibility: Rewriting the History of Women in Ancient India", in S. Jay Kleinberg, ed.,

*Retrieving Women's History: Changing Perspectives of the Role of Women in Politics and Society*, Berg/UNESCO, 1988, p. 319.

98. The post-Mauryan period witnessed the rise of dominant goddesses who had independent cults and powerful imagery such as the Mātṛkās, Hāritī, Mahiṣāsuramardinī.

99. Seema Bawa, *Religion and Art of the Chamba Valley*, New Delhi: Agam Kala Prakashan, 1998, p. 154.

100. P. Jaini, op. cit., p. xi.

101. Rita M. Gross, *Buddhism After Patriarchy: A Feminist History, Analysis, and Reconstruction of Buddhism*, Albany: State University of New York Press, 1993, pp. 60-62.

102. Ibid., p. 62; she says that both Theravāda and Mahāyāna Buddhism existed in context of a patriarchal society strongly informed by andocentric values and modes of thought.

103. Alan Sponberg, "Attitudes toward Women and the Feminine in Early Buddhism", in Jose I Cabezon ed., *Buddhism, Sexuality and Gender*, 1985, pp. 3-35.

104. Kumkum Roy, op. cit., pp. 88-89.

105. Padmanabhan Jaini, op. cit., p. 13.

106. Ibid.

107. M.K. Dhavalikar, *Masterpieces of Terracotta*, Bombay: Taraporevala, 1977, p. 26, pl. 28.

108. James Fergusson, *Tree and Serpent Worship*, London: India Museum, 1873 (2nd edn), p. 10. where commenting on transparent dress of women says "Everywhere, indeed, before the Mohammedan conquest, nudity in India conveyed no sense of indecency. The wife and mother of Buddha are at times represented in the same manner."

109. Ananda Coomaraswamy, *Early Indian Iconography, II, Eastern Art*;. also fn. 10; idem, "Early Indian Terracottas", *Museum of Fine Arts Bulletin*, vol. XXV, 1927, p. 96, he observes "Such (nude) forms are by no means peculiar to India, but it is a remarkable illustration of the continuity of Indian culture that the old and spontaneous conception of fruitfulness and beauty as inseparable qualities have survived throughout the late artistic evolutions where it explains and therefore justifies the expansive and voluptuous warmth of the characteristically feminine types of Indian literature and sculpture."

110. Tapti Guha Thakurta, "What Makes for the 'Authentic' Female Nude in Indian Art?", in *Towards A New Art History: Studies in Indian Art*, ed. Shivaji K. Panikkar, Parul Dave Mukherjee and Deeptha Achar, pp. 358-84.

111. Female nakedness denotes gender and then women clothed. Stewart, op. cit., says that male is free, natural and naked while women clothed and under male control. Clothed and adorned female figures are enhanced by what they wear — both delight in it and increases her seductive impact she has on men.

112. *Atharvaveda*, ed. Damodar Satwalekar, XX.136.5-12; P.K. Agrawala, *Mithuna: The Male-Female Symbol in Indian Art and Thought*, Varanasi: Prithvi Prakashan, 1983, p. 9, on basis of the Atharvavedic text has explained that "in the primeval wilderness, both the archetypal Nudes wander of their own sweet will. The Nude Goddess chases the Nude God and offering him a dish of food invites: 'come, come you, O darling, come! Let you consume this food and unite with me.'"

113. Also see infra, Chapter V, Section on Nuns.

114. Pratapaditya Pal, *Indian Sculpture*, vol. I, Los Angeles: Los Angeles County Museum of Art, 1986, p. 177.

115. V. Desai, "History and Historiography of the Male Sexuality" in V. Dehejia, ed., *Representing the Body*, Delhi, pp. 42-55.

116. Ibid., p. 52.

117. In this context it may be pointed out that except in Jaina canonical literature, male nudity is not discussed. Thus there are no proscriptions against this practice, either because it was not conceived in negative terms or did not exist or did not evoke sexual arousal in the viewer of this nude male form in the same terms as it did for the female body.

118. According to J.N. Tiwari excluding female in erotic compositions in medieval Hindu temples, which, however, belong to an independent genre and need a different explanation, completely

nude female figures are not at all common in Indian art. J.N. Tiwari, *Goddess_Cults in Ancient India*, Sundeep Prakashan, Delhi, 1985, p 45.

119. Czuma, *Kushena Sculpture: Images from Early India*, pp. 85-86 commenting on the *nāginī* sculpture says that she is a voluptuous goddess that represents the traditional Indian ideal that perceives women as symbols of fertility (he does not explain how or why). Apart from characteristics defining her attributes of fecundity and fertility — heavy breasts, narrow waistline and broad hips — she displays the same somewhat massive, robust modelling.

120. I.B. Horner, *Women in Early Buddhism*, p. 224. Also See supra, Chapter 5, for attitudes towards nuns.

121. *Aṅguttara Nikāya*, V. XXII.10 (PTS edn.), vol. III, p. 256.

122. *atheka mṛcchaditthika yakkhini aceta hutva dve hatthe pasretva jihvam ninnametva dasabalassa puruto atthasi* — *Manorathapūraṇī*, vol. III, p. 329.

123. The same story is related also in the Bhaiṣajya Vāstu section of the Gilgit Manuscripts, with the difference that this naked goddess of Mathurā is called *devatā* instead of *yakkhiṇī*, see *Gilgit Manuscripts*, ed. Nalinaksha Dutt, vol. III, pt. 1, 2nd edn. New Delhi: Sri Satguru Publications, 1984, pp. 14-15.

124. *Buddhacarita*, Canto IV. 29-35.

125. Ibid., Canto IV.54-60.

126. *AS.*, 3.III.155, p. 176: *nagne vinagne nyaṅge 'pitṛke 'mātṛke ityanirdeśana vinayagrāhaṇam*; In Kangle's edition the first two words are *naste, vinaste*.

127. *Mbh.* 37.23, 37.22-23. Also R.S. Sharma, *Perspectives in Social and Economic History of Early India*, New Delhi: Munshiram Manoharlal, 1983, pp. 36-7.

128. *Mbh.*, 128.9-15.

129. Ibid., Śānti-Parva, IV. 7.

130. *Bṛhatsaṁhitā*, XIX.22

131. *Rājataraṅgiṇī*, IV.173-76

132. *Saptaśatī*, VI, 69. I, VI.2: *raktadukūlāntaritaḥ stananakhalekh iva navavadhvāḥ*.

133. Ibid., VII.20: *dvacyaṅgulakakapātapinaddhasaviśesanīlakañculikā, darśayanti stanasthalavarṇikāmiva taruṇīm yuvajanebyyaḥ*.

VI.45: *grāmataruṇyo hṛdayam haranti vidagdhānām stanbhāravatyaḥ* । *madane kusumbhrāgayuktakañkukābhranbhrāntāḥ* Cf. Altekar, p. 287, fn 3.

134. *na nābhim darśayedāgulphādvasaḥ paridadhyāt; na stanau vivrtau kuryāt* — *Śaṅkhasmṛti* (page and verse not given), Cf. Altekar, p. 282, fn. 3.

135. S.J. Czuma, op. cit, pp. 85-86; Bénjamin Rowland, *Art of East and West*, Boston: Beacon Press, 1959, p. 19.

136. An article published in *The Hindustan Times* on 18-04-2004 reported that women in the lower foothills of Nepal were stripping themselves naked and tying themselves to the straps of the plough in order to avert an impending drought.

137. *AŚ*, 3.III.156, p. 177.

138. *Rājapraśnīyya Sūtra*, pp. 66-67: *tesi naṁ dārāṇaṁ ubhayo pāse duhaau ṇisīhiyāye solasa solasa sālabhanjiyāparivādio paṇṇattau taau* । *ṇam sālabhanjiyāu līlāttiyāu supaittiyāu sualankiyāu ṇāṇāviharāgavaṇāu ṇāṇāmallapiṇadvāu mutthigicjhasumajshāu āmelagajamalajuyala vaṭṭiya abbhuṇṇayapiṇara-iyasan*.

139. *MWSE*, *prakṛti*: nature, character, essential.

140. *MWSE*, *puruṣa*: male, man, manhood.

141. Infra, Preface.

142. A.K. Coomaraswamy, Eastern Art, II, p. 185.

143. "Das weibliche Schön-heits ideal der indischen Kunst, mit seinen inneraus betonten Formen, hat in der Kunst der ganzen Welt keine bessere Schwester als die paläolithische Venus von Willendorf. . . . Es ist zweifellos ein vorarisches Ideal körperlicher Vollendung zu einer Schönheit, die gleichbedeutend mit Fruchtbarkeit ist." Stella Kramrisch, *Grundzuge der indischen Kunst*, Avalun-Verlag, Hellerau bei Dresden 1924, pp. 29-30. with reference to the Bharhut relief fig. 4.

144. "die äussere Erscheinung ist dem Inder ein getreuer Spiegel seelischer Struktur." H. Zimmer, *Kunstform und Yoga im indischen Kultbild*, Berlin: Frankfurter Verlags-Anstalt, 1926, p. 158.

145. Devanagana Desai, *Erotic Sculpture of India*,

Bombay, 1985, p. 18 says Cults of Fertility, specially the cult of Goddess Śri, have a direct bearing on the depiction of *mithunas* in religious art. She goes on to say that *yakṣas* and *yakṣīs* were the deities of fertility and vegetation cults worshipped for wealth, prosperity, children, etc. In the art of Bharhut, preceding that of Mathurā by about 200 years, the *yakṣas* represented the cultic characteristics in their solemn poses and typical hand gestures like *tarjañī-mudrā*. But the voluptuous female figures of Mathurā are devoid of cultic significance and suggest a secularisation of the original divinities.

146. A. Foucher, *On The Iconography of The Buddha's Nativity*, MASI, no. 46, Delhi: Manager of Publications, 1934.

147. A.K. Coomarawamy, *Yaksas: Essays in The Water Cosmology*, New Delhi: Indira Gandhi National Center for the Arts, 1993; Infra; Chapter 6.

148. J. Ph. Vogel, *Archaeological Museum at Mathurā*, Delhi: Indological Books House, 1971 (rpt.); James Fergusson, *Tree and Serpent Worship*, London: India Museum, 1873 (2nd edn.)

149. See Infra, Chapter 6 sub-section, Śālabhañjikā.

150. See supra, Chapter 4.

151. *NŚ*, II.84-85: *citrakarmaṇi cālekhyāḥ puruṣāḥ strījanāstathā* | | *latābandhāśca kartavyāścaritaṁ ātmabhogajaṁ* |

152. *NŚ*, II.95: *dharaṇīdhāristāste ca śālastrībhiralamkṛtā.*

153. See Infra, Chapter 2, Section on Aditi / Lakṣmī.

154. Supra, Introduction, for the historical context in which post-Mauryan art was produced and consumed.

155. Anna Libera Dallapiccola and Stephanie Zingel Ave Lallemant, eds., *The Stupa: Its Religious, Historical and Architectural Significance*, Wiesbaden: Franz Steiner Verlag, 1980.

156. Himanshu Prabha Ray, *Monastery and Guild: Commerce Under The Satavahanas*, Delhi: Oxford University Press, 1986 pp. 193-94.

157. Jeannine Auboyer, *Daily Life in Ancient India*, New Delhi: Munshiram Manoharlal, p. 76.

158. *Mṛchh.*, Act III.86

159. V.K. Thakur, *Historiography of Indian Feudalism*, Patna: Janaki Prakashan, 1989, pp. 38-39; the account of the Kali Age in the *Mahābhārata* and the Brāhmanical Purāṇas with its myth of the four ages did provide a schematic framework for the expression and awareness of changes in material conditions and traditional values that occurred with the beginning of land grant economy.

160. Ibid.

161. *Saundarānanda*, XVIII.63-64 : *prāyeṇālokya lokaṁ viśayaratiparaṁ mokṣātpratihataṁ kāvyavyājen tattvaṁ kathitamih mayāmokṣaḥ paramiti, tadbudcva śāmikaṁ yatradavahitamito grāhyaṁ na lalitaṁ pāṁśubhyo dhātujebhyo niyatamupakaraṁ cāmī karamiti* [64].

# 2

# The Essential, Reproductive Woman

Biology predetermines that men and women are reproductive beings. Socialisation, on the other hand, ensures that the discourse of reproduction essentially defines women by their body, thus primarily equating women with their reproductive potential. These notions are effectively essentialised and internalised. This potential has then been abstracted and transformed into many layers of meaning that range from physical fertility to universal prosperity. The ability to increase and perpetuate the human species — and, through sympathetic association, plant and animal species[1] — has on the one hand been located biologically within the female body and on the other is personified by the feminine in religio-artistic discourse[2] by associating it with universals such as fertility.

Two sites are especially important for the construction of the reproductive female. (The reproductive woman being necessarily contiguous with the sexual female.) These are the genital and the "pectoral" regions — sites associated with reproduction and nurturing respectively. In the ancient textual tradition too, female*ness* is located in the *yoni* and *stana*. The Jaina text, *Malyagirivṛtti* (CE 1150), in describing the female and the feminine as *strīveda* enumerates seven characteristics or (*lakṣaṇa*s) of the feminine. These are: *yoni* (genitalia and womb), *stana* (breasts), *mṛdutva* (softness), *asthairya* (instability or impermanence), *mugdhatā* (innocence/attractiveness), *abalatā* (weakness) and *puṁsakāmitā* (desire to mate with the male).[3] The first two refer to biological and the latter five refer to social symbols of sex/gender. *Yoni* and *stana* represent the primary and the secondary female reproductive organs. Breasts and vulva remain very important symbols for married Indian women in many parts of India.[4]

Representational types that emphasise attributes special to the female body are significant in the light of the fact that nudity is one of the most noticeable features of the entire post-Mauryan art, especially with regard to female figures.[5] This period and its art can also be considered seminal in defining notions of womanhood and femininity, both in textual and visual traditions — notions that are perpetuated, replicated or transformed in subsequent centuries. This makes the manner in which reproductive female bodies are constituted during this period, significant for studying gender relations and art.

It may be observed that the majority of female figures in the art of the "Śuṅga-Kuṣāṇa" period display prominently marked genitalia (openly or covered by transparent drapery) and prominent, round, full breasts. In this book I seek to recover the physical constitution of the female and feminine along with the meanings associated with their representation. In pursuing this argument, I examine first two sets of sculptures that privilege both the genital and the pectoral elements of a female body, resulting in a "feminisation" of the body/representation. The examples analysed below belong to the period of the first century BCE through the third century CE. They encompass disparate art traditions, such as free-standing sculptures, narrative reliefs and terracottas. These examples assist us in constructing a comprehensive picture of the manner in which the female body was composed within the visual discourse of the period.

The first representational types defined are those emphasising the genitalia, epitomised by a nude lotus-headed figure with outspread legs. The second kind is epitomised by the breast-offering woman. Both figural types emphasise biological reproductive potential on the one hand and female sexuality, with its inherent erotic possibilities, on the other.

An element common to both the above types of representations is their sharing attributes of the Vedic goddess Aditi. Aditi is simultaneously considered a source of life and the universal nourisher. This goddess seems to have influenced the concept of the "divine feminine" in early Indian Art. Significantly, during this period the first sculptural representations of the female (excluding those under the terracotta tradition and certain Mauryan pieces), are produced. Pṛthvī, the earth goddess, shares the nurturing element and also the wish-fulfilling ability, and is often identified with Aditi, a goddess who is further associated with water, fruitfulness, and life-supporting functions. These characteristics are well suited to the imagining of the fertile, reproductive divine feminine image at a time when such visual and textual imagery was beginning to be envisaged and assembled. These very elements are later absorbed into the cult of Śrī-Lakṣmī, who is invoked and celebrated in the Śrī-Sūkta (a *khila* of the *Ṛgveda*) and later texts, which associate Lakṣmī with lotuses, moisture, procreation and universal prosperity.

### 2.1 Lajjā-Gaurī

A divine feminine represented in early Indian art remains enigmatic in identity and intriguing in significance. This personification of the genitalia exhibits a *yoni*[6] or a pudendum, set within

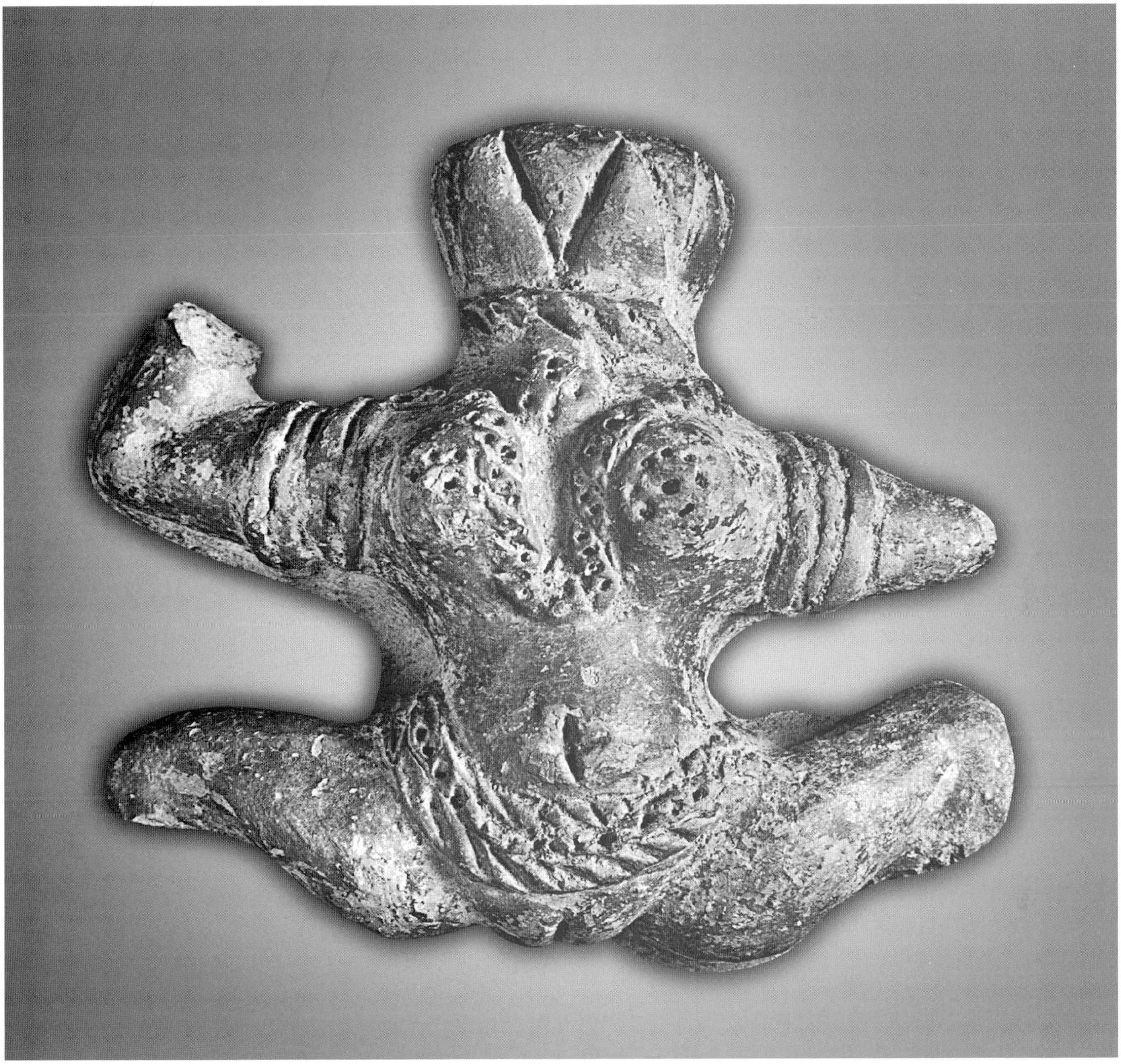

2.1.1 Nude goddess/Lajjā Gaurī, hand-modelled terracotta, second-third century CE, Jhusi, Allahabad district, UP. AM No. Jh. 4617.

outspread legs, signifying "birth-giving." An interesting aspect is the absence of a human face on top of the torso that is often being replaced by a lotus. This deity is crucial to recovering the essentially "feminine" from art. It is difficult to identify this image with a name, since classical sources are silent on the identity or iconography that would approximate to this imagery. Yet, its spread in space and time seems to suggest that she is a popular goddess in the society of the early period. For the sake of convenience she is referred to here as Lajjā-Gaurī, a name acquired from art historians.

## 2.1.1 SCULPTURAL EVIDENCE

A recent monograph on the Lajjā-Gaurī figures has noticed up to 124 sculptures, spread over the entire country; of these 62 each are assigned to north and south India.[7] Of the northern examples, as many as 48 images are in stone and 14 are in terracotta. In southern India the preponderance of stone is even more marked, with 51 sculptures compared to 11 terracotta plaques. The terracotta pieces seem to have been concentrated in the Upper Gangetic Valley, in and around the Kauśāmbī, Bhītā and Jhusi regions. Another terracotta tradition exists at this time in the Maharashtra, north Karnataka and Andhra Pradesh area,[8] a region that coincides largely with the Sātavāhana and Ikṣvāku rule. Later manifestations of similar sculptures abound in Tamil Nadu, Andhra Pradesh and Karnataka, frequently published examples being the Ālampur and Bādāmi images datable to the eighth century CE.[9]

Unfortunately the dating of the terracotta pieces is a contentious issue since, except for one example from Nāgārjunakoṇḍa, no inscription with a positive date accompanies any of these pieces. The dating is therefore largely dependent on stratigraphy of the excavated sites, and comparative stylistic analysis. Even this is often hampered by the fact of these terracottas having been surface finds. Nevertheless, a consensual dating of the Upper Gangetic Valley has been achieved which places them between the first century BCE and the second century CE.[10] The Andhra-Karnataka-Maharashtra finds from Ṭer,

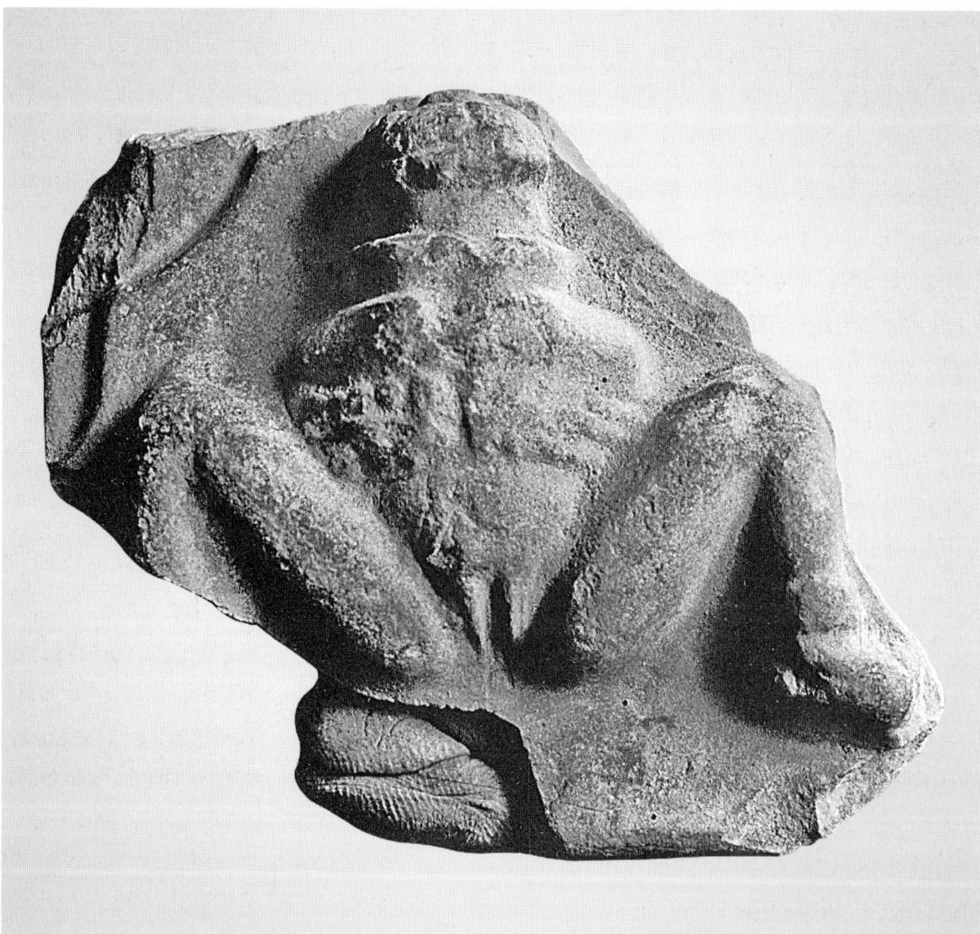

2.1.2 Lajjā Gaurī, headless, armless, no decoration, terracotta, first-third century CE. Ter Museum.

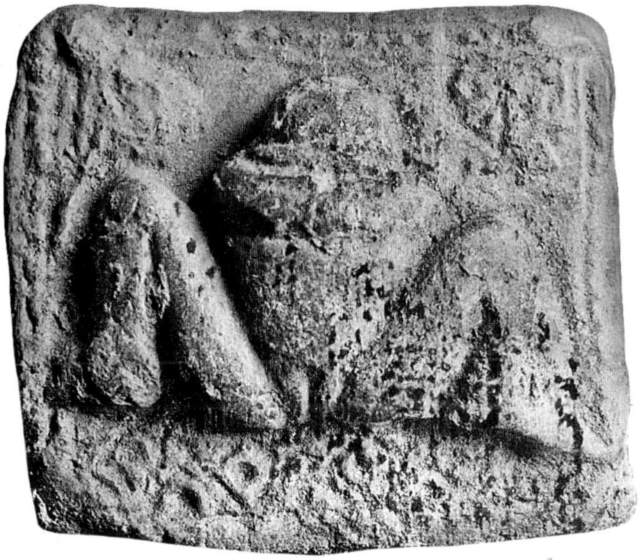

2.1.3 Lajjā Gaurī plaque, headless, armless, decoration below at corners, Sātavāhana, terracotta, *c.* first-third century CE. Ter Museum.

Nevāsā, Sannati, etc. have been dated to the first three centuries of the Christian Era on basis of their association with Red Polished Ware and Black and Red Pottery.[11]

In terms of typology, sometimes even within the same site, the personified *yoni* image exhibits variety. Carol Radcliffe Bolon has typologically classified the corpus of Lajjā-Gaurī stone sculptures and terracotta plaques into four groups.[12]

*Form I* — *Uttānapāda Pot*: a pot-like torso with human legs (*Pl.* 2.1.2), the legs outspread to reveal the pubic mound. This may be topped by a lotus (*Pl.* 2.1.10?) like the one seen emerging from the brimming vase (*pūrṇaghaṭa*) in early *art.*

*Form II* — A lotus-headed deity without arms but with the torso having breasts (*Pl.* 2.1.4).

*Form III* — A lotus-headed deity with arms (*Pl.* 2.1.1), perhaps holding lotus stalks in its hands (*Pls.* 2.1.6, 2.1.8).

*Form IV* — An anthropomorphic type having a human head, the only attribute linking it to the personified *yoni* being a seated posture with outspread legs.

This section concentrates on the first three forms, which fall within our period. A large number of lotus-headed figures have been found in the Kauśāmbī region. One of these (Form II) terracotta image[13] sports a circular object with vertical rising lines and pin-prick grooves, which may represent a petalled flower, instead of a neck and face. The breasts are prominent. The legs are spread out in the birth-giving position and the pudendum bears a genital cleft. One cannot make out any arms (possibly the image was intended to be armless) and the feet are broken off (not illustrated). Another fragmentary (Form II) female image from Kauśāmbī[14] displays (the essential characteristics) of updrawn legs with clearly marked genital cleft. She wears a *mekhalā* of two or three strings of pearls, which accentuates the rounded contours of the abdomen, approximating to a *pūrṇaghaṭa* or a pregnant woman (*Pl.* 2.1.5). The legs and part of

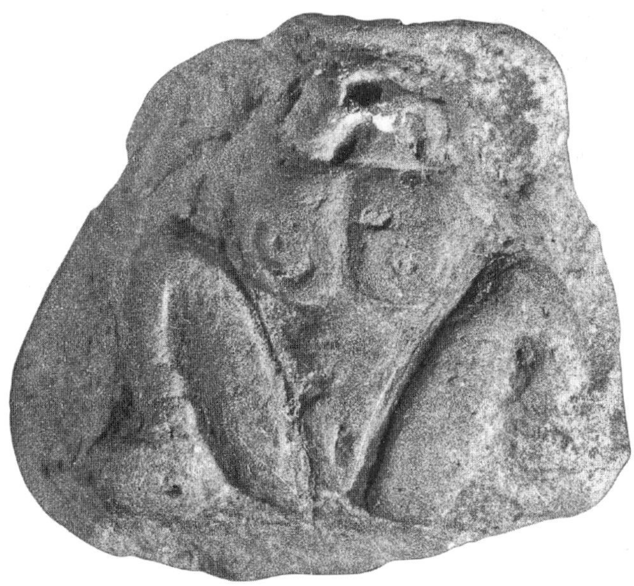

2.1.4 Hand-modelled terracotta, first century CE, Kauśāmbī, UP. Allahabad district. AM No. K 3904.

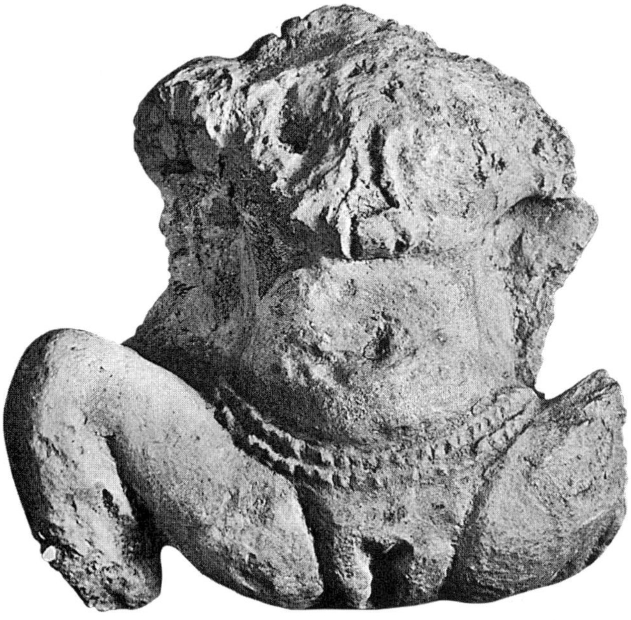

2.1.5 Nude goddess, torso, hand-modelled terracotta, second-third century CE, Kauśāmbī, Allahabad district, UP. AM No. K 5214.

the lotus-face are broken. Two other fragments of female figures from the same site[15] have the same birth-giving posture and the pudendum with a *mekhalā* on the torso, but the rest is badly damaged.

One of the best-preserved representations of the lotus-headed deity of the Form III variety has been found at Jhusi in Uttar Pradesh and is currently in the Allahabad Museum (*Pl.* 2.1.1).[16] It is a hand-moulded terracotta with red-coloured slip. The head, of cushion-like form, has a recurring triangular design incised on it, which may represent the petals of an upturned lotus. The left arm is stretched to the side while her right arm is raised from the elbow in L-shape. Both legs of the figure are stretched out in M-shape, revealing the genital mound with the pudenda clearly marked by a slit. The figure is adorned with a torque and a necklace, the latter dangling between the breasts. Besides these, she is shown wearing a series of armbands and a rope-patterned *mekhalā* or girdle. The breasts have tiny groove marks in concentric circles and a shallow cross indicates the navel. Parts of the arms and legs of the figure are broken.

Two of (Form III) female busts, also from Kauśāmbī,[17] are preserved only from the waist up. One has stump-like arms stretched out to the sides; a thick roll replaces the head, it is decorated with triangles which may signify a lotus. A double grooved line is visible on the neck. She wears a necklace bearing punched circlets, and traces of an armlet can be seen on the right arm (*Pl.* 2.1.10). In the other bust, a lump of clay resembling a basket, its outer surface decorated by incised overlapping petals, can be seen in place of the head. There are incised lines on the neck, below which there is a five-strand torque that partly covers her breasts. A punched circlet indicates nipples. It is highly likely that the now missing lower portion consisted of outspread legs with an exposed, raised pudendum. One terracotta fragment, painted with red slip, from Kauśāmbī and now in the Lucknow Museum,[18] has a lotus head in the form of a half-open flower worn like a crown. The figure leans slightly forward and is shown wearing a lotus filament necklace. The breasts are quite carefully formed. The surviving upraised hand wears a number of bangles and the curved frame has a ridged edge. At the Patna Museum there is another figure from Kauśāmbī made of red sandstone with a lotus head and outspread legs.[19]

John Marshall published a terracotta figure from Bhītā that may be categorised as Form III.[20] This is a circular plaque, datable to the late Kuṣāṇa or early Gupta period. On one side of the plaque a female figure with arms and legs outstretched is depicted. In place of the head there is a lotus flower with its petals falling over the shoulders and a lotus-*mekhalā* over the womb. A similar figure is reported from Kosam.[21] A

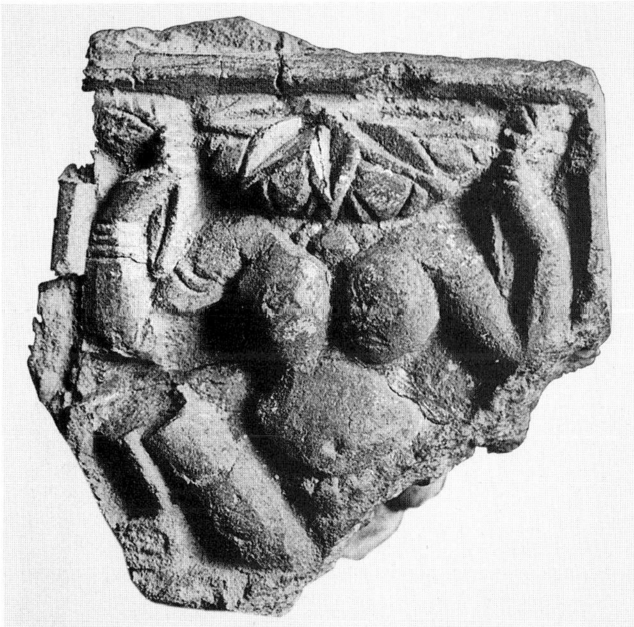

2.1.8 Lajjā Gaurī plaque, floral head, front, red sandstone, *c.* first-third century CE. Ter Museum.

described at length. Made of pink sandstone, datable to the Sātavāhana-Vākāṭaka period, all these four display the birth-giving position with the pudenda clearly delineated. The face is in the form of a full-blown lotus[33] or a conical bud-like form with four petals,[34] tapered at the top and with two curved projections on either side. This may also represent a coconut, which is traditionally placed on top of ritual pots (*kalaśas*). The lotus-face also takes the form of a series of circular bands arising from the neck region.[35] Additional motifs observed are a seated bull and lion on the left and right sides respectively. Two long stalks ending in lotus buds are also visible.

A unique figure from Mathurā, dated to the second century, now in the Victoria and Albert Museum, London,[36] has a frog on one side and a female figure on the other. Seated in a rather cramped *uttānapāda* posture, her arms are upraised. The pudendum is not visible; instead a stippling effect covers the genital mound. Above the mound is a *mekhalā* of incised medallions or large pearls. The breasts are well formed. She wears a necklace fitted closely around the neck. A lotus with a conical top crowns her face. A full human face, seen on one side of this work is very unusual, both for this period and also within the Lajjā-Gaurī terracotta tradition.

Some iconographically similar sculptures belonging to a later period of Caḷukyan lineage from Bādāmi, dated to the seventh century CE, and of the late Coḷa period from Dārasuram and Tanjore district, have been published by Nagaswamy.[37]

A Cāḷukyan stone image from Ālampur had been discussed in detail by Stella Kramrisch, who dates it to *c.* CE 600.[38] Carol Radcliffe Bolon too has published many late Vākāṭaka-Cāḷukya-Coḷa figures.[39]

The above survey of the known terracotta and stone images belonging to the post-Mauryan period suggests that the representational type enjoyed considerable popularity.

There are no analogous figures which emphasise only the male genitalia during the

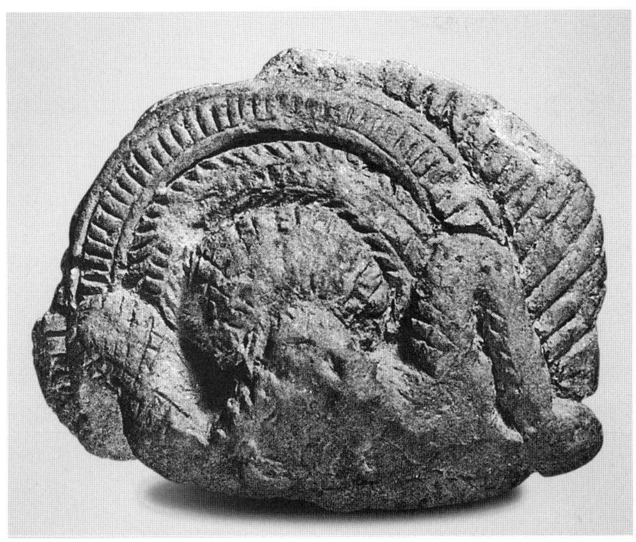

2.1.9 A nude goddess with a flower, torso and head, mould made terracotta, first century CE, Kauśāmbī, Allahabad district, UP. AM No. K 5033.

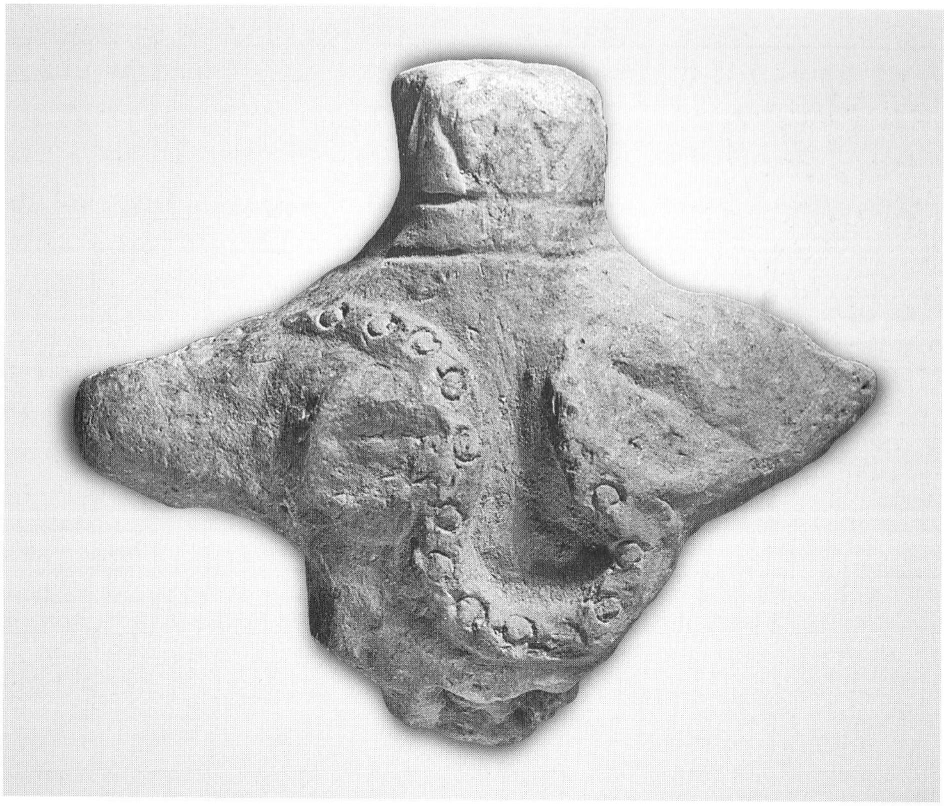

2.1.10 Nude Goddess, torso fragment, hand-modelled terracotta, first-third century CE, Kauśāmbī, Allahabad district, UP. AM No. K 3849.

2.1.11 Nude goddess, stone, first-second century CE, Bhīta, UP. AM.

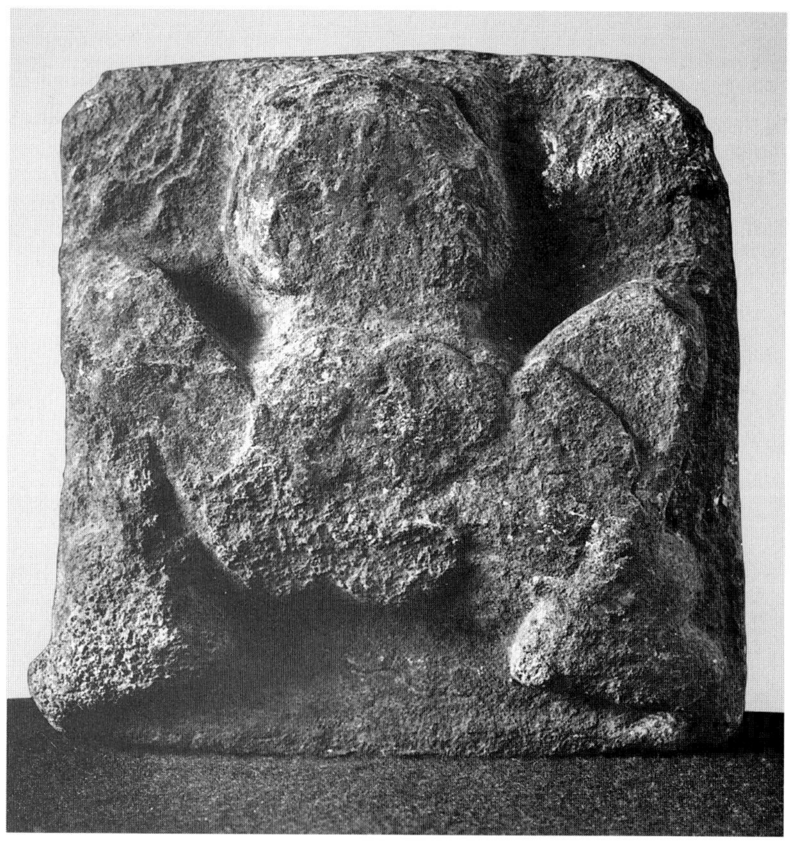

period. The *liṅga*, though valorising the phallus, as a class of sculpture (found prolifically from the Śuṅga period onwards) cannot be compared to the personified *yoni* type. First, the *liṅga* has rarely been found in terracotta. Secondly and more importantly, the *liṅga* belongs to a separate category of religious imagery partly because it can be firmly located within the Śaiva tradition, a tradition that is well established, popular and visible. The same cannot be said of the personified *yoni* type, which indeed does not seem to belong to any mainstream religious sectarian tradition.

I have been able to trace only two pieces that may in some way be considered male counterparts of the personified *yoni* images in the sense that they represent nude figures with exposed genitalia. However, considering the fragmentary condition of the pieces, this claim is very tentative.

One of these, a terracotta from Sārnāth which is datable in the second century CE, is hand modelled,[40] and depicts a male figure with prominent genitalia but whose head is now broken off. From the neck downwards one can see drooping lotus petals (or this feature might be a thick mane), and its arms are akimbo. The other is also a terracotta figure from Shahabad in Hardoi district, Uttar Pradesh.[41] It is a mould-made sculpture, now a headless nude male. Below a V-shaped torso the erect phallus is prominently shown because the legs are stretched outwards, the figure being seated in *lalitāsana* (*Pl.* 2.1.16).

### 2.1.2 ORIGIN AND IDENTIFICATION

The sheer number of Lajjā-Gaurī figures and their geographical spread bear testimony to their popularity and influence in our period. The interesting fact is that some of the terracotta representations are mould-made therefore indicative of replication reinforcing the perception of the prevalence of Lajjā-Gaurī worship. There is very little doubt that this image-type represents a female divinity, since it is frequently found associated with divine symbols such as lotuses, animals, *vāhana*s and pedestals. In absence of any textual reference that provides a definitive description of a lotus-headed nude

2.1.12 Nude goddess, hand-modelled terracotta, *c.* first-third century CE, Kauśāmbī. AM No. K 4865.

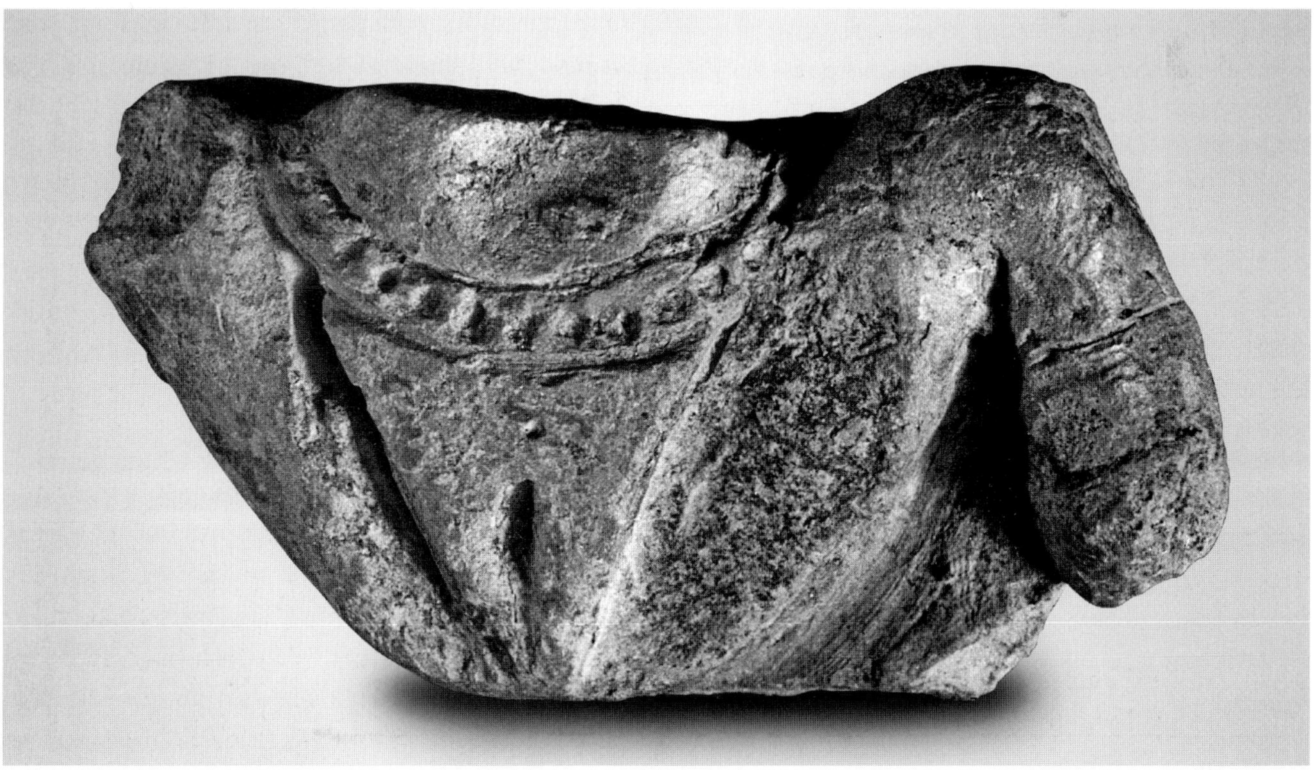

female figure, the identification of this deity has been a matter of controversy.

In most of the early pieces, the deity is two-armed; apart from confirming their early date, this feature indicates that the images are not part of the larger Brāhmanic pantheon. By the end of the Kuṣāṇa period (third century CE), images of gods and goddesses having four arms or more became the norm in the Brāhmanic iconographic tradition, especially in north, central and western India.

An essential distinguishing feature common to all the sculptures of Lajjā-Gaurī is the outstretched legs.[42] This position has been termed *uttānapāda*, which derives from *uttāna*, meaning stretched out, spread out, lying on the back, sleeping supinely or with the face upwards. *Uttānapāda* implies one whose legs are extended in parturition. The term is also associated with creative agency, vegetation and creation of upward germinating plants.[43] This posture and the term for it have been ascribed to Aditi:

> In the first age of the gods, the existent was formed from the non-existent. After this regions were born. This [existent] was born of her with the legs spread open (*uttānapāda*). The world was born of her with the legs spread open. From Aditi, Dakṣa was born and from Dakṣa, Aditi.[44]

Aditi is invoked as granter of wishes, the far-spreading, the Earth, the mother.

> We call for aid verily on the great mother of them of good courses, the spouse of righteousness (*ṛta*), on her of mighty authority, not growing old, wide spreading, on the well sheltering, well conducted Aditi."[45]

Also, the well preserving earth, the unenvious sky, the well-sheltering, the well-conducting Aditi, with well-oared ship of the gods.... Now in the impulse of might (*vāja*) will be commemorated with utterance (*vacas*) the great mother Aditi by name, whose lap is the broad atmosphere, may she confirm to us thrice defending protection.[46]

Besides being *uttānapāda* in the sense that her legs are well spread out and broad (a characteristic shared by Pṛthvī, the earth mother), Aditi is also conceptualised as the universal mother and creatrix.

The second element, special to the Lajjā-Gaurī representational type, is the prominently exposed pudendum. This element is very difficult to identify with a particular deity since no text mentions this as an essential attribute of any goddess. Though this is seen in the female figures on stone discs (see *pls.* 2.1.13 to 2.1.15). We have to assume that it signifies the reproductive potential of women in general and of the deity represented by this image in particular. In the *Atharvaveda* one hymn is devoted to the intercourse between *Mahānagnī*[47] and *Mahānagna*[48] (the Great Female Nude and the Great Male Nude) which is symbolic of the fertility of the plant, animal and human world.[49] However, it does not indicate the worship of a Female Nude alone. Exposed pudenda is often encountered in female figures that belong to the art of this period but not in this "birth-giving" position and not without a human or animal head.

The other distinguishing feature of Lajjā-Gaurī or the personified *yoni* images is the lotus head and lotus stems that surround her. The lotus would ideally connect her with Śrī-Lakṣmī, as suggested by J.N. Banerjea.[50] In the Śrī-Sūkta, Śrī is associated with lotuses. The lotus is her symbol and it also serves as her seat; she stands/sits on a lotus (*padmasthitā*); which serves as the centre of

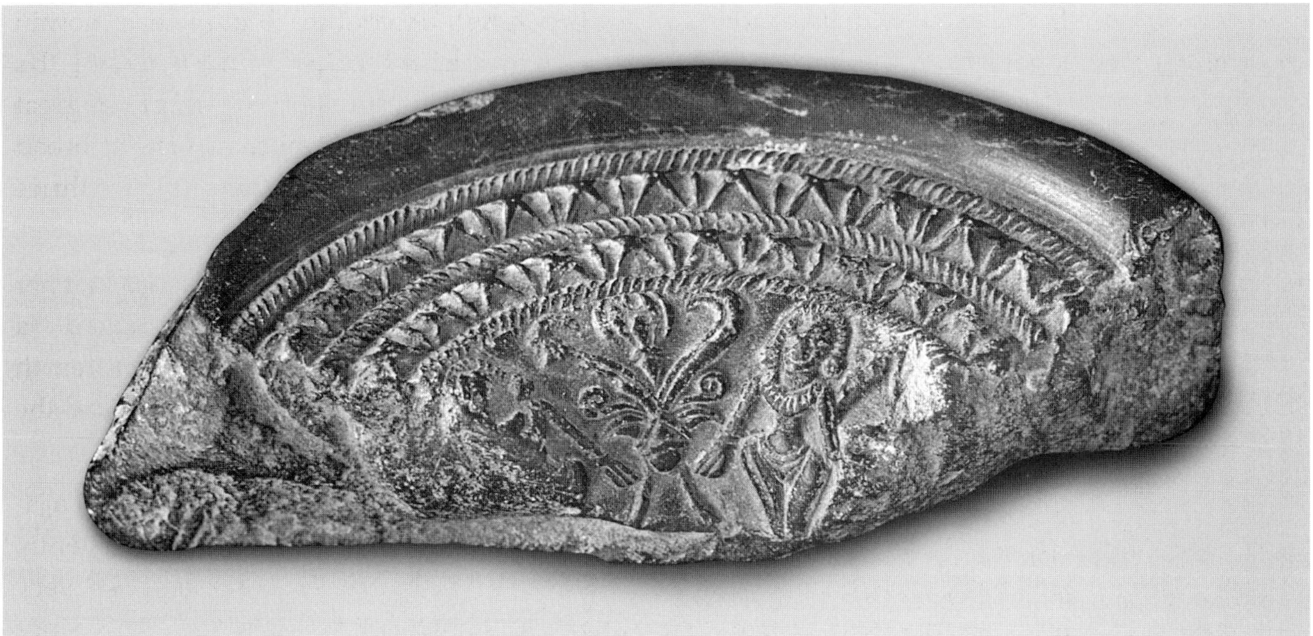

2.1.13 Stone disc Kauśāmbī, stone, *c*. third century BCE, Allahabad district, UP. AM 23.

2.1.14 Stone disc Kauśāmbī, stone, *c*. third century BCE, Allahabad district, UP. AM Mor. 28.

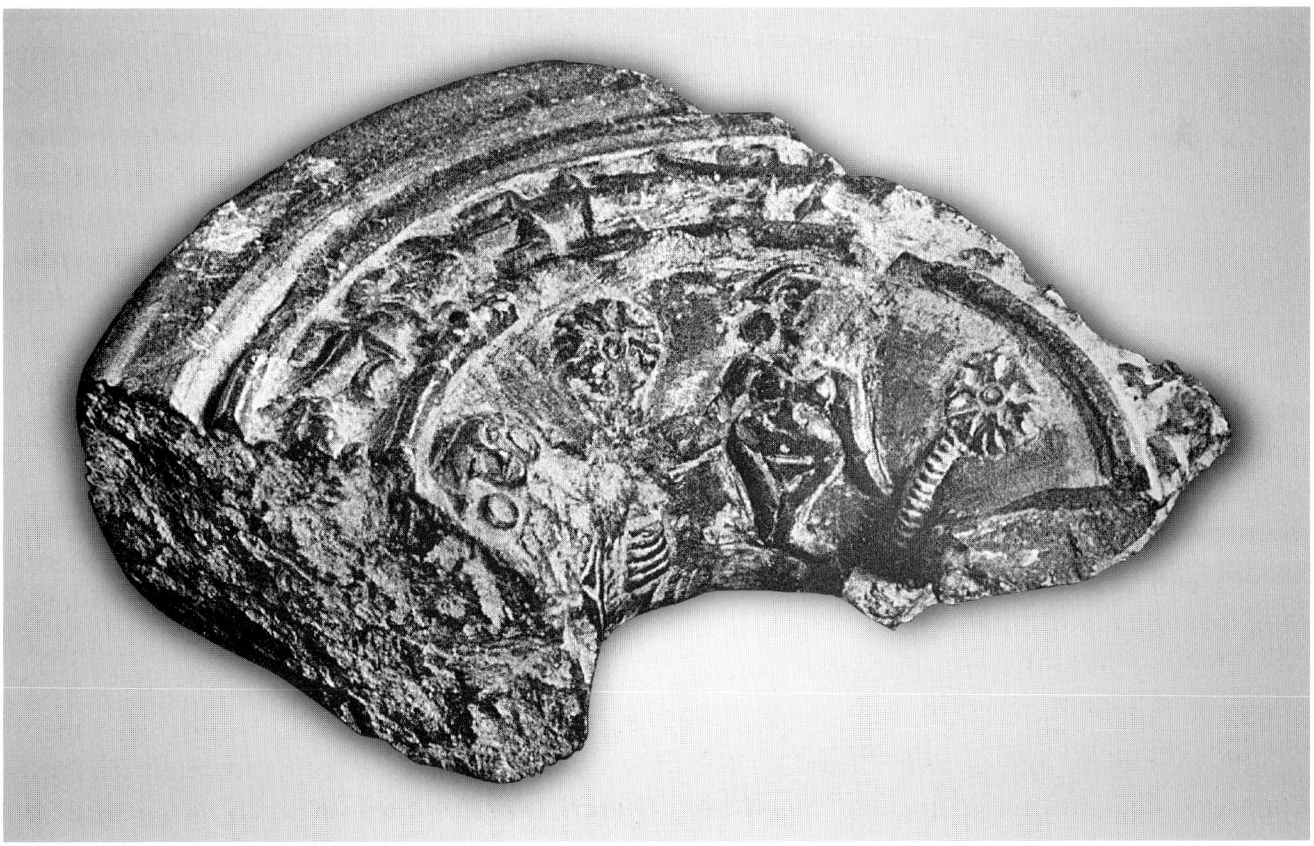

the disc (*padmanemī*); and as its encircling garland (*padmamālā*). She is born from the lotus, which springs from the waters (*adbhyaḥ padmasambhava*) surrounded by lotus buds and leaves. She is the goddess of prosperity (*dhanadāyī* and *mātṛ-dhana*) and fertility (*prajānām bhavasi mātā, putra pautraṁ dhanaṁ dhānyaṁ karetu me* ).[51] A word of caution may be added here: though at later stages the lotus became the special attribute of Śrī-Lakṣmī (a goddess who assimilated many features of Vedic Aditi in the post-Mauryan period), in art the lotus is not exclusive to Lakṣmī. Nor is the lotus-head ever prescribed to Lakṣmī — she is never called *padmamukhī* or *kamalamukhī*,[52] for example. It may be added here that though we frequently encounter animal-headed goddesses in post-Mauryan art,[53] plant-headed deities are hard to come by.

Who, then, is this enigmatic goddess? Stella Kramrisch proposes one of the earliest and most influential opinions on the identity of the goddess by calling her Aditi-Uttānapāda. Similar to the Lakṣmī of the Śrī-Sūkta, she has a lotus-face and lotus-thigh, she is also the "Lady of Abundance." She has a "billowing" form and has "wetness" of water in her element. Using later Vedic literary references, Kramrisch explains the significance of the lotus in the context of Indian art in general and in the context of the Ālampur figure in particular. The lotus, symbol of creativity, blooms above the water. The waters in turn nourish and sustain plant life. She is also the earth, Pṛthvī, the Broad One, spread on the water, the support of all living beings, (Śrī-Sūkta 9).

Marshall was of the opinion that the Bhītā terracotta plaque could be identified with Pṛthvī,[54] though he did not provide any reasoning to support this claim.

P.K. Agrawala agrees with Marshall and Kramrisch that the nude goddess represents Earth Mother.[55] According to him, her posture is such as to receive the seed of the male Sky God and her legs being spread apart suggests a birth-giving posture, which implies that she causes all life to originate from her inexhaustible womb. He identifies her lotus as the *bhū padma* or Earth Lotus.

Sankalia combines ethnographic study with archaeology to arrive at the conclusion that the series of terracotta from Maharashtra and Karnataka represent Lajjā-Gaurī, goddess of childbirth. He translates Lajjā-Gaurī as the "shameless woman" since she is not concerned about covering her nudity.[56] He further notes the current practice of childless women worshipping the Lajjā-Gaurī deity by applying red lead and butter to the breasts and vagina of the image of the goddess.

Sankalia classifies Lajjā-Gaurī as one of the mother goddesses that have enjoyed worship all over Asia and Europe since early proto-historic times. The nude goddess of the "shameless woman" type is seen to approximate to the Egyptian goddess Baubo,[57] remains of whose images have been found up to the Roman period.[58] According to him, Stella Kramrisch's identification of the figure as representing Aditi-uttānapāda is a later apotheosis of an idea or symbolism which was originally foreign.[59] However, Sankalia is unable to explain the significance of the lotus replacing the face in the majority of Lajjā-Gaurī representations. The goddess is lotus-headed and not "headless" as he describes her. This imagery may have its origins in early terracottas in the Mathura Museum that depict a female figure standing with a lotus stalk growing up her back and with lotus flower blossoming on top of her head.

In an exhaustive monograph on the Lajjā-Gaurī, Carol Radcliffe Bolon has based her identification of the goddess on epithets used in current practice. Many of the local names used for this deity are descriptive of the icon, such as Nagna Kabandha or Kamalamukhī, respectively meaning Nude Goddess or Lotus-Faced. Other names, such as Śākambharī or Ellamā, are based on elements of her persona.[60]

Using considerably later textual material (the *Lalitāsahasranāma*, the *Kalpasūtra* and Bhāskararāya's commentary), R. Nagaswamy has identified images from the Cāḷukyan and Coḷa regions as representing *Mahākuṇḍalinī Śakti* in its abstract and physical forms.[61] In his view, most of the figures of "Lajjā-Gaurī" with lotus heads can be dated from the beginning of the Christian Era, when the concept of *yoga* with *Mahākuṇḍalinī* at its centre had taken deep root and was further assimilated into all sub-sects of Indian religion. By derivation, the image type being discussed here coincided with that of *yoginī*s. However, it must be mentioned that there is no textual description of a *yoginī* or of the *kuṇḍalinī* which matches the iconographic features of the Lajjā-Gaurī series.

V.S. Agrawala has published a dozen terracottas from Ahicchatra, which he classifies as nude females, analogous to Lajjā-Gaurī figures. However these depictions are of standing women with human heads.[62] He has identified these with Koṭṭavi,[63] a goddess worshipped in south India who is described as being nude and inauspicious. This raises the question as to whether we can posit a connection between nudity and the evil and ominous nature of the goddess.

In Paurāṇic texts Lajjā is equated to Modesty, the daughter of Dakṣa, wife of Dharma and the mother of Vinaya or good behaviour. The associations here are with qualities considered to be womanly virtues. On the other hand, Gaurī is the brilliant one who is the wife of Viṣṇu or Varuṇa and as such associated with life-giving waters. Gaurī as a class of goddesses is seen as Śiva's wife, such as Umā, Rambhā, Totalā, Tripurā and Śrī. Taken together, something akin to Modest or Innocence, and wife of Śiva would be the meaning of Lajjā-Gaurī.[64] None of these is actualised in the iconography of the personified *yoni* type of goddess.

According to Carol Radcliffe Bolon all evidence points towards the identification of Lajjā-Gaurī images as symbols of fertility. She sees them as part of the Hindu religion and Śaiva sect, and that by the sixth-century Lajjā-Gaurī is considered to be the Śakti of Śiva.

She further traces four distinct iconographic forms of Lajjā-Gaurī, each broadly corresponding to a period and a region.[65] She has divided the known images into the *uttānapāda* pot-form, lotus-headed without arms, lotus-headed with arms and the anthropomorphic deity. These are seen respectively as conforming to a personified symbol, the brimming vase, an incomplete female form with plant parts, and a fully female form with a human, not a lotus, head in a chronologically evolving pattern. She views this as a development from the original village goddess, worshipped for fertility in the form of a pot, which was then elaborated in the second century to include legs. In the third century in south India the goddess further evolved to include arms, culminating into a fully anthropomorphic form in the Deccan under royal patronage in the mid-sixth century.

There is however a problem with this kind of schematic evolutionary model, as Radcliffe Bolon herself acknowledges. At many sites such as Ṭer and Kauśāmbī, the first three forms are found from the same layer or the same period. The other contentious issue is that the Śaiva association, while probable, is not always apparent in the pieces from the Jhusi-Kauśāmbī lineage of the early period. The only firm evidence of this imagery being linked to Pārvatī-Gaurī in the second-third century comes from Vaḍgāon, where the goddess is shown with a bull.

It is difficult to ascribe Lajjā-Gaurī a specific sectarian identity, since the personified *yoni* depictions have been found at both Buddhist and Brāhmanical sites.[66] We find no direct references to her iconography or cult practice in any text relating to the religions mentioned above. It is probable that Lajjā-Gaurī continued to have a widespread cult at the popular level, stemming from a common cultural matrix, a matrix from which the iconography of the goddess has been assembled. Elements such as lotuses and the *pūrṇaghaṭa* womb-like torso also probably emerged from the same matrix.

### 2.1.3 GENDER DELINEATION

The depiction of the *yoni* with or without human appendages such as breasts and limbs can be located within the discourse of reproduction considered to be an exclusively feminine domain.[67]

One would imagine that the stark depiction and worship of female sexual organs valorises the woman or indicates a symbolic valorisation of women. This is, however, not universally true. One has to view such veneration within a social system where women are essentialised as reproductive tools. Her right of reproduction and her reproductive potential become her principal identity, as reflected in the fact that the goddess is "reduced" to a vulva and related symbols such as the *pūrṇakumbha* pot-like womb, water being a universal indicator of life-giving force. The

2.1.15 Ring stone, Dia. 8.1 cm, stone, second-third century BCE, Taxila, Gandhāra. NM Acc. No. 59.534/3.

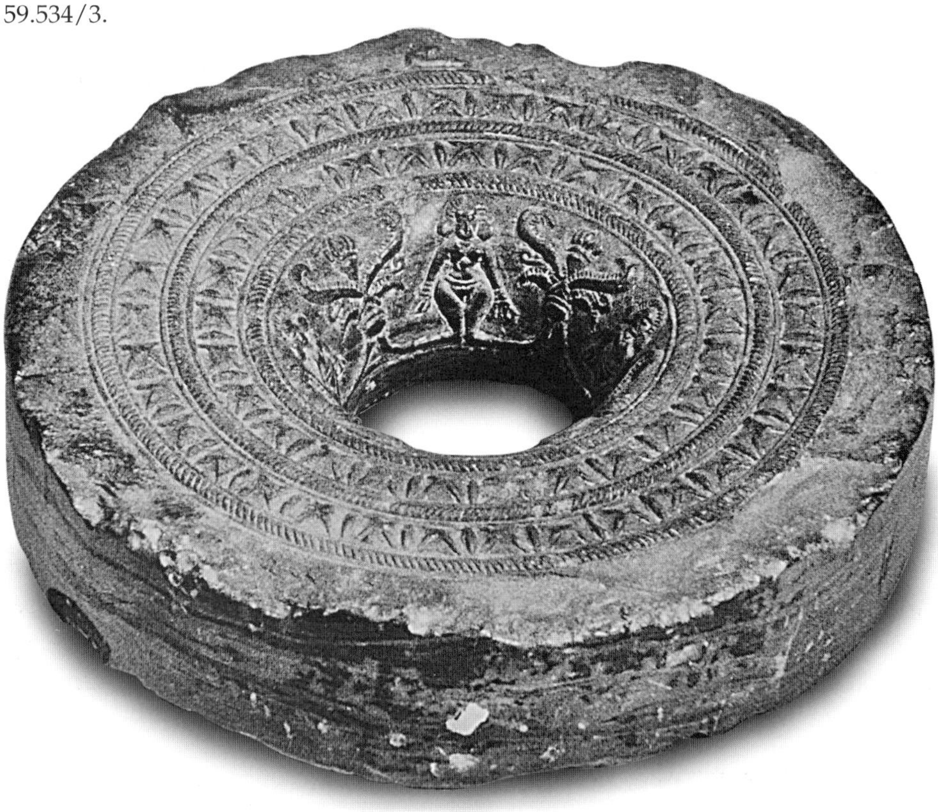

rounded bloated form may also suggest pregnancy.

In Forms II and III, limbs and breasts are shown, suggesting emanation of female power from these secondary sexual organs as well. The evolved forms of Lajjā-Gaurī imply the idea of motherhood encompassing both aspects of reproduction and nurturing.[68]

Anthropological data published by Chapeker and Carol Radcliffe Bolon seems to suggest that it is principally women wishing to be blessed with a child who worship Lajjā-Gaurī in her many manifestations, be it as Koṭṭavi or Nagna Kabandha. Chapeker reports that women worship the goddess by rubbing butter and red arsenicum on the vulva,[69] a practice that would suggest belief in some kind of sympathetic reproduction and fertility. The goddess Lajjā-Gaurī is also worshipped exclusively by women in north India as a symbol of *suhāga* — married status — and in hope of fecundity. Such is the power associated with female reproductive organs, that the vulvic form as represented by a cowrie shell is considered to be a protective device as well and tied around the wrist or waist of an infant to ward off evil and disease.

In other ancient societies such as the Mesopotamian, where the vulva was worshipped as a symbol of goddess Ishtar, both men and women made offerings, seeking her intervention to grant fertility and alleviate distress.[70]

Both Buddhist and Brāhmanical texts are records of patriarchal religious practice and beliefs that marginalise the feminine ritual domain. The only surviving references to these would be in cases where the feminine ritual domain infringes on to the territory of the dominant discourse. In such cases the autonomous feminine cult is assimilated within the Brāhmanic/Buddhist fold through various strategies, one of which may be termed spousification. Spousification indicates a process by which independent and powerful goddesses are converted into the wives of male gods. This decreases their importance, depriving them of their independent devotional base, including institutionalised patronage, and brings the goddess within the ambit of hegemonic patriarchal religious control. The Lajjā-Gaurī escapes spousification and the sculptural series is independent of, or at least not attested by or preceded by, any equivalent representation or description by any concretised religious ideological system. Nor is, as far as our current knowledge goes, the goddess connected through myth or kinship to any major system or male god during the post-Mauryan period.

A solitary clue to the functions attributed to the deity can be gathered from an inscription attached to the Lajjā-Gaurī figure from Nāgārjunakoṇḍa. This is a partially damaged marble image which shows a nude seated figure with legs spread apart laterally, leaving the pudendum clearly marked. A series of anklets on each leg and several elaborately carved girdles encircle the waist. Similarities between the Ṭer and Nāgārjunakoṇḍa terracotta plaques as well as the Nevāsā and Vaḍgāon stone images suggest that there must have been a lotus in place of the head. The figure[71] is not tall, or long, as in the Bhītā and Kosam figures, rather the torso seems shortened. There is a brief, one-line Prākr̥t inscription at the base written in Brāhmī characters of around the third century CE. The epigraph declares that the image was caused to be made by Mahādevī Khaṁḍuvulā, the wife of Siri Ehavala Chāṁṭamūla, who was *avidhava* and *jīvapūta*, i.e. not widowed and with living children.[72]

This inscription indicates first and foremost

that married women, whose children were living, worshipped this goddess, presumably to partake in this good fortune. Secondly, it reinforces the notion that the primary identity of the goddess is linked to maintaining or obtaining the status of married, fertile women. Thirdly, we can infer, at least in this one instance, the existence of a public religious practice of installing such images by royal (and presumably also ordinary) women.

In the absence of documentary evidence from the ancient past one will have to assume that in India, worship of the deity was confined to women, as is the current practice. The agency of women in the patronage of the nude-goddess cult and its perpetuation through ritual practice would also explain the silence of classical sources regarding this deity. At this point it may be relevant to observe that women are admonished in Aśoka's Major Rock Edicts for indulging in useless excessive ritualism and festivals (also at births and marriages), referring perhaps to rituals associated with feminine cults, rather than following true *dhamma*.[73]

Perhaps the cult of Lajjā-Gaurī was a secret cult such as that of Lakṣmī mentioned in the *Milindapañha*; if so, this would further account for the silence within the dominant religious textual discourse. It is also possible that Lajjā-Gaurī worship was confined to unwidowed mothers or married women. Even though in the earlier period many of the terracotta and stone images were small in size which may have been employed in private or local cultic practices, there is evidence of large-sized stone images that were put up in public.

One significant factor that needs to be considered when analysing the imagery of Lajjā-Gaurī is that it is not decorative, rather it has clear ritual and religious functions. This is indicated by the red slip attributed to the majority of the terracotta figures under consideration. The construction and composition of the stone and terracotta plaques, with the figure laterally placed within a square platform, is such that would enable the worshipper to view it standing above the image and looking at it lying flat on the ground or raised platform. This becomes even more apparent in the Vaḍgāon figure where the goddess is supine and the bull is upright. It is also consistent with other cult objects produced during the post-Mauryan era such as the *śilāpaṭṭa*s and the *āyāgapaṭṭa*s, which were also to be viewed horizontally. However, one cannot posit uniform applicability of the horizontal position for Lajjā-Gaurī imagery, given that a pedestal is visible under some of the figures, suggesting that they were set up vertically. P.K. Agrawala has suggested that when the supine figure of the headless goddess, with legs raised and spread apart, was placed directly on the ground, it was supposed that her invisible or louts-head was buried, assimilated into the Earth itself.[74] However, the ornamentation and the care

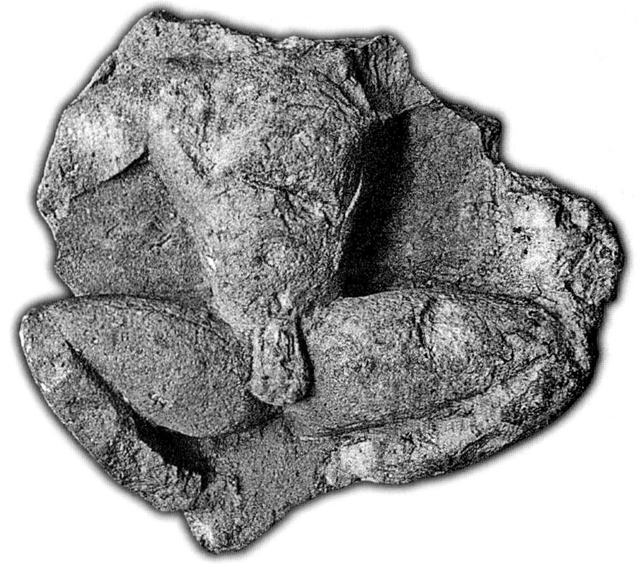

2.1.16 Headless male, mould-made terracotta, third century CE, Shahabad, Hardoi district, UP. Dr. Jagdish Gupta Collection.

in carving the lotus-head suggest that it is meant to be viewed rather than concealed.

The practice of carving female figures with legs spread apart to reveal reproductive organs continues up to the early medieval period, when such figures are found in temples. Thomas Donaldson thinks that such figures performed propitious or apotropaic functions.[75] They indicate *maṅgala* (auspiciousness) to the devotee on the one hand, while their blatant exhibitionism protected the building from disasters such as lightning and floods on the other.

The next significant aspect of the Lajjā-Gaurī imagery is that the earlier sculptural tradition found at mid-Gangetic Valley and to an extent at Ṭer and Nevāsā is divorced from sensuality even though it is strongly sexual in its nudity. The *tribhaṅga* posture, which lends a degree of erotic flexibility to a feminine figure, is entirely absent here. The breasts, when present, are not generally emphasised or sensualised; they may be indicated through incisions or pin marks, or be represented relatively flat in comparison to the *yakṣī-śālabhañjikā* images of the period, which typically exhibit round, full breasts. Alternatively a blooming flower takes the place of breasts in some specimens. The symbolic lotus also

2.1.17 Vegetation growing out of outspread legs, leaf-shaped medallion, first century BCE, Bharhut. IM 233.

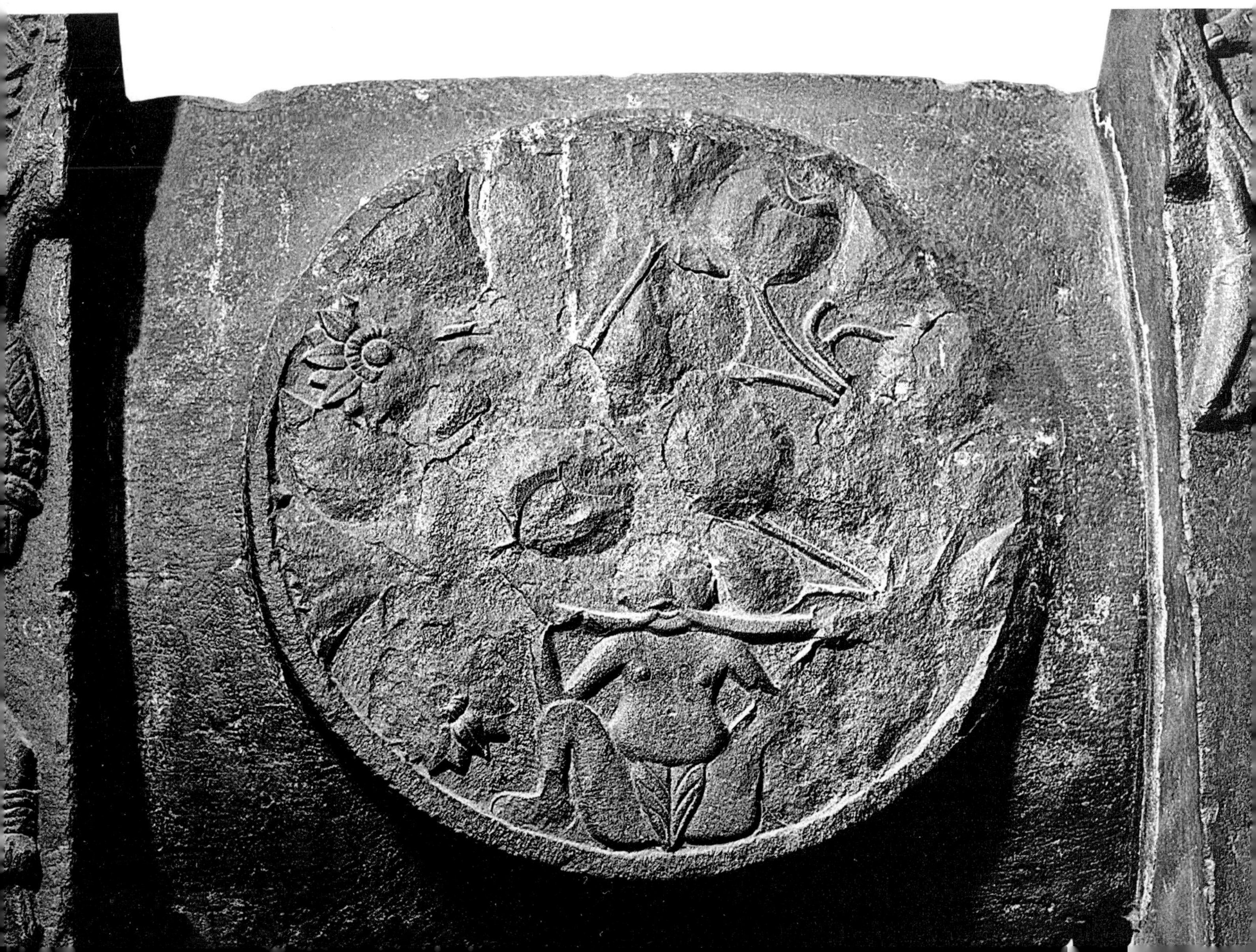

replaces the third potentially sensual element, the face. The factor of beauty associated with the face is absent and thus the potential for casting an alluring gaze is abstracted. There is a complete de-personification of the goddess, making her an anonymous carrier of reproductive potential.

Despite the mystery that surrounds the identity of the goddess and the cult practice associated with her, it is clear that she can be placed within the discourse of reproduction and fertility. Her associations with Aditi and Śrī reinforce the fertility element.

### 2.2 From Aditi/Lakṣmī to Dugdhadhāriṇī: Transforming Imagery of a Goddess

Based on the understanding of the body, especially the female body, as the most crucial site for the construction and delineation of gender, the discussion in this section will concentrate on one such type of representation that privileges the breast in post-Mauryan art. This is the breast-offering or breast-touching figure, the so-called Dugdhadhāriṇī,[76] also identified as Māyā and Lakṣmī, a sculptural type that recurs over a period of almost 500 years. Until now the secondary literature has focused on motifs

2.2.1 Gaja-Lakṣmī in breast-touching pose, first century BCE, Bharhut. IM 208.

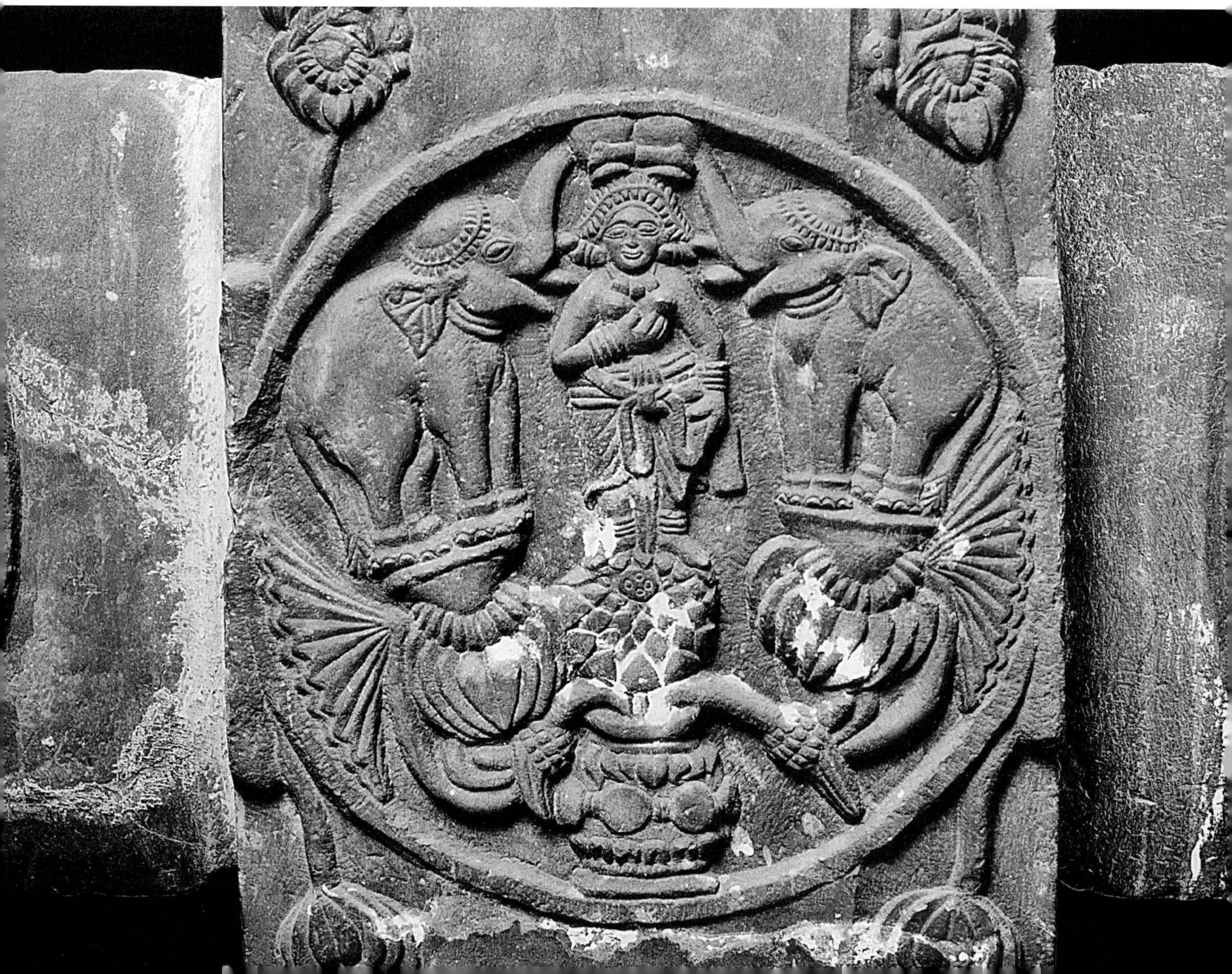

associated with the deity, such as lustrating elephants, or has tried to provide a theological interpretation of it.

The gender implications of breast-offering have been ignored.

There are two issues, which are crucial to this study, that arise in connection with representational types such as the breast-offering female figure. These are (1) the question as to how such imagery contributed to the construction of gender identity during the post-Mauryan period, and (2) the more subjective issue of how these sculptures were perceived and consumed by the viewer of the time. As in the case of the Lajjā-Gaurī series, any interpretation of the breast-offering imagery can only be largely subjective, since contemporary literary sources do not help us in identifying the image with any particular deity. Epigraphic sources are also silent on this matter; even at Bharhut, among the plethora of donative and label inscriptions, none of the breast-touching figures is accompanied by an identifying epigraph.

Representations of the breast, especially in images representing a woman offering her own breast to the viewer or devotee, become important in the feminist discourse, since bio-deterministic theories privileging the notion of woman-as-nurturer are based on the biological fact that only a woman can breastfeed an infant. From a gender perspective, a visual analysis lays emphasis on the fact that breasts are objects of the male gaze, a gaze that sexually commodifies the female body for male voyeuristic gratification. Thus dominant patriarchal art produces and consumes images of women in provocative postures and apparel.[77] In the popular conception, the breast is considered an object both of desire and of nurture.

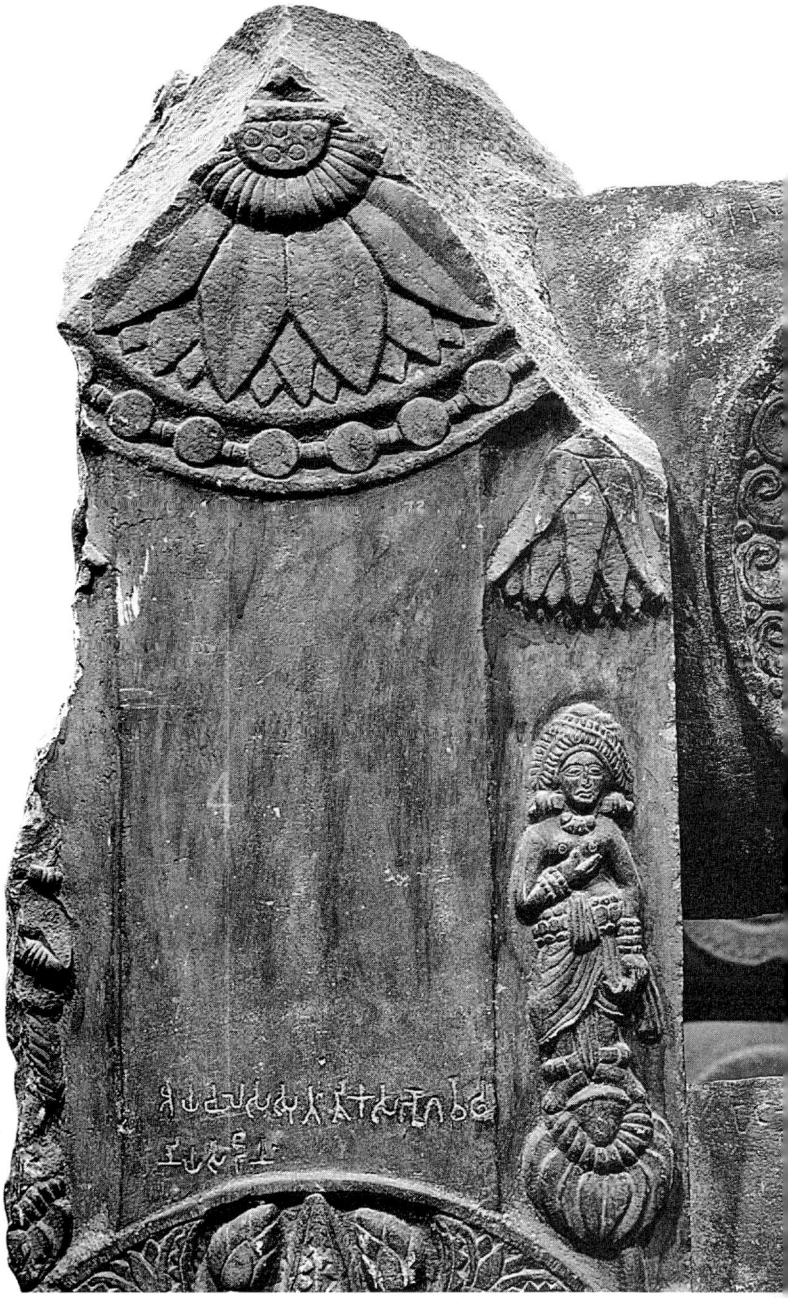

2.2.2 Woman on lotus in breast-touching pose, first century BCE, Bharhut. IM.

However, the [mother-figure, desire, nurture] juxtaposition is not universally applicable to the whole of the post-Mauryan visual tradition. Women are depicted in many other functional models besides mother-nurturer; and women who nurture infants are not necessarily biological mothers. We may have to re-examine the representation-function model in relation to breast-offering motherhood.

### 2.2.1 SCULPTURAL EVIDENCE

The figure of the woman as breast-giver (offering) is not numerically prolific in the whole corpus of *yakṣī-śālabhañjikā*s. The figure is nevertheless significant as attested by its repetition in the art of the early phase up to the later Kuṣāṇa period. Iconographically, the breast-touching figures are often (in the manner of *yakṣī-śālabhañjikā*s) depicted as voluptuous women, in a *tribhaṅga* posture, but with the added element of placing the right hand under the left breast, in an offering gesture.

The available sculptural specimens can be classified into four types:

A. Female figures seated or standing on lotuses and offering their breast, accompanied (*Pl.* 2.2.1) or unaccompanied (*Pls.* 2.2.2, 2.2.3) by elephants, carved on *stūpa* railing pillars and medallions.

B. A breast-touching female figure, akin in treatment to *yakṣī-śālabhañjikā* figures (*Pls.* 2.2.8 to 2.2.11), sometimes with a child (*Pls.* 2.2.8, 2.2.12, 2.2.13), carved on railing pillars.

C. Terracotta plaques with a *pañcacūḍa*-type figure touching her breast.

D. Breast-touching as part of male-female dyad or female-female dyad (*Pls.* 2.2.15, 2.2.16).

*Type A*

The earliest representations of breast-offering figures are found on the railing pillars of the Bharhut *stūpa*, dating back to *circa* second century BCE. There are four such examples, where a female is shown either seated or standing on a lotus, the stem of which may be issuing out of a vase, a *pūrṇaghaṭa* (*Pls.* 2.2.1 to 2.2.3).[78] On both sides of these females are elephants, also standing on lotuses, pouring water over the deity from pots (*ghaṭa*s) held in their trunks.

In the seated figures mentioned above, the female is depicted with one arm akimbo and the other placed under her breast.[79] Some figures are also found with hands folded together in *saṁpuṭita-mudrā* under the breasts. These are shown as squatting on a full-blown lotus springing from a *pūrṇaghaṭa.* On either side, an elephant standing on a lotus pours water over her from a vessel held in its trunk. The lotuses on which the elephants stand issue from the same *pūrṇaghaṭa*.

In two of the standing images from Bharhut, the figures are dressed in elaborate apparel and stand on a full-blown lotus springing from a *pūrṇaghaṭa*. One is shown touching her left breast with the right hand (*Pl.* 2.2.1). In other versions, the female figure either holds the stem of a lotus bud or holds her breast in the left hand (not illustrated). The breast-touching gesture can also occur outside the frame of the medallion: one female attendant figure, standing on a lotus rising from the top of the medallion, is seen touching her left breast with her right hand, while opposite her is her male counterpart, now much defaced.[80] Though the Gaja-Lakṣmī or Śrī-Lakṣmī motif continued at Bodh-Gayā, Sāñcī and Kauśāmbī, the breast-touching action of the female was not depicted here.

At Sāñcī the Gaja-Lakṣmī motif occurs on

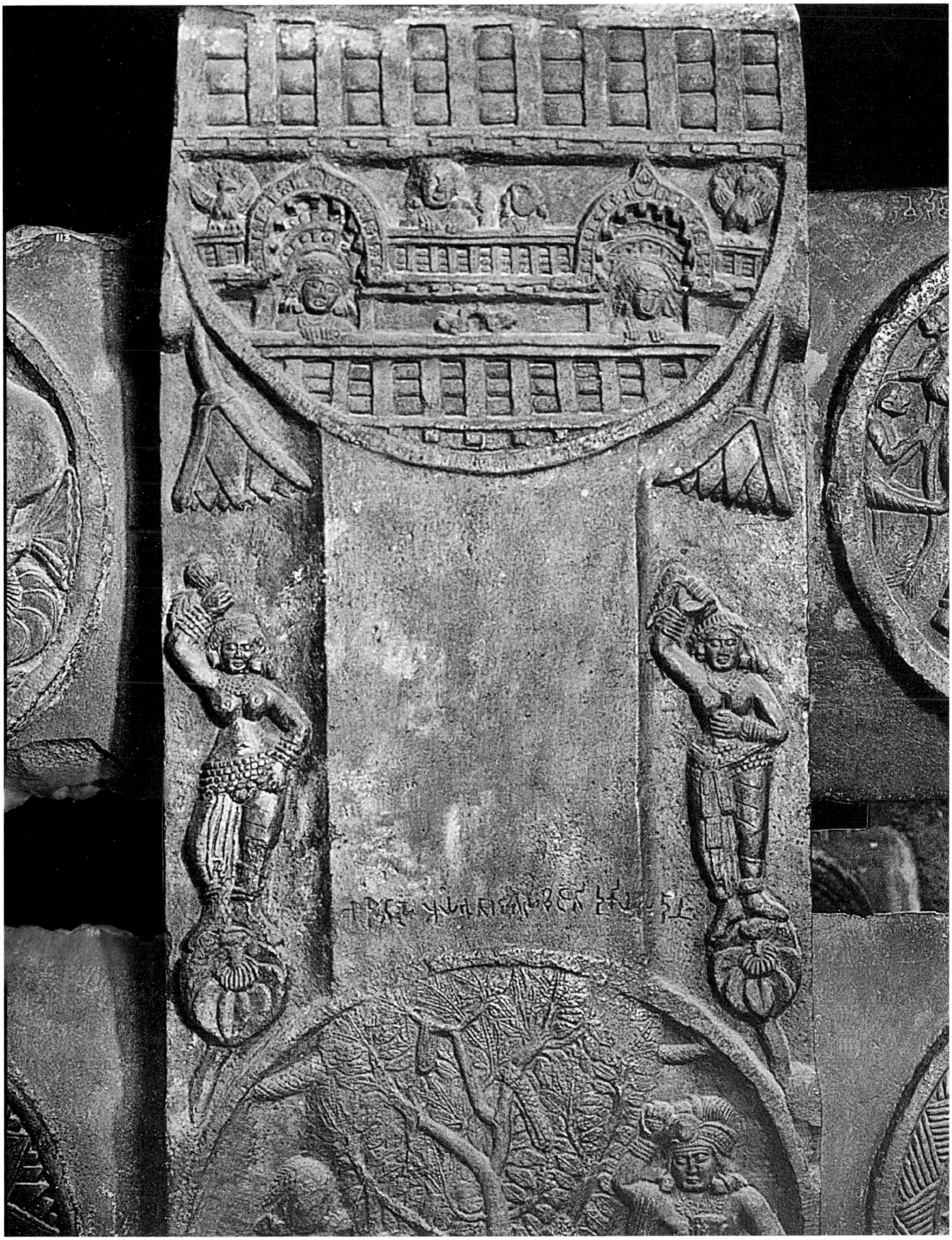

2.2.3 Woman on lotus in breast-touching pose, first century BCE, Bharhut. IM.

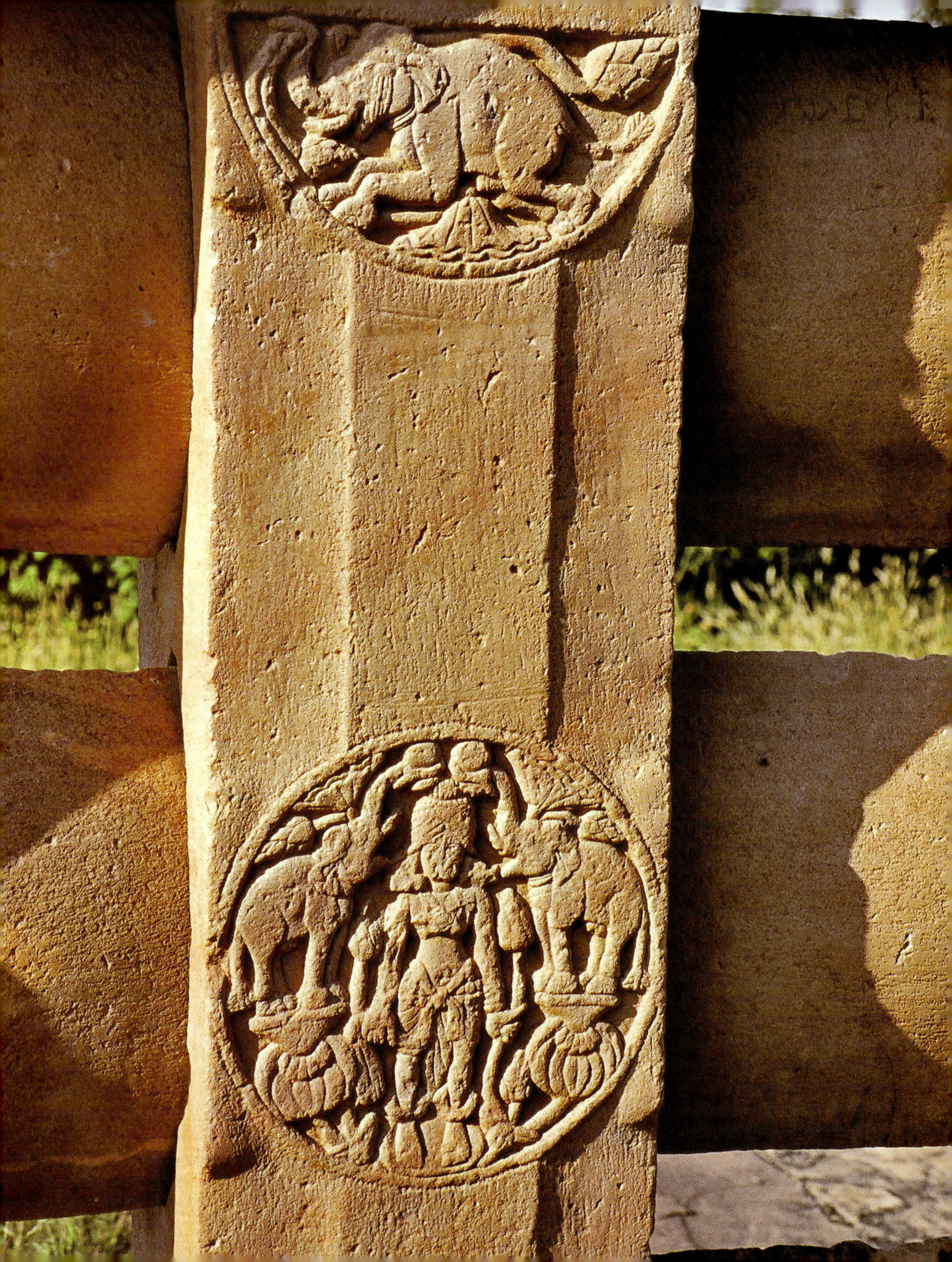

*stūpa*s 1 and 2.[81] The goddess is shown with one arm akimbo and the other hand in *abhaya-hasta*, or without a lotus under her feet, or holding lotus vines but unaccompanied by elephants. The breast-touching is not found in any of these, though there are many combinations of the female figure and lotuses (*Pls*. 2.2.4 to 2.2.7).

Similar representations of the deity are found at Bodh-Gayā (second-first century BCE),[82] also without the breast-offering posture. A contemporary sculpture from a Kauśāmbī *toraṇa* fragment also has the iconography of Gaja-Lakṣmī (Pl. 2.2.20).[83] The right hand is raised in *abhaya-hasta*, while the clenched left hand is placed on the hip. She stands on a large lotus from the sides of which issue stalks, the tallest of which support two elephants that lustrate the goddess with water from long-necked vases held in their trunks. The nudity of the goddess is emphasised through the diaphanous lower garment which is secured by a girdle consisting of a single strand of beads. She is heavily ornamented. A railing pillar from Kauśāmbī[84] depicts a standing female figure holding two lotuses on which two elephants stand lustrating her. She stands on a lotus flower that emanates from the seedpod of another lotus below it, which in turn grows out of a *pūrṇaghaṭa*. At Mathurā, too, elephants lustrating the goddess continued without the breast-offering element in the panels. It is apparent that from the late first century onwards the iconography of Gaja-Lakṣmī becomes fixed and certain features such as breast-touching, first seen on the Bharhut *stūpa*, are abstracted from her portrayal.

2.2.4 Gaja-Lakṣmī, goddess lustrated by elephants, railing medallion, first century BCE, *stūpa* 2, Sāñcī, Madhya Pradesh.

*Type B*

Another kind of depiction, differing in terms of treatment and physical attributes, occurs at Mathurā and Sanghol. These belong to the Kuṣāṇa period. One such sculpture is found on a monolithic pillar, carved in the round, from Maholi near Mathurā (*Pl*. 2.2.9) and now in the National Museum, New Delhi.[85] Here the female is shown standing on a *pūrṇaghaṭa* from which two *padma* flowers emerge, on each of which she places a foot. The left hand cups her right breast. Her right hand holds the knot of a ribbon-like sash tied at her waist above the *mekhalā*. Her face is tilted downwards with eyes directed towards her right breast. She is profusely ornamented with cylindrical earrings, *ekāvalī*, a torque or thick necklace, bangles, *keyūra* and *nūpura*. Carved on the reverse is a rich vegetative tableau with a number of lotus shoots and vines emerging from a pot, throwing out more flowers and buds as they climb up the pillar. In the middle of these one can see two peacocks seated on a lotus pericarp.

Two railing pillars in the Mathura Museum have similar female figures touching their breast. One, slightly eroded, shows a figure standing under an *aśoka* tree and holding her right breast with her left hand, with the thumb touching the nipple. The other hand is placed on the *mekhalā*. Her *dhotī* is transparent and the genital cleft is exposed. The head is tilted slightly towards her right shoulder and the gaze is fixed on her breast. The other Mathura Museum example of the breast-touching figure is found on a railing post from Isapur.[86] The left hand of this figure is shown cupping the right breast while the right hand touches the *mekhalā*. There is a mango tree in the background. This is part of decorative railing around a *stūpa* on which many other female figures of the *yakṣī-śālabhañjikā*s are carved (*Pl*. 2.2.10). A similar example of a breast-touching

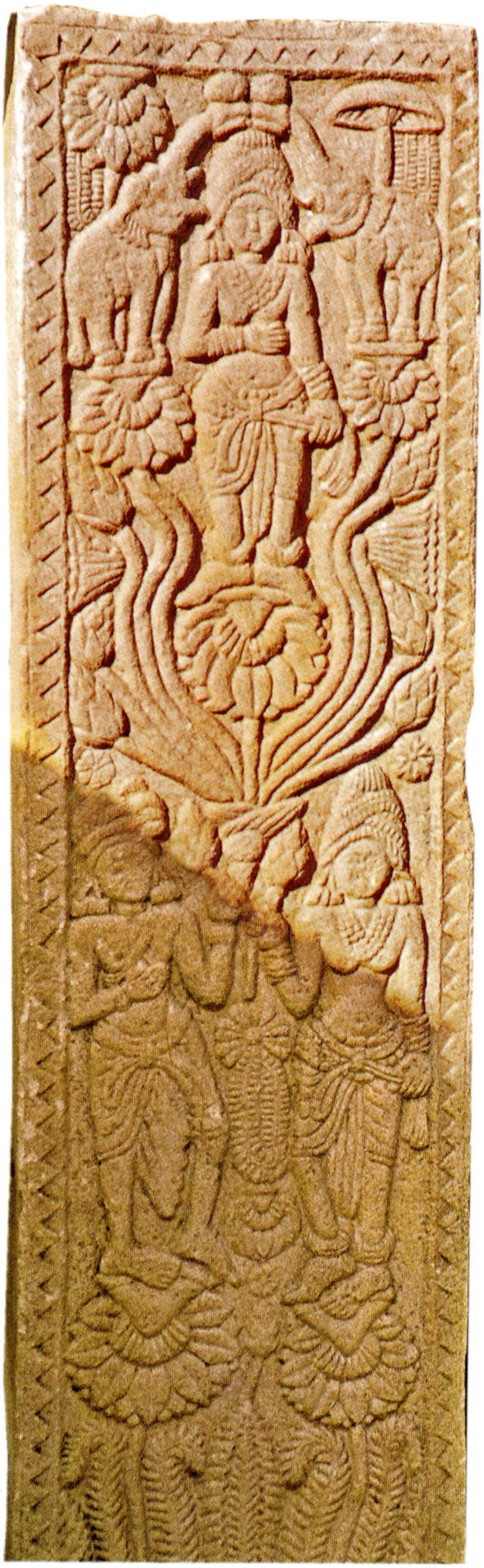

figure from the Mathurā region is in the Cleveland Museum.[87]

There are two railing pillars from Sanghol (first-second century CE) which display a woman in a breast-touching posture. One depicts a woman with a child[88] and the other appears without a child (*Pls.* 2.2.11, 2.2.13): in the Sanghol sculpture catalogue they are labelled "Mother and Child" and "Dugdhadhāriṇī" respectively. The former representation shows a woman with a child straddled on the left hip, with the left hand supporting the child (*Pl.* 2.2.13).[89] The right hand is shown touching the left breast. The child too is touching the left breast of the female figure. The mother gaze is towards the child, while the child has his concentration fixed on the breast (also see *pl.* 2.2.12). The figure is also profusely ornamented and shown in a sensuous stance and wears a *dhotī*, over which a five-stringed *mekhalā* is tied. Her sensuousness is like other *yakṣīs* shown on railing pillars. Interestingly, the folds of the *dhotī* cover the pubic area, an interesting contrast to the usual practice at Sanghol where the female has normally exposed genitalia. The base is broken off, and instead of a peeping spectator at the top, an elaborate window (*gavākṣa*) is shown.

In the other Sanghol instance of the breast-touching female figure, the child is abstracted from the imagery,[90] but the female is shown holding the breast in a more provocative manner, with one of the hands squeezing the breast, one of the fingers very near the nipple and the gaze fixed on the breast (*pl.* 2.2.11). Here too the folds of the *dhotī* cover her middle lower portion. The Dugdhadhāriṇī is standing on a dwarfish *yakṣa*. On the upper portion of the pillar is a spectator, a

2.2.5 Gaja-Lakṣmī, goddess lustrated by elephants, railing pillar, first century BCE, *stūpa* 2, Sāñcī, Madhya Pradesh.

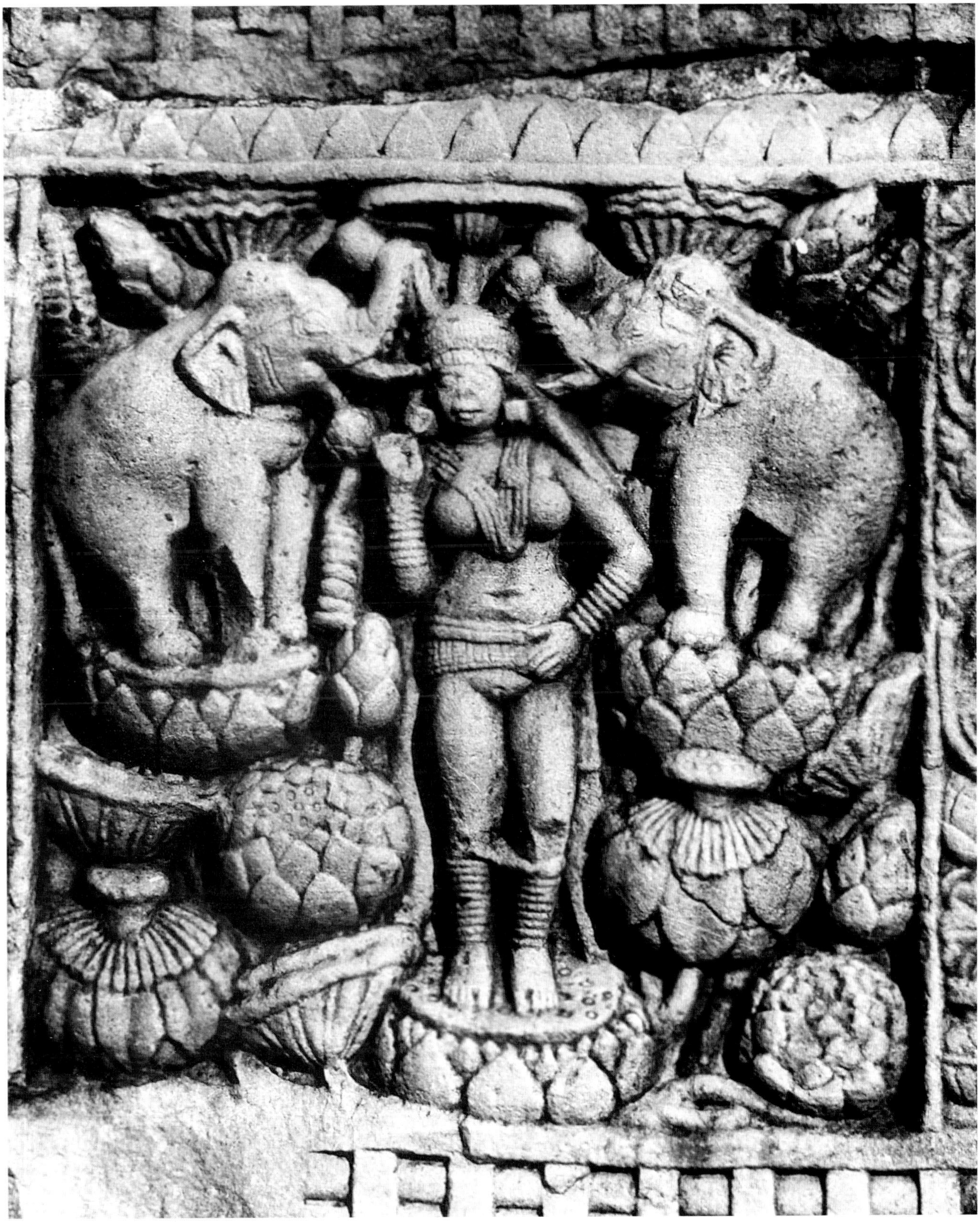

2.2.6 Gaja-Lakṣmī, standing on a lotus, *toraṇa* upright, first century CE, *stūpa* 1, Sāñcī, Madhya Pradesh.

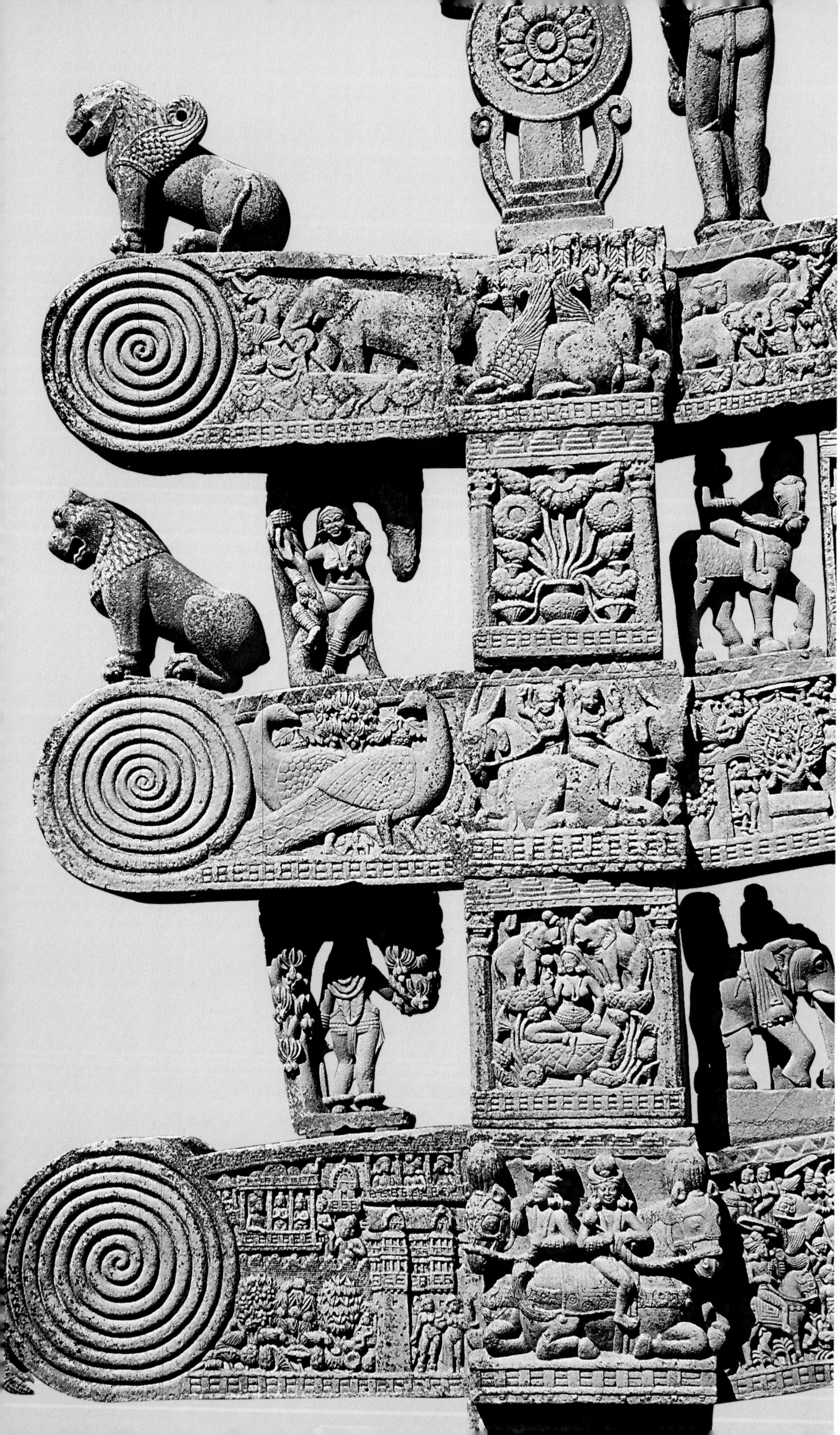

2.2.7 Gaja-Lakṣmī, seated, surrounded by lush vegetative landscape, *toraṇa* architrave, north gateway, first century CE, *stūpa* 1, Sāñcī, Madhya Pradesh.

woman with the right arm raised that can be interpreted as hailing someone (the viewer?) to look at the breast-offering figure below. It is interesting to note that both of these Sanghol figures emphasise only the breast and not the pubic area, while most of the other female figures at Sanghol and Mathurā have both exposed.

One example of a woman offering her breast and accompanied by a child (*Pl.* 2.2.8) is in the Museum of Indian Art, Berlin.[91] She holds a child in her right arm, apparently balancing it on her hip. She offers the right breast with the left hand. The provenance of this piece is not known; it is carved in spotted red sandstone and in a style typical of Mathurā of the mature Kuṣāṇa period. There is also a representation of a *nāgakanyā* (part of an *abhiniṣkramaṇa* episode) in the same museum who is shown holding her right breast with the right hand.[92] The figure stands with the right leg crossed over the left and touches her girdle with her left hand. She is a squat figure with a fat face, looking upwards. There seem to have been scales with flames behind. The provenance of this fragment is not clear. Fischer[93] says Indian women are usually depicted with bare abdomen decorated with a *mekhalā* (a girdle with a front clasp), well known in Kuṣāṇa-period art. Bactrian terracottas also show nude figures of women wearing only a girdle with a leaf ornament. In ancient Indian costumes, such a decoration is seen either below or above a garment. *Nāgakanyā*s sometimes have their leg covered and their hip-girdle closed with a decorative leaf that covers the pubic area.

An exquisitely carved fragment of a woman holding her breast has been discovered at Kauśāmbī and recently published as Śrī-Lakṣmī (*pl.* 2.2.21).[94] All that remains is a fragment of the torso showing a hand, presumably of the woman herself, lightly holding the nipple between the

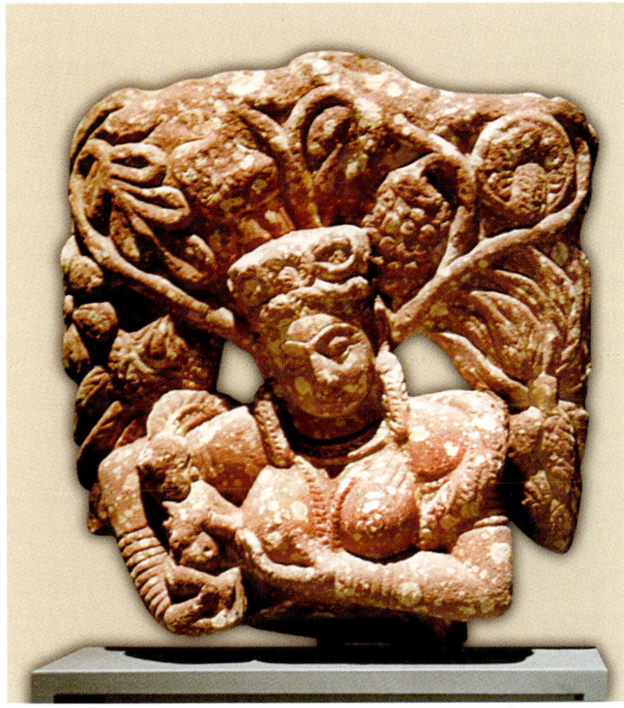

2.2.8 Woman with child in breast-offering pose, second century CE, Museum für Indische Kunst, Berlin. MIK I 10168.

thumb and the edge of the forefinger. Due to the fragmentary nature of the piece, it is not possible to say whether or not a child was associated with the figure. Nevertheless one can see that in this naturalistically delineated sculpture, the breasts are full and globular and the fingers of the hand long and tapering.

### *Type C*

Two terracotta figures now in Mathura Museum[95] are illuminating, in that they combine the so-called *pañcacūḍa* goddess[96] with the breast-touching gesture (*pl.* 2.2.14). Both are low-relief plaques containing a single female figure in the centre. The outer edges of one of the plaque are in the form of a doorway surmounted by a circular arch that forms a kind of a *prabhā*. The figure itself is shown standing and wearing a two-layered skirt. The overskirt terminates almost at the knees, while the underskirt has thick vertical folds that cover the ankles but reveal the feet. She wears a thick torque-like necklace, multiple bracelets and thick earrings of the *kuṇḍala* type. An elaborate headdress surmounted by a circular floral ornament can be seen. On both sides of this are two plaits or *veṇīs*. Five auspicious symbols are clearly shown above these, of which an elephant goad, *aṅkuśa* and a *triśūla* (trident) are identifiable. Her right arm hangs down and holds a bejewelled bag (?) while the left hand touches the left breast.

A fragmentary terracotta plaque found during the Kauśāmbī excavations[97] may be mentioned here, although it does not precisely adhere to the type discussed here. The face and legs of this female figure are unfortunately now broken. However it is clear that the figure holds the sides of her breasts with her two hands as if pushing them towards the centre. The necklace and the *mekhalā* or waistband of the *dhotī* are not very elaborate. The gaze of the goddess is fixed outwards, towards the viewer.

*Type D*

Besides these single-figure pieces we also have other depictions in terracotta which show a couple in which the male is touching the breast of the female partner, especially from the early Śuṅga period. In one of these, the male on the left has his left hand under the chin of the female partner whose face is turned upwards. The right hand of the male clasps her around the shoulder and touches her right breast.[98]

In more than one representation from Begram, a dyad consisting of two female figures (*Pls.* 2.2.15, 2.2.16) is shown. In one such piece the figure on the left is standing in a *tribhaṅga* posture

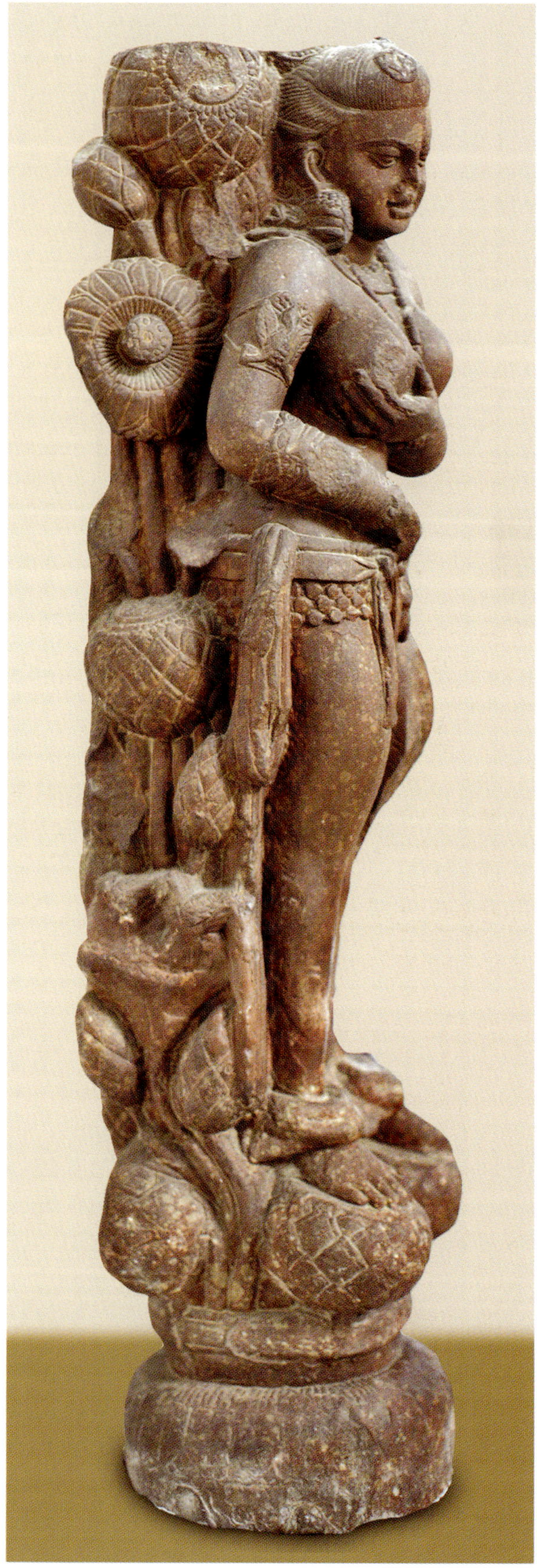

2.2.9 Śrī-Lakṣmī, second century CE, Kuṣāṇa, stone, National Museum, Acc. No. B. 89.

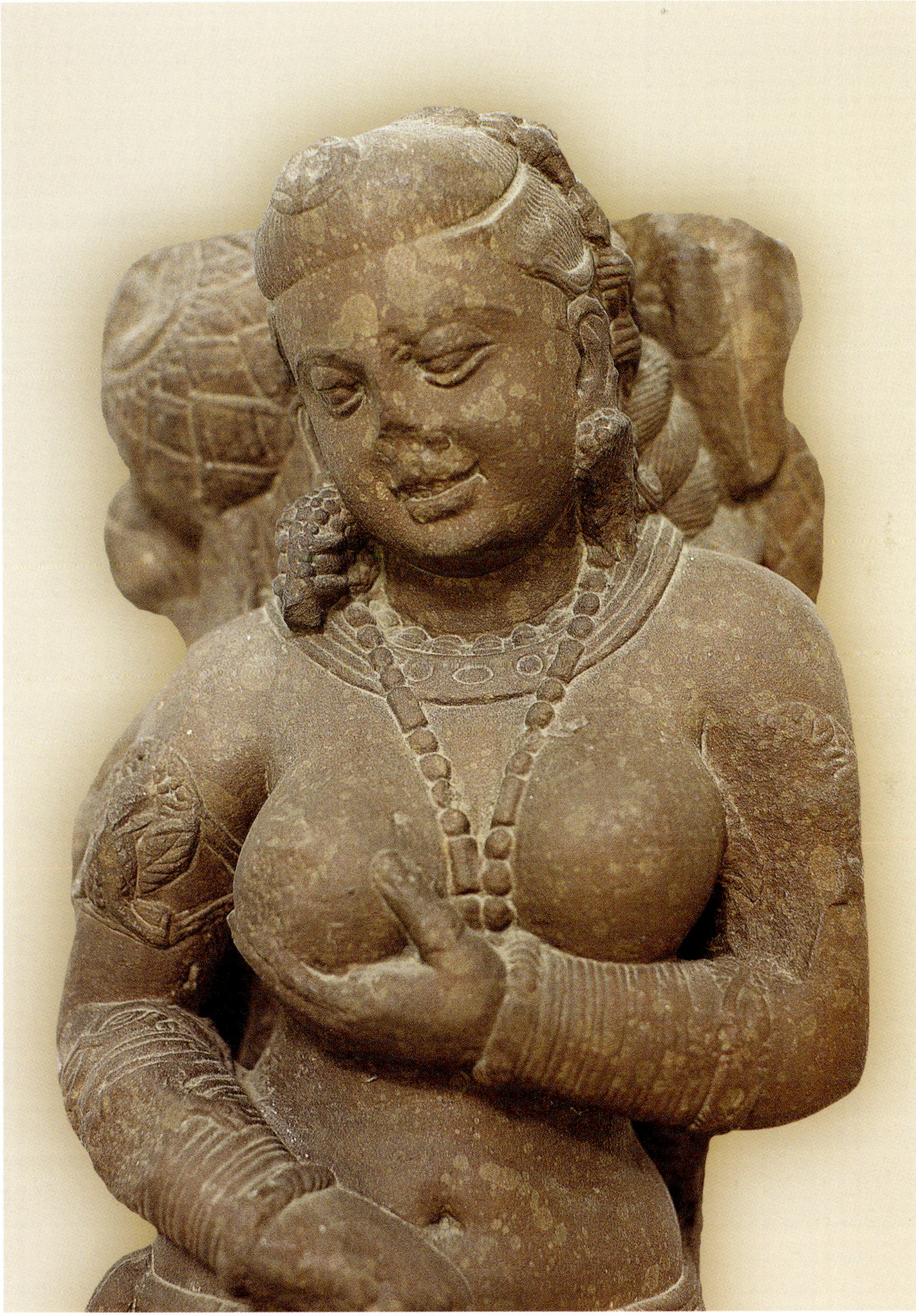

2.2.9a Detail of Śrī-Lakṣmī, second century CE, Kuṣāṇa, stone, National Museum.

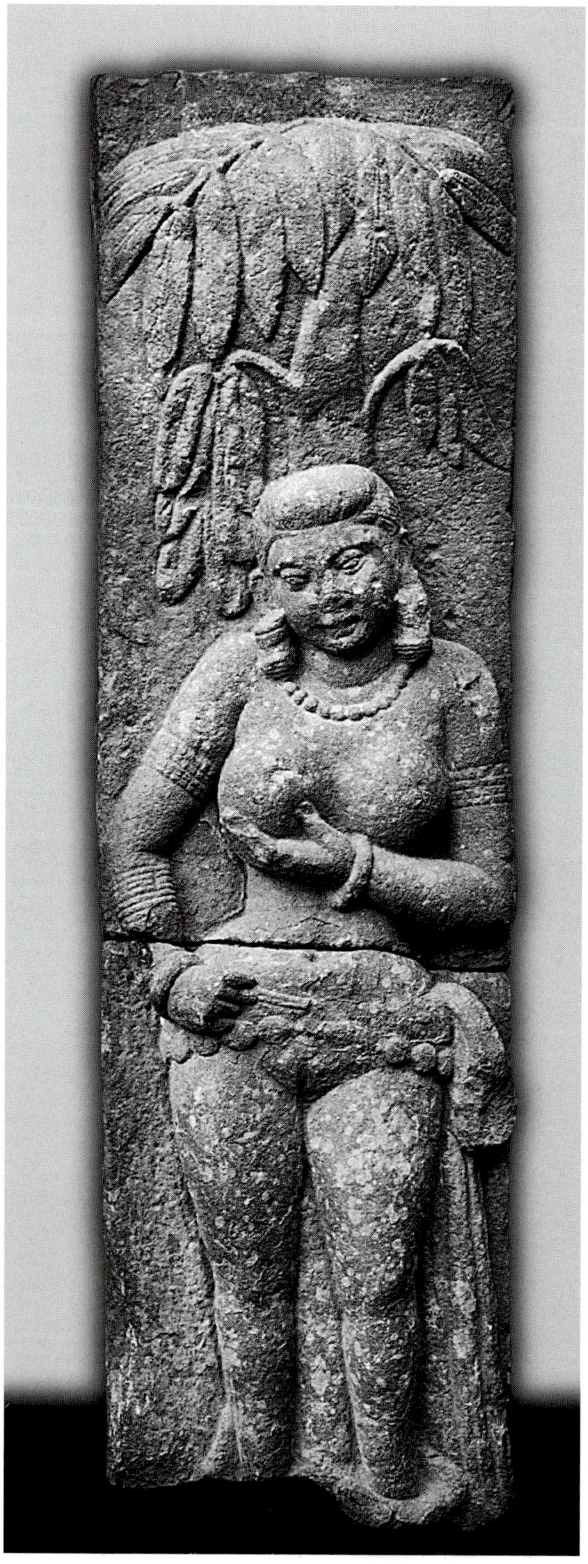

2.2.10 *Yakṣī* under a mango tree, breast-touching pose, standing, railing pillar, Mathurā sandstone, third century CE, Isapur, Mathurā district, UP. GMM No. 13.286.

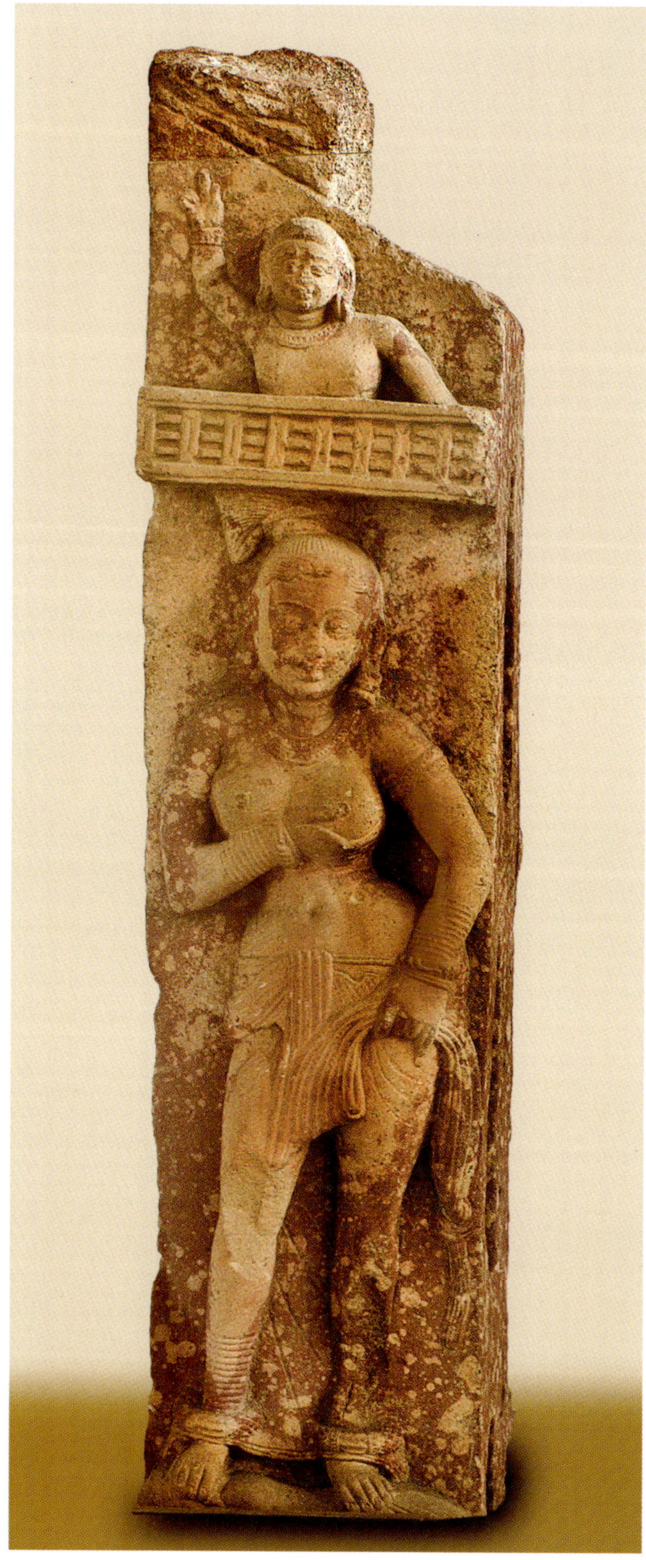

2.2.11 Woman in a breast-offering pose, railing pillar, red sandstone, second century CE, Sanghol, Punjab.

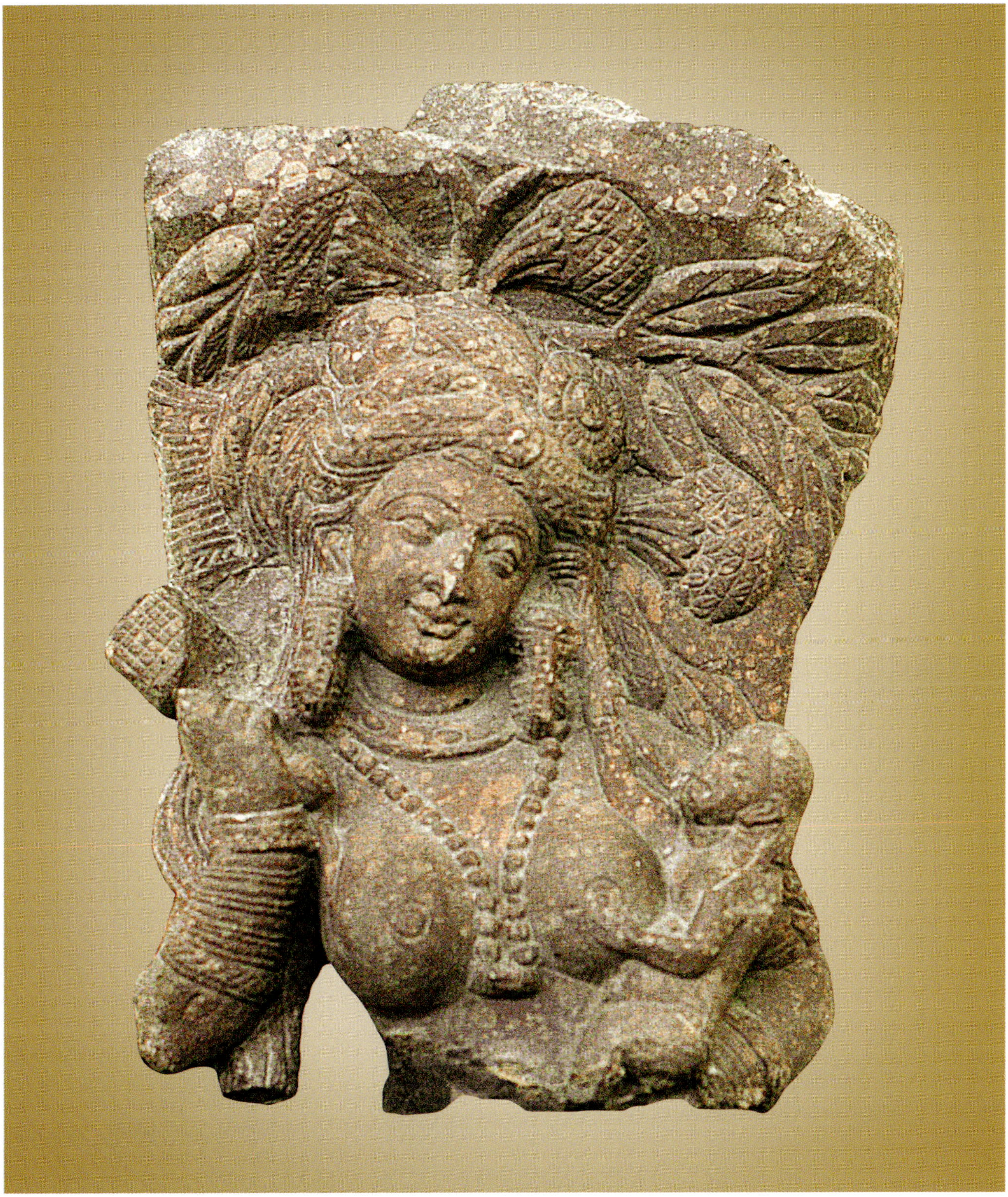

2.2.12 Woman and child in a breast-touching pose, railing pillar, second century CE, Mathurā, GMM.

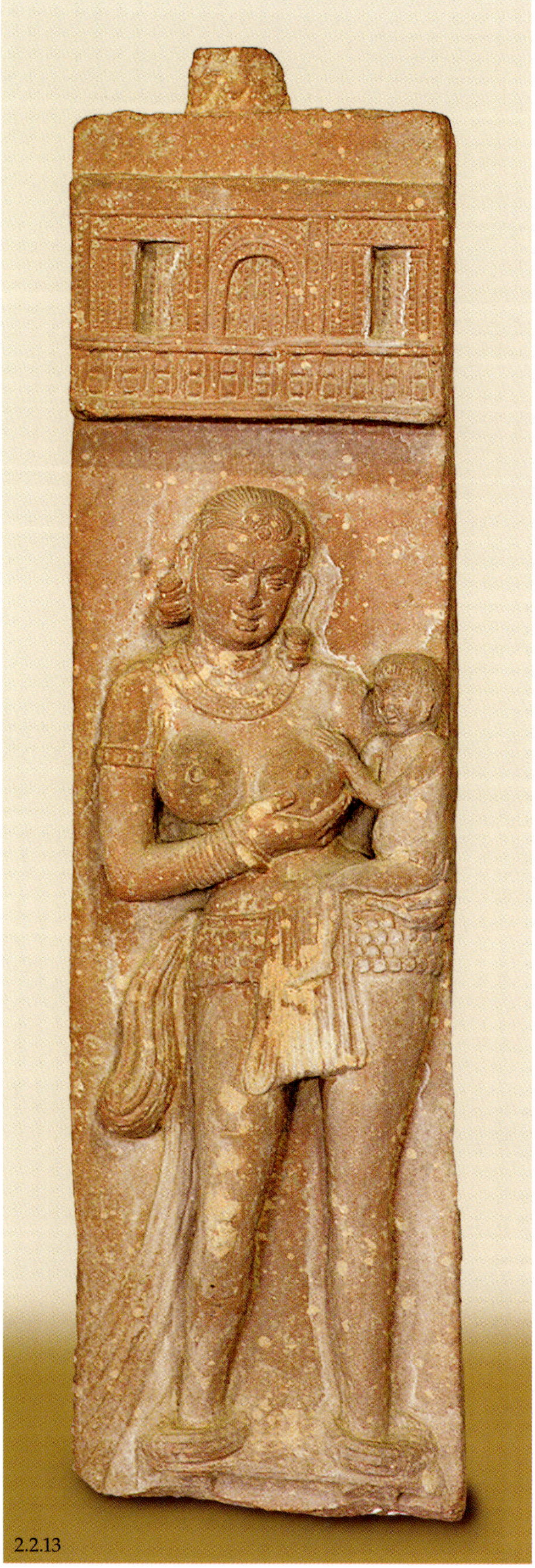

2.2.13

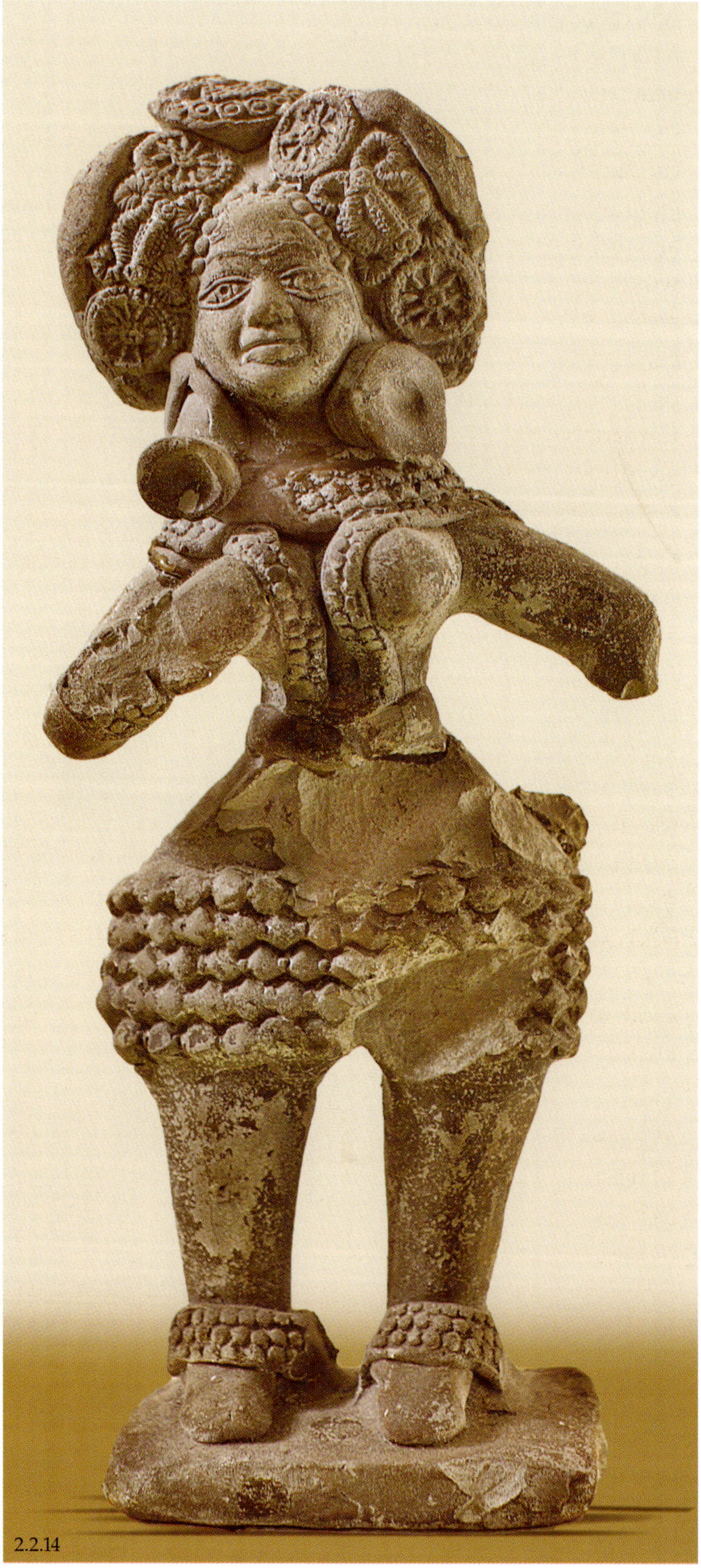

2.2.14

with the hip deflected to the left while the right hand touches the left breast in an offering gesture. Her left hand touches the left breast of the female figure on the right. Another figure on the right, in a less pronounced *tribhaṅga* posture, extends her right arm to embrace the left figure around the shoulder near the neck. Both figures wear nearly transparent *dhotīs* with pearl *mekhalās* around the waist. The pudenda mound can be seen, though it is not emphasised. A vine or bush surrounds them. The two figures are framed by two carved pilasters topped by an architrave in the shape of a *vedikā*.

Type A is found carved on railings; Type B appears both as free-standing sculpture and as part of a *vedikā*; Type C are clearly votive cult objects; and Type D is found as part of pillar reliefs or in "secular" contexts as in the Begram ivories. It is clear from the brief descriptions above that the contexts and the treatment of the various types differ from each other, the breast-touching feature is common to all. Type D continues into the Brāhmanical tradition in the many Umāsahitamaheśvara figures that depict Śiva touching Pārvatī's breast.

### 2.2.2 ADITI/ŚRĪ-LAKṢMĪ/ DUGDHADHĀRIṆĪ

The identification of the breast-touching image is a vexed problem. It has been variously viewed as Māyādevī, the mother of Buddha, as the goddess Lakṣmī[99] and as an unnamed deity of abundance. None of these identifications explain or privilege the special meaning, if any, attached to breast-offering gesture.

It was in the early part of the twentieth century that A. Foucher expressed the opinion that the depiction of a goddess being lustrated by elephants at Bharhut and Sāñcī is related to that of Buddha's Nativity.[100] Perplexed by the absence of representations of the Nativity at Sāñcī and Bharhut, he put forward the theory that these images are depictions of the Buddha's birth in symbolic form. Just as the *aśvattha* tree represented the Enlightenment at Gayā, the wheel represented the First Sermon at Sārnāth, and the tumulus represented the *mahāparinirvāṇa* at Kuśīnagara, the woman seated on a lotus surrounded by elephants represented Nativity.[101] He argued that, since Māyā had dreamt of a white elephant entering her womb, representations which combine lotus and elephant devices were meant to connote the birth of Buddha. In all probability this iconography — two elephants lustrating a goddess seated or standing on a lotus and holding lotus stalks in her hands — was meant to depict the moment after Buddha's birth, when he was washed with two streams of water sent forth by the two *nāga* kings, Nanda and Upananda.[102] In Foucher's reading, the lotus in itself was the symbol of the Nativity, and it also represented moments from the legends that grew around the birth of Buddha, for example that soon after he was born, he took seven steps and lotus flowers grew in his footsteps.

As we shall see in the subsequent chapter, this identification of the Aditi/Gaja-Lakṣmī series at Sāñcī and Bharhut as Māyādevī, the mother of Buddha at the time to his nativity, is difficult to accept. The major question that arises from Foucher's theory is that, when at Bharhut we have a scene that has been labelled as "The Descent of the Lord" and represents the

2.2.13 Woman and child, breast-touching/offering pose, railing pillar, second century CE, Sanghol, Punjab. (facing page left)

2.2.14 Mother Goddess, Śuṅga, second-first century BCE, terracotta, Mathurā, GMM. (facing page right)

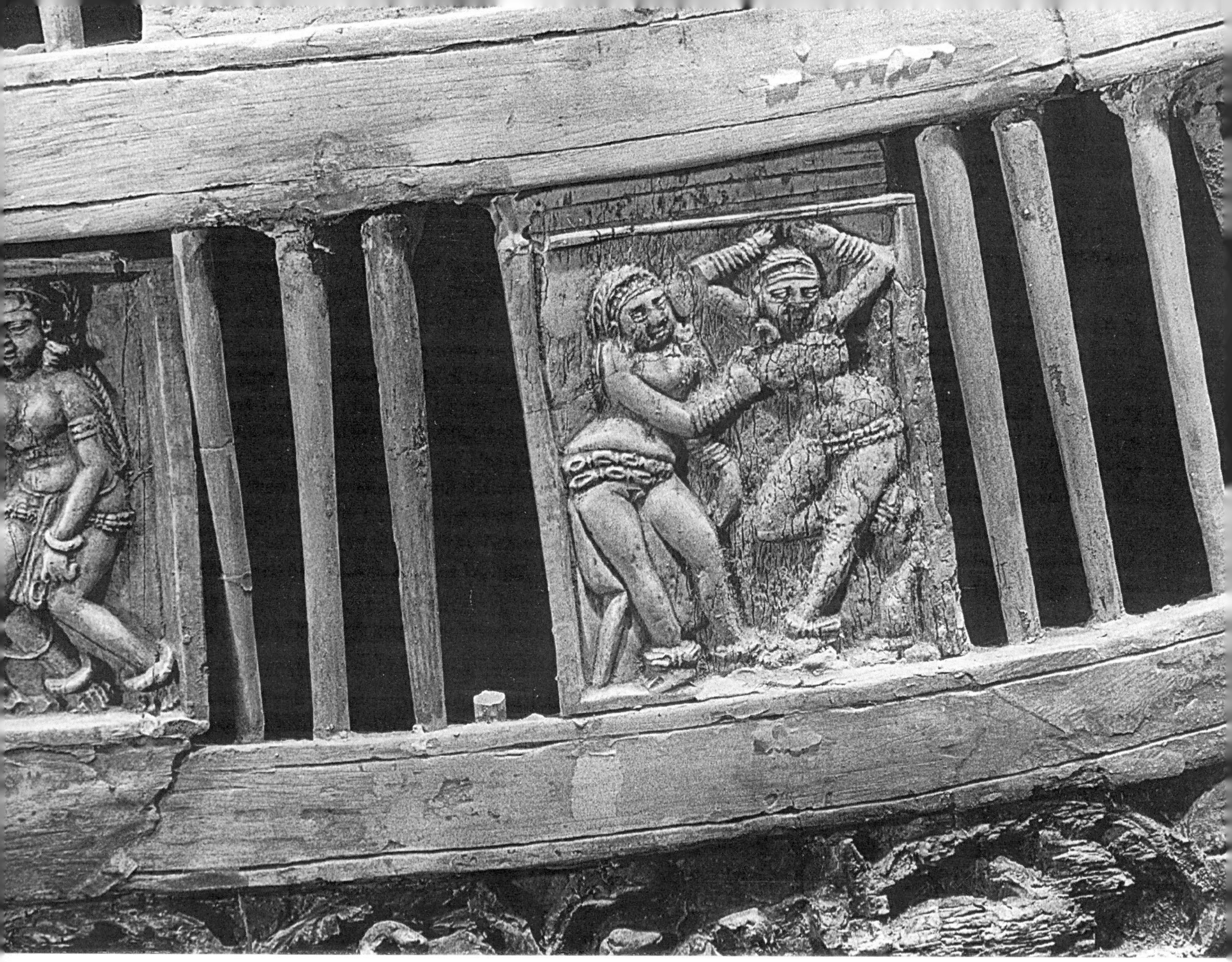

2.2.15 Two women, one touching the breast of the other, part of a large back piece of a royal throne, ornamented with thirteen plaques with carving of women in various modes, ivory, late first to third century CE, Begram, Kabul Museum.

conception of the Buddha, why would the sculptors depict his birth in symbolic terms using devices that have no clear and direct connection with the story of his birth? The second important question that remains unanswered by Foucher's theory is why and how the canonical iconography of Buddha's Conception and Delivery is so different from the Lady among the lotuses lustrated by elephants in all subsequent representations, be these from Gandhāra or Mathurā.

Coomaraswamy, with many later supporters, relates this imagery to the later canonical description of the Gaja-Lakṣmī form.[103] Curiously, we have a large and nearly independent representation of the Sirimā Devatā at Bharhut[104] (*pl.* 2.2.17) which has been also identified with Siri or Śrī, a form of Lakṣmī. However, Sirimā in terms of depiction is akin to other representations of *nyagrodhaparimaṇḍala yakṣī*s or *devatā*s[105] rather than to Gaja-Lakṣmī in a breast-offering posture as presented on the relief medallions of the railing pillars and railings of the Bharhut *stūpa*.

Coomaraswamy identified the female deities of this type as Gaja-Lakṣmī, a form of Śrī-Lakṣmī,[106] irrespective of the fact that they may or may not be shown in the breast-offering pose. According to him, in her representations, Śrī-Lakṣmī is associated with the lotus in three ways: (1) she is *padmahastā* (holding a lotus in her raised right hand, while the left rests on the hip); (2) she is supported on a *padmāsana* or *pīṭha*; and (3) she is *padmavāsinī* or *kamalālayā* (dwelling in the lotus) i.e. surrounded by flowering stems and leaves. Although he concedes that (1) and (2) might be shared by other figures, the third element conclusively identifies her. Coomaraswamy holds that the Sirimā Devatā figure is to be identified with Mother Siri who holds in her raised right hand a lotus flower. He further classifies the Śrī-Lakṣmī images into the *abhiṣeka* type or the Gaja-Lakṣmī type. In this depiction the goddess is shown having one or all of the three characteristics described above. Additionally, there are to be two elephants standing on two lotuses emerging out of a *pūrṇaghaṭa*, lustrating the goddess with water flowing from two pitchers held in their trunks that represent clouds and rain. The breast-touching, when it occurs, is for him a characteristic of Lakṣmī as Lady of Abundance, signifying fertility and wealth. It may be pointed out that, at least in Jaina *sūtra* texts, there are references to the *abhiṣeka* in association with women other than Lakṣmī. The *Jīvājīvābhigama Sūtra*, while describing the qualities of human women living on the *Ekoruka Dvīpa*, after a description of the extraordinary beauty of its female inhabitants, provides a list of 27 signs or *lakṣaṇa*s that are associated with them: *chattra, dhvaja, yuga, stūpa, dāminī, kamaṇḍalu, kalaśa, vāpi, svastika, patākā, yava, matsya, kumbha, śreṣṭha ratha, makara, śuklasthāna, aṅkuśa, aṣṭa-padavī-cighuta-phalaka, supratiṣṭhaka sthāpanaka, mayūra, śrīdāma,*

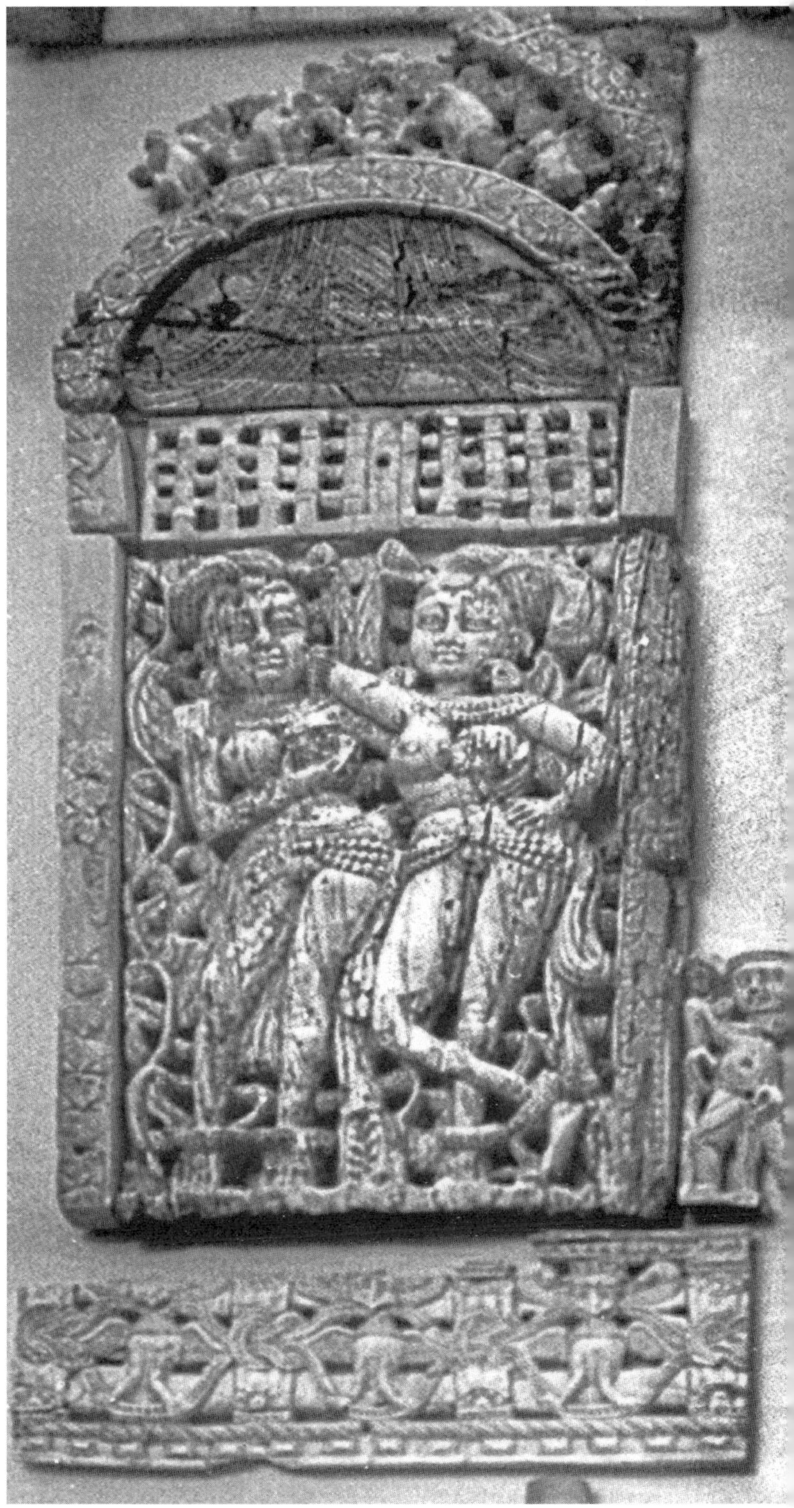

2.2.16 Two women, one touching the breast, furniture back, ivory, late first to early third century CE, Begram, Musee Guimet, Paris.

*abhiṣeka, toraṇa, medinīpati rājā, samudra, bhavana, prāsāda, darpaṇa*, beautiful elephants, bullocks, 32 lions, and 32 *cāmaras*.[107]

While Coomaraswamy may well be correct in his identification of the woman in breast-offering posture as Gaja-Lakṣmī/Śrī-Lakṣmī, there is a critical flaw in his reasoning if it is applied universally to all the breast-touching figures of the early period. In early Buddhist art at Bharhut we have the existence of the breast-touching posture with and without the lustrating elephants, both within the railing pillar medallions and on *toraṇas*.[108] But curiously we also have a similar representation outside the medallion, on a lotus rising above it on a stalk, as a decorative element. Such a depiction is one among many of female and male figures that are suspended on lotus stalks around the medallions, holding auspicious objects in their hands or simply standing with hands folded in adoration or *namaskāra hasta*. This imagery is more in keeping with the *yakṣī*s that adorned the facades of late *stūpa*s at Sanghol and Mathurā. Unless we are willing to accept the fact that the figures inside the medallions and those outside it represent the same deity (which is also seen to correspond to a large, nearly life-sized figure of Sirimā Devatā) we will have to review the suggestion that Sirimā = Śrī = Lakṣmī, irrespective of placement, size or iconographic detail.

The third possibility is that the image represented Aditi, since it matches some elements attributed to the goddess in later Vedic descriptions. Later, the *gaja abhiṣeka* form of Lakṣmī may have appropriated some attributes, such as association with the waters which were considered the domain of Aditi. In later Vedic literature, Lakṣmī is not considered to be the wife of Viṣṇu (an identification that takes place first in the Epics) but Aditi. In the *Taittirīya Saṁhitā* of the *Yajurveda* she receives an oblation as the wife of Viṣṇu[109] and is called "the heavenly of all quarters, the easily milked, the rich in milk, the goddess . . . the lady of Viṣṇu, the mild . . . ruling this world . . . may Aditi be auspicious to us!"[110] She is the mother (once the sister) of the Ādityas, mother of Mitra and Varuṇa, mother or daughter of Dakṣa, sometimes of other gods and kings and of sons generally; motherhood is her essential characteristic. Sometimes she is identified with the Earth (*Pṛthvī*). She is asked to bestow wealth; her gifts are pure, intact, divine, and imperishable. Sometimes she is spoken of as a cow[111] with reference to her milk; the terrestrial milk that is mixed with the *soma* is hers, the *soma* itself is like her milk.

It is in the *Mahābhārata* that Pṛthvī, (Earth) often addressed as the Great Mother, is also imagined as a divine cow giving milk to her children. As a nurse of all, she provides wealth and rejoices to give corn to all men.[112] Like Pṛthvī, Śrī-Lakṣmī is also associated with the cow and the zoomorphic form of the Lakṣmī is the cow — the wish-fulfilling and ever-productive cow. From this we can deduce a link between the divine feminine — whether as Aditi, Pṛthvī or Śrī — and fertility/giving/nurturing and the mammary apparatus.

The attribute of bestowing prosperity linked with Śrī-Lakṣmī is also referred to in other texts of the period. In early Buddhism, Siri-Lakkhi is regarded as a synonym for the goddess of beauty and prosperity. In the *Salikedasa*, *Dhajavihetha* and *Siri Kalakanni Jātaka* she is regarded as the goddess of fortune, wisdom and virtue.[113]

However, none of the textual descriptions of Śrī-Lakṣmī or, later, Gaja-Lakṣmī link her to the breast, either by making prominent breasts her

2.2.17 Sirimā Devatā, great railing, pillar, first century BCE, Bharhut. IM. (facing page)

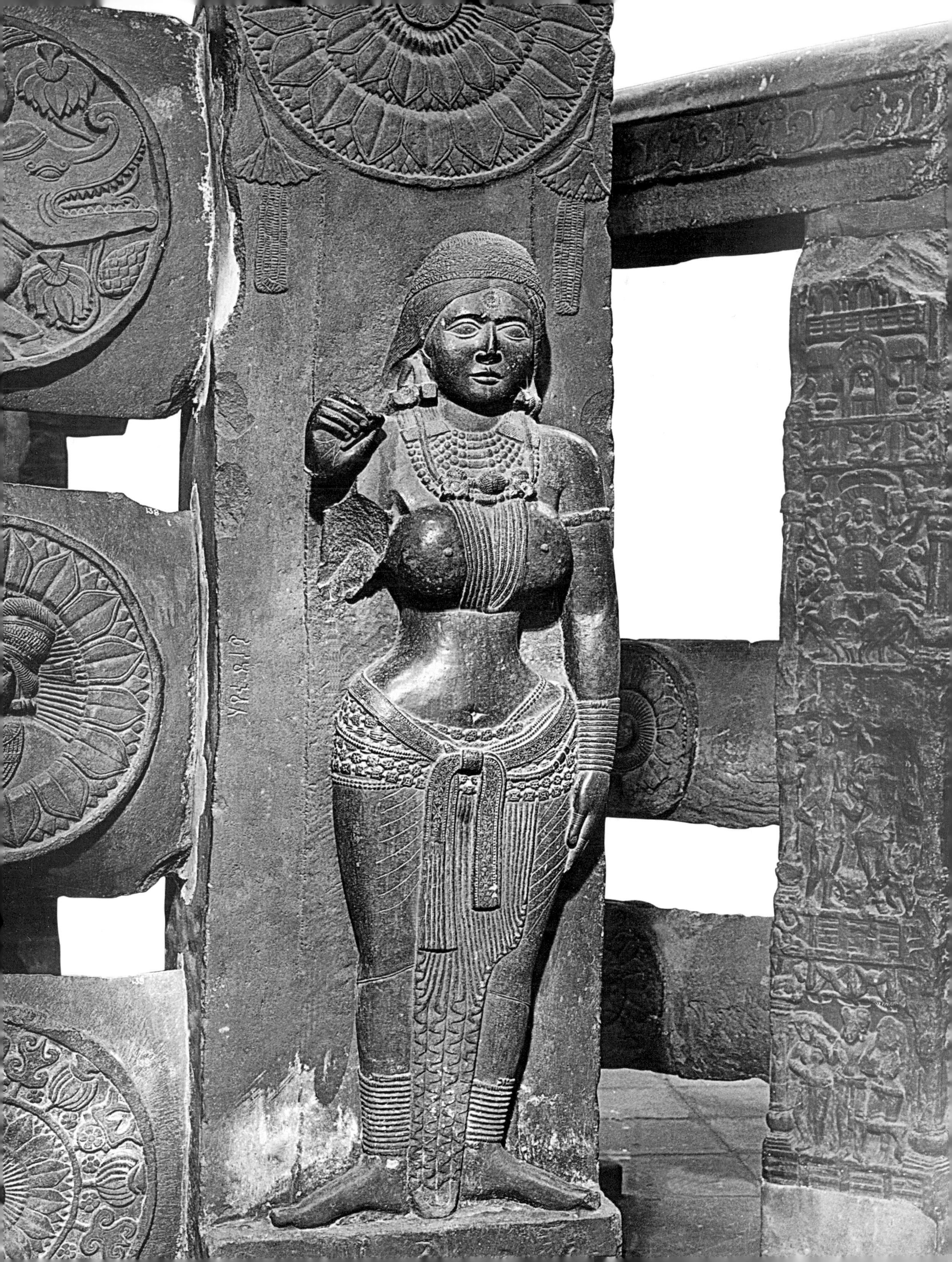

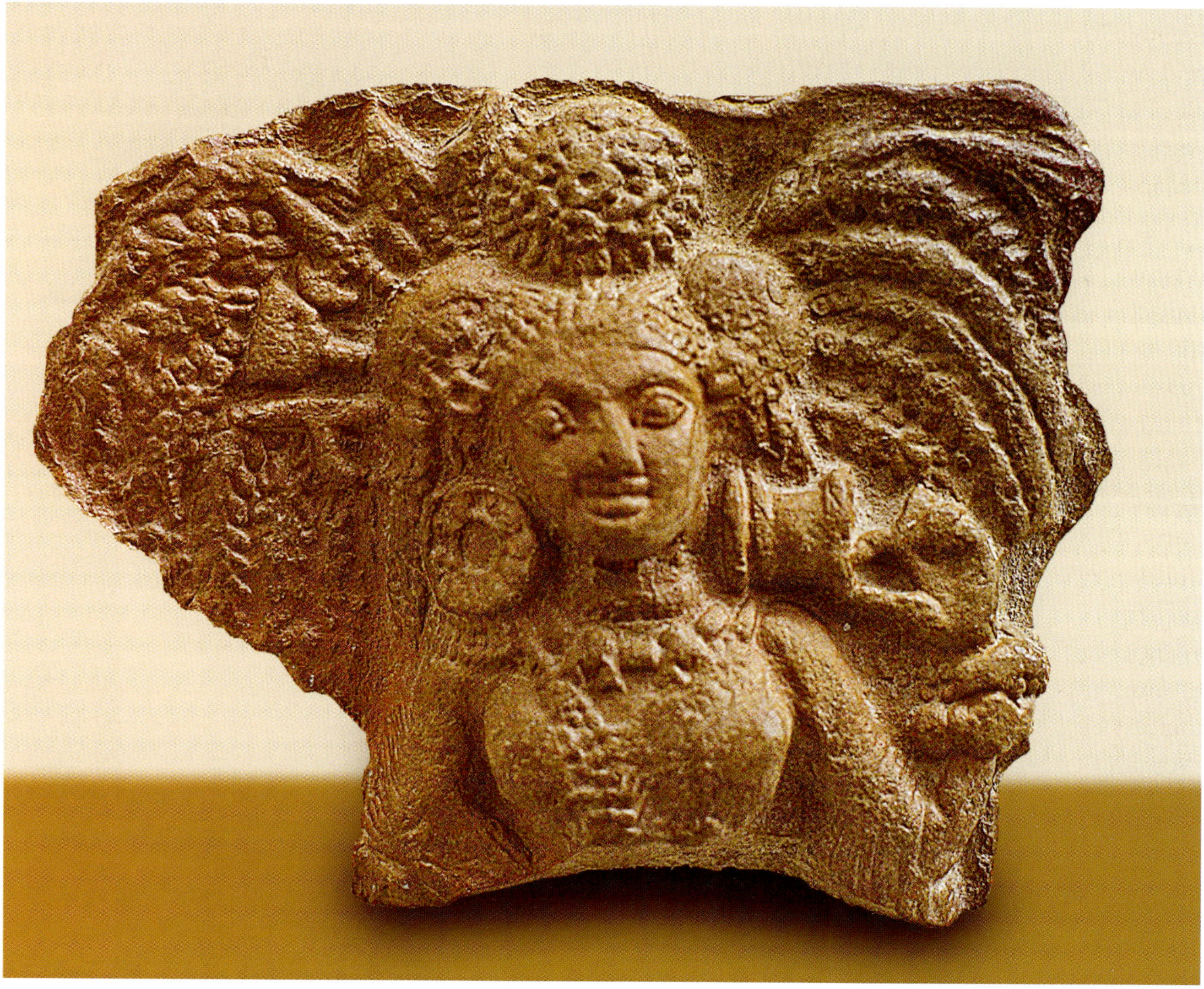

2.2.18 Śrī-Lakṣmī, terracotta, first century BCE.

special or exclusive attribute or by attaching special significance to Lakṣmī's breasts. Rather, her association with the lotus and, in her Gaja-Lakṣmī form, with a pair of elephants is emphasised. Beauty is also her characteristic and it is prescribed that she be depicted as richly ornamented and as beautiful. She is described as well-dressed, decked with various ornaments and having such physical traits as fully developed breasts, a narrow waist and heavy buttocks.[114] Iconographic texts refer to her two, four or (rarely) many-armed variety. In our period we come across the two-armed form only.[115]

One source of inspiration for the development of the early iconography of the breast-touching figure, with or without the child, may be Isis, the Egyptian fertility deity who is often shown offering her breast and in association with Horus, who is depicted as touching her breast, or as a suckling infant.[116]

We notice that in Mathurā art of the Kuṣāṇa period the image, which probably represented Aditi or Gaja-Lakṣmī/Śrī-Lakṣmī in the Śuṅga period, becomes disassociated from the elephants and the lotuses and becomes simply the Dugdhadhāriṇī, the milk-giver. Thus both the element of fertility associated with the lotuses and water, and the divinity accorded by the elephants offering oblation through the *ghaṭas* or waterpots, are abstracted, leaving only the prosperity and boon-bestowing ability.

A later text from Orissa datable to the ninth century, the *Śilpa-Prakāśa*, regards the mother-and-child depiction as one of the *Alasākanyās*. It gives the description of sixteen kinds of *Alasākanyā* or indolent maiden. In local terminology, this is called *Nārībandha,* a band of sculptures containing depictions of women which is considered indispensable to a building. "As a house without a wife, as frolic without a woman so without (the figure of) woman the monument will be of inferior quality and bear no fruit. . . . Woman is most beautiful, when adorned with all ornaments."[117]

The *Śilpa-Prakāśa* then goes on to elaborate on the *mātṛmūrti* (image of the mother).

> Afterwards hear the description of the beautiful image of a mother. The head is placed standing upon the middle line, and so is the whole beautiful body. The left arm on the left side is near the left triangle, from the end of the oblique line and the forearm lies on the horizontal middle line. Inside the right triangle is the figure of a child. From face to foot it is on the middle line. Hanging from the right shoulder, the right hand is placed on the thigh. Both feet are placed in an ordinary way.[118]

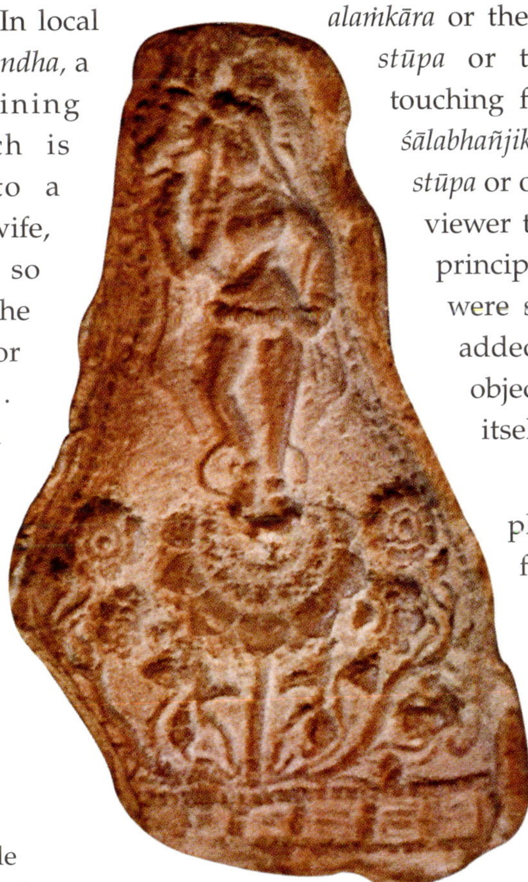

While in the Woman and Child sculptures at Mathurā, Sanghol and various museum collections, the child is often held in this manner, we notice that there is no mention of breast-touching, either by the mother or the child in the textual description.

It is clear from the surviving evidence and from architectural texts such as the *Śilpa-Prakāśa* that mother-and-child figures are parts of *alaṁkāra* or the decorative scheme of the *stūpa* or temple; also the breast-touching figure is one of the *yakṣī-śālabhañjikā* figures that adorns the *stūpa* or other religious edifices. The viewer thus did not view these as principal objects of worship; they were subsidiary ornaments that added value to the principal object of adoration, the *stūpa* itself.

The variation in the placement and size of female figures in breast-offering postures suggests that these figures permeated the entire hierarchy of representations, from the divine to the decorative. At Bharhut, divine imagery is found inside and outside the pillar medallions as subsidiary decorative devices. At Sāñcī, Nāgārjunakoṇḍa and Amarāvatī, as Gaja-Lakṣmī on the railings and *toraṇa* architrave, and at Mathurā and associated sites on railing pillars, it

2.2.19 Goddess standing on a lotus, surrounded by lotus vines, akin to depictions at Bharhut and Bodh-Gayā, first century BCE (?), Kauśāmbī, SML.

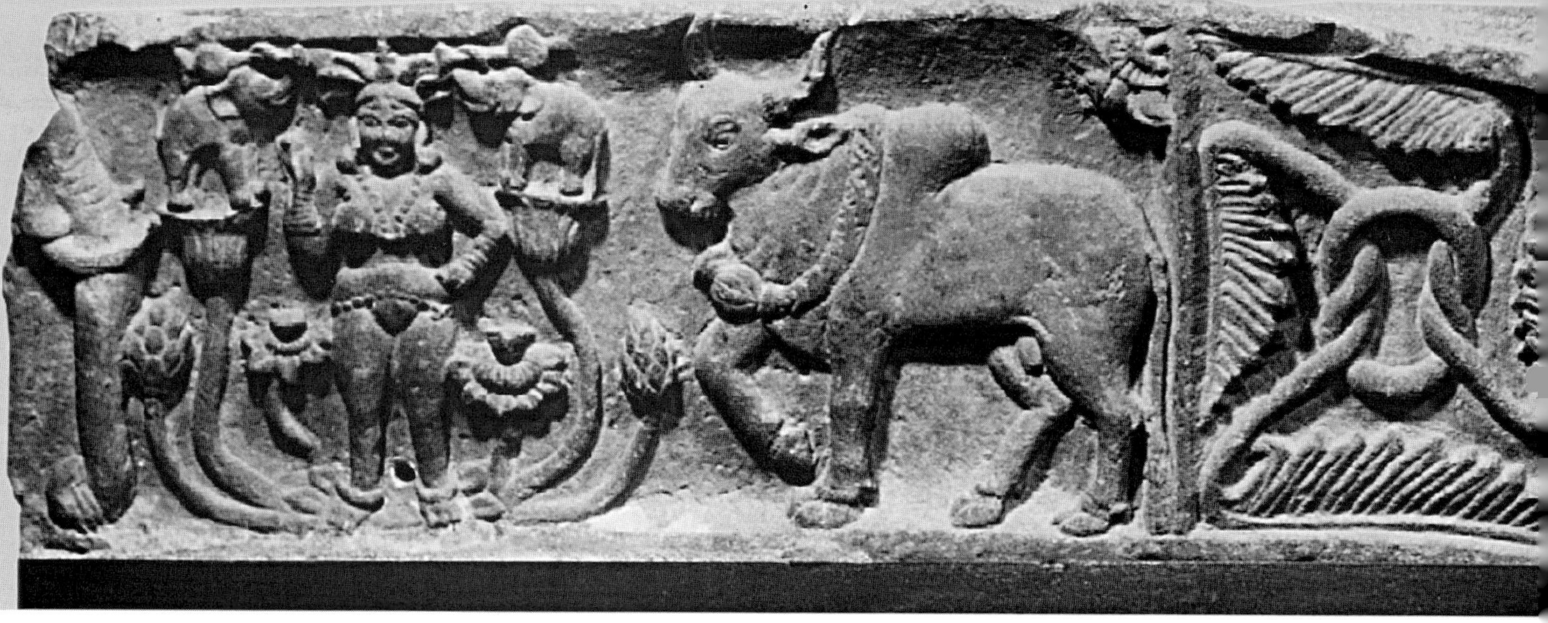

is part of the *alaṁkāra* scheme. This would further imply that breast-touching as a device has a cultural signifier built into it that is not restricted to divine figures only. The other problem that we need to keep in mind is that the breast-touching feature is not the exclusive domain of the hegemonic monumental stone art, but is also prevalent in small terracottas at sites such as Kauśāmbī and Mathurā (*Pl.* 2.2.14) (for without breast touching examples, see *pls.* 2.2.18, 2.2.19). Thus, the representational type is not confined to decorative/symbolic functions on the façades of *stūpa*s and the like, but is also used — as the *pañcacūḍa* representation of the breast-offering goddess — on coins and cult objects. Unless we are willing to accept that the breast-touching gesture is exclusive to the iconography of Śrī-Lakṣmī, we will have to posit that the posture may have signified a common symbolism of wish-fulfilling and granting prosperity that was shared by different divine feminine entities.

Whatever may have been its relative importance with regard to the whole artistic complex of the building and its decorative elements, the choice of the subject in itself has significant gendered implications. I think three possible explanations may be posited to explain the depiction of female figures in a breast-offering posture. One is that it privileged the notion of motherhood and set it up as an ideal. Secondly, that the imagery is linked to and derived from the motherhood function through the act of giving/granting wishes. Thirdly, such a depiction served an erotic and voyeuristic purpose, and is an object of the male gaze within a patriarchal discourse of pleasure and power. These three factors need not necessarily function as separate categories and may in fact overlap.

### 2.2.3 UNIVERSAL NURTURING MOTHER

Feminist studies in general, and feminist art-historical scholarship in particular, has been concerned with the body as the agency through which gender stereotypes are constructed. The most significant female "body" is that of the mother, considering that ideologically the *raison d'être* of women's existence and status has for a very long time been linked to their ability to bear children. This is the basis for the worship of mother goddesses, corn goddesses and other fertility deities. The next significant biological "reality" of females, beyond birth functions, is the demand for lactation to feed their dependent young; yet in practice lactation shows variability

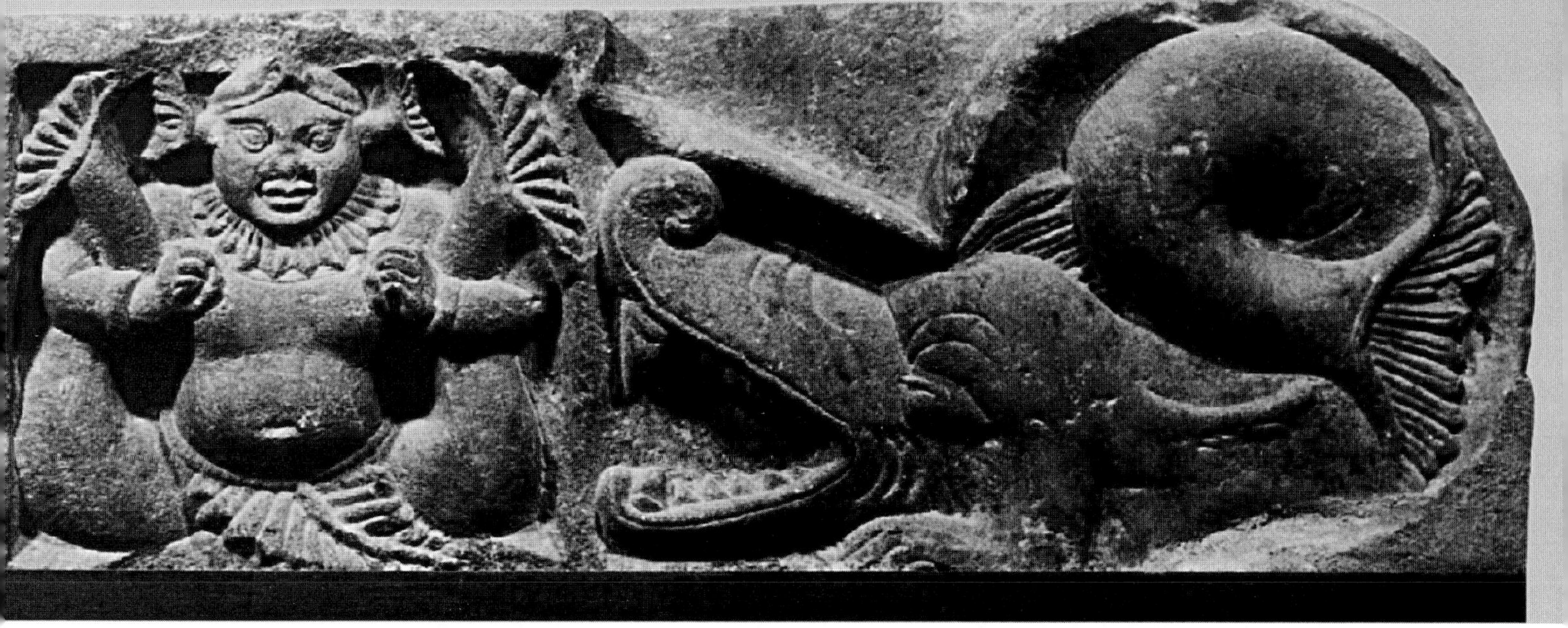

2.2.20 Śrī-Lakṣmī, surrounded by elephants, with a bull, *toraṇa* fragment, first century BCE, Kauśāmbī. AM 65.

at many levels — frequency, length of time, multiple feeders of children,[119] non-biological mothers feeding[120] or alternative food sources[121] — all the options that have been explored in early Indian myths and legends.

It has been argued that in Buddhism there are parallels between the nurturing roles of the Buddha and Mahāprajāpati Gautamī: Gautamī lactates and Buddha preaches. Gautamī's milk shall never quench the thirst of desire; Buddha's will. Gautamī's milk is an extension of her transient body while Buddha's message is an extension of his unchanging textual body. He gives the milk of eternal *dharma* which flows from his *dhammakāya* or body of teaching.[122]

The Śrī-Lakṣmī, Gaja-Lakṣmī or Dugdha-dhāriṇī figures found in post-Mauryan art have been interpreted as fertility figures, symbolising the link between the child-bearing and breast-feeding ability of women and universal fertility. But I would like to subject this notion to further examination to see how far the biological role of child-bearing is converted into a gender role of nurturing through these images.

In this context it is noteworthy that none of the figures is shown as a nursing mother.[123] Such a representation would have established a direct connection between motherhood, nursing and fertility. This is not surprising within the context of ancient Indian texts and mythology, where the primary role model for women is not that of the mother but that of the good wife.[124] None of the mother-son relationships is valorised to the extent that husband-wife relationships are. It is also difficult to find instances in the textual tradition where the breast is the locus of this mother-child relationship or bond. In fact, breast-feeding may even have negative connotations traditionally, as in the case of Pūtanā.[125] Only medical texts such as the *Suśruta Saṁhitā* give us information about certain nurturing aspects of motherhood such as breastfeeding, since they recommend remedies to optimise the feeding of infants.

It can also be seen from the textual references to Aditi, Śrī and Lakṣmī given above that, though we have evidence of a linkage being established between motherhood, fertility and the specific portrayal of Śrī-Lakṣmī, nowhere is the breast-offering posture mentioned. This makes the imagery quite mystifying, since we have instances (at Bodh-Gayā, Sāñcī, etc.) where similar imagery signifying fertility/prosperity was conveyed without the association with the breast.

We also have the notion of fecundity and the protection of children being associated with other deities of the period — Mātṛkās, Hāritī, Ṣaṣṭhī and Naigameṣī.[126] We only have to mention the numerous terracotta figurines of the mother goddess figures recovered from post-Mauryan layers during excavations, and the necessity and choice of such a depiction as Dugdhadhāriṇī becomes even more vexatious.

In the inscriptions too, though we have many references to motherhood, the mother is often mentioned within a conventional framework of the mother-father dyad (*mātapitiho*).[127] In Buddhist texts, the notion of motherhood is associated with the pain of losing one's child and this is further linked to renouncing the world and becoming a *bhikkhuṇī*.[128] The ideal mother is the one who not only cares for her children but also leads them to the right path. Motherhood in fact symbolises attachment, an antithesis of asceticism and one of the elements to be renounced in order to attain *nirvāṇa*.

It seems unlikely that the breast-offering figure is a means of directly reinforcing the ideal of motherhood, especially given the Buddhist context within which the majority of figures have been discovered. It is probable that the biological function of milk-producing breasts is taken up as a symbol to reinforce the gendered ideal of a woman as a giver and nurturer.

### 2.2.4 UNIVERSAL GIVER

The Śrī-Lakṣmī/Dugdhadhāriṇī figure has been interpreted as the deity of prosperity, good fortune and well-being, and this is perhaps the most obvious function of the depiction. The texts of the period, both Brāhmanical and Buddhist, emphasise this particular function.

The adjuncts of the early representations — such as the *pūrṇaghaṭa* (the vase of plenty), the *padma* (red lotus), *padmalatā* (lotus vine) and elephants pouring oblations of life-giving waters — are obviously related to fertility.[129] The goddess is also associated with Kubera, the god of wealth and prosperity,[130] and later with Viṣṇu.[131]

Thus, her ability to grant material prosperity is clear. In a way this reveals the contradiction inherent in the philosophically non-acquisitive religion of Buddhism as it functions through art. While the monks and nuns professed non-acquisition or lack of desire as a virtue, and the laity is encouraged to do the same, one of the desired blessings, as seen in art, is the bestowal of wealth and prosperity. The agency through which this was sought to be achieved is a voluptuous woman that is converted into a symbol of plenty and material prosperity.

### 2.2.5 EROTIC CONNOTATIONS

The breast-offering woman can be considered as an erotic piece of art created for the voyeuristic pleasure of a male audience.

It has been contended that the canonical and pleasing form of the female nude becomes the subject of the male gaze, "posed, objectified, de-humanised and idealised as an erotic sight for male pleasure."[132] This is partly applicable to sculptures such as the breast-offering figures, given the context in which the figures of the Dugdhadhāriṇī have been found. Almost all find-sites are Buddhist *stūpa*s and *vihāra*s, sites of monastic practice and religious devotion.[133] These also developed into major Buddhist centres of pilgrimage, such as Sāñcī, Bharhut, Mathurā and Saṁghapura (Sanghol). A depiction such as the Dugdhadhāriṇī in these contexts — if considered inescapably erotic — reveals the essentially contradictory attitude of heterodox religions towards women, where there is a conflict between the ascetic ideal and sensuous, fecund beauty.

The depiction of the breast-offering pose seems to be exceptional given that almost all textual sources do not recommend even the exposure of breasts to the public gaze, let alone call attention to the secondary sexual organs through the act of touching and looking at them. In fact, the *Nāṭyaśāstra* says that *nāṭyadharma* (dramatic convention) prohibits[134] certain acts on stage including kissing, embracing or any other private acts such as biting, scratching with the fingernails, loosening the knot, *pressings of breasts* and lips. By the time we come to the Dharmaśāstra literature it is clearly laid down that the navel of women should never become visible and legs should be covered down to the ankles.[135] Hala's *Saptaśatī* also seems to indicate that covering the upper part of the body was an accepted convention.[136] Women also wore a bodice called *kañcukī*, the ends of which were tied together under the breasts, or a band called a *kūcabandha*, and this was not entirely removed even in private.[137]

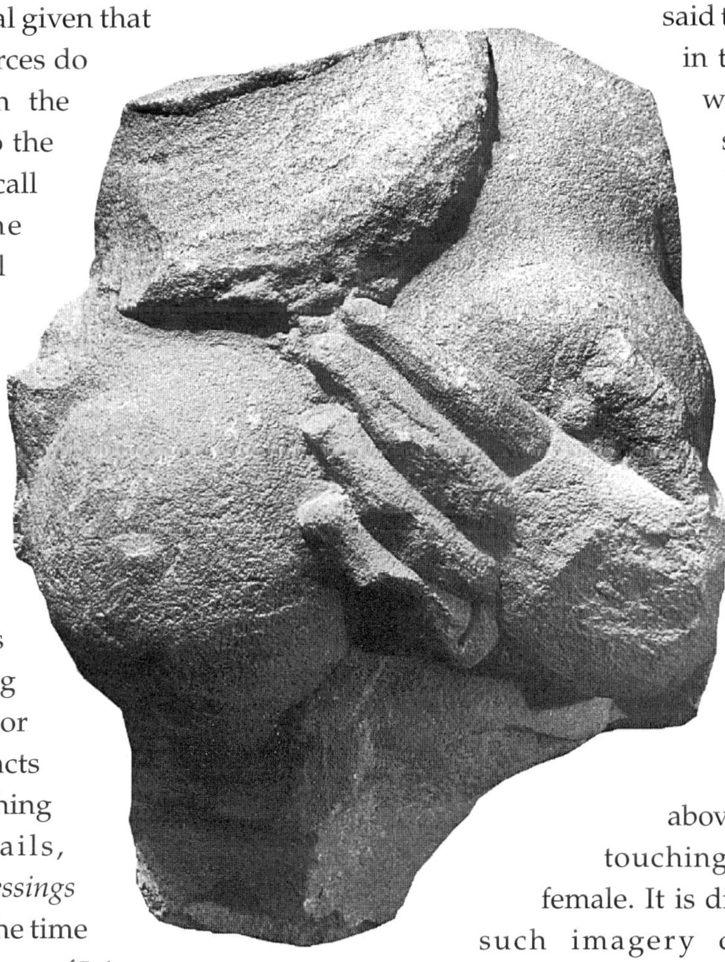

These prescriptions for covering the upper torso were laid down because the erotic potential of exposed breasts was recognised. Aśvaghoṣa exploits their sensuousness to describe the amorous interaction between Sundarī and Nanda in the *Saundarānanda*. Sundarī's beauty is said to be "a very lotus pond in the shape of a woman, with her laughter for the swans, her eyes for the bees and *her swelling breasts* for the uprising lotus bud."[138] She tells her lover that, "as you lie asleep, I shall repeatedly waken you by beating you with my breasts and shall refuse to speak to you."[139]

The erotic element can also be seen in the Type D reliefs and terracotta plaques described above where the partner is touching the breast of the female. It is difficult to imagine that such imagery contributed to the conceptualisation of motherhood. It is more likely that such eroticism was part of some ritualistic cult practice or represented an object of pleasure.

2.2.21 Śrī Lakṣmī, Gupta period, fifth century CE, Kauśāmbī.

While the breast has not been privileged with regard to motherhood in most of the texts (maybe it was such a natural aspect that it was not considered worth mentioning), it is very much part of contemporary and later descriptions of feminine beauty. The Jātakas contain many references to divine and earthly women who are beautiful and full-breasted.[140] The *Jīvājīvābhigama Sūtra*, composed sometime between the first century BCE and third century CE and part of the Jaina Āgama tradition, gives a full description of the breasts of beautiful women inhabiting the Ekoruka Dvīpa. It says that the breasts of such women resemble golden jars (*kalaśa*), are equal and closely set, charming to look at, and seem to be crowned by the nipples set high on the breasts. Both breasts originate and develop together. They are round and set high and their form is such to inspire love.[141] The beauty of the *śālabhañjikā* described in the Jaina text *Rāyapasenīyasutta* is not unlike the Dugdhadhāriṇī figure.[142] The *Mṛcchakaṭika* has a passage in which clouds, *payodhara*, are compared to breasts.[143] We have already seen that in iconographic prescriptions the beauty of Śrī-Lakṣmī lies in her being full-breasted.

Lakṣmī has generally been projected as an ideal of feminine beauty. Her very name is considered synonymous with everything that is charming and lovely. Her association with lotuses, while signifying the fecundity of water, also links her to the allure of lotuses. The lotuses are often employed in similes to describe beautiful bodies, eyes, feet and breasts. Linking it to ornaments and dress enlarges this ideal of beauty. Śrī-Lakṣmī is therefore described as golden-hued[144] and sumptuously and richly ornamented. The depiction of images of such goddesses as Aditi, Śrī-Lakṣmī and Dugdhadhāriṇī did no doubt contribute to the construction of the ideal of the beautiful woman. How far this was transferred to real life is difficult to say, though Sanskrit poetry and drama often compare a beautiful woman to Lakṣmī or a *yakṣī*. Undoubtedly, these beautiful and bountiful maidens added to the attractiveness of the edifice, for the visual gratification of the pilgrims of both genders drawn from all over the country and almost all classes.

If we were to examine the consumers of the visual discourse of which Siri-Lakkhī (Śrī-Lakṣmī) or the Dugdhadhāriṇī forms a part, it would be apparent that it is not only men who were patrons/visitors at these places. More than two-thirds of the inscriptions at Bharhut and about half of the 631 inscriptions at Sāñcī record donations made by women.[145] An analysis of a particular relief sculpture and its corresponding donative inscription does not reveal any particular pattern of patronage in which certain kinds of sculptures are associated with female donations. Given this fact, it would be easy to assume that the sculptures did not have particular erotic connotations linked to the male gaze, and that they functioned merely as ornaments symbolising prosperity and the ability to gratify a wish for the viewer.

However, this does not adequately answer the problem as to why such a depiction is chosen. It is apparent from other feminine representations that female bodies could be shown clothed, as in the Palikheṛā Bacchanalian Scene from Mathurā[146] (*Pl.* 5.17, 5.18) or Māyādevī in the conception and delivery scenes.

The internal evidence is also ambiguous. The viewers' attention is drawn to the full-breasted figure of the woman through the offering or holding gesture, but the gaze of the figure itself is directed towards the breast and not towards the onlooker. This is clearly not a provocative or inviting gaze; rather, it emphasises the object of the gaze — the breast. It does not invite the viewer to participate directly in the act of holding the breast, for the figure appears unself-conscious and unaware of the effect on the viewer.

The depiction of the Dugdhadhāriṇī figure in particular is in keeping with the increasing eroticising or sexualising of both male and female figures during the Kuṣāṇa period. Some work has been done by Vishakha Desai on the obvious depiction of the genitalia in the case of *bodhisattva* and Buddha sculptures of the Kuṣāṇa period. According to her, such imagery conveys the idea of *cakravartin* and the ideal male who is virile and strong. The obvious sexual masculine attributes emphasise the temporal and sacred power of the male deity.

However, in case of such strong sexual/feminine representations as the Dugdhadhāriṇī, one can posit that the function is not to idealise the power of women or the attributes of a woman as the reproducer, but is rather to objectify the woman as the source of giving. The woman here is only an instrument, not an active agent, in the presentation of her own fertility.

There is change over a period of time, from the inception of the image in the Gaja-Lakṣmī portrayal in Bharhut, where she is shown as milk-giver deriving from her ability to be fertile (hence the lotuses and the water).[147] In the interim period we see many experiments with the form. Sometimes she is shown as a goddess touching her breast or as Gaja-Lakṣmī without the breast-touching element, sometimes without the elephants and sometimes standing on a *pūrṇaghaṭa* and *padmapīṭha*. By the time we come to Sanghol, the female becomes a code for universal prosperity and giving; the offering of her breast as a gesture and the power of active fertility are abstracted from her portrayal.

One may suggest that the transformation in the form and function of Sirimā Devatā and Gaja-Lakṣmī to the Dugdhadhāriṇī may be located in the changing politico-social context. These changes had a profound impact on cultural and religious formations that determined and prefaced iconography, mythology and gendering of art. This is reflected in the various experiments and combinations witnessed in the figures of goddesses.

Though in the case of both Lajjā-Gaurī and breast-touching figures we are trying to recover meanings that have been lost, this opens us to both problems and possibilities, and any interpretation offered is fluid and to an extent subjective.

This section has examined the essentialising of the feminine as it has occurred through one type of representation of the female body. It has mapped the varying tendencies within the discourse of reproduction by tracing continuities in this essentialising through its primary and secondary reproductive functions. The two figure types, the Lajjā-Gaurī type and the breast-giver, differ widely in their nature and depiction. The first, being a cult figure, becomes a symbol for the degree to which the female body was seen as controlled by reproductive functions. But this imagery is compatible with many views of female physical strength and of cultural definitions of the female body as a repository of mysteries and fertility. That this cult remains outside the dominant discourses, and is not co-opted through spousification or otherwise, is significant.

The second figure is more ubiquitous in that it varies widely from cult representations to those which are decorative (*alaṁkāra*). The female body through the representation of the breast-giver, the breast itself and the gaze directed towards its offering, makes the breast a central site to posit a multiplicity of meaning ranging from the fertile to the woman as the ultimate giver of all, including pleasure. A process of the sensualising of the female body over the period has been highlighted in the shedding of the fertility symbols from the representation of the figure in the breast-giving gesture. This creation of the gender identity of the essential woman as the reproductive fertility symbol with erotic voyeuristic possibilities is part of the crystallisation of gender identities and roles during the period.

### Notes and References

1. Vedic rituals such as the *puruṣamedha* and *aśvamedha* associate coitus between the chief queen and a stranger or a dead horse as signifying ongoing fertility.
2. One concept that encompasses this notion of female as reproducer is that of *prakṛti*. The union of *prakṛti* and *puruṣa* is considered essential for the perpetuation of life, in which *prakṛti* is nature and feminine while the term *puruṣa* in itself means male. *MWSE*, p. 654, defines *prakṛti*, (f), as the original producer of (or rather passive power of creating the natural world) consisting of three constituent essences or *guṇas* called *sattva, rajas* and *tamas*; nature; woman or womankind; the original or natural form or condition of anything original or primary substance; cause, origin, nature, character. On the other hand, *MWSE*, p. 637, *puruṣa* means a man, a male, human being (pl. people, mankind), a male person; the primeval man as the soul and original source of the universe; the personal and animating principle of men and other beings, etc.
3. *Malyagirivṛtti*, cf. *Jīvājīvābhigama Sūtra*, p. 117. Puruṣaveda, i.e male and masculinity is described as having a *mehana* (penis), *kaṭhoratā* (hardness), *dṛḍhatā* (firmness), *śūratā* (bravery), *smaśru* (facial hair), *dhīratā* (patience and control) and *strīkāmitā* (desire to mate with a female).
4. One would like to observe here that men do not have any analogous symbols of married status either at the time of the wedding or later. This is reflected in Dharmaśāstras. *Manu*, 2.63, 2.67, p. 24, tr. Wendy Doniger, Penguin Books, for example, decrees that there is *upanayana* for men which marks their passage into adulthood and knowledge, a second birth. For women there is no *upanayana* and marriage should be considered a second birth for them.
5. Supra, see previous chapter on Gender and Art.
6. In the lexicons *yoni* is given as a womb, uterus, vulva, the female organ of generation; any place of birth or origin. *MWSE*, p. 858.
7. Carol Radcliffe Bolon, *Forms of the Goddess Lajjā-Gaurī*, Pennsylvania: Pennsylvania State University Press, 1992.

8. H.D. Sankalia, "The Nude Goddess or 'Shameless Woman' in Western Asia, India and South East Asia", in *Artibus Asiae*, XXIII, 1960, pp. 111-23.
9. Stella Kramrisch, "Aditi-Uttānapād", in *Artibus Asiae*, vol. XIX, 1956, pp. 259-70.
10. Carol Radcliffe Bolon, op. cit., p. 12, assigns a later date of third-fourth century.
11. H. D. Sankalia, op. cit., p. 113.
12. Carol Radcliffe Bolon, op. cit., p. 11.
13. Allahabad Museum No. K.3904, Size: .030 × .030m. Also see S.C. Kala, *Terracottas in the Allahabad Museum*, New Delhi: Abhinav Prakashan, 1980, p. 65.
14. Allahabad Museum No. K 5214, Size: .088 × .085m. Also see S.C. Kala, op. cit., p. 65.
15. Allahabad Museum No. 5034 and No. 48.65 Size: .160 × .120m and .080 respectively.
16. Allahabad Museum No. Jh.4617, Size: .120 × .135m. Also see S.C. Kala, op. cit., p. 64, fig. 164.
17. Allahabad Museum No. K.3849, Size: .090 × .150m. Also see S.C. Kala, op. cit., p. 65; Allahabad Museum No. K.3894, Size: .110 × .070m. Also see S.C. Kala, op. cit., p. 65.
18. State Museum, Lucknow Museum, 79.15.6, Late Kuṣāṇa;. Carol Radcliffe Bolon, op. cit., p. 22.
19. Patna Museum, 7606, red sandstone, 5"; Carol Radcliffe Bolon, op. cit., p. 22, fig 40.
20. *ASIAR*, 1911-12, Plate, XXIII.40, p. 40.
21. Ibid., p. 67. Now in Indian Museum, Calcutta.
22. Carol Radcliffe Bolon, op. cit., p. 22, fig. 36.
23. Bhītā, single mould, terracotta, State Museum, Lucknow No. 67.343; S. P. Shukla, "Some Interesting Kuṣāṇa Terracottas in State Museum, Lucknow", in *Bulletin of Museums and Archaeology in UP*, December 1969, p. 34, LD. 3.
24. Allahabad Museum No. K 5034 Size: .030 × .055m.
25. Similar arrangements have been found in stone discs found from Taxila and Uttar Pradesh. See Pramod Chandra, "The Cult of Śrī-Lakṣmī in Four Carved Discs in Bharat Kala Bhavan", in *Chhavi*, pp. 140-41, figs. 286 and 291.
26. H.D. Sankalia, op. cit., fig. 3.
27. *IA-AR*, 1957-8, p. 23.
28. H.D. Sankalia, op. cit., fig. 4.
29. Ibid., fig. 9.
30. Ibid., fig. 10.
31. Ibid., fig. 8 and Carol Radcliffe Bolon, op. cit., p. 16.
32. C. Gupta, "Some Interesting Plaques of Lajja from Paunar", in A.V. Narasimhamurthy and K.V. Ramesh, eds., *Essays in Ideology: Dr. G.S. Dikshit Felicitation Volume*, 1987, pp. 45-50.
33. Ibid., p. 47, fig. 1.
34. Ibid., p. 48, fig. 2.
35. Ibid., fig. 4.
36. R. Codrington, "Iconography: Classical and Indian", *Man*, XXXV, 1935, No. 70, p. 65; Sankalia, op. cit., p. 113; Carol Radcliffe Bolon, op. cit., figs. 66-68.
37. R. Nagaswamy, "From Aditi to Kundalini (From Prehistoric Visiṟikkal to Historic Śrīcakra", in Lokesh Chandra and J. Jain, eds., *Dimensions of Indian Art: Pupul Jayakar*, Delhi: Agam Kala Prakashan, 1986, pp 323-31, figs. 6 and 9.
38. Stella Kramrisch, op. cit., p. 260.
39. Carol Radcliffe Bolon, op. cit., pp. 74-76.
40. Sarnath Museum No. 328, Size; ht. .070m.
41. Allahabad, Dr. Jagdish Gupta Collection. Size: 6 × 6 cm.
42. An early example of a figure in this position is found at Bharhut where we have at least two railing-pillar medallions containing pot-bellied figures from whose navel two vines emanate to fill up the roundel (*Pl.* 2.1.17). Here the triangular area between the thighs is covered with a leaf, so that the sex of the figure is not revealed, possibly it was deliberately androgynised.
43. *MWSE*, p. 174.
44. *Ṛgveda*, X.72.3-4, *bhūr jajña uttānapado bhuva āśā ajāyant* I

    *aditer dakṣo ajāyata dakṣād v aditiḥ pari* [4].
45. *Atharvaveda*, VII.6, 7 [Whitney].
46. *AV*, V11.7.1-2.

47. A.A. Macdonell, *Vedic Index*, p. 396, classes *mahānagnī* with *puṁscalī*, thus rendering both as harlots. (*AV*, XIV.1, 30); XX.136.5) Also a courtesan. *MWSE*, p. 796 also translates *mahānagnī* as a courtesan or a harlot.

48. *MWSE*, p. 796 renders *mahānagna* as quite naked, a paramour, an athlete and a king of a harlot.

49. *AV*, XX.136. Many translators such as Whitney (New Delhi: Munshiram Manoharlal) and Griffith have omitted translating this passage due to its purported obscenity. Damodar Satwalekar has also left it untranslated in his Hindi version due to its esoteric nature. Pt. Khemkaran Das Trivedi and Pt. Jaidev, followed by Devi Chand have translated it in a manner that would render it socially acceptable, by translating it as a game between the king and the queen, but which is completely incorrect and not keeping with the spirit of the text.

50. J.N. Banerjea, *The Development of Hindu Iconography*, Calcutta: University of Calcutta, 1956, p. 375.

51. V.S. Agrawala, *Indian Art*, Varanasi: Prithvi Prakashan, 1965, pp. 81-82.

52. In the *Viṣṇudharmottara* it is said "On the head of the goddess (Lakṣmī) a beautiful lotus is to be made which is to be known as *saubhāgya*". Cf. P.K. Aggarwala, p. 70.

53. See N.P. Joshi, *Mātṛkās in Kuṣāṇa Art*, New Delhi: Kanak Publications, 1986; in Haṛappan civilisation, predating the present area of study by more than 2000 years, one does have a long-leaved plant issuing from the head of a mother goddess terracotta figure. Sometimes, the goddess is also seen to be giving birth to a plant. See, Subhanga Atre, *The Archetypal Mother*, Pune, 1988.

54. J. Marshall, op. cit., p. 40.

55. P.K. Agrawala, "The Headless Nude Goddess and her Identification", in T.S. Maxwell, ed., *Eastern Approaches: Essays on Asian Art and Archaeology*, New Delhi: Oxford University Press, 1992, p. 71.

56. Carol Radcliffe Bolon, op. cit., p. 63, feels that a correct appellation for shameless should be *lajjāhīna* Gaurī.

57. These Baubo figures were carved with an outward spread of the thighs in the shape of a frog. The position of the arms varied: sometimes they were raised in an "attitude of prayer" and sometimes held forward as in invitation, sometimes the hands were laid on the thighs to stretch the legs apart, emphasising the pudenda. In India, Sankalia believes, such figures were received from Egypt through the mediating agency of the Romans in the beginning of the Christian era. As this was the period of heightened trade between the Roman Empire and India, such exchanges cannot be ruled out. Baubo's worship would subsequently have been Indianised and she may have been absorbed into both the Brāhmanical and the Buddhist pantheons.

58. R. Codrington, "Iconography: Classical and Indian", *Man*, XXXV, 1935, no. 70, p. 65; H.D. Sankalia, op. cit., p. 113.

59. H.D. Sankalia, op. cit., p. 121.

60. Carol Radcliffe Bolon, op. cit., p. 63.

61. Nagaswamy, op. cit., pp. 326-29; Size: diam. 4". Coarse buff clay with slip and red paint.

62. V.S. Agrawala, "Terracotta Figurines from Ahichchhatra, District Bareilly, Uttar Pradesh", *Ancient India*, no. 4, p. 252 and figs. 202-7.

63. V.S. Agrawala, *Ancient Indian Folk Cults*, Varanasi: Prithvi Prakashan, 1970, pp. 159-60. According to Agrawala this Koṭṭavi is none other than the Jaina goddess Koṭṭakiriyā in whose honour a festival called Koṭṭakiriyāmahā is celebrated. He further links this goddess to the mother of Bāṇāsura called Koṭara who has been described in the *Bhāgavata Purāṇa* and in Bāṇa's *Harṣacarita* as nude and with dishevelled hair. This is a singular instance of a nude goddess being invoked in later Sanskrit literature. Neither an *uttānapāda* posture nor a lotus head is mentioned, and the fact that dishevelled hair is referred to suggests that the image had a face.

64. Carol Radcliffe Bolon, op. cit., p. 64.

65. Ibid., p. 67.

66. Radcliffe Bolon is of the opinion that Lajjā-Gaurī started off as a village goddess, a *grāmadevatā*, who was then absorbed into Śaiva and Buddhist

pantheons. The existence of Gokumāra, who is worshipped with a pot attached with a penis and worshipped with butter (semen) has been observed by Prof. S. Settar. Gokumāra is taken around, at spring, by village *jogatis* to collect gifts. He observes that both Lajjā-Gaurī and Gokumāra are female and male fertility deities.

67. Gerda Lerner, *The Creation of Patriarchy*, New York: Oxford University Press, 1986, pp. 142, 273 ff., suggests that in ancient Mesopotamia the worship of the vulva celebrated the sacredness of female sexuality and its mysterious life giving force which included the power to heal.
68. Carol Radcliffe Bolon, op. cit., p. 17.
69. B.N. Chapeker, *Report on the Excavations at Ter*, 1958, Poona, 1969.
70. Gerda Lerner, op. cit., p. 142.
71. The figure was found near the Nāgasvāmin temple (site 127). An inscription on the *dhvajastambha* (temple pillar) found at the same site says that the temple came into existence during the rule of Ehavala Chāṁṭamūlam which helps confirm the date of the image.
72. *EI*, XXIX, p. 139: *Sidha[m] mahādevīya a-vidhavāya j[i]vaputāya, mahārāja siri [Ehavala] cāṁtamū la patiya Khaṁḍuvulāya kāritāti.*
73. Romila Thapar, *Asoka and the Decline of Mauryas*, New Delhi: Oxford University Press, 1985, 2[nd] edn., pp. 253-54.
74. P.K. Agarawala, "The Headless Nude Goddess and her Identification", in T.S. Maxwell, ed., *Eastern Approaches: Essays on Asian Art and Archaeology*, New Delhi: Oxford University Press, 1992, p. 71.
75. Thomas Donaldson, "Propitious/Apotropaic Eroticism in the Art of Orissa", in *Artibus Asiae*, 37, nos. 1-2, pp. 75-100.
76. Actually the Dugdhadhāriṇī may be a bit of a misnomer since we have not been able to trace this term in any of the contemporary texts though it has been used in secondary literature. See S.P. Gupta, *Kuṣāṇa Art at Sanghol*, Delhi: National Museum, 1985. The first use of the term may be attributed to V.S. Agrawala who used the term *dugdhadhāriṇī-mudrā* to describe the breast offering gesture. See V.S. Agrawala, Masterpieces of *Mathurā School*, Varanasi: Prithvi Prakashan, 1965, p. 14.
77. See John Berger, *Ways of Seeing*, New Delhi: Penguin Press, 1975, pp. 45, 47.
78. A.K. Coomaraswamy, *La Sculpture de Bharhut*, Paris: Vanoest 1956. Pl. XL, figs. 122, 123, 124, p. 83. N.G. Majumdar, *A Guide to the Sculptures in the Indian Museum*, Archaeological Survey of India, 1937, pp. 21-22, Pls. IV and VI.
79. A.K. Coomaraswamy, op. cit., Pl. 40, fig. 124. Barua, *Bharhut*, p. 47, fig. 79.
80. Bharhut, Indian Museum Acc. No. 73, Calcutta.
81. J. Marshall, *Monuments of Sanchi*, vol. III, New Delhi: Swati Publications, rpt. 1982, Pls. LXXXIII.49a, XC.85b, LLXXXVIII.76b, LXXIX.26b.
82. A.K. Coomaraswamy, "La Sculpture de Bodhgaya" *Arts Asiatica* XVIII, Paris, 1935 Pl. XI, LVI.
83. Pramod Chandra, *Stone Sculptures in the Allahabad Museum: A Descriptive Catalogue*, American Institute of Indian Studies, 1970, pp. 58-59, Pl. XXX.
84. Railing pillar, pinkish sandstone, 95 × 20 cm, Kausambi Museum No. E/7, Allahabad, Kauśāmbī near shrine of Hāritī, Śuṅga; Aruna Tripathi, *The Buddhist Art of Kauśāmbī (From 300 BCE to CE 550)*, New Delhi: D.K. Printworld Pvt. Ltd., 2003, pp. 59-60, fig. 19.
85. R.C. Sharma, *Mathura School*, New Delhi: Wiley Eastern Ltd., 1996, pp. 93, 126, fig. 16 National Museum no. B 89.
86. UP, Isapur, Mathurā district, Railing Pillar, *c.* third century CE, size; ht. .650 × .wt .185m, GMM No. 13.286.
87. V.S. Agrawala, *Masterpieces of Mathurā Sculpture*, Varanasi: Prithvi Prakashan, p 14. Also S.J. Czuma, *Kushana Sculpture: Images from Early India*, Cleveland, 1986, p. 97.
88. This is not the only woman with child combination depicted at Sanghol. In one portrayal a woman is shown straddling a child on her hip while climbing a pile of rocks or a hill. In another example, the woman is holding a child high above

her head, with her back towards the viewer. *Kuṣāṇa Sculptures from Sanghol*, New Delhi: National Museum, 1985, fig. 11.

89. Ibid., pp. 70-71, fig. 10.

90. Ibid., pp. 78-79, figs. 17, 17a.

91. Woman with child in breast offering pose, Museum für Indische Kunst, Berlin, MIK I 10168.

92. Berlin, MIK I 38. K. Fischer, "Why has a Gandharan Sculptor Depicted the Nagaradevata Semi-nude in the Abhiniskramana Scene", in M. Yaldiz, and W. Sebo, eds., *Investigating Indian Art*, Museum für Indische Kunst, Berlin, 1987, p. 63, fig. 3.

93. Ibid.

94. Kauśāmbī, Kausambi Museum No. 782/s, Allahabad University, buff sandstone, Size: 24 × 17 cm, Gupta period. Aruna Tripathi, *The Buddhist Art of Kauśāmbī*, New Delhi: D.K. Printworld Pvt. Ltd., 2003, p. 180, fig. 299.

95. Terracotta, GMM No. 36.2720. Size. ht. .095m, *c.* first century BCE, and Katra Keshav Deo, Mathurā. GMM No. 58.46696, *c.* first century BCE, ht. .120m.

96. Stella Kramrisch, "Indian Terracottas", *Journal of Indian Society of Oriental Art*, vol. VII, 1939, p. 95.

97. Female Torso, Kauśāmbī, Allahabad District, Terracotta, *c.* second century BCE, size: .70 × .80 m, Allahabad Museum, No. 71.

98. *Mithuna*, Mould made Terracotta, Jhusi, Allahabad district, first century CE, size: 100 × .070m. Allahabad Museum, No. Jh. 4568. Also see *Mithuna*, Patna City, Patna District, second century CE, Patna Museum No. Arch. 8178 (Patna Museum Catalogue, p. 18, No. 6, Pl. VI and Wadell, *Report on the Excavation at Pataliputra*, 1903, Pl XX; *Mithuna*, Isapur, Mathurā, U.P., GMM No. 13.286, *c.* CE 200, red sandstone, size: .650 × .185m.

99. For detailed studies on the origin and development of Śrī-Lakṣmī see C. Sivaramamurti, *Śrī-Lakṣmī in Art and Literature*, New Delhi: Kanak Publications; also see Suvira Jaiswal, *Origin and Development of Vaiṣṇavism*, New Delhi: Munshiram Manoharlal, 1985; J. Gonda, *Aspects of Early Viṣṇuism*, New Delhi: Motilal Banarsidass 1st edn., Leiden, 1954, rpt. 1993.

100. A. Foucher, "On the Iconography of the Buddha's Nativity" *MASI*, no. 46, ASI, New Delhi, rpt., 1999 (Original, 1934).

101. Ibid., pp. 1-2.

102. Ibid., p. 3.

103. A.K. Coomaraswamy, "Early Indian Iconography, II: Śrī-Lakṣmī", *Eastern Art*, vol. I, no. 3, 1929, pp. 175-89.

104. N.G. Majumdar, *A Guide to The Sculpture in The Indian Museum*, Delhi: Manager of Publications, 1937, p. 26, Pl. VII. This image can be seen within the complex of *yakṣī/devatās* that have been carved on the railing pillars at Bharhut such as Culakokā and Sudarśana. It has very little in common with the seated and standing figures in pillar medallion identified as Śrī-Lakṣmī identified by Coomaraswamy. There are many references to Siri or Śrī in the Jātakas such as the *Śrī Jātaka* where Siri is considered a goddess of good fortune and prosperity.

105. J.N. Banerjea, op. cit., p. 374. Also S.J. Czuma, *Kushana Sculpture: Images from Early India*, Cleveland, 1986, p. 97.

106. A.K. Coomaraswamy, "Śrī-Lakṣmī", *Eastern Art*, 1927.

107. *Jīvājīvābhigama Sūtra*, Part I, Beawar: Sri Agam Prakashan Samiti, 1989, 3.111.14, pp. 304-6.

108. For an example of *gaja-abhiṣeka* of a female figure seated on a lotus in *bhadrāsana*, see J. Marshall, *Monuments of Sāñcī*, Pt. II, Pls. 41, 3 which is identified here as Māyā. This is carved on the front of the eastern gateway, south end.

109. *Yajurveda*, *TS*, V.ii, 514, vv., 29, 60.

110. Ibid., *TS*, iv. 4, 12.

111. Ishtar is also visualised as a cow.

112. N.N. Bhattacharyya, *The Indian Mother Goddess*, Columbia: South Asia Books, 2nd edn., 1977, p. 102.

113. J.R. Haldar, *Early Buddhist Mythology*, New Delhi: Manohar Books, 1977, pp. 106-8.

114. T.A. Gopinath Rao, *Elements of Hindu Iconography*, vol. I., New Delhi: Motilal Banarsidass, 1968, p. 337.

115. J.N. Banerjea, op. cit., p. 376.

116. Cf. Kazimierz Michalowski, *Art of Ancient Egypt*, New York, 1978, fig. 68.

117. *Śilpa Prakāśa*, ed. and annotated A. Boner and S.R. Sarma, Leiden: E.J. Brill, 1966, p. 46. While we are aware of the difficulty in using this work as a completely authentic text, the spirit of this passage reflects the sentiments expressed in a much earlier text, *Rājapraśnīya Sūtra*, which has been discussed in detail later in the chapter 6, on *yakṣīs*.

118. *Śilpa-Prakāśa*, p. 50.

119. Kathleen M. Bolen, "Prehistoric Construction of Mothering", in Cheryl Classen, ed., *Exploring Gender Through Archaeology: Monographs in World Archeology*, No. 11, Wisconsin: Prehistory Press, 1992, p. 52.

120. For example, Kṛṣṇa and Yaśodā; Buddha and Mahāprajāpati Gautamī.

121. Alternative food sources are suggested in the Uttarakuru legend; See chapter 4, section on *Mithuna*.

122. Liz Wilson, *Charming Cadavers: Horrific Figurations of the Feminine in Indian Buddhist Hagiographic Literature*, Chicago: The University of Chicago Press, 1996, p. 142.

123. A *mātṛkā* figure as a nursing mother exists in the Mathurā art tradition, datable to the Kuṣāṇa period. GMM F.31, Kaṅkālī Ṭīlā, Mathurā. Cf. N.P. Joshi, op. cit., p. 111, fig. 19.

124. Uma Chakravarti, "Development of the Sita Myth: A Case Study of Women in Myth and Literature", in Sanya Shakti, 1, 1983, pp. 68-75.

125. Legend has it that Pūtanā was an ogress who killed babies by suckling them at her breast which contained poisonous milk.

126. See infra, Chapter 3, Section 2. Hāritī was an ogress in Rājagṛha who used to devour children. One day Buddha hid her youngest child under his alms bowl, thus making her realise the loss she was causing. Henceforth she was converted and was transformed into the protector of children. She is often depicted as the consort of Kubera-Pañcikā, the god of wealth. Cf. A.K. Coomaraswamy, *Yakṣas: Essays in Water Cosmology*, New Delhi: Indira Gandhi National Centre for the Arts, 1997, pp. 37-42; Also Gail Sutherland, *Disguises of the Demon: Yakṣas*, Chicago: University of Chicago Press 1989, pp. 143-44. Infra, chapter 3, section 4, Ṣaṣṭhī is regarded as the deity of childbirth. Infra, chapter 3, section 5, Naigameṣī or Harigameṣī is associated with Jainism and is also a guardian of children and childbirth.

127. H. Lüders, *Mathurā Inscriptions: Unpublished Papers*, ed. K.L. Janert, Vandenoeck and Ruprecht, Göttingen, 1961, Nos. 1, 26, 27, 67, 90, 109, 110, 126, 135, 180. Of these only two mention the mother, the rest have used the more conventional form of "the spiritual benefit of mother and father."

128. Susan Murcott, *The First Buddhist Women: Translations and Commentary on the Therīgāthā*, Berkeley: Parallex Press, 1998, pp 74-91. Also see I.B. Horner, *Women under Primitive Buddhism*, Delhi: Motilal Banarsidass, rpt. 1999, pp. 1-18.

129. A.K. Coomaraswamy, *Eastern Art*, vol. II, pp. 175-78; J.N. Banerjea, op. cit., p. 110. R.C. Sharma, op. cit., pp. 93, 126; C. Sivaramamurti, op. cit., pp. 34-35.

130. Kubera with Lakṣmī and another *mātṛkā*, Manoharpur, Mathurā, GMM C. 30; also GMM 61. 5371 and GMM. No. 72.16 and SML. No. 0.241.

131. J.N. Banerjea, op. cit., p. 370.

132. C.L. Lyons and Ann Olga Koloski-Ostrow, *Naked Truths about Classical Arts: An Introduction*, http://www. Stoa.org/diotima/essays/naked truths.html. According to the authors the depictions of female and male bodies can be used to decode the social meaning attached to nudity and dress as indicators of social status. . . . The symbolism of clothing and jewellery, whether employed to conceal, accent or expose the body beneath carried clear and immediately legible messages for the viewer concerning not only the reproductive or erotic availability of the wearer but also her or his position within the community, social and family hierarchy.

133. Vijaya Ramaswamy, *Walking Naked: Women, Society and Spirituality in South India*, Shimla: Indian Institute of Advanced Studies, 1997, p. 77,

points out that "In their rejection of worldly pleasure and family life and emotional attachments arising out of a male cognisance of female sexuality Buddhism and Jainism are more anti-female than Hinduism." She emphasises the essentially misogynist nature of Buddhist and Jain monasticism and in this context , the sensuous depictions on these monuments are even more contradictory. The sensuality of the female figure in early Indian art has been commented upon by authors on Indian art such as Benjamin Rowland and A.K. Coomaraswamy. See Vishakha Desai, "Reflections on the History and Historiography of Male Sexuality in Early Indian Art" in Vidya Dehejia, ed., *Representing the Body: Gender Issues in Indian Art*, New Delhi: Kali for Women, 1997, pp. 44-48.

134. *Nāṭyaśāstra*, XXIV.291-93.

135. *na nābhim darśayedāgulphādvasaḥ paridadhyāt; na stanau vivṛtau kuryāt* — *Śaṅkha Smṛti* page and verse not given, Cf. Altekar, *Position of Women in Ancient India*, p. 282, fn. 3.

136. Hala's *Gāthā Saptaśatī* : *raktadukūlāntaritaḥ stananakhalekha iva navavadhvāḥ* (VI, 69). *Balādākṛṣṭavastrādharntiprasthate mantharaṁ tvam vraja* (II, 62). *Nīlapatapravṛtāṅgītī mā khalvenam tvam parihara* (VI.20).

137. Ibid. VII.20: *dvacyāṅgulakakapātapinaddhasavisesa-nilakañculikā, darśayati stanasthalavarṇikāmiva taruṇīm yuvajanebyaḥ*. VI.45: *grāmataruṇyo hṛdayam haranti vidagdhānām stanabhāravatyaḥ, madane kusumbhrāga yukta kañncukābharaṇabhrāntāḥ*. Cf, Altekar, op. cit., p. 287.

138. Ibid. IV. 4: *hasahaṁsa nayanadvirepha pīnastananatyunnatāpahmakośo*.

139. *Saundarānanda*, IV.35.

140. Cowell, *Jātaka*, vol. V-VI no. 527, ed. and tr. E.B. Cowell, New Delhi: Munshiram Manoharlal, rpt. 1990.

141. *Jīvājīvābhigama Sūtra*, 3.111.14, pp. 304-5.

142. *Rājagraśaiya Sūtra*, 126, pp. 66-67.

143. Śūdraka, *Mṛcchakaṭika*, with commentary of Pṛthvīdhara, ed. M.R. Kale, New Delhi: Motilal Banarsidass, 1972, p. 193.

144. It is recommended that Viṣṇu be also shown as golden in order to emphasise his control and connection with the material world.

145. Kumkum Roy, "Women and Men Donors At Sanchi: A Study of The Inscriptional Evidence," in L.K. Bajpai, ed., *Position and Status of Women in Ancient India*, vol. I, Varanasi, Banaras Hindu University, 1988, pp. 209-23.

146. J. Ph. Vogel, *Archaeological Museum at Mathurā*, New Delhi: Indological Book House, rpt. 1971, p. 25, no. C.2

147. Gerda Lerner, op. cit., 160, feels that the portrayal of goddesses in itself is significant. She contends that "no matter how degraded and commodified the reproductive and sexual powers of women was in real life, their essential equality could not be banished from thought and feeling as long as goddesses lived and were believed to rule human life." P. Chris Whitcome remarks on the changing character of goddess worship, "For a while in Ancient Egypt, women were regarded as embodying an identity and power which was derived from and was based upon the female, of which the mother goddess and ultimately all female goddesses were its manifestations. It was a power acknowledged and respected by men which resided in the female and could be claimed by all women. It was not, as it subsequently became in later Egyptian, Greek and Minoan periods and has remained ever since, a power defined and delimited by men. Chris Whitcome, *Memory, History and State*, http://www.Arthistory.sbc.edu/images women.

# 3

# Mothers

## Child Producers, Child Rearers and Protectors

The constitution of a woman's body in the visual discourse centres on what are conceived of as her principal functions, reproduction and fertility, as is evident in the two image types privileging the female genitalia and breasts.[1] Thus, a woman's potential for motherhood is central to creating a gendered female identity. This is reflected in the fact that almost all divine feminine figures in the post-Mauryan period are hailed as mothers and conceived of as mother goddesses[2] visually, metaphysically and philosophically, based on their function as producers-givers-providers.

The principal goddesses are all referred to as mothers — *mā*, *mātā* or *mātṛkā* — thereby implying the inter-changeability, or sharing of identities and the universalising of motherhood. This phenomenon is seen in the invocation of a goddess by referring to and comparing her to other goddesses, as is the case with Ṣaṣṭhī, who in the Ṣaṣṭhī Kalpa of the *Mānava-Gṛhyasūtra* is also called Lakṣmī, Śrī, Jayā, and so forth.[3] Within the figural representations of goddesses, one can recover certain specific maternal types even though all goddesses are not directly connected with motherhood. Other maternal female representations are derived from mother archetypes be they historically human, semi-divine or divine. These images illustrate an overwhelming concern with motherhood; and an examination of the art forms for the ideology and practice of motherhood-fertility, pregnancy, childbirth and child protection, reveals, however partially, a visual discourse of maternalness informing the art of the period. It is also significant that by mediating their biology to create offspring, women as mothers form families; families form the conjugal bond. Therefore women, through motherhood, are imperative to and influence almost all aspects of organised social structures, especially the forming and perpetuating of gender identities.

The mother-child dyad is considered the most basic one throughout history. The mother and child bond is of great significance given that the prolonged infancy, immaturity and helplessness of the child necessitates the assistance of others for survival. The need to organise the feeding and socialising of the child after weaning requires complex social and cultural moulding considered essential for survival. This depends upon "maternal" care and yet, contrary to the dyad argument, it does not require woman as mother. The child can grow and flourish with fathers, siblings and other adults in place as caregivers, as is the case of many primitive and tribal societies where childcare is a male bastion. Nevertheless, the concept and practice of motherhood is by definition gendered — women, through biology, are mothers, in so far as only the female, not the male, of the human species can conceive and carry the child in her womb till delivery. Further only she can breast-feed the child until it is capable of independent survival by generating food through gathering-production and ensure protection for itself.

It is therefore easier for the woman and child dyad to be socialised and internalised in patriarchal ideologies of settled agricultural and urban civilisations.[4] Given the socio-economic and cultural context of the period, it is not surprising that the aspect emphasised in the post-Mauryan literature, which coincides with the crystallisation of the written tradition, is that of woman as mother. Women as mothers and mothering figures are archetypes that are directly or indirectly constructed in visual representations as well. In contrast, men do not figure in art as fathers. Rarely, when male as father does appear, as in the case of Vessantara and Gautama, it is in connection with their sons, whom they discard in order to reach their personal goals of Buddhahood or *bodhisattva* status. Fathers are perceived to be more callous towards their children while women as childbearers and rearers are shown as having a permanent and strong bond with their children.[5] However, art is at times independent of hegemonic patriarchal control and it is in this field that we can investigate inversions and resistances to overarching patriarchal portrayals of motherhood; males may be seen in a mothering role, albeit rarely, and women may discard motherhood.[6]

At the ideational level, motherhood integrates bio-procreation and social processes; it includes notions of sexuality, reproduction, personhood, childcare, social order, domestic organisation and power.[7] For conceptual clarity, two aspects of motherhood are often distinguished: biological mothering (in the birth relation) and social mothering, although such divisions and categories must remain fluid and permeable, especially in early Indian societies where both adoptive and biological mothering models are encountered in texts and images. The case of Balarāma and Kṛṣṇa being born to Devakī and brought up by Rohiṇī and Yaśodā is one famous example, another being the Buddha who is born to Māyādevī, his natural mother, and raised by Mahāprajāpati, his foster-mother.[8]

Activities that commonly define motherhood are producing, raising, feeding, protecting and caring for children.[9] As will be demonstrated, these practices can be seen in the art of the post-Mauryan period. There seems to have been an overwhelming concern with pregnancy and childbirth, connected with actual birth on the one hand, and child protection and care associated with mothering on the other. This reflects a picture that is somewhat contrary to the one seen in the literature of the period, where the primary role constructed for women is that of wifehood.[10] If we view the evidence of artefacts and art production from early India, it will be clear that mothers, mostly deified, play a crucial role from which they were not dethroned until at least the third century CE. This is in contradistinction to Western religious art, where with the rise of monotheism, which was overwhelmingly patriarchal, the role of multiple mother goddesses declined and faded. The only surviving legacy is the Madonna figure, which remains in the shadow of the powerful and all-encompassing figure of her son and his pantheon.

Having said that, despite the sheer number and variety in representations of the divine feminine in India, most of the mother-goddess images remain enigmatic figures that can open to contesting identifications and interpretations. The relative silence of the mainstream patriarchal religious discourse with regard to the identity and characteristics of most of these female deities is also significant. This may reveal an attempt to make invisible and marginalise powerful feminine images of veneration — images that were not, or could not be assimilated into major pantheons as wives and consorts. This did not stop the production of mother goddess figures, especially in clay, that were seen in natural connection with women. It has been observed by Gerda Lerner too that women play an important symbolic role in agricultural societies, both because their work is valuable in the fields and also because they have control over nature's ritual and reproductivity.[11] It is not surprising that they are ritually enshrined and celebrated in all religious systems in early India.

A popular scholarly approach to understanding the status of women in early Indian society, is analysing and delineating them as mothers. Altekar undertakes this project for Hindu civilisation[12] and concludes that women are venerated because of their sacred role as child-bearers.[13] This is linked to the imperative concern of a Hindu male to produce sons to light his funeral pyre and daughters to give in marriage. For this he needs a wife who would be fertile and legitimate.

Isabel Horner in her seminal work on women in Buddhism wrote an entire chapter on laywomen as mothers, dealing with their status, duties, responsibilities and burdens as reflected in literature.[14] In conclusion, she observed that Buddhism, on the one hand, raises the position of mothers in society by valorising it; and on the other hand frees them from the bonds of motherhood by allowing them to join the order of nuns after discarding motherhood. However, it has been observed that while the bonds of marriage and fatherhood (either actual or intended) often acted as a catalyst that drove men into entering a state of homelessness, i.e. becoming monks within the Buddhist set-up, the same observation does not apply to women. In the stories of *therīs* or nuns, the birth of children is rarely the point of entry into renunciation; often it is only after the death of their child(ren), that they are inspired to join the *bhikkhuṇī saṅgha*,[15] thus proving that the identification of women with the parenting function was stronger than that for men.

The primary object of creation for the artist is not the status of a mother or a mothering figure. One can, however, recover important information regarding the relatively important position that mothers and mothers-in-law (along with their husbands) enjoyed in the familial set-up from the donative inscriptions on sculptural remains.

Another aspect that is highlighted is the popular understanding that equates femaleness with motherhood[16] and, following from this, the universal benevolence ascribed to mother goddesses. This, as will be demonstrated in this chapter, is not an unproblematic approach. The formulation of motherhood as a historic or divine mother/goddess may not be free from terrific or malignant characteristics, as seen in the cases of both Ṣaṣṭhī and Hāritī. The association of these goddesses with a male deity, often one belonging to the organised religious system, is an attempt to tame or control these malignant qualities. The explanation for such a phenomenon may lie in various local cultic beliefs within which these goddesses rose to prominence[17] and the attempt to assimilate these into mainstream religions.

In this chapter I have discussed four sets of representations connected with childbirth and child-rearing that encompass human, semi-divine and divine entities. Māyā and Mahāprajāpati are the natural and adoptive mothers of the Buddha, Hāritī is an ogress and as Bahuputrikā, the mother of many children who under the influence of the Buddha becomes a child protector; while Naigameṣa and Naigameṣī ensure safety of childbirth; and Ṣaṣṭhī both protects and inflicts disease on children. Besides the individual deities who are considered to be mothers, or who have mothering functions ascribed to them, there was a set of goddesses called the Mātṛkās who were venerated as a group. I will not be discussing these in detail since they have received much attention from scholars, but will only touch on their importance in the construction of the ideal of motherhood in art and society.

### 3.1 Māyādevī: Buddha's Mother

It may be natural to assume that Māyādevī would be the perfect candidate for the construction of a model of ideal motherhood in Buddhist art. Māyā as the mother of the future Buddha should have an enormous importance in the Buddhist artistic and ideological scheme. However, we see that such is not the case. A survey of early Buddhist art reveals that quantitatively there are very few depictions of Māyā within this visual tradition. Nor does she seem to have been constructed as the epitome of motherhood; Māyā may be a biological mother but social mothering is not associated with her persona.

I would like to posit that in Buddhism, through the persona of Māyā, a rather non-threatening model of motherhood is constructed. On the one hand, all sexual connotations are subtracted from the conception of the Buddha, thus removing any threat or contradiction to the monastic ideal that was being valorised in art and literature. On the other hand, the human bond between a son and mother is also removed by the convenient death of Māyādevī, the mother of Siddhārtha, six days after his birth. Her role is only to be the carrier of the future Buddha. An additional observation can be made here that, interestingly, no immaculate or magical elements seem to be associated with the conception of Gautama's own son, Rāhula. Nor is any special

3.1.1 Conception of the Buddha by Māyādevī, railing medallion, first century BCE, Bharhut. IM 93. The inscription reads *bhagavato ukrānti*.

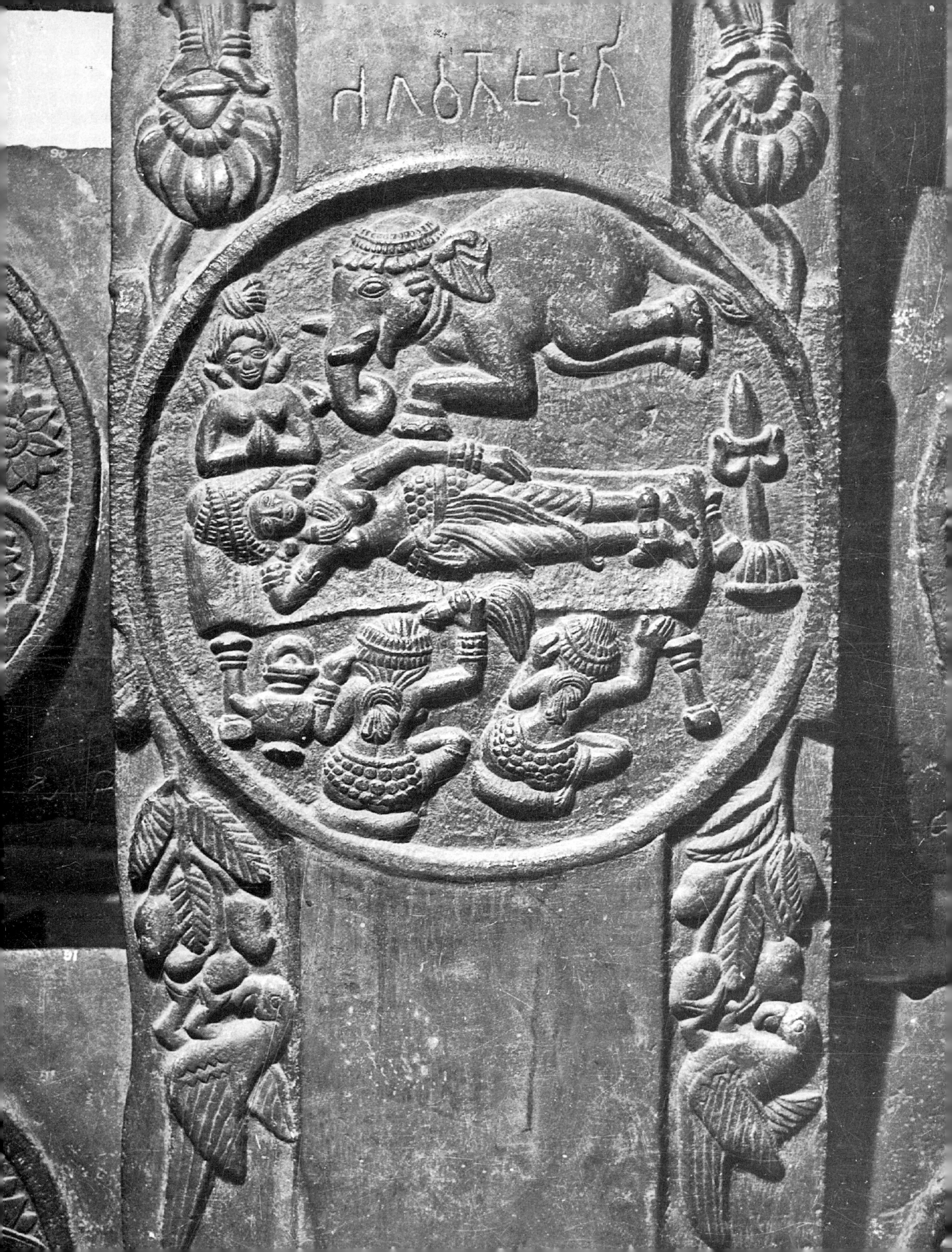

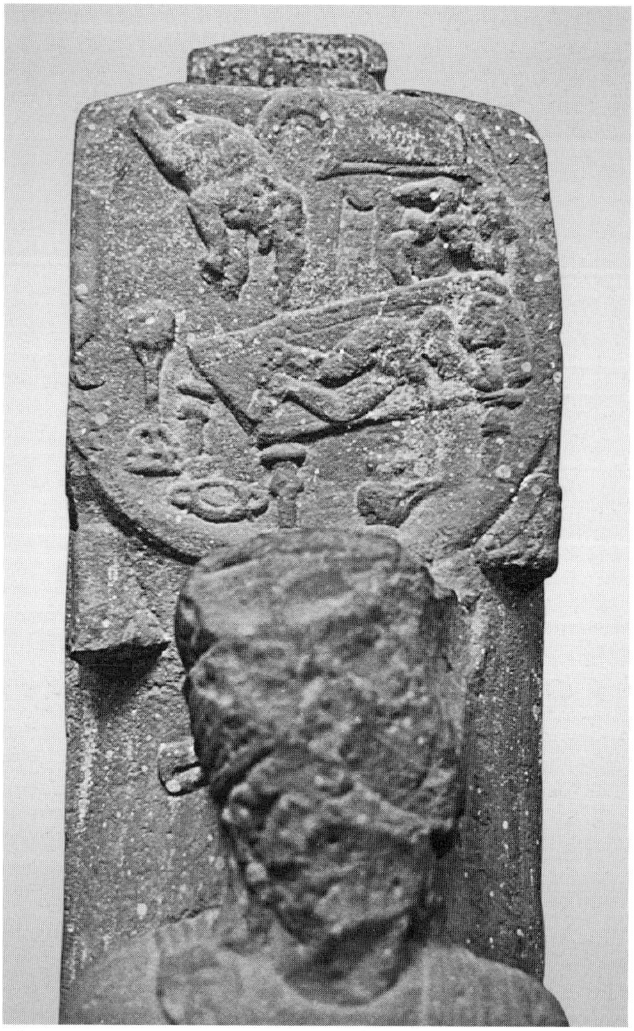

3.1.2 Conception of the Buddha by Māyādevī, railing pillar, late first century BCE, Hathin, Haryana.

element of celibacy related to this episode in the Buddha's life, probably because Rāhula is not meant to be projected as divine or supermundane being.

The mother of Buddha does not disappear from Buddhist lore after the birth of the Buddha. On reaching Enlightenment the Buddha does not forget his filial duty but ascends to the Tuṣita heaven to preach her and thirty-three gods before descending back again to earth at Sankisa. In the visual tradition, Māyā does not appear personally in this episode; the Buddha or his symbol is shown climbing down a ladder with the nun Utpalavarṇā kneeling at the lower end (*Pl.* 5.3).[18]

Māyādevī appears in first of the "Four Great Miracles," the four crucial episodes in the Buddha's life — his Birth, Enlightenment, First Sermon and Death. These coincide with four sites — Lumbinī, Bodh-Gayā, Sārnāth and Kuśīnagara — which are recommended as the "four great pilgrimages" by the Buddha to his followers before his death.

In this scheme Lumbinī emerges as a major pilgrimage site as is proved by Aśoka's inscription found at the site.[19] This particular inscription describes Aśoka's visit and the concessions he made to the villagers at the site to mark the auspicious occasion and place.

After examining the available material from early Buddhist art, I view Māyādevī's encounter

3.1.3 Conception of the Buddha by Māyādevī, detail, railing pillar, late first century BCE, Hathin, Haryana.

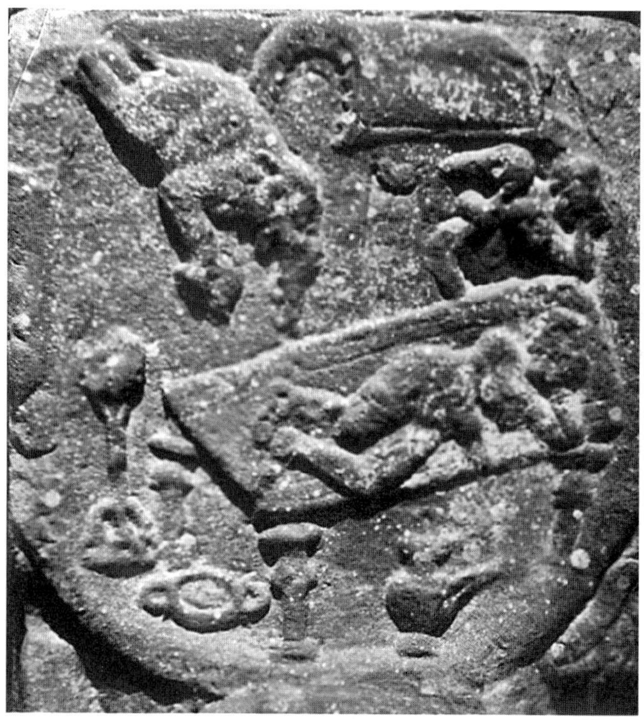

with motherhood in two representational types, that of conception and of delivery of Prince Siddhārtha, the future Buddha.

### 3.1.1 MĀYĀDEVĪ: IDENTITY AND CONNOTATIONS

Māyādevī, the mother of the Buddha, is described in the following terms: "That counterpart of Indra (Śuddhodana) has a queen, a very Śacī, whose splendour corresponded to his might. In beauty like Padmā, in steadfastness like the Earth, she was called Mahāmāyā, from her resemblance to the incomparable Māyā."[20] In the *Saundarānanda*, Aśvaghoṣa identifies the Buddha's mother Māyā with Māyādevī, referring to her as *mayeva divi devatā*,[21] a goddess in heaven called Māyā who is devoid of the vices of anger, ignorance and deceit.[22]

A goddess named Māyā is mentioned in the *Śatapatha Brāhmaṇa*[23] as *asura vidyā* and who elsewhere is believed to be *prakṛti*.[24] V.S. Agrawala is of the opinion that the power of *asuras* is believed to be *māyā*, which was deified as goddess Māyā. This notion is confirmed by a passage in the Śānti-Parva of the *Mahābhārata* that views Māyā as representing the *daityas*, through as beautiful as Śrī.[25] Agrawala further asserts that Māyā, the goddess, predates Śrī; the latter in fact assimilates some elements of Māyā's cult.

E.H. Johnson by referring to an Egyptian papyrus dated to around the third century CE has thrown some light on the identity of the goddess.[26] In this document in an invocation to Isis, she is equated with all the mother goddesses known to the Graeco-Roman world such as Cybele Atangatis, Astorte, Nanaia and many others. Among this list is mentioned Maia, i.e.

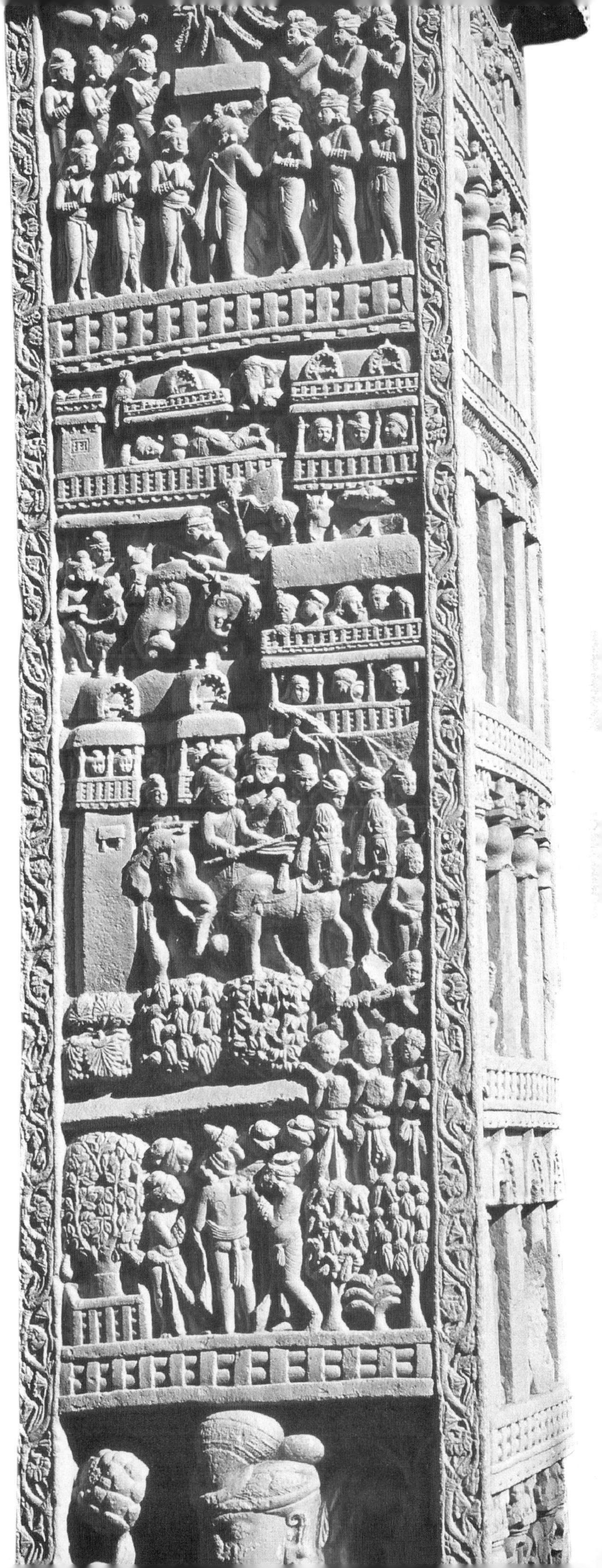

3.1.4 Visit to Kapilavastu and conception of the Buddha by Māyādevī, *stūpa* 1, first century CE, Sāñcī.

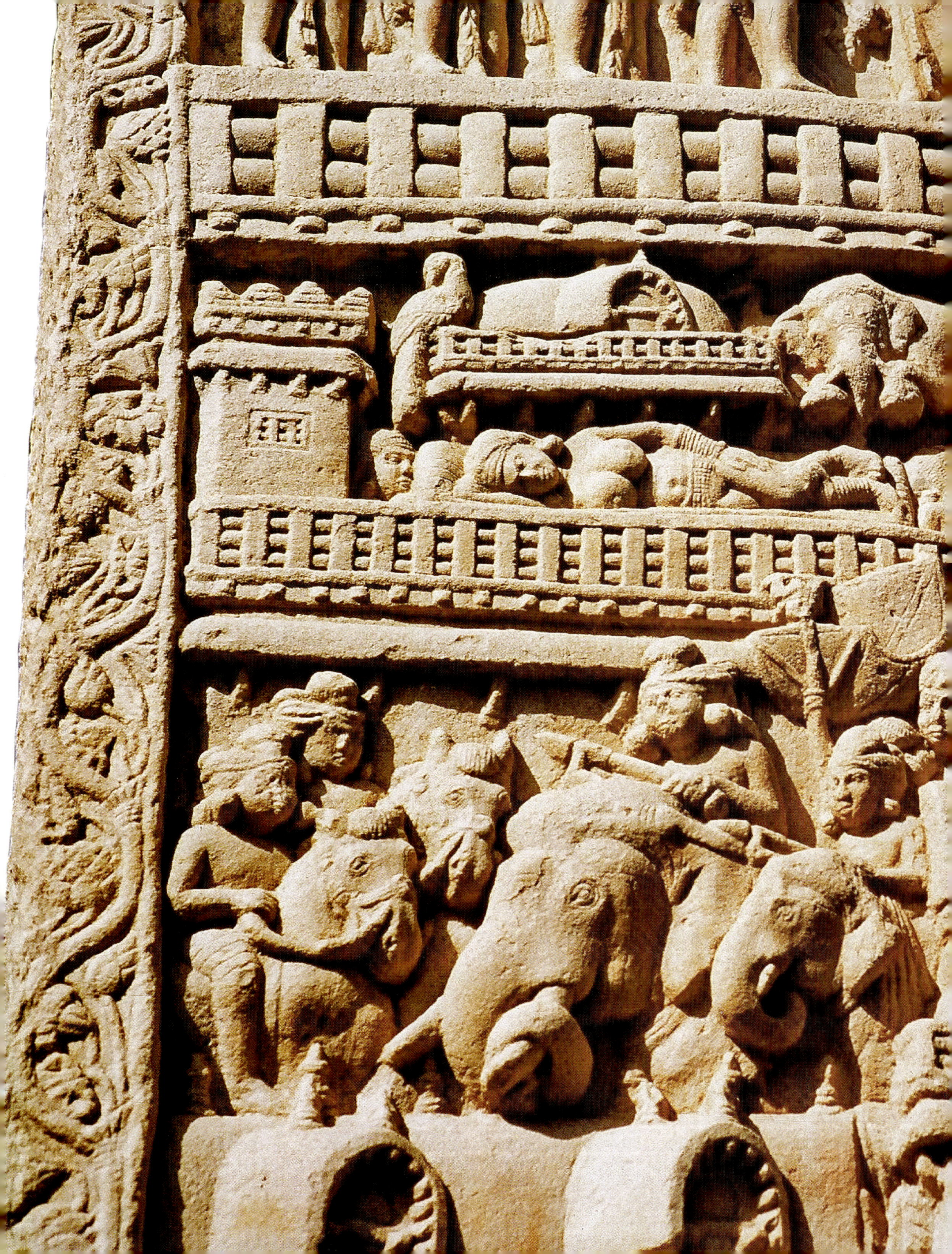

Māyā, in India and Johnson suggests that the goddess mentioned by Aśvaghoṣa and this are the same. It is also suggested in the papyrus that this goddess seems to be specially associated with water, is probably being worshipped in the Gangetic valley, "thou lady of the land, bringest the flood of rivers . . . and in Egypt and Nile, in Tripolis the Eleutherus, in India the Ganges . . . and exists through all rain, every spring, all dew and snow and all things forever."[27] This suggests that in the Gangetic valley, Māyā, to whom the Buddha's mother is being compared, was being worshipped as a fertility goddess who may also have been like Isis, a mother deity.

Positing another theory regarding the identity of Māyā, D.D. Kosambi asserts that at Lumbinī, Buddha's birthplace, there exists a shrine of Rumindei, a form of mother goddess who is none other than Māyā at the time of nativity.[28] He has made a tentative (but very significant) suggestion linking Māyā to Ṣaṣṭhī, since Māyā died on the seventh day after Buddha's birth, which is very close to the sixth night that is the special time for the worship of goddess Ṣaṣṭhī and celebration of the infant's survival.

Given the absence of any inscription or iconographic text that describes either her characteristics or her precise functions, the exact identity of the original mother goddess Māyā remains a mystery. *Māyā* as a phenomenon, however, is often discussed in all the major religio-philosophical systems, generally to describe mysterious forces that

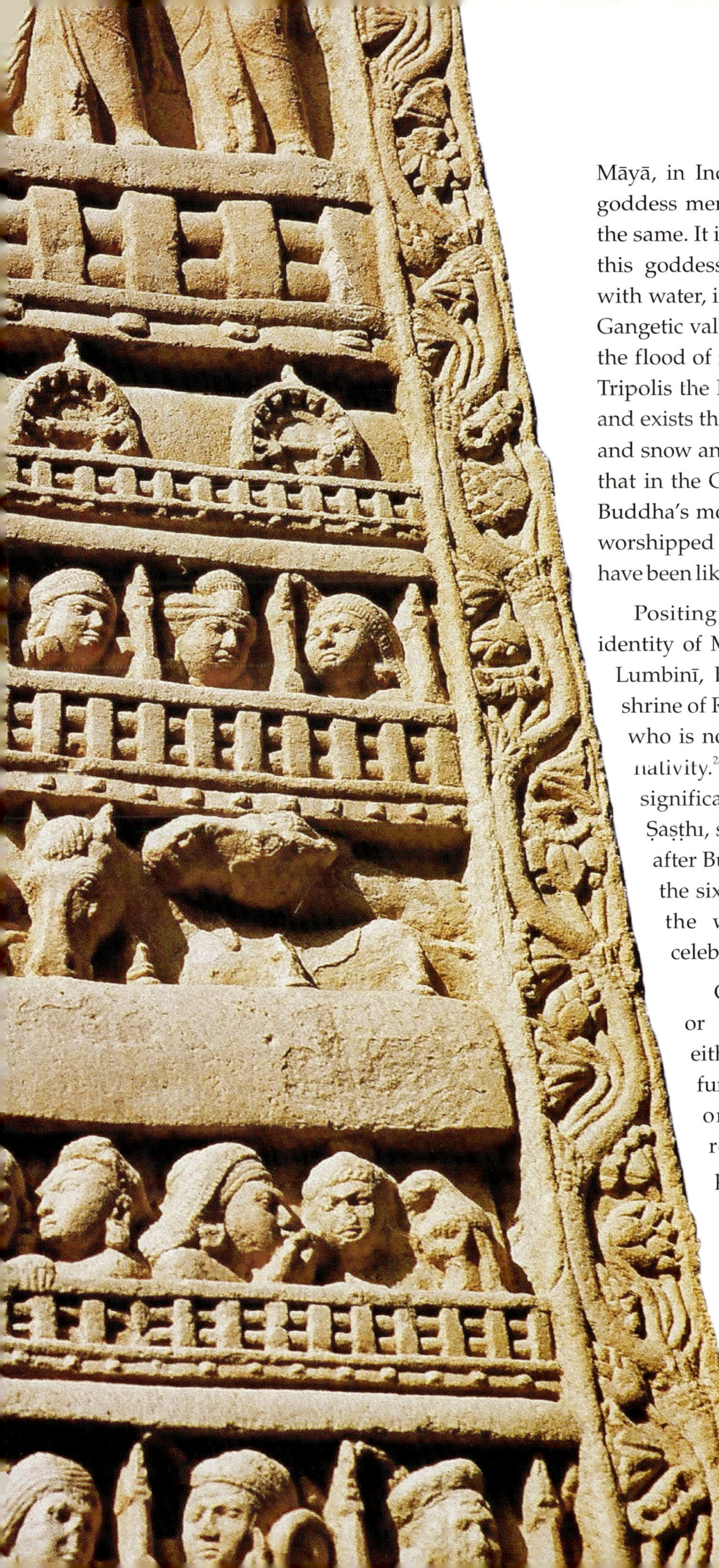

3.1.5 Conception of the Buddha by Māyādevī, detail, *stūpa* 1, first century CE, Sāñcī.

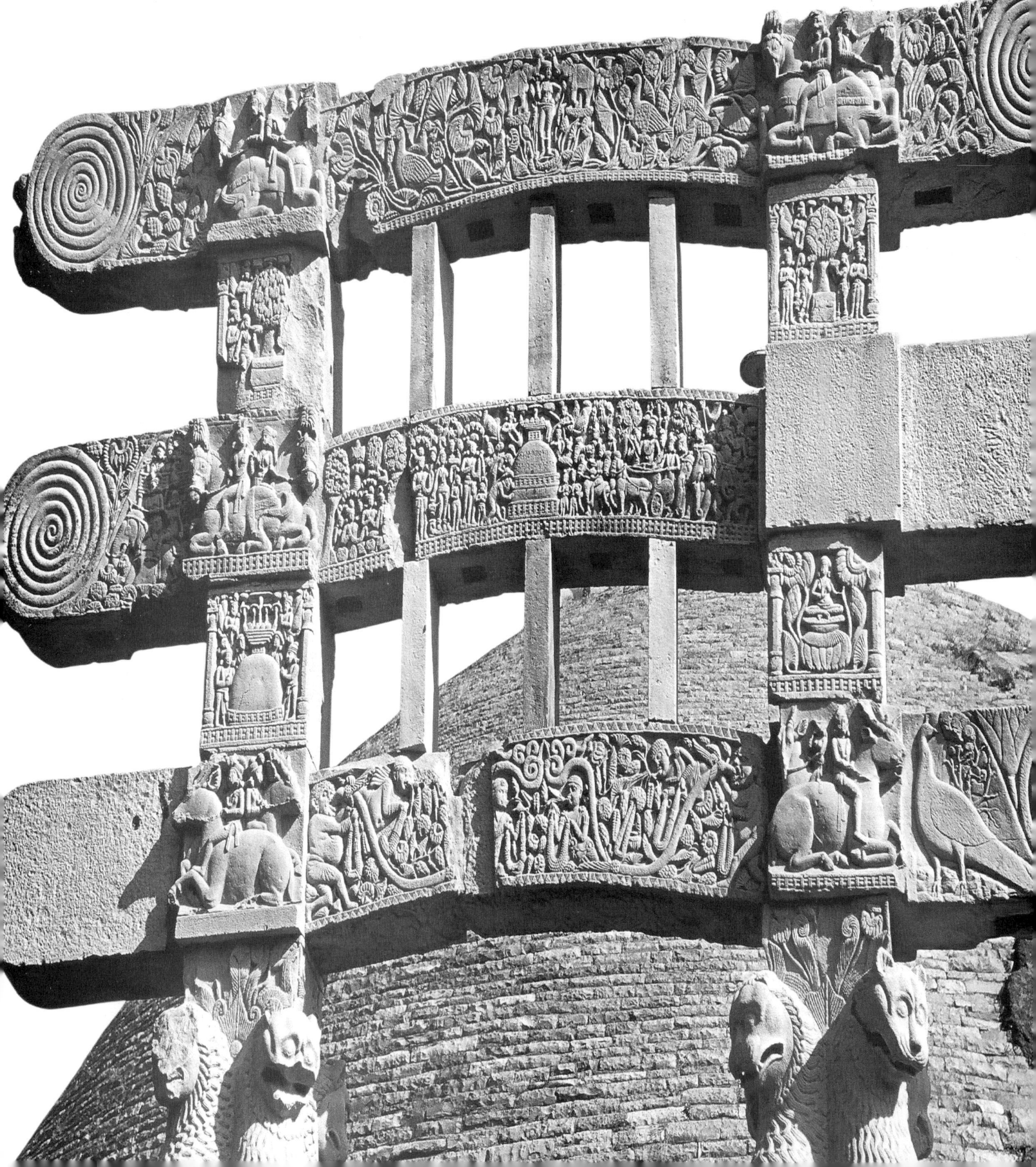

permeate the world, mundane and sacred. This unknown power is not always conceived of as benign or positive. Aśvaghoṣa attributes these words regarding *māyā* (whom he compares to woman-temptress) to the Buddha addressing a recalcitrant Nanda: "... understand this world to be unstable, a mere phantasmagoria, a magician's kaleidoscopic show (*māyā*). Abandon the snare of delusion (*mohajāla*) . . . and the snare of suffering (*duḥkhajāla*)."[29] In the Jaina tradition, vices such as cheating and wickedness are called *māyā* and indulging in these vices is one of the fundamental causes of rebirth of a woman.[30]

Zimmer has explained *māyā* as the highest divine principle, the divine life force in and by itself, centring on the phantasmagoria of the world process. The fluctuating mirage is a display of cosmic power, but the fundamentally changeless supra-mundane source and the being of power is not implicated in the mirage.[31] To the Supreme Being and to the enlightened devotee the whole spectacle is but a cosmic dream, a convincing yet delusory reflex of the force of *māyā*.

It has been described by Monier-Williams[32] as art, wisdom, extraordinary or supernatural power (in the earlier language); illusion, unreality, deception, fraud, trick, sorcery, illusion, magic; an unreal or illusory image, phantom, apparition; duplicity. The Buddhists consider *māyā* as one of the 24 minor evil passions. In philosophy it is identified in Saṁkhyā with *prakṛti* or *pradhāna* and in the Vedānta it is regarded as the source of the visible world. With Śaivas it is one of the four *pāśa*s or snares that entangle the soul. With Vaiṣṇavas it is one of the nine *śakti*s or energies of Viṣṇu; illusion personified (sometimes regarded as the daughter of *anṛtta* and *nṛttī* and mother of *mṛtyu* or as a daughter of Adharma). It is also used as a name for Mother of Buddha and also for goddess Lakṣmī. Apte[33] agrees and gives similar epithets emphasising the illusory nature of *māyā*. He adds that the term may also connote unreality, the illusion by virtue of which one considers the unreal universe as really existent and as distinct from the supreme spirit. The *Pāli-English Dictionary*[34] identifies *māyā* as "(a) Deceptive appearance — fraud, deceit, hypocrisy, (b) as a mystical formula or a magic trick."

3.1.6 Gaja-Lakṣmī, *stūpa* 1, first century CE, Sāñcī, Madhya Pradesh. Erroneously identified as representing the birth of Buddha.

Certain visual representations that have been specifically identified with Māyā/Māyādevī occur only in Buddhist art. These images may, however, share certain devices and symbols that belong to a larger cultural matrix of the post-Mauryan art; symbols such as the lotus or the *śālabhañjikā*-like posture of Māyādevī (where she is shown in *tribhaṅga*, with her hip projecting onto one side, holding a branch of a tree). This has led to a certain degree of controversy concerning the number and type of sculptures that portray the Buddha's mother.

A. Foucher, perplexed by the absence of representations of the Nativity at Sāñcī and Bharhut, propounded the theory that the Buddha's birth was depicted in a symbolic form. Just as the *aśvattha* tree represents the Enlightenment at Gayā, the wheel the First Sermon at Sārnāth, and the tumulus the *mahāparinirvāṇa* at Kuśīnagara, according to Foucher, the woman seated on a lotus surrounded by elephants (*Pl.* 3.1.6) represented Nativity.[35] He argues that since Māyā has seen a white elephant entering her womb, medallions in which a combination of lotus and elephant devices appear connote the Birth of the Buddha. Similarly, he asserts that the words *nāga* and *nāga-*

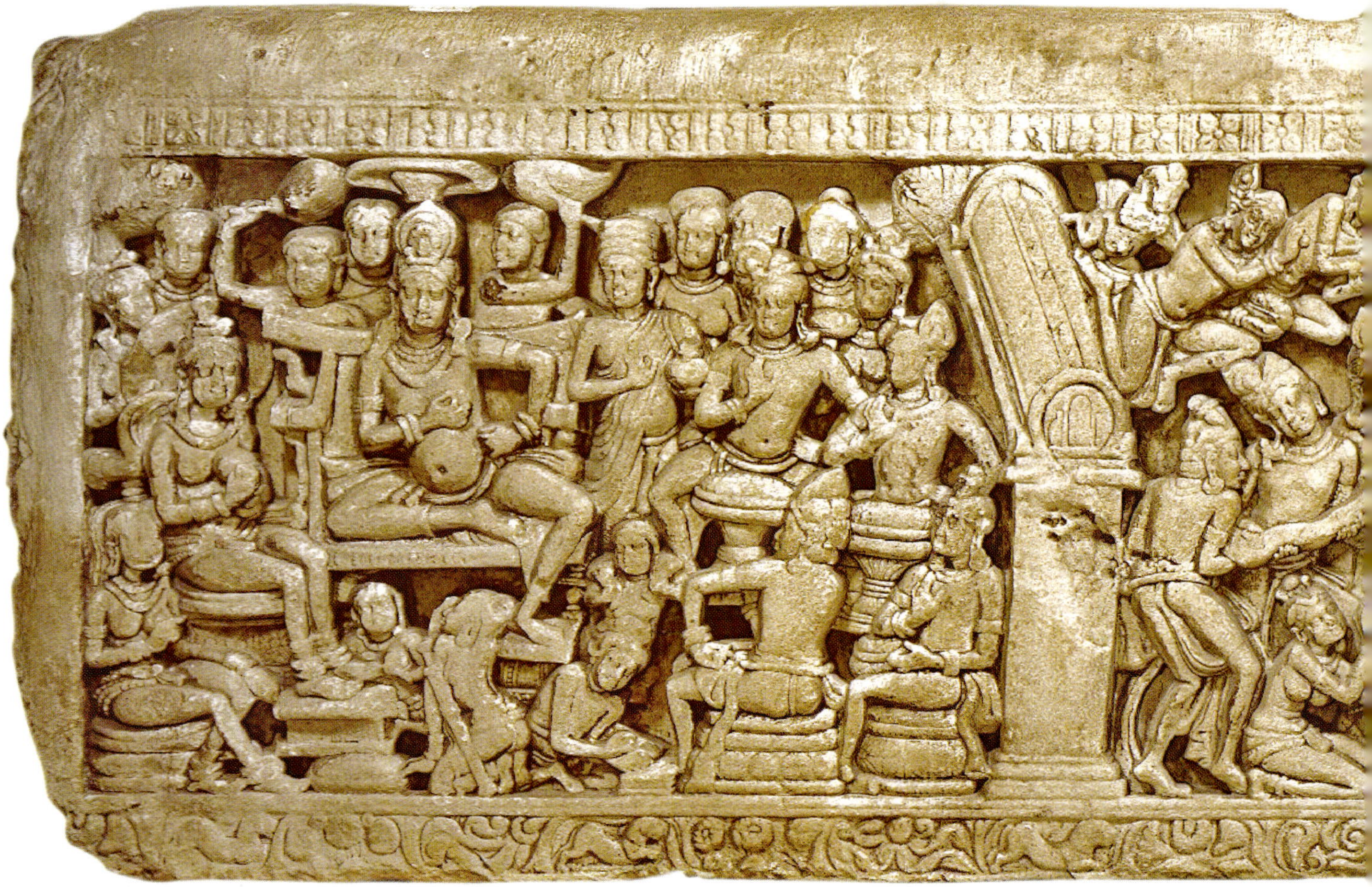

3.1.7 From left to right. Interpretation of the Dream of Māyā, Birth of Buddha and Prince Siddhārtha in harem of the Kapilavastu palace, inner face of a coping stone, second century CE, Amarāvatī.

*nāsā* (trunk of an elephant), both meaning an elephant, denote the same Event. Thus in Foucher's schema, the two elephants lustrating a goddess seated or standing on a lotus, holding lotus stalks in her hand, are meant to depict the moment when, after the Buddha's birth, he is washed with two streams of water sent forth by the two *nāga* kings Nanda and Upananda.[36] In this reading the lotus is the symbol of Nativity and it also represents moments from the legends that grew around the birth of the Buddha, for example, that soon after his birth, the baby Buddha took seven steps and lotus flowers appeared under each of his footsteps.

As we have seen in the previous chapter, this identification of the Aditi/Gaja-Lakṣmī series at Sāñcī and Bharhut as Māyādevī, the mother of Buddha at the time to his Nativity, is difficult to accept. Coomaraswamy was the first to challenge Foucher's view and posit an alternate identification as Śrī-Lakṣmī. One vital question that arises from Foucher's argument is that when at Bharhut we have a scene that has been labelled as the Descent of the Lord and represents the conception of the Buddha, why would the sculptors depict the Birth scene in symbolic terms, using devices that have no clear and direct connection with the story of his birth? The second important question that remains unanswered by Foucher's theory is why and how the

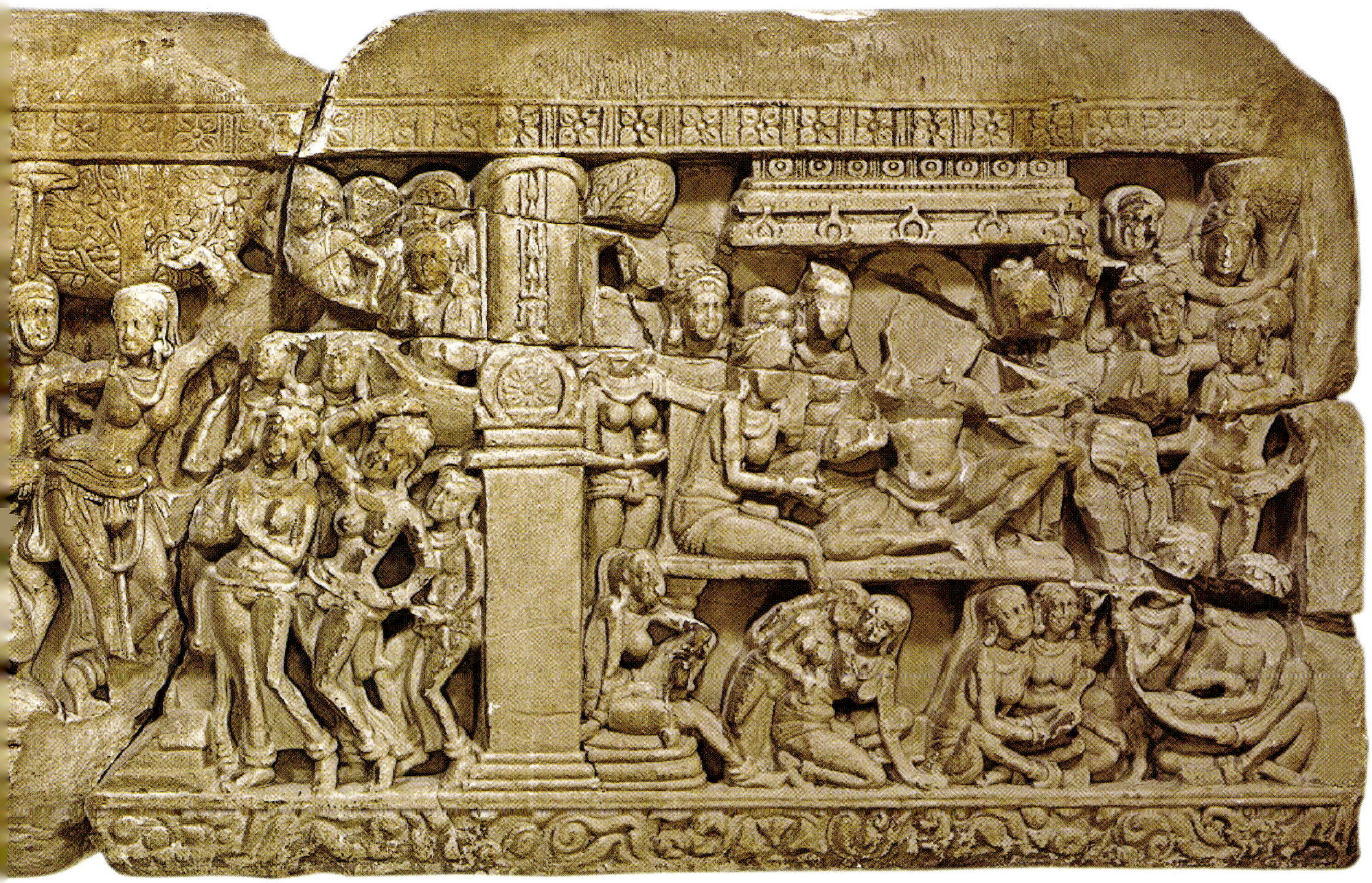

iconography of the Buddha's Conception and Delivery evolves in ways that are not linked to the goddess seated on the lotus in any form or manner in all subsequent representations, be these from Gandhāra or Mathurā. This may be explained by the fact that the art of the earlier and later periods represents two separate traditions that chose to depict this episode in differing ways.

Another representation associated with Māyādevī is a terracotta figurine of the *pañcacūḍa* type,[37] now in the Ashmolean Museum, as Māyā, the original goddess to whom the Buddha's mother is compared by Aśvaghoṣa.[38] Here again one may argue that terracottas of the *pañcacūḍa* type may have been fertility goddesses not necessarily identifiable as Māyādevī.

Nevertheless there are some unequivocal representations to which we can ascribe the identification of the mother of the Buddha: these are the conception and delivery scenes. As observed above, Māyā occurs generally in scenes connected to portrayals of the Buddha's life, especially his birth. In the earlier period, at Bharhut, Sāñcī and Gandhāra, his conception in the form of the dream of Māyā is often found. In later art at Gandhāra, Mathurā, Amarāvatī and Nāgārjunakoṇḍa, depictions of the delivery seem to be more popular, especially in the north-western region. Two more episodes, depicted more often in the art of Deccan, that feature Māyā are Asita's interpretation of Māyā's dream along with his prophecy regarding the Gautama's future, and the presentation of the Buddha to the tree-*yakṣa* soon after his birth (*Pl.* 3.1.8).

### 3.1.2 CONCEPTION

The divine conception of the Buddha by Māyā is believed to have been revealed to her in a dream of a white elephant with six tusks coming down from heaven and entering her womb. This has often been labelled in secondary texts as Māyā's Dream. Both the *Saundarānanda* and the *Buddhacarita* contain descriptions of this episode, and later texts, such as the *Lalitavistara*, also mention it. The *Saundarānanda* says, ". . . then in due season she (Māyā) saw in a dream a white six-tusked elephant, mighty as Airāvata enter her womb."[39] According to the *Buddhacarita*, "the night before she conceived she saw in her sleep a white lord of elephants entering her body, yet she felt thereby no pain."[40]

In early Buddhist art this episode is usually visualised as a female figure lying laterally on her side, facing the viewer, on a couch surrounded by her waiting-women who are asleep. An elephant is shown, sometimes touching her side with his trunk and sometimes hovering over her, or in the centre of the composition.

The earliest known example of such a depiction has been discovered at Bharhut (*Pl.* 3.1.1). Here the Buddha's birth as Prince Siddhārtha is found carved in a railing-pillar medallion.[41] The couch on which Māyā is reclining divides the panel into two parts; on top is the elephant, while the lower portion contains the attendant women. Māyā is shown wearing an opaque *dhotī* tied at the waist with a multi-stringed pearl *mekhalā*. One can also see heavy anklets, multi-layered bangles and an elaborate necklace. The coiffure is heavy and twisted. She lies with one hand folded under her neck and the other stretched along her side. Parallel to the side of the couch is a tall standing object, like a stick with a taurine on top. On top can be seen a large elephant that is approximately three-quarters of the size of Māyā. The elephant is crouching and seems to be wearing a tasselled head ornament. It is to be noted that the elephant has only two tusks. In the left-hand corner the bust of a waiting woman with folded hands is visible. Below the couch, in the foreground, two seated women are shown with their backs turned, probably asleep. The woman on the left has a *cāmara* in her hand. Beside her is a *kamaṇḍalu* or a water vessel. Below the medallion two parrots peck at two bunches of mangoes with leaves hanging underneath. Above the medallion rise two lotuses, atop which stands a female figure to the right and on the left a male.

A short inscription in Brāhmī that says *bhagvato ukanti*, or the Descent of the Lord[42] is carved on the top portion of the railing pillar. The epigraph unequivocally identifies the panel as the *bodhisattva*'s descent from heaven into Māyā's womb, i.e. the conception of the Buddha by Māyā. Since the actual birth is not shown at Bharhut and the label implies descent, therefore the relief may stand for both conception and birth. It is also probable that the representation of delivery of the baby Buddha had not been iconographically fixed yet, because even at Sāñcī, the birth was not depicted in the way it was done in later centuries.

Two similar depictions are found on the

3.1.8 Four events from life of Buddha. Top right: Māyā's Dream; Top left: Interpretation of the Dream; Bottom right: Birth of Buddha; Bottom left: Presentation to the *yakṣa*, drum slab, second century CE, Amarāvatī.

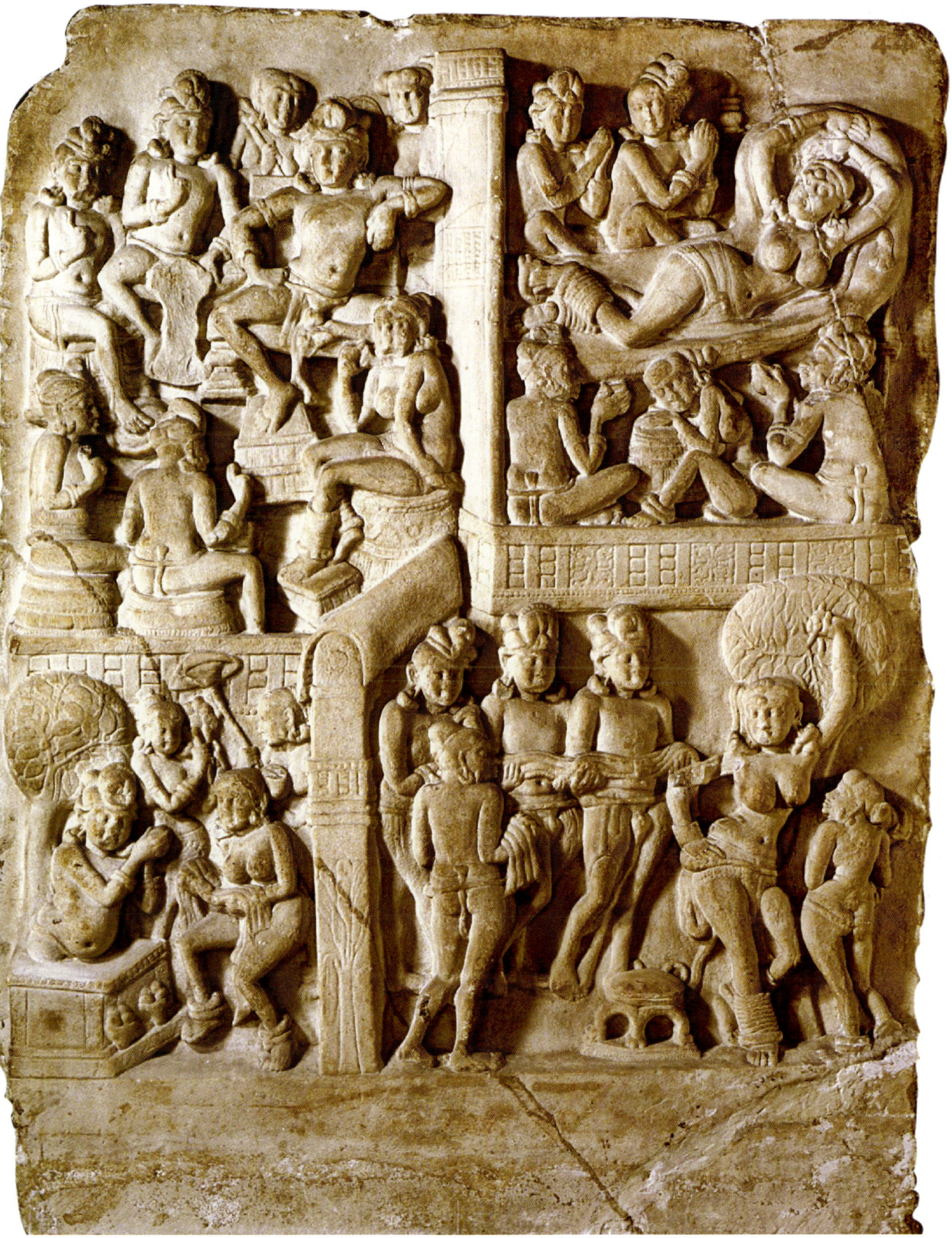

railing of a *stūpa* at Andher, near Sāñcī and at Hathin in the Gurgaon district of Haryana.[43] At the latter site Māyādevī's Dream is carved on the half-medallion on the upper register of a railing pillar (*Pls.* 3.1.2, 3.1.3). The queen is shown lying on her side on a couch, with two sleeping attendants above. A lamp and an ewer are also visible. The elephant is shown hanging vertically on the right side. The scene is more elaborately delineated here than at Bharhut, with Māyādevī lying in a *kūṭagaraśālā* (domed pillared pavilion). The representation on the pillar from Hathin shows remarkable similarities in treatment as well as style with the Bharhut version and may be dated to the first century BCE. A date close to Bharhut and Hathin may be posited for the Andher specimen as well.[44] Here the episode of the Conception of the Buddha is carved on the upper portion of a railing upright. The queen lies on her right side on a couch flanked by tall lamps. An elephant with a long trunk appears above Māyā, flying towards her feet. As at Hathin, on either side of this divine being float celestial creatures bearing garlands; two female attendants are seated at the bottom of the panel. It may be noted here that at Andher, given the preponderance of the lotus motif in the decorative scheme of the railing, it may be termed a *padma vedikā*.[45] The rare finds of portrayals of the Conception of the Buddha may be due to the relative insignificance of the episode in the iconographic scheme of the early period or a reluctance to portray this episode in his life.

According to Ratan Parimoo, the portrayals of solitary elephants holding lotus stalks in their trunk on *stūpa* II at Sāñcī (dated to around the middle of the first century BCE and earlier than *stūpa* I) perhaps can be identified as young Siddhārtha, since some texts describe him as carrying a lotus in his trunk as he appeared to Māyādevī in her dream.[46]

At a slightly later site of *stūpa* I at Sāñcī, datable to the middle of the first century, we have a single, summary depiction of the Conception of the Buddha. On the north pillar (south face) of the eastern *toraṇa* (gateway) the episode is depicted on a small panel (*Pls.* 3.1.4, 3.1.5). Part of the side of the pillar is carved in two scenes demarcated by the use of two *vedikās* (balcony railings). On the right, three faces are shown peering down at the procession shown below from the windows of a pavilion or a balcony. In the middle is a flying crouching elephant at the level of the roof structures. On the left, under a cylindrical roof with a *caitya* window, a female figure is lying on what seems to be a couch, quite like the depiction at Bharhut. The difference from Bharhut-Hathin-Andher scheme is that here the attendant figures are absent. However, as at Hathin and Andher, the elephant appears above her feet and not above her waist as at Bharhut. The elephant is undoubtedly carved in large proportion compared to Māyādevī than the one at Bharhut. The Conception of the Buddha does not seem to enjoy the same significance at *stūpa* I and is clearly dwarfed by a large rectangular panel illustrating the procession to Kapilavastu after Buddha's enlightenment,[47] which is carved just below it.

The Conception theme travelled to the Gandhāra region, where we find a number of reliefs showing a female reclining on a couch and an elephant hovering above her. Here the elephant is smaller and encircled by a halo-like disc, and his position is inclined so that his trunk touches the right hip of the mother.

Among the profusion of themes from the Buddha's life in Gāndhāran art, that of the Conception is often found on architectural members such as railing posts and architraves. In one such depiction Māyā, wearing a skirt-like

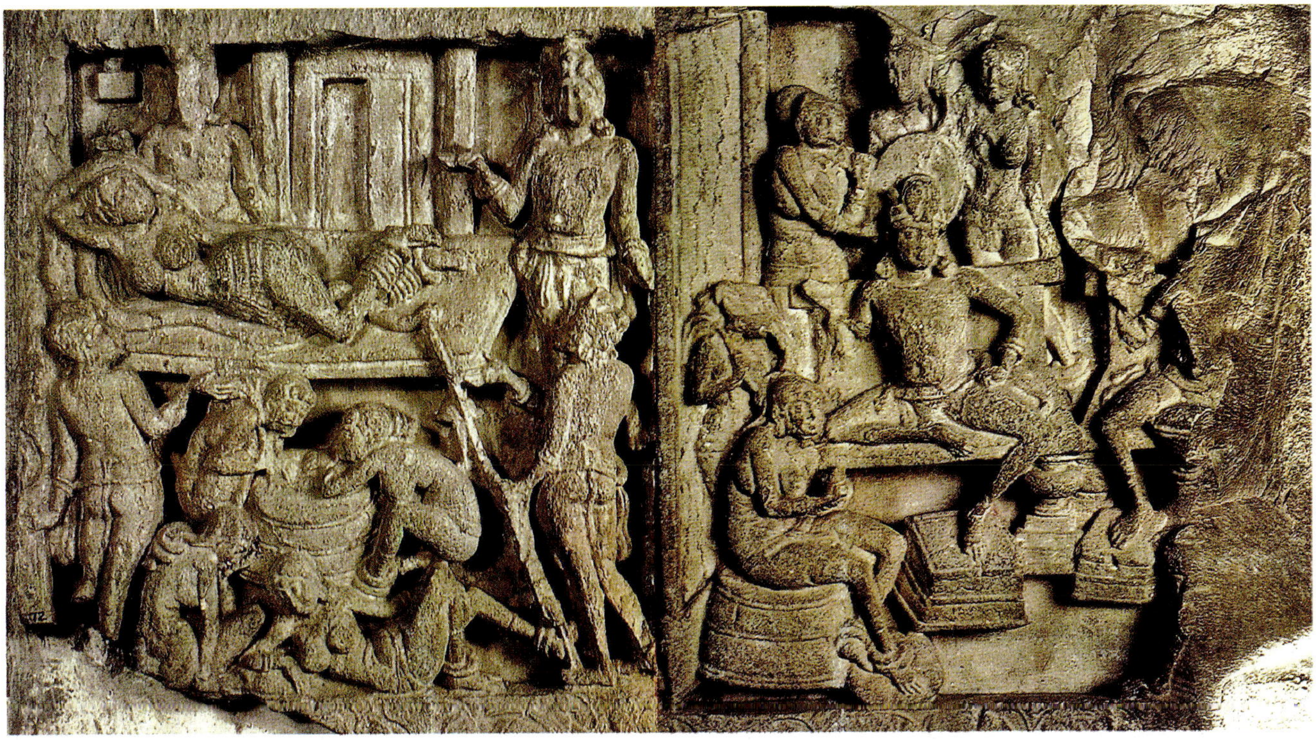

3.1.9 Conception and Birth of Buddha, second century CE, Amarāvatī, Indian Museum, Kolkata.

lower garment, is lying laterally on a couch, her body turned towards the viewer.[48] An elephant surrounded by a full halo is seen with his trunk touching and seemingly piercing Māyā's side, on the point of entering the womb.[49] Two attendants/worshippers, probably Śakra and Brahmā, watch from above.

In a later version, also from Gandhāra, we see the queen and the elephant in the centre with two attendant figures on each side; the composition being set in what seems to be a pavilion in the centre of the relief. On the left is the scene that reveals the interpretation of the dream by the sage Asita (recognisable by the matted hair in the manner of an ascetic) for the future Buddha's father, Śuddhodana. Śuddhodana is seated on a bench with his right hand raised in gesticulation and behind him stand two attendants.

The same episode is carved at Amarāvatī,[50] the difference here being that the elephant is shown in outline, with hardly any relief modulations, and confined to the frame. There are a number of women attendants above, and below the couch. At the four corners are four male figures. A snake-like object is shown lying beside her; this may suggest the embryo in the womb, the child to be born. The snake and the fish are two well-known symbols of fertility and progeny. The snake suggests superior types of progeny, while the fish is indicative more of passion than of eminence and purity.[51]

In another slab from the same site,[52] Māyādevī is present in all four scenes that combine four continuous moments of the birth story in four compartments, ingeniously divided by railings and uprights, beginning with the dream or conception on the right (*Pl.* 3.1.8). However, the elephant seen on the *kūṭagara* roof is carved in miniscule proportions. Māyā is watched over by the four gods of the quarters. The next panel

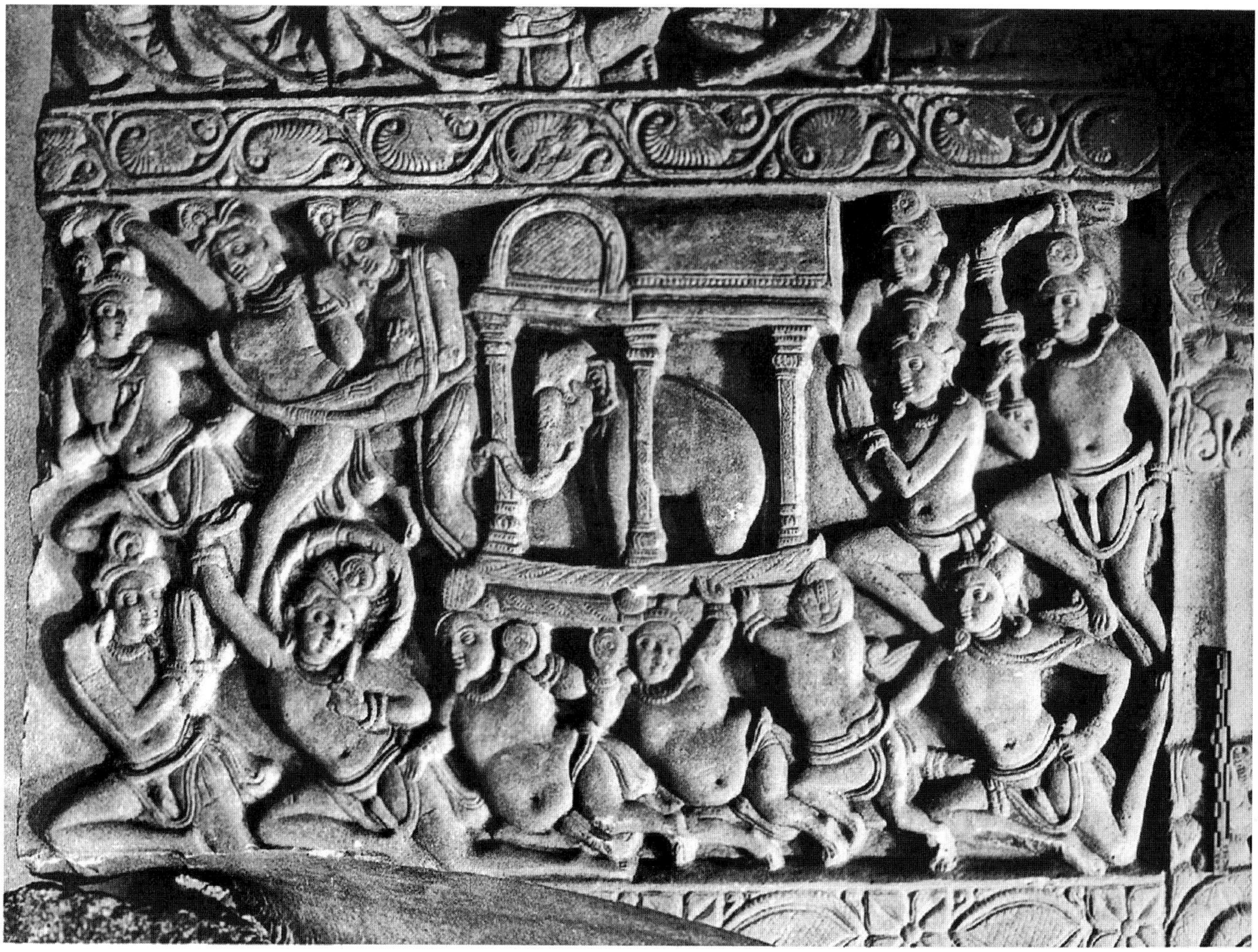

3.1.10 Descent from the Tuṣita Heaven, conception of Buddha, third century CE, Ikṣvāku, Nāgārjunakoṇḍa.

illustrates the king's court, where Māyā is present again, and the priests who have been called upon to interpret the dream make *vitarka-hasta* gestures. The third section shows the birth itself and the last the presentation of the newly born Siddhārtha by Māyā to the *yakṣa* or tree spirit. This episode is not mentioned in the *Nidānakathā* or in the *Buddhacarita*. The *Lalitavistara*, a much later text, mentions that the boy Siddhārtha was carried to the *yakṣa* shrine in a grand procession.[53]

In a depiction at Nāgārjunakoṇḍa,[54] only one part of the episode is shown, in which the Buddha-to-be in the form of an elephant is being carried through the sky in a palanquin by dwarf-*yakṣa*s in the Tuṣita heaven (*Pl.* 3.1.10).[55] Around this are various adoring figures of deities. This is clearly a moment before he appears in Māyādevī in her dream. In the *Saundarānanda* this episode is described thus: "Then the *bodhisattva*, descending to earth from among the Tuṣita gods, decided to become incarnate among the family of that monarch (Śuddhodana)."[56]

### 3.1.3 DELIVERY (BIRTH)

It is said after 10 months of pregnancy, Māyā delivered Siddhārtha Gautama standing up rather than lying down. In the Buddhist belief system the standing delivery is a special feature of the birth of *bodhhisattvas*.

At Bharhut and Sāñcī we do not find the episode of the Delivery carved on the *toraṇas* and *vedikās* of the *stūpas*. It is only from the late first century onwards that it appears at Amarāvatī, Mathurā and Gandhāra. A typical Delivery scene shows Māyādevī holding the branch of a *śāla* or *plākṣa* tree[57] with her right hand, while the left hand rests on the waist. She stands in *tribhaṅga*, and from the right side of her waist issues the baby Buddha. This may be indicated by the actual form of a child or through Buddha's footprints (*buddhapāda*) on a cushion. As he emerges, Indra and Brahmā hold him on a roll of cloth or a cushion. Usually on the left of Māyādevī her attendant women can be seen. Above this scene often gods, *kinnaras* and such-like heavenly entities may be portrayed in attitudes of adoration and thanksgiving with folded hands.

It seems that in imagining the scene of the delivery or actual birth of the Buddha, the *śālabhañjikā* motif was adapted and further elaborated. It is clear from the above description that Māyādevī giving birth and *śālabhañjikā* imagery share certain elements relating to trees such as clutching the *śāla* or *plākṣa* branch and standing under a tree more or less in a *tribhaṅga* posture. It is difficult to say definitively whether the former borrowed from the latter as has been postulated by Parimoo.[58] On the basis of the evidence available to us, the *śālabhañjikā* imagery predates the imagery of the Buddha's birth. However, we must keep in mind that we have a rather complete portrayal of the event carved on one relief sculpture from Kauśāmbī datable to the first century CE. It is also true that at Kauśāmbī, Mathurā and other sites, the Birth of the Buddha and the *śālabhañjikā* continued to be carved simultaneously. The *śālabhañjikā* image, that seems to have served as the prototype for Māyā delivering the baby Buddha, is, however, not the Bharhut *yakṣī* such as the Chandra Yakṣī (*Pls*. 6.28, 6.29). Rather it may have been derived from a more voluptuous kind, similar to the bracket figures at Sāñcī (*Pl*. 6.34), found prolifically later in Mathurā art.

The *śālabhañjikā* figure that functions as the symbol of universal fertility[59] became connected to birth of Buddha. Perhaps the Birth-of-the-Buddha in some way was supposed to confer the boon of children/prosperity on the devotees, though this is not mentioned in any text. In any case the common imagery places both the *śālabhañjikā* figures and Māyādevī in the delivery posture within the discourse of reproductivity.

Contrary to the textual description of the

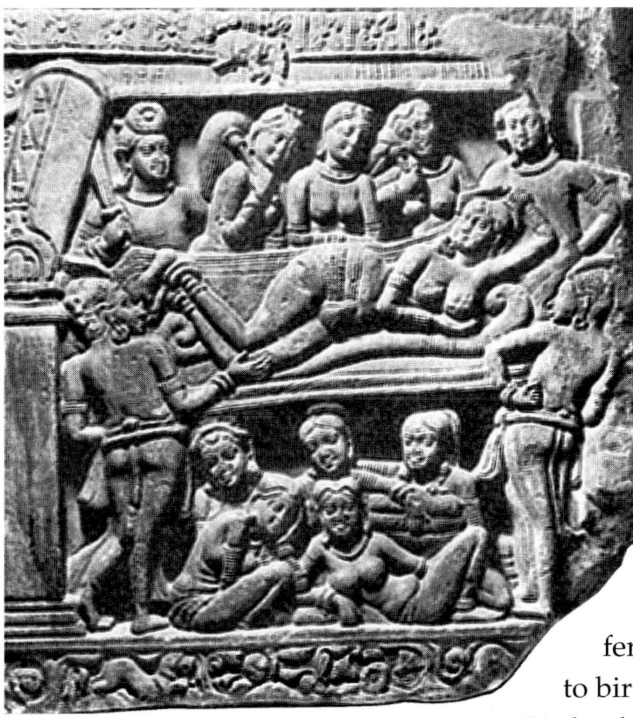

3.1.11 Conception of Buddha in Māyā's dream, second century CE, Amarāvatī, Indian Museum, Kolkata.

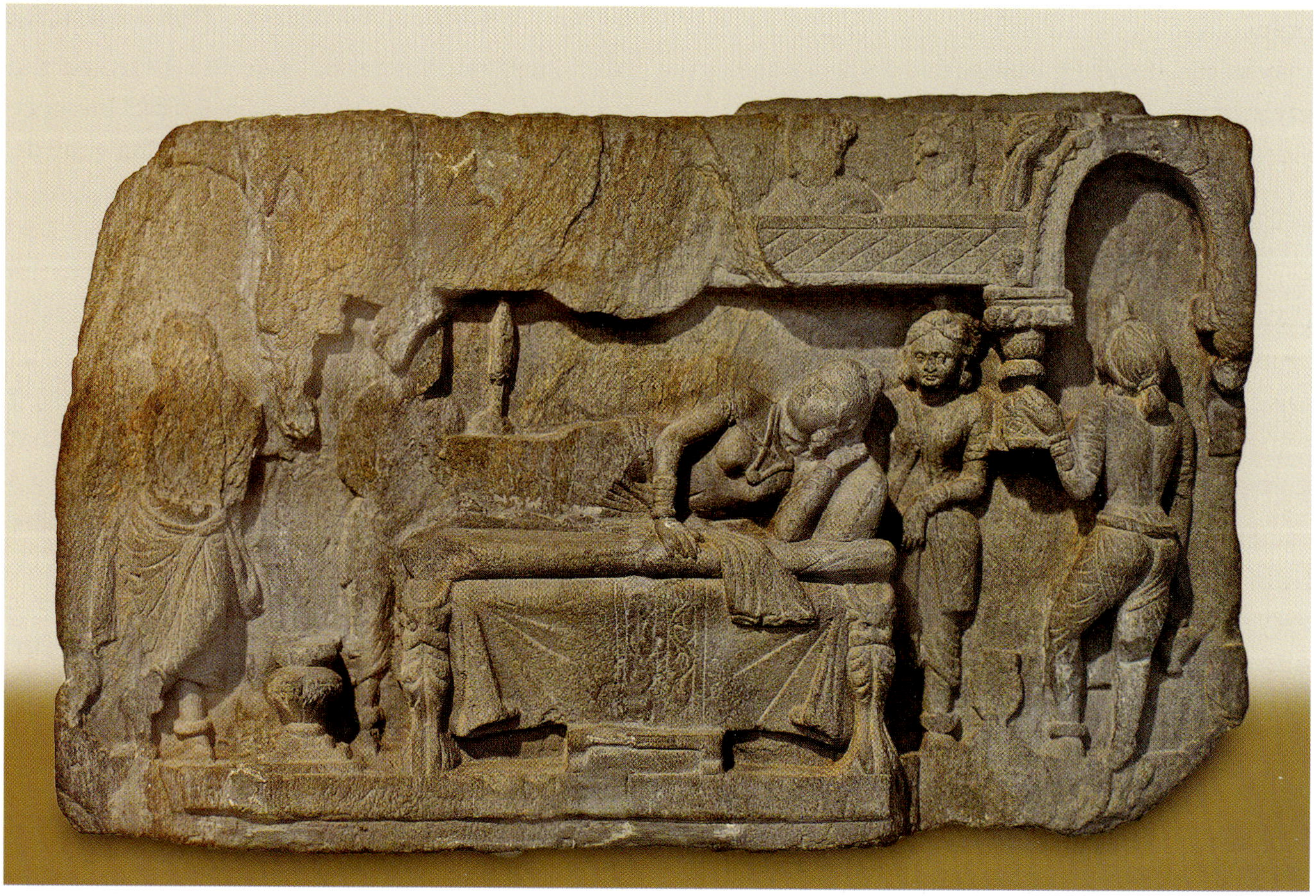

3.1.12 Scenes from the Life of Buddha, third century CE, Ikṣvāku. Nāgārjunakoṇḍa, NM.

Buddha's birth given in the *Buddhacarita*, the actual iconography shows Māyā standing. In all other aspects the text seems to match the visual representation. According to Aśvaghoṣa,

> Māyā, the queen of that god-like king bore in her womb the glory of her race and *being in her purity free from weariness, sorrow and illusion* (emphasis mine) she set her mind on the sin-free forest (Lumbinī). In her longing for the lonely forest as suited to trance, she asked the king to go and stay in the grove called Lumbinī, which was gay, like the garden of Caitraratha with trees of every kind. In that glorious grove the queen perceived that the time for her delivery was at hand, and, amidst the welcome of thousands of waiting women proceeded to a couch overspread with an awning. Then as soon as Puṣya became propitious from the side of the queen,[60] who was hallowed by her vows, a son was born for the weal of the world, without her suffering either pain or illness.[61]

It is clear from this passage that Māyā lay on a couch as she gave birth and that Indra and Brahmā were not present at that particular moment to receive the child. In the matter of the couch, the description comes close to the couch seen invariably in Conception scenes.

In a slightly later text, the *Mahāvastu*, the position of delivery described approximates to the actual portrayal. It says that Māyādevī coming to Lumbinī grove playfully held on to a branch of the *plakṣa* tree with her arm and playfully stretched herself at the moment of giving birth to the glorious one (the Buddha). According to the *Nidānakathā*, the tradition of the Lumbinī Grove near Kapilavatthu relates that Māyā on her way to her natal place, Devadaha, expressed the wish to play in the *śāla* grove (*śālavanakilaś kilitukāmata*). She approached a branch of a *śāla* tree which bent itself down towards her. Māyā reached out and held it, on which labour pains came upon her and she delivered the child.[62]

The transformation in the position of delivery from reclining on the couch to a standing position may have a basis in the evolution of the belief that during the birth of a *bodhisattva* his mother remains in a standing posture.[63] Such a notion may have been further developed by the artists to establish an iconographic relationship between Māyādevī and *śālabhañjikā*. It was further believed that after his birth, the Buddha did not touch the earth but was received by four gods on a golden cloth woven in Kāśī.[64]

The earliest surviving example of the representation of the actual birth of the Buddha may have come from the Kauśāmbī atelier.[65] This is carved on a *sūcī* railing on which a panel in low relief, now damaged, is divided into two parts arranged one above the other. In the lower section, the central figure is that of Māyādevī standing beneath a tree whose bough she is holding with her left hand. The tree itself, with

3.1.13 Detail, Birth of Buddha, third century CE, Ikṣvāku, Nāgārjunakoṇḍa. NM Acc. No. 50. 17.

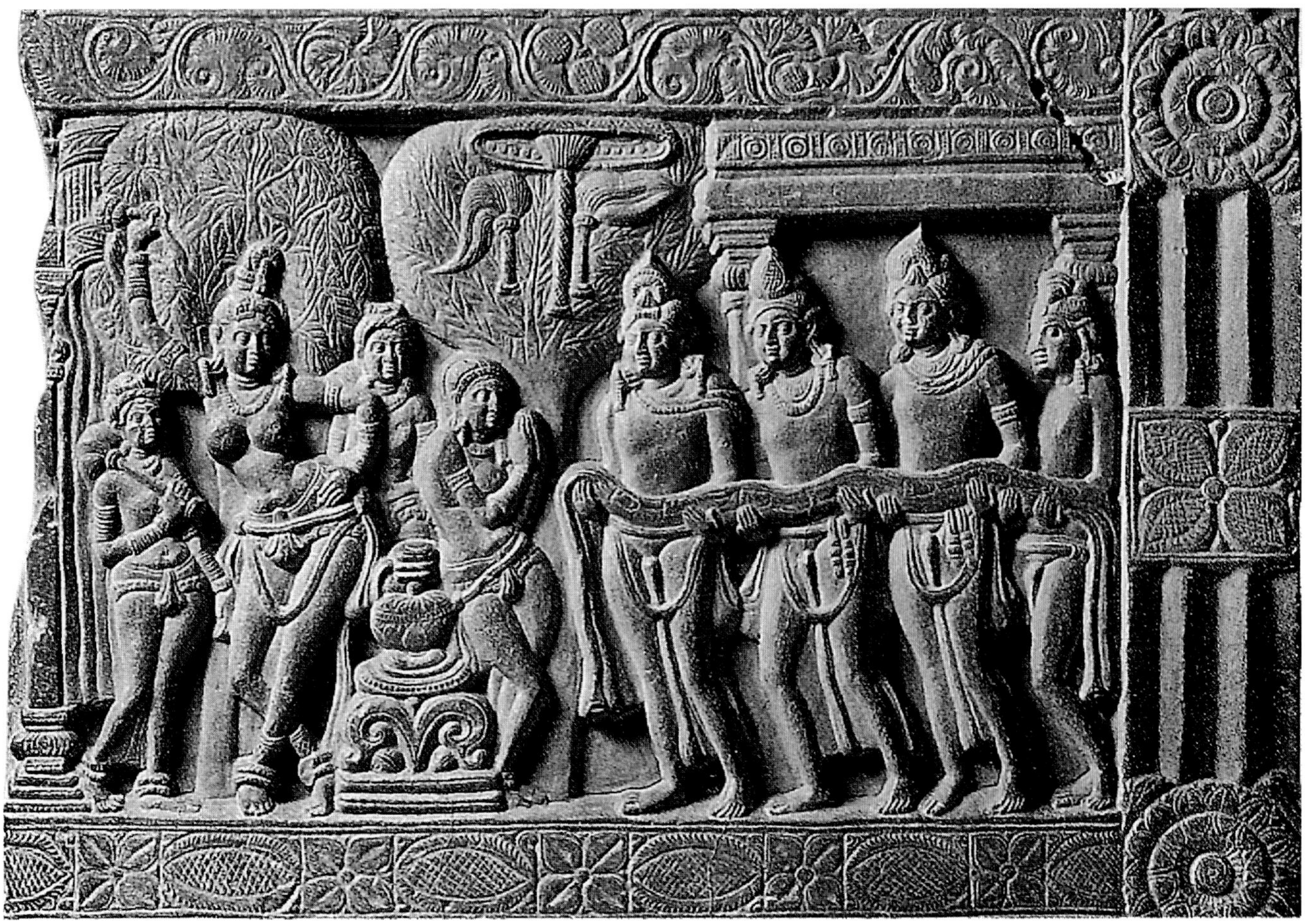

leaves and fruits and flowers, is shown spreading in an arch over her head. The right hand of the figure is damaged but may have been placed on her waist or have been shown embracing the tree trunk. The left leg is raised, giving the figure a somewhat *tribhaṅga* appearance. Māyādevī can be seen wearing thick anklets and a number of bangles cover her forearm. On her left, three male figures are visible, of whom the first to her left is probably Indra wearing a high crown and holding an object that looks like a piece of cloth. On the back slab, between this figure and Māyādevī, are carved a *chatra* and *cāmara* (an umbrella and a fly whisk) symbols of universal paramountcy. On her right are two female figures, probably attendants given that one is in *añjalī-hasta*. On the upper panel are two seated female figures playing instruments. The figure on the left may be a serpent goddess (*nāgī*) since below the *mekhalā* her legs have been replaced by snake-like coils.

The largest number of sculptures portraying the Delivery of the Buddha survive from the Gandhāra area (*Pls.* 3.15, 3.16, 3.17), testifying to the popularity of the theme in the region. In most of the sculptures Buddha Gautama is seen emerging from the right side of the standing Māyā, who is wearing a knee-length skirt-like *dhotī*. She holds a *śāla* branch with her right hand while her left arm is around her sister Prajāpati/female attendant on the left or it rests on her waist. The infant is received on a cloth by one or two male figures (with or without halo) representing Indra and Brahmā. Additional royal female attendants are usually depicted carrying a water vessel with a spout and a bag/casket and fly whisks. Also male attendants with or without a *cāmara* are sometimes seen. At the top, heavenly flying adorers are often shown to emphasise the momentousness of the divine event.[66]

One such frieze, now in the Freer Gallery, is divided into three panels.[67] In the middle panel Māyā is shown with the left leg crossed over the right. One hand grasps the tree above, on her right is the three-eyed Indra holding a cloth on to which the haloed infant emerges from the right side of the waist. On the left is a slightly depressed panel in which there are two female attendants, one of whom is holding a mirror, while the other has a casket/box with a handle and a peacock-feather fan. A tree at the back and an adoring flying figure above are visible. On the right there are two male adorants, the *uttarīya* of the one on the far right flies upwards to the sky.

At Mathurā too, this episode from the life of the Buddha became a popular theme in art[68] as is attested by a relief panel in red sandstone (*Pl.* 5.3), datable to the Kuṣāṇa period. This slab is divided into levels. On the upper level, on can see the five major events; these are, from right to left, the Birth, Enlightenment, Descent at Sankisa, *mahāparinirvāṇa*, and Worship of the *stūpa*; on the lower panel are carved the worship of the Buddha by *nāga*s and Māra's temptation. The Birth scene here depicts a female figure, legs crossed over one another, standing under a heavily foliaged tree. With her upraised hand she holds a branch of the tree and with her left hand she is seen embracing another female figure as if taking her support. On her right side appears a male figure wearing a high crown receiving a baby in both his hands.

In the early Buddhist art of the Deccan region, from Amarāvatī[69] (*Pls.* 3.1.7, 3.1.8) and Nāgārjunakoṇḍa,[70] (*Pls.* 3.1.13, 3.1.14) the Birth scene, like the Conception episode, is usually part of a composition illustrating three or four events related to the Birth. Starting with Māyā's Dream, Interpretation of the Dream by Asita, the composition includes the Birth of the Buddha and concludes with the presentation of the baby to the tree-*yakṣa*. In one relief from Nāgārjunakoṇḍa (*Pl.* 3.1.13), Māyādevī stands on the left side of the composition in reverse *tribhaṅga*, i.e. her left hip projects. The motif of the child cannot be seen here, and the presence of the *boddhisattva* is evoked by the presence of a female attendant folding her hands or holding the royal umbrella and fly whisk. The baby is presumably received by the four *deva*s, or guardians of the quarters, on a piece of cloth on which are seven tiny foot-marks indicating the seven steps of the *bodhisattva*. Here the *deva*s stand in one row, in comparison to Amarāvatī, where the four *deva*s are in a circular group and one figure is portrayed in a difficult back view creating a suggestion of movement.

At Nāgārjunakoṇḍa, there is a frieze showing the *yakṣa* peering out of his shrine, hands folded in *añjalī-hasta* (*Pl.* 3.1.14). Unlike Amarāvatī, where the *yakṣa* is shown peering out of a tree, the moment carved here is when baby Siddhārtha is brought near him by Māyādevī. She is attended by three maids, two of them waving *cāmara*s while a third crouches at the feet of the *yakṣa*. In the second section of the relief the sage Asita carries the infant, indicated again by a horizontal roll of cloth on which are carved the *buddhapāda*. The composition is arranged in such a manner that the gaze of each person within it is riveted to the invisible child.

In the *Buddhacarita* the presentation to the *yakṣa* is not mentioned though it does say, "Māyā lay on a couch with a glorious canopy with feet of beryl and framework glistening with gold and

3.1.14 Presentation of the Buddha to the *yakṣa* at birth, details, third century CE, Ikṣvāku, Nāgārjunakoṇḍa.

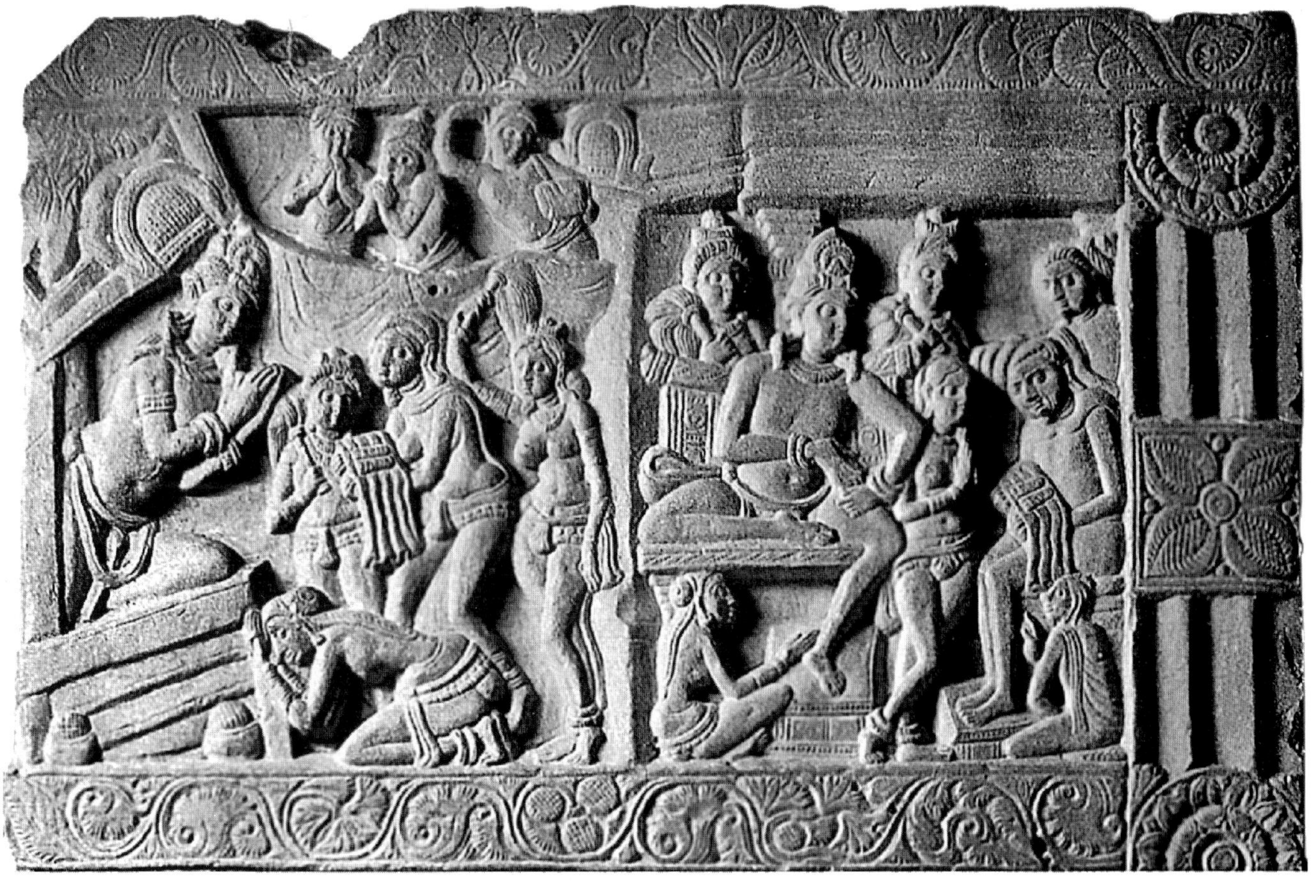

round him the *yakṣa* lords stood reverently on guard with golden lotuses in their hands." As for the seven steps just after his birth there is no specific reference in the text. Of the Buddha it is said: "Looking at the four quarters with the bearing of a lion, he uttered a speech proclaiming the truth, 'I am born for Enlightenment for the good of the world, this is my birth in the world of phenomena'." At this moment, "two streams of water, clear as rays of the moon and having the virtue, one of heat, one of cold, poured forth from the sky and fell on his gracious head to give his body refreshment by their conduct."[71] There is no mention of *nāga* kings, Nanda and Upananda, performing this office, an episode which is mentioned only in the *Lalitavistara*, a later text.

The *Buddhacarita* however does describe the incident of *deva*s welcoming the sight of the new-born Master, often illustrated in Buddhist relief sculptures.

> The dwellers of heaven, themselves remaining invisible, held up in the sky a white umbrella and bowing with their heads in obeisance before his majesty . . . the highest blessing that he might obtain enlightenment. The mighty snakes with their thirst for the most excellent Law fanned him, and with eyes shining with devotion, bestrewed him with *mandāra* flowers, offices they had performed for the Buddhas of the past.[72]

After the birth of the Buddha, Māyā departs from the scene and from life, though this is never depicted in art. The explanation given in the textual tradition is that the parents were overjoyed at the birth of such a mighty son, and Māyā died of happiness.[73] Śuddhodana, made of sterner material, "saw him (the Buddha) resting on the nurse's lap, like the son of Agni on Devī's lap, the tears flickered on the eyelashes and sighing, he looked up to heaven."[74] It is probable that Māyādevī died as a result of the delivery, nevertheless, the differing and gendered responses attributed to the mother and father are noteworthy.

3.1.15 Birth of Buddha, West Pakistan, second century CE, Gandhāra style, Museum für Indische Kunst, Berlin.

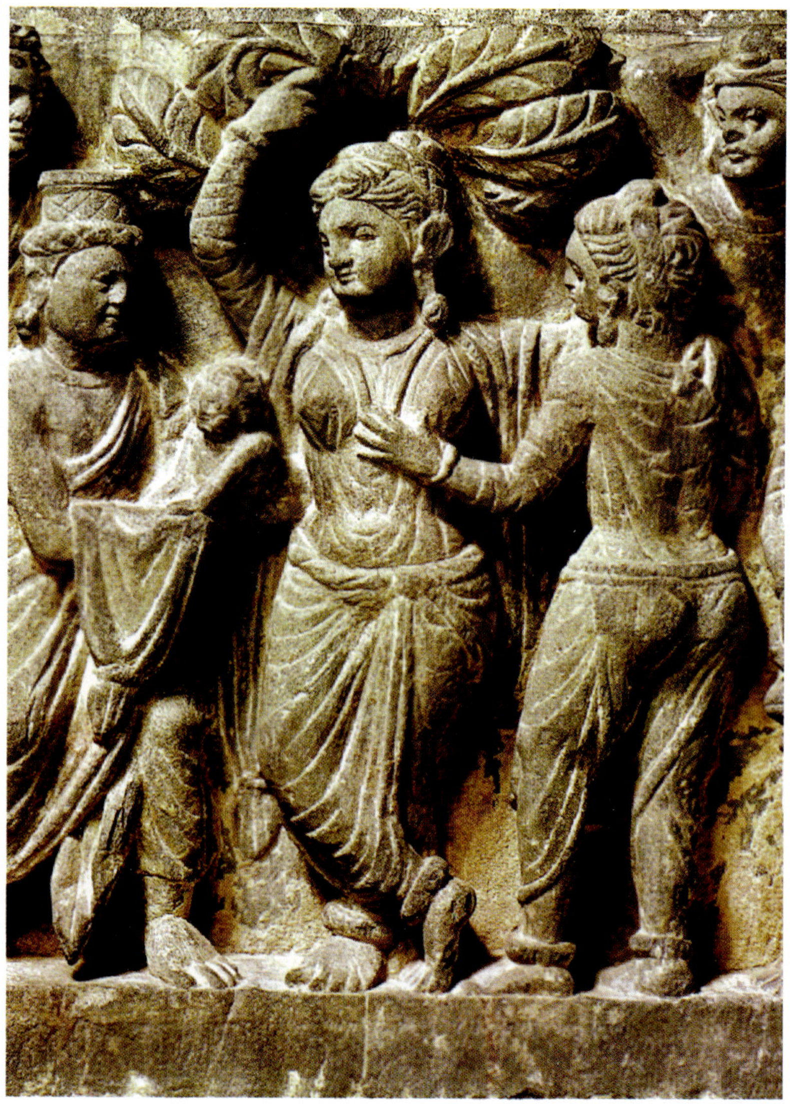

### 3.1.4 ENGENDERING MĀYĀDEVĪ

The rendering of Māyādevī in terms of numbers and treatment is crucial in analysing contemporary discourses on birth and motherhood, especially within the Buddhist ideological set-up. The idealisation of Māyā in text and image, in my opinion, combines the biological imperative, which is also seen as a social imperative of mothering, with the religious imperative of celibacy (non-contamination) and renunciation enunciated and valorised in Buddhist thought.

The role of sexuality on the part of Māyādevī and Śuddhodana, the parents of Prince Siddhārtha, are abstracted from the conception of the future Buddha. It is revealed to Māyā in a dream that an elephant is entering her womb through the left side. Thus the actual sexual and reproductive act between a man and a woman is rendered unnecessary. In the *Buddhacarita* the episode is described like this:

> Then *without defilement* (emphasis mine) she received the fruit of her womb, just as knowledge united with mental concentration bears fruit; before she conceived she saw in her sleep a white lord of elephants entering her body, yet she felt thereby no pain.[75]

The absence of pain is also a significant element in the discourse of motherhood associated with the birth of the Buddha. A list of woes specific to women existed in early Buddhist literature and was circulated among the believers in the form of Jātakas and hymns of *therī*s and *thera*s. Thus, it permeated stories and the consciousness of both men and women. I.B. Horner cites a list of five woes which are women's lot: having to leave her family at an early age, menstruation, pregnancy, childbirth and having to be subservient to a man.[76]

The *Therīgāthā* reiterates this notion:

> Woeful is a woman's lot
> . . . woeful when sharing home with hostile wives
> woeful when giving birth in bitter pain
> woe too when mother murdering embryo
> comes not to birth, and both alike find death.[77]

There are references to the pain of losing a child in many psalms in the *Therīgāthā*. These psalms also highlight the freedom from such pain and anguish enjoyed by the *therī*s consequent on their renunciation of familial ties and worldly desires and their realisation of the True Path. Paṭācārā, a senior nun who herself was widowed and whose children died in tragic circumstances, maddened by grief, was counselled by the Buddha to consider these as mere worldly ties. Thus, she reached Enlightenment and further consoled and counselled 500 other women who had lost their children.[78]

In the *Aṅguttara Nikāya* it is pejoratively mentioned that women can never get enough of two things — intercourse and childbirth.[79] This misogynist notion is based on the conception of the fundamentally evil and uncontrolled inherent nature of women — *strīsvabhāva*.[80] The implications of this statement seem significant in the light of the imagery of the Buddha's birth in so far as during the process of conception Māyādevī herself is not associated with intercourse. As explained above, according to Buddhist belief, she was impregnated by the white elephant who is none other than Buddha himself who has decided to descend from the Tuṣita heaven to bring enlightenment to the earth.

Similarly, neither the birthing position, nor the actual birth, is imagined as "normal." This

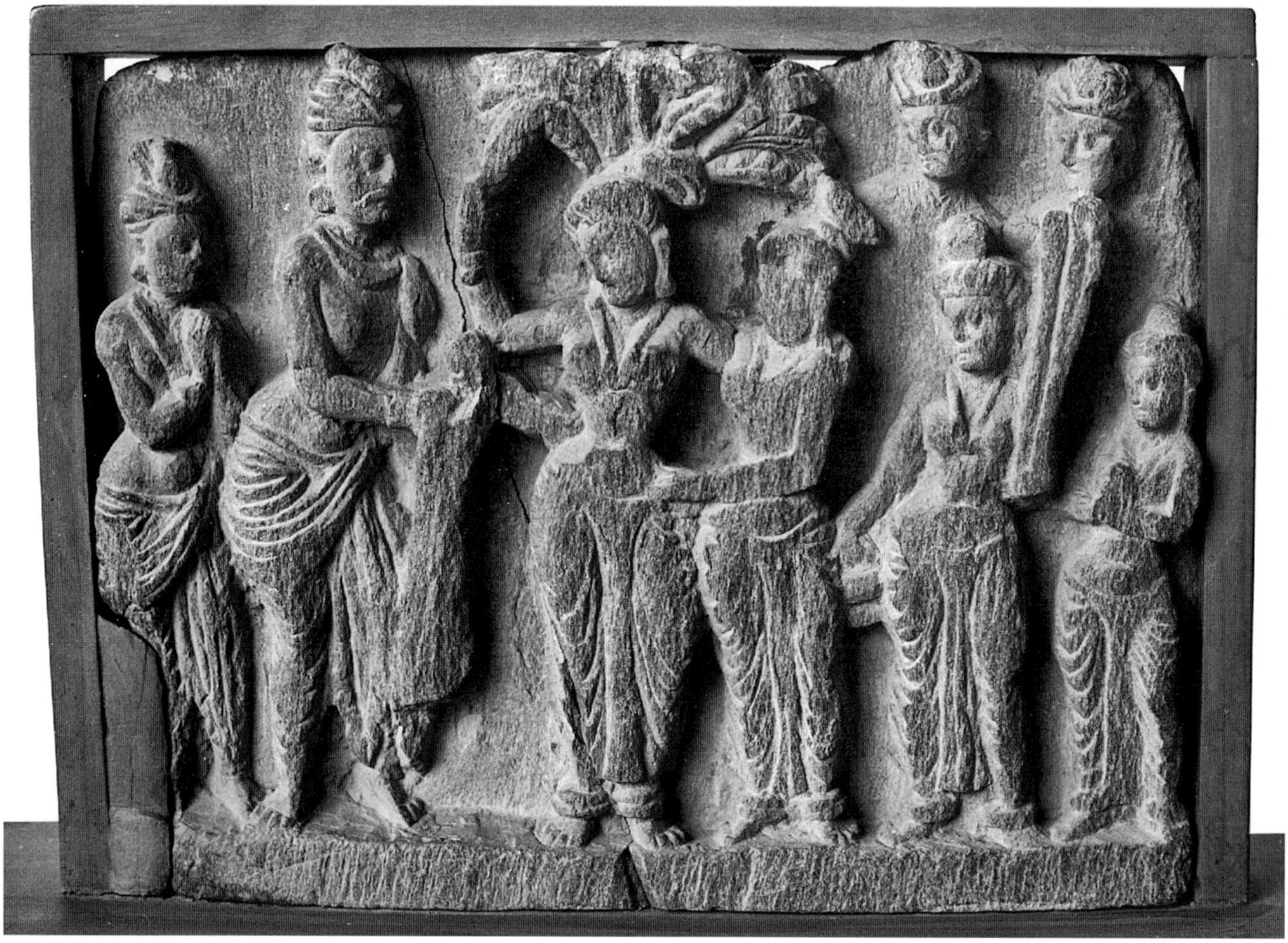

3.1.16 Birth of Buddha, Gandhāra style, blue schist, first-second century CE, West Pakistan, Bharat Kala Bhavan, Varanasi. BKB. 755. 788.57.

becomes evident if we compare the standing posture of Māyādevī with the outstretched legs of the Lajjā-Gaurī images where a female figure with a lotus head is shown in a birth-giving position.

These references from Buddhist literature, which precede or are contemporaneous with the depictions of the Buddha's Conception and Birth, may provide the reason for the belief that he was conceived immaculately and that his mother had a special birth position. Both of these specific conditions are linked with attitudes towards women's sexuality as a negative element leading to the pain and suffering of childbirth. Māyādevī as the mother of Buddha, and thus also the Buddha himself, are freed from the taint of sexuality and regular childbirth.

We can see from the above survey that the numbers of images depicting the moment of the Buddha's conception are rather few, especially in the earlier art at Bharhut and Sāñcī. Even with the rise of Mahāyāna, the conception was a theme that did not enjoy the same relative popularity as did depictions of the actual birth.

An additional observation may be made here. Māyādevī is never shown completely nude. In the earlier depictions at Bharhut, Kauśāmbī and later at Mathurā, she is always clad in a *dhotī* that covers her body below the waist. Unlike the *yakṣī-śālabhañjikā* imagery, the garment is not carved in a transparent manner to reveal the genital region. In accordance with the conventions of the Gandhāra tradition governing female bodies, Māyādevī is shown fully clothed, with both the primary and secondary sexual characteristics well covered. One may posit that the portrayal of Māyādevī is considered special; inspired by no other intention than to illustrate an important historical moment and to evoke devotion in the viewer, untrammelled by the distractions of a naked female body. The clothing on Māyādevī's person also highlights the fact that female nakedness is not a universal phenomenon in sculptures of the post-Mauryan period. We should keep in mind that for the viewer the images discussed in this section are meant to portray a historical moment which had significant religious value.

Two other devices add to Māyādevī's prominence in the relief discussed above. First, in both the conception and birth series, she is attended by royal servants who serve to highlight her position as a queen. Even her sister and co-queen, Prajāpati, attends to her. Within the relief, Māyādevī occupies the centre, and despite the presence of gods like Indra and Brahmā, she remains the focus of the composition. Secondly, the white elephant is associated with her. The

3.1.17 Birth of Buddha, Māyādevī in Lumbinī Grove, first-third century CE, Gandhāra. GMAG.

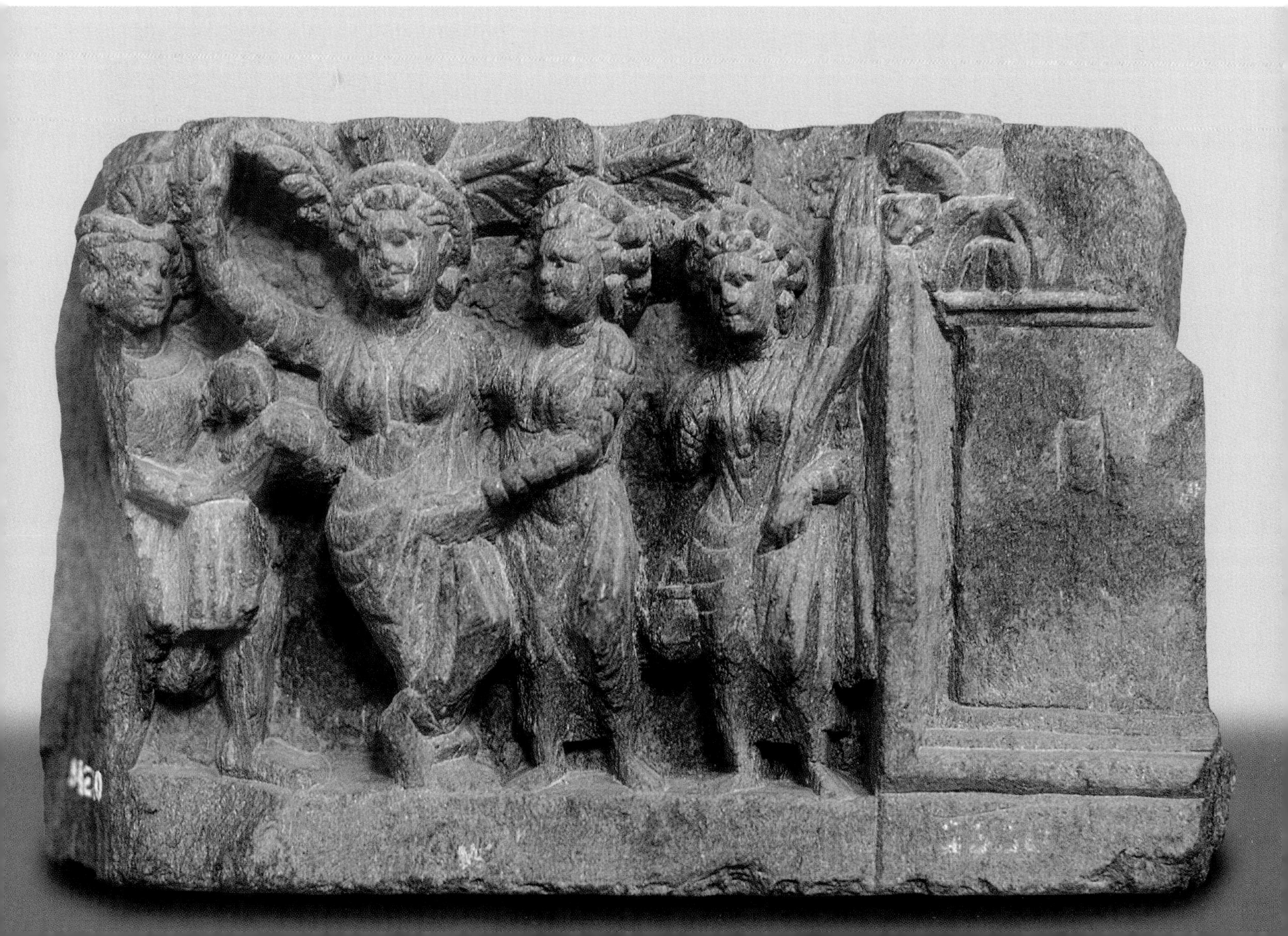

white elephant is the supreme imperial mount; it is part of the jewels or *ratna* of the state and part of the patrimony of any universal monarch or *cakravartin*. This is illustrated in the *Vessantara Jātaka*,[81] where Prince Vessantara gifts the royal elephant to some brāhmaṇas as *dakṣiṇā*; consequently there is distress in the kingdom and he is banished for his wanton generosity.

In friezes depicting Māyādevī as a mother, the *raison d'être* of such carvings is undoubtedly the glorification of the miraculous powers of the Buddha, emphasising his superiority over all other gods. The proximity of her relationship to the Buddha must have conferred respect and reverence on Māyādevī. It is nevertheless important that in these narrative panels she, as a woman, is treated with respect and veneration by the artists of the period, which cannot be said of all representations of women. Such a contradictory approach may reflect a multiplicity of attitudes towards women and femininity in early Buddhism, mirroring the multiplicity of voices found in Buddhist texts.

One can read the presence of three entities in Māyā. The first is the phenomenon *māyā* which is an illusion of the world, a mysterious spirit. Second is the goddess Māyā, epitome of beauty and prosperity. The historical and mundane Māyādevī, mother of the divine Buddha, was linked to the goddess Māyā on the basis of the similarities of their virtues by ancient hagiographers. One wonders if this was a mere coincidence or whether Māyādevī as the mother of the Buddha was part of *māyā*, the web of illusion?

### 3.1.5 MAHĀPRAJĀPATI

I have not been able to discover any significant visual that represents Mahāprajāpati.[82] For the sake of completeness I nevertheless give a brief account here of her role as the Buddha's foster-mother.

Subsequent to Māyā's death, six days after the birth of the Buddha, the mothering role is taken up by the co-wife and sister of Māyā, Mahāprajāpati, who brings up Gautama Siddhārtha.[83] The initial details of his upbringing are not provided, and the role of his surrogate mother becomes significant only after his enlightenment when she implores him to found the *bhikkhuṇī saṁgha*, allowing women to enter the homeless state.[84]

In this case, her surrogate motherhood becomes important because Ānanda, the favourite pupil of Buddha, who has taken up the cause of Prajāpati and her followers, invokes the duty of a son towards the mother.

The name Prajāpati is derived from Sanskrit *prajā* which means procreation, propagation, birth, offspring, children, family, race, posterity, descendants, after-growth (of plants), etc. Prajāpati, feminine, also means a matron, lady and as a nun it is used to denote Gautama Buddha's aunt and nurse.[85]

She is also the mother of Nanda, the Buddha's cousin, and the protagonist of Aśvaghoṣa's *Kāvya Saundarānanda*, whom he converts to the faith.

### 3.2 Hāritī

In the post-Mauryan religious complex, especially that of Buddhism, Hāritī has a unique and very important position. This Yakṣī-Goddess traverses the spectrum between malevolent cannibalism and benevolent motherhood on the one hand and that between the divine and the human worlds, on the other. A study of Hāritī as a mother-goddess is also interesting because she is a biological mother herself, and is actually depicted with children around her person. Further, she is projected in literature both as a real mother and as an abstract universal one: a mother to her own children and a mother who looks after all children.

One of the more popular goddesses of the Buddhist pantheon in the post-Mauryan era, Hāritī has been subjected to numerous scholarly studies.[86] These studies have focused largely on dating images of Hāritī and on describing their stylistic affiliations. Hitherto, Hāritī has rarely been placed within the complex of motherhood and mothering figures that predominate in the religious art of the period. Nor has there been an attempt to analyse the significance of the varying representations of Hāritī in the art of the period.

Further the studies seem to assume that the cult of Hāritī was largely prevalent in and around the Taxila region since we have numerous images from the Gandhāra region. A closer scrutiny, however, makes it clear that she was also

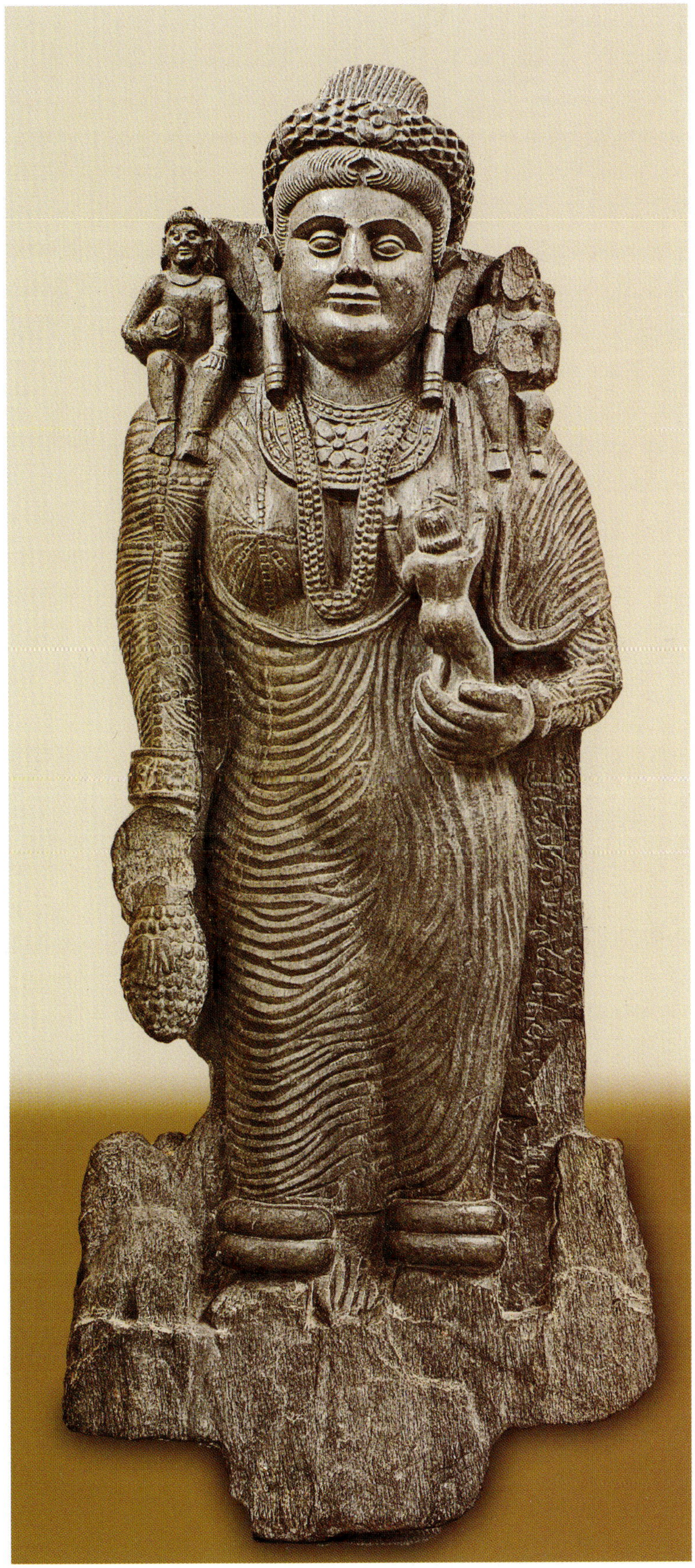

3.2.1 Inscribed image of Hāritī, first-second century CE, Skarah Ḍherī, Gandhāra. GMAG No. 1625.

worshipped both in the Gangetic plains and the Deccan regions as well. In fact, "Hāritīputra" is the phrase used by dynasties that ruled Deccan, from the Sātavāhanas to Kadamba-Cāḷukyas.

### 3.2.1 SCULPTURAL EVIDENCE

Hāritī can be recognised by the children depicted around her. She is sometimes shown seated with a child resting in her lap and playing with her necklace and at times being nursed on her breast. She is also depicted in a standing posture having numerous children around her. There are two broad types of Hāritī representation:

*Type A*: She is carved individually with children around her. The images may be further classified into seated and standing figures.

*Type B*: She is accompanied by a male figure, as part of a couple. Both figures are generally seated.

Type A depictions emphasise her solid, statuesque posture, standing with her legs slightly apart, balancing her many children around her. One such example comes from Skarah Dehri, Pakistan (*Pls*. 3.2.1, 3.2.2), which is now housed in the Government Museum and Art Gallery, Chandigarh.[87] The goddess wears an over-garment, a tunic with long sleeves. On her feet one can see double ankle bands. She stands holding a bunch of grapes in her right hand, while she cups the feet of a small child standing on her left hand. The back view of this child is seen as he touches the left breast of the deity. Two other children are seated on her shoulders, and near her left foot there is evidence that another child was carved here who must have also had a counterpart on the right, which is now lost. The folds of the tunic are incised with fine lines. Her hair is arranged with a bun tied on top of her head, and a fringe high on the forehead parted in a way to reveal an almond- shaped space. She wears a wreath on her head, and a number of necklaces, among other jewels. Her oval face has large, wide-open eyes with incised pupils. Below Hāritī's left hand is an inscription in Kharoṣṭī. In a somewhat similar representation from Takht-i-Bahi, now in the Peshawar Museum, she is shown (like Lakṣmī) standing on a *pūrṇaghaṭa* (a pot of plenty) under a canopy of leaves, carrying the younger child on her left hip.[88] The Sikri image in the Lahore Museum is also similar[89] with children clambering over her and playing between her feet. Similar figures have been reported from the north-western region of India (*Pl*. 3.2.6).[90] In two such figures[91] the child is not only shown clambering over her breast but being suckled at it, establishing a clear mother-infant relationship within the sculpture.

At Mathurā, perhaps due to the popularity of a general cult of the mother through Mātṛkā worship, Hāritī retains her maternal character, as she is represented with numerous children around her (*Pls*. 3.2.3 to 3.2.5). At Mathurā, Hāritī has been depicted seated in the typical posture of a Mātṛkā.[92] Seated on a stool-like throne, she is cradling a child in her lap (*Pl*. 3.2.3). Below her, between her legs, at least two other children/diminutive figures are visible. Also seen seated to the right of the female figure is a portion of a pot-bellied male figure holding a cup in his left hand, perhaps Kubera or one of his *yakṣa*s. The broad pedestal underneath this composition contains a number of dancing and rejoicing figures. In a somewhat similar representation of a seated female figure,[93] probably belonging to the central Gangetic Valley, we can see two male children: one seated on her left thigh and another between her legs (*Pl*. 3.2.4). She holds the seated child in a protective embrace, clutching him with her left hand. In this

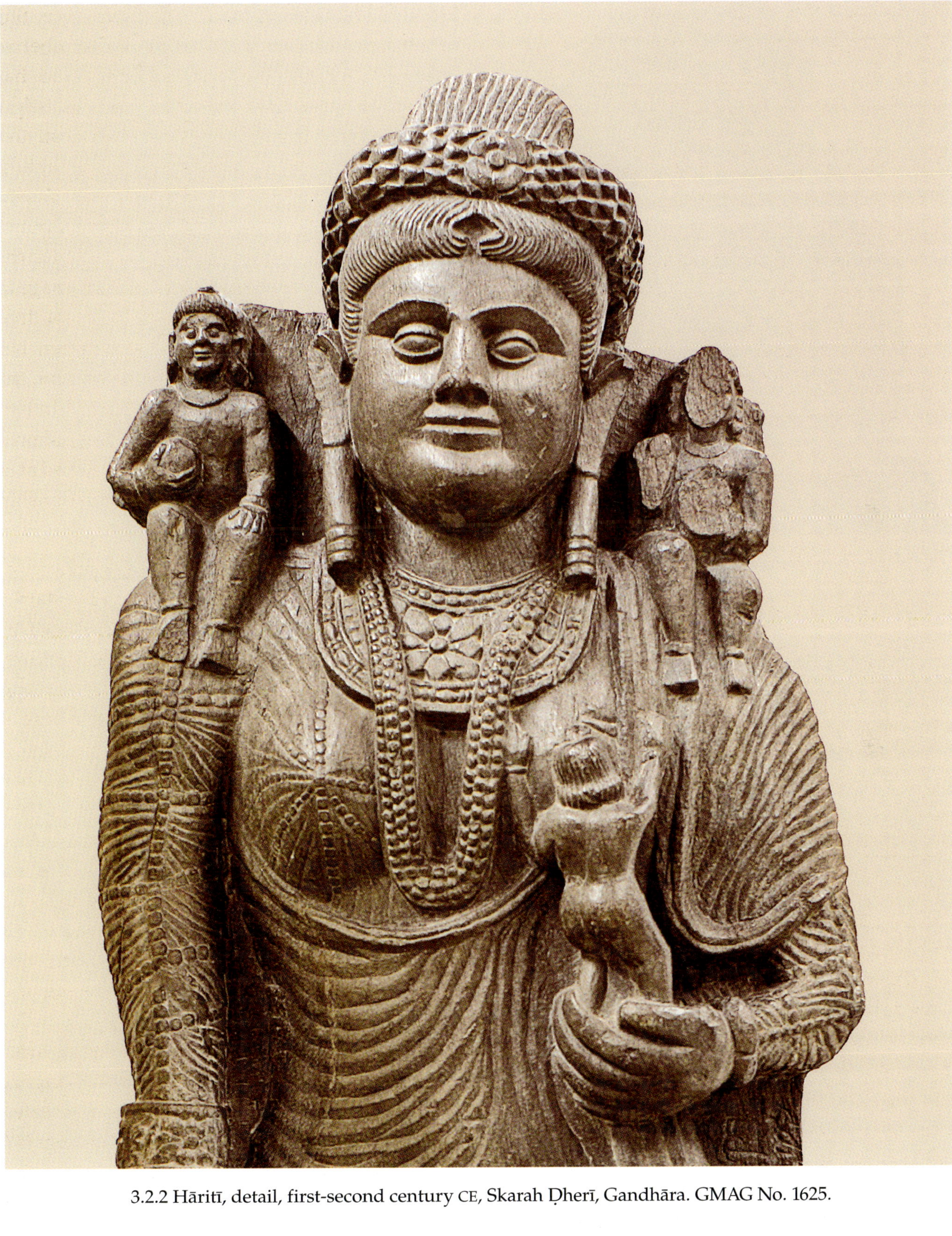

3.2.2 Hāritī, detail, first-second century CE, Skarah Ḍherī, Gandhāra. GMAG No. 1625.

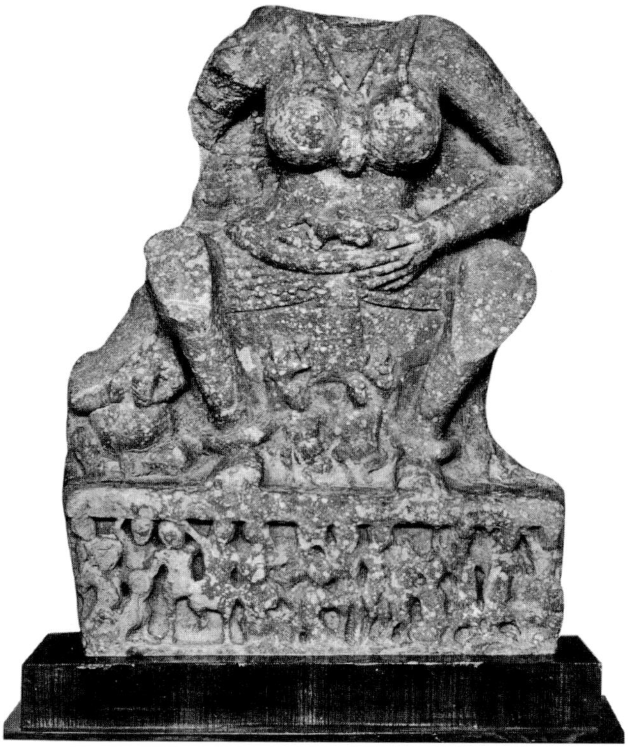

3.2.3 Hāritī seated, red sandstone, third century CE, Tayapur, Mathurā district, UP. GMM No. F 30.

identified as Ghoṣitārāma.[95] The figure is seated in *pralambapādāsana* with hands placed on her knees (*Pl.* 3.2.20). She looks straight on at the viewer. Surprisingly, there are no child(ren) associated with this figure.

Hāritī is perhaps the first female Buddhist divinity in art that is associated in a spousal relationship with a male deity. She is associated with Jambhala, Vaiśrāvaṇa, Pañcika or Kubera the first three being manifestations of Kubera, a Vedic deity with fertility associations who is

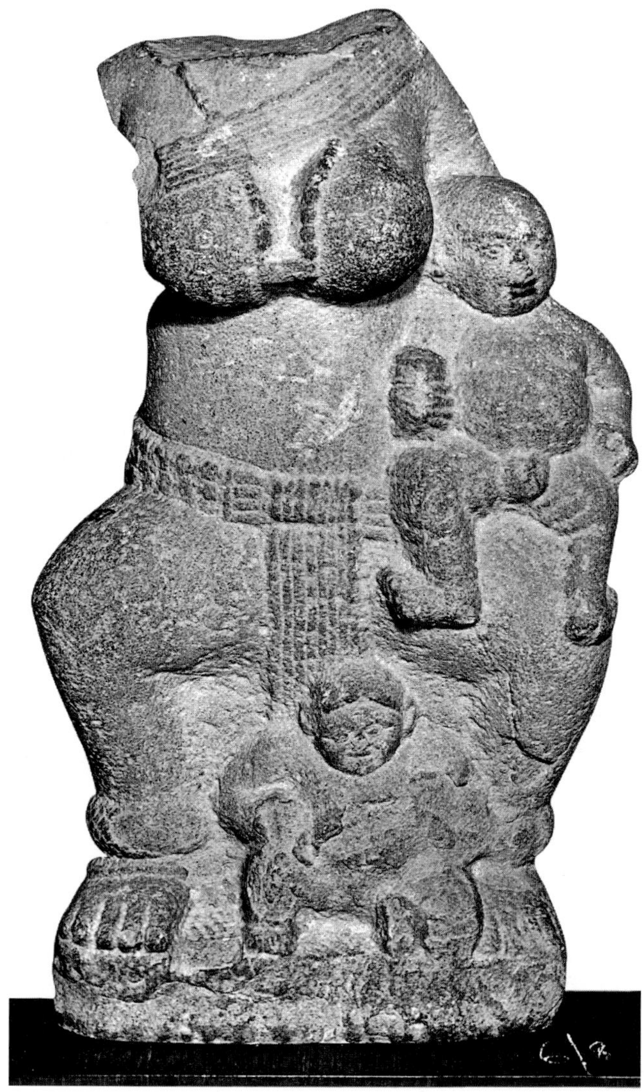

3.2.4 Hāritī, seated, with children on her lap and between her legs, red sandstone, second century CE, Mathurā. GMM

sculpture, besides the usual *dhotī* tied with a thick *mekhalā*, a band of the upper garment passing over her upper chest is clearly visible. Images of Hāritī continue well into the early medieval period. At Sārnāth there is a seated figure of the goddess with a child in her left arm that was unearthed near the north-west of Jagat Singh Stūpa. Another figure of the goddess was found in the Nālandā ruins, seated in *lalitāsana* with a child on her left knee and a fruit in her right arm.

At Nāgārjunakoṇḍa, a so-called temple of Hāritī (*Pl.* 3.2.18) was discovered within which was found a seated image of a goddess (*Pl.* 3.2.19).[94] Unfortunately only the lower portion of this figure is now extant. There is no evidence of a child or children around the goddess.

During the excavations at Kauśāmbī a terracotta seated image of Hāritī was discovered in a shrine within the monastic complex

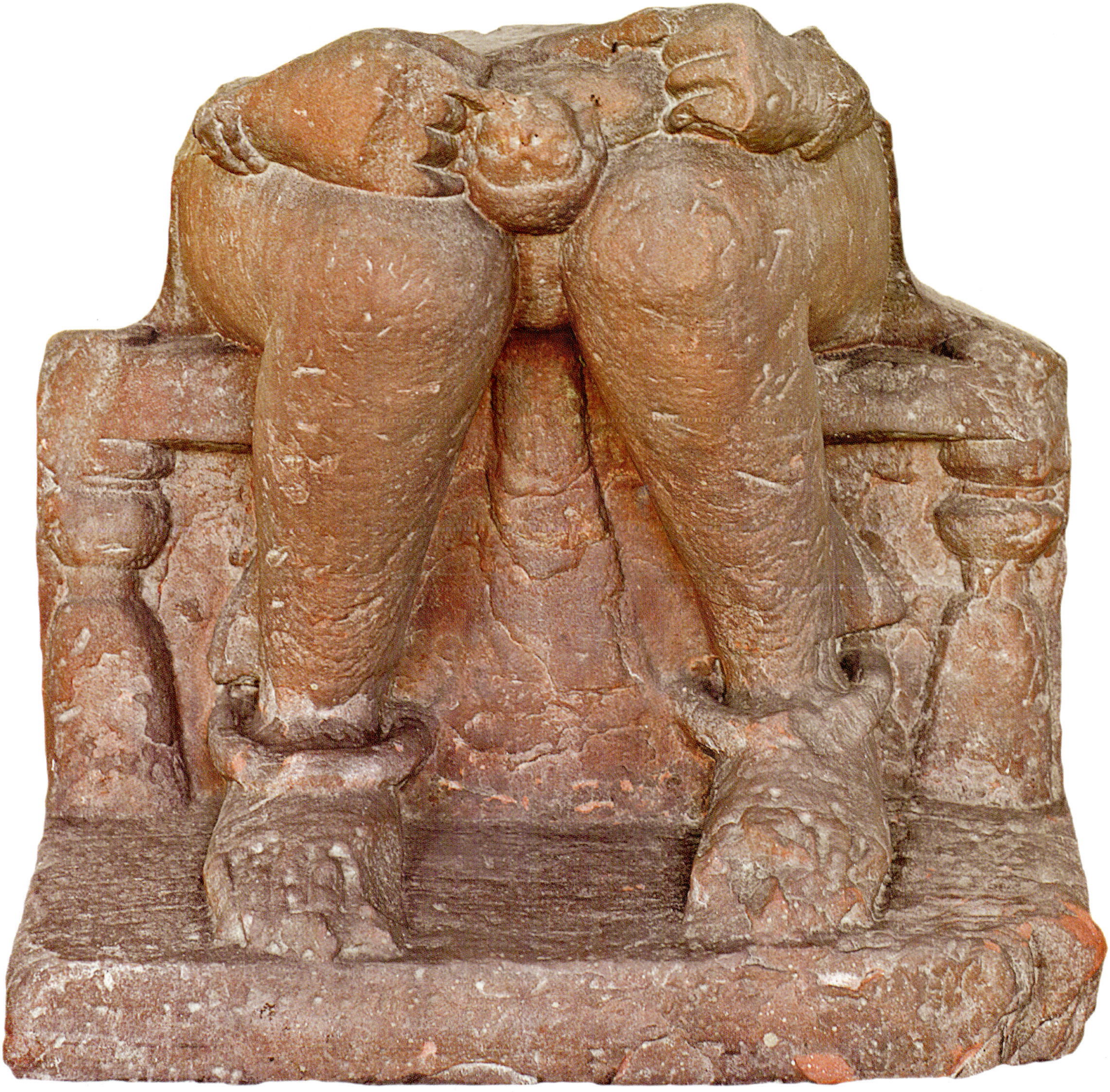

3.2.5 Mātṛkā-Hāritī, seated with child on her lap, red sandstone, second century CE, Mathurā. GMM.

appropriated by the three main traditions, Buddhist, Jaina and Brāhmanical. Jambhala/Pañcika or Kubera usually shares a pedestal with his consort, both being seated in *pralambapādāsana*.

Type B figures are far more prolific in and around Mathurā, in almost the whole of the central Gangetic Valley, and in the Gandhāra region. In most of these compositions the goddess is seated to the left of the male and holds a child in her lap or in the crook of her left arm. Often she is shown holding aloft a lotus in her right hand. The male partner holds a lance in his right hand and a purse or goblet in his left. He is shown as corpulent. At Mathurā, Hāritī and her male consort are generally in a squatting position (*Pls.* 3.2.7 to 3.2.10),[96] while in Gandhāra, Hāritī is usually in the *pralambapādāsana* and Kubera/Pañcika in *lalitāsana* (*Pl.* 3.2.12).[97] In the latter, both the male and female figures are fully clad in long flowing garments. In rare cases there is a slight diminution of the female partner in comparison to the male,[98] though the norm is to depict both in equal proportions. At Mathurā, interestingly, there are instances of a crowd of worshippers being included in the composition, sometimes to the right[99] (*Pl.* 3.1.12) and sometimes to the left[100] of the couple. From the latter example, where we can make out the sex of the worshippers, it is clear that all of them are women.

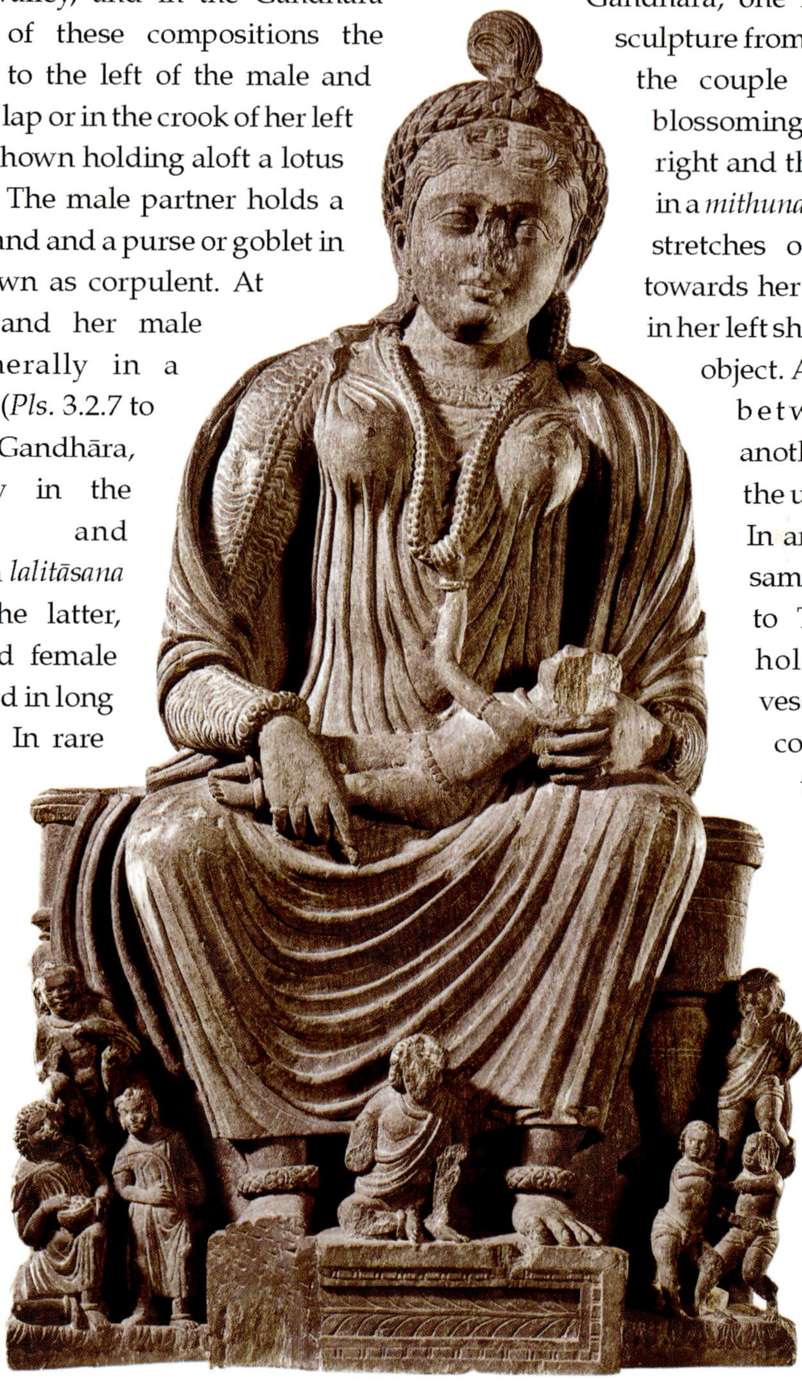

Among Type B representations from Gandhāra, one represent-ation is a sculpture from Jamālgaṛh showing the couple standing under a blossoming tree, the male on the right and the female on the left in a *mithuna* composition. Hāritī stretches out her right hand towards her male partner while in her left she carries a noose like object. A naked child stands between them and another child is visible in the upper background.[101] In another group of the same school belonging to Type B the female holds a pan-shaped vessel, evidently containing food.[102] In the best preserved figure of this type, from Sahri Bahlol,[103] Hāritī and Pañcika are placed side by side, the male holding a lance in his right hand and in his left, a money bag; but Hāritī, rather than holding children, holds

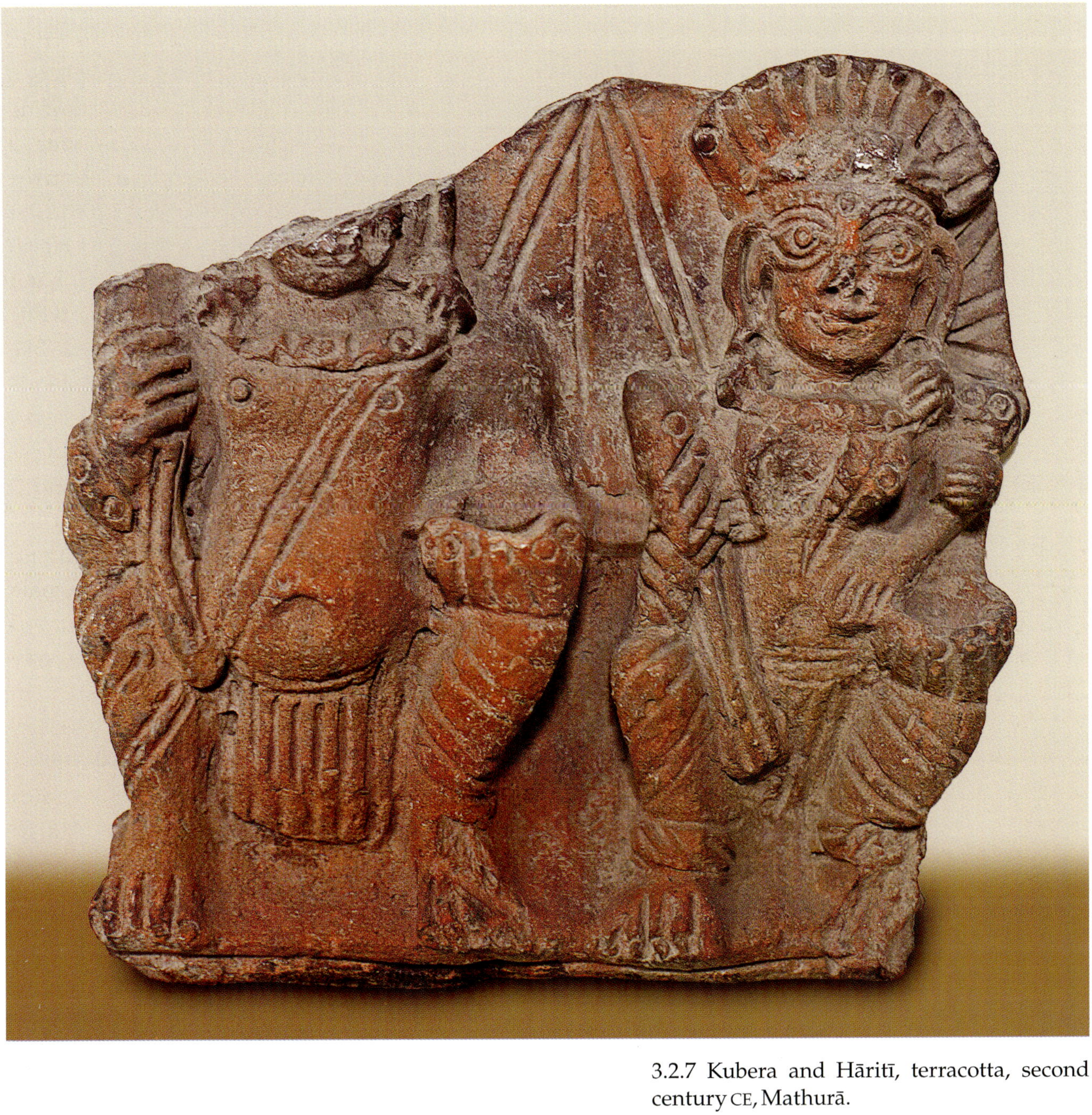

3.2.7 Kubera and Hāritī, terracotta, second century CE, Mathurā.

3.2.6 Hāritī, third century CE, Gandhāra, Yusufzai, West Pakistan, British Museum. OA 1886/6-11. (facing page)

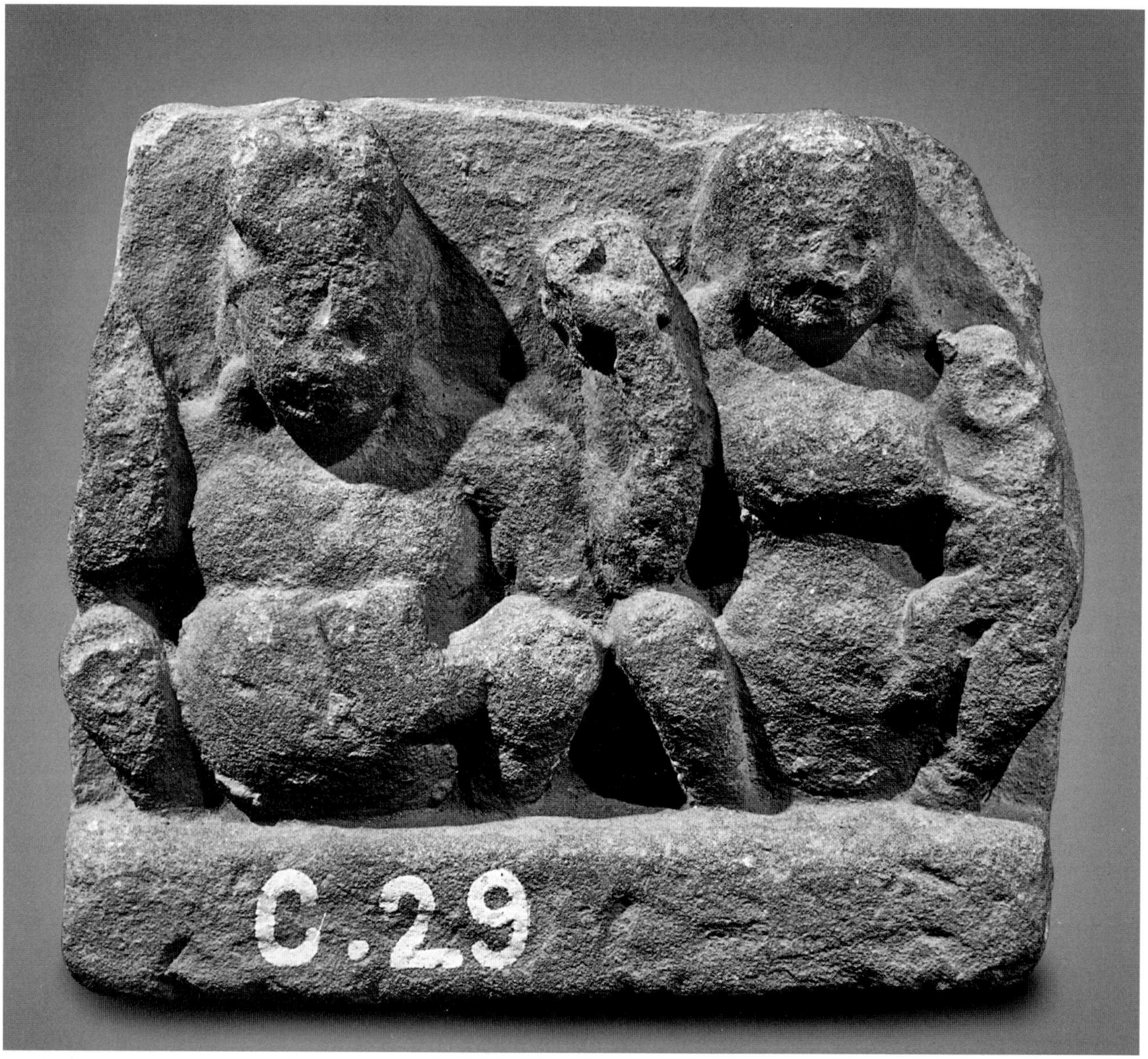


3.2.8 Kubera and Hāritī, Mathurā sandstone, third century CE, Kervai, Mathurā district, UP. GMM No. 00.C29.

a cornucopia, the abstract symbol of wealth and prosperity. The fecund mother, here, becomes the universal giver.

The male partner in these Type B images has been identified with Kubera who had an independent cult[104] of his own at least from the first century onwards. At Bharhut a large male figure with his hands folded in adoration, labelled as Kupiro (Kubera) Yakṣa (*Pl.* 3.2.14), is carved on one of the corner *vedikā* pillars. The tradition of the image continued all over north India where the iconography of Kubera as the god of wealth and prosperity became crystallised over the next 300 years. At Mathurā he is depicted as a squatting pot-bellied deity[105] (*Pl.* 3.2.15) associated with various *nidhi*s (attributes) of wealth such as a cornucopia, a purse, a mongoose,[106] or even a lotus.

It is as the lord of wealth that he became associated with Śrī-Lakṣmī in the *Mahābhārata* and other texts.[107] In actual art production too, especially at Mathurā, Kubera is often associated

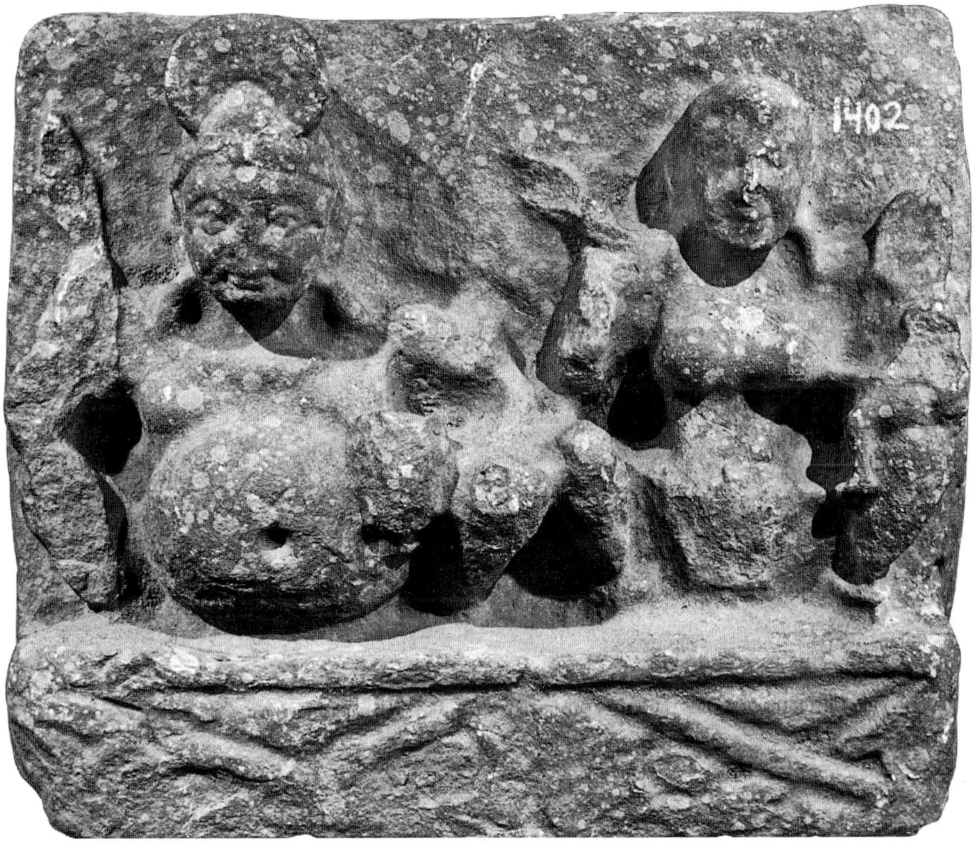


3.2.9 Kubera and Hārītī, Mathurā sandstone, third century CE, Mathurā district, UP. GMM No. 18.1402.

with a lotus carrying Lakṣmī[108] (*Pls*. 3.2.17, 3.3.5) and other Mātṛkā goddesses (*Pl*. 3.3.7).[109] At Mathurā Hārītī is portrayed not only with Kubera but also with Lakṣmī. In an image that is now in the Lucknow Museum,[110] a goddess identified as Lakṣmī is seated at the right holding a lotus in her right hand and her left hand is in *abhaya-hasta*. In the centre is Kubera and in the left corner is Hārītī (another example in *Pl*. 3.3.5 but with the goddess seated to the right). This is a unique representation because Kubera is also considered to be the husband of Lakṣmī. A sculpture such as this suggests that Kubera and his consorts are not only considered to have the power to grant prosperity but also to embody, through association, the power to grant and protect the property and children of his worshippers.

### 3.2.2 ORIGINS AND IDENTIFICATION

The identity of some of the images of Hārītī has been unequivocally established thanks to the inscriptions carved on the Skarah Dehri and Nāgārjunakoṇḍa sculptures. The second line of the Skarah Dehri epigraph clearly states that ". . . I ask for protection of the children."[111]

The epigraph explains her function as an abstract mother whose blessings are sought to protect all children from disease. This is undoubtedly linked to her status as an actual mother which is described in Buddhist literature.

In the Buddhist legend, Hārītī was an ogress, or a *yakṣī* with malevolent propensities, who inhabited the city of Rājagṛha. In one version of the story, given in the *Vinaya Piṭaka* of the

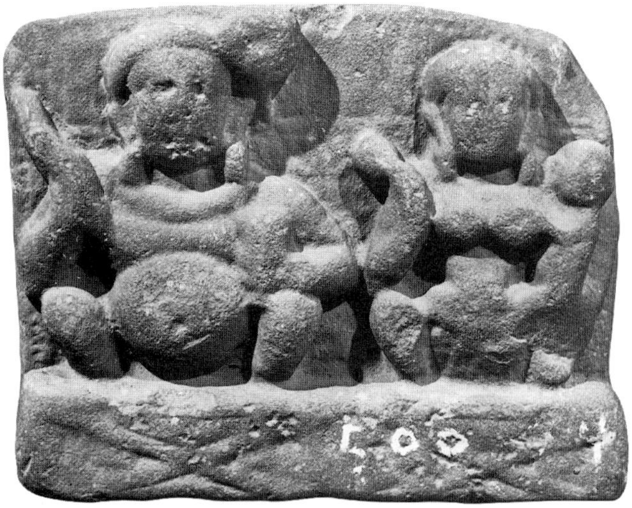

3.2.10 Kubera and Hāritī, Mathurā sandstone, third century CE, Gopālpur, Mathurā district, UP. GMM No. 14.500.

Sarvāstivāda School, Hāritī is reborn as the *yakṣī* of Rājagr̥ha, called Huanśī, who becomes the mother of 500 strong children.[112]

I-tsing narrates a similar story, identifying Hāritī as a mother, who due to some cause or the other, made a vow to devour all the babies of Rājagr̥ha. She is reborn as a *yakṣī* who eats one child every day. The Buddha, in order to cure her of her cannibalistic appetite, conceals her favourite and youngest child under a miraculously enlarged begging bowl. The Buddha restores her child to the frantic *yakṣī*, but before doing so he makes her realise the pain and suffering she was inflicting on other parents, and thus brings her to awareness of her cruelty. In exchange for giving up cannibalism, the Buddha grants her a boon that she and her children are to partake of offerings left at Buddhist establishments. The Chinese traveller adds that a figure of Hāritī was found at the corner of the dining hall or the porch of the monastery where such offerings were left for her and her children. I-tsing further states that Hāritī had the power of

3.2.11 Hāritī and Pāñcika, red spotted sandstone, second century CE, Indian Museum, Calcutta. IM A 25083/9282.

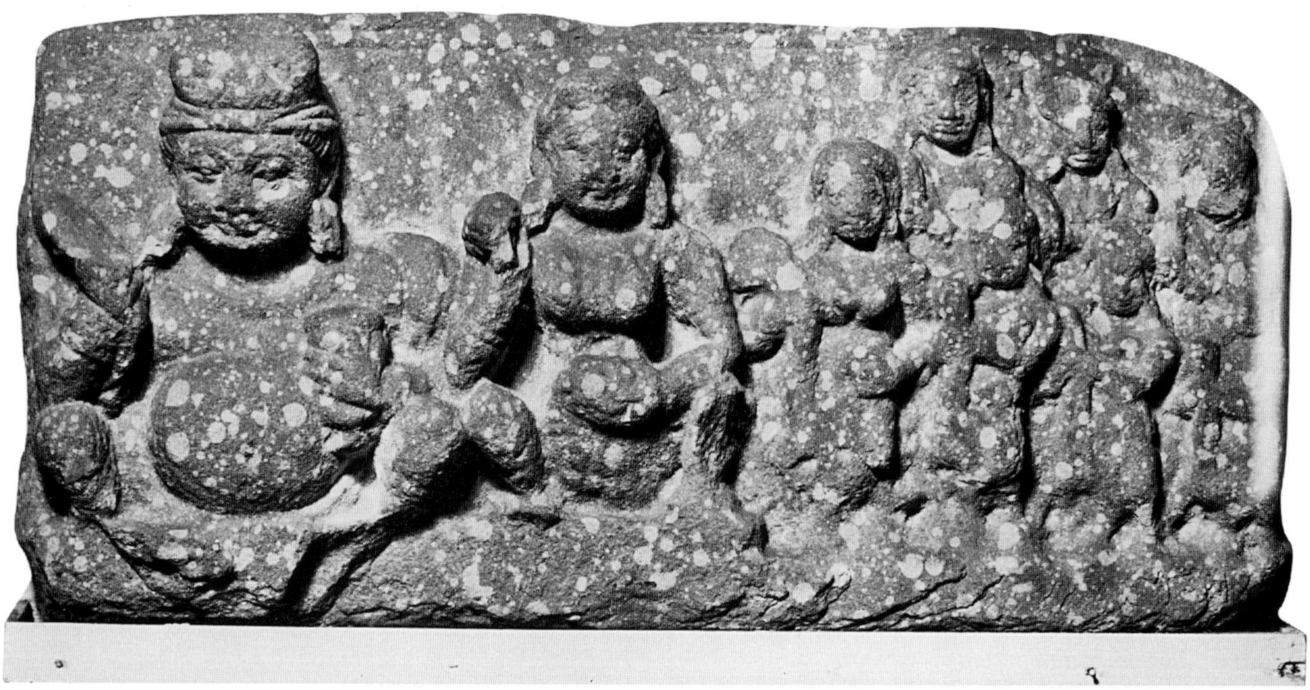

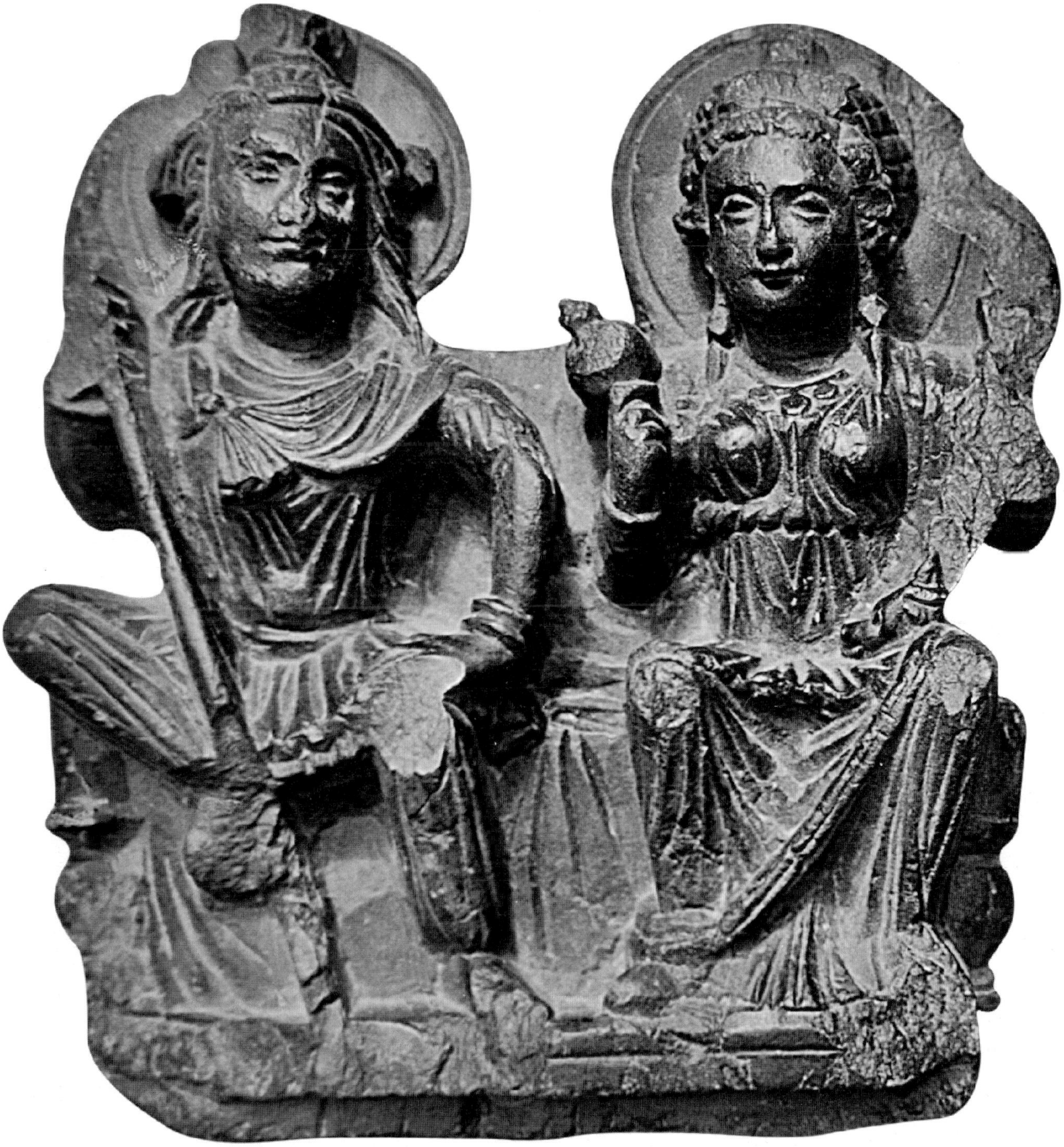

3.2.12 Hāritī and Pāñcika, stone, second-third century CE, Gandhāra. NM Acc. No. 49.2/5.

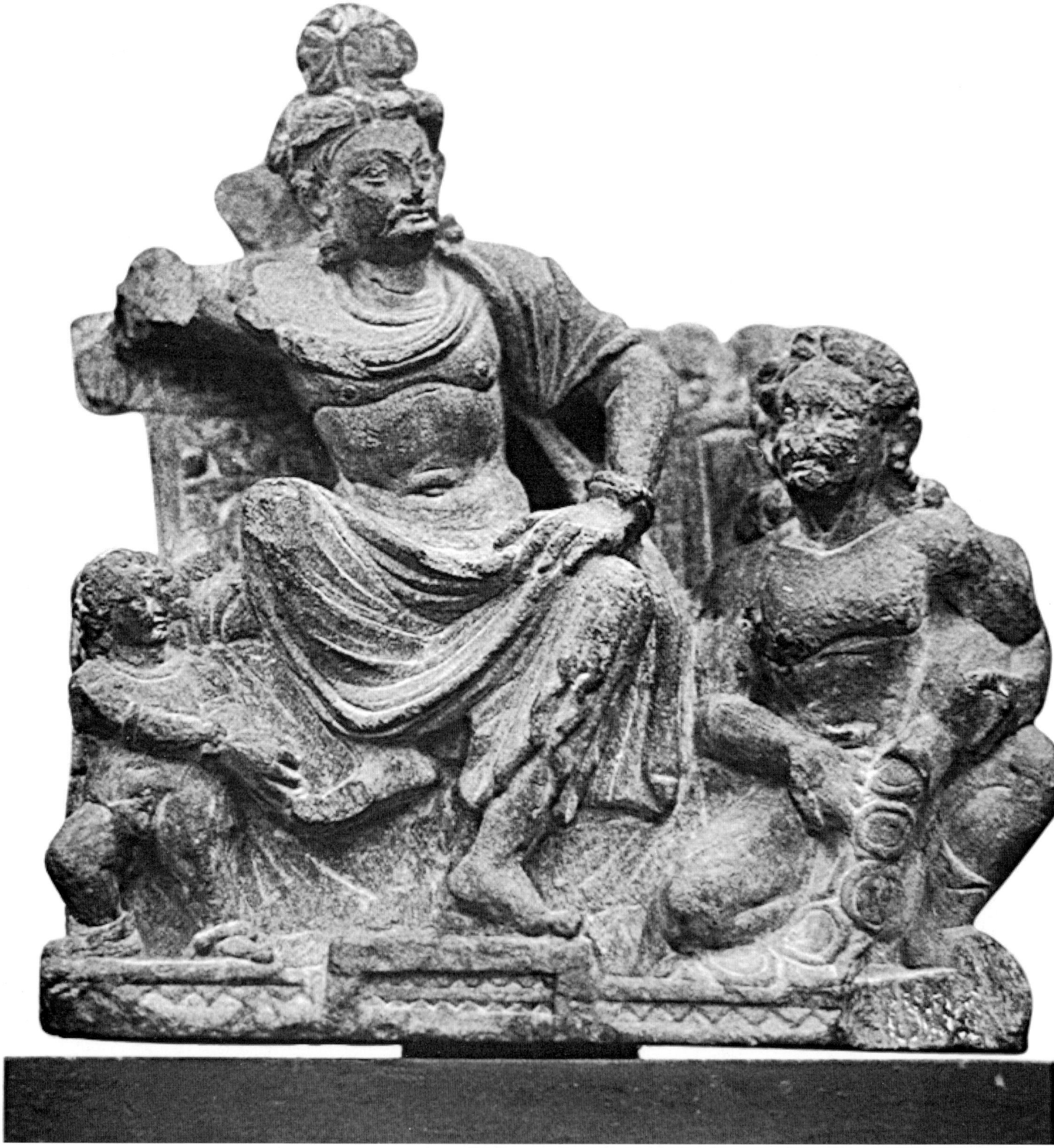

3.2.13 Kubera with associates, seated, second century CE, Gandhāra. GMAG 606.

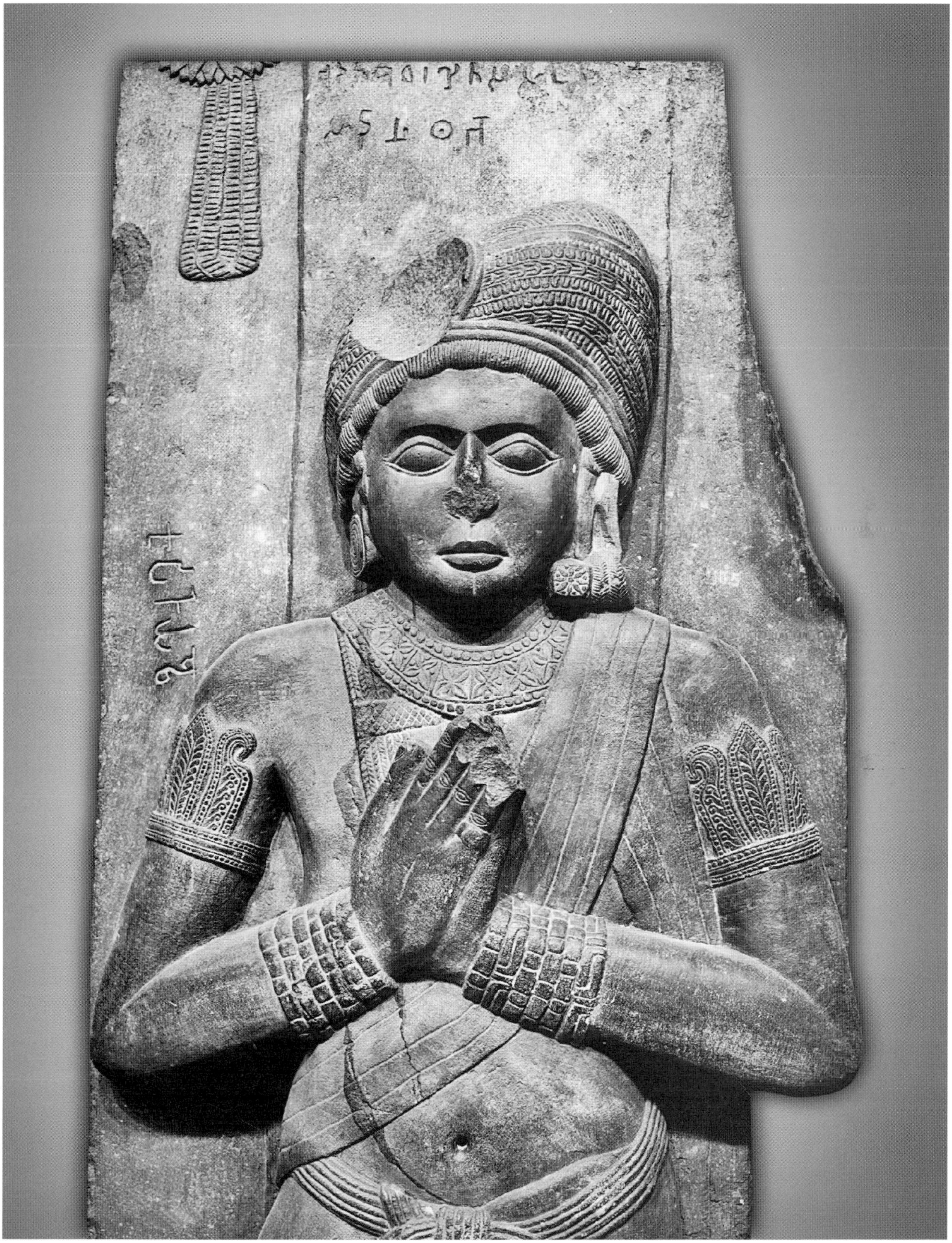

3.2.14 Kupiro *yakṣa*, north gate, corner, railing pillar, first century BCE, Bharhut. IM 105.

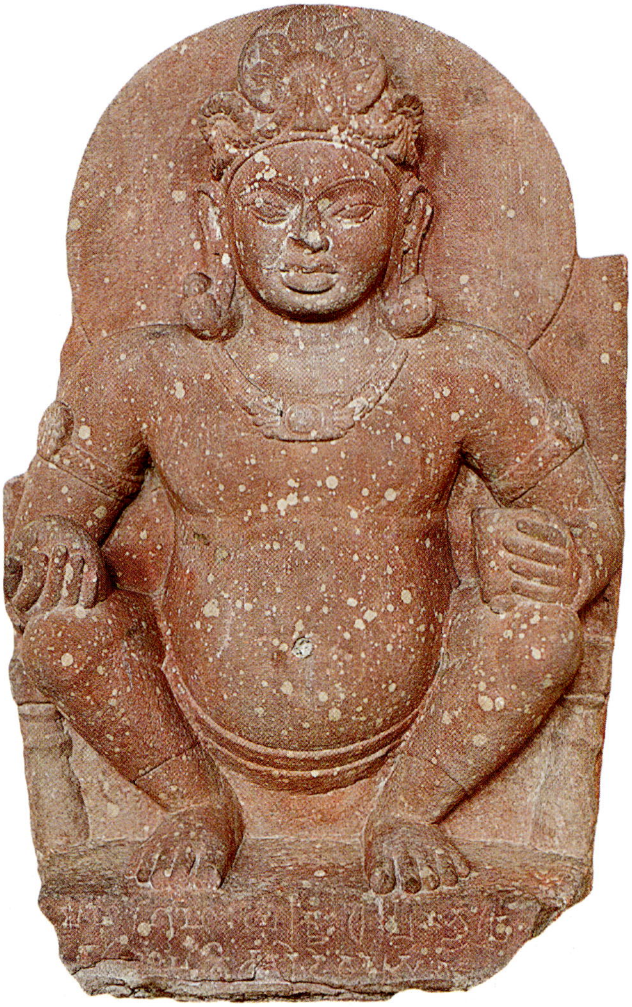

3.2.15 Kubera seated, inscribed, Mathurā sandstone, third century CE, Kaṅkālī Ṭīlā, Mathurā district, UP. GMM No. 46.3232. 351.92.

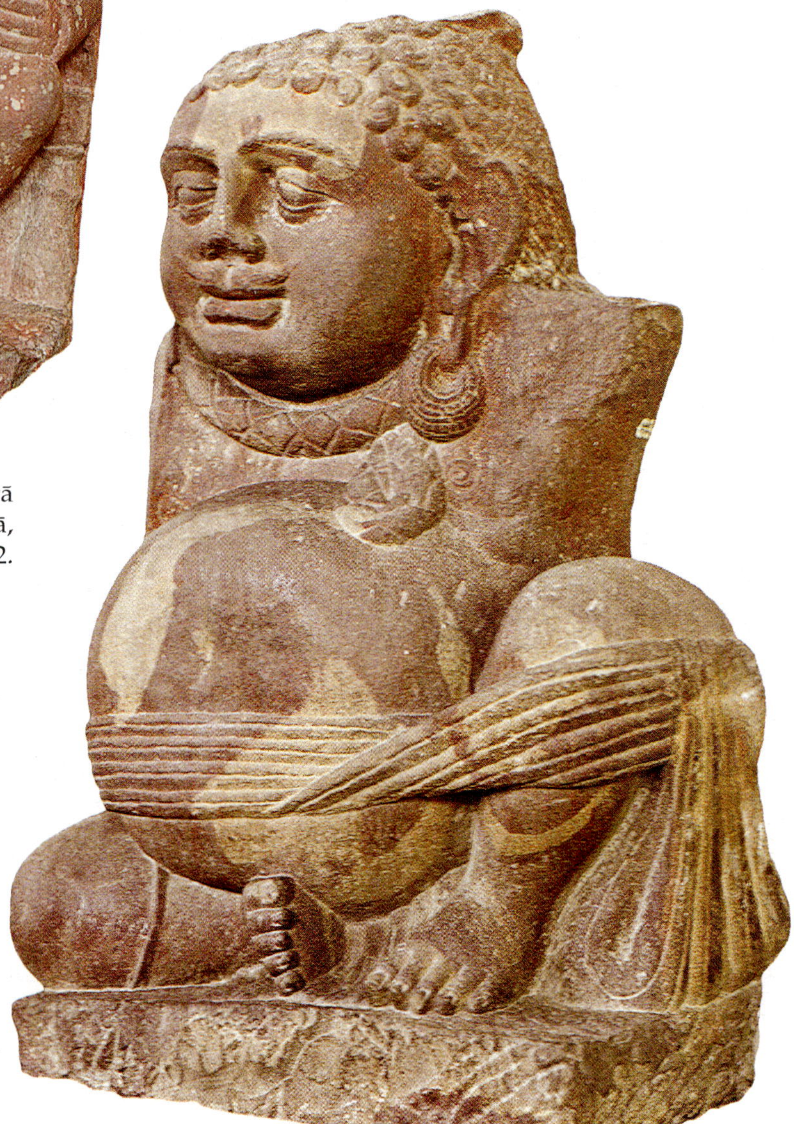

3.2.16 Kubera, red sandstone, second century CE, Mathurā, GMM.

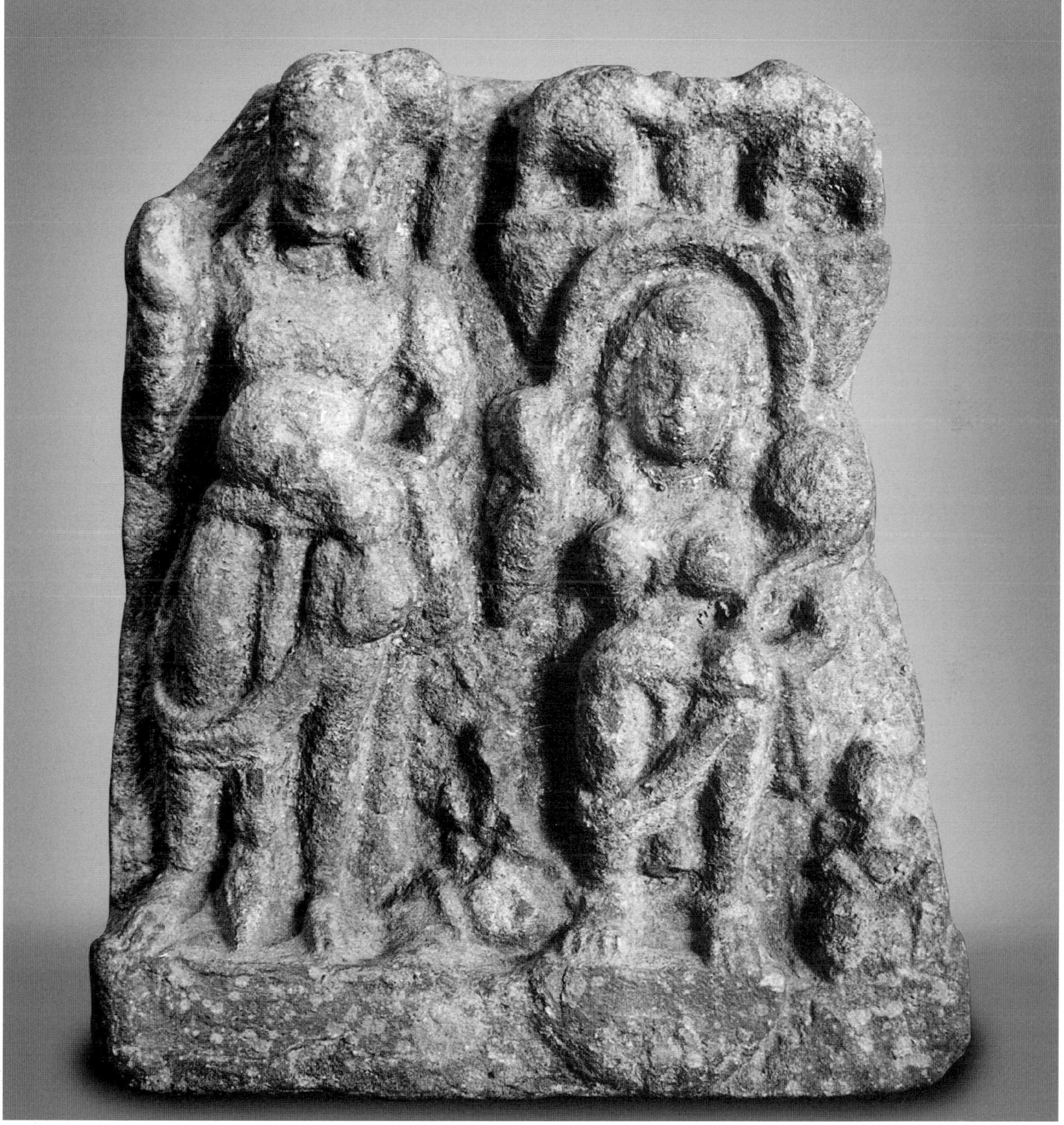

3.2.17 Kubera and Gaja-Lakṣmī, standing, pink sandstone, third century CE, Mathurā district, UP. GMM No. 44.3145.

granting wealth and children. She was usually depicted as holding one child in her arms and with three or five children around her knees.[113] This is confirmed by the account of Hiuen Tsang, who writes that the common people of Puṣkalavatī, modern Peshawar, offered sacrifices to the goddess in order to obtain children.[114]

Her marriage with Pañcika, the *yakṣa* Protector of Gandhāra, is mentioned in *Saṁyuktavastu*.[115] Here she is referred to as Abhiratī, the sister of *yakṣa* Śatagiri. In order to cure her of her child-eating propensities Śatagiri marries her to Pañcika with whom she has 500 children. Thus, she becomes *bahuputrikā* (mother of many sons).

The legend regarding her child-eating also explains the name Hāritī, which means stealer or someone who takes away, deriving from *hāra*,[116] meaning to steal. Her other names such as Huanśī and Abhiratī, on the contrary, imply her more benevolent character as the bringer of joy and happiness.

Hāritī appears first in the Buddhist pantheon as an independent deity, who is gradually spousified as the wife of Pañcika, a form of Vaiśrāvaṇa or Kubera *yakṣa*, by the first century of

3.2.18 Hāritī Temple, third century CE, Ikṣvāku. Nāgārjunakoṇḍa (After ERS).

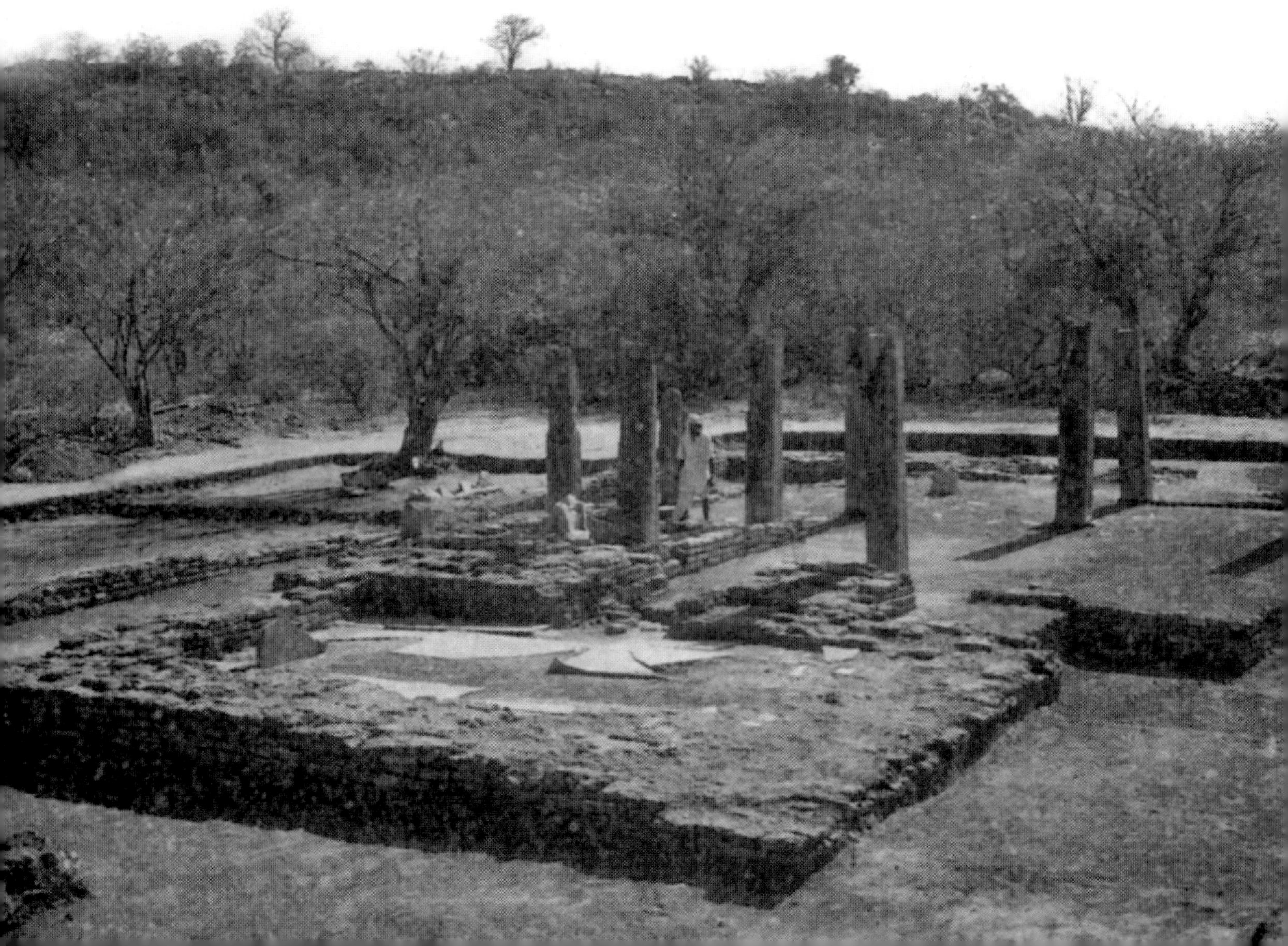

the Christian Era. In their manifestation as tutelary deities the couple, Bahuputrikā Hāritī and Pañcika, was probably preceded by the pair Maṇibhadra and Bahuputrikā, two figures who enjoyed some cult prominence and worship.[117] This transformation and absorption of folk cults centring on *yakkhinī*s and *rākkhasī*s such as Hāritī occurred over a period of time as the mythology of demonic folk gods and goddesses was brought into the ambit of mainstream religions.[118] These ancient cults of *yakṣī*s form the basis of the cult of Hāritī and the worship of a very similar Jaina goddess, Ambikā, given that the iconic forms as well as the origin myths are linked to the *yakṣa/yakṣī* complex. The other major influence on the development of the concept and iconography has been Mātr̥kā worship, in terms of their association with both children and motherhood.

### 3.2.3 MOTHER PAR EXCELLENCE

Hāritī is obviously a fertility figure associated with the generation of children, but also with their destruction. She is the mother of 500 demon-like sons who are thought in some versions to be bearers of pestilence and responsible for the death of children.[119] As a malevolent goddess she is akin to the *bālagraha*s described in the medical treatises and may be compared with goddesses like Jātahāriṇī[120] and Ṣaṣṭhī discussed later in this chapter.

In both the Type A and Type B depictions, Hāritī is shown with children around her. This iconographic element coalesces with her identity as a mother *par excellence*. She is also known as *kumāradhārī* (or carrier of children), which confirms her position as a mother.

Hāritī figures, like other mothering figures, are clothed, especially from the waist down (in a *dhotī*), perhaps as a mark of respect and divinity. When standing, the posture is *samabhaṅga* and the positioning straight and both seated and standing figures are solid and looking straight. Type A depictions emphasise the goddess's solid statuesque structure, standing with her legs slightly apart, balancing her many children around her. Type B compositions reflect a more intimate family setting with the couple and one or more infants around them. It may however be noted that it is Hāritī who is depicted as holding the child or who has the frolicking child on her lap; the male partner, it seems, does not shoulder any child-nurturing functions. This seems to mirror the familial structuring within a patriarchal household, which is further reinforced by the *dampati* (married couple) positioning with the female deity on the left of the male, with few exceptions.

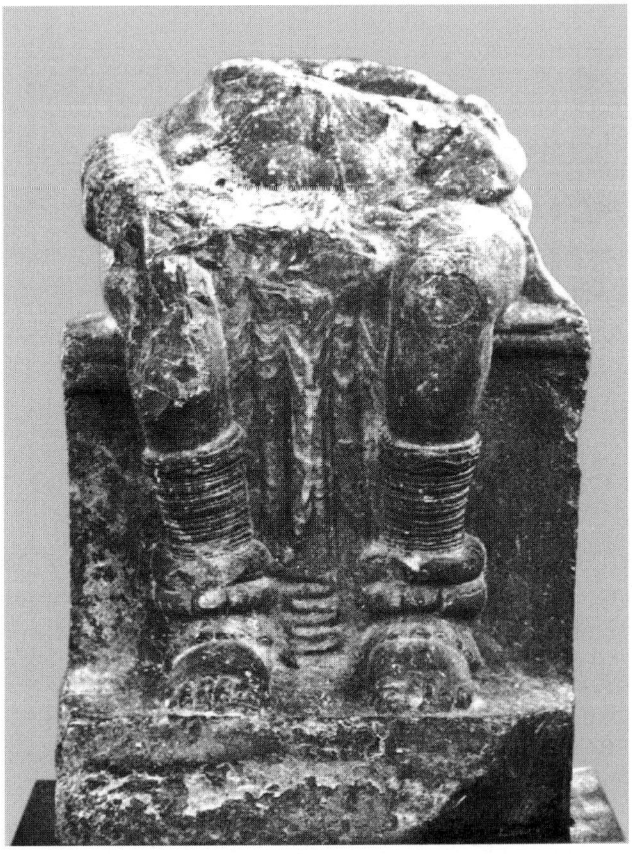

3.2.19 Hāritī seated, Hāritī Temple, third century CE, Ikṣvāku, Nāgārjunakoṇḍa. (After ERS)

Hāritī is located within the twin discourses of motherhood and prosperity; she is perceived as a mother and as a child-protector figure. Thus, iconographically, she is invariably shown with children on her lap or in her vicinity. There is a strong element of fecundity in the construction of Hāritī, clear in its linkage with Kubera, the deity of wealth. Hāritī, especially, exhibits the ambivalent nature of *yakṣa/yakṣī*s as benevolent and malevolent deities, as derived from their non-Vedic roots.

The very brief introduction to Hāritī given above makes it clear that she is an important Buddhist deity with an independent cult of her own. The beginnings of her worship lie in her origins as a *yakṣī* who is feared and appeased for her cannibalistic character. Later she is associated with fecundity and as such becomes linked to Kubera-Pañcika-Jambhala and together they become harbingers of abundance and embodiments of charity. The epithets *bahuputrikā* and *kumāradhārī* emphasise her maternal aspects and place her within the discourse of fertility. The third aspect is her transformation into a benevolent goddess who assumes the character of child-protector. She is also linked with *bālagraha* deities mentioned in medical texts of the post-Mauryan period. However, as the Skarah Dehri inscription indicates, the malevolent character is not entirely suppressed, as she continues to be worshipped as the deity of disease.

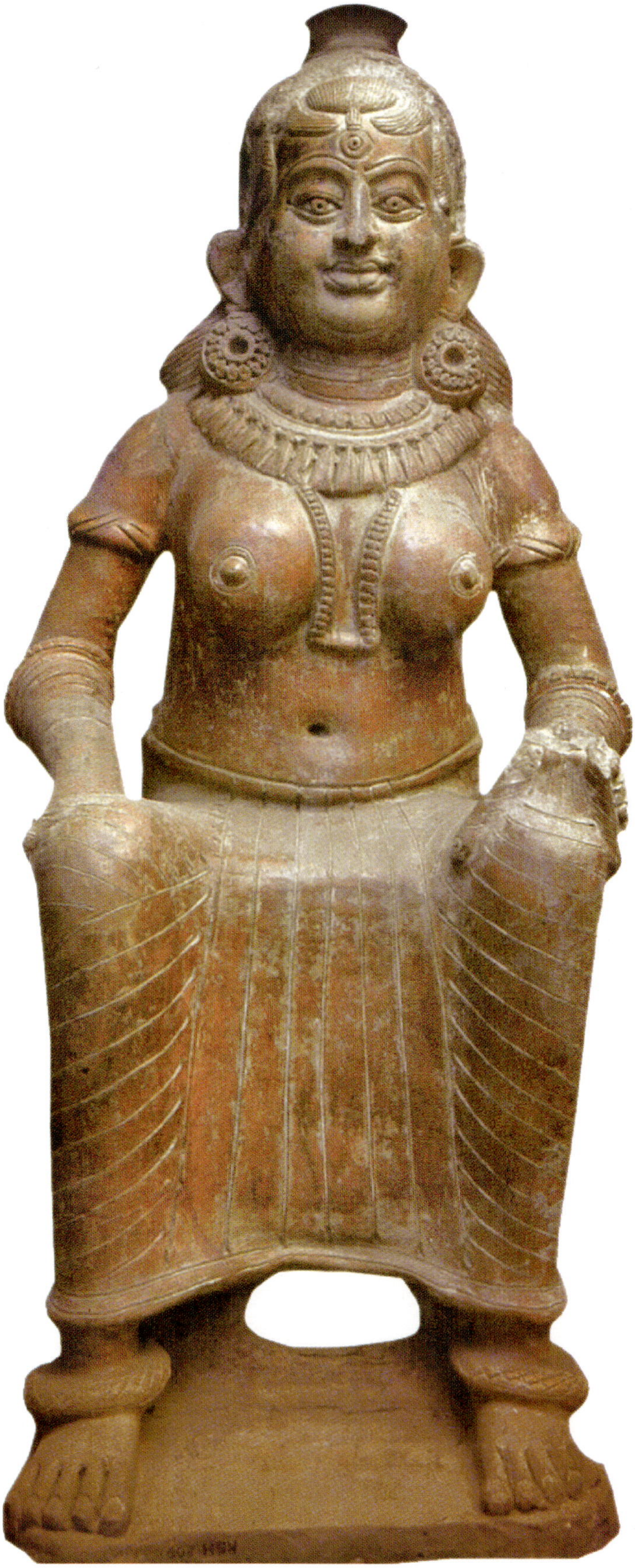

3.2.20 Hāritī seated, terracotta, Kauśāmbī, UP.

### 3.3 Mātṛkās

The Mātṛkās, as a set of mothers, were another important image type, especially at Mathurā. However, I will not be discussing these in detail since they have received adequate scholarly attention.[121] I would like to point out that the Mātṛkās, as a group, are remarkable in that they represent a complex of mother-goddesses depicted individually and as a collective.

They represent a group of generic mothers who embody mothering functions in their conceptualisation and imagery. The iconography of the Mātṛkās is not developed and included in a canonical system during the post-Mauryan period. Thus they are not identifiable with the later Gupta tradition of the Saptamātṛkās or Aṣṭamātṛkās found in the Hindu-Pauraṇic pantheon of deities, as has been pointed out by Shivaji Panikkar.[122] They seem to have an independent cultic status that was also associated with male gods such as Kubera, Kārttikeya and Balarāma-Saṁkarṣaṇa, but these goddesses are not their *śakti*s or female versions of them.

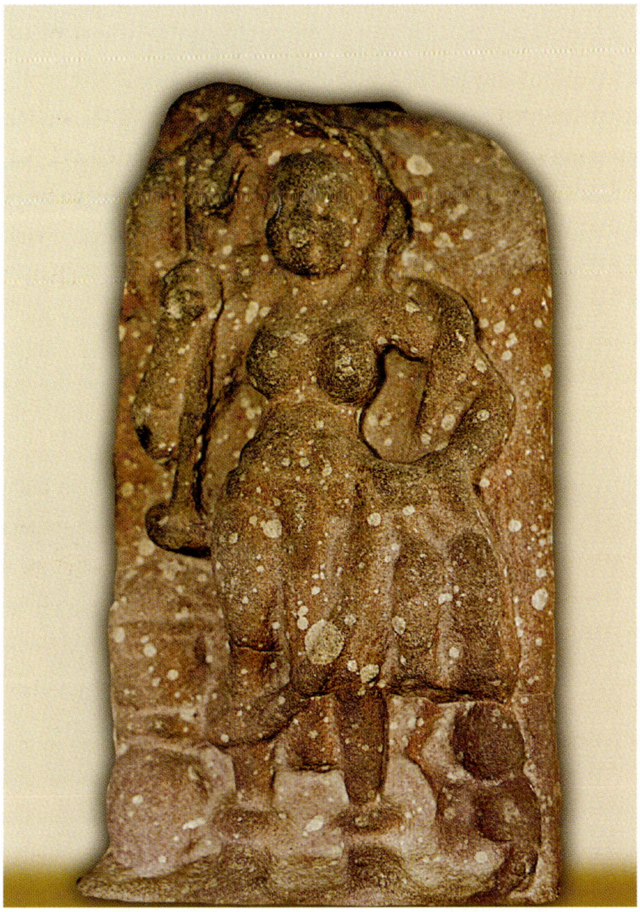

3.3.1 Devī Vasudharā, standing, holding lotus parasol with her emblems: two vases and three fish, first century CE, Mathurā sandstone, Yamunā River bed, Mathurā district, UP. GMM No. 27.28.1695.

There are a large number of Mātṛkā images which would suggest that it was a significant image type. Of the 104 images, almost all of them from the Mathurā school and post-Mauryan layers; only 2 are of bronze, the rest being of stone. From this corpus of evidence N.P. Joshi has identified many types of Mātṛkās.[123] These types includes:

1. Mātṛkās with a human face, seated with a cradled child (*Pl.* 3.5.15).
2. Mātṛkās with faces of birds, animals or human beings seated in a line with cradled children (*Pl.* 3.3.6).
3. Mātṛkās seated with cradled children but further associated with one or more *yakṣa*s.
4. Mātṛkās, one or more, sitting and carrying a grown-up child (*Pl.* 3.3.4).
5. Mātṛkās with a lizard (*godhā*) in hand.
6. Mātṛkās sitting without children.
7. Mātṛkās seated by the side of Kubera (*Pl.* 3.3.5).
8. Mātṛkās in association with Skanda-Kārttikeya.
9. Mātṛkās with wings (*Pl.* 3.3.3).
10. Mātṛkās without children, standing in line.
11. Female divinity, perhaps a Mātṛkā, standing alone. (*Pls.* 3.3.1, 3.3.2).
12. Unidentified Mātṛkā, perhaps of malicious

nature, Ṣaṣṭhī or Jātahāriṇī Ṣaṣṭhī, the chief Mātṛkā associated with children.

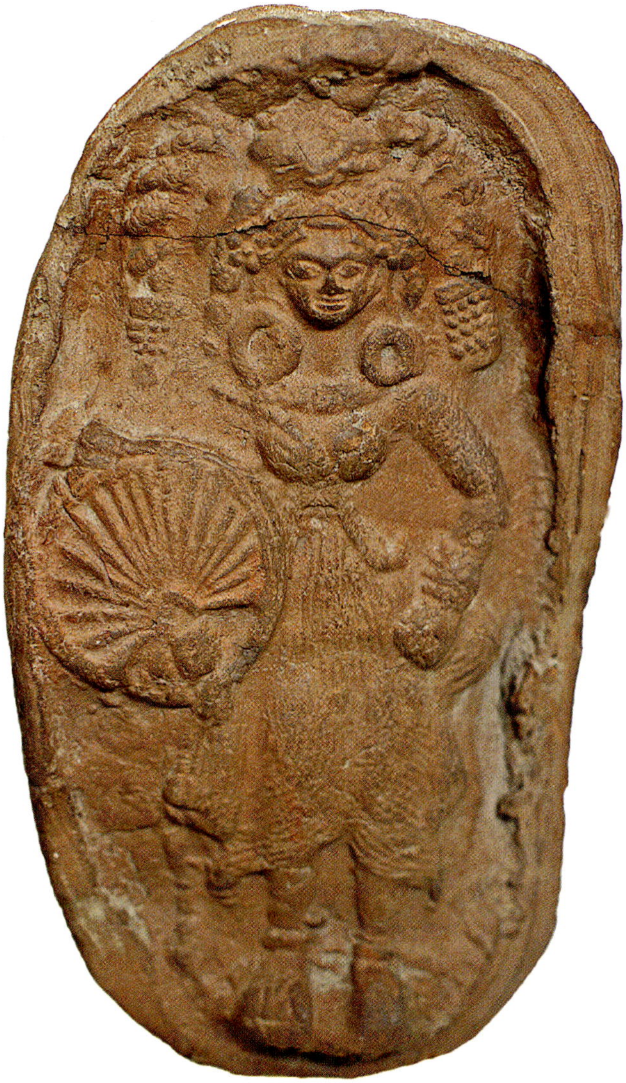

3.3.2 Goddess with palm-leaf, pañcacūḍā (?), terracotta, first century BCE, Mathurā, GMM.

It is clear from the above classification that the representational type termed Mātṛkā is not exclusively used to denote female figures with children. Iconographically, however, the most significant sculptures associate human, animal and bird-headed females with children, either cradled in their laps or in other mothering postures such as suckling a baby (GMM. No. 2331) or playing with an infant (GMM. No. F.31). Though some mothering activities, such as holding a child on the hip or playing with a baby, are also associated with the *yakṣī* figures carved on the *vedikā* pillars, these cannot be considered divine Mātṛkā figures. The latter are non-sensualised and non-provocatively delineated in comparison to the female figures associated with children in the *yakṣī* series. The Mātṛkās also are shown in *abhaya-hasta*, suggesting protection and care on the one hand and a divine status (on

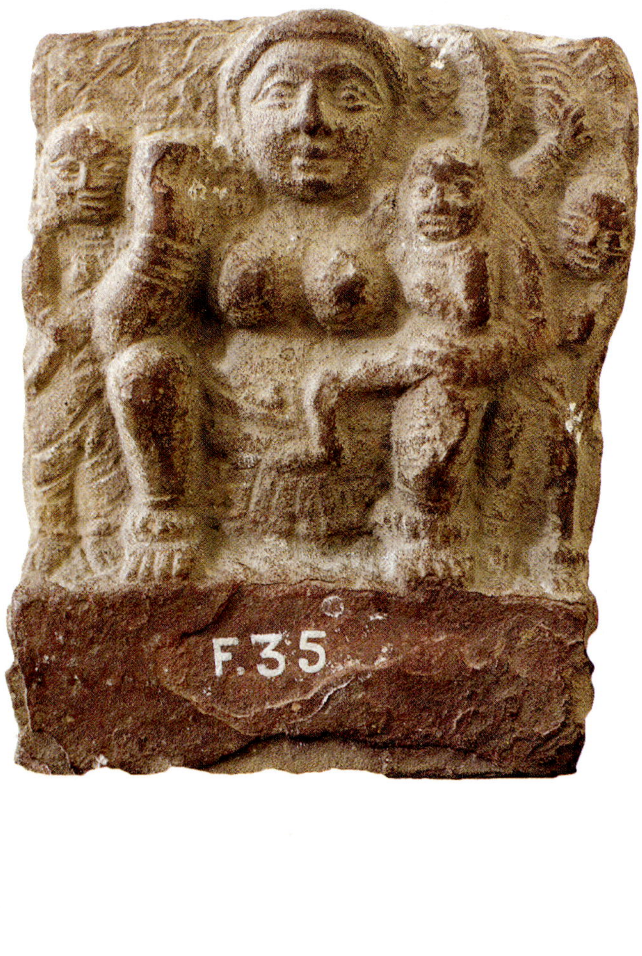


3.3.3 Mātṛkā seated in *bhadrāsana, abhaya-hasta*, with child on lap, red sandstone, second century CE, Mathurā district, UP. GMM F.35.

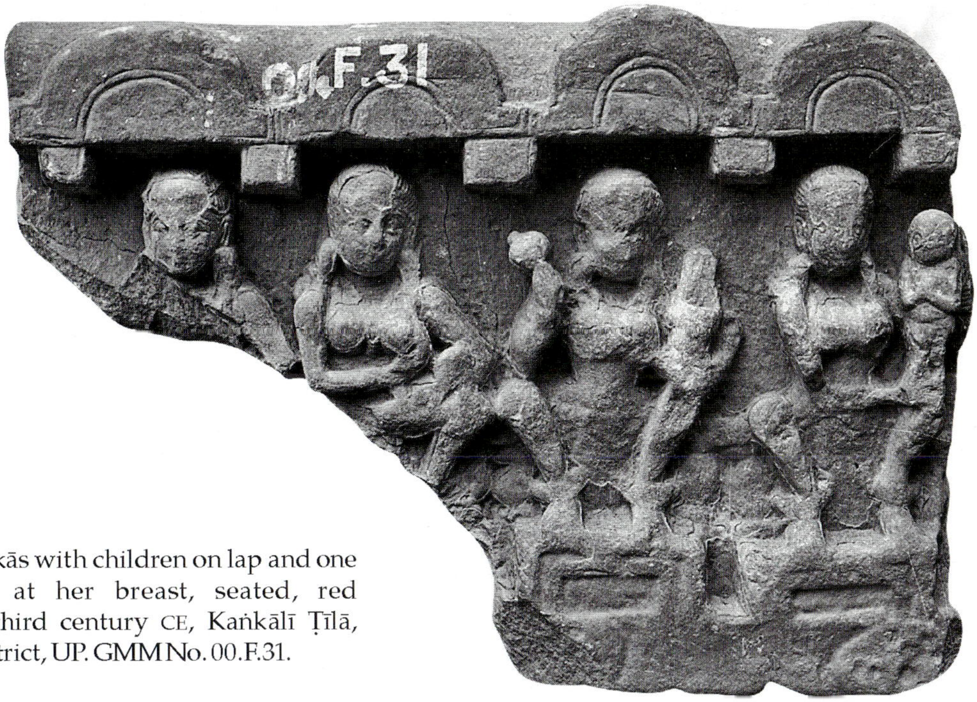


3.3.4 Four Mātṛkās with children on lap and one with child at her breast, seated, red sandstone, third century CE, Kaṅkālī Ṭīlā, Mathurā district, UP. GMM No. 00.F.31.

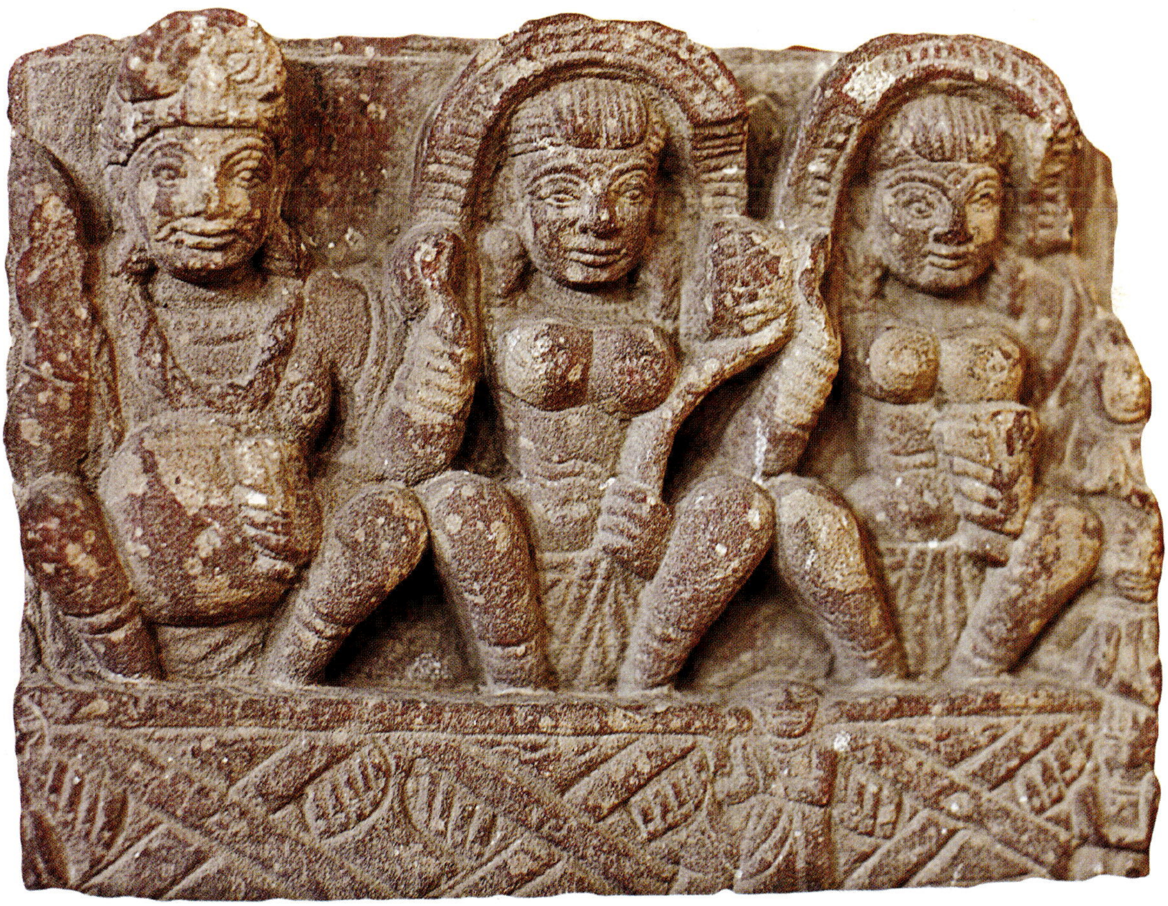

3.3.5 Kubera with Lakṣmī and Hāritī, seated, red sandstone, third century CE, Manoharpur, Mathurā district, UP. GMM No. C.30.

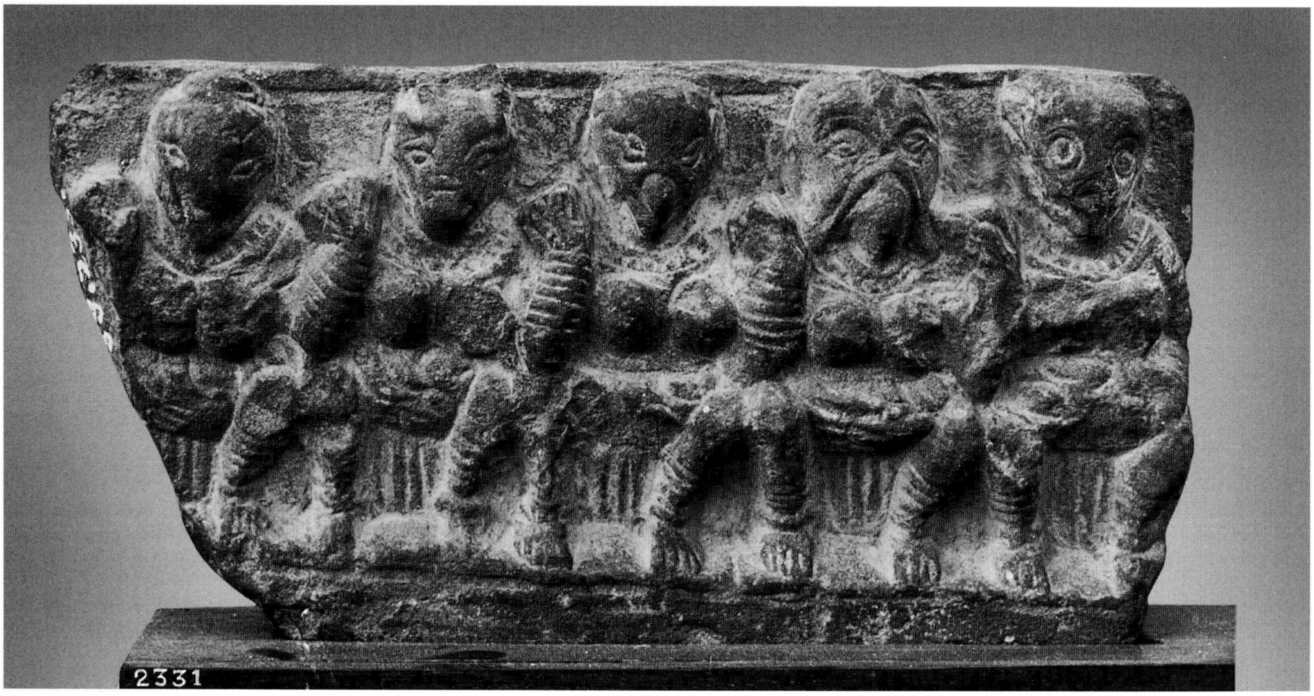

3.3.6 Mother goddesses with bird and animal faces, seated, red sandstone, third century CE, Mathurā district, UP. GMM No. 33.2331.

account of their ability to grant protection) on the other. They are often shown with attributes such as full pitchers, palm-leaf fan or lotuses or flames held in their hands.

The relatively small size of the Mātr̥kā panels suggests that these were votive objects used in rituals to ward off evil spirits in some cult practice related to children. This would relate well with the main function of protection of children associated with the Mātr̥kās in the medical texts, *Suśruta Saṁhitā* and *Kaśyapa Saṁhitā*, where they are classified as *bālagraha*s or diseases afflicting young children.

In the *Mahābhārata*, the Mātr̥kās are associated with the protection only of the young Skanda. This is due to the relationship of the Mātr̥kās with Skanda-Kārttikeya in mythology regarding his origin.[124] Broadly, the Mātr̥kās are linked to the six Kr̥ttikās who raised Kārttikeya as surrogate mothers, suckling him. The seven daughters of the fire god, *tapa*, asked and received the boon of being worshipped as benevolent and respected mothers of the entire world.[125] Skanda also granted the task of afflicting and protecting children to female *bālagraha*s. He is the natural son of Svāhā, to whom he grants the status of mother; but he is also considered the son of Śiva and Pārvatī. Thus, the two main characteristics of Skanda are son-ship and the ability to grant the status of a mother to a deity. Though iconographically not all Mātr̥kās are linked with Skanda Kārttikeya, his cult is closely related to the cult of the Mothers.

We will now discuss three specific types of Mātr̥kā: Ṣaṣṭhī, Naigameṣin/Naigameṣī and Jātahāriṇī.

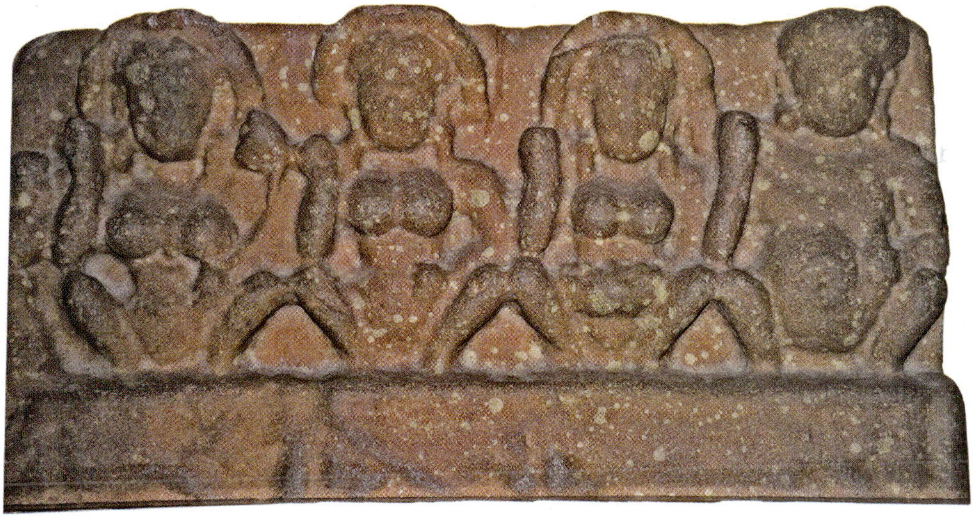

3.3.7 Kubera and Mātṛkās seated in row, hands raised in *abhaya-hasta*, second century CE, red spotted sandstone. SML.0.241.

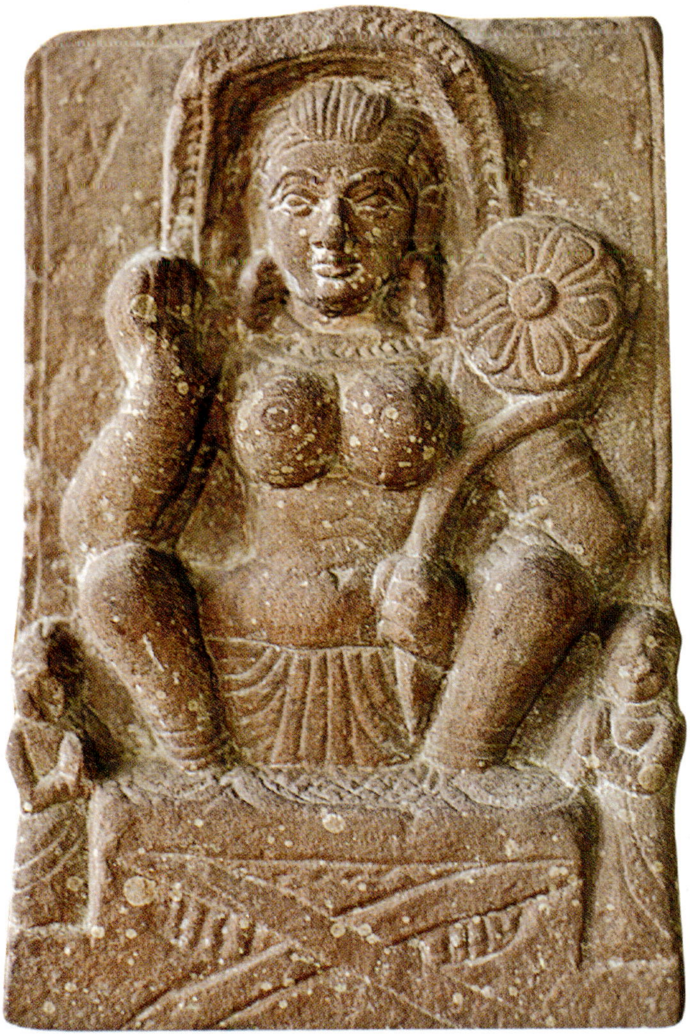

3.3.8 Lakṣmī, seated with lotuses in her hands, second century CE, red spotted sandstone, Mathurā.

### 3.4 Ṣaṣṭhī

The inclusion of Ṣaṣṭhī as a mothering figure may be considered problematic from a cursory study of the texts and images, given that she is neither described as a biological mother in the textual tradition nor associated with children in the visual tradition.

However, she is primarily associated with birth and protection of children and especially invoked on the sixth day after childbirth. Like many other feminine deities who perform the mothering role, her worship during the early period is limited to the area in and around Mathurā. Ṣaṣṭhī belongs to the complex of deities such as Naigameṣī, the Mātṛkās, and Jātahāriṇī who collectively comprise the *bālagraha*s, forces that pose a danger to children and are connected to Skanda, the principal *bālagraha*.

Ṣaṣṭhī is the goddess who is worshipped on the sixth day of the month, which is also her *mahātithi* (special day) this is recorded in medical texts as well the *Mahābhārata*, both of which

3.4.1 Ṣaṣṭhī, red sandstone, second century CE, Mathurā district, UP. GMM No. 00.F2.

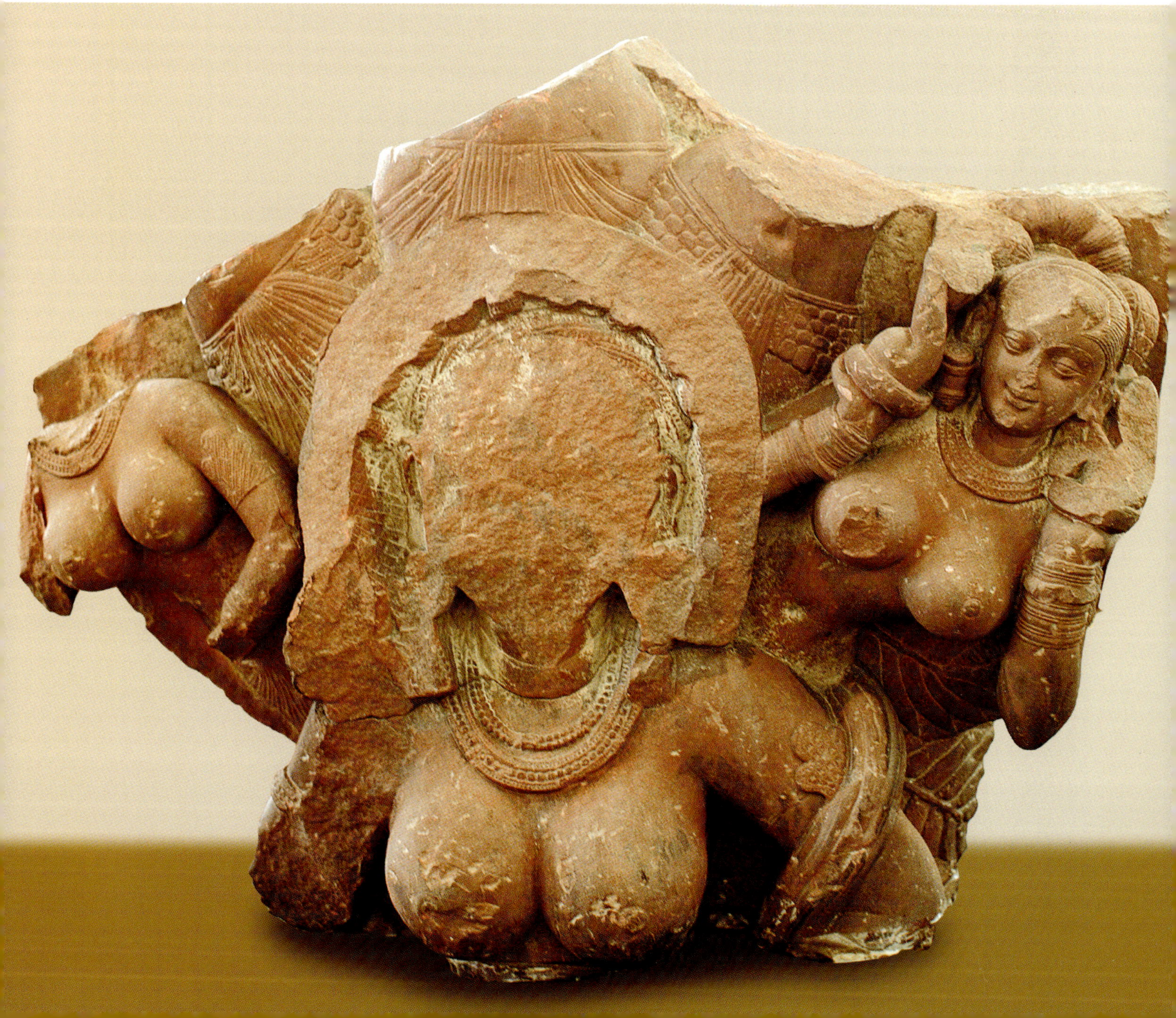

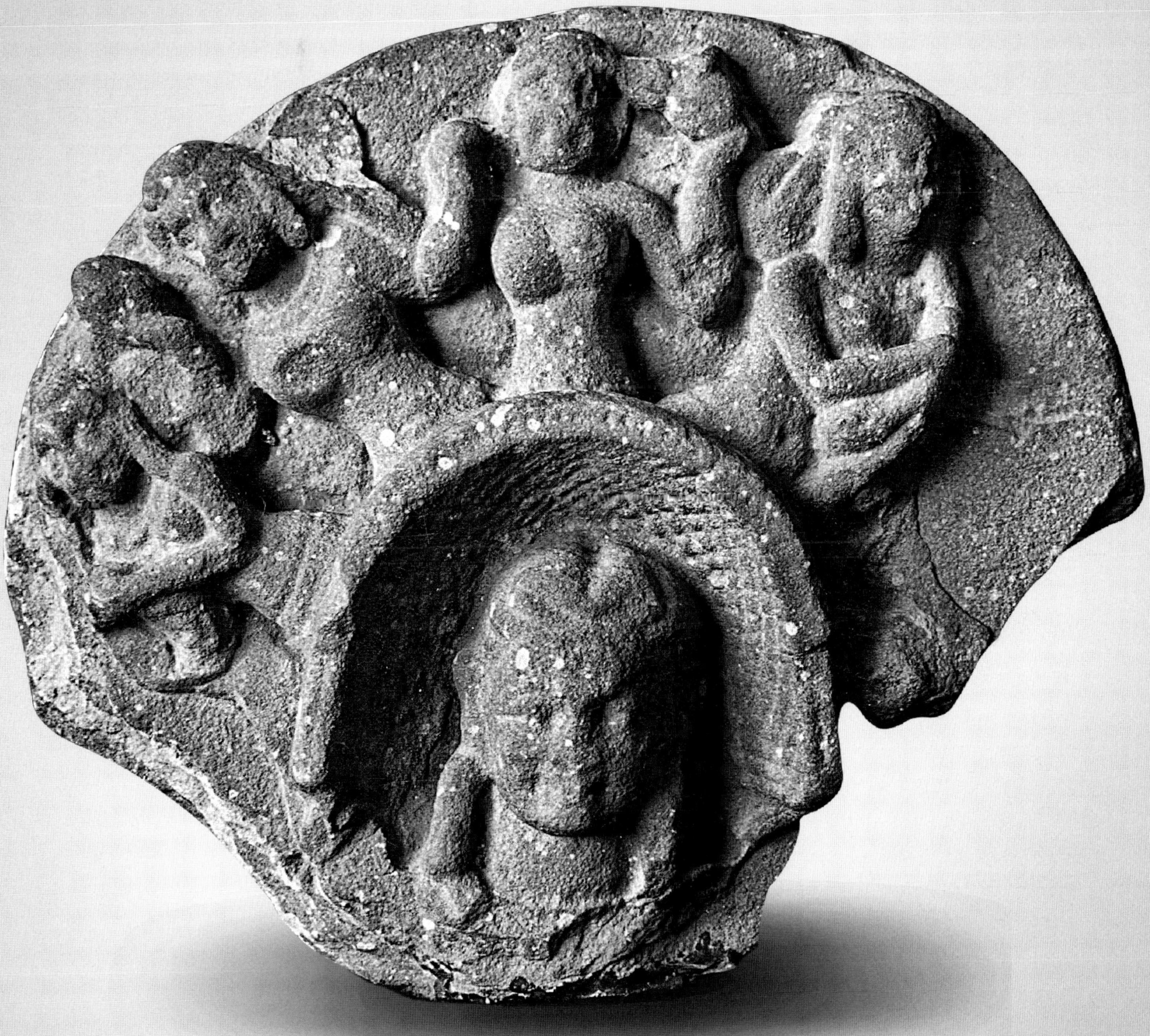

3.4.2 Ṣaṣṭhī, Mathurā sandstone, second century CE, Potra Kuṇḍ, Mathurā district, UP. GMM No. 54.3763.

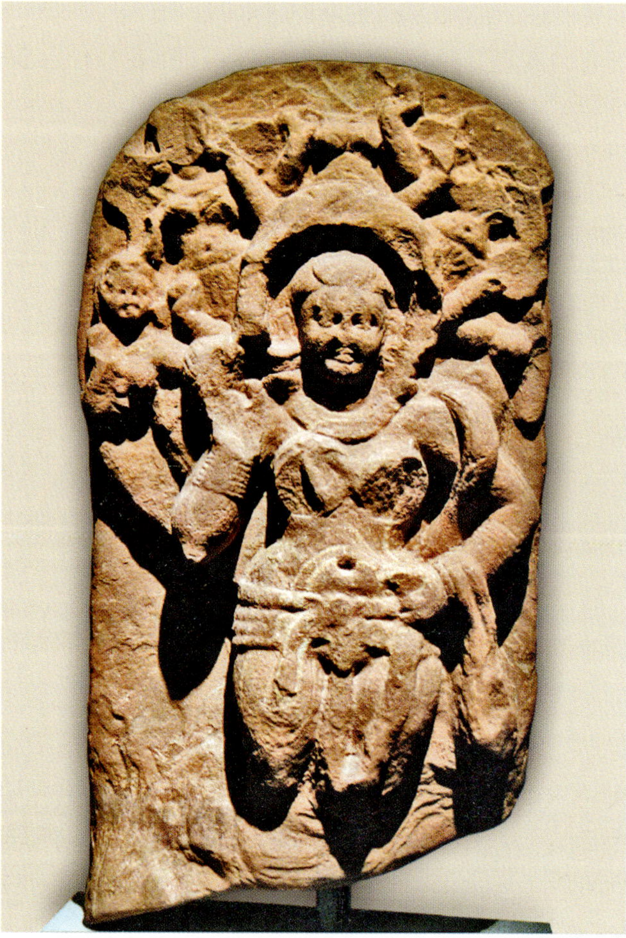

3.4.3 Ṣaṣṭhī, red sandstone, second century CE, Mathurā, Musuem für Indische Kunst, Berlin. MIK I 5924.

belong to the early historical period. She is worshipped on the *chaṭha* (the sixth day) śukla *pakṣa* of Kārttika month in Bihar and Uttar Pradesh. A festival of the same name is held on the sixth day after Dīwālī in which Ṣaṣṭhī is invoked. As Sūtaka[126] Ṣaṣṭhī she is the goddess who presides over the sixth day after child-birth. This takes many forms, for example in central Uttar Pradesh a mother is fed cereal on the sixth day after childbirth by the women of the household in a ceremony presided over by a male Brāhmaṇa. However, the male does not approach the new mother since she is considered to be impure.

Ṣaṣṭhī is an important goddess in eastern India whose extensive worship is not recorded in the canonical literature, perhaps because she is worshipped almost exclusively by women in domestic religious ceremonies rather than in public temples. In Bengal, Ṣaṣṭhī protects infants, and in villages her terracotta image or just a stone is set up under a tree, in most cases under a jackfruit tree as it has an abundant yield. In the ceremony that follows, an amulet made of *caurī* shell, resembling a vulva is tied around the wrist or the waist of the infant to ward off evil and to protect it from illness.[127]

### 3.4.1 SCULPTURAL EVIDENCE

In the present state of our knowledge, there are eleven sculptures that may be identified with Ṣaṣṭhī and which have been published; all of them are datable to the Kuṣāṇa period and are in Mathurā style.

These may be classified into two types:

#### *Type A*

This type has a standing female figure along with another five subsidiary, radiating figures. The main figure is located in the centre of the panel in a *samabhaṅga* (straight posture). Visible over her head is an arched "canopy-like" structure that rises from her shoulders and loops a little distance above her coiffure (*Pls.* 3.4.1 to 3.4.4).[128] She is always shown wearing an opaque *dhotī* tied with a thick cloth belt and/or a *mekhalā* at the waist. Her ornaments include armbands, bangles and necklaces. Usually an *uttarīya* comes over the shoulder and under her arm. Either this *uttarīya* or the end of a cloth tied around the waist is draped over her left wrist.

#### *Type B*

Within this configuration a six-headed goddess is found in conjunction with two male deities; sometimes, only one of the two male figures is depicted. These form a group of three figures, the central figure being female, bearing five female heads arranged above her canopy in a semi-circle (*Pls*. 3.4.5 to 3.4.7). She stands with her feet set slightly apart, wearing a thick *dhotī*, and other accoutrements of Type A figures. Her right hand is raised in *abhaya-hasta* and the left hand rests on the knot of the waistcloth. On both sides are two male figures, usually, though not always, shown with a *śakti* in one hand while holding up the other hand in *abhaya-hasta*.

The use of a canopy over divine feminine figures is a significant element in art of the period, as are the *abhaya-hasta* gesture and *śakti* attribute.

One of the most discussed examples of the Type A images now housed in the Mathura Museum (as Antiquity No. F.2) is much abraded.[129] This is a standing female figure, a large part of which is carved in the round. Of what remains, it can be said that the main figure was two-armed, with well-defined full rounded breasts. She wears a broad multi-stringed necklace hanging just below her neck and rounded earrings. She is shown also wearing *keyūra*, armbands and thick bracelets. One can make out an ornamental *uttarīya* falling over her left arm. Over her head she bears a canopy, behind which can be seen five radiating female figures from the waist upward. Two of these figures rise from behind her shoulders, two from

3.4.4 Ṣaṣṭhī, Mathurā sandstone, second century CE, Yamunā River bed, Mathurā district, UP. GMM No. 31.2101.

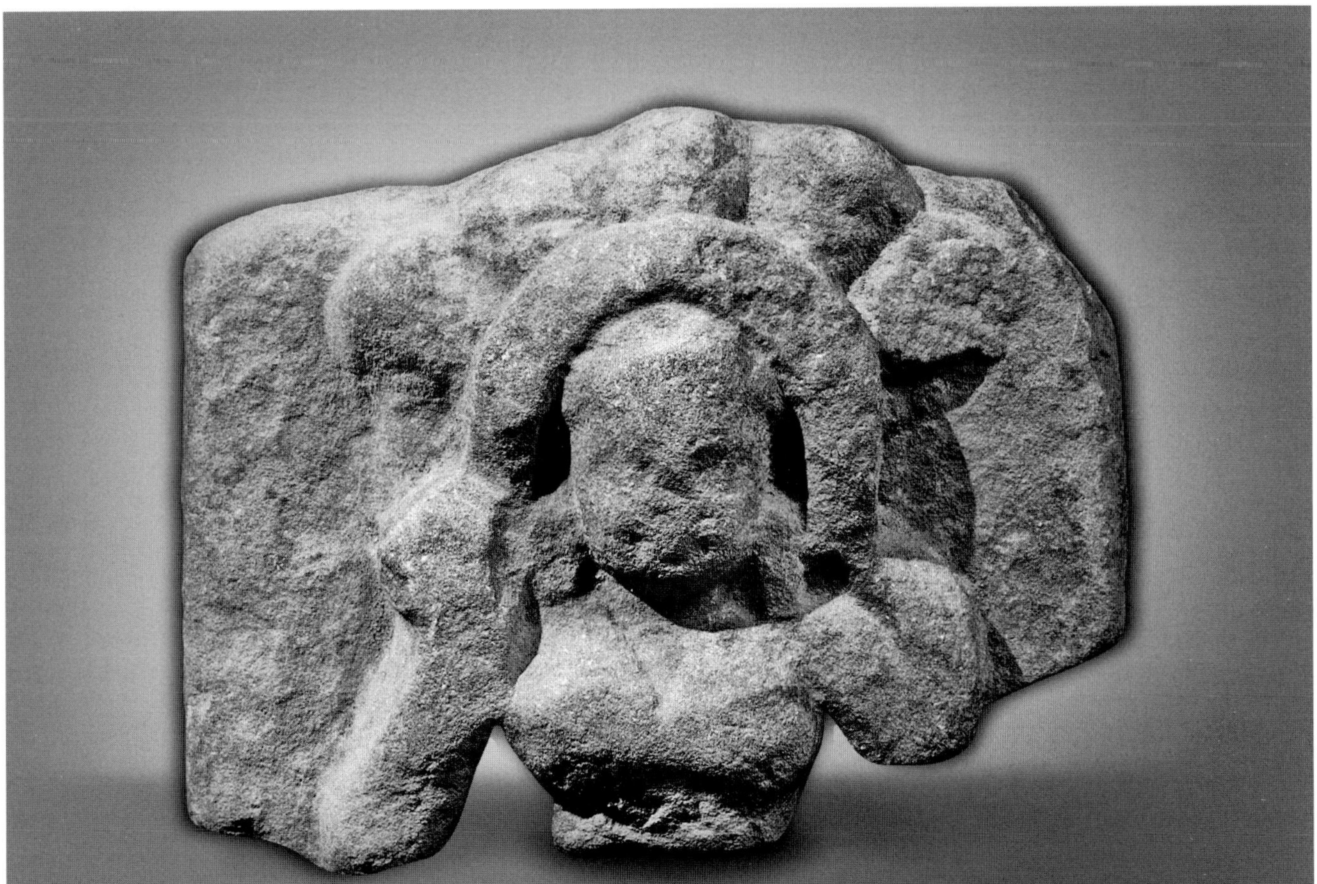

the side of the head, and one is above the head. Only the lower figure on the proper left has her head and the attributes held in her hands extant in all details. Apparently she carries bowls of flames or rather torches in her upraised arms.[130] The corresponding figure to the right, though badly mutilated now, probably did not carry torches. The other three subsidiary figures are so damaged to make a credible reading of the attributes in their hands difficult. The reverse shows an *aśoka* tree with branches emanating from its trunk and a squirrel climbing up its trunk. This sculptural piece seems to have been deliberately defaced so that its facial features are abraded and both hands of the deity are broken.

The next example of Type A is again in a fragmentary condition, revealing only the upper part of a multi-headed female figure (GMM No.54.373).[131] One can make out her face topped by a canopy from which emerge what must have been five auxiliary figures. These female figures have been crafted from the waist upwards, of which only four are now extant. Unlike the above-mentioned sculpture belonging to Type A, in this specimen the radiating figures do not rise upwards from behind the shoulder, rather they are arranged in a fan shape above the canopy (*Pl.* 3.4.2). The figure immediately above the main face is in full frontal view, while the one on the right is in three-quarter profile. Of the two subsidiary female figures on the left, one is almost in full frontal view, though the one to the extreme left is in profile as was probably her counterpart on the other side. The hands of these figures are all upraised though the objects they held are not distinct. Since the canopy is further away from the face, the cross-hatching pattern under it is evident. Another figure with similar elements, now much defaced, has also been found in Mathurā,[132] the difference being that it may have been circular in shape (*Pl.* 3.4.4).

A female figure of Type A, now preserved in the Berlin Museum, is in a relatively better state of preservation (*Pl.* 3.4.3). Carved in bold relief, this standing figure of the goddess survives from above the knees. She is clad in a *dhotī*, and holds her right hand in *abhaya-hasta* while her left hand is held akimbo. Around her one can see five female figures radiating forth, occupying the entire halo, underneath which relief ground is visible. The figures hold some object in their left hands, which is not distinct enough for credible reading.[133]

Among the Type B figures, one of the more complete depictions is now in the Mathura Museum (GMM. No. F.3).[134] Carved in relief on a squarish slab one can see the goddess standing in the middle, her right hand raised in *abhaya-hasta*, while the left hangs near her hip holding a vessel of some kind (*Pl.* 3.4.7). She is dressed in the usual *dhotī*, which is tied at the waist with a thick band of cloth that ends on the left side of the figure in a loop that droops from her elbow. The *uttarīya* wraps itself around the left arm. Above her face there is a canopy, and five radiating heads are visible here. On her right and left stand the male deities, both of whom hold a *śakti* in the left hand while the right is raised in the *abhaya-hasta* posture. They lean outwards towards the edge of the slab, thus making space for accommodating the five faces that rise above the central figure. A similar composition but smaller in size has been discovered from Girdharpur near Mathurā.[135] In this, only one male figure is now extant who is shown with his right hand in *abhaya-hasta*.

Another similar piece is of a canopied goddess standing between two male figures with five female heads emerging above the canopy, now in the Museum für Indische Kunst, Berlin.[136] In this depiction, the canopy starts from the edge of her shoulders and above this the five heads are

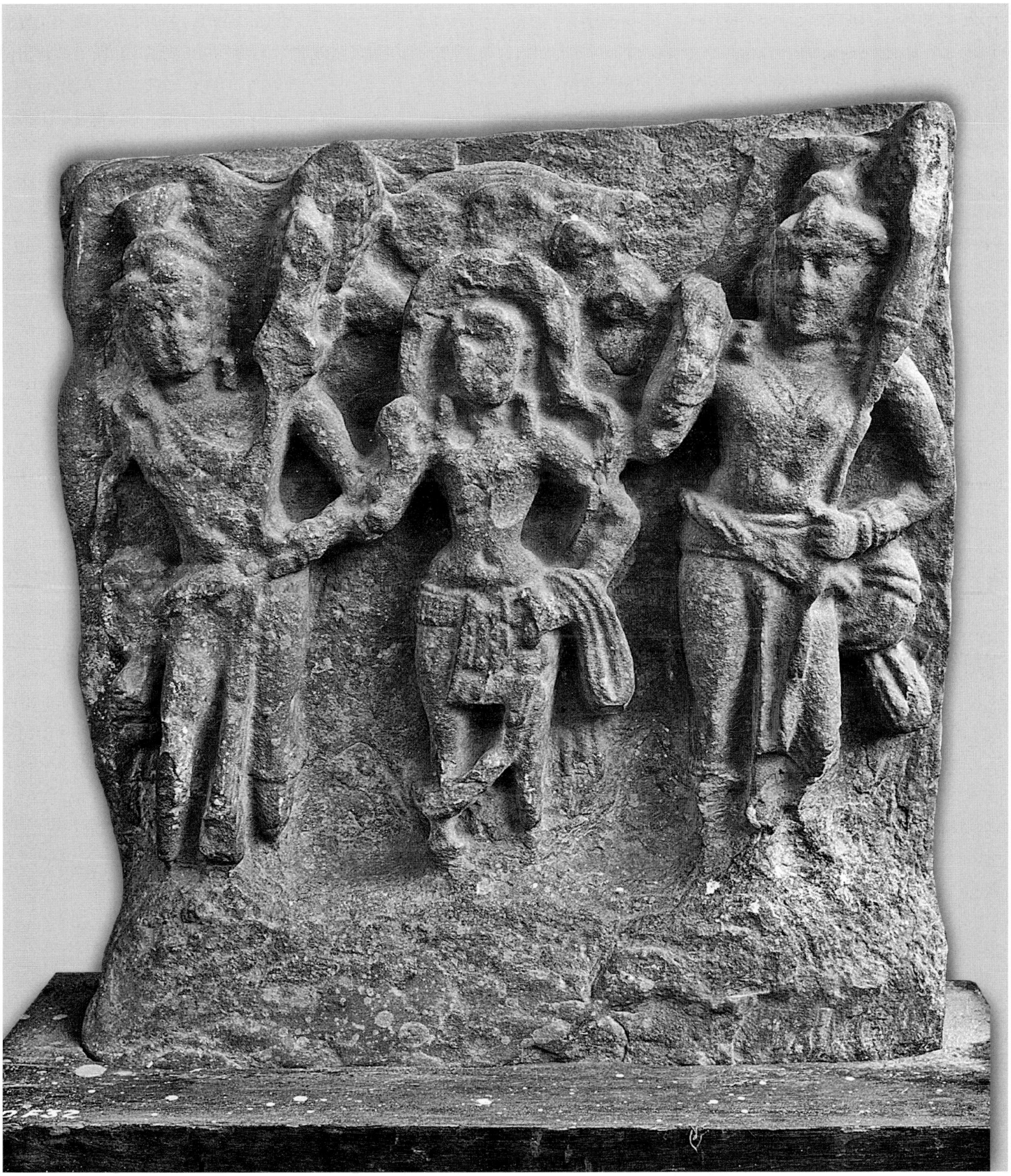

3.4.5 Ṣaṣṭhī with two male attendants, Mathurā sandstone, second century CE, Mathurā district, UP. GMM No. 00F.22.

arranged in a semi-circle. The coiffure of these busts is very well preserved in this piece, and links them with the *yakṣī* figures made in the Mathurā style. In a fragment from Mathurā,[137] we have another composition of the same lineage that shows Ṣaṣṭhī on the left of a male figure who is shown holding a *śakti* in his right hands while his left hand rests on his waist. The presumably central figure is that of the goddess and a male figure stands to her left. In the present state, the female figure can be seen from the waist upwards. Above her face a portion of the canopy is visible, atop which rest two female heads; the one to our left seems to be resting on the shoulder of the male figure (*Pl.* 3.4.6). A small fragment[138] shows the upper part of a male deity, perhaps Skanda with his *śakti* in his right hand. Ṣaṣṭhī has a canopy over her head but only one of the five heads survives.

In another example of Type B, now in the Mathura Museum, one can see a goddess with five subsidiary heads and flanked by two male companions standing on a low platform-like pedestal (*Pl.* 3.4.5).[139] The right hand of all three figures is raised in *abhaya-hasta*. All of them are seen standing in a balanced posture with feet slightly apart, as in GMM F.3. The central female figure wears a *dhotī* with pleats in the centre, while a looped end of either the *dhotī* or her *uttarīya* falls in loop over her left wrist. She is shown wearing thick *nūpuras* (anklets).

An important variation in the Type B figures is a relief of a female goddess bearing miniature heads over the canopy. Of the original five, only three of the subsidiary heads are now distinct.[140] Though she stands between two male figures as in the other sculptures, the important point of difference here is that the male deities are shown shorter than the main female figure in the centre.

Also of Type B is a female figure[141] that stands perfectly balanced like her male companions with her feet slightly apart. The *uttarīya* curves from behind the shoulders to emerge from behind her right leg to fall over her *dhotī*, perhaps ending in a loop that she holds over her left wrist. Her right hand is raised, probably in *abhaya-hasta*. She is shown wearing thick *nūpuras*. It seems that there was a large halo behind her, on which were carved five heads in low relief. The two male deities carried long sticks in their left hands and raised the right hands in *abhaya*. The pedestal of this piece has two vertical lines between which are horizontal wavy lines.

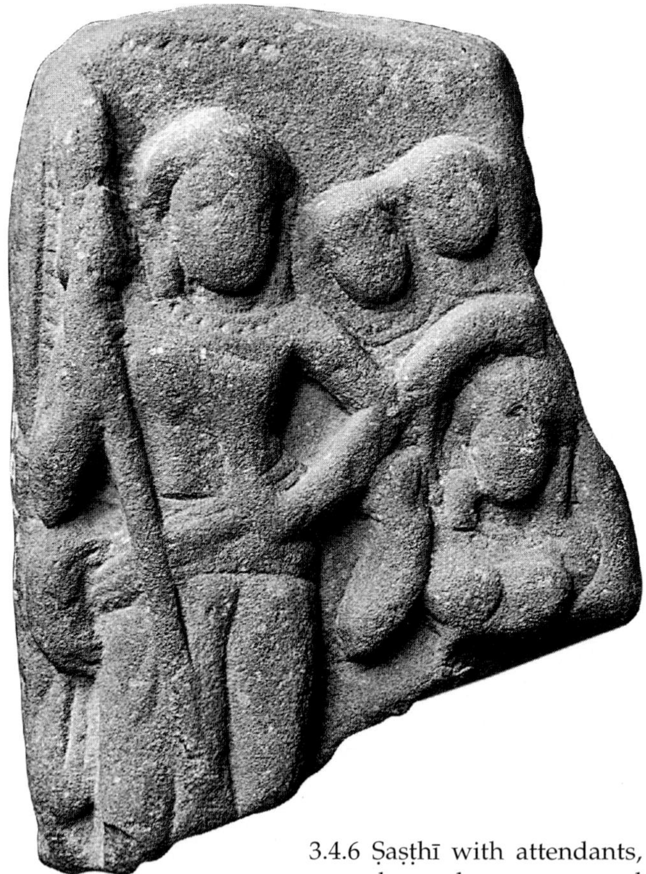

3.4.6 Ṣaṣṭhī with attendants, red sandstone, second century CE, Mathurā district, UP.

3.4.7 Ṣaṣṭhī with two attendants, red sandstone, second century CE, Mathurā district, UP. GMM No. 00F.3. (facing page)

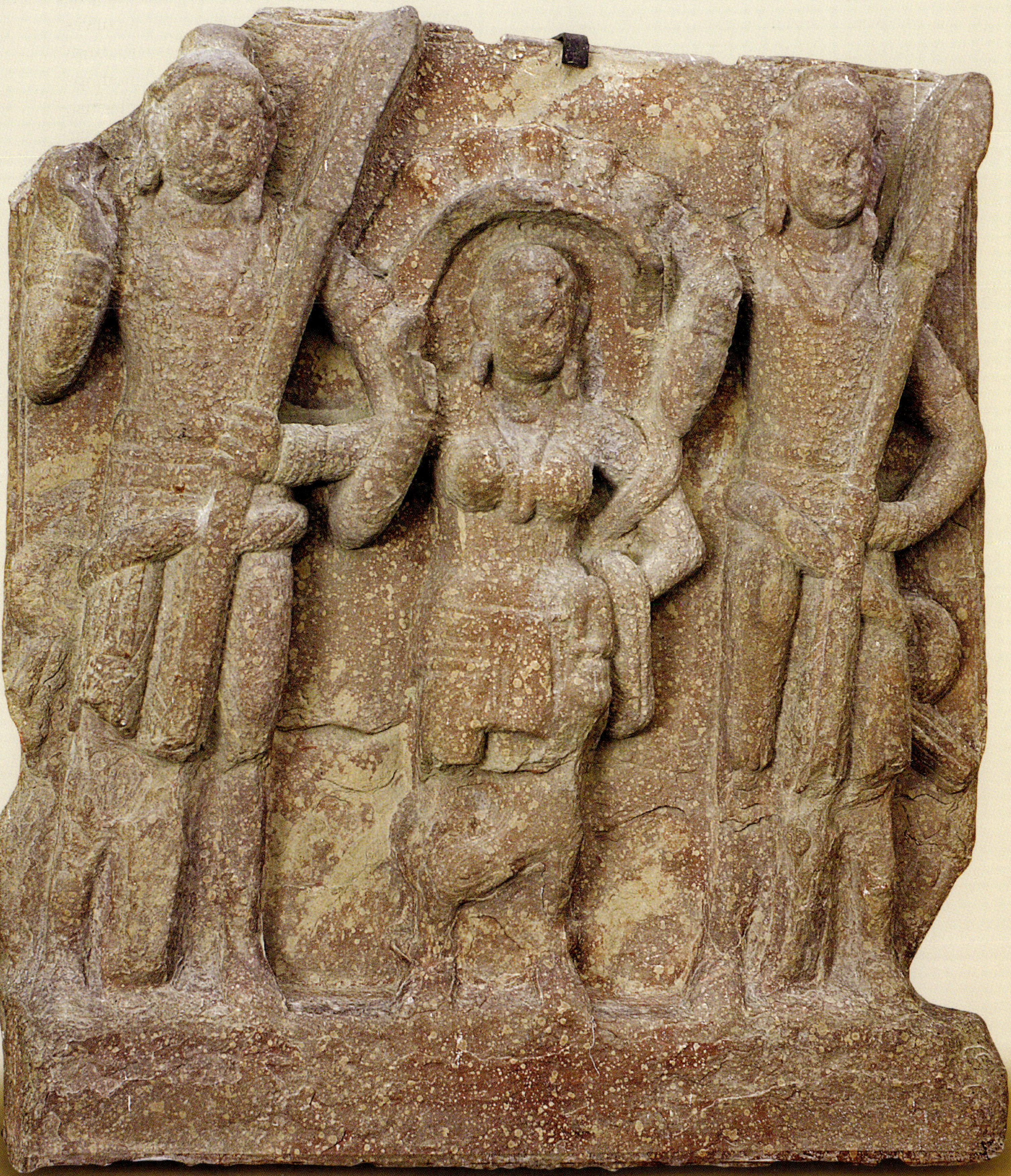

Yet another variation of Type B is a bas-relief also from Mathurā region, now in the State Museum, Lucknow (SML J.84).[142] In this important specimen, the female figure is shown without a canopy over her head. Instead, two (of which only one to the right survives in its entirety) of the originally five female figures can be seen rising from behind the shoulder and side of the head. The radiating figures are shown from the bust upwards though they are rather miniaturised in comparison to the ones in the Type A series; the one that is extant being smaller in size than the head of the principal figure. The principal figure is clad in a *dhotī* with a small fan-like pleated end hanging in the centre from the waist, rather like the costume worn by *mohiniāṭṭam* dancers today. The *uttarīya* passes from above her left arm, over the back of her shoulders to emerge in front of the knees, to end at the waist where it forms a loop held in the left hand of the deity. The position of or the attributes held in her right hand have been obliterated, but presumably the hand was in *abhaya-hasta*. The figure is ornamented with a number of bracelets and bangles clearly visible on her left arm, an armband, thick cylindrical earrings, a torque-like necklace and a long stringed necklace hanging between her breasts and she wears a dot like *ṭīkā* mark in the middle of the forehead. The presence of a line of pearls above and below her breasts suggests that she may have been shown wearing a blouse, *kūcabandha*.[143] To her left one can make out the body of a male figure, now headless, who is shown carrying a thick, long stick, probably a *śakti*, in his left hand, with the right raised in *abhaya-hasta*.

At Sonkh, a site near Mathurā, a flatly cast bronze of a standing divine couple has been discovered during excavations.[144] The piece shows the couple in frontal posture standing on a low pedestal, framed by columns and an architrave made of double rods. The frame gives the impression of a *toraṇa* with S-shaped brackets inserted in the angle between the pillar and lintel on both sides, and a central ornament consisting of a tripartite symbol like a *nandyāvartta* above the beam with a ring below it. The figures are joined to each other as well as to the frame by a small bar. The male figure is to the right of the female. The latter is dressed in a short garment and has an animal head with large round eyes and ears, with hair bristling around the head. Her right arm is bent upwards holding the hand with its palm turned inwards in *vyāvṛtta-mudrā*. The male figure raises his right arm and also holds the hand with its palm turned inwards. In his left hand he carries a bowl. He is shown dressed in a *dhotī*, the knotted end of which is visible in folds between his legs. A broad necklace runs from shoulder to shoulder. His hair appears to be piled up high (like the *jaṭāmukuṭa* seen on the six-faced male figure on Yaudheya coins) and is decorated with a diadem. According to the excavator, these conjoint figures represent Skanda and a cat-headed mother goddess, Carcikā Ṣaṣṭhī.[145]

### 3.4.2 INTERPRETING THE ṢAṢṬHĪ FIGURES

Despite the fragmentary condition of most sculptures, one can make out the faces of many. In terms of size, many of these are almost life-sized. At least two of the Ṣaṣṭhī figures are about three-fourths of a metre tall and carved in the round, suggesting that they were housed in shrines of their own.

In the Type B series, but for one, Ṣaṣṭhī is shorter and smaller than the male deities. With her canopy she stands shoulder-high to Skanda and Viśākha, while she is only chest-high up to her coiffure. The reverse is true of only one piece, GMM 62.19 (described above), where Skanda and Viśākha reach up to Ṣaṣṭhī's upper chest.

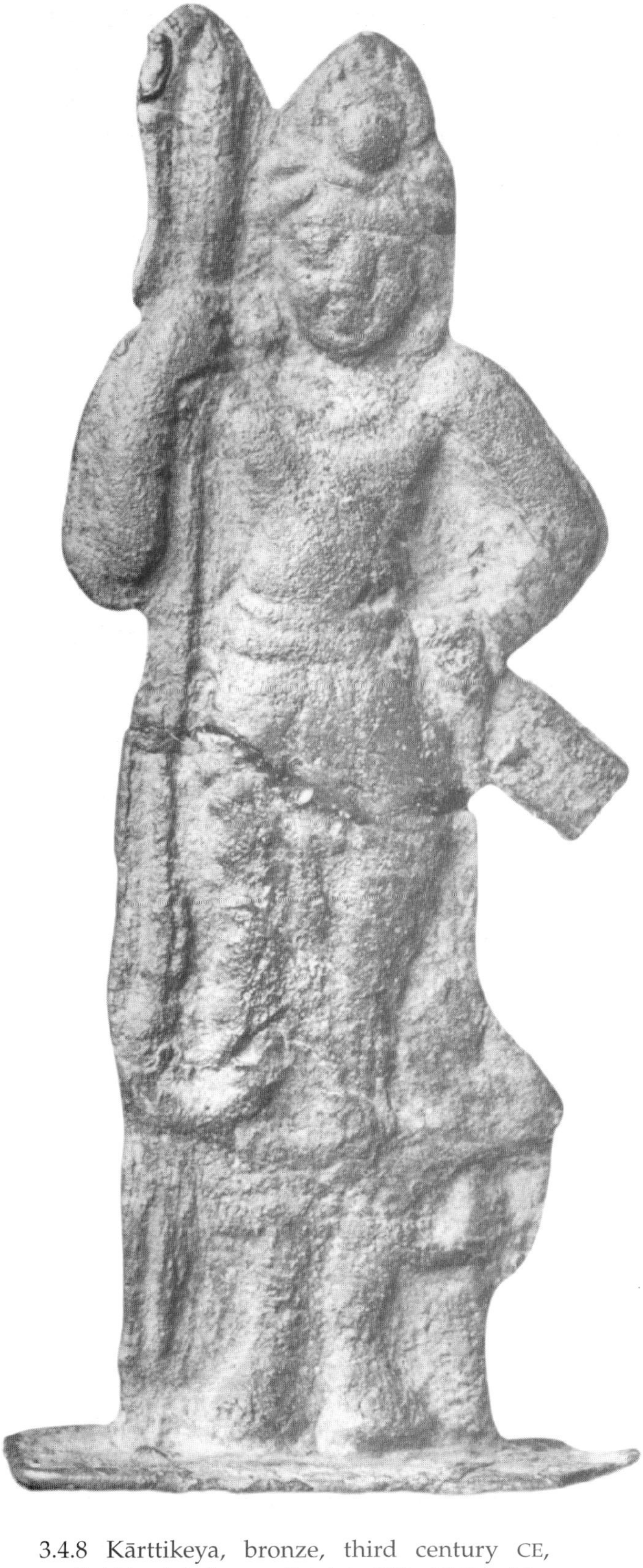

3.4.8 Kārttikeya, bronze, third century CE, Soṅkh, Mathurā district, UP. GMM No. SOI.118.

A question that may be pertinently raised is whether Type A and Type B represent the same deity/combination of deities or whether these were two separate deities or complex of deities. The most significant link between these two types may be traced from SML J.84 which combines features of both Type A and Type B. Here, the triad of figures (though only two survive in this particular piece) is combined with the radiating scheme. In this particular sculpture the canopy seems to be missing, replaced by a halo carved on the back slab. However, in almost all the other pieces discussed above, the canopy is an integral part of the representation. The evidence presented by J.84, described above, seems to suggest that six figures and six heads were different devices used to represent the goddess Ṣaṣṭhī. It must be mentioned here that it is the six-headed form, rather than the configuration with five busts and one whole female figure, that comes closest to her Ṣaṇmukhī (six-headed) figure discussed below. This canopy, a kind of a veiled nimbus, over the head of Ṣaṣṭhī is a distinct feature of Mathurā art of the Kuṣāṇa period. It is like a semi-circular arch with a shallow scalloped under-edge, which rises above the coiffure; this is seen above the images of the divine feminine such as Mātr̥kās, Hāritī,[146] Bhadrā and Lakṣmī.[147]

Scholarly opinion on the issue whether or not the five radiating figures emerging from the main figure and the five heads above the "canopy" of the main figure represent the same deity, or whether each of these figures/heads has a different identity somehow connected with the main figure is divided. According to R.C. Agrawala, P.K. Agrawala and others all the six, including the main face, were meant to portray a single polycephalous deity. In almost all the pieces these subsidiary bodies/heads have been arranged just above the canopy, sometimes in a miniaturised form. P.K. Agrawala is of the opinion that representing subsidiary deities as heads instead of as half-figures marks the second phase in depicting polycephalous images such as Ṣaṣṭhī, Vaikuṇṭha-Viṣṇu and Skanda. In the first phase the sculptors tried to translate the myth of multi-headed gods by representing them through half-bodies or busts amalgamated with the main image. In the second stage these were reduced to only heads.[148] T.S. Maxwell has argued that the five subsidiary figures in the case of at least one sculpture, GMM F.2, may each represent a different deity.[149]

One of the arresting features of Ṣaṣṭhī iconography is the five radiating[150] figures that can be seen in both individual and group sculptures. In the case of at least two of the sculptures, GMM 00.F2 and SML J. 84, the five subsidiary deities are shown rising from behind the shoulder. These are shown from the waist upwards, two on both sides of the shoulder, presumably two from behind the head and one rising from above the head. This radiating structure was seen also in what R.C. Agrawala and P.K. Agrawala have called the Viṣṇu-Vaikuṇṭha imagery[151] where Saṁkarṣaṇa is seen to emerge from behind the shoulder of Viṣṇu.[152] Maxwell has identified the same as Caturvyūha form of Viṣṇu.[153] The difference is that in the Viśvarūpa kind of depiction we have other deities than the main figure seeming to emanate, symbolising the *vyūha*s of Viṣṇu.

### 3.4.3 IDENTIFICATION

Originally the six headed/bodied figures were identified as Nāgarājñī or Queen of the Nāgas by Alexander Cunningham who first published the Mathura Museum F.2 piece.[154] J. Ph. Vogel and V.S. Agrawala accepted this classification and attributed the same nomenclature to subsequent finds of similar figures.[155] The Nāgarājñī identification is based primarily on the canopy above Ṣaṣṭhī being understood as a snake-hood and the emanating figures as attendants of the *nāga* deity.

V.S. Agrawala was the first to identify goddess Ṣaṣṭhī on the coins discovered in a hoard found in Chakrātā near Dehradun in Uttarakhand.[156] According to him the so-called "tribal" coins of the Yaudheyas depict six-headed and one-headed figures of Ṣaṣṭhī in conjunction with Skanda. The majority of these coins show a standing male figure on the obverse with a goddess on the reverse. Among these, some coins depict Kārttikeya on the obverse and Ṣaṣṭhī on the reverse, both having six heads, which are arranged in two rows of three each. The difference between the male and female portrayals is that Kārttikeya seems to sport a crest of matted locks resembling a *jaṭāmukuṭa*. The legend on the coins reads *bhāgavata svāmino brahmanasya devasya kumārasya*.[157] This confirms the identity of at least the male deity on the coin as a form of Ṣaṇmukha Skanda (six-headed Skanda).[158] V.S. Agrawala has proposed that Kārttikeya-Skanda was also known as Brahmaṇya, Kumāra in the *Mahābhārata*, therefore in all probability the female figure of the reverse is Skanda's spouse Devasenā or Ṣaṣṭhī discussed in the *Mahābhārata*.

N.P. Joshi[159] and R.C. Agrawala[160] extend the Ṣaṇmukhī–Ṣaṣṭhī identification to the sculptural series. In the Vana-Parva of the *Mahābhārata*, Devasenā is designated as the wife of Skanda.[161] Skanda is called Devasenāpriya and Ṣaṣṭhīpriya (the beloved of Devasenā and Ṣaṣṭhī) in the same text, which would suggest that they were meant to denote the same goddess.[162] Devasenā is the daughter of Prajāpati and perhaps being the husband of Devasenā, Skanda is also called the commander of the divine army. Devasenā is identified with Ṣaṣṭhī but also with Lakṣmī, Āśā, Sīnīvālī and Kuhū in this section of the *Mahābhārata*.[163] Ṣaṣṭhī, as the name implies, is the goddess who presides over the sixth day. In the Vana-Parva, the sixth day is mentioned as her special date. It is stated that Skanda married and united with Devasenā, the very incarnation of Lakṣmī, on the fifth day which is therefore Śrī Pañcamī. He obtained his object on the sixth day, Ṣaṣṭhī, of the lunar month.[164] This is confirmed by the *Kaśyapa Saṁhitā* and the *Mānava-Gṛhyasūtra*.

The *Mānava-Gṛhyasūtra* of the Maitryāna School has an entire hymn devoted to Ṣaṣṭhī and the ritual surrounding her worship, known within the text as Ṣaṣṭhīkalpa.[165] This hymn invokes Ṣaṣṭhī in order to obtain children, especially male children (*putra*), cattle (*paśu*), and wealth (*dhana*), through a special ceremony designed for the purpose. It recommends that the devotee should make certain preparations on the fifth night of the *śukla-pakṣa* of the lunar month such as sleeping on a bed of leaves and practising celibacy (*brahmacarya*). On the following morning, i.e. the sixth day, the devotee/ performer of the ritual should bathe and adequately prepare for the worship by smearing the ground, *lepa*, etc., then thinking of Ṣaṣṭhī he should start the *āhuti* with an invocation to Ṣaṣṭhī. In the passage she is compared to Lakṣmī, Śrī, Nandī, Sarasvatī, Puṣṭi, Śrī-Sirimā. She is invoked as wish-fulfilling (*kāmadā sarvakāminām*) pure and famous (*puṇyaṁ yaśasvinīm*) *devī*. She is described as lotus-footed, *padmacāriṇī*. She has also been referred to as the wife of Kāma,[166] Kāmapatnī Ṣaṣṭhī. Gonda has summarised this passage as invoking Ṣaṣṭhī, the goddess who is connected with new-born children and "who gives treasures, possesses goods, grants the fulfilment of wishes, which is propitious and full of splendour."[167] He also observes that the passage intermingles the identity of Ṣaṣṭhī with the Śrī of the Śrīsūkta, as certain verses in the Ṣaṣṭhīkalpa and Śrīsūkta are similar.

Significantly, she has been called *kāmapradām*[168] *rajanīm*[169] *viśvarūpām*[170] *ṣaṣṭhīm upavartatu me dhanam.*[171] The above invocation apparently requests the wish-fulfilling, dark (?) and all-formed Ṣaṣṭhī to bring wealth closer (to the devotee). The fact that she is referred to as *viśvarūpā* (having all forms) may indicate the many forms that are seen emanating from the main figure in the sculptures mentioned above.

Besides the *Mānava-Gṛhyasūtra*, medical treatises composed during the post-Mauryan period like the *Suśruta Saṁhitā* and, in the era that immediately followed, such texts as the *Kāśyapa Saṁhitā* give some iconographic details regarding Ṣaṣṭhī. A passage found in the Revatīkalpa of the *Kāśyapa Saṁhitā* suggests that Ṣaṣṭhī is also known as Revatī, by which name she finds mention in the *Suśruta Saṁhitā*. In the former text, Ṣaṣṭhī is referred to as Ṣaṇmukhī (six-headed) and is called the sister of Skanda,[172] contrary to the evidence from *Mahābhārata* where she is his wife. The text does not explain why she is endowed with six heads. We know that Skanda acquired his six heads either during the process of his conception or after his birth.[173]

In both the Revatīkalpa of the *Kāśyapa Saṁhitā* and the Ṣaṣṭhīkalpa of the *Mānava-Gṛhyasūtra*, Ṣaṣṭhī is referred to as Kāmarūpiṇī, Kāmapatnī. It is difficult to interpret this appellation: does it imply that Ṣaṣṭhī is another form of Rati, the consort of Kāma (the god of love), or does it emphasise her ability to fulfil desires and wishes?

The identification of these sculptures is not universally accepted. An alternative identification of at least one of the series of

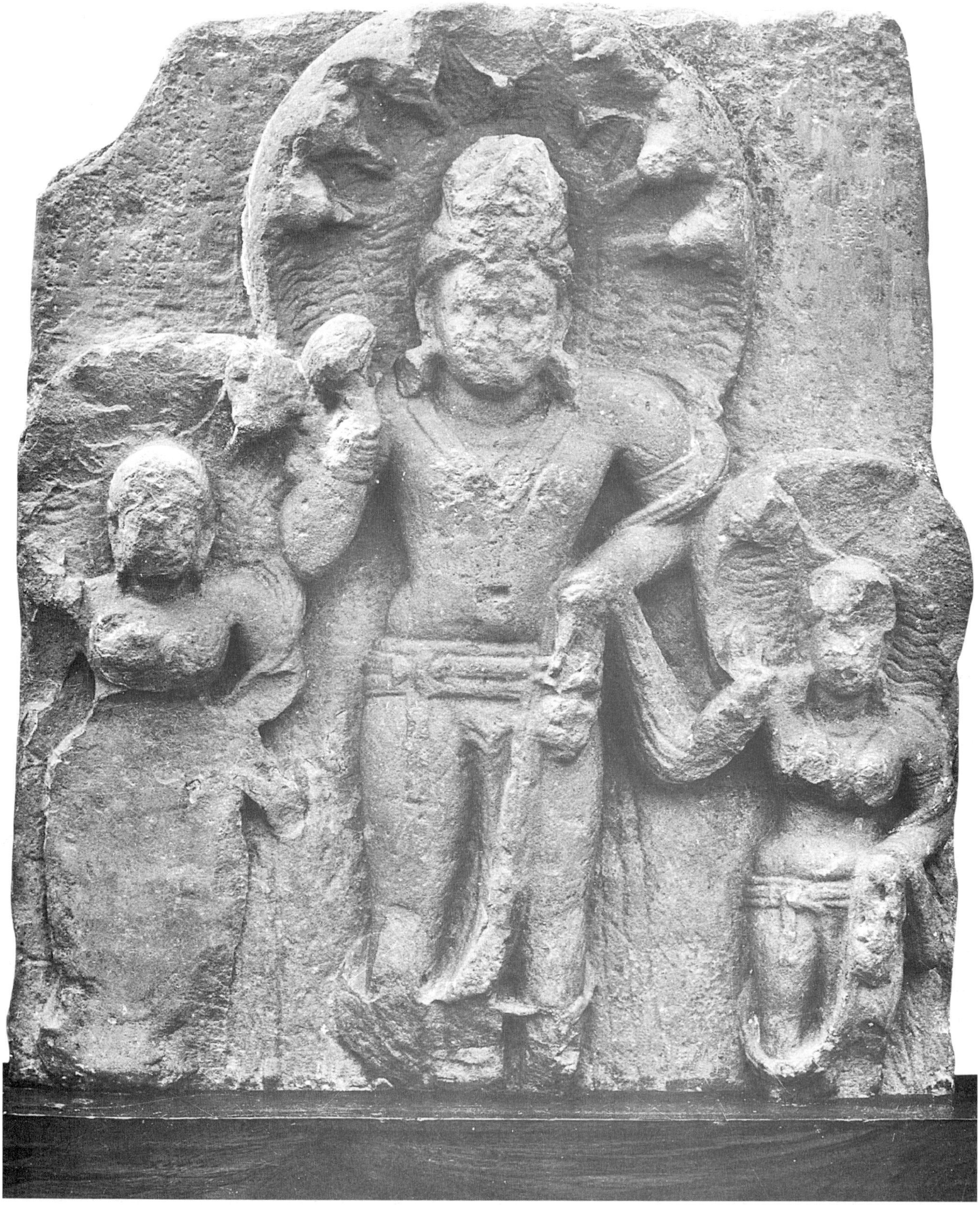

3.4.9 *Nāga* flanked by two *nāginī*s, inscribed on the lower pedestal, red sandstone, dated in the 8th year of Kaṇiṣka, *c.* CE 152?, Bhador village, Mathurā district, UP. GMM No. 12.211.

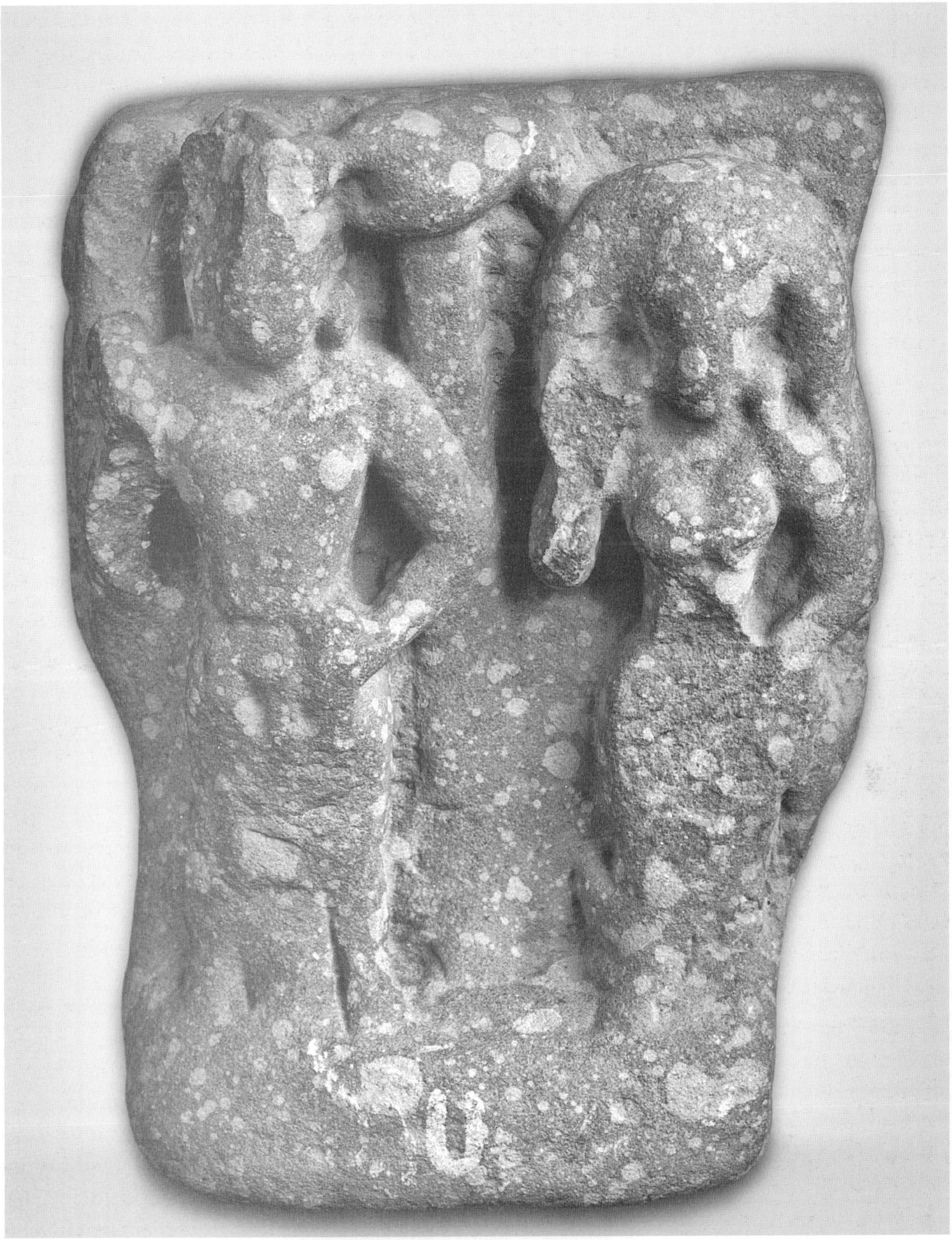

3.4.10 Balarāma and Ekānaṁśā, standing, Mathurā sandstone, third century CE, Mathurā district. GMM No. OOU.45.

sculptures here, GMM 00.F2, has been posited by Maxwell.[174] He suggests that this sculpture represents exactly the same construct as that of the Viṣṇu-Caturvyūha image (GMM No. 14.392-395), but with a triplication of the apical figure.[175] He opines that the most fitting name for the sculpture as the counterpart of a Caturvyūha image may simply be Caturvyūha-Śakti.[176]

Until now it was thought that there were only two radiating forms available to us from Mathurā datable to the Kuṣāṇa period; a male image representing Caturvyūha-Viṣṇu and the other female representing Ṣaṣṭhī/Caturvyūha-Śakti. However, recently an auction house catalogue published a photograph of a main female goddess with seven figures radiating from her (*Pl.* 3.4.12).[177] The principal goddess is carved in the usual Mathurā style with the right hand raised in *abhaya- hasta* and the left akimbo. Above her head there is a canopy carved as seen in the Ṣaṣṭhī images. There are three figures on each side of the goddess and one above her head, raising the number of subsidiary figures to seven instead of the usual five. On the reverse is carved a leafy tree in relief. It is difficult to identify this goddess, the only probable explanation perhaps being that this sculpture represents some form of the Aṣṭamātṛkās. Hitherto, groups of "mothers" have been found depicted in a row, in panels, or carved individually, but never in a radiating form such as in this figure.

Despite the limitations of the evidence available to us, I would argue for the identification of images of a feminine divinity with five radiating figures/heads as Ṣaṣṭhī. References to Ṣaṣṭhī in literature composed approximately prior to or contemporary with the period when the images were being created lend credence to this identification. The appellations *viśvarūpā* (multi-formed) and *ṣaṇmukhī* (six-headed) used in the *Mānava-Gṛhyasūtra* and the *Kaśyapa Saṁhitā* respectively to describe Ṣaṣṭhī match both Type A and Type B sculptures.

### 3.4.4 SKANDA AND ṢAṢṬHĪ

Ṣaṣṭhī is associated with Skanda-Kārttikeya at two levels: within a familial relationship as his wife or sister, and as a *bālagraha*.

The worship of Skanda was popular in the Mathurā area during the Kuṣāṇa period, as is attested by the archaeological material. An image datable to CE 89 with a dedicatory inscription addressed to Kārttikeya has been discovered.[178] Many other images of Skanda-Kārttikeya from the same area, dating to the early centuries of the Christian Era, have been recovered. One such image is a bronze statue of Skanda, holding a *śakti* in the left hand, discovered by Herbert Härtel during excavations at Soṅkh and belonging to the Vasudeva III layers[179] (*Pl.* 3.4.8).

A major antiquity linked to the Skanda cult during the Kuṣāṇa period is the Lala Bhagat pillar,[180] named after the village near Kanpur in Uttar Pradesh where it was discovered. The pillar carries a dedicatory epigraph, *kumāra varasa*, invoking Kumāra-Skanda. This octagonal pillar is carved on one side in low relief, depicting series of images in a vertical order, all probably related to Skanda. At the top are a pair of flying geese (*haṁsa mithuna*) with a pole held between their beaks on which is tied a cylindrical object. Next in a descending order is a male deity, probably Sūrya driving a chariot drawn by four horses. Two female attendants can be seen on either side of the god, one holding a *chattra* over his head and the other a *cāmara*. Under the hooves of the horses is a dwarf with a terrible face. Below this are three females, identified tentatively by P.K. Agrawala as Uṣā, Pṛtyūṣā and Chāyā.[181] Underneath these are 13 dwarfish figures with grotesque faces and pot-bellies. Just under this is shown a dancing peacock in frontal view, the circular fan of its tail forming a kind of a halo. Just below this, one can see an elephant in profile, enveloped in a cloud, standing in a pond of lotuses and holding a lotus vine in his trunk. A blank space follows that ends in a small composition. On the left, a pillar with a cock capital and a dwarf *yakṣa* at the base are depicted. On the right of this pillar is a standing female figure worshipping it with folded hands. This figure is being lustrated by two elephants, one on each side of her. She has been identified as Gaja-Lakṣmī.[182] A cock capital was found within a radius of 8 ft. of the pillar, and no doubt originally sat atop it in the manner depicted on the pillar relief.

The accompanying inscription on the upper side of the obverse confirms the identity of the deity in whose honour this pillar was erected as Skanda. Ṣaṣṭhī is not depicted, unless we concede that the iconography of Ṣaṣṭhī approximated that of Lakṣmī. As we have seen in both the *Mahābhārata* and *Mānava-Gṛhyasūtra*, Ṣaṣṭhī is identified with Śrī-Lakṣmī. The cock is a well-known *vāhana* of Skanda, as is the peacock. The elephant no doubt stands for Indra who confers the title of *senāpati*, the commander of his army, on Skanda.

We do know from textual tradition that Skanda-Kārttikeya was considered a *graha* deity who combined both child-protecting and child-destroying functions in his divine persona.[183] As we will see in the section on Naigameṣa, Skanda is believed to be the head of a host of demons, most of whom have Śaiva affiliations, who destroy children. In this scheme of child-protecting and child-injuring functions, Ṣaṣṭhī is allied to Skanda as his sister. And Skanda is the *bālagraha par excellence*.

Kārttikeya is also found in association with one or more of his brothers on the coins of the Kuṣāṇa king Huviṣka; on one coin type Skanda and Viśākha appear, each carrying a *śakti* in his hand. On one gold coin there are three similar *śakti*-carrying male figures which are named in the legend as Skanda, Kumāra, Viśākha, and Mahāsenā. The presence of three figures but four names suggests that at least one represented a conjoint deity, probably Skanda-Kumāra, as has been cited in Pāṇini's *Aṣṭādhyāyī*. As mentioned above he is often found depicted on Yaudheya coins also.[184] On the reverse of this coin is Śiva standing next to Nandikeśvara.

### 3.4.5 ANALOGOUS SCULPTURES

The sculptural arrangement of Ṣaṣṭhī in the centre with a male deity on either side is not unique in post-Mauryan art (*Pl.* 3.4.9), especially around Mathurā. Similar sculptures of Ekānaṁśā with Baladeva and Vāsudeva flanking her have been discovered (*Pl.* 3.4.10).[185] It is related in the *Ghaṭa Jātaka* that Balarāma and Vāsudeva were younger brothers of Añjanā Devī, the black goddess,[186] who, according to Suvira Jaiswal, is none other than Ekānaṁśā.[187] Kaṁsa is supposed to have ruled over the city of Asitañjanā, the city of Añjanā and it is also mentioned that as a result of the curse of Kānhādipāyana (Kṛṣṇa Dvaipāyana) all the Vṛṣṇis perished except Añjanā Devī. In the Vana-Parva of the *Mahābhārata*, which also mentions Ṣaṣṭhī, she is identified with Kuhū, a dark goddess.[188] It has been mentioned in the *Bṛhat-Saṁhitā* of Varāhmihira, composed sometime around the sixth century, that the image of Ekānaṁśā should be flanked by Baladeva and Kṛṣṇa.[189] Even today Ekānaṁśā is identified with and worshipped as Bhadrā/Subhadrā along with Balarama and Keśava in Orissa.

3.4.11 *Bhisa Jātaka*, great railing, coping stone, first century BCE, Bharhut, Indian Museum, Calcutta. IM 362-63.

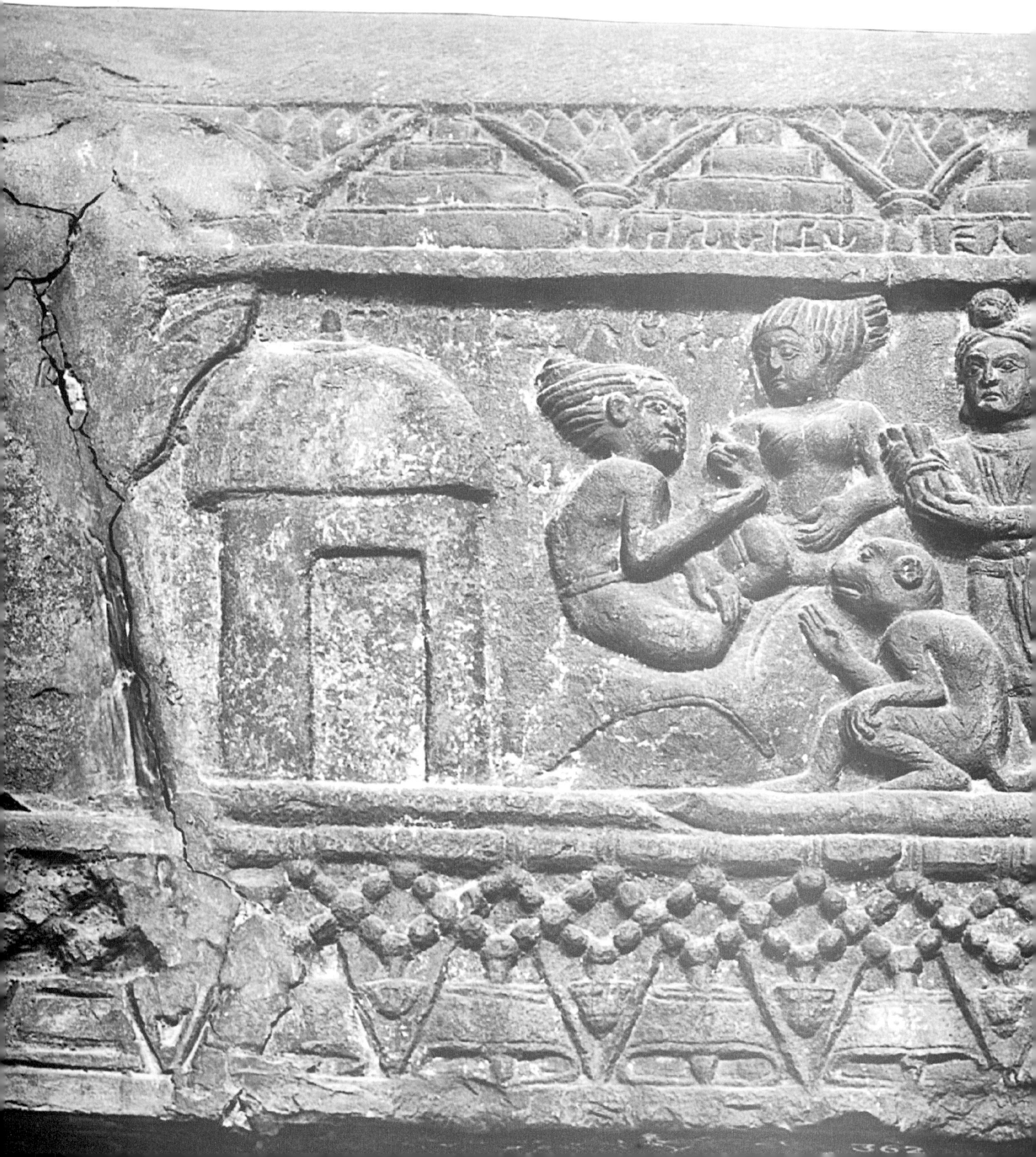

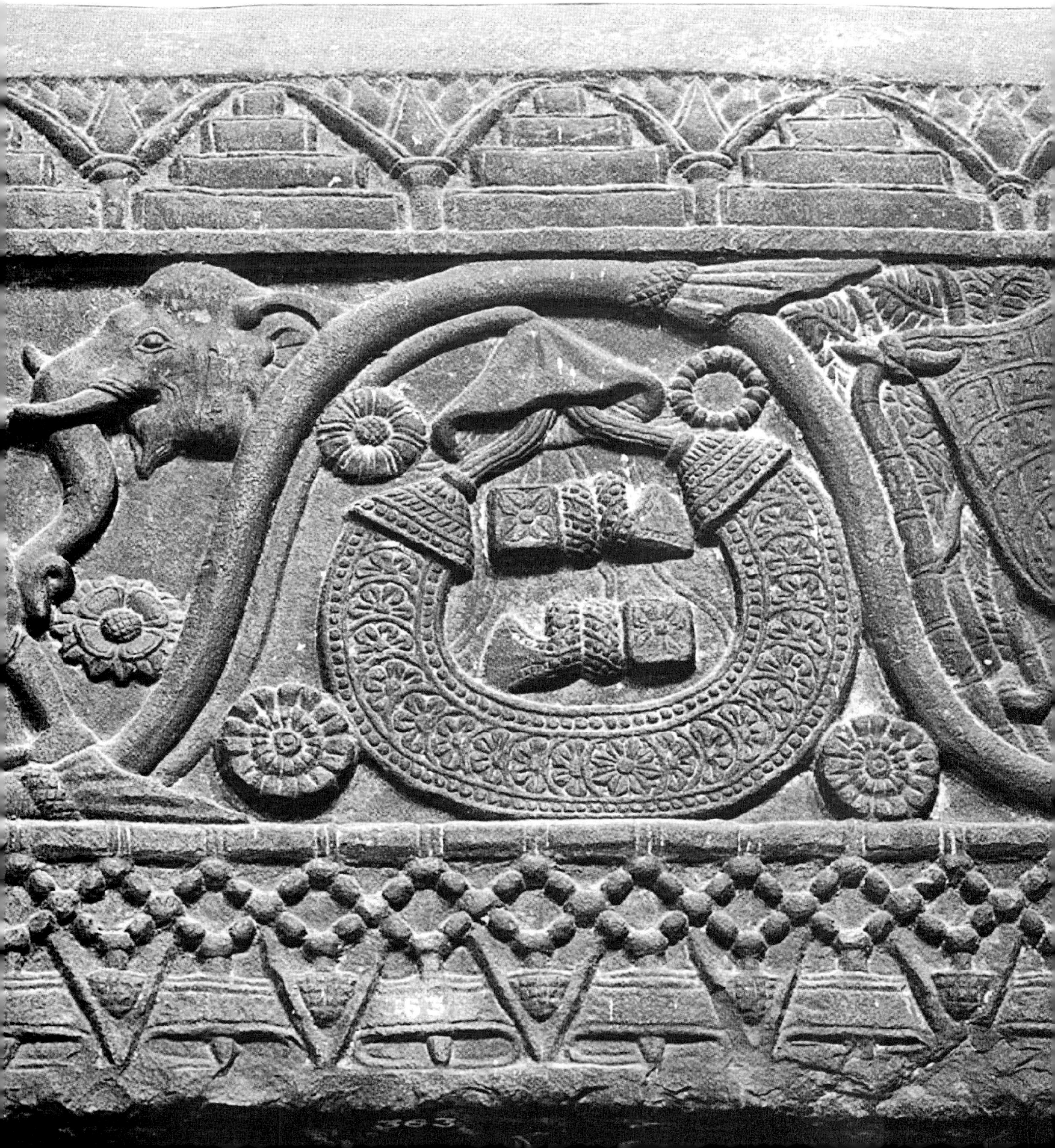

An inscription found at the Mora Well within Mathurā city mentions the worship of Bhāgavataṁ *pañcavīrāṇāṁ* (the five heroes of the Vṛṣṇis (Bhāgavatas)) in a stone temple, *śailadevagṛha*, built by Tosa.[190] The images are described as glowing and handsome in appearance. Lüders identifies these five heroes with Baladeva, Akrūra, Anadhṛṣṭi, Śaraṇa and Viduratha on the basis of Jaina sources.[191] J.N. Banerjea suggests that these can be associated with Vāsudeva, Sāmba, Pradyumna, Baladeva and Aniruddha.[192] Balarāma and Vāsudeva, along with Sāmba, Pradyumna and Aniruddha are part of the *pañcavīra* of Vṛṣṇis (five eponymous heroes of the Vṛṣṇi tribe) who seem to have been worshipped both as a group and individually during the Kuṣāṇa period. Suvira Jaiswal suggests that all, except Sāmba, developed into the *vyūha*s of Viṣṇu and were worshipped as such in a cult which represents an intermediate tradition of Vaiṣṇavism coming between the worship of Ekānaṁśā with two associate gods and the emergence of Vāsudeva as all powerful, supreme god.[193] She is also of the opinion that in the depictions of Ekānaṁśā with Vāsudeva and Balarāma, the goddess was the most important figure, and that her significance declined with the changeover from a matriarchal to a patriarchal state.

Here one can add the evidence from the Bhiṣa Jātaka which is illustrated at Bharhut and labelled as *Bhiṣa Jātaka* (*Pl.* 3.4.11). In the relief one can see the god Śakra with a bundle of lotus fibres placing these before the *bodhisattva*; in the background can be seen the sister, the elephant, the monkey and the hermitage.[194]

In *Daśaratha Jātaka*, Sītā is described as the sister of Rāma and Lakṣmaṇa who later marries Rāma.[195] This is reminiscent of the Skanda-Viśākha-Ṣaṣṭhī and Baladeva-Ekānaṁśā-Vāsudeva triads who are also believed to be siblings. It may be suggested that in familial politics, sibling bonding (the famous example being that of the Pāṇḍavas) was considered to be important and celebrated. In this familial complex, the sister too is significant and integral and was often associated with fertility and prosperity. We know that Sītā is considered an agricultural deity.[196] Ekānaṁśā was also considered to be a goddess associated with fertility and protection of the baby Kṛṣṇa, and was worshipped with parched grain, unhusked rice and flowers.[197] Placing Ṣaṣṭhī within this context might help us posit an alternate male-female dyad, of a brother-sister that was finally overtaken by the dominant husband-wife pairing in the familial as well as religious discourse. The brother-sister portrayal survives in sculpture and in popular literature of heterodox sects' traditions, while it has been silenced or marginalised in the mainstream Brāhmanical textual tradition where many sibling relationships are converted into marital bonds.

### 3.4.6 ṢAṢṬHĪ AS A BĀLAGRAHA

Ṣaṣṭhī has been mentioned in the medical texts as one of the *bālagraha*s, diseases that afflict young children. She is invoked on the sixth day after the birth of a baby and is also known as Sūtikā Ṣaṣṭhī.[198] In the *Suśruta Saṁhitā* she is called Revatī and described as a goddess who wears many garments, floral wreaths, pastes and dangling earrings. She is called dark (*śyāmā*) and mother (*mātā*) who is young and is attended by other female deities such as Lambā, Karālā, Vinatā and Bahuputrikā.[199] In the *Kaśyapa Saṁhitā*, Revatī is described as the most dreadful of all *bālagraha*s who commands worship even from the gods. It says that she practised penance to please Skanda and was granted the status of his sister as a reward. She was named Ṣaṣṭhī because she was the sixth sibling, coming after five brothers (Skanda, Guha, Kumāra, Viśākha and Nandikeśvara).[200] She is considered to be the source of life and happiness and also as ever-beautiful (*nityalalitā*) and competent to assume forms at will (*kāmarūpiṇī*). She is also called six-faced (*ṣaṇmukhī*) as mentioned before. Revatī has been given 16 synonyms including Ṣaṣṭhī and Jātahāriṇī by Vṛddha Jīvaka, the author of the *Kaśyapa Saṁhitā*. Jātahāriṇī has the power to take away the children of irreligious, impious and crooked parents.[201]

The inclusion of Ṣaṣṭhī as a mothering figure can be considered problematic given that she is not designated as a biological mother in any text, nor is she depicted in conjunction with child(ren) in images. However, the primary function attributed to her in medical texts is that of protection of children, especially on the sixth day after childbirth, the sixth being her special day, *mahātithi*. She is not only benign but is also seen to be malignant, just like her brother/husband. In the *Mahābhārata*, in the form of Revatī, she is attributed the function of afflicting children unless propitiated with unguents, ablutions, sacrifices and the like.[202]

Despite the Ṣaṣṭhī's usually smaller size in comparison to her male companions, she is undoubtedly the main figure in the triad groupings. It is she who is placed in the middle and she is the only one who has the canopy-like arch over her head. And it is only she from whom subsidiary figures or heads radiate forth. In both the Type A and Type B sculptural series, the depiction of the divine feminine creates considerable visual impact. The five radiating figures emanating from her person mark her as a significant figure among the plethora of divine feminine figures within the Mathurā art tradition.

Ṣaṣṭhī is neither diminutive in size, like the Naigameṣī and Lajjā-Gaurī images, nor is she sensuously delineated like the *śālabhañjikā-yakṣī* figures. It is also noteworthy that unlike the nearly-nude *śālabhañjikā-yakṣī* sculptures, Ṣaṣṭhī is always depicted wearing a *dhotī* and in at least one case, perhaps also a *kūcabandha*. This may imply respect and reverence. This is in contrast to most of the contemporaneous *yakṣī/śālabhañjikā* figures of the Mathurā school of art which are covered with transparent drapery and are frankly sensuous. As has been noted before, the Ṣaṣṭhī

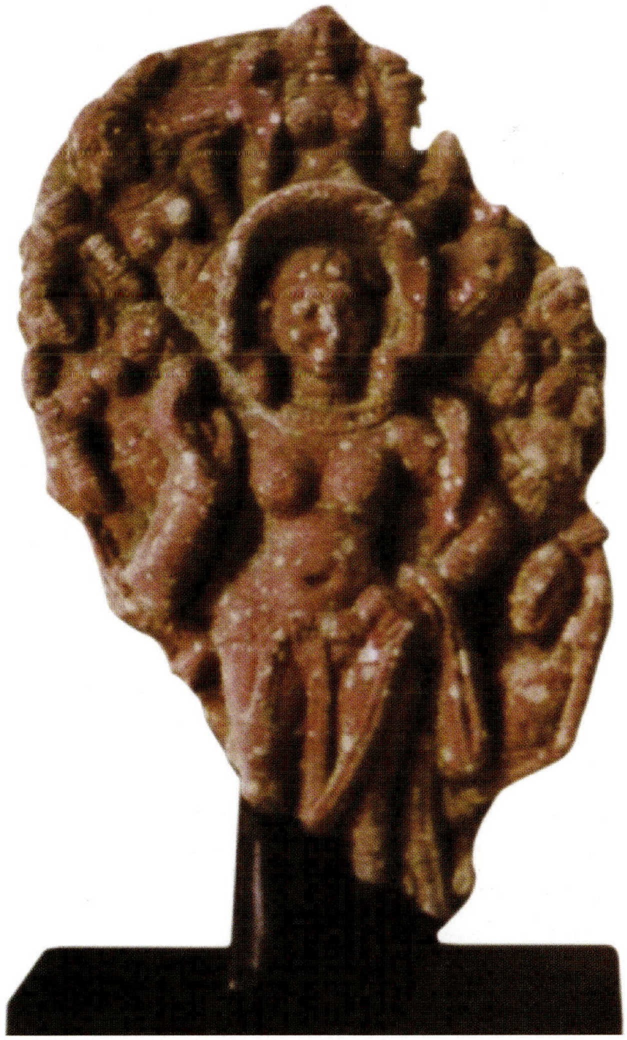

3.4.12 Goddess with six subsidiary forms emanating, second century CE, red sandstone.

figures are standing straight and there is no movement in the body of the sculptures, unlike those of the *yakṣī* figures. While it may be an overstatement to say that clothing was an exclusive attribute of divine figures, it is noteworthy that most of the divine feminine images are shown clothed during the Kuṣāṇa period.

The clothing and composition of Ṣaṣṭhī's images mark her as an enigmatic figure who represents the powerful feminine force which is mysterious, simultaneously benign and malignant. Such a power has to be propitiated through special rites which were spelt out in Ṣaṣṭhīkalpa and Revatīkalpa, texts composed for this specific purpose. Ṣaṣṭhī's imagery and the rites associated with her suggest that during the Kuṣāṇa period she enjoyed an independent cult which was subsequently suppressed and could not develop and flourish as did its compositional counterpart, the Caturvyūha-Viṣṇu.

### 3.5 Naigameṣa and Naigameṣī

Naigameṣa is a fascinating deity in terms of gender roles. Even though there are other male divinities such as Skanda who are associated with protection of children in the post-Mauryan period, Naigameṣa is the only male deity who is actually depicted with children around him.

Further, it is significant that he appears to have a geographically limited cult centring on Mathurā and associated sites. The cultic images of Naigameṣa and his feminine counterpart are found only in the Kuṣāṇa period, even though his cult may perhaps have antedated Kuṣāṇa rule in northern and north-west India.

These images are generally in the form of small objects in stone or terracotta. This would suggest that they were votive objects, perhaps used at the time of childbirth.

#### 3.5.1 SCULPTURAL EVIDENCE

One of the best-preserved pieces from Mathurā shows a goat-headed male figure in profile, with his face turned towards the right[203] (*Pl.* 3.5.1). The body below the neck is in frontal view. The deity is seated on a throne in *lalitāsana* with one leg folded on the throne and the left foot on the floor. There seem to be two baskets on the floor, under the seat. On the right a child touching the right leg of the main figure is visible. To the right of this child there is a fully clothed female figure holding a *cāmara*, and next to her is a winged female figure and a woman with a child cradled in her right arm. The women are bejewelled and their lower body is not nude but covered in a skirt-like *dhotī*. Nine dancing female figures are carved on the reverse side (*Pl.* 3.5.2).

The piece described above is an exception in the corpus of goat-headed deities of a similar kind. Most such deities are represented individually, with or without children, with one hand raised in the *abhaya* or protection-granting gesture (*Pls.* 3.5.4, 3.5.5). These are therefore cultic figures, unlike the figure described above, which is represented as part of a narrative. An example of the larger corpus of goat-headed male divinities is one that was found in the Kaṅkālī Ṭīlā in Mathurā[204] (*Pl.* 3.5.6). The legs beneath the knees and the right arm are now missing. In his left hand he holds two children hanging down about his thigh. Traces of children on each of his shoulders are visible, of which only the legs are still discernible.

Another piece shows a standing figure of a goat-headed male deity[205] with a child on each of his shoulders, and two more children, one on each side at the bottom of the relief slab. The children probably had their hands folded in adoration. The right hand of the deity is held up in *abhaya-hasta*, while the left is holding what seems to have been a purse or the knot of the waistband. A similar depiction of a male goat-faced deity with one child on each shoulder and a child on each side at the bottom was also found from the same area.[206]

Another fragment is part a goat-faced male figure which is depicted carrying four children, two on each shoulder (*Pl.* 3.5.4).[207] The hands of the children are folded in adoration. The deity's own right hand is raised in *abhaya-hasta*. Besides the usual bracelets and necklace, this figure is adorned with a lotus-disc crown with a small horn-like protrusion in the middle.

One of the more interesting images of a male goat-headed god is a rectangular relief slab of the deity with a male child squatting on each shoulder (Pl. 3.5.5). The children hold one horn each in their hands. Two more children, also male, are shown on either side at the bottom. The principal figure holds the left hand of the child on his left while the other child touches his thigh. Overall, the entire composition shows a dynamic interaction between the frolicking children and the principal godhead.

Two other fragments of a similar nature have been noticed. The first, showing the upper part of a goat-headed male figure with children on his shoulders, was uncovered from a well at Palikhera in Mathurā. The other, having only a goat face, is also from the Mansawala well at Palikhera.[208] They are now housed in the Mathura Museum. The latter piece has a very well-defined lotus-disc crown rising above a fillet-like band on the forehead. Some other fragments with a human face and ram's horns have been found (*Pls.* 3.5.7, 3.5.8).[209] But it is difficult to posit that these are anthropomorphic versions of Naigameṣa.

Depictions of ram-headed jars have been found in these regions as well. In one stone plaque now in the State Museum, Lucknow[210] (*Pl.* 3.5.3), a goat-headed jar is found in conjunction with a lance-carrying standing Skanda and a seated bird-faced Mātṛkā with a child in her lap,

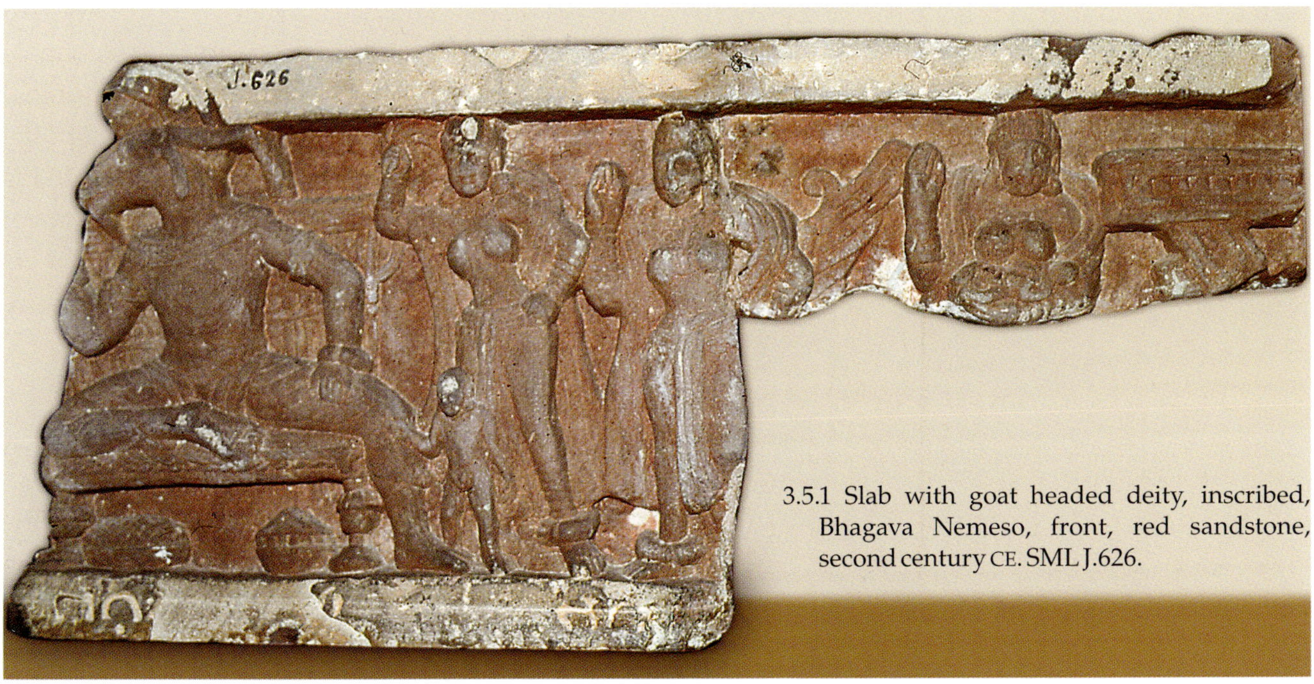


3.5.1 Slab with goat headed deity, inscribed, Bhagava Nemeso, front, red sandstone, second century CE. SML J.626.

placed on a cushion. It has been suggested that the jar either represents the *suvarṇa-kuṇḍa* (the golden lake) in which Svāhā deposited the semen from which Kārttikeya was born, or *suvarṇa* itself, which was born along with him.[211] Or perhaps Naigameṣa is meant to be portrayed through the jar. Carved on the extreme right are a group of worshippers with folded hands.

Also found in the same area, but belonging to an earlier period, are *yakṣa* figures carrying a diminutive male figure in their hand (Pl. 3.5.9).[212] Interestingly, though these small figures may have their hands folded in adoration, at least in one case they are depicted standing on a pedestal. Could it be that these served as prototypes for the later depictions of the goat-headed deity with children?

### 3.5.2 IDENTIFICATION AND ORIGINS

An inscription found on the base of the narrative relief carved on a *toraṇa* architrave from Kaṅkālī Ṭīlā consists of the words *bhagava nemeso*. This provides us with a positive and clear identification of the goat-headed deity as Nemeso, also known as Nejameṣa, Naigameṣa or Hariṇaigameṣa. The relief in all probability illustrates the episode of the transfer of the embryo[213] from Devanandā to Triśalā, as elucidated below.

Naigameṣa of the Vedas is benefic in character. In the *Mahābhārata* he is seen as both a *graha* and a commander of Skanda's army. In the *Suśruta Saṁhitā*, however, he is a *graha* who is malefic in nature and poses danger to children.

The antecedents of the goat/ram-headed deity can be found in Vedic texts. In the *Atharvaveda* Naigameṣa is a *yakṣa*.[214] In the *Śatapatha Brāhmaṇa* it is said that Prajāpati sacrifices a goat for Kumāra-Agni. The goat seems to have been considered an animal sacred to Agni. There seems to be also a connection to Aja-ekapāda,[215] an one-footed goat-deity who is also connected with the number six.[216] This Aja-ekapāda is associated with the Rudras, which perhaps would have led to his association with Skanda. Naigameṣa seems to be intimately connected with Skanda-Kārttikeya.[217] Both the deities have the peacock as their *vāhana* and are considered to be the head of the divine army of Indra.

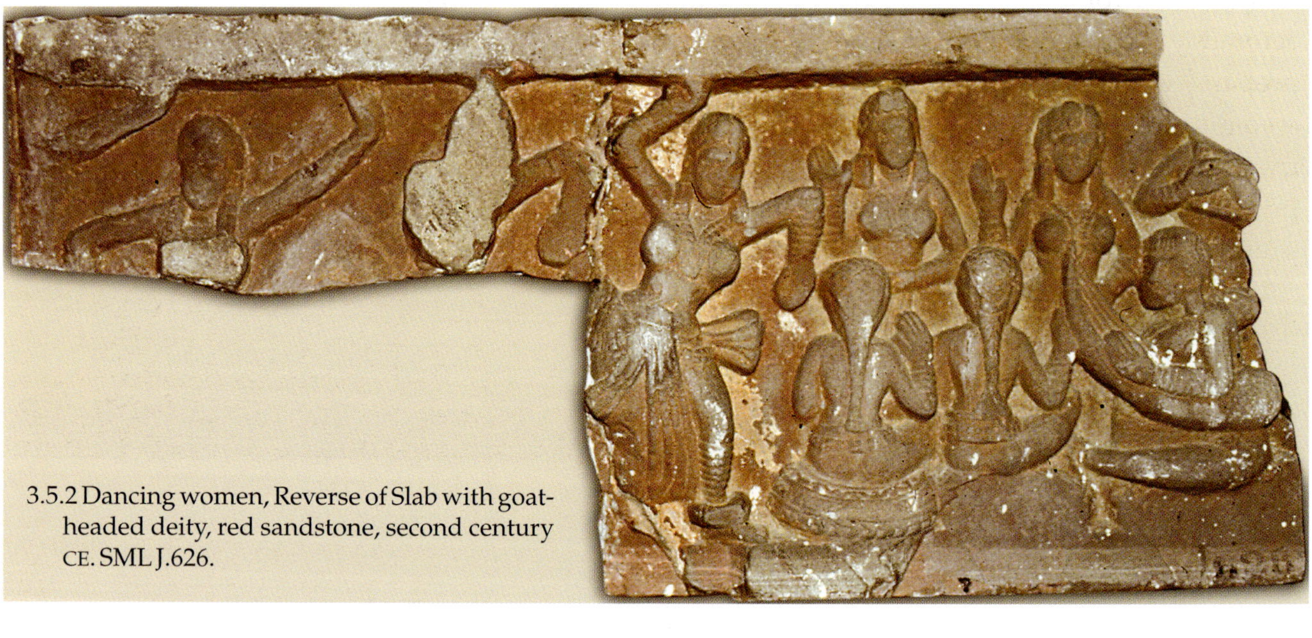

3.5.2 Dancing women, Reverse of Slab with goat-headed deity, red sandstone, second century CE. SML J.626.

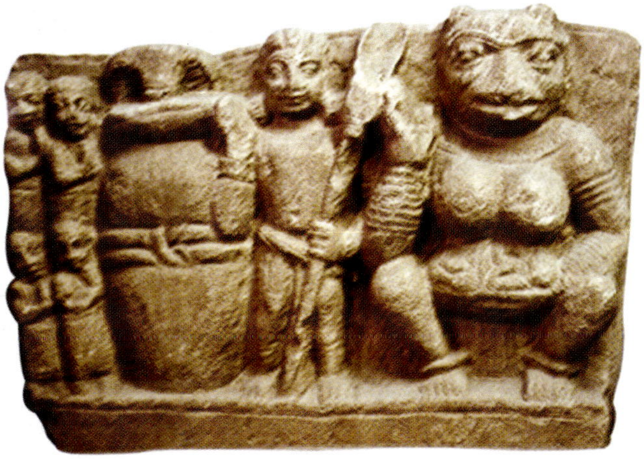

3.5.3 Ram-headed jar, standing lance-carrying Kārttikeya, animal-faced Mātṛkā seated, second century CE, red sandstone. SML. 0.250.

The Gṛhyasūtras prescribe the worship of Naigameṣa in a ceremony known as *sīmantonnayana,* in which the pregnant woman's hair is parted by her husband during the fourth month of her pregnancy.[218] In course of the ceremony Nejemeṣa is prayed to thus: "Nejemeṣa, fly away, and come back with an excellent son. Make me, who longs for a son, pregnant with a male child." Though the stanza itself suggests that this prayer to Nejemeṣa is spoken by a woman desiring male offspring, the ceremony itself is performed by a man who prepares the *sthalipāka* and offers it to the god, enjoining him to produce pregnancy.[219] These rites are combined with others asking for the protection of the embryo from demons and the prevention of miscarriage.[220]

This function is reinforced in Jaina texts, and in the early Jaina pantheon Hariṇaigameṣin occupies a special place. The Jainas associate Hariṇaigameṣin with the legend of the "Transfer of the Embryo" related in the *Kalpasūtra* of the Śvetāmbaras. Here it is stated that when Mahāvīra descended from heaven (as the Buddha descended from the Tuṣita heaven), he entered the womb of Devanandā, a woman belonging to the brāhmaṇa *varṇa.* Upon investigation by Indra/Śakra, no precedent for the birth of an Arhat or a Cakravartin or a Vāsudeva or a Baladeva in a degraded brāhmaṇa family was found. Therefore he called upon Hariṇegameṣin, divine commander of the infantry, to switch the Divine Embryo into the womb of Triśalā, a woman who belonged to an acceptable kṣatriya *varṇa.*

Naigameṣin as a deity who controls childbirth is also associated with Kṛṣṇa. U.P. Shah quotes two such incidents from Brāhmanical and Jaina texts.[221] In the first legend,

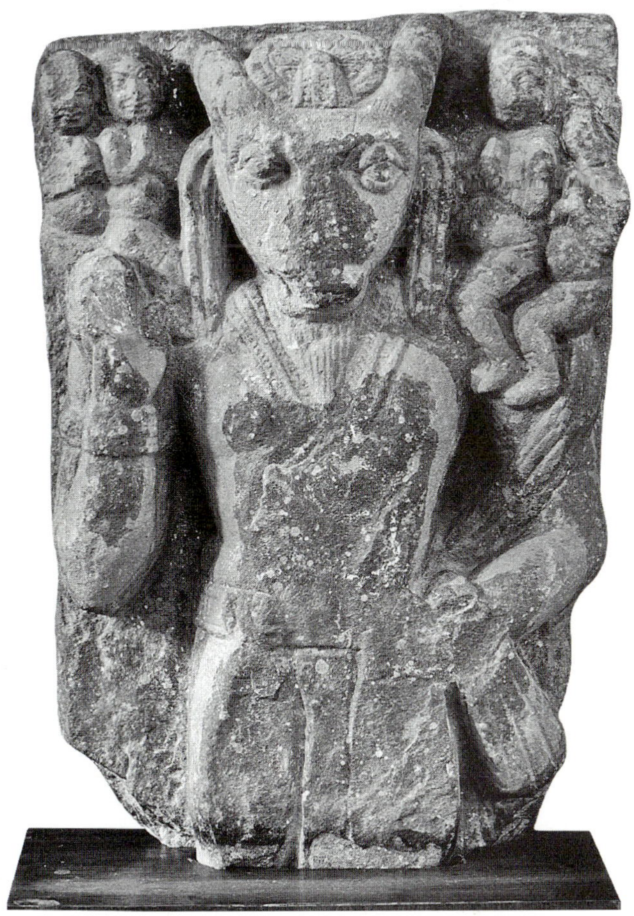

3.5.4 Harinaigameṣa, red sandstone, third century CE, Mathurā district, UP. GMM No. 34.2347.

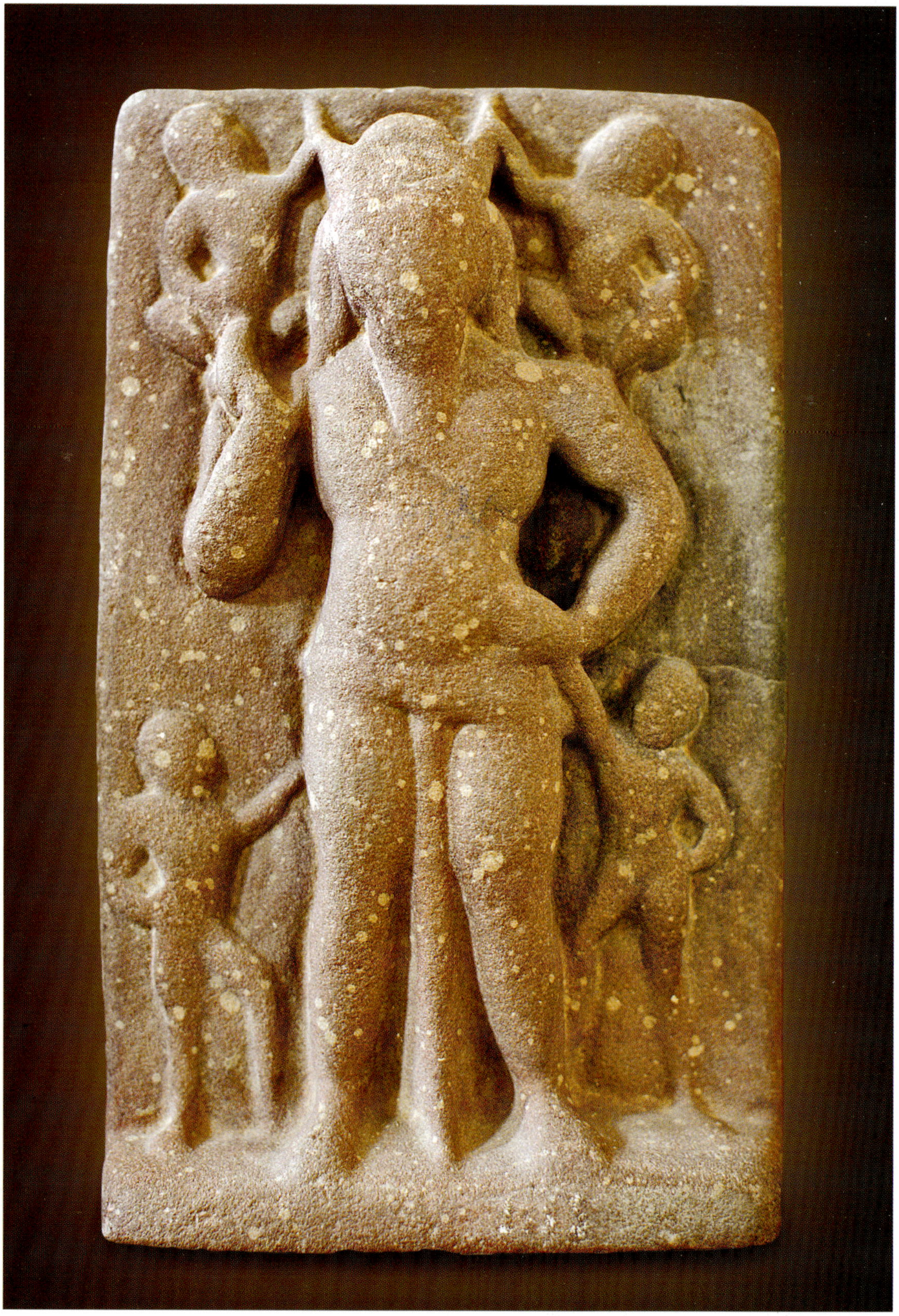

3.5.5 Harinaigameṣa, Mathurā sandstone, third century CE, Yamunā Bed, Mathurā district, UP. GMM No. 15.115.

narrated in Gajasukumāra-adhyayana of *Antagadasao*, a certain lady called Sulasā is informed that she would be able to deliver still-born babies only. To avert this calamity she starts worshipping Hariṇaigameṣī, who, pleased with her devotion, switches her lifeless embryos with Devakī's living embryos. Thus, Sulasā delivers healthy sons and Devakī only still-born babies. Ultimately it is Kṛṣṇa himself who propitiates Hariṇaigameṣī by fasting in a *poṣadhaśālā* and gains the boon of being born as Devakī's eighth son.

The iconography of Naigameṣa is given in Suśruta's *Uttaratantra* section which deals with diseases that inflict children through the demonic deities called the *bālagraha*. Naigameṣa is one of the nine principal *bālagraha*s in Skanda's pantheon. He is supposed to have a goat's face with ever-moving eyes and eyebrows, *calākṣibhrūḥ*.[222] He has also been called *kumāradharā*, the carrier of children, a role which can be seen illustrated in representations of the deity where he is depicted with children.

Another legend found in both the *Neminātacaira* and *Vasudevahiṇḍī* relates the manner in which Kṛṣṇa invokes Naigameṣin in order to gain a son for Satyabhāmā. Naigameṣin grants the boon, and presents a necklace to be worn by the queen. U.P. Shah ascribes an iconographic significance to this necklace, as some goat-faced images from Mathurā are shown wearing elaborate necklaces. However, it is difficult to accept Shah's view given that similar necklaces adorn almost all the *yakṣa* figures found in the same area. At the most, one might concede that the ornament could have acquired some symbolic value in the case of Naigameṣin.

In Brāhmanical and medical lore Nemeṣa or Naigameṣa is associated with Skanda. In the *Mahābhārata* and in medical treatises both the deities are considered to be *bālagraha*s, or demons dangerous to children. Skanda is the leader (*adhipati*) of the *graha*s, while Naigameṣa is one of the nine *graha*s mentioned in the *Suśruta Saṁhitā* along with Skanda, Skanda-apasmāra or Viśākha, and six female deities: Śakunī, Pūtanā, Andha-Pūtanā, Sītā-Pūtanā, Revatī and Mukhamaṇḍikā. Naigameṣa is also called a *pitṛgraha*. According to the same text, variously-faced (*nānārūpa*) deities were appointed by

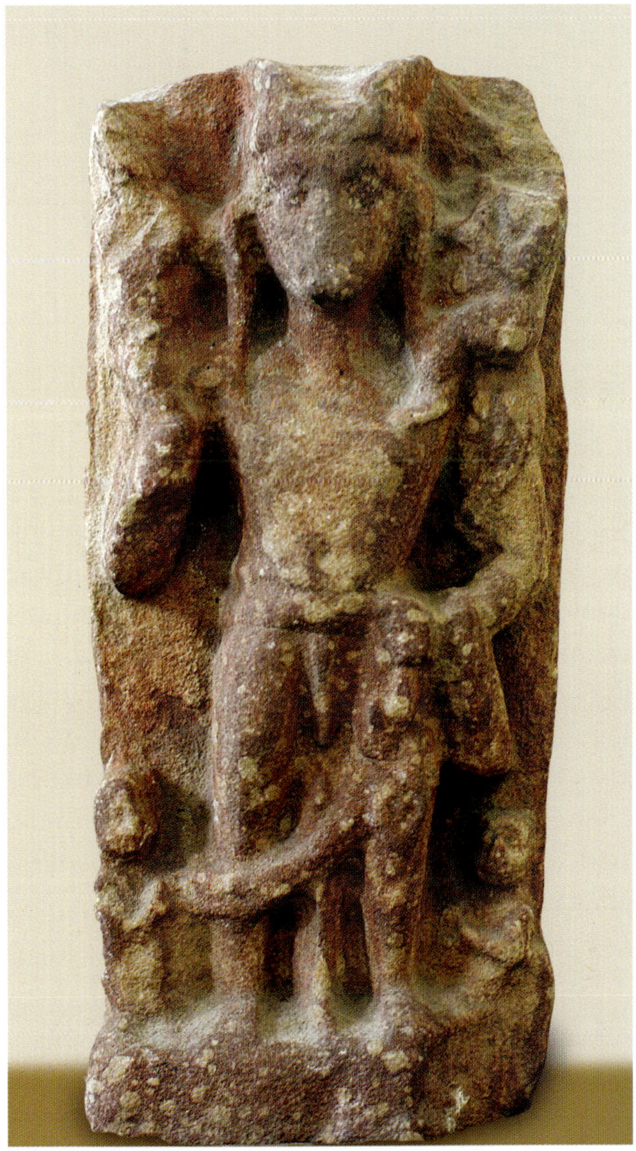

3.5.6 Harinaigameṣa, Mathurā sandstone, third century CE, Mathurā district, UP. GMM No. 34.2482.

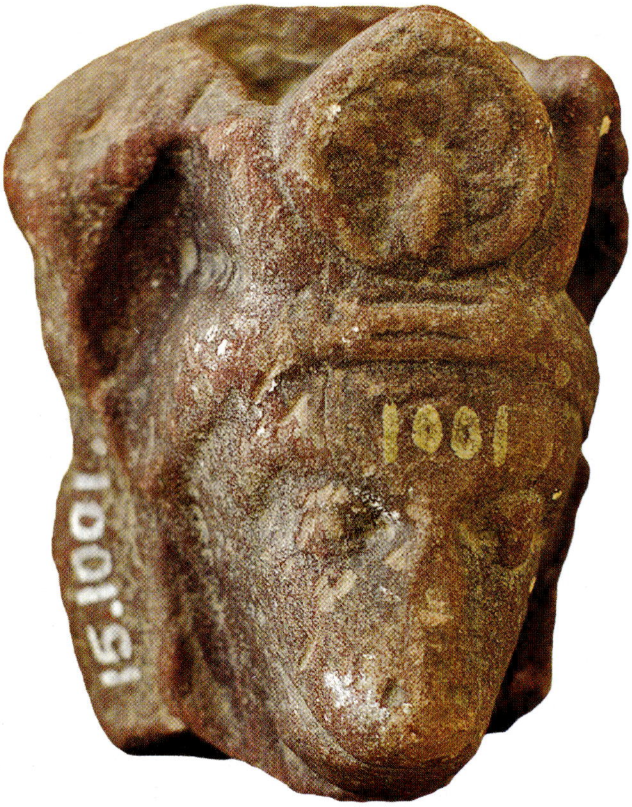

3.5.7 Head of Harinaigameṣa, Mathurā sandstone, third century CE, Mathurā district, UP. GMM No. 15.1001.

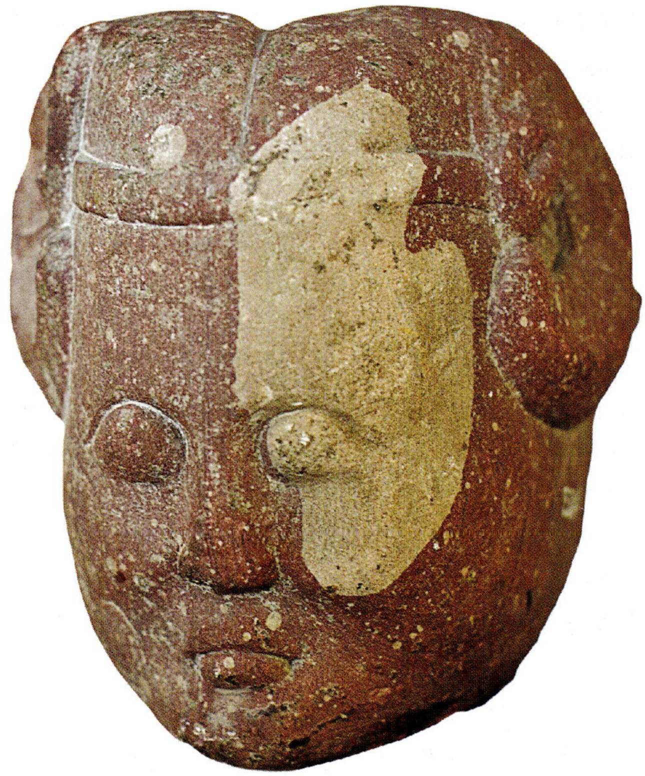

3.5.8 Male head with ram's horns, red sandstone, first century CE, UP, Bhūteśvara Mahādeva, Mathurā district. GMM No. 11.157.

Kūttika, Umā, Agni and others for the protection of baby Guha lying in the reed forest. Of these deities, Pārvatī created Naigameṣa as Meṣānana (ram-faced) and he became a friend of Guha. In the slightly later text, the *Kaśyapa Saṁhitā*, datable to *c.* CE 300-400 at the latest, there is a section on *kumārabhṛtyam* or diseases that inflict children. It contains a hymn devoted to Ṣaṣṭhī known in the text as Revatīkalpa in which, however, Naigameṣa is not mentioned.

According to Bühler, the goat's head excellently suits a deity who has to do with reproduction and children, as the strong sexual instincts of the goat did not escape the notice of the ancient Hindus.[223] It may be inferred that the goat's head was the original attribute of Naigameṣa-Naigameṣin, the brāhmaṇas later substituting a ram's head on account of the seeming connection of the name with *meṣa* (ram). The Jainas, on the other hand, used a deer's head on account of Hariṇegameṣī's possible connection with *hariṇa* (gazelle).

Naigameṣa is associated with the *nyagrodha* tree. His special date is the sixth day of the month, which coincides with that of Ṣaṣṭhī.[224]

### 3.5.3 FEMALE GOAT-HEADED DEITY

Female versions of the goat-headed deity have also been found at Mathurā. These are usually found carved in high relief on rectangular stones; a goat-headed female figure may rarely be found among a row of animal and bird-headed Mātṛkās (*Pl.* 3.3.6).

In one of the best preserved examples, the goat-headed goddess is carved in the round holding with her left arm a child seated on her left knee.[225] Her right hand is in *abhaya-hasta* and there is big halo measuring five-and-a-half inches in diameter round the head. She wears a prominent necklace above her breasts.

One of the better-known depictions of the female goat-headed deity portrays her with prominent breasts. She is holding a pillow with her left hand on which a male child (defaced) is lying with hands joined on its breast (*Pl.* 3.5.11).[226] The right hand of the deity is broken but seems to have been raised to the shoulder, perhaps in *abhaya-hasta*. The goddess wears a beaded necklace and bangles. A similar figure with prominent breasts over which there lies a broad necklace, has been recovered from the Kaṅkālī Ṭīlā in Mathurā (*Pl.* 3.5.12).[227] The child on the cushion here is much defaced but presumably, like the earlier piece, this too was a male child with hands folded in adoration. One variation in the depiction of a goat-faced female figure[228] shows her holding a lotus in her right hand and a goblet in her left; no children are present (*Pl.* 3.5.10).

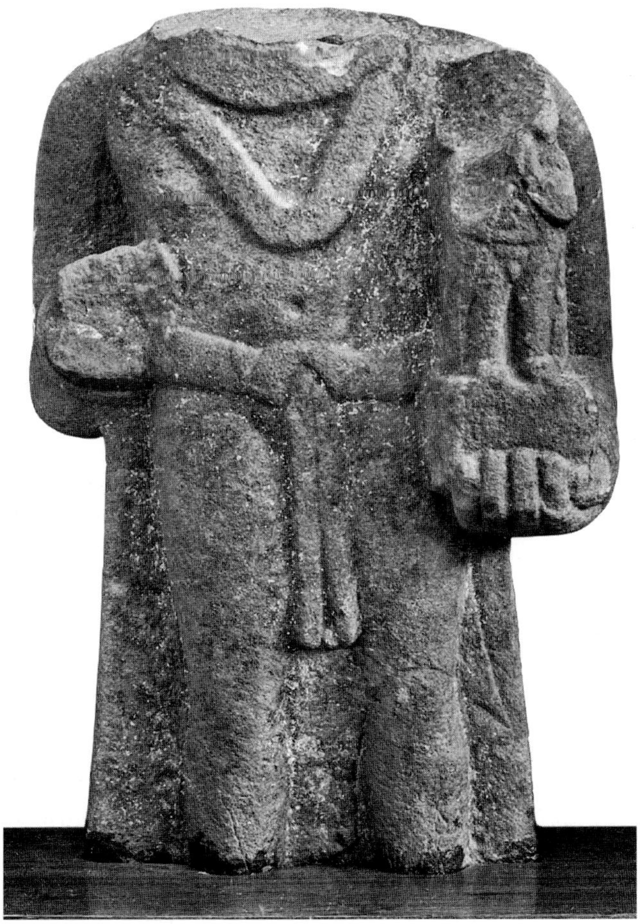

3.5.9 *Yakṣa* with child, standing, red sandstone, third century BCE, Mathurā district, UP. GMM No. 44.3130.

A goat-faced deity is also part of a panel showing at least three seated female figures,[229] though there is a possibility that there were originally at least five deities. Each of the three remaining figures is seated, holding up the right hand in *abhaya-hasta* and cradling a child in left hand.

Female goat-faced figures having long dangling ears and holding children with human faces in their laps, found at Mathurā and associated sites may have been another variation in depicting this goddess (*Pl.* 3.5.13).[230]

### 3.5.4 ENGENDERING MALE AND FEMALE GOAT-HEADED DEITIES

Who is the female goat-headed deity, and why was she conceived and created at the same time and in the same region as a male deity with a goat's head? The male deity, Naigameṣa, is ostensibly ascribed mothering functions, and has a well defined mythic-religious foundation around his person.

V.S. Agrawala offers an interesting explanation for this phenomenon: the supervision of children and childbirth — the function assigned to Naigameṣin — must have made this male deity appear anomalous to the worshippers and sculptors of Jaina art, since "*in all naturalness* (emphasis mine) it should be a female divinity that would understand and sympathise with the aspirations of those who aspired to be mothers."[231] In Agrawala's opinion, the confidential prayers to remove the "curse of infertility" could only have been made to a tender-hearted female divinity. The feminisation of Naigameṣa or Nemeso was achieved with ease since both the Buddhist example of Hāritī and the Brāhmanical version, in the form of Śrī-Lakṣmī, were close at hand. This is illustrated by the fact that later images of Naigameṣī have a human head; and in this form the figures become an ideal of mother-and-child imagery.

Shivaji Panikkar has attributed the change in sexual identity of Harinaigameṣin to the deity's special aspect of association with children: it was this that facilitated the invention of the feminine form of the deity.[232] He also rejects the notion that the female version of the goat-headed deity may be his spouse, as was the case with later Saptamātṛkās such as Vārāhī or Kaumārī.

As stated above, both the male and female figures are to be found in the same period and within the same geographical area. It would thus be safe to assume that the different sexual identities of the deities did in fact signify different functions, and that the female deity is simply not a feminised form of the male.

A clue to their separate identities may lie in their iconography. Most of the male figures that are shown with children have them either riding on their shoulders or near their feet. In one case, the male deity is depicted with the children hanging above his thighs in what seems to be a threatening posture. This could suggest that the deity combined both benevolent and malefic qualities in his person. In contrast, the feminine counterpart is usually shown cradling the child on a cushion, denoting her benevolent nature and ability to nurture and care for the child, as is also indicated in her posture.

It is pertinent to observe that a *dhotī* always covers the lower portion of the body, both of the female and male goat-headed deities. This is a trait shared by most other divine figures, which further disproves the popular notion that most female figures in post-Mauryan art, especially in Mathurā, were created nude or semi-nude. Divinity is further suggested by the *abhaya-hasta* or protection-granting gesture, and by the associated children, who have their hands folded in worship and directed towards the deity. Additionally, the gaze of both the male and female figures is focused outward and not on the child(ren). This seems to suggest that the sculpture includes the viewer in its range of protection. Other attributes associated with some of the figures, such as the purse, goblet and lotus, suggest additional meanings including prosperity and fecundity.

The females have full, rounded and close-set breasts, suggesting nurture through lactation, one of the elements of motherhood. Though generally found as an independent object of worship, the female goat-headed deity can also be found among the mothering figures (Mātṛkās).

The relatively small size of the figures recovered, in comparison to the *yakṣa-yakṣī*, Hāritī or Ṣaṣṭhī sculptures, and the fact that most of them are carved in relief rather than in the round, would suggest that these were votive objects. Perhaps they were created and/or donated during a particular ceremony such as the *sīmantonnayana* or during actual childbirth as a protective/apotropaic device. The small pedestals underneath the figures also suggest that these were vertically placed, maybe against a wall or in a niche. It is doubtful that they were placed in large structural shrines.

In the textual tradition, Hariṇegameṣin or Nemeso is directly linked to protecting the embryo, to ensuring safe childbirth, and also to

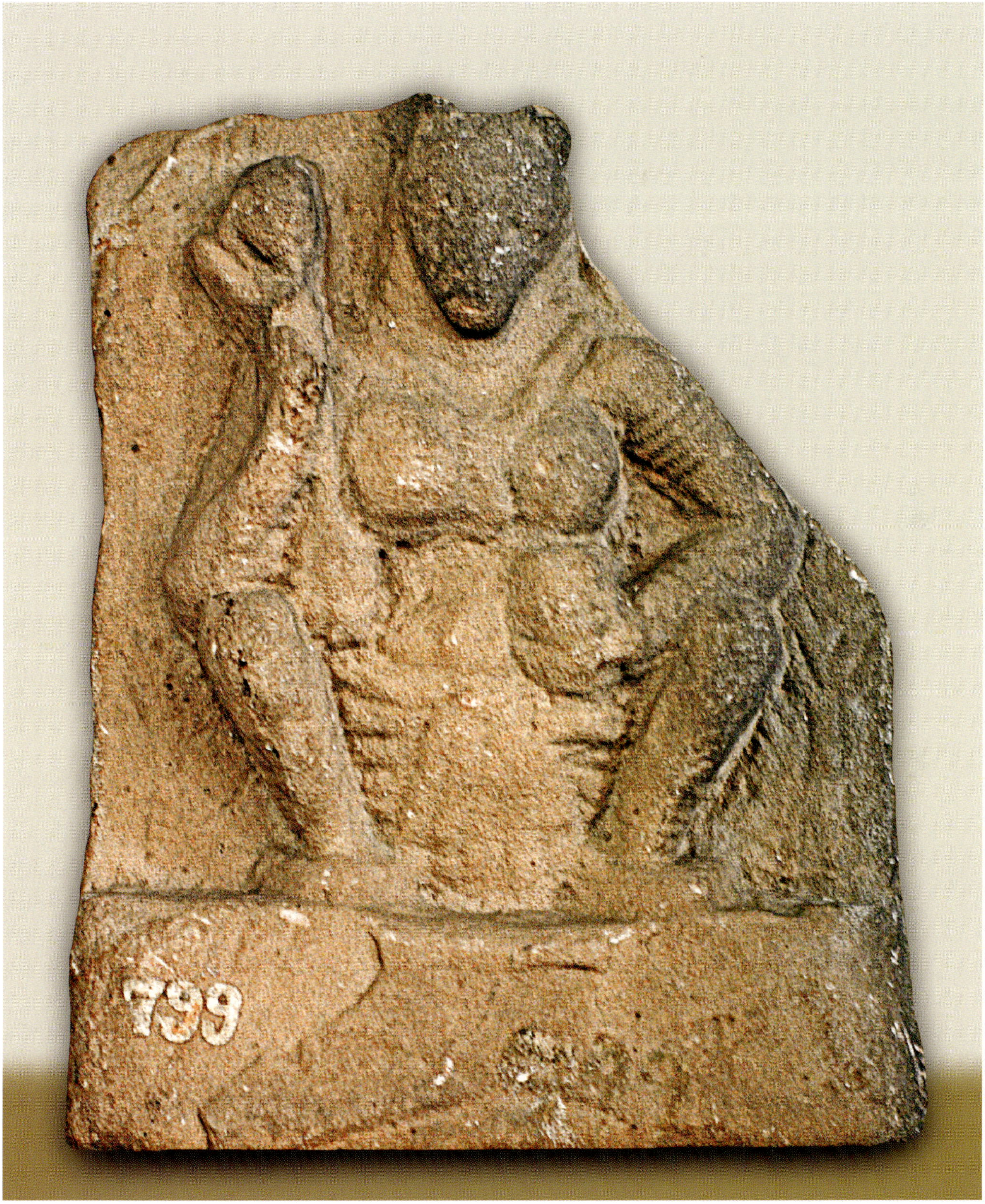

3.5.10 Female goat-headed deity, with a child in her lap, second century CE, red sandstone, Mathurā district, UP. GMM

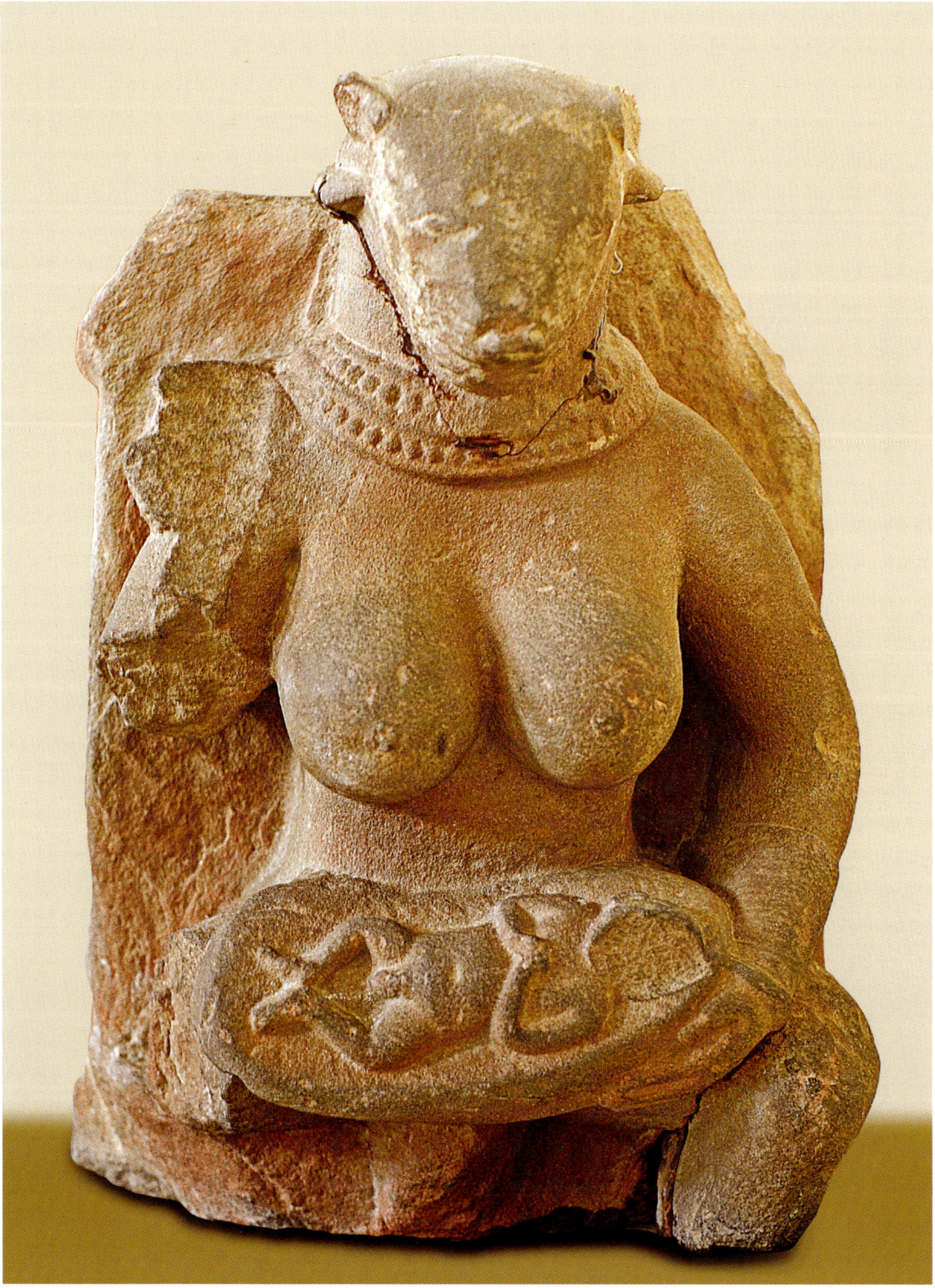

3.5.11 Female goat-headed deity, Naigameṣī, red sandstone, second century CE, Mathurā district, UP. GMM No. E 2.

fulfilling the desire for the birth of children. The textual tradition as well as the iconography of the male and female versions of the goat-headed deity locates them within the domain of fertility, pregnancy and childbirth. The male grants wishes for offspring, protection and care, while the female embodies nurture and care.

### 3.6 Malignant Goddess

There are not many examples of negative deities among representations of the divine feminine in the religious complex of the post-Mauryan period. Amongst the plethora of mother-goddess figures found at Mathurā, there is a rare four-armed goddess seated on a hillock made of rocks and rubble, which is visible to the right of the deity (not illustrated).[233] Both her legs can be seen in front, as if she were squatting over this pile of rocks. Unfortunately her head and extra forearms are no longer extant. Locks of her hair can be seen hanging over her shoulders, rather like *jaṭā*s. In each hands she holds up a child (who actually looks quite grown up), by its neck. A third child can be seen lying face-down near her feet. On the lower left arm of the figure is a coiled snake-shaped armlet, *keyūra* can be seen.

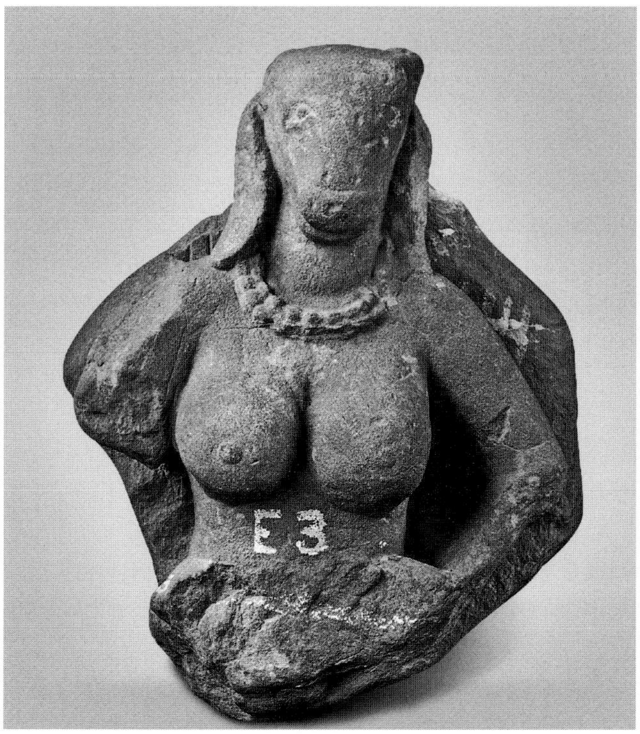

3.5.12 Naigameṣī, Mathurā sandstone, second century CE, Kaṅkālī Ṭīlā, Mathurā district, UP. GMM No. 00E.3

This figure has been identified as Jātahāriṇī, one of the malignant *bālagraha*s found enumerated in the *Suśruta Saṁhitā* and the *Kaśyapa Saṁhitā*. Jātahāriṇī is not evil but, according to the belief stated in the texts, she has the power to take away, *hāra*, young children of irreligious, impious and evil parents. In the image described above, she seems to have killed at least three children. The snake armlet on her upper arm also suggests her association with *nāga*s and the power to take away the life of children. Her appearance is terrific, unlike benign goddesses such as Bhadrā.

The redemptive mothering qualities of child protection and care, evident in goddesses like Hāritī, are not seen in this image. The children here are not cradled in the lap of the goddess as if she were a Mātṛkā, nor do they frolic around and clamber up her person as they do in Hāritī figures.

### 3.7 Conclusions

The number and variety of "mother" figures delineated in this chapter suggests there was an overwhelming concern with motherhood and a need to project it through imagery in the period under discussion. This anxiety of post-Mauryan society over maternity exhibits itself in the production of myriad mother-goddess figures concerned with fertility, pregnancy, childbirth and child protection. The anxiety, however, does not seem excessive keeping in view the transitional and turbulent times.

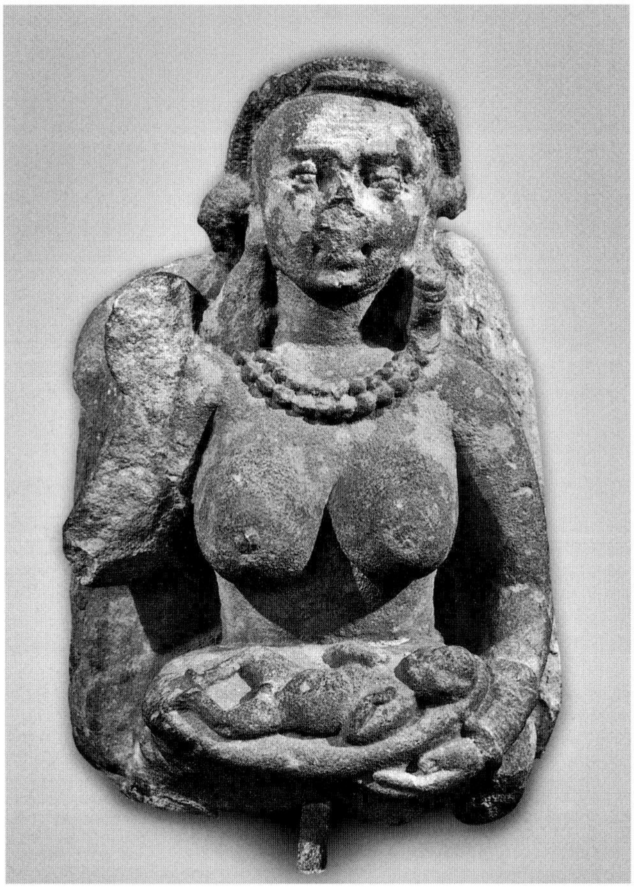

3.5.13 Naigameṣī, red sandstone, second century CE, Manoharpur, Mathurā district, UP. GMM No. E 4.

The imperative, especially among the higher echelons, to have an heir, is reflected in Jātaka stories such as the *Kuśa Jātaka*. Here the king Ikṣvāku, anxious to have a child but being presumably impotent, sends first dancing girls, then the court ladies, and finally the chief queen Śīlavatī, out into the streets of his kingdom with the command that they conceive a child, keeping *dharmanāṭaka*, the dictum of righteousness, in mind while having sexual intercourse with a stranger.[234] This story is illustrated at Bharhut as well.[235] The entire episode sheds light not only on the significance of reproduction but also on the ambivalence towards patriarchal norms of faithfulness versus ensuring fertility of women.

It is within this context that one can place the Buddhist attitude towards childbirth and maternal emotions as being symbols of suffering and bondage. The lament of many nuns (*therīs*) such as Ubbirī and Paṭācārā's Five Hundred,[236] that motherhood is a sad task and that they became stream-enterers after the death of their children, is significant. This is an indication of the high infant mortality rate, and it also provides an explanation for the relative proliferation of mother-goddesses/child-protectress figures in the religious art of the period.

The above discussion of some of the mothering figures available from the post-Mauryan period reveals that not all of them were seen as biological mothers. In fact, there exist alternative models of adoptive motherhood or social mothering that are associated in myths with divine motherhood, as is the case with the Mātṛkās and Naigameṣi/Naigameṣī. In Buddhist and later Jaina traditions, both textual and visual, biological mothers such as Māyādevī, Hāritī and Ambikā are deified. In the Brāhmanical tradition, abstract deities such as the Mātṛkās become connected with motherhood.

A child makes it possible for a woman to be mother. A number of mothering images discussed above are shown with children, but this is not universally applicable to all mothering figures as is seen in the Ṣaṣṭhī figure.

Another important element that marks the mothering figures in art is their solidity. Irrespective of their size, in the treatment there is a degree of massive immobility associated with them. This impression is partly projected by the sitting or standing posture with the gaze focused outward and partly by the hands raised in *abhaya* (protection). It may also be noted that, unlike the *yakṣī-śālabhañjikā* images, the divine mothers are always depicted as clothed figures with a *dhotī* and/or a blouse, perhaps to indicate their supra-mundane status and as a mark of respect and reverence. It also reinforces my view that nude feminine figures were not the norm in early Indian art; rather, there is a differentiation in clothing that is linked to the function and nature of the sculpture.

Thus, within the discourse of motherhood in art, nurture and duty, along with protection, form significant elements.

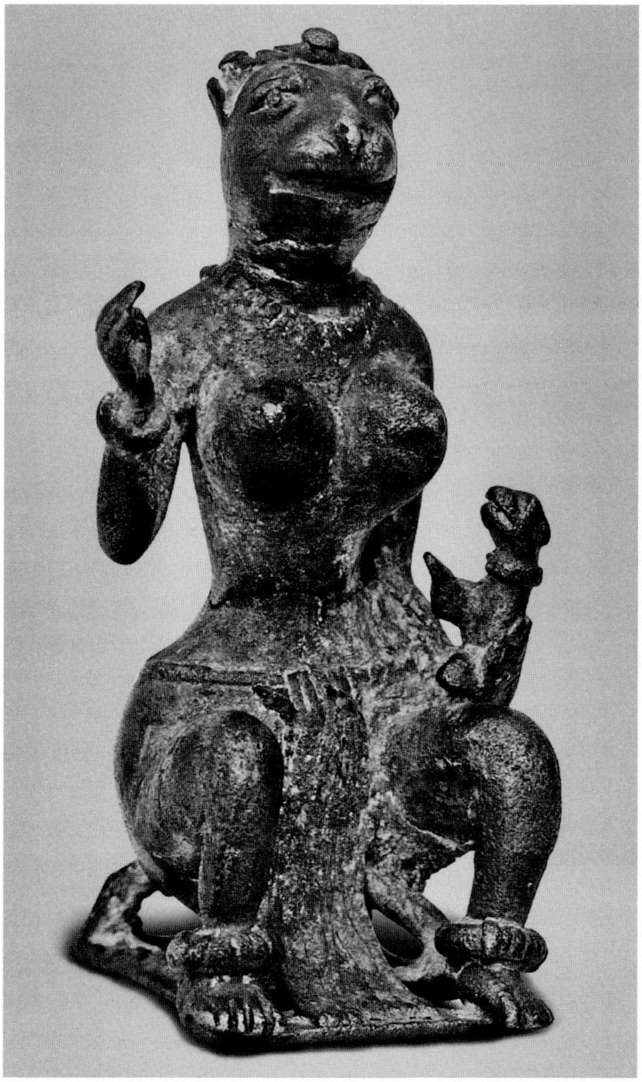

3.5.14 Mother Goddess, animal-headed with baby on lap, bronze, first-second century CE. AM.

## Notes and References

1. See supra: Chapter 2.
2. D.T. Meyers, S. Mater, J. Kristeva, eds., *Feminist Thought: A Reader*, Routledge, New York, 1997, p. 303 have observed that consecrated representation of femininity is absorbed by motherhood. However, this motherhood is a fantasy that is nurtured by the adult man or woman, of a lost territory, what is more, it involves less an idealised archaic mother than the idealisation of the relationship that binds us to her, one that cannot be localised, what in psychological terms can be termed primary narcissism. Christianity as a religious discourse is focused on Maternality.
3. *Mānava-Gṛhyasūtra*, 2.13.9; for Ṣaṣṭhī see below.
4. It has been argued that private property results in a greater control of men over female sexuality, through marriage and family. This includes making pregnancy and childcare a woman's domain.
5. I.B. Horner, *Women Under Primitive Buddhism*, Delhi: Motilal Banarsidass Publishers Pvt. Ltd., 1999 (reprint), pp. 11-13 gives examples from early Buddhist Pāli literature where mothers of criminal, deformed and other less privileged children refused to give them up, even though the fathers readily abandoned them.
6. Ibid., p. 4 observes that with the rise of Buddhism and the admission of women into the *bhikṣuṇī saṁgha*, the order of the nuns, the popular conviction that child-bearers were the only women of any account and that motherhood was not only their natural and almost sole function, but their primary duty as well, was vanishing.
7. Kathleen M. Bolen, "Prehistoric Construction of Mothering", in Cheryl Classen, ed., *Exploring Gender Through Archaeology: Monographs in World Archeology No. 11*, Wisconsin: Prehistory Press, 1992, pp. 49-50.
8. Infra, Section on Māyā.
9. Kathleen M. Bolen, op.cit., p. 49.
10. Uma Chakravarti, "Preliminary Observations on the Impulse Control of Women in Early India:

Ideology, Kinship and The State As Mechanisms of Control", in K.D. Bajpai, ed., *Position and Status of Women in Ancient India*, Varanasi, 1992, p. 127.

11. Gerda Lerner, *The Creation of Patriarchy*, New York: Oxford University Press, 1986, p. 50.

12. See Uma Chakravarti, "Beyond the Altekarian Paradigm: Towards a New Understanding of Gender Relations in Early Indian History", in Kumkum Roy, ed., *Women in Early Indian Societies*, New Delhi: Manohar, 1999, pp. 72-81, for an analysis of Altekar's nationalist project of valorising and celebrating the status of Hindu women.

13. A.S. Altekar, *The Position of Women in Hindu Civilization*, New Delhi: Motilal Banarsidass, 2nd edn.: 1959 (rpt. 1995), pp. 100-103.

14. I.B. Horner, op. cit., pp. 1-18.

15. Kumkum Roy, "Of Theras and Therīs: Visions of Liberation in the Early Buddhist Tradition", in Vijaya Ramaswamy, ed., *Researching Indian Women*, New Delhi: Manohar, 2003, p. 83.

16. See, Shashi Bhushan Dasgupta, *Aspects of Indian Religious Thought*, Calcutta: Firma KLM, 1977, p. 105.

17. J.N. Tiwari, *Goddess Cults in Ancient India (With Special Reference to the First Seven Centuries AD)*, New Delhi: Sundeep Prakashan, 1985, p. xi.

18. For the depiction of this episode see infra, Non-Wives: Prostitutes and Nuns. The nun Utpalavarṇā received Buddha when he descended at Sankissa.

19. Romila Thapar, *Cultural Pasts*, New Delhi: Oxford University Press, 2000, p. 426.

20. *Buddhacarita*, I.1-2.

21. *Saundarānanda*, II.49: *tasya devī nṛdevasya māyā nāma tadābhavat* । *vīta kroddhatamo māyā māyeva divi devatā* ॥

22. Ibid.

23. *Śatapatha Brāhmaṇa*, II.4.3.11.

24. *Śvetasvatāra*, 4.10: *māyām tu prakṛtim vidyat māyinām tu maheśvaram*. Quoted in V.S. Agrawala, *Ancient Indian Folks Cults*, Varanasi: Prithvi Prakashan, 1970 p. 149.

25. Ibid., p. 150.

26. E.H. Johnson, "A Terracotta Figure at Oxford", in *JISOA*, vol. X, 1942, p. 101.

27. Ibid., ll. 103, 222-231; Oxyrhychus Papyrus No. 1280 (ed. Grenfell and Hunt, part XI, pp. 190-220); Cf. E.H. Johnson, "A Terracotta Figure at Oxford", p. 101.

28. D.D. Kosambi, *Myth and Reality: Studies in The Formation of Indian Culture*, Bombay: Popular Prakashan, 1962, pp. 101-2.

29. *Saundarānanda*, V.45: *tatsaumya lolam parigamya lokam māyopam citramivendrajālam priyāmithyām tyaja mohajālam chettum matiste yadi dukhajālam* ॥

30. Padmanabhan Jaini, *Gender and Salvation: Jaina Debates on the Spiritual Liberation of Women*, New Delhi: Munshiram Manoharlal, 1992, p. 15

31. H. Zimmer, *The Art of Indian Asia: Its Mythology and Transformation*, vol. I, New Jersey: Princeton University Press, 1960 (3rd Imprint of 1908 original), p. 106. For detailed analysis see H. Zimmer, *Maya den indische Mythos*, Rascher Verlag, Zurich, MCMLII.

32. *MWSE*, p. 811.

33. V.S. Apte, p. 757.

34. *Pāli-English Dictionary*, p. 529.

35. A. Foucher, *On the Iconography of the Buddha's Nativity*, MASI, No. 46, ASI, New Delhi, rpt. 1999 (original, 1934), pp. 1-2.

36. Ibid. p. 4.

37. *Pañcacūḍā* literally means five buns of hair. It implies a depiction of a female figure with five hair bunches ornamented with five or more devices such as the *aṅkuśa, darpaṇa, dhvaja, paraśu, śrīvatsa,* etc. Many such figures in terracotta have been discovered from post-Mauryan layers at sites such as Mathurā, Kauśāmbī, Candraketugaṛh, etc.

38. E.H. Johnson, op. cit., pp. 94-102.

39. *Saundarananda*, II.50, *svapane atha samaye garbhmavisantam dadarsa sa, saddantam varanam svetameravatamivaujasa*.

40. *Buddhacarita*, I.4.

41. Bharhut, Madhya Pradesh, great railing,

medallion, Indian Museum, Calcutta No. 93; Also, N. Majumdar, *Guide to Indian Museum*, Part I, p. 41.

42. LL. No. 801; Sanskrit- *garbhāvakrānti.*

43. Hathina, Gurgaon Railing pillar, Size: 57" x 10", red sandstone. Now in Chandigarh Art and Sculpture Gallery; D.S. Punia, "New Evidence of Pre *Kuśāṇa* Sculpture from Gurgaon District (Haryana)", in *East and West*, New Series 31, 1981, pp. 134-34.

44. Kurt Behrendt, "An Unnoticed Relief from Bhilsā Topes and its relationship to the Sculpture at Sāñcī", in *South Asian Studies*, vol. 16, 2000, pp. 1-9, figs. 1-4. I was unable to see this relief sculpture when I visited Andher, apparently it was placed face down on the ground to prevent further erosion.

45. *Rājapraśnīya Sūtra*, 154-155, pp. 85-86.

46. Ratan Parimoo, *Life of Buddha in Indian Sculpture Ashta Maha Pratiharya: An Iconological Analysis*, New Delhi: Kanak Publications, 1982, p. 6 , fig 2.

47. Manjushree Rao, *Sanchi Sculptures*, New Delhi: Akay Book Corporations, 1994, Pl. 10; Also J. Marshall, *The Monuments of Sanci*, vol. II, Pl, 50a, 1.

48. Western Pakistan, Sculptured slab, first-third century CE. Gandhāra style, schist, size: .200 × .130m, Prince of Wales Museum 3.

49. Emfagnis, Schist, Gandhāra, third century, size: .290 wide. MIK I 63, *Museum für Indische Kunst, Berlin: Catalogue 1986*, Staatliche Museen Preussishcer Kulturbesitz, Berlin, Plate 178.

50. Amarāvatī, second century CE, Chennai: Government Museum.

51. C. Sivaramamurti, *Sri Lakshmi in Indian Art and Thought*, New Delhi: Kanak Publications, 1982, p. 3, fig. 4, x.

52. Now in Indian Museum, Calcutta; for other depictions of Māyādevī's Dream from Amarāvatī see Robert Knox, *Amaravati: Buddhist Sculpture from the Great Stupa*, London: British Museum Press, 1992, pp. 100, 138, 139, 144, 146 & 150.

53. Edward Conze, *The Life of Buddha: As Legend and History*, New Delhi: Motilal Banarsidass, 1993, p. 48.

54. For other views of Dream of Māyādevī at Nāgārjunakoṇḍa see Elizabeth Rosen Stone, *The Buddhist Art of Nāgārjunakoṇḍa*, New Delhi: Motilal Banarsidass, 1994, figs. 36, 41, 65 & 83.

55. Ibid., fig. 192, p. 71.

56. *Saundarānanda*, II.48.

57. The *śāla* tree of the Lumbinī grove near Kapilavastu is mentioned in the *Nidānakathā* of the Jātakas and the *plakṣa* tree in the later texts such as the *Mahāvastu* and *Lalitavistara*: cf., Gustav Roth, "The Woman and Tree Motif", in *JAS, Letters and Science*, vol. XXIII, no. 1, 1957, p. 98.

58. Ratan Parimoo, *Life of Buddha in Indian Sculpture Ashta-Maha-Pratihara: An Iconological Analysis*, p. 11.

59. Stella Kramrisch, *Indian sculpture in Philadelphia Museum*, Philadelphia, 1961, p. 16. She observes that in *śālabhañjikā* motifs, the vegetative and the feminine coalesce so organically as to transmit the creative generative energy from one to the other.

60. *Buddhacarita*, I.10: this is likened to the birth of Aurva from the thigh, of Pṛthu from the hand, of Māndhātṛ, the peer of Indra, from the head, of Kakivat from the armpit, as such wise was his birth.

61. Ibid., 1.5-I.9.

62. Gustav Roth, op. cit., p. 98.

63. *Majjhima Nikāya*, 23.2, 8 quoted in U.N. Roy, *Śālabhañjikā in Art Philosophy and Literature*, Allahabad: Lokbharati Publications, 1979, p. 4.

64. Gustav Roth, op. cit., p. 98.

65. Kausambi Museum No. E/27, Allahabad University, buff sandstone, Size: 56 × 70.5 cm, Śuṅga; Aruna Tripathi, *The Buddhist Art of Kauśāmbī*, New Delhi: D.K. Printworld Pvt. Ltd., 2003, p. 70, fig. 31.

66. Some examples of the Birth of Buddha in Gāndhāra style — West Pakistan, first-second century, schist, Size: 180 × .225m, Bharat Kala Bhavan No, 755, Varanasi; Pakistan, first-second century, schist, Indian Museum, Calcutta, this example is set in a half medallion; Pakistan, green schist, .140 × .140m, Prince of Wales Museum No. 5, Mumbai-set in a *caitya* window; West Pakistan,

second century, blue schist, .320 × .18m, Allahabad Museum No. 126; Pakistan, second-third century Blue schist, .320 × .270m Government Museum and art Gallery No. 2306, also No. 2315, size: .150 × .120m and No. 1593 size: .180 × .155m, Chandigarh; Western Pakistan, third-fifth century, blue-gray schist, size: .150 × .220m, Mathura Museum No. 34.2530, GMM, Mathurā; Schist, second-third century, size: breadth, 46.5 cm, MIK I 52, Museum für Indische Kunst, Berlin.

67. Pakistan, Nativity of Buddha, *c.* CE 150 Gāndhāra style, dark gray blue slate, size: ht. 670m. Freer Art Gallery No. 49.9, Washington. Part of a frieze.

68. GMM. Antiquity no. 00.H2; also GMM. N2; N.P. Joshi, *Archaeological Museum, Mathura*, 1966, pp. 56-57, figure 49.

69. For birth of Buddha scenes at Amarāvatī see Robert Knox, op. cit., pp. 33, 100-19, 136, 138, 144, 146, 150.

70. For Birth of Buddha scenes at Nāgārjunakoṇḍa see Elizabeth Rosen Stone, op. cit., figs. 36, 65, 83, 158, 162, 188, 209, 210; pp. 28-30, 42, 63-65, 70, 73.

71. *Buddhacarita*, I.17, I.15, I.16.

72. *Buddhacarita*, 1.18-19. Similar rejoicing is recorded in *Saundarānanda*, II.52-55.

73. *Buddhacarita*, II.18. And when the queen Māyā saw the vast power of her son, like that of the divine seer, she was unable to bear the joy it caused her and she went to Heaven to dwell there.

74. Ibid., I.61.

75. Ibid., I.3-4.

76. I.B. Horner, *Women under Primitive Buddhism*, pp. 28, 48.

77. *Therīgāthā, Psalms of the Early Buddhist*, PTS, (1[st] edn. 1909), rpt., 1964, LXIII verses 216-217, p. 109. *Therīgāthā*, tr. and ed. Vimalkirti, New Delhi: Samyaka Prakashana, 2003, p. 189. *Dukkho itthibhavo, akkato purisadammasarathina, samttikampi hi dukham, appekacca sakim vijatayo. Galake api kantanti sukhumaliniyo visani khadanti, janamarkamjjhgata, ubhopi byasanani anubhonti.*

78. *Therīgāthā*, verse L, 127-129, p. 78. Paṭācārā said, "Why mournest thou for him who came to thee, lamenting through thy tears: "My Son, My Son!", Seeing not the way he came, Not yet the manner of his leaving you? . . . As man to die, and pass on to other births — so hither and so thence — why should you weep? . . . And that consuming grief for my dead child, that poisoned all the life in me is dead." Also see Sundari's *gāthā*, verses 312-315 and also Gotami's verses, Appendix, *Saṁyutta Nikāya*, 3.

79. See supra, Chapter 1: Gender and Art: Paradigms and Problematic.

80. Ibid., sub-section on Nakedness.

81. Cowell, *Jātaka*, No. 547.

82. Sometimes one of the attendant figures in the Birth of Buddha series is considered to be Mahāprajāpati. For example see *Gandhara Sculpture in the Government Museum and Art Gallery*, Chandigarh, 2002, pp. 116-26, figs. 386, 526.

83. *Buddhacarita*. Then the queen sister, who equalled her in majesty and did not fall below her in affection and tenderness, brought up the prince, who was like the scion of the gods as if he were her own son (2.19).

84. Her own verses are given in *Therīgāthā*, LV, pp. 87-89, where she is called the daughter of Sakyan Anjana of Devadaha.

85. *MWSE*, p. 658.

86. Anna Maria Quagliotti, "An inscribed image of Hāritī in the Chandigarh Museum and Art Gallery", in *Silk Road Art and Archaeology*, 6, 1999/2000, pp. 51-60; Ludwig Bachofer, "Die Hāritī von Skarah Dehri", in *Ostasiatische Zeitschrift*, 1936, pp. 99-101; K. Walton Dobbins, "A Note on the Hāritī Image from Skarah Dehri, Year 399", in *East and West*, vol. 17, nos. 3-4, 1967, pp. 268-72; Bhagwat Sahai, *Iconography of Minor Hindu and Buddhist Deities*, New Delhi: Abhinav Publications, 1975, pp. 253-58; Alice Getty, *The Gods of Northern Buddhism*, New Delhi: Munshiram Manoharlal, 2[nd] edn., 1978; K. Krishna Murthy, "Vestiges of Hāritī Worship in Andhra", in Amita Ray and et al. eds., *Indian Studies: Essays Presented in the Memory of Prof. Niharranjan Ray*, New Delhi: Caxton Publications, n.d., pp. 57-58.

87. Government Museum and Art Gallery, Chandigarh, No. 1625.

88. Bhagwat Sahai, op. cit., p. 255.

89. Ibid.

90. For other examples see Anna Maria Quagliotti, op. cit., pp. 51-60, figs. 4-8; for seated examples see fig. 3.

91. For other examples see Anna Maria Quagliotti, op. cit., pp. 51-60, figs. 5 and 8.

92. UP, Tayapur, Mathurā district, Hāritī, seated, third century, red sandstone, GMM No. F. 30.

93. Now in Patna Museum, third century, Hāritī, head and arm missing.

94. Elizabeth Rosen Stone, op. cit., fig 24; *Indian Archeology: A Review*, 1954-55, pp. 22-23.

95. Aruna Tripathi, op. cit., fig. 166.

96. For example, UP, Kervai, Mathurā district, Kubera and Hāritī, third century, Mathurā sandstone, GMM No. 00.C29; UP, Mathurā district, Kubera and Hāritī, third century, Mathurā Sandstone, GMM No. 18.1402; Gopalpur, Mathurā district, Kubera and Hāritī, third century, Mathurā Sandstone, GMM No. 14.500.

97. West Pakistan, grey schist, National Museum No. 49.21/5, Now in the National Museum; also Zwalf, *Catalogue of the Sculptures in the British Musuem*, Hāritī, British Museum. OA 1886/6-11; Indian Museum, Calcutta, IM A 25083/9282.

98. For example Soṅkh, Mathurā district, Kubera and Hāritī, second century, Mathurā Sandstone, GMM No. 5; Mathurā, now in Indian Museum, Calcutta, second century CE seated.

99. UP, Mathurā district, Kubera and Hāritī and worshipers, third century, Mathurā Sandstone, GMM No. 15.1179.

100. Mathurā, now in Indian Museum, Calcutta, second century CE seated.

101. Bhagwat Sahai, op. cit., p. 256.

102. Ibid.

103. Ibid.

104. A.K. Coomaraswamy, *Yakṣas*, pp. 35-44.

105. UP, Kaṅkālī Ṭīlā, Mathurā district, Kubera seated, inscribed, third century, Mathurā Sandstone, GMM No. 46.3232.

106. A.K. Coomaraswamy, op. cit., p. 37.

107. J.N. Banerjea, *The Development of Hindu Iconography*, Delhi: Munshiram Manoharlal, 2002 (5th edn.), p. 372.

108. See AIIS; No. 362.11

109. N.P. Joshi, *Mothers, Mat̥rkās in Mathurā Art*, p. 128 ; UP Girdharpur Ṭīlā, Mathurā District, Kārttikeya and female deity standing, inscribed "Pravarikasa", third century, Mathurā Sandstone. GMM No. 17.1316.

110. State Museum, Lucknow, No. 0.241.

111. Sten Konow, *CII: Kharoṣṭhi Inscriptions with the Exception of Those of Asoka, II*, pt. I, Calcutta, 1929, pp. 124-27.

112. Bhagwat Sahai, op. cit., p. 253.

113. I-tsing, *A Record of the Buddhist Religion as Practised in India and the Malay Archipelago CE 671-695*, tr. J. Takakusu, New Delhi: Munshiram Manoharlal, rpt. 1982, p. 37.

114. Si-yu-ki. *Buddhist Records from the Western World*, tr. S. Beal, 1884, London, Delhi: Orient Books Reprint Corporation, rpt. 1969, pp. 110-11.

115. Alice Getty, op. cit., p. 84.; Also GMM No. 2520 which is a stone plaque with Ardhanārīśvara, Viṣṇu, Gaja-Lakṣmī and Kubera all with right hand raised in *abhaya-hasta*.

116. *MWSE*, p. 1289: *hāra*, means bearing, carrying, carrying away, stealing.

117. Gail Sutherland, *Yakṣas: Disguises of the Demon*, New York: SUNY, 1991, p. 144.

118. Ibid., p. 143.

119. Ibid., pp. 144-45.

120. Shivaji Panikkar, *Saptamāt̥rkā Worship and Sculpture*, Delhi: D.K. Printworld, 1997, p. 47, *fig.* 12.

121. Ibid.; N.P. Joshi, *Māt̥rkās: Mothers in Kuṣāṇa Art*, New Delhi: Kanak Publications, 1986; N.P. Joshi, "Two Māt̥rkā Plaques in the State Museum, Lucknow", in *BMAUP* 1, March 1968; N.P. Joshi, *Catalogue of Brāhmanical Sculptures in the State*

*Museum, Lucknow*, part I, Lucknow, 1972; R.C. Agrawala, "Mātṛkā Reliefs in Early Indian Art", in *East and West*, vol. 2, nos. 1-2, March-June 1971; pp. 79-90; Katherine Anne Harper, *Seven Hindu Goddesses of Spiritual Transformation*, New York, 1989; Moti Chandra, "Studies in the Cult of the Mother Goddess in Ancient India", in *BPWM*, no. 12, 1973.

122. Shivaji K. Panikkar, op. cit., p. 42.

123. N.P. Joshi, *Mātṛkās: Mothers in Kuṣāṇa Art*, p. 104.

124. For the various versions of the myths relating to the origin of Mātṛkās see Shivaji K. Panikkar, op. cit., Chapter 2.

125. *Mahābhārata*, Vana-Parva, CCXXVII.

126. In Hindu belief system, *sūtaka-pātaka* are periods of impurity shared by the entire family. Both birth and death mark these periods and in the duration of *sūtaka-pātaka* Brāhmaṇa priests do not accept any cooked food or perform any *yajña* in the affected family.

127. N.N. Bhattacharya, *The Indian Mother Goddess*, New Delhi: Manohar, 1977, pp. 46-47.

128. I am using the term canopy to denote an arched object visible above the head of main female figure. This may have been an *uttarīya* or a scarf worn high above the coiffure like a modern day *oṛhanī* or a kind of a *cattra*. It has been suggested by T.S. Maxwell, *Vishvarupa*, Delhi: Oxford University Press 1988, p. 37 that it may have been a *śūrpa* or a winnowing fan associated with Sītalā (the goddess of small pox). In the current rituals associated with Ṣaṣṭhī, *śūrpa* is used by women as a receptacle for offering made on Chaṭha, or Ṣaṣṭhī *tithi* to the Sun god.

129. Mathura Museum No. F 2, red sandstone, size: ht. 74 cm or 29". Kuṣāṇa period, *ASR*, XX, pp. 34-35, Pl. III; A.K. Coomaraswamy, *History of Indian and Indonesian Art*, 1927, fig. 82; V.S. Agrawala, "Miscellaneous Fragmentary Figures", *Journal of The U.P. Historical Society*, vol. XXIII, 1950, pp.202-3; P.K. Agrawala, "Identification of The So-Called Nagi Figures As Goddess Ṣaṣṭhi", *East and West*, vol. 21, 1971, pp. 325-29, fig 10, also pp. 325-29: N.P. Joshi, op. cit., p. 126, figs. 39a-b.

130. V.S. Agrawala, op. cit., pp. 102-18. However, Maxwell is of the opinion that the objects held in the hands of this subsidiary figure may be coiled snakes. See Maxwell, op. cit., pp. 39f.

131. Potrakuṇḍa, Kaṭrā, Mathurā, Mathura Museum No. 54.3763, red sandstone, size: 18 × 20 cm or 8 × 7". Kuṣāṇa period; N. P. Joshi, op. cit., p. 126, fig. 40.

132. Rānīmaṇḍī, Mathurā, Mathura Museum No. 54.4266, Red sandstone, Size: 12 × 14 cm, Kuṣāṇa period. N.P. Joshi, op. cit., p. 126-27.; *BMA*, 11-12, p. 66.

133. Mathurā, Museum für indische Kunst, No. MIK I.5924, red spotted sandstone, size: 67.8 cm, Kuṣāṇa period, catalogue No. 49, p. 32, Berlin; N.P. Joshi, op. cit., p. 127, fig. 40.

134. Mathurā, Mathura Museum No. F.3, red sandstone, size: 1.7m or 3'10", Kuṣāṇa period; N.P. Joshi, op. cit., p. 127, fig. 40; V.S. Agrawala, op. cit., p. 205; *EW* 21, fig. 2.

135. Girdharpur, Mathurā, Mathura Museum No. F.32, Red sandstone, size: 47 cm or 18 ½", Kuṣāṇa period, N.P. Joshi, op. cit., p. 128; *JUPHS*, XXII, p. 203.

136. Probably Mathurā, Museum für Indische Kunst, No. MIK I 10196, red spotted sandstone, Kuṣāṇa period. Catalogue No. 49 p. 32 Berlin; Kuṣāṇa period, N.P. Joshi, op. cit., p. 128.

137. Salempur Well near Mathurā, Mathura Museum No. 15.739, red sandstone, size: 17 cm or 6 ½". Kuṣāṇa period, N.P. Joshi, op. cit., p. 128, fig. 44; V.S. Agrawala, op. cit., p. 205; *BMS*, p. 230

138. Mathurā, Baroda Museum, Vadodara No. AC 2251, red sandstone, size: 6 cm, Kuṣāṇa_period; N.P. Joshi, op. cit., p. 128, Line Drawing 13.

139. Mathurā, Mathura Museum No. 1244, Red sandstone, Kuṣāṇa period; N.P. Joshi, *Mothers (Mātṛkās) in Kuṣāṇa Art*, p. 127, fig. 40; JUPHS, XXII; EW 21, fig. 3.

140. Mathurā, Mathura Museum No. 62.19 Red sandstone, Size: 14.5 × 13 cm, Kuṣāṇa period, N.P. Joshi, op. cit., p. 127, fig. 41; BMA., No. 4, pp 50-51.

141. R.C. Agrawala, op. cit., No. 21, fig. 1.

142. Kaṅkālī Ṭīlā, Mathurā, State Museum Lucknow, Museum No J. 84, red sandstone, size: 18 x 20 cm

or 8 × 7", Kuṣāṇa period, N.P. Joshi, op. cit., pp. 127-28, fig. 42.

143. A *kūcabandha* is a flat band of cloth to tie the breasts. Cf. J.N. Banerjea, *The Development of Hindu Iconography*, p. 295.

144. Soṅkh, Bronze, Size: Ht. 10.6 cm, wd 8.5 cm, Kuṣāṇa period; Herbert Härtel, *Soṅkh Excavation*, Berlin, p. 281, Pl. 18.2.

145. Ibid., p. 218; the report quotes P.K. Agrawala, *Early Indian Bronzes*, 1977, p. 64 "from the iconographic evidence provided by some stone plaques from Mathurā itself and by certain texts, we have no doubt that this goddess is Carcikā Śaṣṭhī, a mother goddess presiding over childbirth and assimilated with Devasenā Śaṣṭhī, wife of Skanda."

146. Mathurā, GMM.C.30.

147. Mathura Museum No 17.1301, red sandstone, Kuṣāṇa period.

148. P.K. Agrawala, East and West, 1971, p. 328.

149. T.S. Maxwell, op. cit., pp. 41-45, fig. 1.3.

150. The term ramifying has been used by Maxwell, op. cit., to describe GMM F.2 and SML J.84 along with Caturvyūha Viṣṇu image of GMM 14.392-5.

151. P.K. Agrawala, op. cit., 1971, p. 329.

152. Mathura Museum No 14. 392-5, red sandstone, Kuṣāṇa period.

153. T.S. Maxwell, op. cit., pp. 41-43.

154. A. Cunningham, Report on a Tour in Eastern Rajputana in 1882-83, *ARASI*, XX, pp. 34 ff. Pl. III.

155. J. Ph. Vogel, *Mathura Museum Catalogue*, Allahabad, 1910, p. 11; idem, *La Sculpture de Mathura*, Paris, 1930, p. 47, Pl. XL; V.S. Agrawala, *Mathura Museum Handbook*, Allahabad, 1939, p. 38; idem, A Catalogue of Brāhmanical Images in Mathura Art, *JUPHS*. 1951.

156. V.S. Agrawala, "Goddess Shashthi on the Yaudheya Coins," *JNSI*, p. 29.

157. John Allan, *Coins of Ancient India*, p. 270, Cf. V.S. Agrawala, op. cit., p. 31. Kārttikeya and his pantheon seem to have been worshipped by the Yaudheyas who ruled over most of Punjab, Haryana and north Rajasthan in the third and early part of the fourth century. Their capital was probably Rohhitaka, modern Rohtak in Haryana, where a mint of Yaudheya coins was discovered by Birbal Sahni; K.K. Dasgupta, *Tribal History of Ancient India: A Numismatic Approach*, Calcutta: Navabharat Publishers, 1974, p. 107.

158. P.K. Agrawala, *Skanda-Kārttikeya*, Varanasi, 1967, p. 33.

159. N.P. Joshi, "Devi Ṣaṇmukhī ya Ṣaṣṭhi", in *BMA* in UP, June 1969, pp. 38-41.

160. R.C. Agrawala, op. cit., pp. 79-90.

161. Vana-Parva of *Mbh.* 229.49-50: *evam skandasya mahiṣī devasenām vidurjanam, ṣaṣṭhi vam brāhmaṇam prahurlakṣmīmasaṁsukhapradam.* Cf. R.C. Agrawala, op. cit., p. 6.

162. Vana-Parva of *Mbh.*, 232.6 and 232.8.

163. Suvira Jaiswal, *Origin and Development of Viṣṇuism*, New Delhi: Munshiram Manoharlal, 1985 (2nd edn.), p. 99.

164. *Mbh.* III.V.3; Cf. Suvira Jaiswal, op. cit., p. 99.

165. *Mānava-Gṛhyasūtra*, II.13.

166. *MWSE*, p. 271 Kāma can be understood as desire or as the God of Love.

167. J. Gonda, *Aspects of Early Viṣṇuism*, New Delhi: Motilal Banarsidass, 1st edn., Leiden 1954, rpt., 1993, p. 218.

168. *MWSE*, p. 272, gives the meaning of *kāmapradā* as fulfilling wishes.

169. *MWSE*, p. 863 gives *rajanī* in MānGr. as a particular personification; in a general sense it means dark or blue.

170. *MWSE*, p. 993 gives *viśvarūpa* as a noun signifying various forms; wearing all forms, variegated, manifold.

171. *Mānava-Gṛhyasūtra*, II.13.d.

172. *Kāśyapa Saṁhitā*, Cikitsā Sthāna; Balagraha Cikitsādhyāya: *bhrātā tvam bhagin ṣaṣṭhī loke khyāta bhaviṣyasi* | [9, p. 467] *ṣaṇmukhī nityalalitā varada kāmrūpiṇī.* [11, p. 467] Also *bhaginī jajñe ṣaṣṭhī skandasya dhīmataḥ* [12, p. 467] *uddisya ṣaṇmukhī saṣṭhī tathā lokeṣu nanditi.* [13, p. 467]

173. For a fuller treatment of the myths connected to

the birth of Skanda see P. K. Agrawala, op. cit. To summarise some myths connected to the birth of Skanda, it was believed that Skanda was born from the union of Agni and Svāhā. However, Svāhā took the form of the six of the wives of the seven *ṛṣis* and after each union went and deposited Agni's seed in the Himalayas. From this was born Skanda and therefore he acquired six heads. Another tradition suggests that he was raised by six Kṛttikās and developed six faces to suckle the six mothers simultaneously. In Mathurā art tradition from the Kuṣāṇa period Skanda is often found with a set of Mātṛkā figures.

174. T.S. Maxwell, op. cit., pp. 46, 39-45.

175. Ibid., fig. 1.2.

176. Ibid., pp. 41-42; he bases his analysis in the Pāñcarātra cosmogony as represented by Lakṣmī Tantra. According to Pāñcarātra texts, Śāntī is spawned from the mind of Vāsudeva, with Saṁkarṣana; from Saṁkarṣana's left side Śrī is born; Pradyumna is her son, from whom emanates Sarasvatī with Aniruddha, whose Śakti is Rati.

177. Mathurā, red mottled sandstone, *c.* second century, size: 21.5 cm high; *Christie's Catalogue*, South and South-East Art, London, 2000, No. 19

178. Mathurā, GMM no. 2949, Kuṣāṇa period, P.K. Agrawala, op. cit, Pl. VIII, IX, p. 47.

179. H. Härtel, op. cit., p. 218, Pl. 18.2.

180. P.K. Agrawala, op. cit., figs. III-VI.

181. Ibid., pp. 48-50.

182. Ibid.

183. Ibid., p. 10 attributes this to his varied parentage. Agni, who was believed to be Skanda's father was prayed upon for a son and he bestowed progeny on his faithful votaries (*ṚV* 3.1.23; 1.64.4) and he also rendered the womb of a woman capable of conception (*ṚV* 3.3.10; 10.51.3) in a hymn called *garbhadoṣanivāraṇam*. He also protected babies in the womb (*ṚV* 10.162). Rudra on the other hand was considered to be a terrible being and he was asked not to inflict children with diseases and not to injure them (*ṚV* 7.46.2; 1.114.8 and *VS* 16.16; *AV* 11.2.9).

184. For more information on the cult of Skanda-Kārttikeya in ancient India see P.K. Agarawala, op. cit.

185. N.P. Joshi, "Devī Ekānaṁśā kī Kuṣāṇa Kālīna Mūrtiyāṅ", in *BMA in UP*, March 1968, pp. 21-24; R.C. Agrawala, "Krishna and Baladeva as attendant figures in early Indian Sculpture", in *IHQ*, XXXVIII, no. 1, 1962, pp. 86-88.

186. Cowell, *Jātaka*, no. 454. the *jātaka* contains a portion of the *Mahābhārata* story and it narrates that Añjanā was the sister of ten brothers of whom the two eldest were Vāsudeva and Baladeva. The rest were Canda deva (Candra), Suriyadeva (Sūrya), Aggideva (Agni), Varuṇadeva, Ajjuna (Arjuna), Pajjuna (Parjuna or maybe Pradyumna), Ghaṭa Paṇḍita and Aṁkura. Añjanā lived with her natural parents while her brothers spent their initial years living with Nandagopa for the fear of Kaṁsa who was killed eventually by Vāsudeva and Baladeva. Baladeva is considered a great wrestler while Vāsudeva wields the wheel, as we see in Brāhmanical texts. At the end of the story the latter is killed by Jara. It is not clear from the story whether Añjanā was married to the ten brothers or not. It is however stated that she ruled and lived with them and received an equal share in the Dwarikā kingdom.

187. Suvira Jaiswal, op. cit., p. 68.

188. *Mbh.* III.208.8. In Paurāṇic texts, she is identified with Amāvasyā and Sīnīvalī (*Vāyu Purāṇa*, II.8.82) Ekānaṁśā is also seen as Yoganidrā or Viṣṇu's power of illusion, who was incarnated as the daughter of Nanda and Yaśodā and was dashed against the wall by Kaṁsa. She then rose to the sky and forecast the coming of Kṛṣṇa (*Harivaṁśa* II. 2.34f). It is also said that she did not die but was brought up like a son among the Vṛṣṇis and was worshipped by them for having protected Kṛṣṇa (*Harivaṁśa* II.2.46, 100.13-4). This belief is confirmed by the *Vāyu* and *Brahmāṇḍa* Purāṇas that state that she was the daughter of Nanda and was brought up among the Vṛṣṇis who worshipped her. *Vāyu Purāṇa*, Bibliotheca Indica edn. II. 34.203-5; *Brahmāṇḍa Purāṇa*, III.71.220f).

189. *Bṛhat Saṁhitā*, 50.37.9. Cf. Suvira Jaiswal, op. cit., p. 66.

190. *EI*, XXIV, No. 27, pp. 194-97.

191. *EI*, XXIV, No. 27, pp. 199.

192. J.N. Banerjea, *JISOA*, XIII, pp. 64f.

193. Suvira Jaiswal, op. cit., p. 68.

194. N.N. Majumdar, *Guide to The Indian Museum*, Calcutta, p. 33.

195. Cowell, *Jātaka*, No. 461. The Jātaka tells the story of Daśaratha's children — Rāma-paṇḍita, Lakṣmaṇa, Sītā and their step-brother Bharata — the exile of the former three, the death of the father, the reign of Rāma through his slippers, his eventual return from exile and his marriage with Sītā who becomes his queen consort. That Rāma and Sītā were first brother and sister and later became husband and wife is quite unequivocally stated, since at the end Buddha declares that in their former births, Daśaratha was Śuddhodana, Rāma-paṇḍita was he himself and Sītā was Rāhula's mother (i.e. Siddhārtha's wife).

196. Her name means the furrow of a plough and in myth her birth is from the earth.

197. *Harivaṁśa*, Poona edn. II.3.14. Cf. Suvira Jaiswal, op. cit., pp. 127-28 considers Sītā and Ekānaṁśā cults to be parallel developments.

198. *Kāśyapa Saṁhitā*, Cikitsā-Sthāna, Bālagrahacikitsā-adhyāya, verse 13, p. 467; *tasmācca sūtikāṣaṣṭhīṁ Rakṣaṣaṣṭhī ca pūjayate.*

199. *Suśruta Saṁhitā*, Uttaratantra, 31.10 : *nānavastradharādevī citramālyanulepanā, calatkuṇḍalinī śyamā revatī te prasīdatu* 31.11 । *lambā, karālā, vinatā tatheva bahuputrikā, revatī suṣkanāmā yā sā te devī prasīdatu* ॥

200. *Kāśyapa Saṁhitā*, Cikitsā-Sthāna, Bālagrahacikitsā-adhyāya, verses 3-5, pp. 466-67; *nāmabhinrbahubhiścaeva tvā vaksyantī janā bhuvi*। *vāruṇī revatī brāhmī kumārī bahuputrikā* [3]. *śuṣkā ṣaṣṭhī ca yamikā dharanī mukhamandikā*। *mātā sītāvatī kaṇḍūh pūtanādha nirujeikā*। [4] *raudanī bhutamātā ca lokamātāmahītī ca*। *śaraṇyā puṇyakīrtiśca nāmāni tava vinśatiḥ* [5].

201. Ibid.

202. *Mahābhārata*, Vana-Parva, CCXXIV.

203. U.P. Kaṅkālī Ṭīlā, Mathurā district, Relief fragment, first century, red sandstone. 25 × 55 cm. Lucknow Museum No. J 528/626 (obverse), Also see G. Bühler, *EI*, II, p. 314, Pl. II; V. Smith *Jaina Stūpa at Mathurā and Other Antiquities*, p. 25, Pl . XVII; J. Burgess, *Ancient Monuments*, p. 25, Pl. CLVI.

204. Kaṅkālī Ṭīlā, Mathurā, Mathura Museum No. E1, Size: 1'3¼". Kuṣāṇa period. V.S. Agrawala, "Miscellaneous Fragmentary Figures", *JUPHS*, vol XXIII, 1950, p. 66. Also *ARASI*, vol. XX, Plate IV, 5; G. Bühler, *EI*, vol. II, p. 314, plate II; V. A. Smith, op. cit., plate XVIII.; *JRAS*, for 1895, p. 153. comparable to GMM No. 2547.

205. Mathura Museum No. 1046, red sandstone, size: ht. 8½", Kuṣāṇa period, from the Yamuna; V.S. Agrawala, op. cit., p. 68.

206. Mathura Museum No. 2482, Red sandstone, Size: ht. 9½", Kuṣāṇa period. V.S. Agrawala, op. cit., 1950, p. 69.

207. Mathura Museum No. 2547, red sandstone, size: ht. 1'5", Kuṣāṇa period. V.S. Agrawala, op. cit., p. 69. Presented by Pt. Govind Charan.

208. Mathura Museum No. 909 and 1001, red sandstone, size: ht. 4½ and 5", Kuṣāṇa period, V.S. Agrawala, op. cit., p. 68. Both are found from the site of Palikhera which was an important Buddhist site from which a colossal *yakṣa* as well as the figure of Kubera set within a bacchanalian scene have been discovered.

209. U.P., Bhūteśvara Mahādeva, Mathurā district, male head with ram's horns, first century, red sandstone. GMM No. 11.157.

210. Stone plaque, SML. No. 0.250, Lucknow.

211. N.P. Joshi, *Catalogue of the Brāhmanical Sculptures in the State Museum*, Lucknow, Part I, State Museum, Lucknow, 1972, p. 59.

212. UP, Mathurā district, *yakṣa* bearing a club and small male figure, standing, second century BCE, red sandstone. GMM No. I.18; UP, Mathurā district, *yakṣa* with child, standing, second century BCE, red sandstone. GMM No. 44.3130.

213. See G. Bühler, op. cit., U.P. Shah, "Harinegameṣin", in *JISOA*, vol. XIX, 1952-3 and

Shivaji Panikkar, op. cit., p. 44.

214. Winternitz, "Nejamesha, Naigamesha, Nemeso", *JRAS*, 1885, pp. 140ff.

215. A. MacDonell, *Vedic Mythology*, Varanasi, Indological Book House, 1963, p. 75.

216. *ṚV*, 1.164.6; *AV*, 13.1.6.

217. *Mbh.* 1.66.2566.

218. J. Gonda, "The Sīmantonnayana as Described in The Gṛhyasūtras", in *East and West*, vol. VII, 1956, pp. 20-22; *Āśvalāyana-Gṛhyasūtra*, i. 14.3; *Sāṁkhāyana-Gṛhyasūtra*, i.22.7

219. *Mānava-Gṛhyasūtra*, II.8.

220. J. Gonda, op. cit., pp. 21-22.

221. U.P. Shah, op. cit., pp. 21-22.

222. *Suśruta Saṁhitā, Uttaratantra* 36.II: *ajānanaḥ calākśrībruḥ kāmarūpī mahāyaśāḥ, bālaṁ bālapitā devo naigameso abhirakṣitu.*

223. *EI*, vol. II, pp 314ff; *Āpastamba Dharmasūtra*, II.13.

224. *Suśruta Saṁhitā, Uttaratantra*, 36.10: *bali nyagrodha vṛkṣoṣu titho śaṣṭhyāṁ nivedayat.* For Ṣaṣṭhī see supra.

225. Mathura Museum No. 1210, red sandstone, size: ht. 10", Kuṣāṇa period. V.S. Agrawala, op. cit., p. 68. Recovered from the Yamunā.

226. Mathura Museum No. E.2, red sandstone, size: ht. 1'4", Kuṣāṇa period. V.S. Agrawala, op. cit., p. 67; also *ARASI*, XXX, plate. IV. 2.

227. Mathura Museum No. E.3, red sandstone, size: ht. 1'½", Kuṣāṇa period. V. S. Agrawala, op. cit., p. 69.

228. Mathura Museum No. 799, red sandstone, size: ht. 8½", Kuṣāṇa period. From Shah Qazi Isapur Well, Mathurā. V.S. Agrawala op. cit., p. 67.

229. Mathura Museum No. 60.4844, red sandstone, size: 9½ × 5" Kuṣāṇa period; N.P. Joshi, *Mothers (Mātṛkās)* in *Kuṣāṇa* Art, p. 107. Also *BMA*, No. 4, p. 57 no. 12; 11-12, p. 68.

230. V.S. Agrawala, "Terracottas of Ahichchhatra", *Ancient India*, no. 4, 1947-48, pp. 130-33.

231. V.S. Agrawala, "Presiding Deity of Childbirth Amongst the Ancient Jainas, with special Reference to Figures in the Mathura Museum", *Jaina Antiquary*, vol. II, no. VI, March, 1937, p. 78.

232. Shivaji Panikkar, op. cit., p. 45.

233. Mathurā, Mathura Museum No 17.1357, red sandstone, size: 185 × 57 cm or 33½ × 22½", Kuṣāṇa period; N.P. Joshi, op. cit., p. 125, fig. 38.

234. Cowell, *Jātaka* No. 531; ultimately queen Silavati conceives through Indra. This is similar to the story of Kuntī's and Mādrī's impregnation through divine agency.

235. B.M. Barua, *Bharhut II*, p. 150, Scene 133 on a coping stone.

236. I.B. Horner, op. cit., p. 194; also see section on Māyādevī above.

# 4

# Lovers, Married Couples and Wives

In early Indian art, it is difficult to posit any single model of the "Ideal Wife." Marriage is the single most important institution for women, and there is thus a concomitant centrality of marriage in structuring gender relations. In such a situation, only the devoted and faithful (*pativratā*) wife should ideally be extolled and reiterated in visual representations. Instead, we find a range of portrayal of women as wives and female partners with a multitude of meanings attached to these. These comprise wives/female partners forming one half of divine couples with overtones of fertility; devotee couples; *mithuna*s denoting propitious/ apotropaic elements; or erotic *mithuna*s connected with fertility and sexuality. Wives in visual narratives are perceived either as the embodiment of temptation and evil, or as ideals reinforcing socially sanctioned norms. In the depiction of "women as wives," their roles change in relation to the context and intentionality of their portrayal. "Men as husbands" do not share the same range of signification, even though there are similar variations in the context within which they are represented.

## 4.1 The Ubiquitous Couple

The *mithuna* (the loving pair) is a ubiquitous symbol found in the art dating to the Śuṅga-Kuṣāṇa-Sātavāhana period. The *mithuna* can be depicted in a straightforward passive fashion or in myriad permutations and combinations of activities. These depictions of *mithuna* transcend size and medium, ranging from small terracottas to life-size stone reliefs. There are human *mithunas*, *haṁsas* (geese) *mithunas*, also *matsya* (fish pairs) along with *mṛga*- (deer-) *mithunas*.

*Mithuna* literally means paired, forming a pair; pairing, copulation; a pair or a couple; also twins. It can also signify the other part, complement or companion of anything.[1] A synonym of *mithuna* used mainly in texts is *yugala* or *yugalika*, which also means a pair or a couple.[2]

In Jaina texts the *yugala-jugala* are said to be born as twins of man and woman.[3] The *yugala-jugala* unites together by free will, but as yet, bears no burden of sharing the responsibility of procreation. Depicted in ideal untainted bliss, by nature *yugala* are simple and auspicious in action. No worldly passions such as selfish (*rāga*), lust (*kāma*), wrath (*krodha*), greed (*lobha*), wilful delusion (*moha),* hinder their life of freedom. Each pair dallies with inexhaustible pleasure and fulfils its desires. They live in ideal, healthy and beautiful conditions. They suffer neither death nor disease.

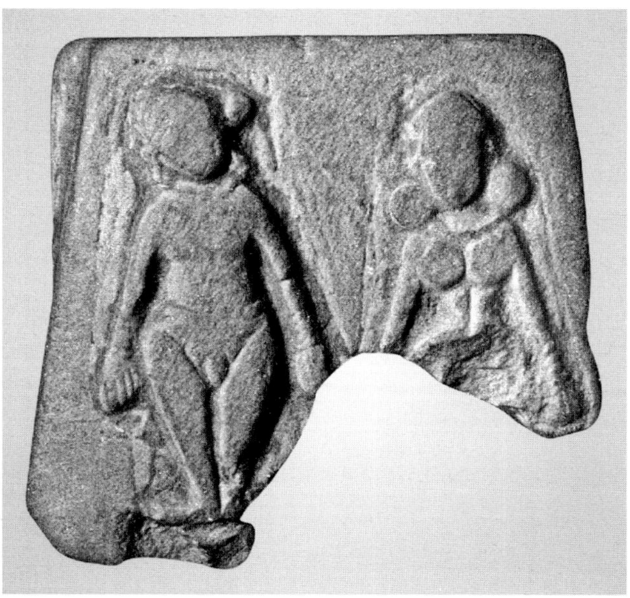

4.1 Plaque of goddess with consort, perhaps Mahā-Nagna and Mahā-Nagnī, third century BCE, Kauśāmbī. AM.Mor 6.

Another variant of the *mithuna* depiction is the *dampati*. *Dampati* is derived from *dama*, which in Ṛgvedic terminology means a house presided over equally by husband and wife as *dampati*.[4] It is in this sense that the term is understood in classical texts,[5] though by the post-Mauryan period *dampati* becomes a conventional term that does not carry connotations of equal social status within the household.

Like the *mithuna*, *dampati* is also a male-female dyad depicted often on the façades of *stūpas*, *vihāras* and temples. As a motif it is distinguished from *mithuna* only by the arrangement of the figures: unlike the *mithuna*, in a *dampati* composition the female is always to the left of the male. This arrangement is a visual manifestation of the belief that legitimately women in general and wives in particular belong to the left side (*vāma*). Women were supposed to sleep on the left side; they occupied the left position in rituals.[6]

### 4.2 Sculptural Traditions

Post-Mauryan art marks an efflorescence of *mithuna* depictions, exhibiting a variety of forms found within various contexts which are enumerated below.

#### 4.2.1 TYPE A: GODDESS WITH CONSORT

A standing nude man-woman dyad on a stone plaque from Kauśāmbī[7] (*Pl.* 4.1) has been identified as a Mother Goddess and her consort,[8] or a nude God with his partner.[9] Here the goddess is shown on the right with large breasts and broad hips, with hands hanging to her sides and wearing two heavy circular earrings. The portion below the hips is broken off. The male is depicted in a similar posture, and his head is tilted to give

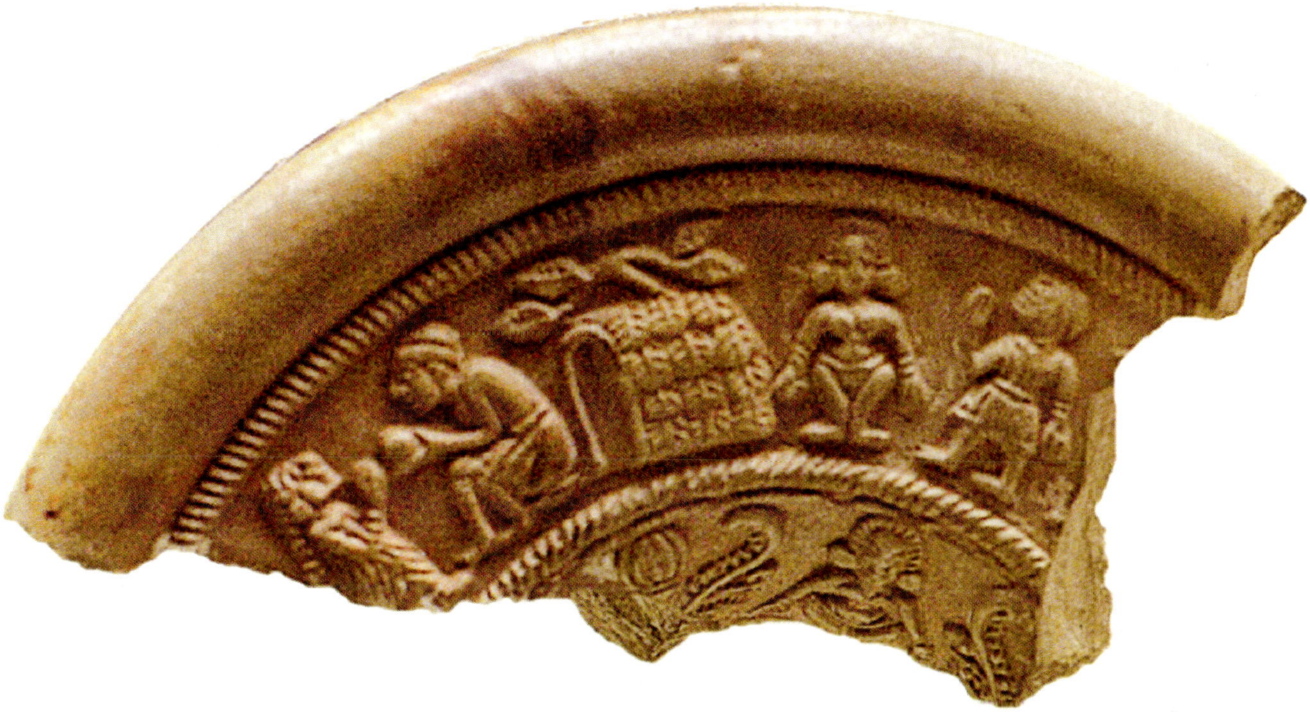

4.2 A nude goddess being worshipped by male partner with offerings. A hut shrine to the right, second-third century BCE, Ropar, Punjab.

the impression that he is looking at the female. His maleness is emphasised by the clearly visible phallus and lack of breasts, and he does not appear to be wearing earrings; a knot of hair to the left side is visible. Though frontally nude, there appears to be long, cloak-like drapery carved behind the figures. The couple, especially the female, is very similar to figures carved on a stone disc found in the middle Gangetic valley and from Ropar in Punjab.

On the Ropar stone disc (*Pl.* 4.2), the female figure is shown in association with a male worshipper or partner standing next to a hut, interpreted as a shrine in the forest.[10] The goddess is completely nude and standing in hieratic *samabhaṅga* pose, while the male is shown wearing a long coat reaching the knees. His hair is secured with a fillet. On the other side of the hut is a female figure with a male figure facing and holding a spherical object in his hand, perhaps an offering of fruit. Pramod Chandra has identified the Ropar disc and other similar discs (*Pls.* 4.3, 4.4) as *Śrī-cakra*s with the Goddess Śrī-Lakṣmī as the object of worship carved on them.[11] P.K. Agrawala suggests that the nude figures on the Kauśāmbī plaque may represent the *Mahā-Nagnī* and *Mahā-Nagna* mentioned in the *Atharvaveda*.[12] A comparison of the Kauśāmbī plaque with the stone discs shows that the female figure was depicted with a prominently marked genital cleft, and that she represented a divine feminine figure, being surrounded in the discs by sacred symbols such as palm trees, *śrīvatsa*, lotuses and the like. The male figure and the female figure are depicted in a deity-and-worshipper relationship.

The worship of sacred *mithuna*s is seen in steatite plaque found at Rājgīr near Patna and datable to *c.* 245-105 BCE.[13] This plaque is divided into three compartments, each with a couple in it. The lowermost panel has the nude female figure standing on the left in a *samabhaṅga* posture which is also typical of the nude goddess seen at Kauśāmbī and on the stone discs noted above. She is being offered a cup, perhaps containing wine, by the male figure that is also nude. The upper two panels contain couples who are fully clothed. In one of these panels, the male offers a cup to the female, while a jar is visible nearby. In the other panel the female is dancing while the male plays a musical instrument. Representations of wine-drinking/offering on early plaques, accompanying nude goddesses, suggest that this was associated with cultic rituals.[14]

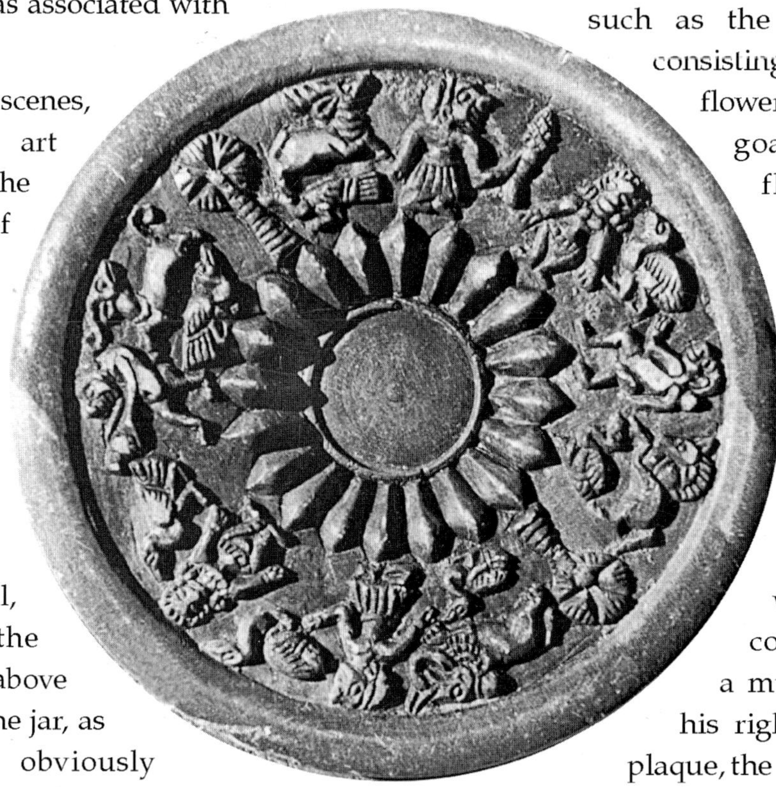

These and other scenes, from Mathurā art belonging to the Kuṣāṇa period, of women being offered wine by their male partners (*Pl.* 4.17) suggest that wine-drinking could take place in a secular setting, in a normal social ritual, as probably in the panel mentioned above with the cup and the jar, as well as in more obviously religious-cult settings. This presents a social picture of a sophisticated and mature society in relation to wine, in which it is used to ease social relations (including sexual relations) and also as part of religious rites. In later periods, however, wine-drinking by women was associated with the deviant behaviour of women, who were regarded as sexually uncontrolled.[15] In the art of the post-Mauryan period depictions such as the Vasantasenā series where the woman is shown being offered wine in one scene (*Pl.* 5.7) and keeling over as if drunk in another (*Pl.* 5.6) seems to associate the potentially negative side of wine-drinking with women — but not with men. In both early and later depictions, wine drinking by women connoted the deployment of female sexuality.[16]

Another form of the divine *mithuna* is seen in terracotta plaques from Candraketugaṛh and also from the mid-Gangetic valley, depicting the *pañcacūḍa* goddess[17] with a male partner. Divine status is indicated by the sacred ornament such as the *pañcacūḍa* hairpin consisting of an axe, a trident, a flower and an elephant's goad or *aṅkuśa* in a floriated headdress worn by the female.[18] In the plaques from Ahicchatra[19] (*Pl.* 4.5), the female divinity has three attributes, *āyudhas*, in her headdress. She is shown touching the waist of her male companion who holds a musical instrument in his right hand. In another plaque, the figures are posed in a manner that has the woman on the left of the man in the traditional grouping seen, for example, at the Buddhist cave site of Kārle (*Pl.* 4.13); they are shown standing together, each with left hand on hip.[20] The male wears an asymmetrical turban, an upper scarf, and a *dhotī* held up by a knotted sash, as well as other

4.3 Stone disc with nude goddess, male partners/worshippers, animals and palm trees, third century BCE, Murtaziganj, Patna, Bihar. Patna Museum 10738.

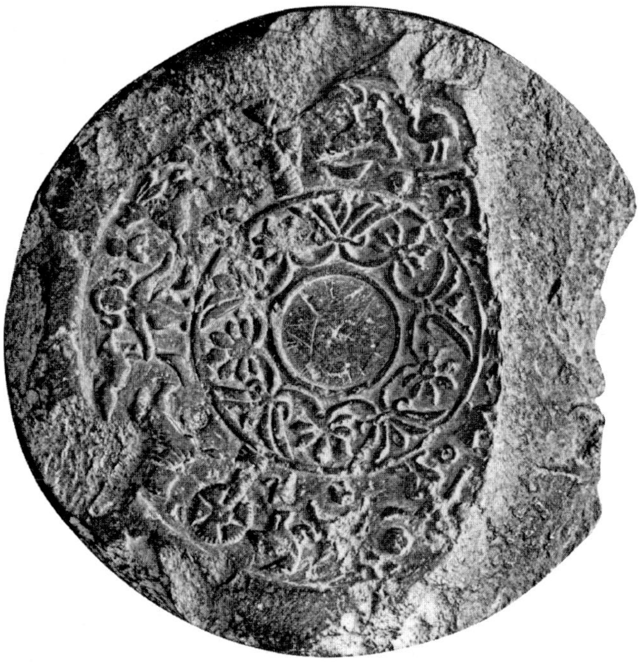

4.4 Ring stone, with nude goddess, third century BCE, Varanasi. Bharat Kala Bhavan.

jewellery of a richly appointed male in typical Śuṅga-period attire. The female is seen wearing fine ornaments, jewellery and closely fitted drapery and has *āyudhas* in her headdress of the *pañcacūḍa* type.

Plaques with the nude goddess and her partner and those with the *pañcacūḍa* couple seem to be independent cultic objects that have not been found in architectural contexts. The nudity of the former image-type, and the association with sacred motifs of both *mithunas*, suggests a fertility element in connection with the former image-type. It is probable that the representation of this female divinity with her male partner may have had a cultic significance related to performance of fertility rites, which in the ancient past included actual sex play.[21]

Why is the female divinity in these depictions to be considered the principal deity and the male as the subsidiary partner? How are the representational types under discussion different from later divine couples such as Umāsahitamaheśvara-mūrti or Lakṣmī-Narāyaṇa? These are questions that may legitimately be raised in connection with the above premise. It may be suggested that both the nude goddess in *samabhaṅga* posture, and the *pañcacūḍa* goddess, may be found alone without the male partner, on stone discs and terracottas. This implies an independent autonomous status. Another observation in this context is that the male partner in many cases is shown in a suppliant posture that may suggest obeisance and subservience, and make the female figure the dominant one in the relationship. Significantly, there is no diminution in the size of the female, such as we notice in later divine couples, in this or most other *mithuna* depictions.

### 4.2.2 TYPE B: SACRED SYMBOLS WITH MITHUNAS

The concept of sacred *mithunas* being associated with fertility rites is strengthened by a terracotta plaque from Awra in Mandsaur district, Madhya Pradesh, datable to *c*. 100 BCE – CE 300.[22] It is divided into three vertical sections, of which the central one is occupied by a female divinity, identified as Śrī,[23] who stands on a lotus and touches her right earring. Her *yoni* is visible below the thick *mekhalā*. She stands between two elephants, and jewels and sheaves of corn surround her. On either side of her are *mithunas* "engaged in what appears to be sexual union."[24] There are pitchers in the foreground, perhaps denoting the presence of wine. Moti Chandra suggests that this proves that ritual coitus and wine rituals associated with the goddess presage later Tāntric sexual rites. He also points to the existence of a secret cult of Śrī, mentioned in the *Milindapañha* (*c*. first-second century CE) that may have included sexual rites.

The ritual importance of the couple associated with sacred objects is carried through in the decorative scheme of sacred buildings such as *stūpa*s. This is well articulated in a panel carved on a corner pillar of *stūpa* II at Sāñcī, dated to the second-first century BCE.[25] On this vertically aligned composition, the upper portion is occupied by a divine female figure standing on a lotus being lustrated on each side by two elephants standing on lotuses to each side of her.[26] Below her are a human couple standing on lotus leaves. The woman, to the right of the male, seems to hold a cup in her right hand while with her left she holds a loop tied at the end of the waistband. The man stands in similar position, but holding a lotus vine ending in a bud in his right hand. *Pūrṇaghaṭa*s or vases of plenty are visible near their feet as is seen from the rounded shape with a narrow neck of the pot. Underneath this are two rearing lions whose lower legs are placed on a single lotus. At the bottom is a pair of horned cattle rearing on their hind legs, and underneath that are two lotus blooms that rest on a tortoise (see *Pl.* 2.2.7 for *mithuna* at Sāñcī). Thus we see that the whole complex of motifs here are *māṅgalya* (auspicious) in nature, stressing the abundance and fertility of productive couples in association with elements of the "water cosmology."

A somewhat similar arrangement is depicted on a railing pillar from the same monument, but in association with a sacred tree enclosed by a low *vedikā*.[27] Below this tree is a human *mithuna,* and beneath this is a pair of cranes.

### 4.2.3 TYPE C: DEVOTEE MITHUNAS

At Bharhut (*Pl.* 4.7), and *Stūpa* II at Sāñcī has depictions of *mithuna*s, combined with sacred symbols, mainly in adoring postures. On one corner-pillar a human *mithuna* is seen standing on both sides of the pillar with a short donative inscription on it.[28] The female is to the right of the pillar, holding a lotus vine with a bud in one hand, while the male on the left folds his hands in *añjali-hasta*. Underneath the pillar is a pair of bulls.

Also at the same site, a sculpture delineates a couple paying respect to a *dharmacakra* mounted on a pillar with three lions supporting the wheel. The male and female stand on each side of the pillar with hands folded in adoration. Similar depictions of couples adoring a sacred tree are found at the same site.

Another depiction of the same theme, with more than one devotee-*mithuna* worshipping the *dharmacakra,* is also available from the *stūpa* II railing. In this panel, the bottom consists of a

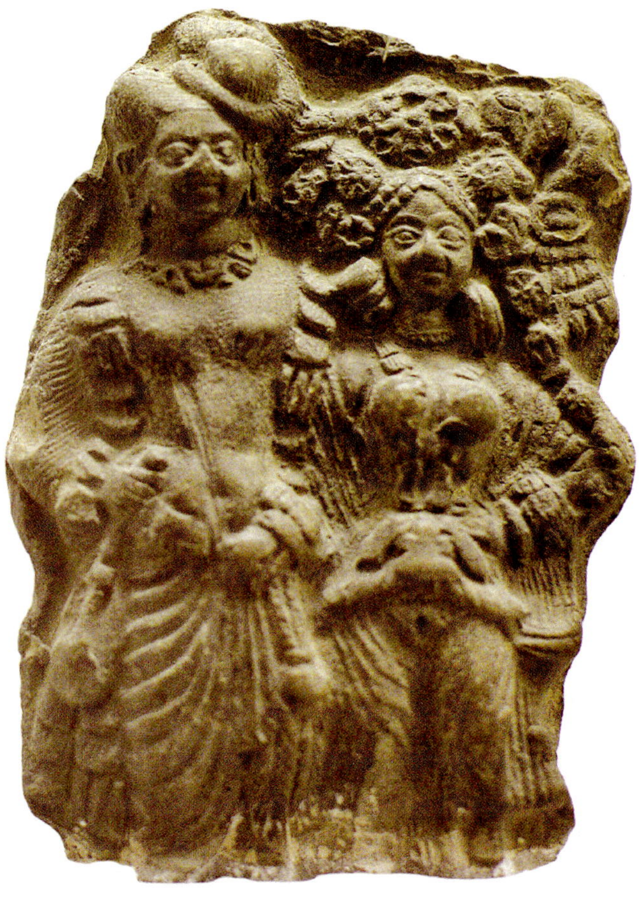

4.5 *Mithuna*, 15.8 × 10.2 × 2.6, Terracotta, Ahicchatra, UP. NM Acc. No. 62. 248.

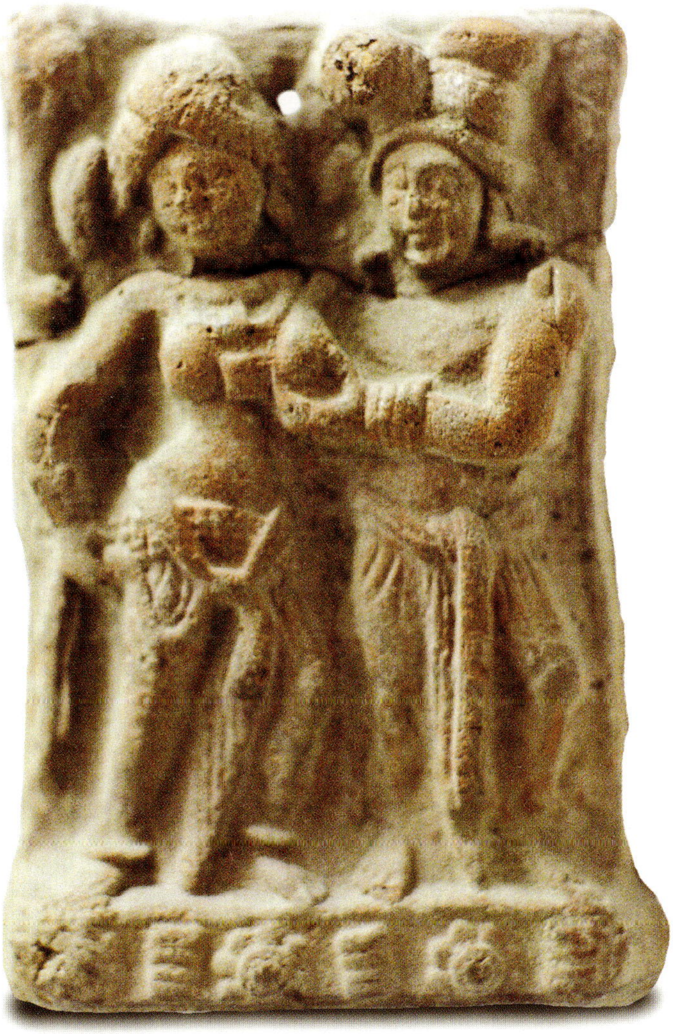

4.6 Amorous *mithuna*, terracotta, Śuṅga period, Kauśāmbī, NM.

*vedikā* in relief.[29] Above that in the centre, set on a tiered pedestal, is a *dharmacakra* adorned with a garland. On both sides of this are "adoring couples." The females kneel at the base of the pedestal on both sides with heads bowed in obeisance, hands folded in *añjali-hasta*. The males are depicted as standing and holding objects in their hands such as a *cāmara* and a garland as offerings.

The tradition of *mithuna*s paying respect to a sacred object continues at all major Buddhist and Jaina sites, at Amarāvatī, Nāgārjunakoṇḍa and Mathurā.

### 4.2.4 TYPE D: LOVERS/MARRIED COUPLES

Probably the largest range of *mithuna* depictions is of couples seated and standing without being associated with a sacred object within the composition, though representations are found carved on religious structures. Some of these may be delineated as slightly amorous pairs.

A *dampati* pair *par excellence* is Hāritī and Kubera who are usually set within a familial composition.[30] Hāritī is placed on the proper left of Kubera (*Pls.* 3.2.9, 3.2.10, 3.2.13). Children surround Hāritī, while Kubera sits regally aloof by her side.

Often the male and female are carved standing next to each other, with an arm around the shoulder or waist of the partner, or touching the *mekhalā* or waistband (*Pl.* 4.6). These figures are more often than not standing straight and looking at the viewer rather than each other. Such pairs are seen in terracottas exemplified by the two plaques in the Lucknow Museum,[31] of which one is a typical *mithuna* with the woman on the right of the man and the other is a *dampati-mithuna* with the woman on the left. Interestingly, both these show the figures wearing thick pleated *dhotī*s that cover the body below the waist, which is not a universal convention in *mithuna* representations.

Such images are also found on the railings of *stūpa*s belonging to the early period of Buddhist art. At Bharhut, we find a *dampati-mithuna* on a medallion[32] (*Pl.* 4.9) carved on a railing pillar. Also at Bharhut, on a coping of the great railing, are found four scenes carved between undulating vines (*Pl.* 4.10) showing idyllic family life. This depiction appears to be a natural progression of pairing in a sequential manner. In the first scene a woman is shown harvesting rice on the right of a tree and on the other side a woman tending a pot over a stone hearth. The next scene shows the

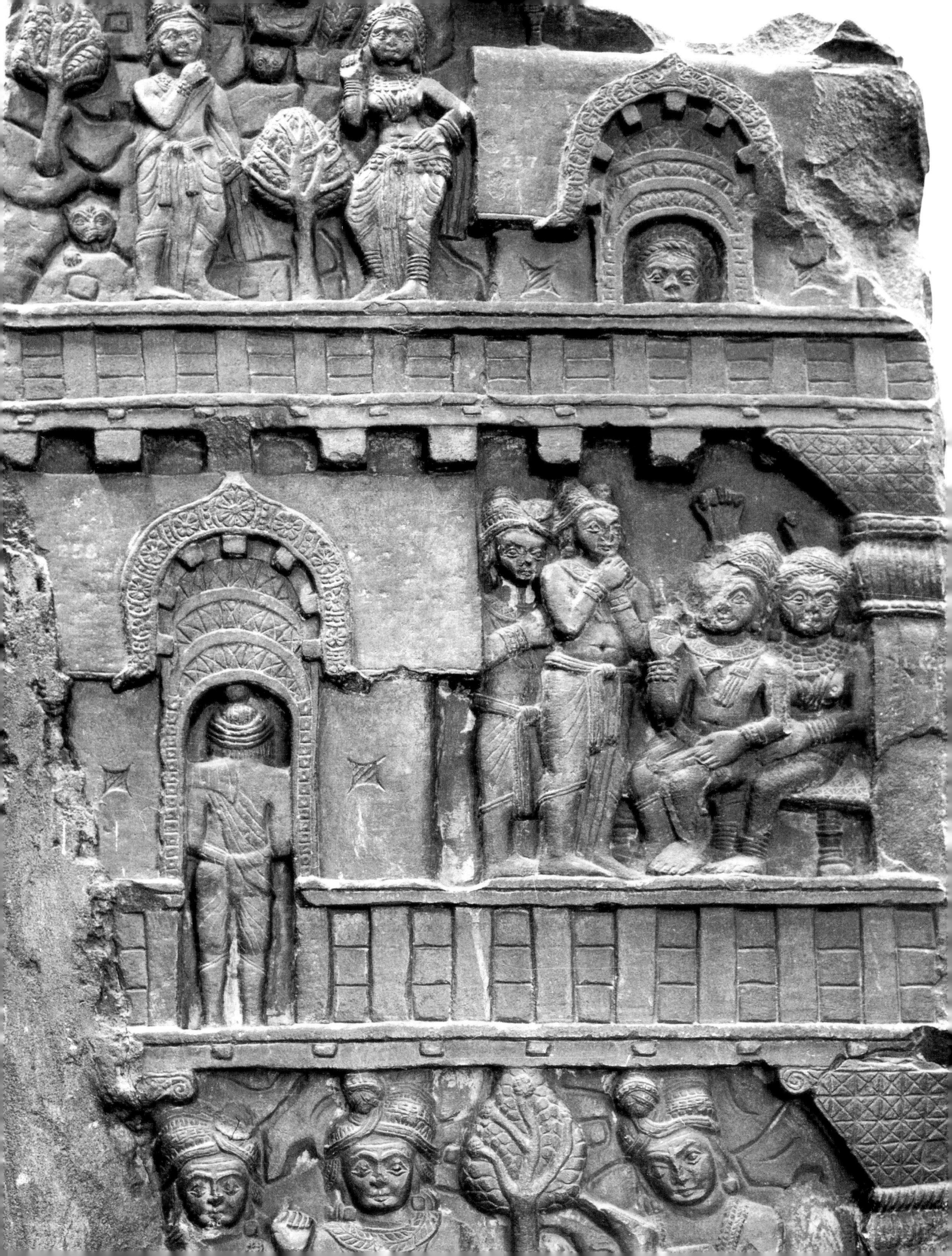

enjoyment of various fruits by a group of women; followed by a man and a woman, each holding out the fingers towards two children; and in the last scene, a man stands on the left with two other scenes on the other side. Foucher identified this series as representing Uttarakuru, the land of plenty described in Brāhmanical and Buddhist texts such as the *Mahābhārata*, *Dīvyāvadāna* and *Mahāvastu*.[33] In this mythical land rice is plucked and cooked directly without any fire beneath the pots; food is available in plenty; children are nourished through sucking on the fingers of adults; and the dead are carried to the sacred mountain by birds.

Similar scenes of men and women disporting with each other in Uttarakuru are also found on *stūpa* I at Sāñcī (*Pl.* 4.11).[34] Here the couples are seated on elephants or on low couches near gushing waterfalls, under umbrella-shaped trees, rich and thick vines, flowering trees and near lotus ponds and with musicians entertaining them.

At Kauśāmbī, on the face of a pillar divided into two parts, the upper half shows male and female figures. The female is standing with her body turned slightly towards the male who is on the left of the female.[35] The right leg of both figures is raised with only the toes touching the ground, and the left leg is straight. The male holds a sheaf of flowers in his right hand, while the left arm is akimbo. He is shown wearing a big turban and the ends of the *uttarīya* come from the back over the forearm to fall at the sides. A knee-length *dhotī* is tied at the waist by ribbon-like waistband, one of its loose ends falling between the legs and the other over the left thigh. As jewellery he wears heavy looped earrings and a multi-strand necklace with spacers like the Mathurā *yakṣa*s. The female is similarly attired in a knee-length sāṛī secured at the waist with a multi-strand pearl *mekhalā*, above which is a ribbon-like waistband knotted over the thigh. The *uttarīya* comes over the right forearm and hangs down at the side. Bangles, *nūpura*s and a torque adorn her; and her hands appear to be folded in adoration (they are slightly damaged). Perhaps in this case the male was a deity and the female a devotee, or alternatively perhaps both are devotees.

4.7 Devotee *mithuna* above Vidhura Paṇḍita Jātaka panel, railing pillar, first century BCE, Bharhut. IM 257-8.

Both at Bharhut and Bodh-Gayā (*Pl.* 4.14) are carved a *dampati-mithuna* with the male tugging at the *uttarīya* of the woman with one hand and also pulling her arm towards him. This has been identified as illustrating the *Candra Jātaka*, which is discussed below in the section on Good Wives.

At Mathurā, there is a fragment of a stone slab showing an amorous couple, *mithuna*, a few buildings and a fine border scroll with auspicious symbols.[36] It seems to be a palace scene, given the elaborate architectural setting, with a *kūṭagara* pavilion on top. The female figure stands to the right with her left arm around the shoulder of the male who holds it with his upraised left hand. His right arm seems to have been behind her shoulder. She is touching her *mekhalā* with her other hand, emphasising the exposed genital mound. Very prominent and globular breasts mark her figure, with a thick necklace around her neck and shoulders. He is dressed in a *dhotī* with a cloth over it, tied with a thick sash and well covered from the waist downward. Both are shown looking at each other, giving the scene an aura of intimacy.

At Mathurā, Bharatpur, and other sites where Kuṣāṇa art of the Mathurā school has been found, *mithuna*s and *dampati-mithuna*s have been

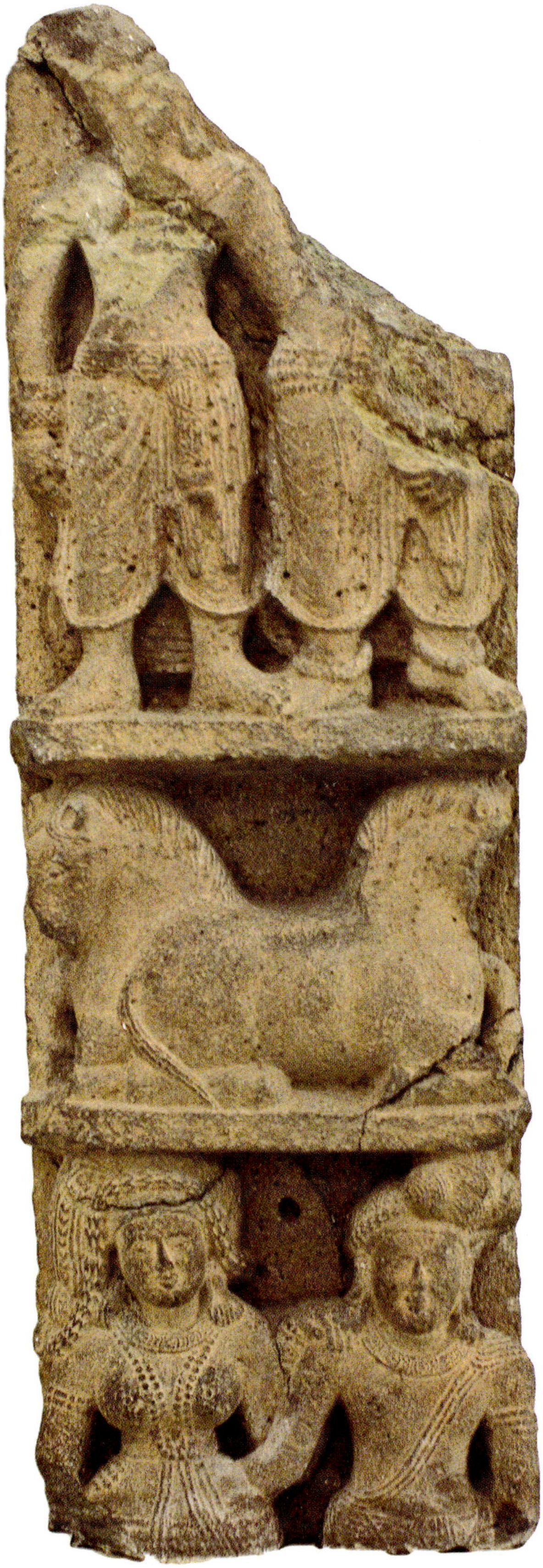

discovered with the figures either standing next to each other in a straight and solid manner or in sensual poses.

The early Buddhist art of the Deccan provides us with many examples of *mithunas*. They are represented both seated and standing (*Pl.* 4.8), and in non-amorous and amorous attitudes. A range of these was found at the earliest monastic site of Pītalkhorā (*Pl.* 4.22),[37] of which the most interesting piece may be the royal couple seated on a decorated octagonal *pīṭha* with a cover, probably of animal hide. The male holds the female from the back with his right arm. He wears a pendant ornament in his right ear. His *dhotī* is worn tightly around the legs but hangs in the centre in a folded loop ending in a tuft. His left leg is flexed and rests on a footstool. The female is seated in *lalitāsana* on the right thigh of the king, and she clasps him around the shoulder with her left arm. She sports rich ornaments: a five-stringed torque, *graiveya*, a two-stringed *stana-hāra*, wristlet and bangles and a seven-stranded *mekhalā*. A *dhotī* with schematic folds covers her lower body. Her head is turned towards the king. In the composition there are also three female attendants, holding indistinct objects. Thick *dhotī*s cover the lower bodies of all the other *mithuna* figures from these sites.

At Kārle, on the entrance façade is carved a series of *mithunas* (*Pl.* 4.15) and *dampati-mithunas*. The latter is a series of flying *mithunas* carved high up the cave near the *caitya* windows. The first series flanks the doorways to the *caitya* and are depicted in very solid, straight and royal

4.8 Railing Pillar *mithuna śākhā*, first century BCE-first century CE, 83 × 25 × 27 cm, stone, Sātavāhana, Pītalkhorā, NM. Acc. No. 67.189.

4.9 *Mithuna* in dancing pose, medallion, railing, inscribed, first century BCE, Bharhut. IM 99. (facing page)

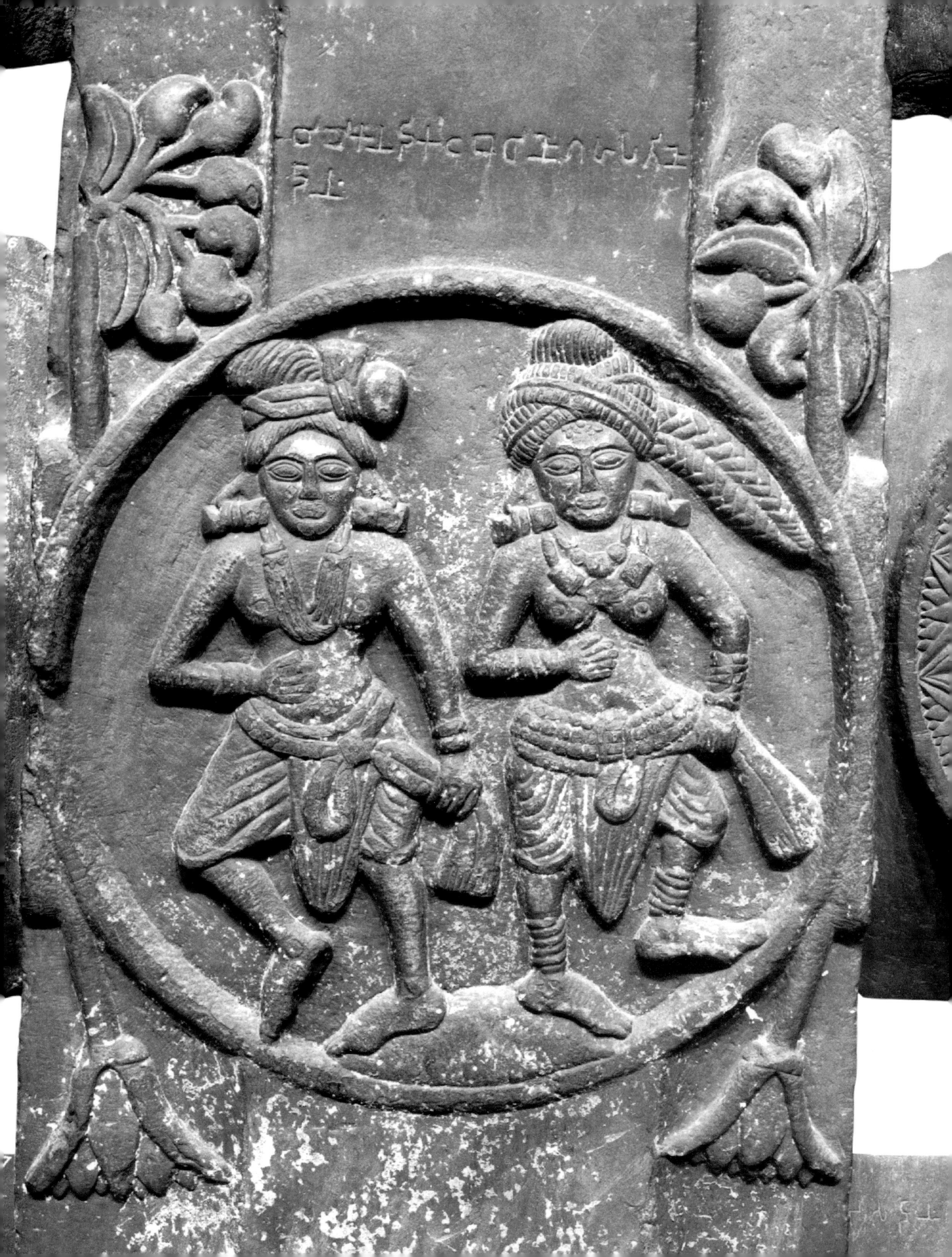

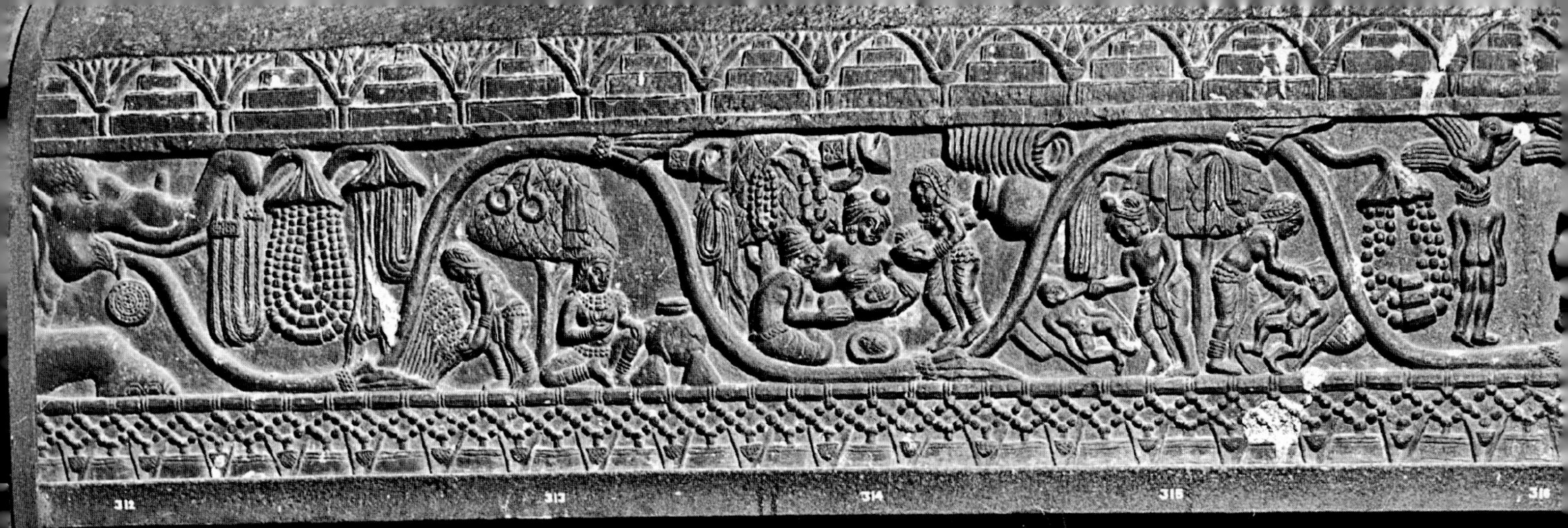

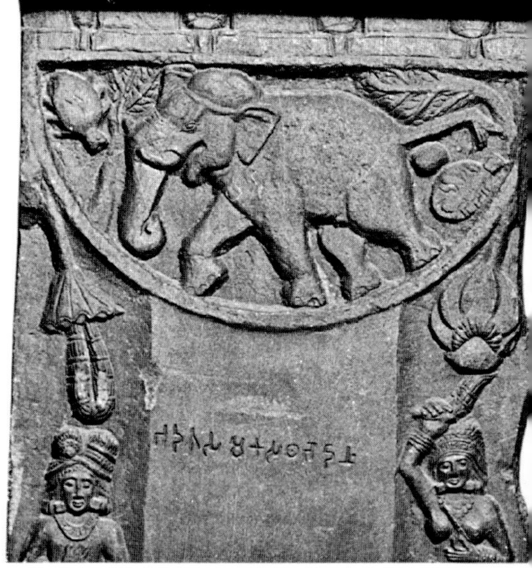

manner. Both the male and female figures are nude from the waist upwards, but a *dhotī* covers the lower body. In the female figure this reaches to the ankles with the central cloth falling in short pleats, while in the case of the male the *dhotī* falls just below the knees. She wears a *mekhalā* as well as a ribbon-like waist tie, and the male has a thick folded waistband. Both have one arm around each other, while the other is either akimbo or holds the *uttarīya* near the waist. Alternatively, the hands may be folded in *namaskāra-mudrā* (as a mark of respect). Inside the *caitya*-cave there are rows of pillars on both sides of the hall, topped by couples seated on elephants. Among the many donatory inscriptions are carved two epigraphs[38] recording the donation of *mithuna*s by one Bhadraśarman, a Buddhist monk. One is carved over the *mithuna* figures on the right of the verandah and the other near the *mithuna* on the inside of the front screen facing them.[39]

At Nāgārjunakoṇḍa, *mithuna*s are carved on uprights (*Pl.* 4.17) that divide various religious

4.10 Scenes depicting the idyllic land of Uttarakuru, coping, great railing, first century BCE, Bharhut. IM 315-16.

4.11 Couples disporting with each other in the ideal land of Uttarakuru, panel on the front face of north pillar of western gate, *stūpa* II, first century CE, Sāñcī. (facing page)

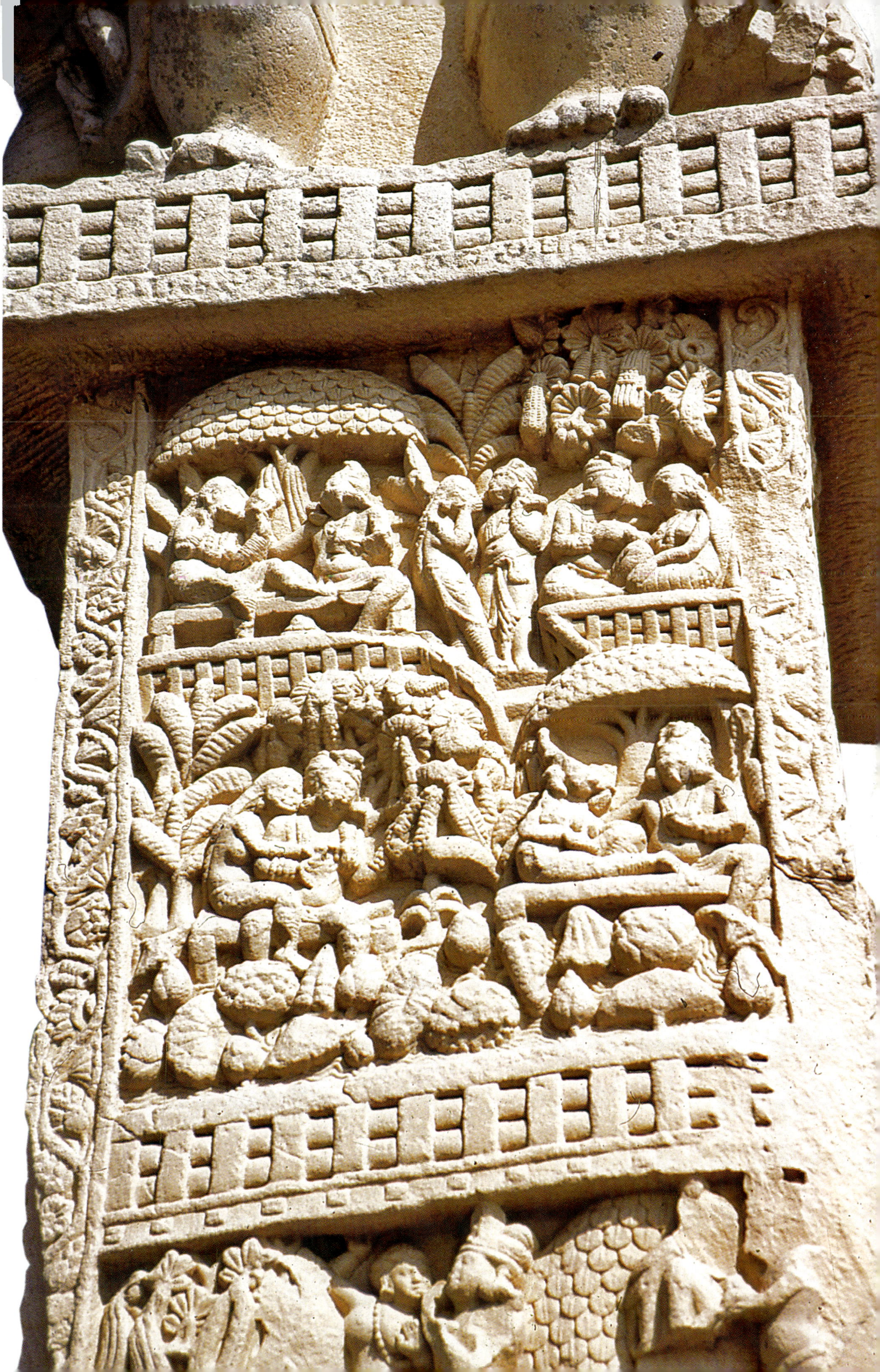

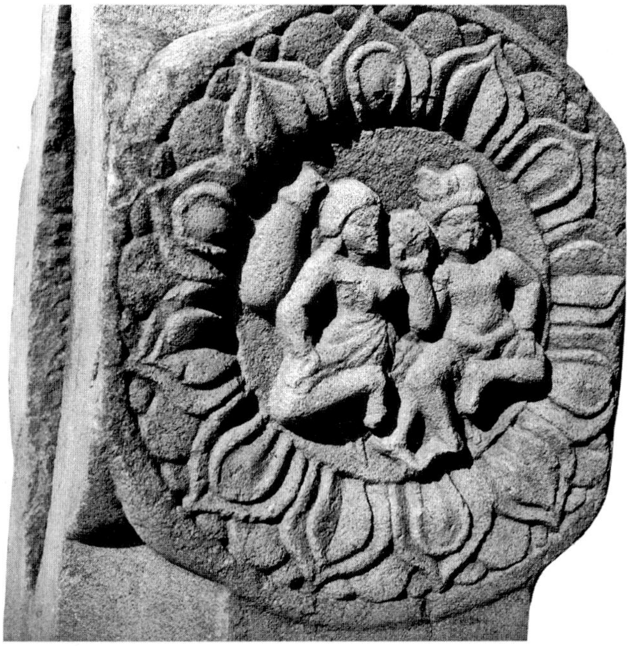

4.12 Seated *mithuna*, within a lotus medallion, first century BCE, Bodh-Gayā.

Amorous scenes are prolific in terracotta. An example is a terracotta plaque found at Kauśāmbī and belonging to the second century BCE, now in the National Museum (*Pl.* 4.23), which shows a couple seated on a low couch.[43] The female figure is seated between the slightly spread out legs of the male, who touches the *mekhalā* of his female partner with his right hand and has his left arm around her shoulders. She touches her earring with her right hand and holds the man in a close embrace with her left arm. The female figure is shown turned towards the male and in this scenes from each other. These are sensuous *mithuna*s in terms both of treatment and content. Here the bodies of male and female figures are constructed as sinuous and fluid, moving into the curves of each other's bodies, creating an intimate whole. Embracing couples are carved in myriad amorous poses such as pinching the chin,[40] holding each other's waistbands and the like. The female figures have the genital cleft clearly exposed.

This sensual treatment has been carried through also in the carvings on the jamb of the doorway of Cave No. III at Nāsik (which seems to be a precursor of the elaborate doorjamb ornamentations of Hindu temples).[41] On both sides of the door are *rūpaśākhā*s, divided into five panels, each containing a couple in an intimate pose. Many of these are scenes of intoxication of the female partner[42] or of offering of cups, presumably containing wine, by a figure of either sex. There are depictions of partial disrobing and intimate touching.

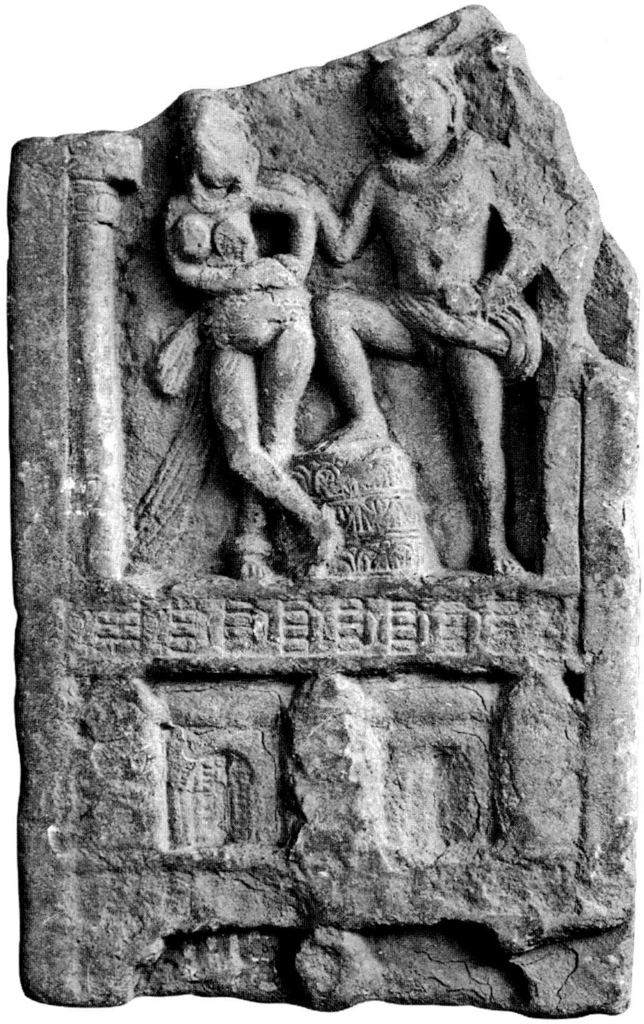

4.13 *Mithuna*, standing, red sandstone, third century CE, Mathurā district, UP. GMM No. I.12.

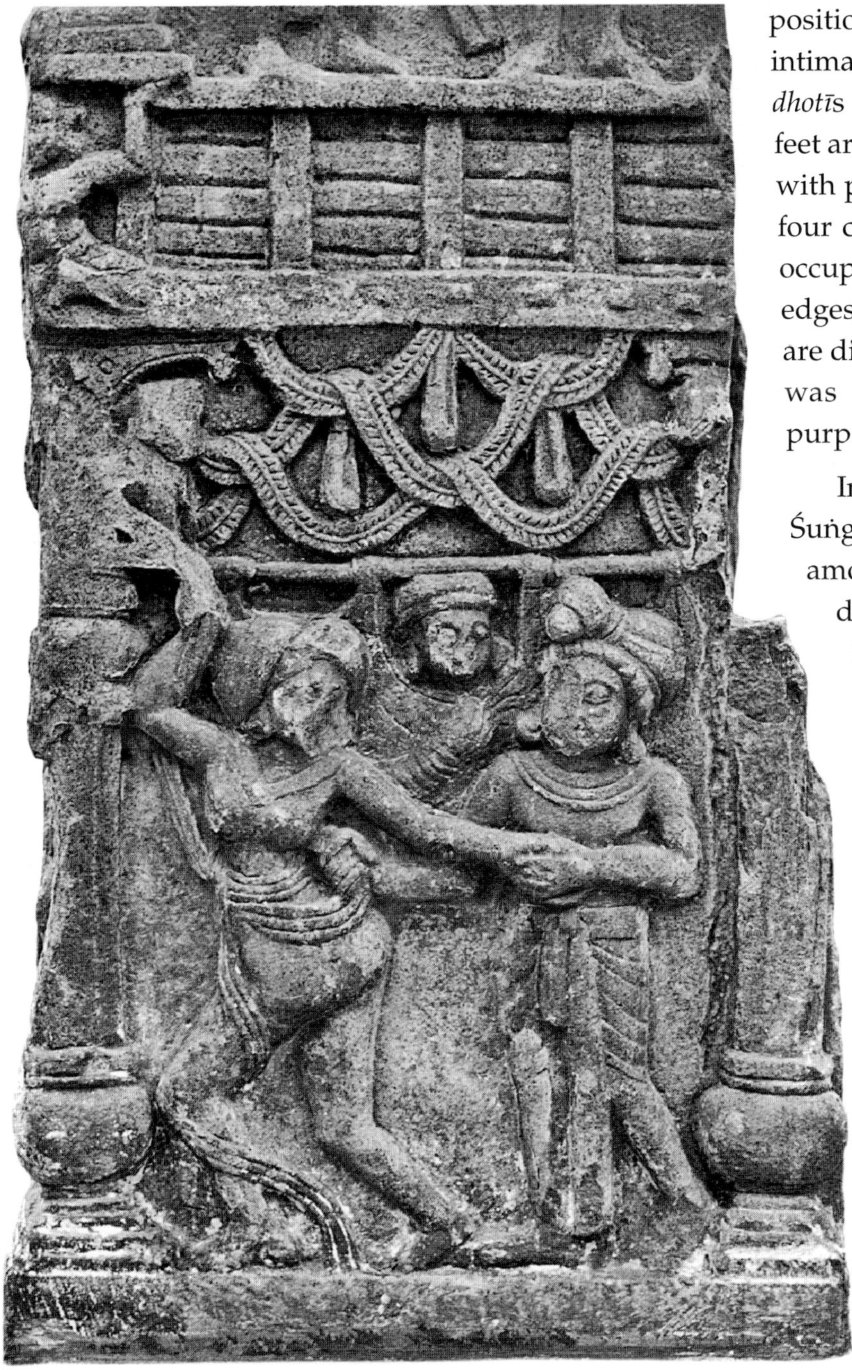

4.14 Amorous couple with the male pulling on the robe and arm of the female, panel on pillar, railing, first century BCE, Bodh-Gayā.

position both can look at each other in an intimate fashion. Both are covered with *dhotī*s from the waist downwards. Their feet are placed on a low footstool. Flowers with protruding bigger blooms visible at four corners surround the couch and its occupants. On the top right and left edges, two holes for hanging the plaque are discernible, suggesting that the piece was used for votive or decorative purposes.

In the terracotta tradition of the Śuṅga period, many *mithuna*s in mildly amorous poses have been discovered. In one example from Kauśāmbī, now in the National Museum (*Pl.* 4.6), the woman is on the right of the male. Both the figures stand in a slightly flexed position. The male holds the left breast of the woman with his left hand.[44] The woman holds the loop of her waistband with one hand while clasping her companion around the shoulder with her other arm. The male seems to be looking at the woman who is looking away towards the right. This terracotta plaque also has a hole at the top as if it were meant to be hung on a nail. Both the pieces described above have obvious erotic overtones, indicating a celebration of sexuality.

Though belonging to the later Gupta period, a terracotta piece from northern India, a *dampati-mithuna*,[45] is very significant. The male is shown seated cross-legged, and the female in half-*bhadrāsana*. Her right arm is extended and rests at

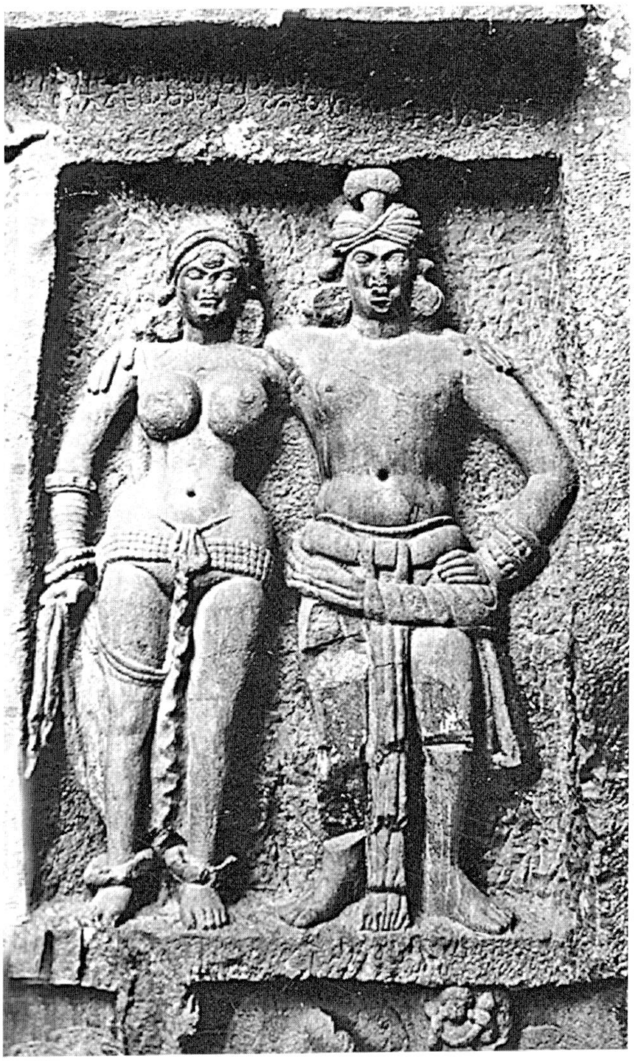

4.15 *Mithuna* carved on the entrance doorway of the *caitya* hall, first century CE, Kārle.

the elbow on the knee of the male. Her left hand is placed on the calf of her folded leg. The male's left arm is folded with the elbow resting on the shoulder of his partner and his other hand is placed on the thigh. This is a very intimate, warm scene. However, its importance lies in the inscription of one word — *ramaṇa*, meaning sensual enjoyment — which is incised in Gupta-Brāhmī characters at the lower left of the piece. Here is clear evidence of the enjoyment of earthly pleasures by both men and women.

### 4.2.5 TYPE E: COUPLES ENGAGED IN PLEASURABLE ACTIVITIES

Drinking and amorous activities are often connected with *mithuna*. In an architectural fragment from Patna city, belonging to the late Śuṅga period (*Pl.* 4.19 another similar is *Pl.* 4.18), a couple is shown standing under a fruit-laden *aśoka* tree.[46] The male on the left offers his female companion a goblet/cup held in his extended left hand. He is shown wearing a fillet-like band in his hair. She has her left arm around his shoulders and her right hand holds the *mekhalā* tied below her waist. The female figure is quite nude with her genitalia clearly visible, while the male wears a discernible *dhotī* through which the male genital organ is indicated. She is shown looking away towards her right though the male is gazing at her.

Also belonging to the Śuṅga period, carved on a stone railing pillar from Bodh-Gayā, is a very fine example of a couple enjoying music and dance.[47] The female carries a lute while the male holds its shell plectrum. The woman is shown standing on the right of the male, with the *vīṇā* in her right hand while the left arm is around the shoulder of the male. She is shown wearing a thick pleated *dhotī* and a prominent headdress, and is ornamented with a *stana-mālā* and earrings. The male has his arm around the waist of the female while clasping the plectrum in his left hand. He is also clad in an opaque *dhotī* with a tall asymmetrical headdress. He is shown standing in *samabhaṅga* while his female companion stands with slightly flexed legs. Both seem to be of about the same size, although in fact the female is slightly the taller of the two. They are looking at each other, giving a very life-like quality to the picture. The scene is set within an architectural setting with pillars on each side, but instead of the usual architrave/*vedikā* pattern,

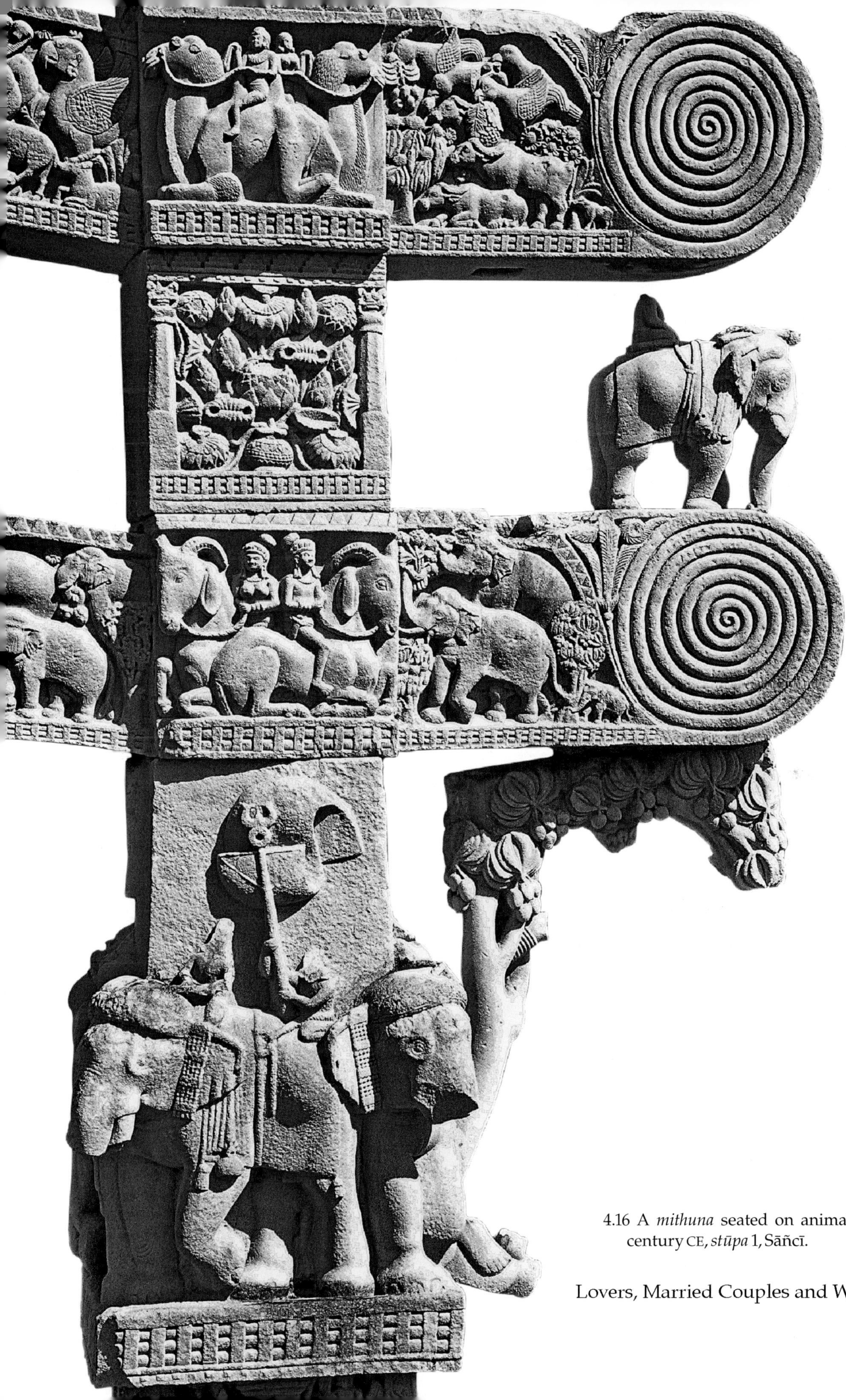

4.16 A *mithuna* seated on animals, *toraṇa*, first century CE, *stūpa* 1, Sāñcī.

garlands suspended from the top of the panel are depicted, giving the scene a festive environment.

A slightly later example, also from Bodh-Gayā (*Pl.* 4.27), is carved on an architectural fragment showing a male-female dyad dancing.[48] The woman is on the left with her left arm extended in a dance movement, and with her right arm she embraces the man, who has his left arm around the female figure. The piece is now partly broken, so that it is difficult to make out the rest of the details. The two figures are looking at each other and are of almost equal stature.

On a stone relief carving from Kosam datable to the first century CE, now housed in the Allahabad University Museum, there is another couple engaged in music and dance.[49] The male seated on the right of the standing dancing female, is depicted playing a harp-like instrument (see Pl. 4.28 for similar treatment). Both are shown wearing *dhotī*s that cover their lower limbs. The setting seems to be a garden with bushes and flowers, and the man is seated on a pile of stones.

Again from Bodh-Gayā, there is a rare specimen of a female figure as a *śālabhañjikā* being assisted by her male partner to cling to or clamber up the tree trunk. She rests her right leg on his lap while the left leg touches the tree (*Pl.* 6.31).[50]

A *dampati-mithuna* terracotta plaque from eastern India with applied ornaments[51] shows a female on the left of the male; her right arm is raised in dance posture, with her left on her hip.

4.17 *Mithuna* in various poses used to separate panels depicting different scenes from one another, third century CE, Nāgārjunakoṇḍa.

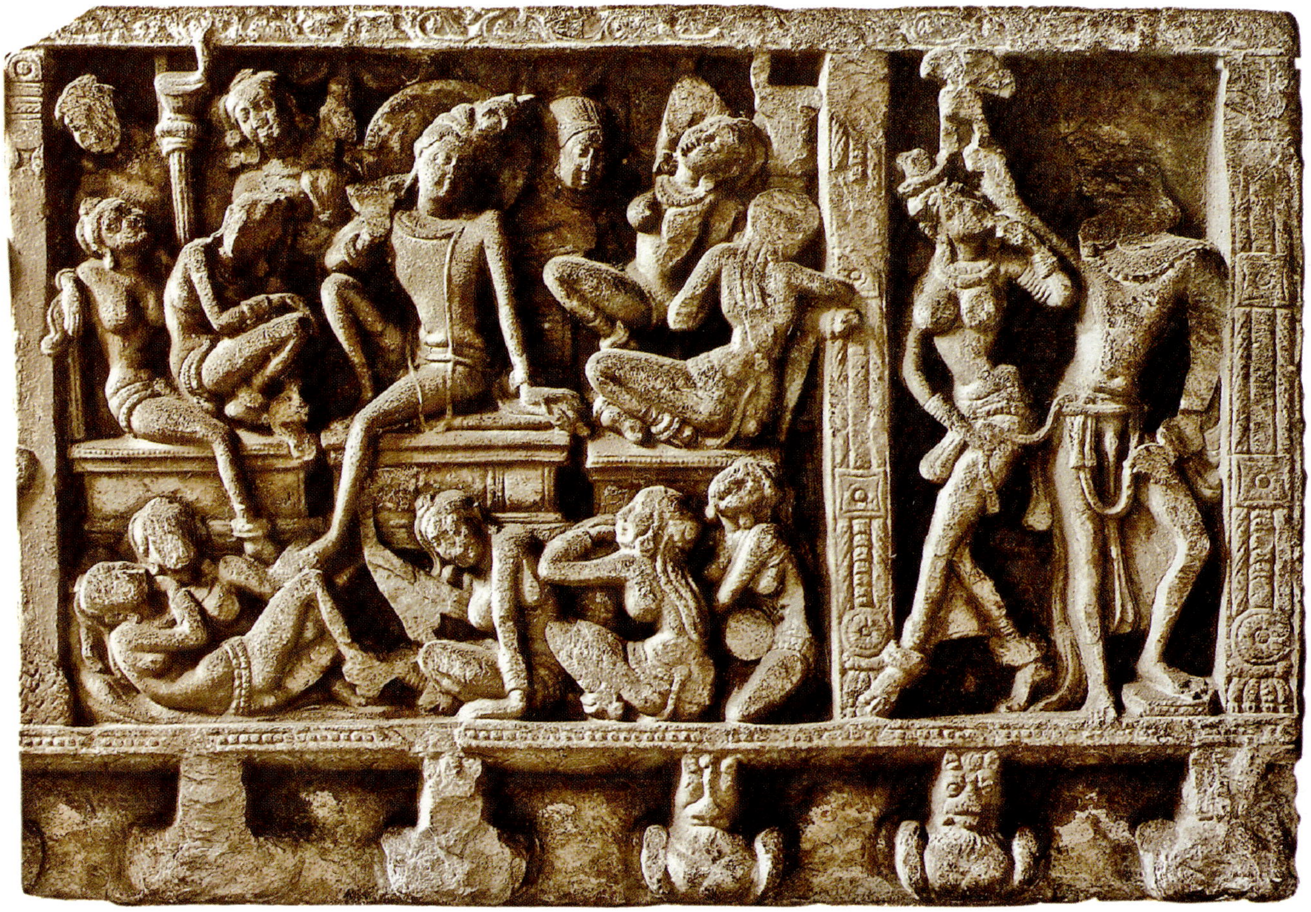

Her right leg is bent at the knee behind the diagonally placed left leg. The face is tilted. Her male partner is seated on a cushion. Both are arranged in graceful postures. He is looking towards the woman, who is looking to the right, not at him. This plaque presents a secularised version of a ritual theme. The courtly and erotic scene shows a male musician playing the *vīṇā* to accompany the lady's dance.[52] Although richly attired, the figures do not wear the ornaments generally associated with sacred terracotta plaques. The pavilion setting evokes the distinctive roof-and-pillar construction of contemporary architecture.

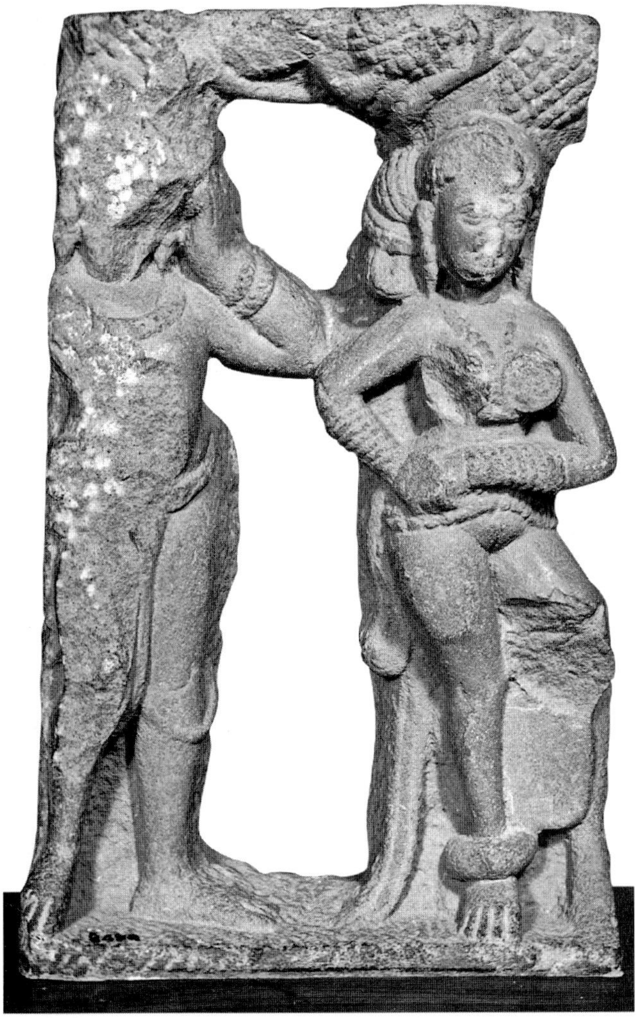

4.18 *Mithuna* under an *aśoka* tree, second century BCE, Patna, Bihar. Patna Museum. Arch 8484.

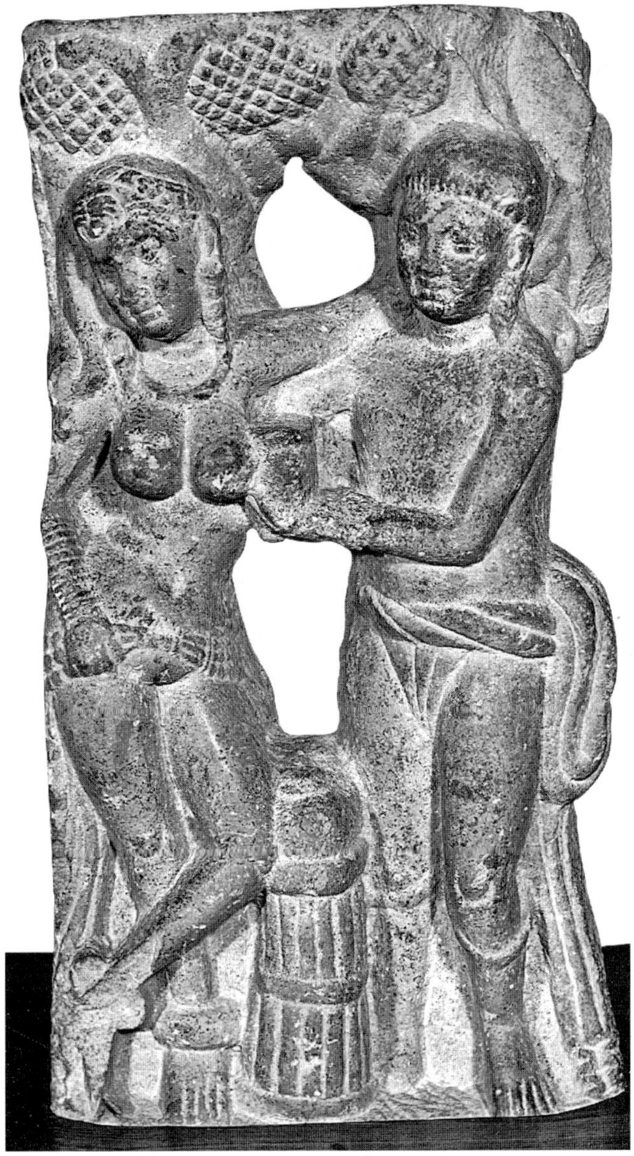

4.19 *Mithuna* under an *aśoka* tree, male offering wine to female, second century BCE, Patna, Bihar. Patna Museum. Arch 8178.

Couples engaged in various leisure and pleasure activities in secular settings are also available, especially in terracotta. On a round plaque from Bhītā having broad margin decorated with oblique incised lines, a couple in a pleasure garden are represented.[53] A little to the left of centre, is a house within a railing which has a gable roof, while in the background are trees and below is a pond filled with lotuses. On the

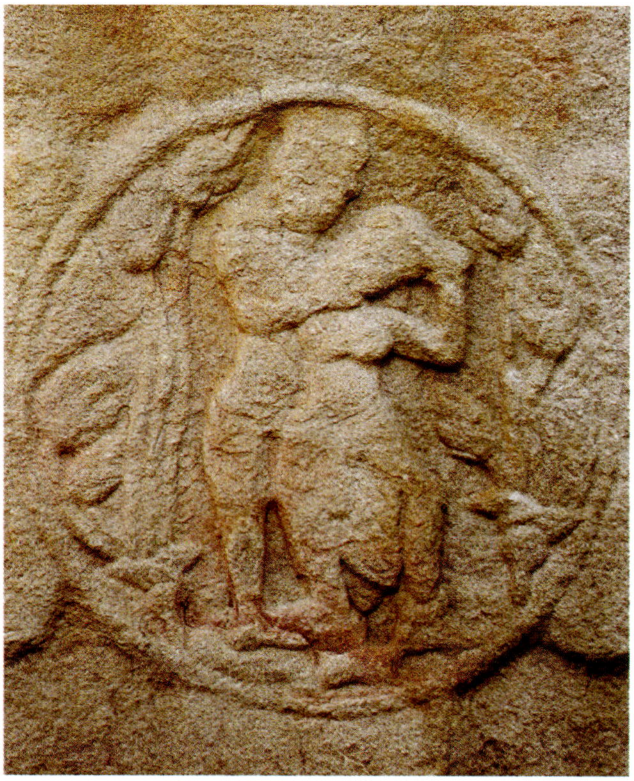

4.20 Amorous *mithuna*, railing, first century BCE, *stūpa* II, Sāñcī.

right is a bullock cart and in the centre, a jungle and the deer. In the uppermost part is a couple inside an enclosure, but the details are not clear. Other interesting secular subjects in terracotta sculptures include a picnic party in a bullock cart and lovers in a garden.

There is also a terracotta tradition, extending all over north India from about the second century onwards, of depicting coital couples, *maithuna*. Many of these are from Candraketugaṛh, now housed in the Ashutosh Museum in Kolkata. The couples here exhibit various positions of sexual congress. Sometimes female attendants assist them in the act. At Kauśāmbī and Bhītā, too, *maithuna* is depicted on terracotta plaques. According to Devangana Desai, these scenes represent *kāmaśāstrīya bandha*s from a pre-Vātsyāyana era.[54] Devangana Desai also sees a transformation in these sexual themes, in that they appear to have a ritual significance in the eastern Indian terracottas, while a more urban and secular sensibility is revealed by *kāmaśāstrīya* themes of the mid-Gangetic plains.

### 4.2.6 TYPE F: SPECTATOR MITHUNAS

On many Kuṣāṇa-period *stūpa* railing-pillars, especially those found at Mathurā and associated sites such as Sanghol, there are figures carved above the main figure, usually a *yakṣī*/*śālabhañjikā*, that seem to be looking at the latter (*Pls.* 6.15, 6.18, 6.22, 6.25). These represent a special class of figures that are difficult to categorise; one can at best call them spectator figures. They are derived from the depiction of citizens that are seen on the balconies and pavilions of multi-storeyed *caitya* buildings witnessing processions and events below, which are carved on the *toraṇa*s and pillars at Bharhut, Sāñcī and Bodh-Gayā. The later spectator figures are generally a male-female dyad, though there are exceptions, such as a female-female pair or three figures. They are visible only as busts.

A brief survey of a single site, Sanghol, reveals the variations in the depiction of these spectator *mithuna*s depicted in a variety of postures. 117 sculptural antiquities found buried together at this site must have constituted a *vedikā* or railing around the *stūpa*. A number of these sculptures are that of *yakṣī*s carved on rail posts, standing in various postures, many of which are also seen in Kuṣāṇa sculptures at Mathurā, datable to the second century.

(a) In one such scene, a *dampati-mithuna* is found above a *yakṣī* with a mirror.[55] They are posed above a *vedikā* that divides the two scenes. Both are looking outwards rather than at the *yakṣī* below, and seem to have no interaction with each other.

(b) In another scene the *dampati*-couple above the dancing *yakṣī* are framed in two separate panels, but both look downwards at the dancer who is balancing a pitcher on her elbow (see *Pl.* 6.26).[56] This pitcher partially covers the female on the left.

(c) In a third variation the couple shown above the *yakṣī* with a child is unique in so far as the female of the pair is larger and has abnormally large, elongated ears.[57]

(d) In a fourth scene, one can see above a *yakṣī*, in a languorous attitude, the *dampati-mithuna* simply looking at each other.[58]

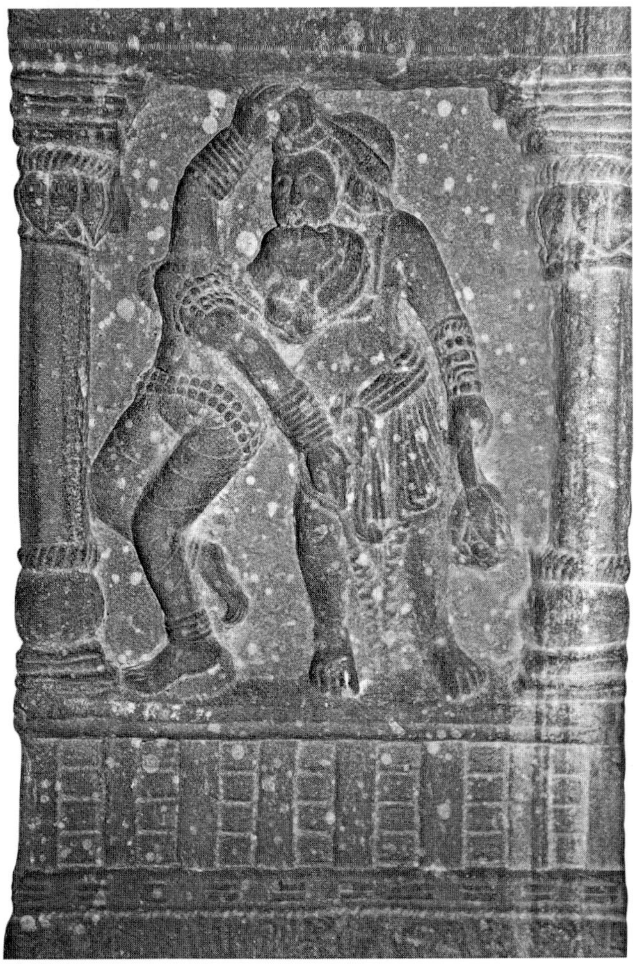

4.21 A couple in an intimate pose, panel on a railing pillar, second century CE. SML.

(e) In a fifth piece, the *mithuna* above the *yakṣī* putting on a thick necklace have their arms around each other's shoulders.[59]

(f) Sixth, a railing post shows a *dampati-mithuna* above a *yakṣī* holding lotus flowers look down at her with their hand under their chin, perhaps in wonderment at her beauty.[60]

(g) Seventh, in the *mithuna* composition above a female figure playing a harmonica-like instrument, the female of the pair is posed slightly in front of the male. Both are looking down at the main figure with smiles on their faces,[61] suggesting joy at the music.

The origins of these figures may in fact lie in the spectators lined up on the balconies and pavilions in the procession scenes seen in earlier narrative art at Bharhut, Sāñcī and Bodh-Gayā. These spectators, belonging to both sexes, witness the activity below such as the Departure of Buddha or the Visit to Kapilavastu and also participate in the action through their presence as urban citizens expressing their sorrow, joy or other emotions at the event illustrated in the narrative. The exact function of the spectators in later sculptures is a mystery, since they are mentioned in none of the contemporary or later texts on architecture. At one level they may have played the role of *sākṣī* (a witness) without which any religious experience is considered incomplete. In the Indian context they probably have the same *sākṣī* function as the flying figures that always appear in the sky, in the top corners of reliefs showing a momentous religious occurrence: they enhance the magic and importance of the moment merely by their presence. In the case of these *nāgarika* couples on railing-pillars they no doubt lend an air of immediacy and reality to the legendary scenes they are shown witnessing: they are the contemporaries of the spectators of this art, or in other words they are depictions of the living people who visited the *stūpas*, shown as in a mirror, but witnessing not a contemporary event but an event from a sacred past, as it were bringing that specific past into the present. The privileging of *nāgarika* couples as witnesses in the reliefs is presumably aimed at arousing the interest of sophisticated materialistic city folk in Buddhism and related supernatural phenomena in general, and at encouraging sponsorship. It may be possible that some of the donors recorded in the inscriptions, or types representing them, might be among these *sākṣīs*. However, in some cases the spectator on top interacts with the figure below, either by pointing at the scene or in one case by holding the neck of a pitcher, *surāhī* that the *yakṣī* balances on her upheld hand. Another noticeable feature is that often the spectator figures are seen suspended above a curved drapery that resembles a curtain.

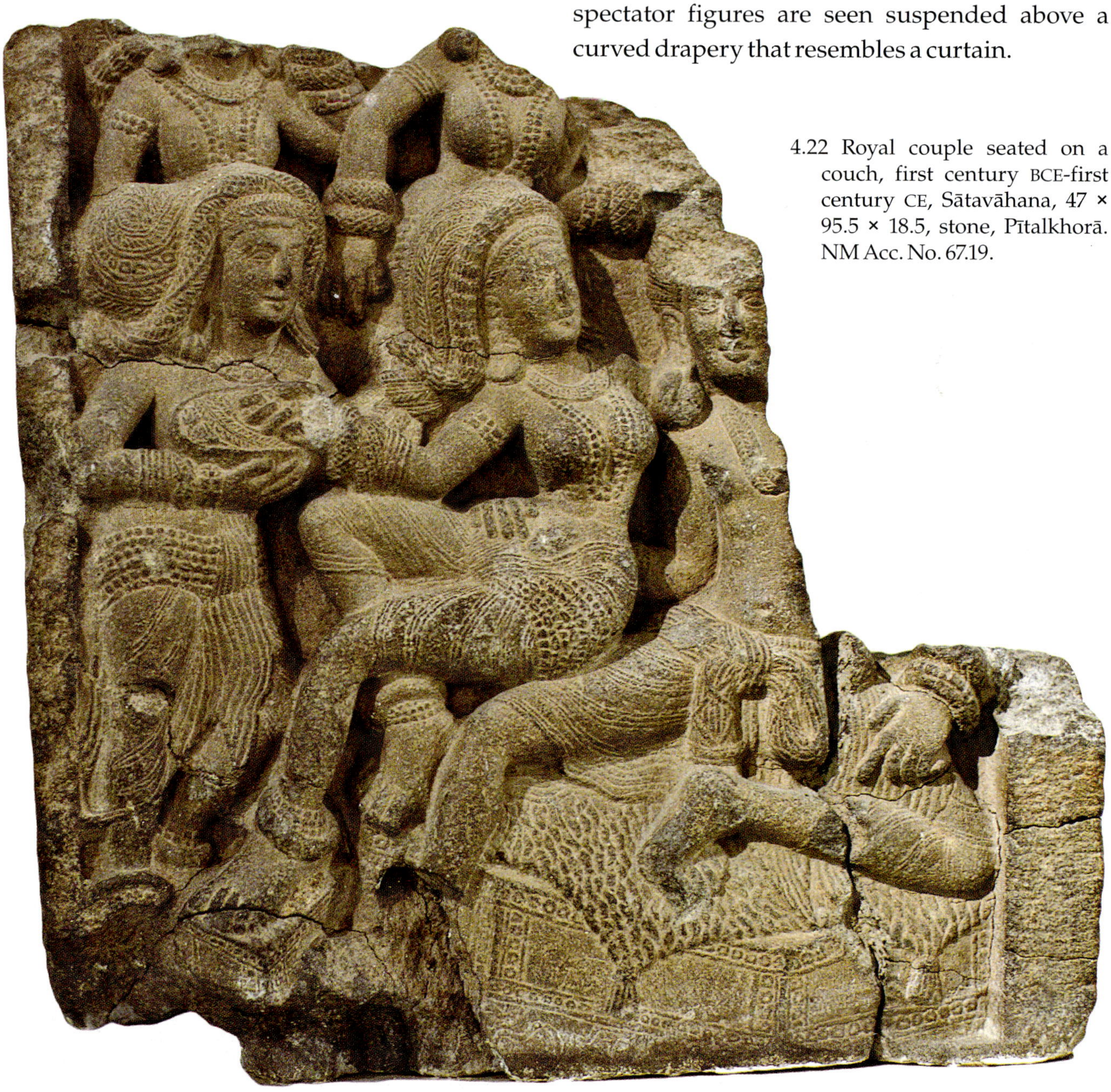

4.22 Royal couple seated on a couch, first century BCE-first century CE, Sātavāhana, 47 × 95.5 × 18.5, stone, Pītalkhorā. NM Acc. No. 67.19.

## 4.3 Meanings and Interpretations

The two inscriptions from Kārle, mentioned above, have facilitated the identification of male-female dyads as *mithunas*. *Dampati-mithuna* is more difficult to locate in inscriptions, as the husband and wife are usually found in the broader familial unit of the *gahapati* donors, where the family includes not only the married couple but also parents and parents-in-law, and siblings.

Post-Mauryan texts do not provide any indication that helps us ascribe a precise symbolic value to *mithuna/dampati* couples carved on contemporary monuments. In the Jaina texts such as *Rājapraśnīya Sūtra* and *Jīvājīvābhigama Sūtra* that may be placed in this

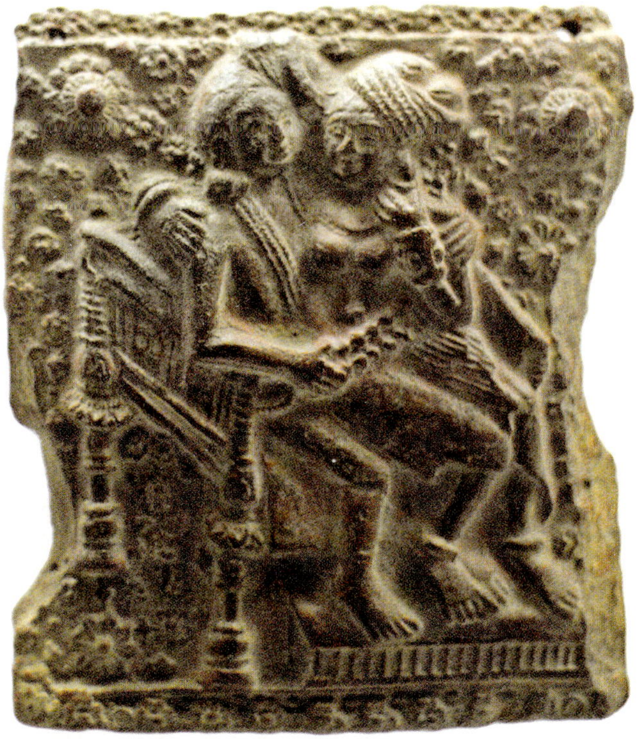

4.23 Lovers seated on a couch, first century BCE-first century CE, Kauśāmbī, terracotta. NM Acc. No. 0.67.

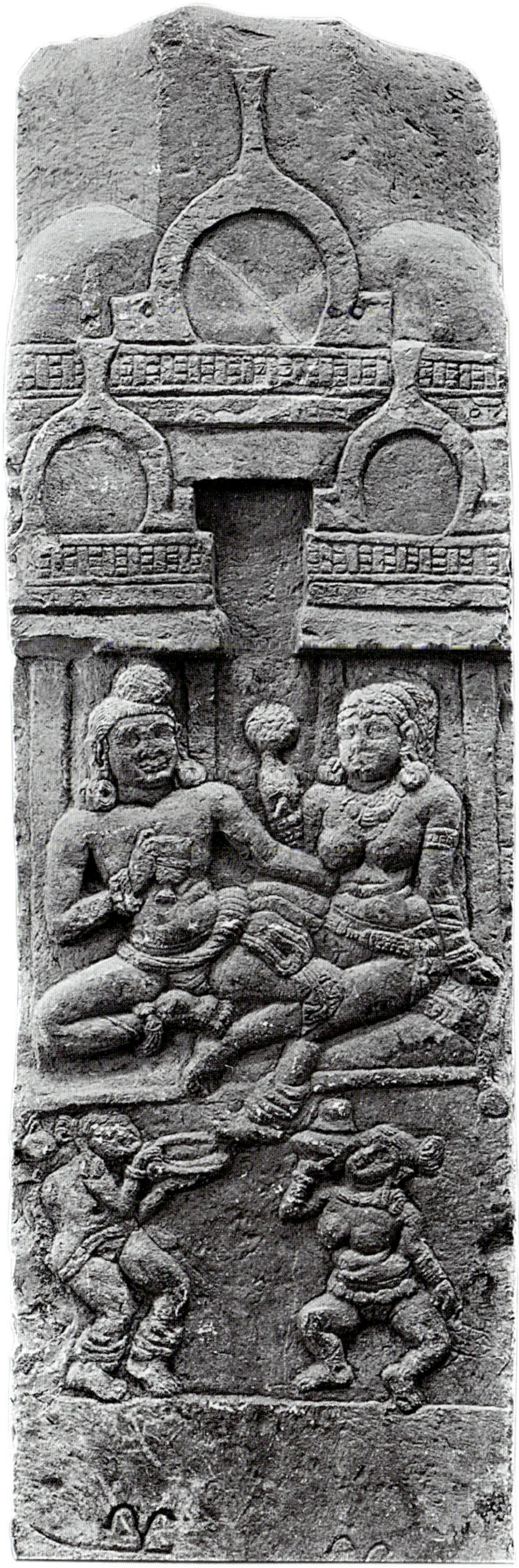

4.24 Royal couple seated, third century CE, Sannathi, Gulbarga district, Karnataka, Bangalore Museum.

period, it is prescribed that *yugalas* (pairs) — human, animal or fish — be carved on the gates, *toraṇas*, and walls, *bhittis*, of the *vimāna-dvāras*.[62] The latter text specifically mentions *matsya-yugala*, (a pair of fish) among its list of eight auspicious symbols, the *aṣṭamaṅgala*,[63] without however explaining the exact significance of each symbol. Therefore we have to rely on Vedic and post-Vedic texts for a clarification of the significance for ritual and social signification of *mithuna* (the pair). From the earlier Vedic textual references one can infer that a certain symbolic meaning must have crystallised into a motif which was transposed on to the symbolic ornamentation of buildings.

From early Buddhist *stūpas* to medieval Hindu temples, the *mithuna*, in both its *dampati* and *maithuna* form, assumed auspicious/apotropaic functions. *Mithuna* (the couple) exists at two levels. First there is the religious-ritualistic level seen in later Vedic literature, and secondly the artistic level at which it became a part of a code of symbols signifying *maṅgala* (auspiciousness). This code was undoubtedly rooted in a philosophy and a theology that viewed *mithuna* or pairing as essential and productive. An early text, the *Śatapatha Brāhmaṇa* informs us that "*mithuna* means a productive couple."[64] The basic concept suggests fecundity

4.25 Royal couple in amorous pose, large back piece of a royal throne, ornamented with 13 plaques with carving of women in various modes, Detail bottom row, 6th plaque, late first century to early third century CE, Begram, Kabul Museum.

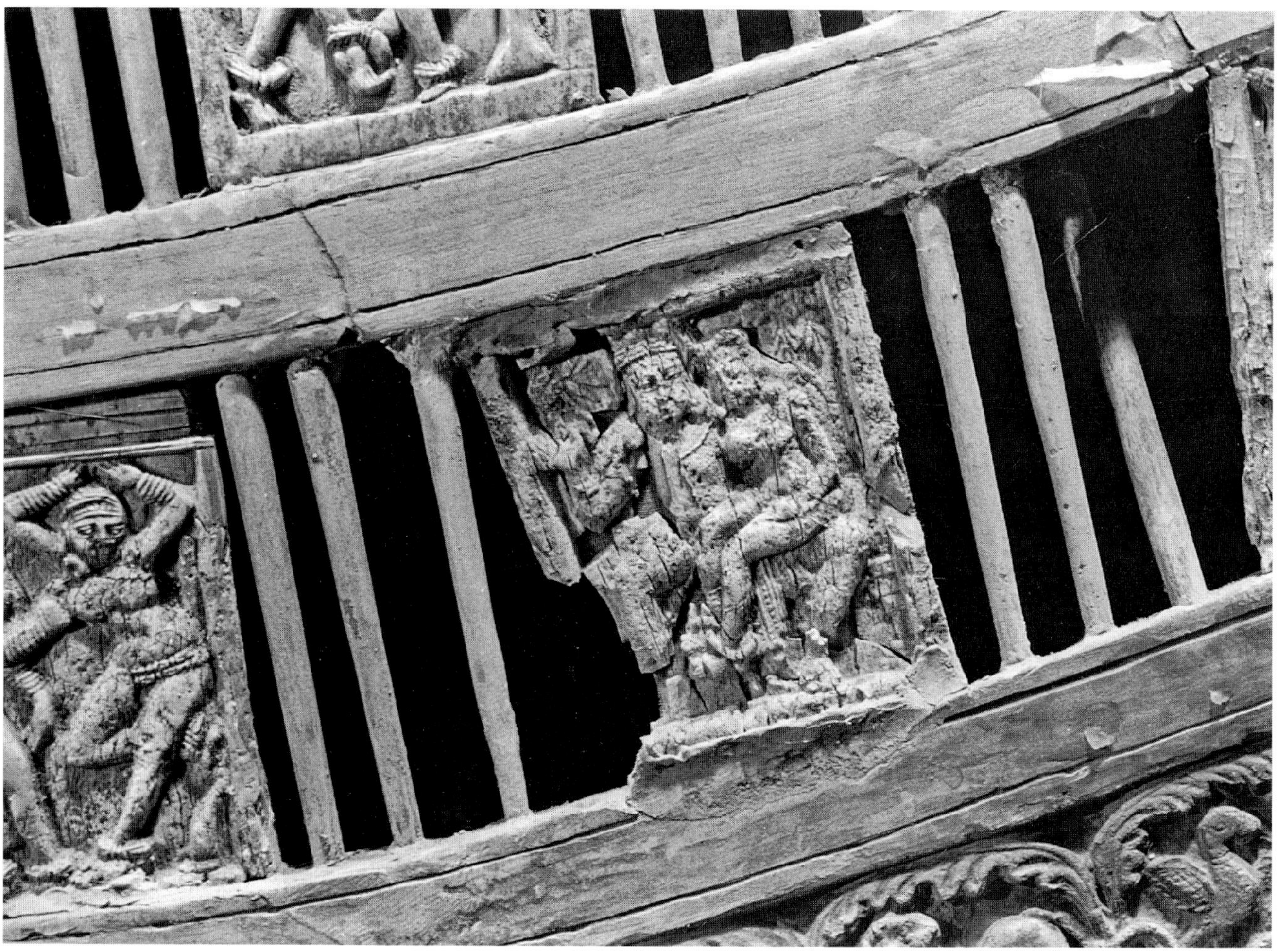

and that coupling leads to life, and that everything exists in pairs; thus a union of opposites becomes imperative for the continuation of life.

Pairing *per se* is an important concept from the Vedic period onwards that becomes visualised in *mithuna* and *dampati* depictions.[65] *Mithuna* in later Vedic poetry is viewed as made up of all pairs, complementing and contradictory, that are perceived as two wombs making up one *mithuna* — ideally a union of Savitar and Sāvitrī. These pairs are Agni and Earth, Varuṇa and Waters, Vāyu and Space, Sacrifice and Metres, Thunder and Lightning, Sun and Sky, Moon and Asterisms, Mind and Speech, Man and Woman.

It can thus be inferred that *mithuna* is accepted as the highest concept of human existence, of beauty, auspiciousness and things aspired to, similar to other symbols such as *kalpadruma*, *kāmadhenu*, *pūrṇaghaṭa*, etc.[66] All such symbols in turn are also associated with the *mithuna*, for example the *mithunas* that exist in the land of Uttarakuru live in a perpetual state of joy, free from worldly longings and needs since all wishes are fulfilled by *kalpadruma*, etc. As we have seen in the case of a coping sculpture from Bharhut (*Pl.* 4.10) and *toraṇa* reliefs from *stūpa* I at Sāñcī (*Pl.* 4.11),[67] there was a similar belief in Buddhism. The themes of Uttarakuru are also reflected in the classical poetic tradition where *mithunas* living in a state of perpetual bliss are idealised. In the description of this land one hears of *kalpalatās* showering bountiful gifts of ornaments, fabrics, cosmetics and drinks in various containers of jackfruit shape among others.

The connection between *mithuna* as a concept and fertility *per se* is well established in later Vedic liturgies accompanying sacrifices. In the *Śatapatha Brāhmaṇa* it says that the altar is female and the sacrifice is male, and that the woman lies embracing the male, whereby through copulation productive offspring are obtained.[68] The significance of pairing for reproduction and continuation of the race and the cattle is well recognised.[69] The *mithuna* is indeed considered an effective tool for generation and multiplication of humans and animals.[70] Thus fertility is implicitly and explicitly linked with *mithuna* or the pair. In the Śānti-Parva of the *Mahābhārata* Janaka explains that "it has been said that the relation between male and female is like that which subsists between the Indestructible and the

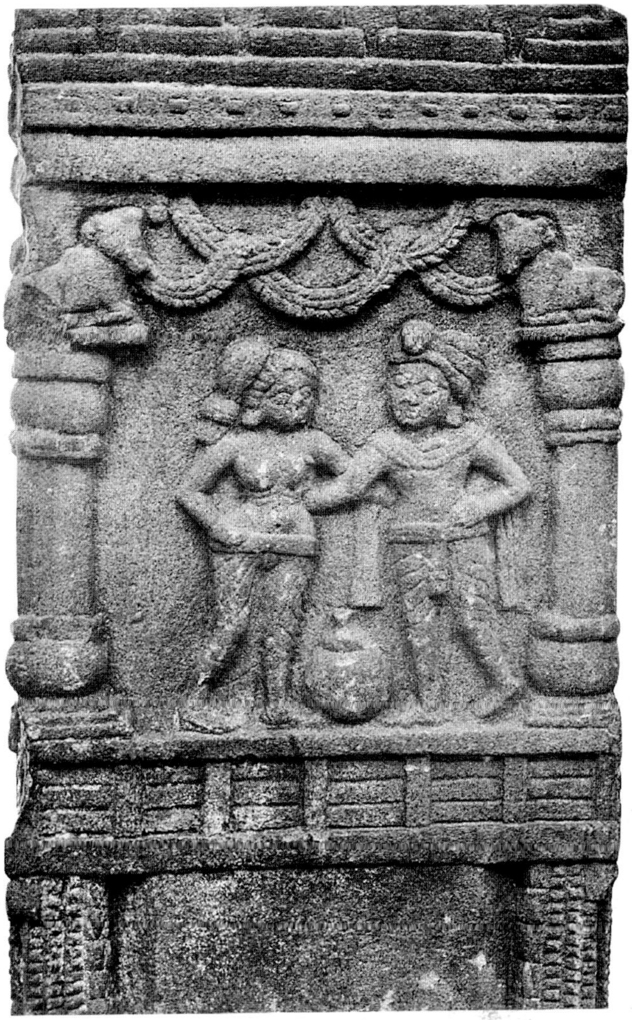

4.26 *Mithuna*, with arms around each other, a vase lying between them. Note: the pudendum is marked, first century BCE, Bodh-Gayā.

Destructible (*Puruṣa* and *Prakṛti*). Without a male, a female can never conceive, in consequence of their union upon each other . . . through each other union for the purpose of sexual congress and through each depending on the attributes of the other, forms (of living creatures) flow in menstrual seasons."[71] However it may be pointed out that despite the interdependence on each other, *puruṣa* and *prakṛti* are deeply gendered concepts. In the same text, it is said that the "learned say that *prakṛti* which is fraught with attributes of Creation and Destruction is called *Avidyā*; while *puruṣa* who is freed from the attributes of Creation and Destruction and who transcends the four and twenty principles is called *Vidyā*."[72]

Nevertheless, *mithuna* is one of the few fertility motifs in Indian art that are well articulated in literature, and in this it is unlike the *śālabhañjikā* figures whose connection with fertility is elusive in textual tradition.[73] This may be due to the symbolic and real regeneration observed in the sexual union of the male and female of the species. Thus human sexuality is integral to *mithuna* depictions, though the symbolism of sexuality is explicitly portrayed only in the case of coital couples.

It is this element of explicit fertility that was emphasised in cultic and votive divine *mithuna*s

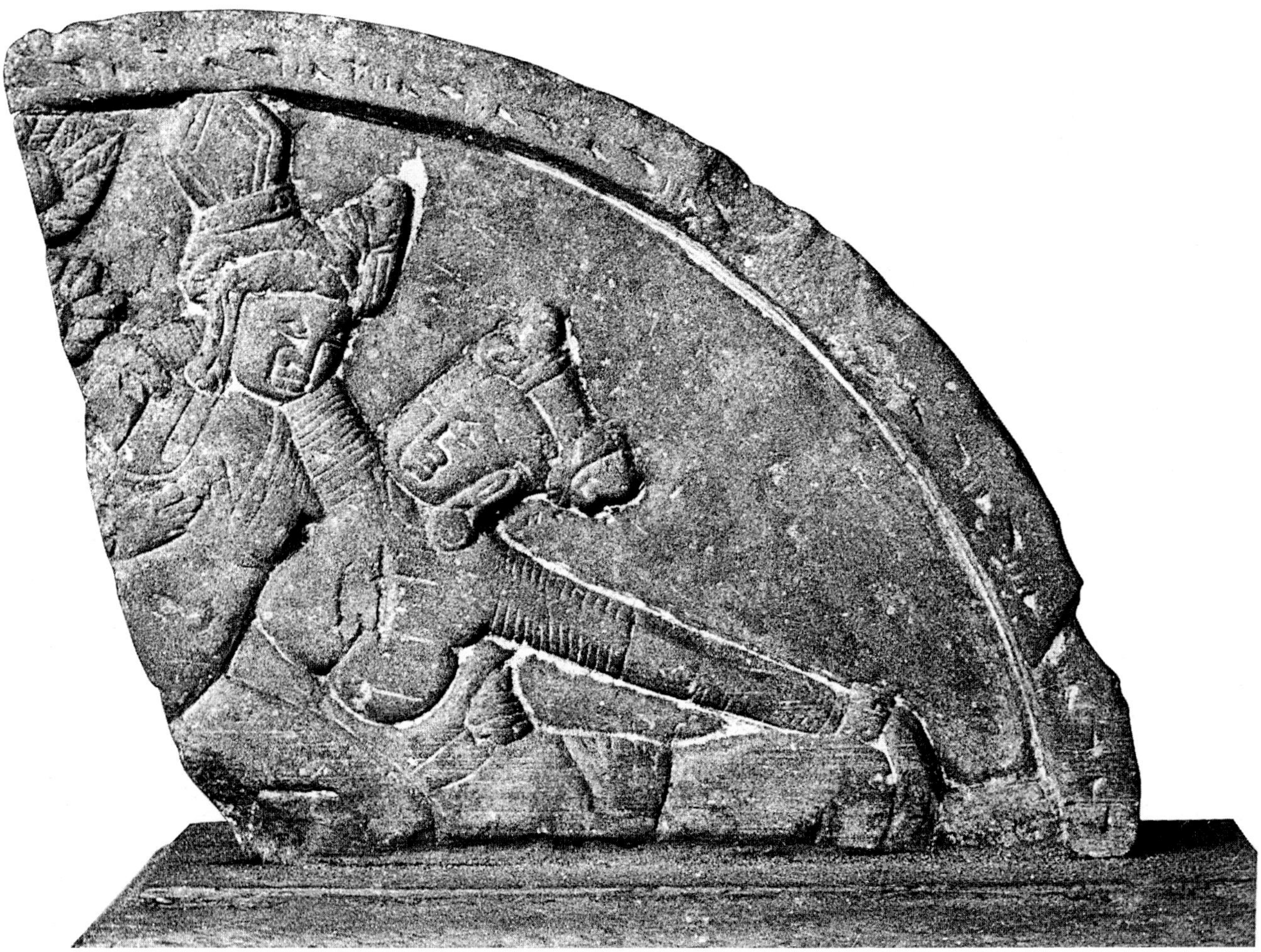

4.27 *Mithuna*, dancing, gray soapstone plaque, ht. 60mm, Bodh-Gayā, second century CE. Patna Museum No. Arch 1524.

seen on the stone discs and terracotta and steatite plaques of eastern India and the mid-Gangetic plains. It is no wonder that many sacred symbols such as *stūpa, liṅga, stambha* and the like are linked with human and animal *mithuna*s. These no doubt not only provided auspiciousness (*māṅgalya*) to a building or a site, but perhaps also the act of viewing it was believed to impart sympathetic fertility to the viewer.

Behind the man-woman pairing, as a concept that was later translated into art, was the belief that *kāma,* or sensual desire,[74] is all-pervasive and as such influences the entire world. It is essential to control and channel this powerful force, preferably to overcome it altogether because it hinders the human vision, thus becoming an obstacle to achieving salvation (*mokṣa* or *nirvāṇa).* Successful transcending of the realm of *kāma* leads to an abode of light.[75] One can achieve this either through destroying desire by renunciation, as did the Buddha and the Jina, or one can follow Śiva's path of a householder who conquered *kāma* along with Pārvatī through *dāmpatya* (married bliss).

### 4.4 Married Couple: Dampati

One may only speculate on the reason behind the popularity of *dampati-mithuna* depictions, since texts do not, of course, refer to this. We can postulate that married couples were considered auspicious as a symbol of legitimate social order, within which sexuality was ordered and controlled, perpetuating the human race. In the texts, *pati-patnī* (the husband-wife pair) is repeatedly eulogised.

In the *Bṛhadāraṇyaka Upaniṣad* the origin and concept of the married couple is well articulated. It explains "in the beginning this world was *Ātman*, soul, alone in the form of a person. Verily, he had no delight. Therefore one alone has no delight. He desired a second. He was, indeed, as large as a woman and a man closely embraced. He caused his self to fall into pieces. Therefrom arose a husband, (*pati*) and a wife *(patnī*)." It was believed that "oneself (*sva*) is like a half fragment as Yājñavalkya used to say. Therefore a wife fills this space, he copulated with her. Therefrom human beings were produced."[76] The man-wife dyad here is an emotional and sexual pair from whom the human race was created and reproduced.

A husband-wife pairing is essential for most successful ritual performances, as is clear from the *Ṛgveda* where the *dampati* is eulogised thus,

> O gods, the husband and wife who with
> one mind offer libations and purify them
> with the *soma* juice ever mixed with milk

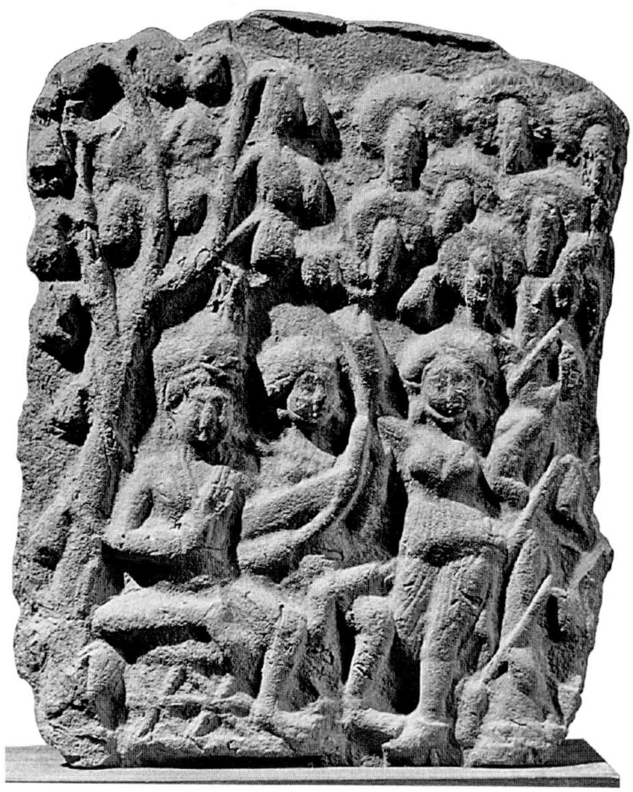

4.28 Couple enjoying music and dance in an arboreal retreat, terracotta, first century BCE-first century CE, Kauśāmbī. NM Acc. No. 60.436.

— constantly associated, they acquire appropriate sacrificial viands and offer sacrifice, and never do they fail in strength . . . blessed with *youthful and adolescent offspring*, they reach their full extent in life, both decked with ornaments of gold. Offering acceptable sacrifices, obtaining the *wealth* they solicit, presenting oblations (to the gods), for the sake of immortality enjoying personal union, they pay due honour to the gods[77] (emphasis mine).

The married couple then is capable of having healthy and legitimate offspring, and of fulfilling their ritual as well as social duties. This is reinforced in the Dharmaśāstras that enjoin that for a householder a "wife is the very root of Human Goals, not only of *dharma, artha* and *kāma*, but even of *mokṣa*. Those that have a wife can fulfil their due obligations in this world; only they truly lead a pleasant life and can be happy and their lives only are full and gifted."[78]

The wife is the source of renewal of the husband, for she provides children that carry on the father's lineage in a patriarchal society. "She, the wife, in sooth is one half of the man's own self; hence as long as he does not obtain her, so long he is not regenerate, for so long he is incomplete. But as soon as he obtains her he is regenerated, for then he is complete. 'Complete I want to go that supreme goal,' thus (he thinks) and therefore addresses his wife."[79] On the one hand the couple in marriage are a symbol of spiritual and physical continuum and renewal, and on the other they ensure legitimate patriarchal succession. An added element in ancient Indian societies is the need to ensure caste purity, the burden of which falls on women. It is desirable that women do not marry into inferior *varṇa*s, thus leading to instability of the caste-based social order.[80]

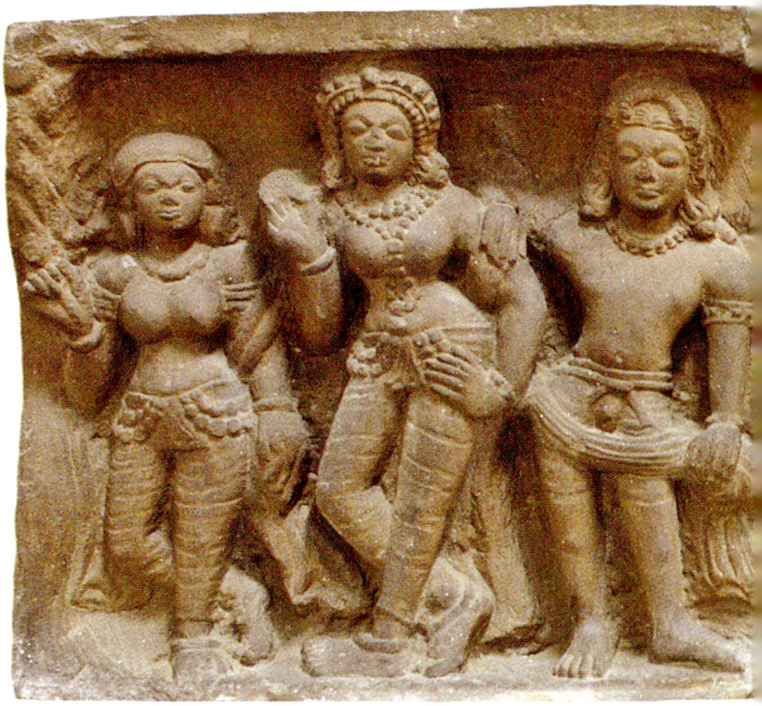

The evolution of the husband-wife motif took two directions in post-Mauryan art. On the one hand, by the beginning of the Christian Era, in both image and text, a male god was paired with a female spouse and vice versa. This was accompanied sometimes by an elaborate myth about the wedding of the divine couple and their subsequent children, as is the case with Śiva-Pārvatī and their children Ganeśa and Kārttikeya.

On the other hand, there are the *dampati* depictions on secular and sacred edifices that may signify the representation of the couple in a manner that conformed to the idea of a legitimate married couple with the husband placed conventionally on the right of the woman. Dhavalikar views the *dampati* as husband and wife, and *mithuna* as representing an amorous couple.[81] For him, *dampati* in standing or sitting postures appear to be respectable citizens and represent the very picture of conjugal bliss. Amorous couples are shown in various postures from dalliance to sexual union, kissing,

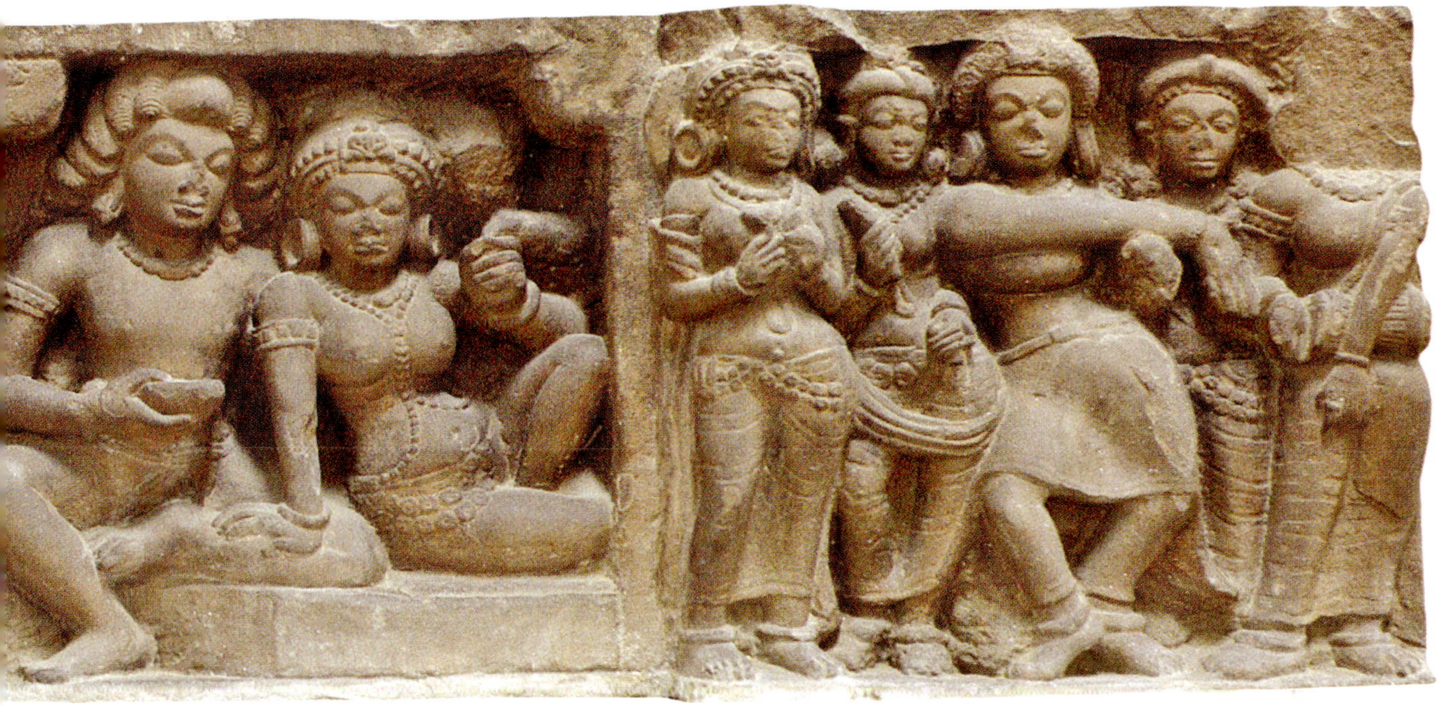

embracing, touching the genital parts of each other. It has been argued by P.K. Agrawala that there is an evolution from the stage of promiscuous *mithuna* into *dampati*. The artist, while trying to show *dampati-mithuna,* seeks social approval for the theme of amorous activity on the part of his male-female characters. Dhavalikar on the other hand has dated the *dampati* plaques to circa 200-100 BCE, whereas in his opinion the *mithuna*s or amorous couples appear only in the layers ascribable to 100 BCE to CE 100.[82] However, it may be contended that from the beginning of Indian art, *mithuna* and *dampati* as motifs were simultaneously deployed, as has been seen above. Devangana Desai has not made a distinction between *mithuna* and *dampati*. In her opinion there is a progression towards greater secularisation and sensualisation of the *mithuna* imagery from the second century to the third century CE due to the changing tastes of the increasingly urbanised population.[83] Perhaps the meanings of the two were complementary but

4.29 Lovers enjoying wine, dance and music, 34 × 185 × 24 cm stone, fifth century CE, Gupta, Deogaṛh. NM Acc. No. 51.184.

conveyed different purposes; *dampati* representations may have been used to depict mytho-historical figures, such as Sundarī and Nanda or to portray actual donors.

At Kārle and Kānheri, as regards the couples depicted at the entrance, the woman is placed on the right and not on the left of the man. They may be either donor couples or praying couples. Inside the Kārle caves the finials of pillars have a pair or more than one pair of couples seated in an embracing posture on an elephant. They are used here more as a decorative motif rather than as a mystic symbol, without any special symbolism which may be attached to the "couples" represented on the side of the doorways of the shrine.[84] The *mithuna* was considered part of the scheme of auspicious symbols, *maṅgala* that signified the concept of everlasting bliss in the

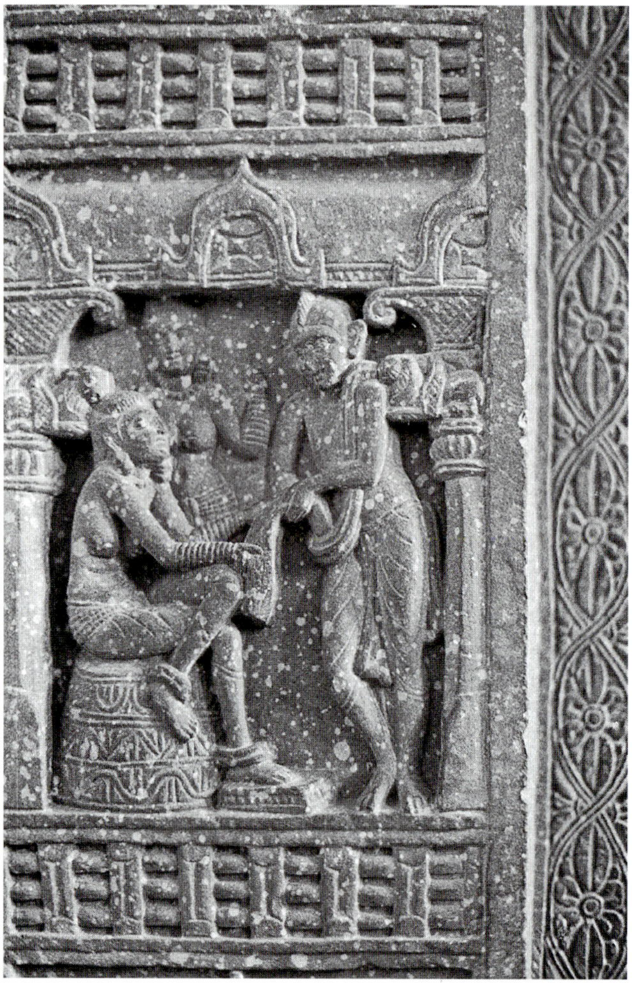

4.30 Detail of scenes projecting amorous interaction between a young royal couple, identified as Sundarī and Nanda, red sandstone, fragmentary doorjamb carved on two faces, second century CE, Mathurā. SML J 533.

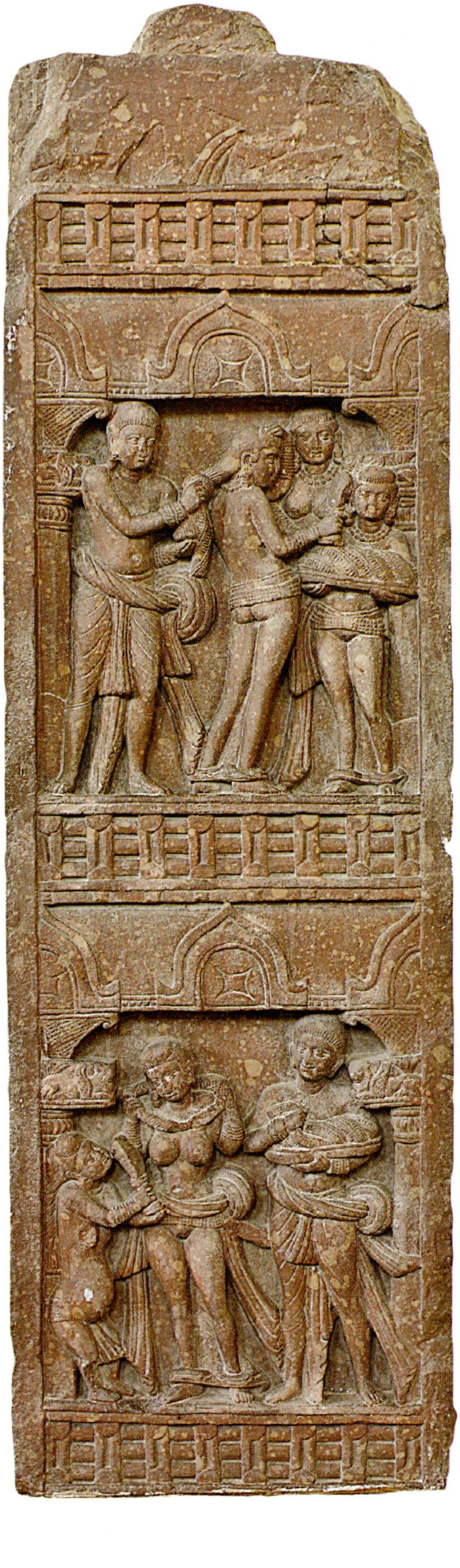

4.31 Scenes projecting amorous interaction between a young royal couple, identified as Sundarī and Nanda, second century CE, Mathurā.

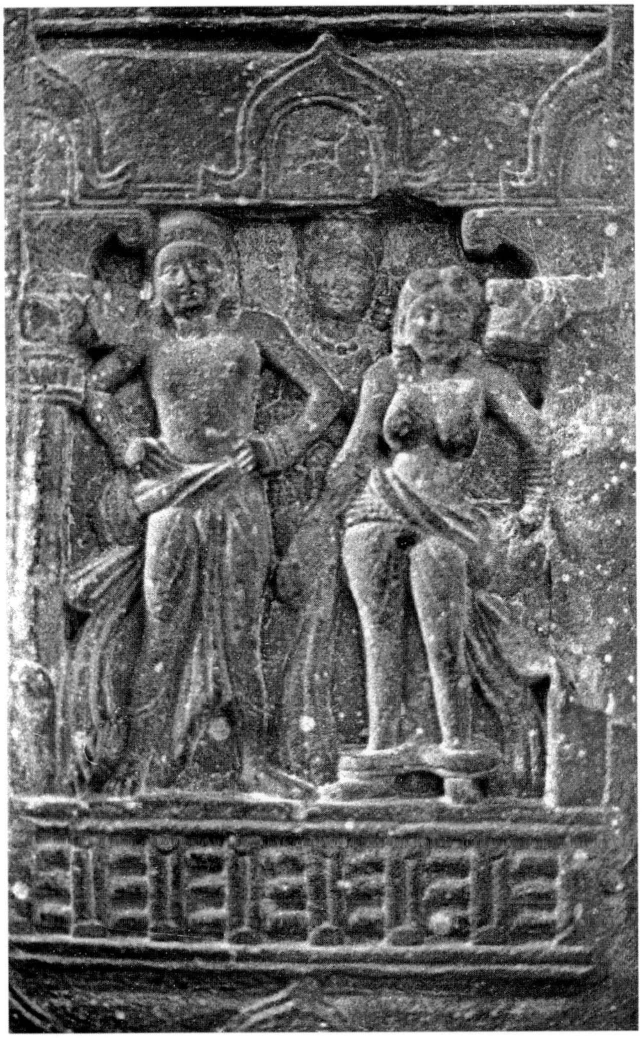

4.32 Detail of scenes projecting amorous interaction between a young royal couple, identified as Sundarī and Nanda, second century CE, Mathurā. SML J 533.

land of Uttarakuru or other celestial places. Jaina texts also reflect this symbolism, containing references to *yugala*s perpetually disporting in the *vimāna* of *Sūryabhū deva* or in the mythical island of Ekoruka *dvīpa*.[85]

*Mithuna* depictions celebrate sexual union; in *dampati-mithuna* representations this union is socialised within a marital relationship. Underlying both representational types is valorisation and codification of the reproductive potential of the couple. However, by reducing the couple to a symbol, the sexuality inherent in the coupling is conveyed in more manageable and palatable form, especially given the monastic contexts in which it was often deployed. The symbol provides an outlet for otherwise unacceptable social and gendered roles or behaviour to be depicted in terms that do not offend or contradict the dominant socio-religious ideology.[86] The imperative to depict the pair in a symbolic form even within ideologies that privilege the ascetic may be sought in the lay public that patronised their community and monuments. This lay public celebrated and participated in fertility and sexual rituals and thus even the monks accepted the couple and coupling as a motif of auspiciousness.

### 4.5 A Specific Couple: Sundarī and Nanda

Along with *mithuna* motifs seen on the facades of religious (and secular) structures, there are specific husband-and-wife pairs depicted. The most prominent pair is that of Sundarī and Nanda, immortalised in a poem by Aśvaghoṣa in his *Saundarānanda*. This story of royal romance and renunciation must have been very popular in the first two centuries CE, being carved on monuments and recorded in the literary tradition, both in the *Jātaka*s and in verse.

Besides Aśvaghoṣa, the Sundarī-Nanda story is also mentioned in the *Therīgāthā*:[87] A *therī* who embraces the path of renunciation after her entire family converts to the Buddha's faith is mentioned as the sister of Nanda and the Buddha, and as the sister of Abhirūpa Nanda and Rāhula's mother and the daughter of Mahāprajāpati Gotamī.

In the sculptural tradition, Nanda's wife Sundarī is portrayed; her dalliance with Nanda is found in two types of sculptural composition. In the first, a toilet scene involving the husband and

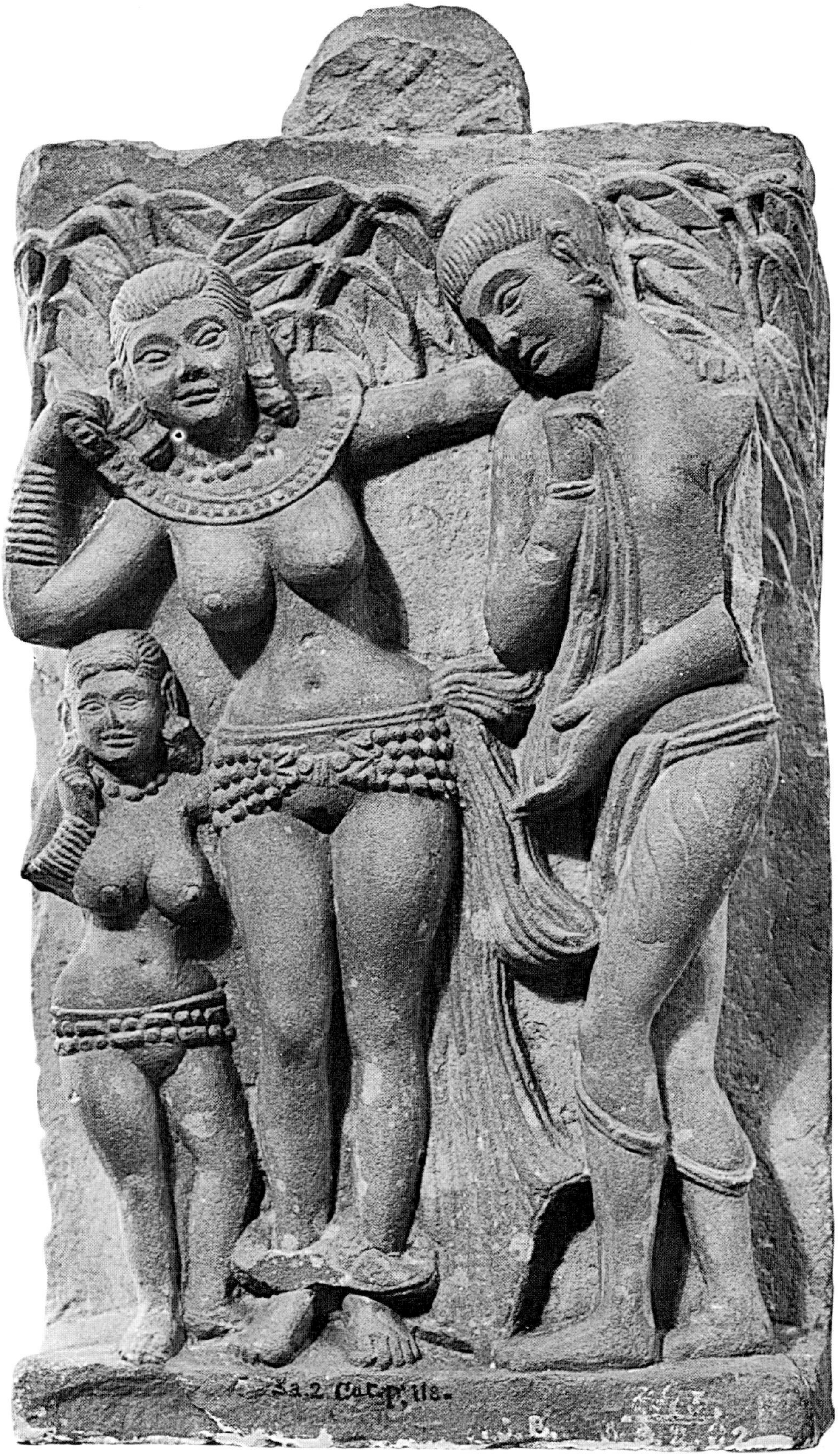

4.33 A female wearing a necklace and a male figure assisting her with her toilet, perhaps Sundarī and Nanda, red sandstone, second century CE, Sankisa, Etah district, UP. IM, No. A 24250/Sa 2A.S.B/5173.

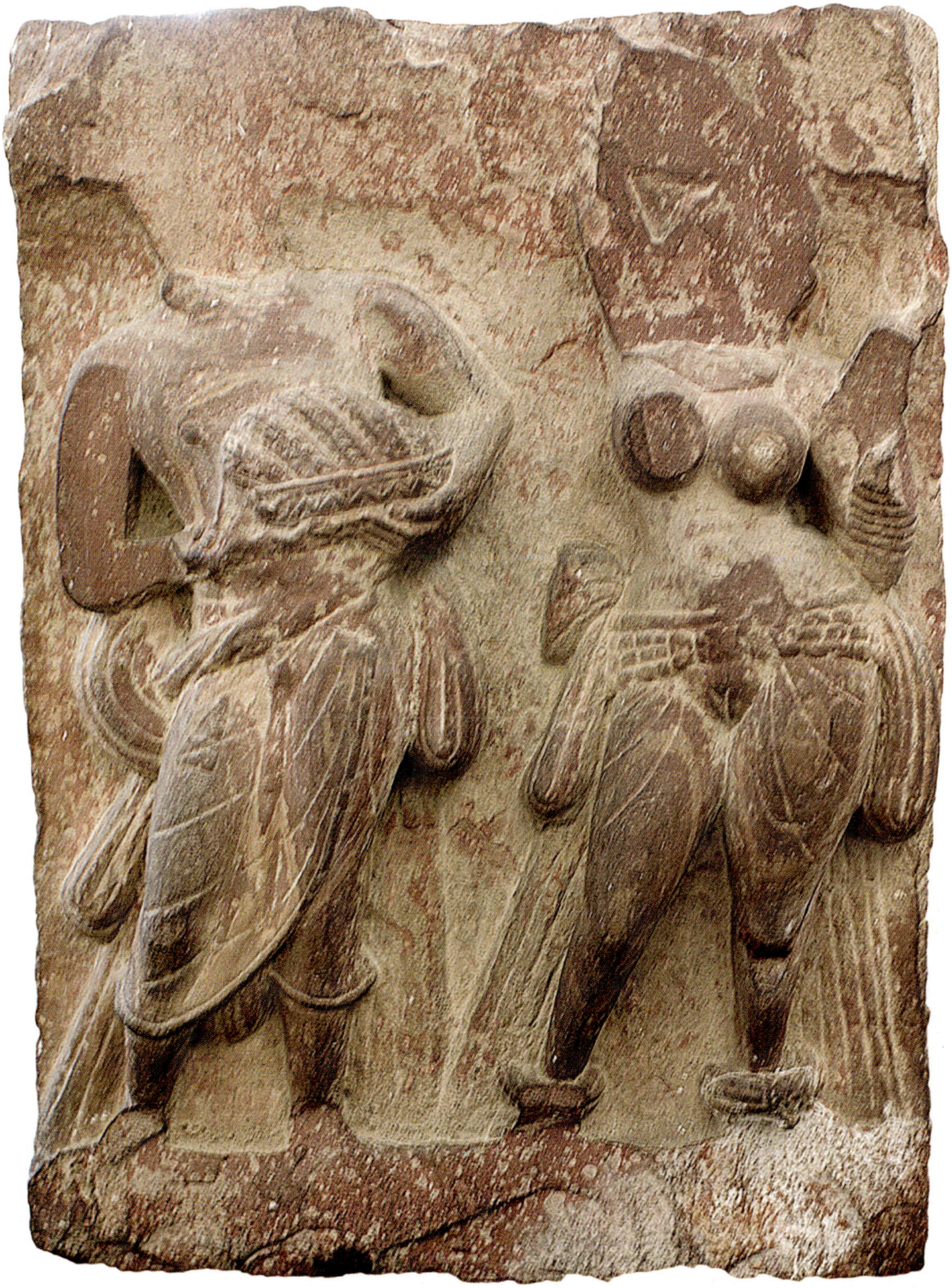

4.34 *Mithuna*, man holding a tray with a garland, standing, red sandstone, first century CE, Mahāvana, Mathurā district, UP. GMM No. 36.2663

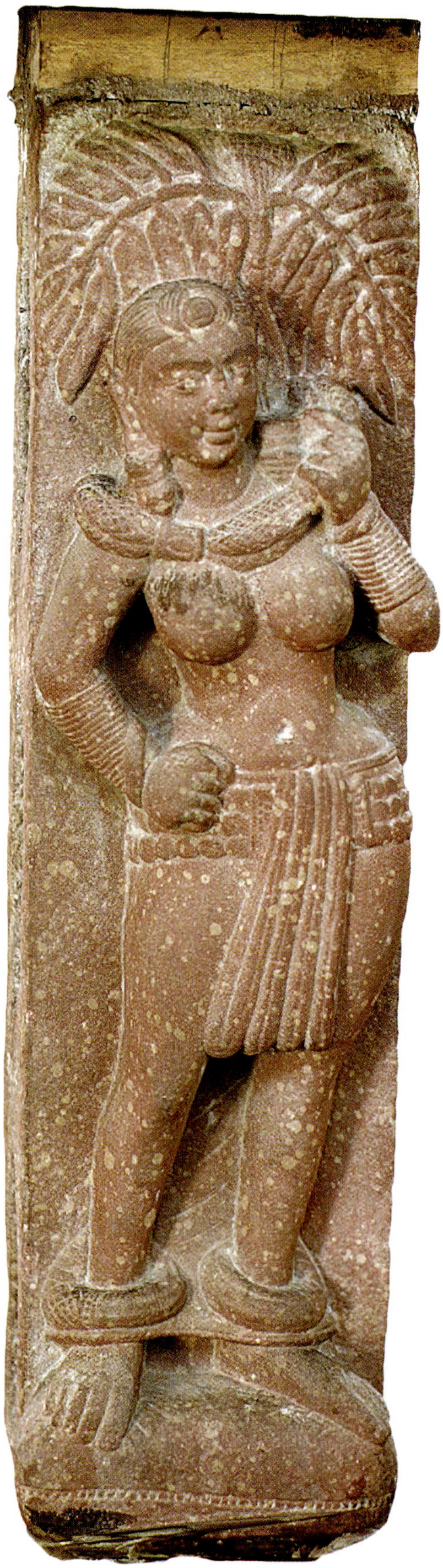

wife is delineated, and the second contains more elaborate palace scenes including one or more mendicants accompanying the royal couple. These visuals share some elements with the descriptions found in Canto 4 of the *Saundarānanda*.

Aśvaghoṣa spent considerable effort in painting a verbal picture of the love between Nanda and his wife, with whom Nanda spent innumerable hours in play and passion. He describes how in the process of love, "he covered her with ornaments, not that she should be decorated but only to serve her. . . ." In response, she put a mirror into her lover's hand, saying, "Just hold this up while I paint myself;" and he obeys her request.[88]

On a second-century jamb from Mathurā, known as the Saundarānanda panel (*Pls.* 4.30 to 4.32)[89] and now in the Lucknow Museum, the reliefs, which are carved on both sides, eight scenes of a couple indulging in various activities have been identified as representing the dalliance of Sundarī and Nanda. These include the male handing a garland to the female, offering her wine, holding her sash as she dresses with the help of a female attendant, holding up a mirror during her toilet, etc.

The depiction of the toilet scenes with a male and female figure does not precisely illustrate the moment from the poem quoted above, yet the atmosphere of intimacy between the principal figures built by the sculptor allows for the identification.

Similar scenes are seen on a railing pillar from Mathurā (*Pl.* 4.31). The exact context in which it was found is not known;[90] in all probability it was part of a Jaina or Buddhist monument. This pillar is divided into two sunken panels enclosed between pillars supporting a long architrave with ogee arches. In the upper panel, a male-female couple occupy the centre. The rear view of the woman is shown, thus her face is in one-fourth profile. She is looking into a mirror, *mandana*

4.35 *Yakṣī* adjusting necklace, railing pillar, red sandstone, second century CE, Mathurā.

4.36 *Yakṣī* adjusting necklace, railing pillar, second century CE, Kuṣāṇa, Sanghol, GMAG. (facing page)

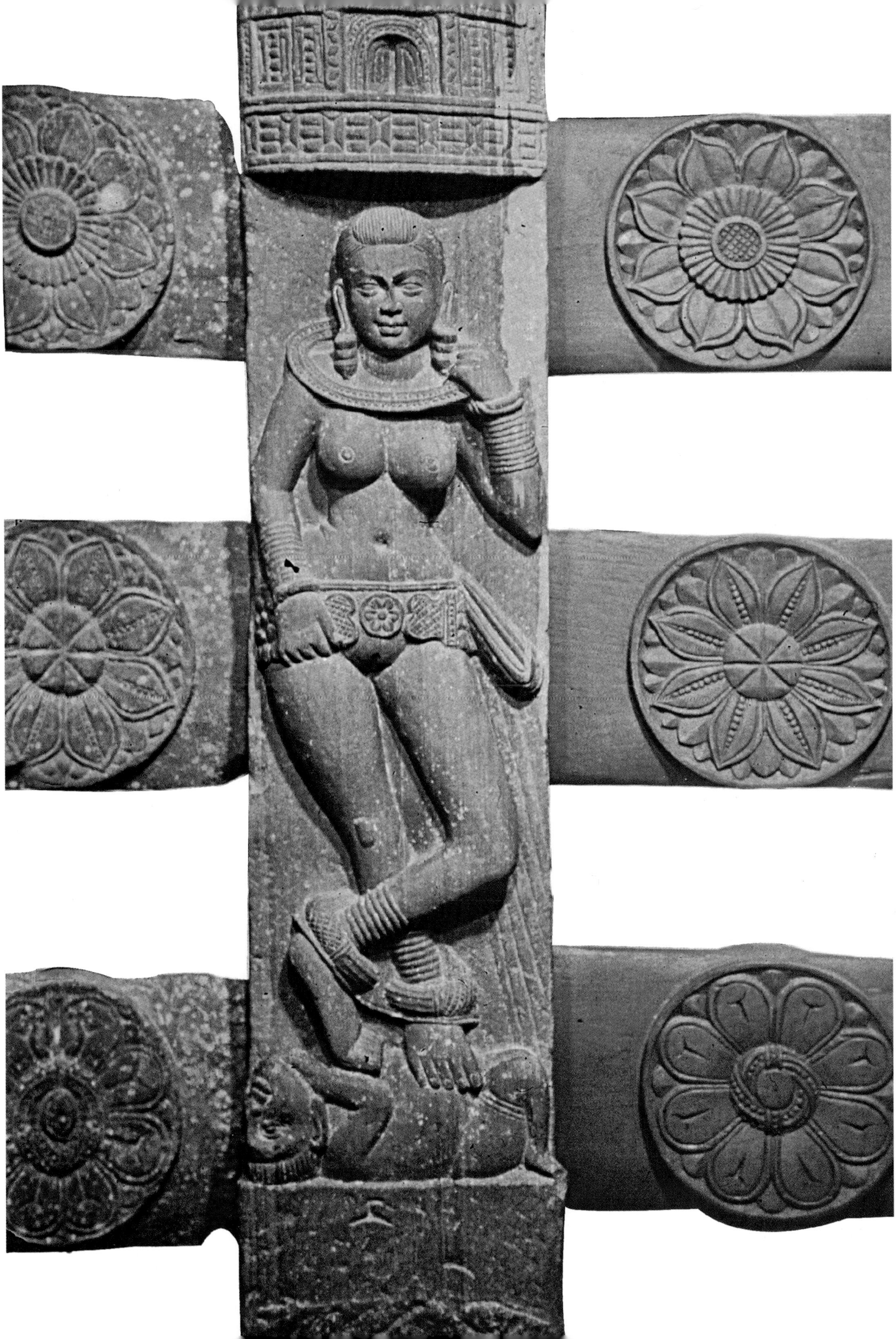

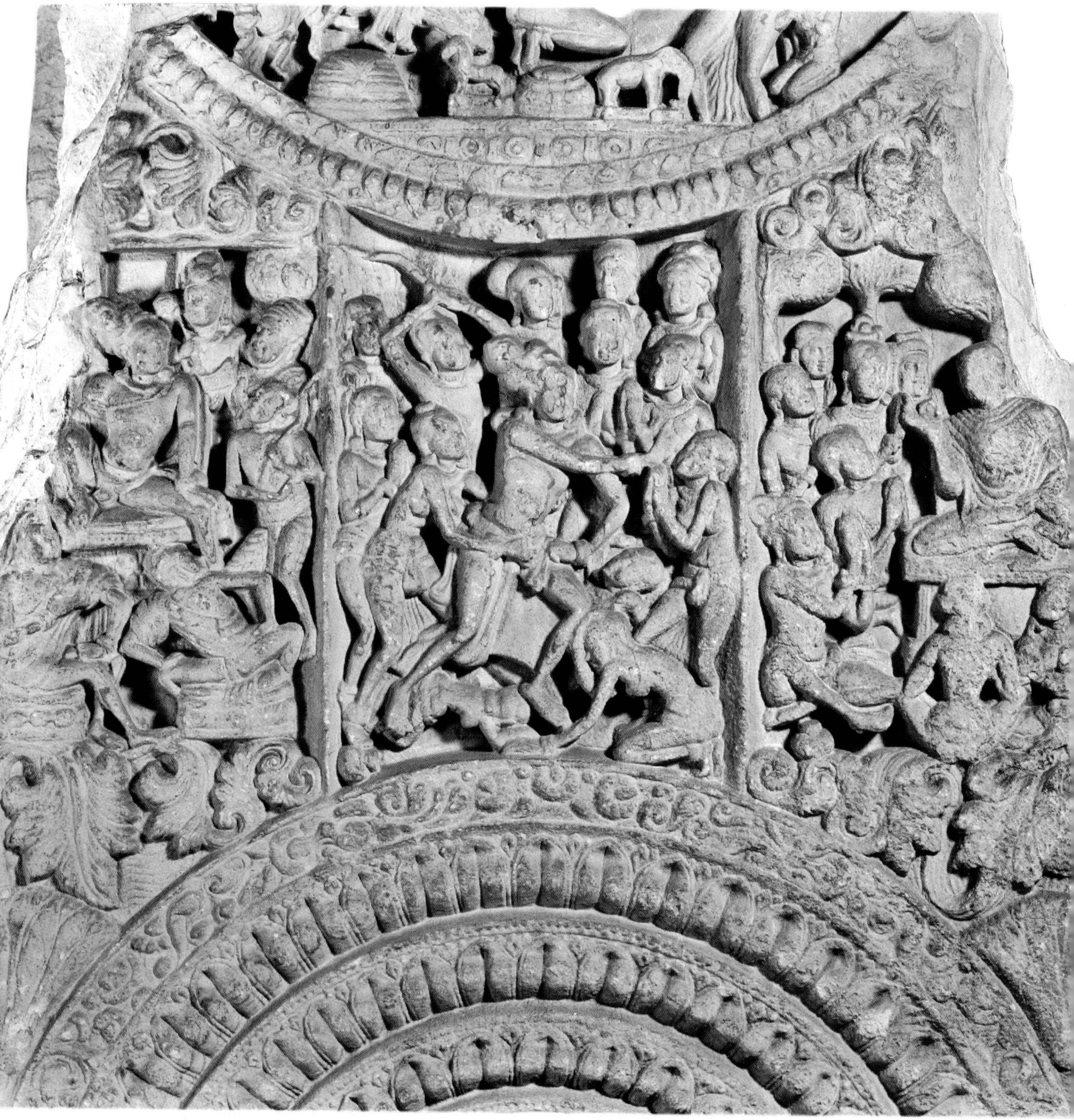

4.37 The conversion of Nanda, lower portion of a pillar, third century CE, Amarāvatī.

*darpaṇa*, held in her right hand, and trying to arrange her frontal hair with her left hand. Her male companion is standing behind her, dressing her braid of hair by interweaving it with a garland of flowers. With his other hand he holds the sash around his waist that is looped at the end in a typical Kuṣāṇa-period manner. Two female attendants are also visible, the one on the far right holding a tray with a garland on it, *utpala-mālābhāriṇī kanyā*[91] (a woman bearing a garland of lotuses).

In the lower panel, another toilet scene with principal male and female figures is repeated. Here the woman is shown adorning her person with a thick garland, thrown over both her shoulders, which she holds with both her hands. She is looking into a mirror held up in front of her face by a dwarfish female figure (or perhaps a eunuch). To her left is a male figure holding a garland tray. The reverse of the pillar shows a *yakṣī* figure. A similar scene has also been recovered from Sankisa (*Pl.* 4.33),[92] with the female figure in a frontal standing position, putting on a thick garland, with a male companion on her left. He seems to be holding a thick, long garment, perhaps an *uttarīya*, in his hands, waiting for her to receive it from his hands. A diminutive female attendant is also seen.

In all these scenes from Mathurā (*Pl.* 4.34) and Sankisa the female figure is delineated with close-set, full and rounded breasts, a thin waist, and broad hips. The lower half of the body seems clothed with transparent drapery since the genital region is clearly visible, with a well-marked cleft. In the constitution of the female body, along with the jewellery that adorns it, such as a thick *mekhalā*, the female figures in the Saundarānanda panels approximate to the *yakṣī* figures of the Mathurā atelier (*Pls.* 4.35, 4.36). However, one notices that unlike the conventionalised *dampati* motif, portrayals of husbands and wives engaged in certain activities are more dynamic in these figures. This is apparent in the arrangement of the male and female *vis-à-vis* each other, in which the female can be either to the left or the right of the male.

At Amarāvatī in the second century CE, the theme of the romance of Sundarī and Nanda and the renunciation of Nanda was a popular subject with the sculptors-designers. They elaborated it to include palace scenes that are described in Canto IV (when Sundarī tries to keep Nanda at her side) and Canto VI (where Sundarī, hearing of Nanda's conversion, wails and becomes prostate with grief). As at Mathurā, the translation into visual is not exact, since it is probable that the sculptor and the poet were borrowing from a commonly-known story rather than from each other.

On the inner face of a railing pillar of the Amarāvatī *stūpa*, the bottom three panels represent scenes from the story of the Conversion of Nanda (*Pl.* 4.37).[93] The left-hand panel shows the prince seated on a throne, with his beautiful wife seated on a cushion at his feet adjusting her robe. To her left is another, smaller figure seated with his back to the viewer, his robe wrapped tightly around his body and left arm. At the top right of the panel is a tree and behind the prince is a *cāmara*-bearer. Also present is a fat old man wearing a turban with a chinstrap. Below him is a male figure in a short, pleated *dhotī* carrying a short, crooked staff. The central panel shows the prince struggling with a group of women. A kneeling woman at the bottom right is trampled under his feet. One holds him by his waist, probably his wife Sundarī, trying to prevent him joining the order. To the right are a number of women, their right hands raised in supplication.

To the left of the panel a male figure raising his bow over his head may be Kāmadeva. The right-hand panel depicts the Buddha on a platform in a grove of trees surrounded by male and female worshippers. The Buddha's right hand is raised in *vitarka-mudrā*.

We have three moments from the story represented here. The left-hand panel shows a happy and contented royal couple, comporting themselves within socially sanctioned roles, with the wife seated on a stool at the feet of her lord and husband. An appropriate royal setting is provided for this scene. The only indication of amorousness in the scene is Sundarī with her hands on her clothes, which is a strategy employed to attract the male. In the central panel among many women are clinging to the waist of the male and it appears that the motif of frivolous and uncontrolled women impeding the path of the pious, and an ascetic (male) is being implied. Appropriately, a female is shown being trampled underfoot, as should be all sense-desires that impede the path towards *nirvāṇa*. Kāmadeva, the

4.38 A royal couple seated in a palace, scene from *Saundarānanda*, third century CE, Amarāvatī.

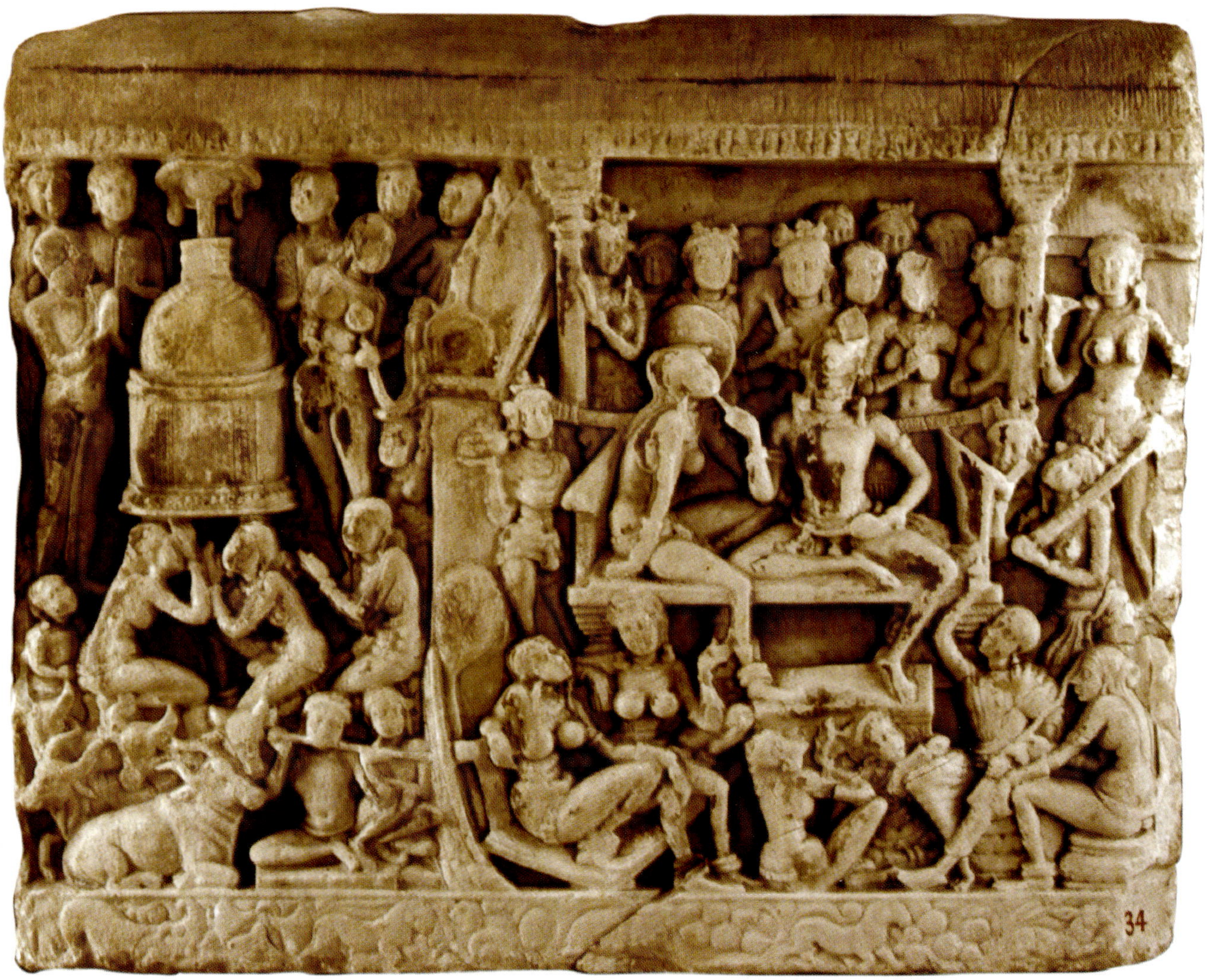

god of love who is also an embodiment of Māra, the Evil one, in the Buddhist religious system, represents the realm of sense-desires and passion.[94] In the right panel, righteousness symbolised by the Buddha triumphs over temptation and as Nanda becomes a monk, on the way to attaining *nirvāṇa*, both men and women with folded hands — presumably, including the ones who had tried to prevent him from achieving this aim — hail the Righteous path.

The same episode is also carved on the railing coping from the Amarāvatī *stūpa* (*Pl.* 4.38).[95] In the main portion of this relief, Nanda and his wife sit regally in a pillared hall on an elaborate throne with three high sides, stepped and cushioned legs and footstool. Behind the throne stand a pair of female attendants with *cāmaras* held over their shoulders. Behind them stand a group of mostly female attendants, with a turbaned male amidst them. To the right of the throne is a *prasādikā*, wearing a shawl and with a round-lidded box in her raised right hand. On the other side are female figures with musical instruments. Other female attendants are ranged around them. Also in the scene is a monk-preacher who is seated to their left on a low stool. With shaven head and covered completely by a pleated gown, he raises his bare right arm and hand in the direction of the seated prince. In his left hand he holds a crooked staff. This is repeated on a frieze of a drum slab.[96]

Undoubtedly in the first two centuries of the Christian era, both in the Upper Doab region at Mathurā and in the Deccan (see *Pl.* 4.40), the love of the royal couple, their idyllic and blissful married life, and the subsequent renunciation of these worldly pleasures by Nanda, were a popular theme for the visual and literary productions of writers, sculptors and designers as well as donors who patronised the production. Perhaps this popularity was linked to the great difficulty faced by Nanda in leaving his beautiful and virtuous wife, his prolonged battle with temptation. This struggle may have struck a chord with the Buddhist brethren who faced similar difficulties in renouncing the material world with its pleasures, as is reflected in the poems of the monks recorded in the *Theragāthā*[97] and also in the tales of many backsliding brothers admonished by Buddha in the *Jātaka kathā*s.[98]

One notices a difference in the treatment of the theme in the northern and southern artistic traditions. At Mathurā there is a greater emphasis on the intimacy and love between the royal couple. This is in consonance with the secularisation and sensualisation of art during the time of the Kuṣāṇas in Mathurā[99] and related centres. At Amarāvatī, on the other hand, it is Nanda's renunciation and the intervention of the monk community that is highlighted, making it closer to the textual version.

The issue here is not only that Nanda, despite temptation, became a monk. The significance of the tale lies in the fact that this act is hailed and set up as an example for the monks and the laity alike. The valorisation of male monks such as Nanda highlights the invisibilisation of all the great nuns who attained spiritual enlightenment against all odds and who are hailed in the *Therīgāthā* and its commentary as *arhant*s of great merit.[100]

The other significant aspect of the Sundarī and Nanda legend is that despite Sundarī's unimpeachable virtue and the couple's contentment within the bonds of marriage, Nanda is constructed as a hero for having left his wife and household where he was very happy.[101] This is illustrated in Aśvaghoṣa's *Saundarānanda*, and it is also emphasised in examples from Amarāvatī, where Nanda is feted for having finally renounced his beautiful wife and the

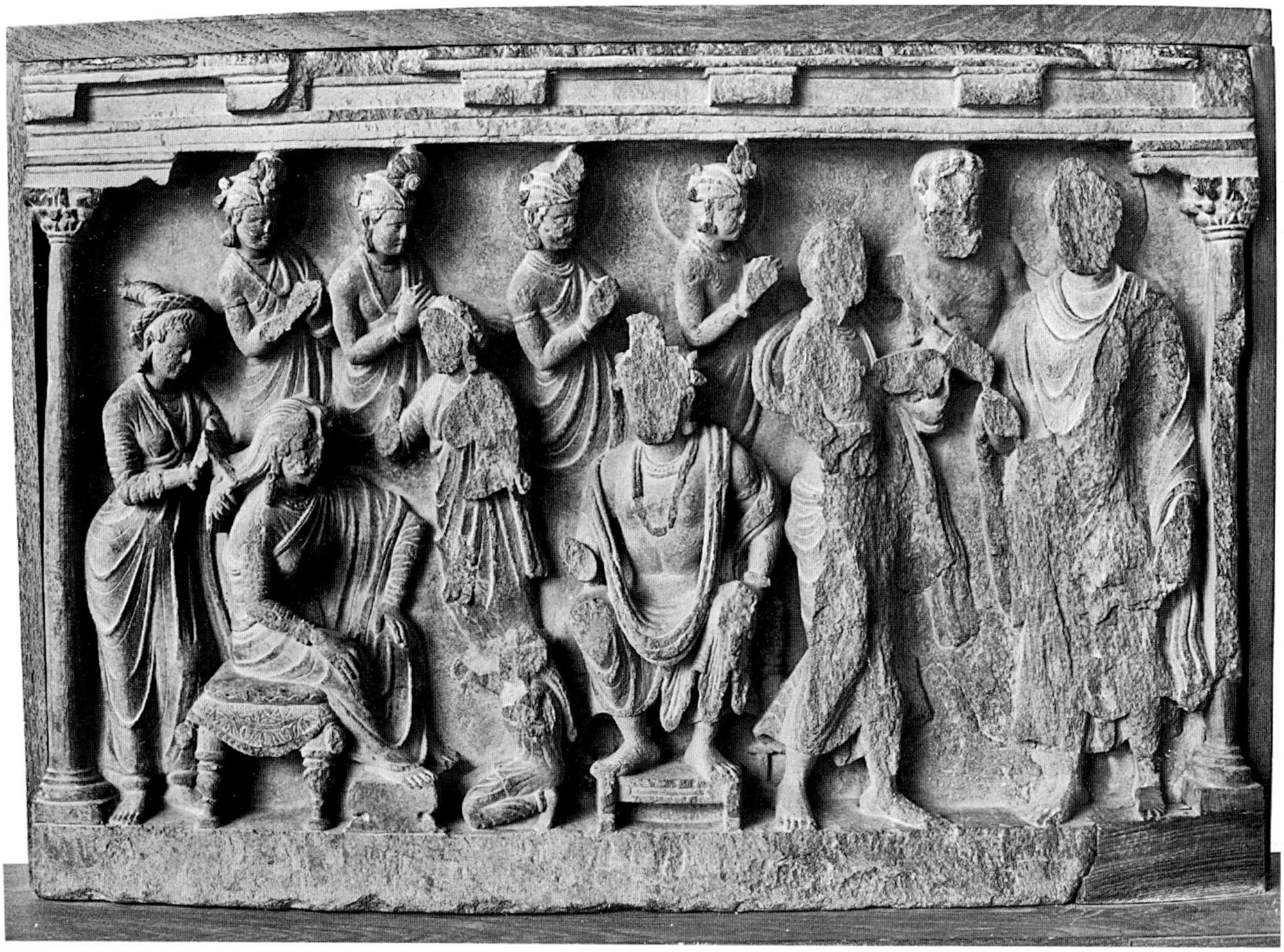

4.39 The conversion of Nanda, third century CE, Gandhāra.

world of sense-pleasures. He is forced against his will to become a monk, and to achieve this end various stratagems are employed, including raising visions of hideous old female bodies to illustrate the impermanent charm of his wife, and of the extraordinary beauty of *Apsaras*es in heaven whose charm casts his wife's loveliness in the shade.

Sundarī herself, in Aśvaghoṣa's version at least, is not only beautiful but also forceful and confident. According to the poet she bore three names, "Sundarī for her majesty and beauty, Māninī for her obstinacy and pride and Bhāminī for her extreme beauty in her love and her spirit."[102] Yet, her husband was encouraged and cajoled into leaving her to join the faith. Thus, social graces, beauty of body and purity of mind and marital fidelity are not sufficient virtue in a woman. In the Sundarī-Nanda episode the ascetic ideals of patriarchal religion are valorised and not feminine virtue.

### 4.6 Wives in Narrative Episodes

As part of a man-woman couple, the woman is viewed as auspicious and good; she is a symbol of prosperity and fecundity. However, as individual and specific wives, women are not perceived to be uniformly and universally benevolent. An investigation into some portrayals of wives found in narrative art carved on the *stūpa*s of Bharhut,

Sāñcī, Mathurā, Amarāvatī and Nāgārjunakoṇḍa is attempted here to illustrate this.

Two observations on narrative art need to be made before one embarks on excavating gendered implications from the stories carved on the *śūci*s, *stambha*s and *uṣṇīṣa*s of the *stūpa*. First, the stories projecting the role of wives are few in comparison to the vast array of narrative and didactic tales expounding Buddhist ideals which range from the impermanence of all life and the virtue of charity to the nobility of the *bodhisattva*s in their previous lives. Secondly, the object of putting up these and other narratives was not to highlight the iniquity of women as a category. These tales are didactic. They are largely hagiographic, meant to instruct the viewer on the greatness of the Buddha in his present and previous lives, and of the Buddhist path, and to tell a story that edifies the audience. Such visual narratives sought to evoke an emotional response in the viewers. However, it is in the same didactic nature of the narrative that one can read the manner in which gender roles were constructed and projected. This was aimed at controlling and restraining women. Ideal wives were set up as an example whose behaviour was to be emulated while the behaviour of faithless wives was to be avoided.

A note regarding the manner in which these visual narratives were constructed may be added here. Vidya Dehejia has recovered myriad forms of narrative in early Buddhist art such as synoptic, continuous narration using mono-scenic, sequential, and conflated modes.[103] All these modes excerpted and represented significant moments from well-known stories, which recalled the whole episode for the viewer. Thus, the viewer is left to narrate the entire story to him/herself and derive a lesson from it; perhaps a monk acting as guide helped him/her narrate/understand this.[104] The visual narratives are contextualised within the socio-ethical world view of the viewer and the monk-sculptors. These relied on prior knowledge of the episode on part of the viewer. We cannot reconstruct the response of the viewer but it must have been conditioned by their class, gender and caste.

A cursory reading of normative texts may suggest that the ideal of *pativratā*, the perfect loyal and obedient wife, was internalised to such an extent as to render the reinforcement of the idea in art superfluous. However, the socialisation of gender roles, especially that of the wife, was partial at best. In the Brāhmanical tradition there is a fear of an inversion of the patriarchal model of a subservient wife which is expressed through the concept of the Kali Age crisis, a symptom of which is that most women lapse into unrestrained behaviour, disregarding the precepts laid down in the *strīdharma*, and flout all moral constraints.

However, it is only in the *Therīgāthā* (a collection of verses composed by *therī*s), senior nuns of the *bhikkhuṇī saṁgha*, the nuns' order, that one can recover women's voices expressing resistance to the idea of wifehood being either the ideal or the goal for womanhood.

In the discourse of the nuns, there is a deep resentment of the treatment and subjugation of women as wives. Amongst the many woes particular to women the following are stressed:

> Woeful is a woman's lot
>
> . . . woeful when sharing with hostile wives
>
> woeful when giving birth in bitter pain . . .[105]

Of the five woes that constitute a woman's destiny — having to leave home at a tender age to live with the husband and his relatives, menstruation, pregnancy, bringing forth, and waiting upon a man[106] — two at least are explicitly consequent on the social order, namely being married at an early age and being subservient to men. Pregnancy, childbirth and menstruation are linked to female physiology. Almost all the ills that a woman suffers in the list given by the *therīs* are the result of the social obligation of marriage; the exception being menstruation, a purely biological phenomenon which may have become more difficult to bear under the pressure of social taboos. Even more apparent is *therī* Isidasi's lament that though she ministered to her husband and his family, including his parents and sisters, he still ill-treated her.[107] Escape from torture and subservience lay in renunciation of the domestic world in order to embrace the relative freedom of the monastic order. It has been observed that for *therīs*, the relationship between renunciation and marriage was more problematical than for *theras*. For the nuns, renunciation was an alternative to marriage that had to be achieved rather than received as an automatic choice.[108]

In such a situation, with patriarchal ideologies stressing obedient and faithful wives as the foundation of all order, the ideologues such as monks and *brāhmaṇa*-priests would have used every opportunity to stress and reinforce the model, be it through text or image. In fact, art may have proven a more effective medium of socialisation of gender roles in view of the fact that it could be viewed by a large number of women (and lower castes) who were otherwise deliberately kept illiterate by the hegemonic Brāhmanical social order. On the other hand, art had a limited audience of pilgrims who could afford to visit the urban centres where most of this art was located. It must have been the upper caste/class women who consumed these messages, as can also be seen in the donative inscriptions that reveal that wives/daughters/ mothers belonging to *gahapati* or merchant families made the maximum amount of donations. In the Jātakas too the errant as well as the good wives are mainly drawn from the ruling and merchant-*gahapati* classes, whose sexuality needed to be controlled; wives of lower castes on the other hand are represented as enjoying pleasure. The anxiety and pressure to preserve the sanctity of caste and the status of class through control over women was more for upper classes/castes than the lower classes.

Control over women's impulse or nature (*strīsvabhāva*) was exerted through three mechanisms — ideology, kinship and state

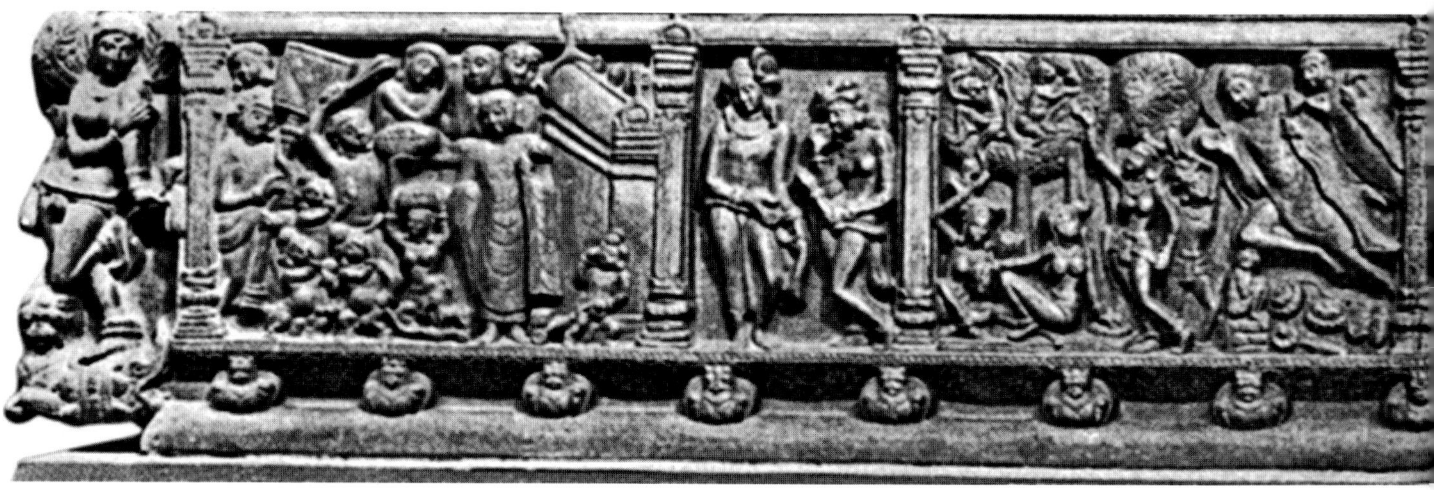

control.[109] Art obviously falls into the category of ideology. Ideology naturally also influenced the structuring of the kin who ensured that a woman was never free, but always under the physical and mental control of her male relatives who enjoyed authority over her body, mobility and resources. Similarly the state, through the agency of the king, had the right to punish errant wives who did not submit to male authority. This could take the shape of physical punishment or the threat of it. In Buddhist literature the primary function of kingship is to punish those who commit crimes against the family (adulterers) and those who commit crimes against property (robbers).[110] Some women escaped the drudgery and humiliation of this stifling control though the path of renunciation in the Buddhist and Jaina religions. (Whether or not this was a solution to their woes is not known. The only text available to us, the *Therīgāthā* seems to assume that "entering the stream" meant the end of all worldly woes.) Those women who did not choose to renounce the world had to conform to the ideal of the good wives, delineated and presented for their edification on sacred monuments, which they were expected to visit in order both to derive religious merit and to reaffirm their faith.

### 4.7 Bad Wives

It is clear from the representations of bad wives in visual narratives that these were imprecatory in nature and intent.

At Bharhut, on a railing pillar of the great *vedikā*, the central medallion depicts the very instructive tale of a brāhmaṇa, his wife and her lover (not illustrated). The side of this medallion carving is cut away, and only the middle portion and the inscription survive. The space is divided into two panels, the upper with a railing and *caitya*-windows, and a lower showing probably the inside of a chamber where the characters of the story are placed.

There are three figures in the composition. A man on the left is seated on a wicker stool with his feet resting on a footstool in front of him, playing a harp resting under his chin, and with a cloth tied around his eyes. In front of him, occupying the centre of the medallion, is the standing figure of a woman arranged almost frontally, holding out her right hand towards the seated male. From behind her right shoulder another arm with a clenched fist bearing down on the male is visible.

4.40 Nanda in Indra's Heaven, third century CE, Ikṣvāku, Nāgārjunakoṇḍa.

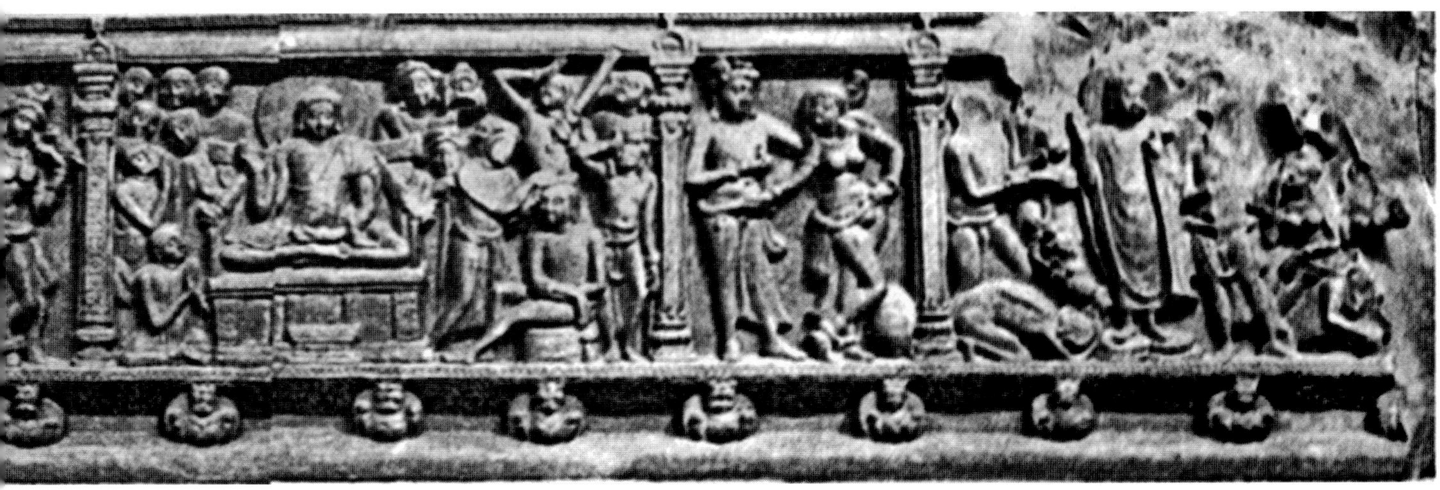

The same female is seen dancing on the right-hand side. Between the two postures of the woman are seen one hand and one leg, indicating perhaps the presence of a second man concealed behind the woman.

The inscription accompanying this scene mentions the Jātaka as *yam brahmano avayesi* (as the *brāhmaṇa* played) *jātakam*. Cunningham[111] was the first to identify this as representing the *Andhabhūta Jātaka*,[112] which has been accepted by Coomaraswamy[113] and Barua.[114] It tells of a brāhmaṇa-chaplain and a *bodhisattva*-king who diced together regularly, the king chanting a verse dwelling on the eternal iniquity of women for luck at every throw, resulting in invariable defeat of the chaplain. In order to reverse his luck in the game and to prove the king wrong, the chaplain decided to bring up a girl in total seclusion. He brought a pregnant woman into his house who delivered a baby girl, who in turn was kept secluded, looked after exclusively by women, and no man but the chaplain was allowed access to this girl. He had complete control over the girl and she was subject to him. He again diced with the king, but this time the king's lucky chant failed, while the brāhmaṇa, using a counter-chant that only his girl was true, won the game, since at least one girl was indeed chaste. The king, realising the truth, sent a clever scoundrel to seduce the girl. With the help of a clever ruse and of the waiting woman of the girl, this man succeeded in entering the otherwise well- guarded house and establishing sexual contact with the girl. He then expressed the wish of giving the brāhmaṇa a punch before he left. So the girl asked the brāhmaṇa to play the lute while she danced, and on the pretext of being shy of dancing in front of the brāhmaṇa, blindfolded him, as seen on the left of the medallion. She then begged permission to strike him, at which her lover smote him on the head, of which act only the arm is visible in the composition. Consequently, in the next dice game the king won, and the brāhmaṇa, suspecting infidelity, asked the girl to undergo a fire ordeal to prove her chastity. The girl tricked the brāhmaṇa by declaring herself ready to perish in the fire if any hand other than that of the brāhmaṇa had touched her. But she also arranged for her lover to try and save her in public. As planned, he came

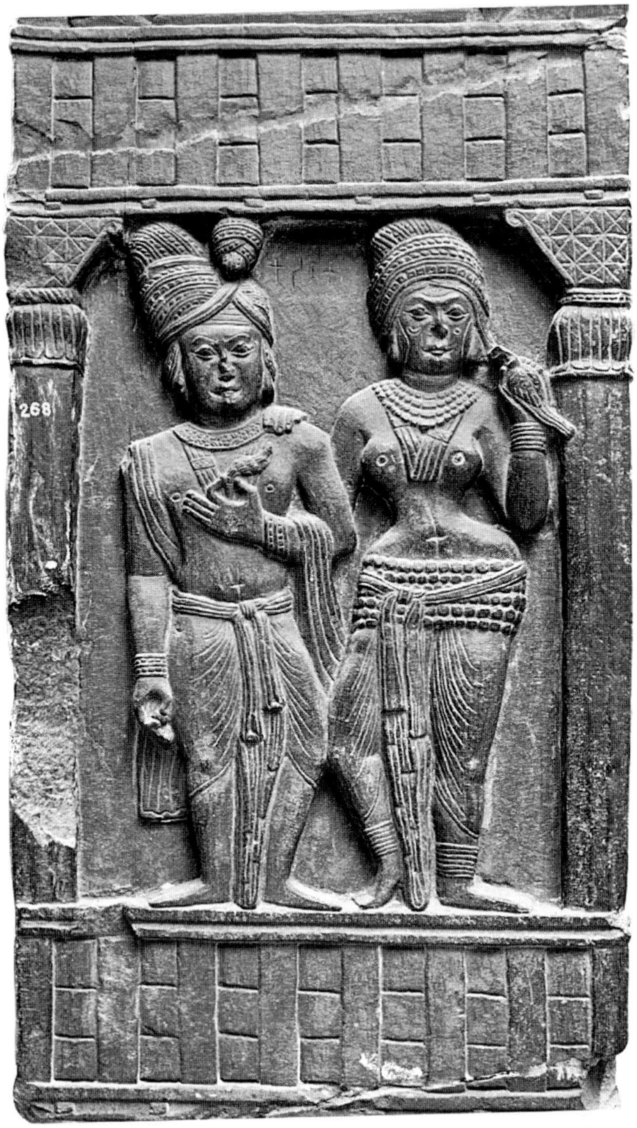

4.41 *Kaṇḍari Jātaka*, panel, south gate, corner pillar, first century BCE, Bharhut. IM 268.

forward and held her hand to stop the brāhmaṇa from forcing her to enter the fire. She then refused to undertake the fire ordeal, saying that she was undone, as another man's hand had touched her. The brāhmaṇa still drove her away with blows. At the end of the *Jātaka kathā* it is clarified that the story is told to illustrate the insatiable nature of women, who despite being closely guarded and swearing oaths of faithfulness, go on seeking mate upon mate.

The depiction here effectively captures the most important events in the story that illustrate the perfidy of the girl, blindfolding the unsuspecting brāhmaṇa, dancing to lure him, and keeping her promise to her lover. Similar episodes that stress the inconstancy of women are seen in the *Rādhā Jātaka* and the *Gahapati Jātaka*.

4.42 *Chaddanta Jātaka*, medallion, railing, first century BCE, Bharhut. IM 291.

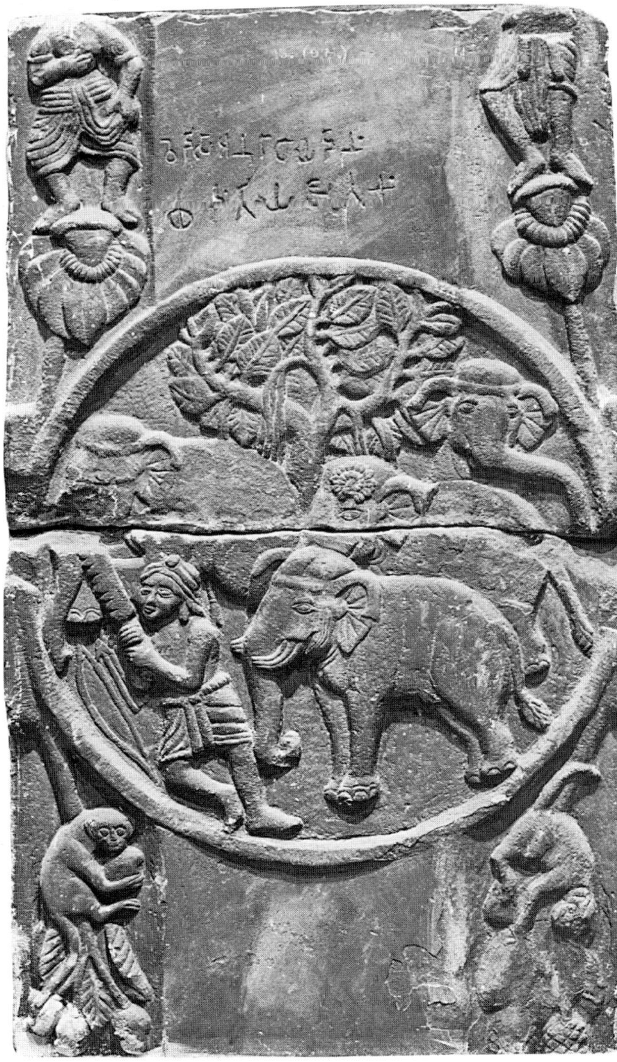

The seated brāhmaṇa-husband is equal in size to the standing female,[115] which effectively manifests the master-subject, husband-wife relationship. The lover is of course male, but nevertheless he is delineated in similar proportions, perhaps because of his complicity in adultery.

The visual is constructed in such a manner that two moments of the narrative are conflated. In front of the blindfolded brāhmaṇa the girl stands, behind whom is her lover in the act of landing a buffet on the chaplain, and on their left is the same girl dancing. The story itself is very instructive in revealing the depth of suspicion, mistrust and condemnation of female sexuality among the Buddhist monk-editors and monk-supervisors, shared perhaps by the laity. The belief that women need to be constantly guarded, and that even then they transgress moral precepts, is clearly delineated here. Manu says that no matter how closely a woman is guarded, she will find ways of committing sexual excesses and that the best-guarded women are the ones who guard themselves.[116] The distinction between the texts of Brāhmanical culture and the more popular Jātaka tales in this respect is only the difference between prohibition and the representation of transgression; in the former, transgression is only implied or viewed as a possibility. In the Jātakas, both in textual and visual versions, it is actually enacted by women. There is a coalescence of the values of high culture and the more popular beliefs about the "essential nature" of women that cannot be guarded.[117]

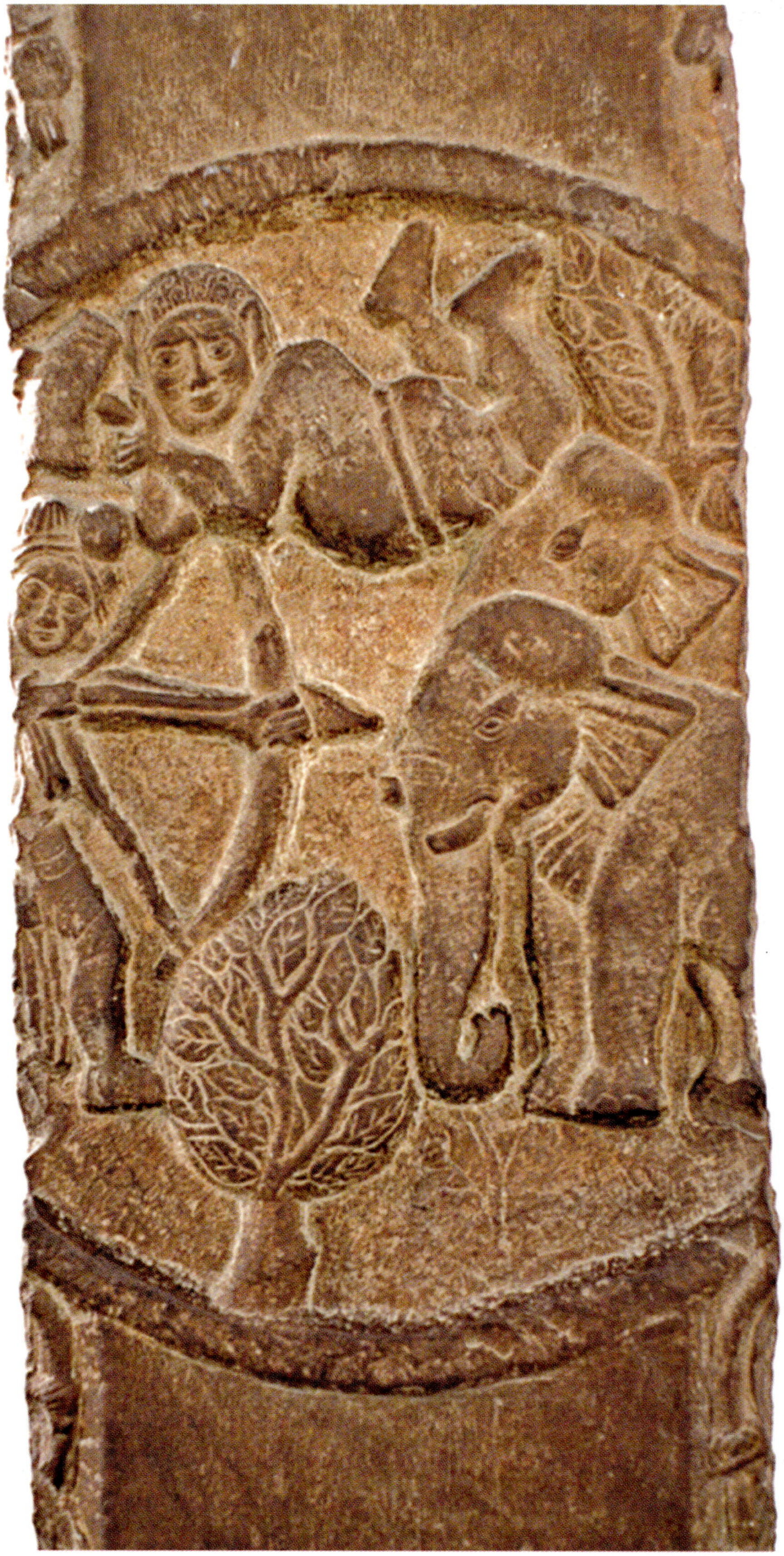

4.43 Probably *Chaddanta Jātaka*, Śuṅga, 205 × 29.5 cm, railing pillar, first century BCE, Bharhut. NM Acc. No. 68.161.

Also carved on a railing pillar at Bharhut, in the middle panel, is the episode of Kandarī and Kinnarā (*Pl.* 4.41), which corresponds to the *Kinnara Jātaka*[118] and is also repeated in the *Kuṇāla Jātaka*.[119] On the face of it the scene looks like an ordinary standing *dampati-mithuna* with the woman placed to the left of the man. Her right leg is slightly bent at the knee, which makes her hip protrude, otherwise she stands upright. She is dressed in a multi-pleated *dhotī* held at the waist with a thick *mekhalā* of multiple pearl-strings. Above the *mekhalā* is a long ribbon-like garment with one end hanging above her leg. She wears an earring only in her left ear according to Barua's reading[120] though this is not immediately discernible. Her right hand is placed on the left shoulder of the man while in her upraised left hand she holds a small bird, which may be a pigeon. The man is shown standing with a slight bend at the knee of his left leg. He is also dressed in a knee-length *dhotī* but without a *mekhalā*. He holds a round object in his right hand, which according to Barua may be an earring, and in his left hand a bird that looks like a tiny hawk in front of his breast. Both the male and female wear *uttarīya*s and a tall headdress adorns the former while the latter sports an upraised coiffure.

The label inscription makes it clear that this relief is supposed to illustrate the story of King Kandariki.[121] This story is one of the many tales told within the *Kuṇāla Jātaka*, a profoundly misogynist collection of instances illustrating the perfidy of women in general and wives in particular. King Kandarī was a handsome young man who was married to a very beautiful lady. The queen, despite having a besotted husband and all the comforts at her command, managed to maintain adulterous relations with a misshapen cripple who lived below the palace by the simple expedient of climbing down a rose apple tree whose branches reached the royal bedchamber. Once Kandarī's glance fell on the cripple and he wondered whether any woman could lust after such a loathsome creature. His chaplain informed him that it is his own queen who has formed a passion for the cripple, and the king confirms the truth of this by spying on the pair. That very night, the cripple being angry with the queen for being late for the rendezvous, strikes her, and in the process her earring slips off and is picked up by the king. To bring the truth out in the open, he ordered the queen to appear in his presence wearing all the jewels he has bestowed on her. After much delay, she appeared in only one earring and the king accuses her of infidelity. The chaplain requested that the queen be spared since she is only a woman and it is in the nature of women to be wicked and vile, as he demonstrated through recounting many similar cases for the edification of the king (and the reader of the tale).

The only indication of this story in the visual discourse is an earring in one ear of the woman, the other being in the hand of the man, as claimed by Barua. However, Dehejia — according to whom the female is wearing both earrings, and the man is not holding an earring in his hand — disputes this.[122] The dove in his hand is difficult to explain; perhaps it is an illusion to the half-bird status of the queen who is called Kinnarā, a class of half-bird, half-human celestial entities. The misogynist nature of the tale cannot be seen in the composition itself and must have lain in the knowledge of the narrative by the spectator or the monk-guide who would explain it to the pilgrim. The text is clear in delineating *strīsvabhāva*, the essentially uncontrolled and uncontrollable sexuality of women.

Pertaining to the animal kingdom[123] one story that is repeatedly illustrated in art is the *Chaddanta Jātaka*.[124] This would suggest that the tale carried a very significant message for the Buddhist community. It has been carved on a medallion at Bharhut (*Pls*. 4.42, 4.43) that shows a male in the foreground sawing off the tusk of an elephant. The right half of the medallion contains four other elephants, one of which has a lotus on its forehead, perhaps representing Mahāsubhaddā. At Sāñcī *stūpa* I, there are three depictions of the story, on the medallion of a railing pillar and a long continuous narrative on the top architrave of the inner face of a *toraṇa* of the northern gateway. The tale is also seen on a terracotta plaque, with elephants in a lotus pond.[125] The latter is a well-planned composition, with four elephants in right and left alternating profiles; to the right, two monkeys climbing a tree function as a decorative motif.

The story is about a previous birth of the Buddha who takes the form of a noble white six-tusked (elephant) *bodhisattva*, living as the leader of a herd of 8000 elephants near the lake in the Himalayas. He has two head queens, Cullasubhaddā and Mahāsubhaddā. Cullasubhaddā in comparison to Mahāsubhaddā feels slighted by her husband, and after praying to the *paceka-buddha*s that she be allowed to avenge this dishonour, lies down and dies. In her next birth, she becomes the chief queen of Videha where she feigns illness, claiming that the only cure is the possession of the tusks of the white six-tusked elephant. A hunter obeys her command but, unable to cut off the mighty ivory, is helped by the magnanimous *bodhisattva* who cuts the tusks himself. At the conclusion of the tale the queen dies of remorse at the death of the noble being.

### 4.8 Good Wives

It may be inferred that only misogynist messages, delineating the evil nature of women, were being carved and displayed for public consumption. This however would be inaccurate as certain illustrations of stories featuring virtuous and chaste wives are also visible within the vast decorative schemes of *stūpa*s and to a lesser extent of *caitya-vihāra*s. Such narratives are no less instructive in bringing out the ideal gendered behaviour prescribed for women as wives. They have to be placed within a gendered discourse that valorised chastity and wifely duty as the highest duty of women, eulogising Sītā, Sāvitrī, Anasuyā, Arundhatī, and others.

Barua has identified one narrative on a railing pillar medallion at Bharhut that is labelled as the *Yavamadhyaka Jātaka*,[126] as illustrating the *Mahā-Umagga Jātaka* (*Pl*. 4.44).[127] It is a crowded composition. At the top of the medallion is a male seated in *pralambapāda* posture on stool/couch. He is shown touching his necklace with his right hand. Seated next to him on his left is another male, and on his right is a standing female figure holding a *cāmara* in one hand. Seen behind the main male figure is a row of male faces. Two men carrying a basket on a pole between them occupy the centre and the left foreground. Another man seems to be carrying a similar basket clasped in front of him. Just below them are three baskets with male faces on them. From one basket a male figure seems to rise. In the right corner of the medallion one can see two female figures, of whom one is an imposing figure dressed in a royal or affluent manner with an elaborate headdress; her left arm seems to be on the shoulder of the other female figure.

The *Mahā-Umagga Jātaka* is a long story consisting of many episodes eulogising the Buddha's omniscience, in the present and also in

4.44 *Yāvamajjhaka Jātaka*, medallion, railing pillar, first century BCE, Bharhut. IM 208. (facing page)

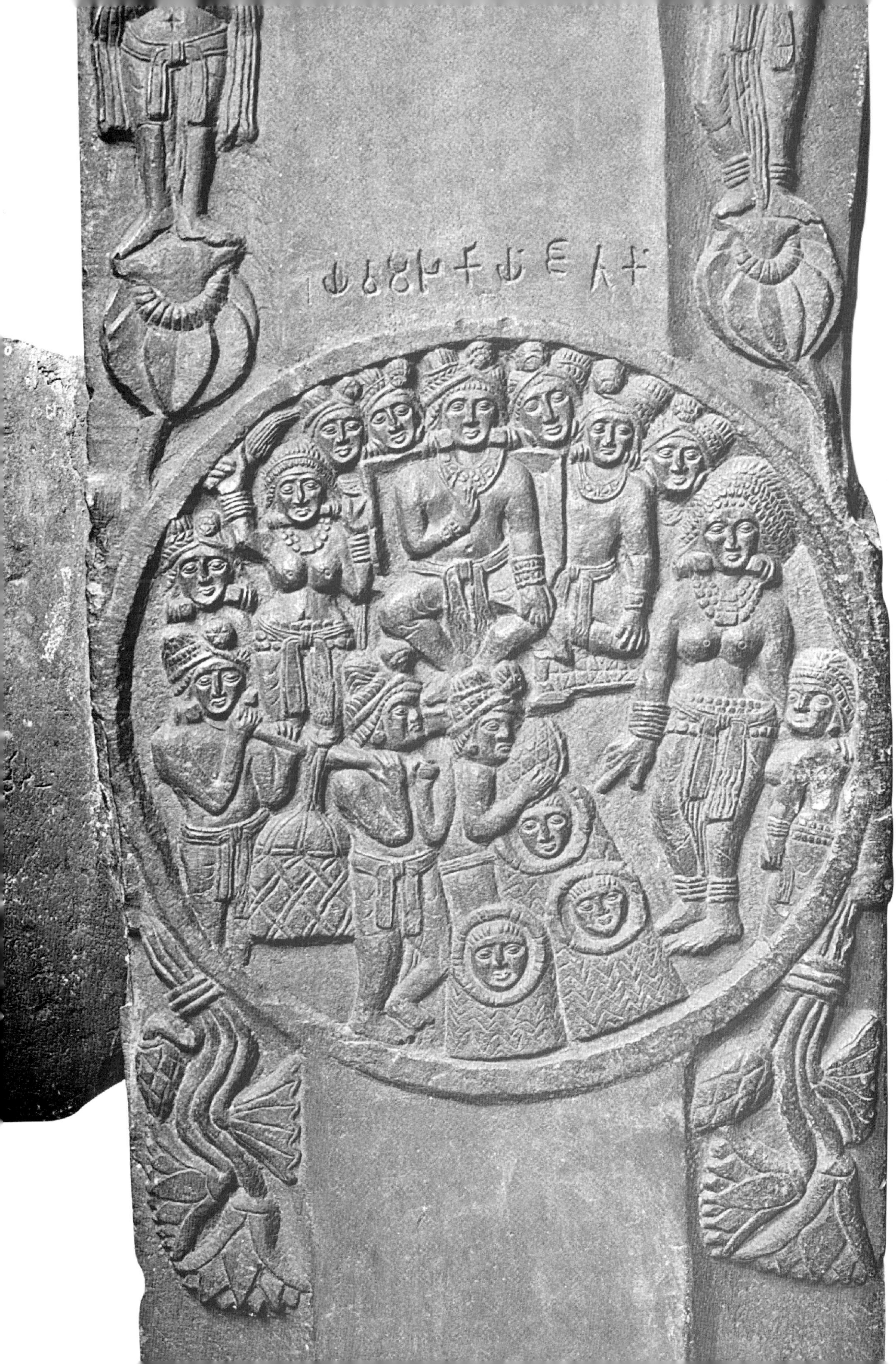

the past, as Bodhisattva Mahoṣadha. In one of the episodes a village on the outskirts of Mithilā called Yavamadhyaka, or Yavamajjhaka as mentioned in the inscription, is the location where an incident involving cattle stealing occurs. This incident is however not the one that is illustrated in the medallion. The episode here is in all probability the one extolling the intelligence and fealty of Amarā, the wife of Bodhisattva Mahoṣadha. Once led by Senaka, four courtiers of the king of Videha, who were jealous of Mahoṣadha's and Amarā's reputation of honesty and intelligence, decide to discredit them. Senaka steals and secretes the king's crest, his golden necklace, his robe and his golden slippers in Amarā's house. Amarā, cognisant of the plot, keeps records of each item and the manner in which it was put in her house. The rogue courtiers inform the king of the theft of his property and accuse Mahoṣadha. Mahoṣadha, apprised of the plot, flees from his home and hides in the countryside. On hearing this, each of the courtiers, unknown to the other, offers to take Mahoṣadha's place in Amarā's heart. She sends for each one separately and has their heads shaved and throws them into jakes or baskets. She then has them wrapped up in rolls of wicker, which are carried into the king's presence, followed by the lady herself with the king's possessions. In the court she discloses the whole story to him and departs. He is then advised by a *yakṣī* who lives in his *chatra* (parasol).

At Bharhut it is the last moment of denouement that is illustrated with the king seated with various courtiers. The lady Amarā dominates the right side of the composition with her regal and confident bearing, while the courtiers are in a discomfited position. Three of them stick out their round, shaved heads from the wicker baskets, while one of them is shown being carried in ignominously. The fifth basket clasped in front of the male figure may in fact represent a moment before the opening of the basket.

The heroine of this depiction is undoubtedly the good and useful wife who saves her husband's honour while keeping her virtue intact. The seated king is appropriately placed at the top of the composition where he plays the role of adjudicator while the discomfited villains are trussed up and play no active part in the scene. A woman's valour and intelligence are celebrated here at Bharhut, when they are deployed within the socially sanctioned role of a wife and for the larger good of her husband and his family.

Another virtuous wife is seen illustrated at Bharhut on a coping stone of the great *vedikā*,[128] which may represent either the *Sambulā Jātaka* or the *Vessantara Jātaka*. It seems to be part of a continuous narrative, set between the loops of a long vine. It shows a tree on the left, probably the rose apple tree of the mountain *narada* (as given in the inscription, *vaduko kathā dohati. jabu noddode pavate*) from which emerge two human hands, the right holding a water jug with a spout and a handle, and the other a bowl which may hold food. In the centre is a man seated on an upturned vessel or a round rock with his arm stretched out as if to receive the water bowl. On the far right is a woman turned towards the right with a *kamaṇḍalu*-like vessel in her hand.

If we were to identify this relief with the Sambulā story, the resemblance between text and depiction would lie in the fruit and water that the lady used to collect and draw for her husband. This visual narrative however could also illustrate the activities of Mādrī, the wife of Vessantara, who looked after her husband and children in the forest related in a Jātaka of the same name.

In the *Sambulā Jātaka* it is said that Sambulā is the devoted and beautiful wife of prince

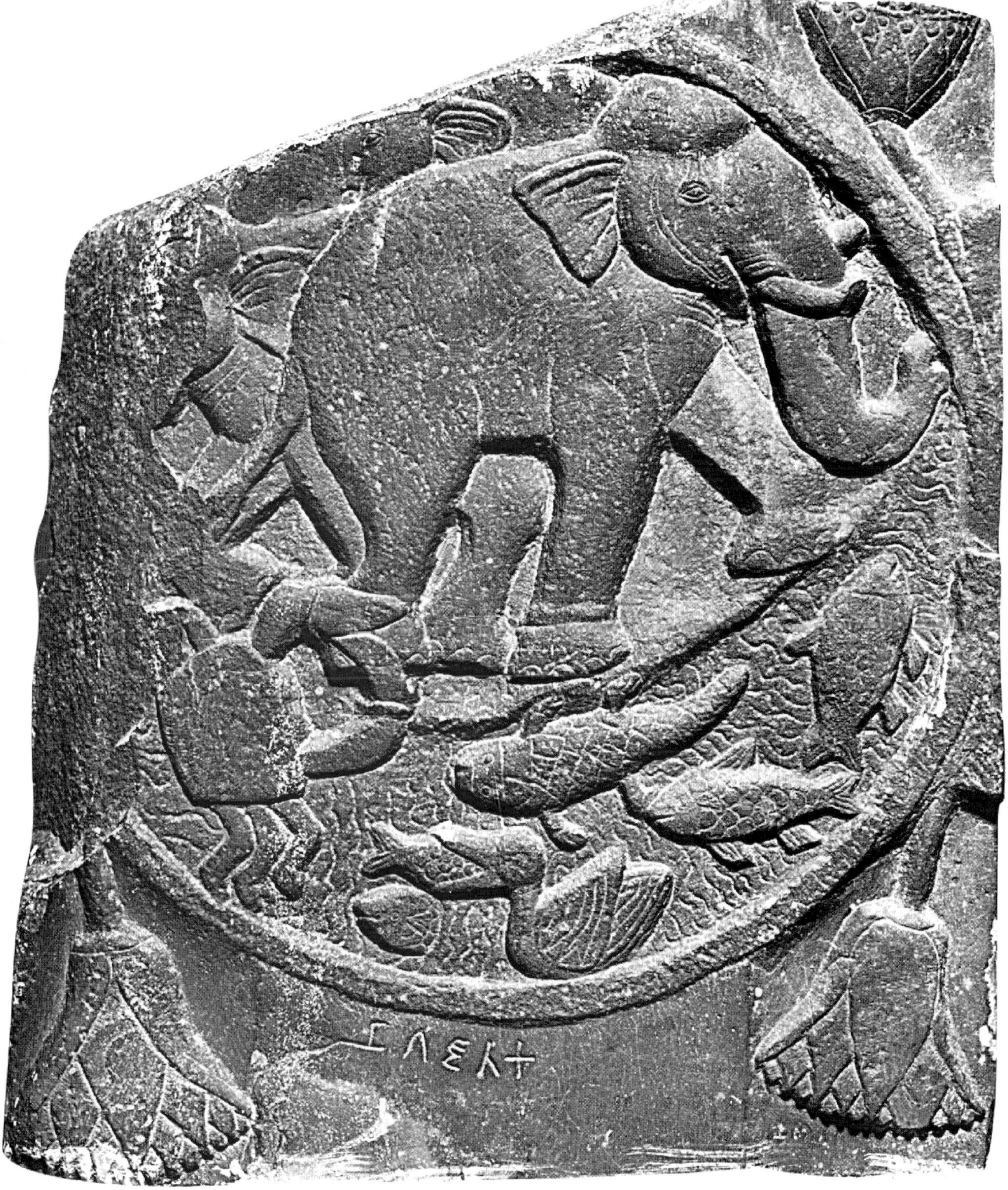

4.45 *Kakkaṭa Jātaka*, medallion, railing pillar, first century BCE, Bharhut.

Sotthisena of Videha. The prince, having been afflicted by leprosy, leaves for the forest. Sambulā insists on accompanying him to care for him in his time of need. In the forest, he builds a hut of leaves and Sambulā devotes herself to his welfare. She prepares a bath for him, gathers fruits of which he has his pick while she eats the leftovers, and she bathes him and dresses his sores. One day while gathering fruit she is accosted by the evil *yakṣa* of a lake who threatens to eat her if she refuses to be his wife. She is saved by the *vajra*-wielding Sakka (Śakra), but the husband refuses to believe that she had not played him false. To prove her virtue, she vows that she will cure him through an Act of Truth. In performing this, she pours water on his head, saying "May Truth for aye my shelter be, As I love no man more than thee, and by this Act of Truth, I pray, May thy disease be healed today." By the power of his wife's virtue Sotthisena is cured and both return to Benares where his father abdicates in Sotthisena's favour. He sets up Sambulā as the chief queen and he himself departs for the mountains. Sotthisena however ignores Sambulā who pines for his attention. The ascetic-father on his return sees Sambulā's condition and counsels his son that virtuous and loving wives are difficult to find and given this paucity he should value his wife, and thus Sambulā is reinstated in the affections of her husband and in the status enjoyed by chief queen.

A similar tale is indicated by the label inscription *Dusito giri dadāti na*.[129] This points to the presence of a relief illustrating the *Suchchapa Jātaka*[130] though the visual narrative is now missing. The Jātaka was narrated to highlight the fruits of a woman's virtue and the importance of Truth. Once, afraid of the machinations of his son the crown prince, King Brahmadatta of Benares banishes him to the forest for the span of the king's lifetime. The prince's chief wife accompanies him to the forest where she serves him devotedly. After his father's death, the royal couple start their journey back, and on the way the wife asks whether, if a mountain were turned to gold, her husband would give her some of it. The prince rudely and openly refuses to consider parting with even a small portion of the hypothetical mountain. Back in Benares, he installs her as the chief queen but otherwise ignores her existence. His minister, who is a *bodhisattva*, decides to rectify this oversight on the part of the king by pointing out the rare virtue of a woman/queen who praises her husband even when he maligns her. The king, realising the truth of this, bestows all power and prestige on her.

Both the *Sambulā Jātaka* and *Suchchapa Jātaka* point towards an internalisation of the norm of obedient and faithful wifehood, *pativratā-dharma*, by women. This is used as the ultimate test of the virtue that increases their value in both society and polity; they are installed as chief queens with all powers. However, the tolerance exhibited by women as wives is not absolute; there are signs of protest at neglect through two mechanisms — pining away into a decline, and complaining to influential relatives/advisers of the male companion. These aspects can be read in the textual version of the Jātakas, but in the reliefs they are not represented.

On a Bharhut railing pillar there is panel showing a couple in which the woman is resisting the advances of the man who is pulling her towards him. She looks towards him. The absence of prominent pendant earrings and large ear-openings distinguishes the male figure as a human being from the *kinnara* and other demi-gods, because, according to Barua, the latter are always shown wearing these ornaments. A similar panel has been found carved on a half-medallion on a Bodh-Gayā *stūpa* railing pillar. If the descriptions are correct, the scene illustrates the *Candā Kinnara Jātaka,*[131] which narrates how an amorous king miserably failed to force into his embrace a *kinnarī* whose husband he had shamelessly wounded. Once a Kinnara and his wife Candā (Candrā) had come down from their abode in the moon-mountain (*candā pabbata*) to disport in the green pastures below. A king who had given up his kingdom and donned the robes of an ascetic arrived at this spot. The king chanced upon the couple, attracted by the music of the flute being played by the Kinnara. Struck by Candā's beauty, he shoots her mate with an arrow and reveals himself to Candā. Candā, frightened yet faithful, flees lamenting her loss, and the king offers to marry her to replace the Kinnara. But Candā refuses and the king departs. She, perceiving that there is still life in her mate, provokes Śakra to restore the Kinnara to life. The couple then depart for Moon Mountain forever.

According to the text, the *Canda Kinnara Jātaka* was recounted by the Buddha to highlight the virtues and steadfastness of Rāhula's mother, Siddhārtha's wife, who behaved in a pious and loyal manner after Siddhārtha gave up the world to seek enlightenment. It identifies Chandā as Rāhula's mother and the Kinnara as the Buddha in a previous birth.

Here again, a wife's faithfulness saves the life of her mate and forces even Śakra to grant her wish in this regard. In the visual, however, a preliminary observation shows a man pulling a woman towards him, using force, which is an unusual feature. This is quite unlike the couples seen in *mithuna* or *dampati* motifs, which are depicted disporting themselves harmoniously.

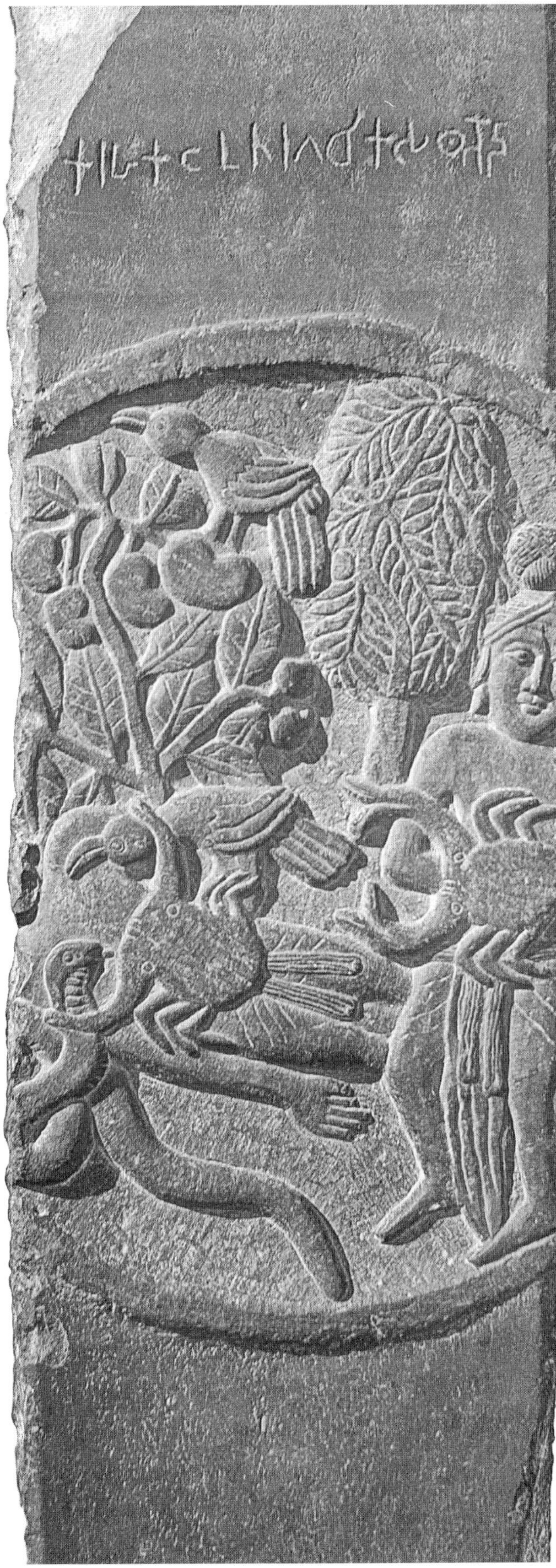

4.46 *Suvarṇa Kakkaṭa Jātaka*, 178 × 27× 32.5 cm, stone, first century BCE, Bharhut. NM Acc. No. 68. 162

Faithfulness was not unknown in the animal kingdom, and in the *Kakkata Jātaka*[132] the story of a *bodhisattva*-elephant is told whom his mate saves from a crab who has jumped on to his back. She attracts the crab with her honeyed voice and he frees the elephant that then steps on the crab and tramples him to death. This story was told by the Buddha when a faithful wife had begged for the life of her merchant husband from a robber chief who wanted to kill him. At Bharhut this tale is illustrated on a railing medallion (*Pls.* 4.45, 4.46), and the scene is titled *Nāga Jātaka*, the *Elephant Jātaka*.[133] A lake is carved on the lower part of the medallion, with a few big fish and a crane or swan swimming in water, and a huge crab emerging from it. The larger elephant has his right hind leg caught in the claw of the crab. On the left side of this elephant is a smaller one, evidently an elephant mare, seen reaching as far as the lower edge of a rock, as Barua claims, though this is difficult to make out.

The preceding text-image study highlights the juxtaposition of two models of wifehood — good wives and bad wives. The former is an exposition of the ideal wife who, through following her *pativratā strīdharma*, overcomes her inherent nature, *strīsvabhāva*. This involves the taming of female sexuality through inculcating virtues of self-sacrifice, fidelity and chastity. The latter, on the other hand, is the unrestrained and immoral behaviour of wives who let their inherent evil nature take over, which leads to infidelity and promiscuity. In the case of Sundarī, however, even her chastity and extreme love for her husband are construed as epitomising temptation and an obstacle in the path of true faith.

On the other hand, on the same edifices are found *mithuna*s portrayed as harmonious and often as amorous and loving couples. In fact, in examples (though not carved on monuments) from the early period, human sexuality is divinised and celebrated through the worship of the goddess and her partner. In the terracotta tradition this tendency is even stronger, with explicitly coital couples being depicted. These are closer to the religious tradition that created and venerated images of Kāmadeva, the god of love, and of fecund mother goddesses — a tradition that evidently propagated the idea that people might have seen pleasure as sustaining, or as a strategy for survival, a view that the *bhikkhu*s perceived as the path of moral degeneration. The discourses of pleasure and reproduction were no doubt fragmented. To the monk-supervisors of the monuments, the *mithuna* may have become a simple motif suggesting fertility and auspiciousness; this is implied in the donation of *mithuna* sculptures by a monk at Kārle. However, we have to bear in mind that these narratives and amorous couples may have been constructed and consumed by the contemporary audience in ways quite different to the intentions of the *bhikkhu*s.

## Notes and References

1. *MWSE*, p. 816.
2. *MWSE*, p. 854.
3. P.K. Agrawala, *Mithuna: The Male-Female Symbol in Indian Art and Thought*, Varanasi: Prithvi Prakashan, 1983 p. 24.
4. A.A. Macdonell, *Vedic Index of Names and Subjects*, vol. 1, Varanasi: Motilal Banarsidass, 1958, p. 340. *St. Petersburg Dictionary* asserts that *dampati* denotes "the master of the house" but Macdonell disagrees and says that it in the dual to designate the "master and mistress" of the house.
5. *MWSE*, p. 469: *dam* means a house; *dampati* means the lord of the house, or as *dvandva* and *dam* in the sense of a wife, therefore "the two masters" — husband and wife.
6. *Śat. Br.*, I.1.1.20, II.5.2.17, IV.4.2.16. As is stated in the *Brāhmaṇa* texts while explaining the sacrificial rituals: the man must sleep on the right side of the female. Cf. P.K. Agrawala, op. cit., p. 23.
7. Plaque, buff sandstone, Kauśāmbī, *c.* third century BCE, Size: .036 x .034m, Allahabad Museum No. Mor 6.
8. Pramod Chandra, *Stone Sculptures in the Allahabad Museum*, vol. I, AIIS, Poona, 1970, p. 37, no. 7, Pl. III.
9. P.K. Agrawala, op. cit., Pl. 95.
10. Y.D. Sharma, "Past Patterns as unfolded in Excavations at Rupar", in *Lalit Kala*, no. 1, 1955-56, Pl. XLVI, No. 13.
11. Pramod Chandra, "The Cult of Sri Lakshmi and Four Carved Discs in Bharat Kala Bhavan", in *Chhavi: Golden Jubilee Volume*, Bharat Kala Bhawan, Benares, pp. 139-48.
12. P.K. Agrawala, op. cit., p.4.
13. *Indian Archaeology — A Review*, 1962-63, pl. XII, pp. 5-6.
14. Moti Chandra, "Recent Sculpture in the Prince of Wales Museum," *BPWM*, no. IX, 1964–66, p 25.
15. *Manusmṛti*, IX.13, 80.
16. See infra, Chapter 5, section on Gaṇikas.
17. In the *Mahābhārata pañcacūḍa* was an *apsarā*, *Mbh*, Śānti-Parva, CCCXXIII.
18. Stella Kramrisch, "Indian Terracottas", in *JISOA*, 7, 1939, pp. 74-75.
19. V.S. Agrawala, "Ancient Terracottas from Ahichchhatra", in *Ancient India*, no. 4, 1947-48, pl. XXXVI, 16; XXXII, 12, 14.
20. Amy G. Poster, *From the Indian Earth: 4,000 Years of Terracotta Art*, The Brooklyn Museum, New York, 1986, p. 99, fig. 29; Mithuna couple, Mathura ? Śuṅga, *c.* 200-50 BCE. Moulded terracotta plaque, 11.0 × 7.0 cm G.K. Kanoria Collection; also p. 104, fig. 35 which shows an enshrined goddess and attendant, Chandraketugarh, first century mould terracotta plaque. T.M.H 1985.
21. Devangana Desai, *Erotic Sculptures of India*, New Delhi: Tata McGraw Hill Publishers Pvt. Ltd., 1975, p. 14.
22. H.V. Trivedi, *JMPIP*, vol. XI, p. 25; D. Desai, op. cit., p. 13.
23. Moti Chandra, "Studies in the Cult of the Mother Goddess in Ancient India", *BPWM.*, no. XII, p. 25, fig. 17; D. Desai, op. cit., p. 14.
24. Moti Chandra, op. cit., p. 25, fig. 17.
25. *Mithuna* panel with goddess; east face of a corner pillar in the southern entrance of the railing of *stūpa* II at Sāñcī, second-first century BCE.
26. For a discussion on this representational type see Chapter 2.
27. Sāñcī, *stūpa* II, North face of a corner pillar in southern entrance of the railing, second-first century BCE.
28. Sāñcī, *stūpa* II, East face of a corner pillar in western entrance of the railing, second -first century BCE.
29. *Mithuna*, devotee couples at a sacred symbol. Relief on a corner pillar on the eastern entrance of the railing of *stūpa* II at Sāñcī, Madhya Pradesh, second century BCE.
30. See Chapter 3: Section on Hāritī.
31. Terracotta plaque, Ahicchatra, size: 12.9 × 8.1 cm, SML No 56.492, Lucknow; Terracotta, SML No. 51.82.
32. Bharhut, Railing Pillar, Great Railing, Indian Museum, Kolkata.

33. A. Foucher, "Sur l'interpretation de quatre bas relief de Bharhut", in *Reveu des Arts Asiatiques*, no. 1, 1939-42, pp. 1-9.

34. *Stūpa* I, Sāñcī, Front face of northern pillar of Western Toraṇa, first century BCE; also West face of western pillar of South Gate.

35. Aruna Tripathi, *The Buddhist Art of Kauśāmbī (From 300 BCE to CE 550)*, New Delhi: D.K. Printworld Pvt. Ltd., 2003. pp. 50-51, *fig*. 10-b. Part of a fragment of a four sided pillar, buff sandstone, ht. 90 cm, Manhai-Kauśāmbī, Śuṅga, Kausambi Museum, Allahabad University.

36. Late Kuṣāṇa, GMM No. 17.1.43.

37. M.N. Deshpande, "The Rock Cut Caves of Pitalkhora in The Deccan", *Ancient India*, no. 15, 1959, pp. 66-93.

38. J. Burgess, *Buddhist Cave Temples and Their Inscriptions*, Varanasi: Indological Book House, 1964 (rpt.), Inscriptions No. 13 and 14, p. 91.

39. Ibid., p. 23.

40. A similar pose is found in earlier terracotta tradition and also includes the male touching the breast of the female. *Dampati-mithuna*, Jhusi, Allahabad district, first century CE. Mould made terracotta, .100 × .070m, Allahabad Museum No. Jh 4568.

41. For example Nachna, Pārvatī temple, Gupta period; M.A. Dhaky, M.W. Miester and Krishna Deva, eds., *Encyclopaedia of Indian Temple Architecture: Foundations of North Indian Style*, vol. II, pt. 1, AIIS & OUP, 1988, Plate, No. 57.

42. For an alternate reading of this posture see Chapter 5, section on Gaṇikas.

43. Terracotta plaque found from Kosam belonging to second century BCE, now in the National Museum.

44. This seems to have been a popular theme, for another example see *mithuna* under an *aśoka* tree, Patna City, second century BCE, Patna Museum No. Arch. 8178: Patna Museum Catalogue, p. 8, no. 6, Pl. VI.

45. Amy G. Poster, op. cit., p. 160, fig. 98. Seated couple, Ahicchatra? Gupta period, fifth century CE terracotta relief tile, 30.7 × 13.0 cm, collection of Robert H. Ellsworth.

46. *Mithuna*; buff sandstone, ht. 51 cm, with traces of paint, from Patna city, first BCE, Patna Museum No. Arch. 8178. The style suggests a transitional phase between Bharhut-Gayā and Mathurā dominated style.

47. *Mithuna*, panel on pillar of sandstone railing from Bodh-Gayā, Bihar, *c*. first century BCE.

48. *Mithuna-dampati*; Grey soapstone, ht. 60 cm, Bodh-Gayā, Patna Museum No. Arch. 1524.

49. *Mithuna*, Kosam, the first century CE, Allahabad: Allahabad University Museum.

50. For a detailed discussion and description see infra, Chapter 6, section on *śālabhañjikā*s.

51. Amy G. Poster, op. cit., p. 105, fig. 36, Dancer and Musician, Eastern India, first century BCE, red mottled terracotta plaque with applied ornaments, 123.7 × 9.2 cm, collection of Samuel Eilenberg. The couples depicted in Śuṅga period plaques do not always signify a religious or ritual function. Terracottas often show scenes of a favourite pastime of the cultured population, this plaque represents a secularised version of a ritual scene. This is a courtly and erotic scene.

52. S.S. Biswas, *Terracotta Art of Bengal*, New Delhi: Agam Kala Prakshan, 1981, pl, xlix, d and e.

53. *Mithuna*, round plaque from Bhītā, Indian Museum Calcutta, No. AAA/1650-74; Dhavalikar, *Masterpices of Indian Teracottas*, Bombay: D.B. Taraporevala, 1977, p. 29, Pl. 35.

54. D. Desai, op. cit., p. 15.

55. Paribogha-darṣiṇī, *Kuṣāṇa Sculptures from Sanghol*, no. 1, p. 61.

56. Ibid., no. 2, p. 62, detail on p. 63.

57. Ibid., no. 4, p. 64. Mother and Child.

58. Ibid., no. 19 A, p. 82. A Languorous Lady.

59. Ibid., no. 19 B, p. 83. *Śṛṅgāra-racaṇa*.

60. Ibid., no. 20, p. 85, detail on p. 84. *Yakṣī* holding lotus flowers.

61. Ibid., no. 21B, p. 86, detail on p. 87. Lady playing harmonica.

62. *Jīvājīvābhigama Sūtra*, 3.130-131.

63. Ibid., 3.130-131, pp. 366-70.

64. *Śatapatha Brāhmaṇa*, X.5, 2, 8.

65. And even the divine world was peopled by gods and goddesses as couples who through their union gave birth to other gods, *asura*s, humans, etc. Exception to the legitimate pairing of gods and goddesses were *gandharva* and *apsaras* pairing that is actually defined to be an exemplar of the *mithuna* ideology; "from Prajāpati, when dismembered, couples went forth in the form of *gandharva*s and *Apsaras*es." *Śat. Br.*, IX.4.1.2, though they conjointly are lauded as presiding over the marital life in all its delights and joy without being bound by ties of marriage. *Atharvaveda* XIV.2.9; XIV2.34-5.

66. P.K. Agrawala, op. cit., pp. 15-16.

67. On the western gateway, north pillar front face of *stūpa* 1, Sāñcī.

68. *Śatapatha Brāhmaṇa*, I.2.5.15.

69. *Tāṇḍya Brāhmaṇa*, XIV.5.4. "At the beginning of the sacrifice he brings about a pairing: for the sake of obtaining progeny"; *Taittirīya Saṁhitā*, II.6.1.4. "he who knows the *mithuna* of the fore-sacrifice is propagated with offspring, with cattle and with *mithunas*."; *Taittirīya Saṁhitā*, V. 6.2.3, "The pots and pans make pairs, for the propagation of pairing; with offspring, with cattle, with *mithuna*s is he propagated for whom these are put down and he who knows them thus."

70. *Maitrāyaṇī Saṁhitā*, I.8.3; I.9.8.; I.10.7; II.3.7; II.5.5. Also *Taittirīya Saṁhitā*, I.6.4.4, "May I be propagated by a *mithuna*."

71. *Mbh.*, Śānti-Parva, CCCVI.

72. Ibid., CCCVIII.

73. See infra Chapter 6, Section on *śālabhañjikā*s.

74 Infra, for Māra as Kāma and as such an epitome of Evil, see chapter 7 ; section on Māra and his daughters.

75. P.K. Agrawala, op. cit., p. 24.

76. *Bṛhadāraṇyaka Upaniṣad*, 1.4.1; 1.4.3; tr. Hume, *The Thirteen Principal Upanishads*, Oxford, 1931, p. 81.

77. *Ṛgveda*, VIII. 31.5-9.

78. *MBh.*, 1.74.40-41.Cf. P.K. Agrawala, op. cit., p.25. *Puruṣārtha* concept is there by the *Sūtra* and Epic literature. *Hiraṇyakeṣu Gṛhyasūtra*, II.19.6; Patañjali on Pāṇini's *Aṣṭādhyāyī*, II.2.34. Also see *AS*. I.7. *Kāmasūtra*, I.2.1-4.

79. *Śat. Br.*, V. 2.1.10 (Eggeling. Oxford 1894).

80. *Manu*, VIII.353 says that *varṇa-saṁkara* or mixture of castes can lead to general destruction.

81. M.K. Dhavalikar, op. cit., pp. 26-27.

82. Ibid., p. 27.

83. Devangana Desai, op. cit., p. 26.

84. O.C. Gangoly, "The Mithuna in Indian Art," in *Rupam*, no. 22-23, Apr.-July, 1925, pp. 54-61, on p. 55 does not consider the *mithuna* to be a sexual couple.

85. *Jīvājīvābhigama Sūtra*, pp. 302-6.

86. For the manner in which patriarchy creates and manipulates symbols to organise and dominate see Gerda Lerner, *The Creation of Patriarchy*, USA: Oxford University Press, 1987, pp. 199-211.

87. *Therīgāthā*, PTS (1964), xli, p. 55.

88. *Saundarānanda*, II.12-13.

89. SML J. 533, red sandstone. Ht: 143.5 × 29 cm, first century CE, Kaṅkālī Ṭīlā, Mathurā. This is a Jaina stele and the depiction of a Buddhist legend here displays its symbolic significance in the post Mauryan period.

90. Railing Pillar, GMM No. 186, Ht. 4'9". Red sanstone, second century CE; V.S. Agrawala, *Catalogue of the Mathura Museum: Architectural Pieces*, Varanasi: Prithvi Prakashan, 1963, pp. 32-33.

91 Ibid., p. 32.

92. Sankisa, Etah district, red sandstone, second century CE, ht: 35.5 × 18.5 cm. Indian Museum Acc. No. A 24250/Sa. 2A.S.B/ 5173. Architectural piece with tenons at the bottom and top to secure it.

93. Robert Knox, *Amaravati Buddhist Sculpture from the Great Stupa*, London: British Museum 1992 p. 60, fig. 12 (inner face).

94. Infra, Chapter 7, section on Māra and his daughters.

95 Robert Knox, op. cit., pp. 99-100, fig. 40.

96. Ibid., p. 139, fig 72, also probably, pp. 150, 152 fig. 77,78.

97. *Theragāthā* (PTS), pp. 32- 48.

98. Jātaka, Cowell, i. 42, 44, 128, 133, 137; ii. 13,23, 79, 81, 89, 81 illustrate the difficulty for the benefit of weak willed monks.

99. Devangana Desai, op. cit., p. 19.

100. For the invisiblisation of nuns Supra, Chapter 2, section on Nuns.

101. *Saundarānanda*, IV.5-9, says, "it seemed that produced by the Creator to surpass mortals without attaining the appearance of gods; for she was like a divinity wandering in the garden of Nandana, while Nanda was the cause of joy to his family." IV. 6 it goes on to say that "Had Nanda not gained Sundarī — the two would have failed to reach the perfection of beauty. . . ."

102. Ibid., IV.3.

103. Vidya Dehejia, *Discourse in Early Buddhist Art: Visual Narratives of India*, New Delhi: Munshiram Manoharlal, 1997, pp. 1-35.

104. Ibid., p. 33 has remarked on the role of monk guides mentioned in *Mūlasarvāstivādin Vinaya*.

105. *Therīgāthā*, PTS, 1964, vv. 214-217.

106. *Saṁyutta Nikāya*, XXXVII, iii, i.3.

107. *Therīgāthā*, PTS, 1964, XV.LXXII.

108. Kumkum Roy, "Of Theras and Therīs: Visions of Liberation in the Early Buddhist Tradition", in Vijaya Ramaswamy, ed., *Re-searching Women*, New Delhi: Manohar, 2003, p. 85.

109. Supra. See chapter 1: Gender and Art, Also E.J. Leslie, "Strisvabhava: The Inherent Nature of Women", in N.J. Allen et al., eds., *Oxford University Papers on India*, Oxford: Oxford University Press, 1986; Uma Chakravarti, "Preliminary Observations on Impulse Control of Women in Early India: Ideology, Kinship and State as Mechanisms of Control," in *Women in Ancient India*, vol. 2, ed. K.D. Bajpai, Varanasi, 1992, pp. 127-44.

110. Uma Chakravarti, op. cit., p. 142.

111. A. Cunningham, *The Stupa of Bharhut, Mahabodhi, Bhilsa Tope*, pp. 65-67, Pl. XXVI, fig. 8.

112. Cowell, *Jātaka*, no. 62.

113. A. Coomaraswamy, *La Sculpture De Bharhut*, Paris: Vanoest, 1956, Planche, XXVIII, fig. 6.

114. B.M. Barua, *Bharhut* Pt. II. 1979 (rpt.), Delhi: Indological Book Corporation, p. 94, Scene 95a.

115. The exigency of balancing the composition may have been also a reason for such an arrangement.

116. *Manusmṛti*, IX.10: and IX.3 Also see chapter 1, section on *Strīsvabhāva* and *Strīdharma*.

117. Uma Chakravarti, *Men, Women and Beasts: The Interface Between High Tradition and Popular Tradition in Cultural Production*, New Delhi: Nehru Memorial Museum and Library, CXV, Second Series, November, 1992, p. 20.

118. Cowell, *Jātaka*, no. 321.

119. Ibid., no. 536.

120. Barua, *Bharhut* II, p. 158.

121. LL .747.

122. Vidya Dehejia, op. cit.

123. Uma Chakravarti, op. cit., p. 13, observes that as reflected in the Jātakas, the animal kingdom had thoroughly internalised the social value system of the humans in terms of hierarchy, labour, inequality, patriarchy and the like.

124. Cowell, *Jātaka*, no. 514.

125. Amy G. Poster, op. cit., p. 107, fig. 40. Eastern India, Śuṅga period, first century BCE, moulded terracotta, 8.7 × 6.7 × 1.8 cm, Ashutosh Museum of Indian Art, Calcutta University. It being moulded proves popularity of the scene.

126. LL. 796; Barua, *Bharhut* II, p. 158.

127. Cowell, *Jātaka*, no. 546.

128. Barua, *Bharhut* II, pp. 162-64, Scene no. 140.

129. Ibid. p. 115.

130. Cowell, *Jākata*, no. 320.

131. Ibid., no. 485.

132. Ibid., no. 267.

133. LL.724.

# 5

# The Non-wives
## Nuns and Prostitutes

It is my contention that in the art and literature of the period, we see the classification of women as wife, mother or non-wife through the categorisation of them as *dampati* or *mithuna* (consort), *mātr̥kā* (mother, whether natural or adoptive), and other women. It seems that it is their gender roles that define the status of women. Superimposed on these are the *varṇa-jāti* divisions. Men are rarely perceived as fathers, husbands or male prostitutes. The categories used to classify men were those of their *varṇāśrama-jāti*, profession and learning. Thus, the identities and roles of men as a category were based on their social or economic status or ability, while those of women were based on their physical and social role within the family as an institution, where their sexuality was controlled and regulated.

In this section an attempt is made to see how the category that I have termed the "non-wife" was constructed, perceived and represented through art. This will involve demarcating sculptures that may represent nuns and prostitutes and examining the question as to whether art constructed and reinforced their gender identity as that of the non-wife.

I define the non-wife as a woman whose sexuality is not used within the socio-religious-legal world for legitimate reproduction, a woman who does not belong to one man in a monogamous marriage. In early Indian art two such classes may be observed: those of the nun and the prostitute. This is not to suggest that either nuns or prostitutes were and could have never married or the latter could not at any point of life give up their profession and join the order of nuns. However, during the time they were nuns and prostitutes, as social entities, they constituted the category of non-wives. While the sexuality of the former is perceived to be restricted and controlled to the extent that it is not permitted any expression, that of the latter is construed as the epitome of unrestrained sexuality[1] that can be utilised by more than one man, for a price. The demarcating feature for both nuns and prostitutes is the fact they appear to function outside patriarchal social control[2] even while interacting with and being at least economically dependent (one for alms and on the other for customers) on that same society.

### 5.1 The Nun and the Prostitute

It is interesting to note how both nuns and prostitutes are viewed in a derogatory manner and were often approximated to one another in the post-Mauryan era as well as in more recent times.

In the *Arthaśāstra* it is recommended that both nuns (*bhikṣuṇī*) and prostitutes (*rūpajīvā, gaṇikā, veśyā*[3]) be employed for similar tasks such as spying.[4] In the *Vinaya Piṭaka* too there are references to *veśyā*s taunting nuns as being akin to prostitutes.[5] There is also a reference in the *Vinaya Piṭaka* leading to a rule being enacted that nuns should not bathe uncovered. On one occasion a group of nuns was bathing naked near a group of prostitutes and they were taunted by the latter who said that the nuns were like the prostitutes themselves because both shaved off their pubic hair.[6]

In later literature such a comparison seems to have become accepted and amplified. One of the recourses open to an old prostitute was to become a *kuṭṭanī* (a procuress/bawd) and the other was to become a *tapasvinī* (a female mendicant).[7]

It has been remarked that a spiritual woman, *ipso facto*, being defined as "deviant," also gets marginalised and ostracised like the prostitute. A Buddhist text, in its reference to a code of conduct for nuns, states that in the eyes of society nuns were creatures of pleasure for monks and hence rigid segregation was imposed upon them.[8]

The approximation of prostitutes to nuns in the popular imagination is not surprising, given that both categories of women are essentially above *jāti* and interact with people from all sections of society. In fact, all such occupational groups that are non-exclusive and interact with the public at large — such as entertainers, physicians and ascetics — are clubbed together in the *Arthaśāstra* and earmarked for spying. This is due to the fact that they have access to information, are mobile, agile and not taken seriously by society.

We find that the *gaṇikā* and the nun are both categories that were not only outside the control of patriarchal society but also seem to have freely negotiated the public and the private spheres. This is highlighted in the first Act of the play *Mṛcchakaṭika* when Maitreya, the *vidūṣaka*, refuses to step out at night, reasoning that the royal roads are beset not only by officials but also by *veśyā*s (prostitutes) so late in the night.[9] Vasantasenā, a courtesan being out in the streets and chased by the villain at night, establishes this within the play. In the same play even the servant girl, Radanikā, refuses to go out without a male escort. In contrast to Vasantasenā, domestic women such as Cārudatta's wife, Dhūtā, do not appear in public places such as roads and gardens. Women's mobility seems restricted to the inner quarters of the house, where

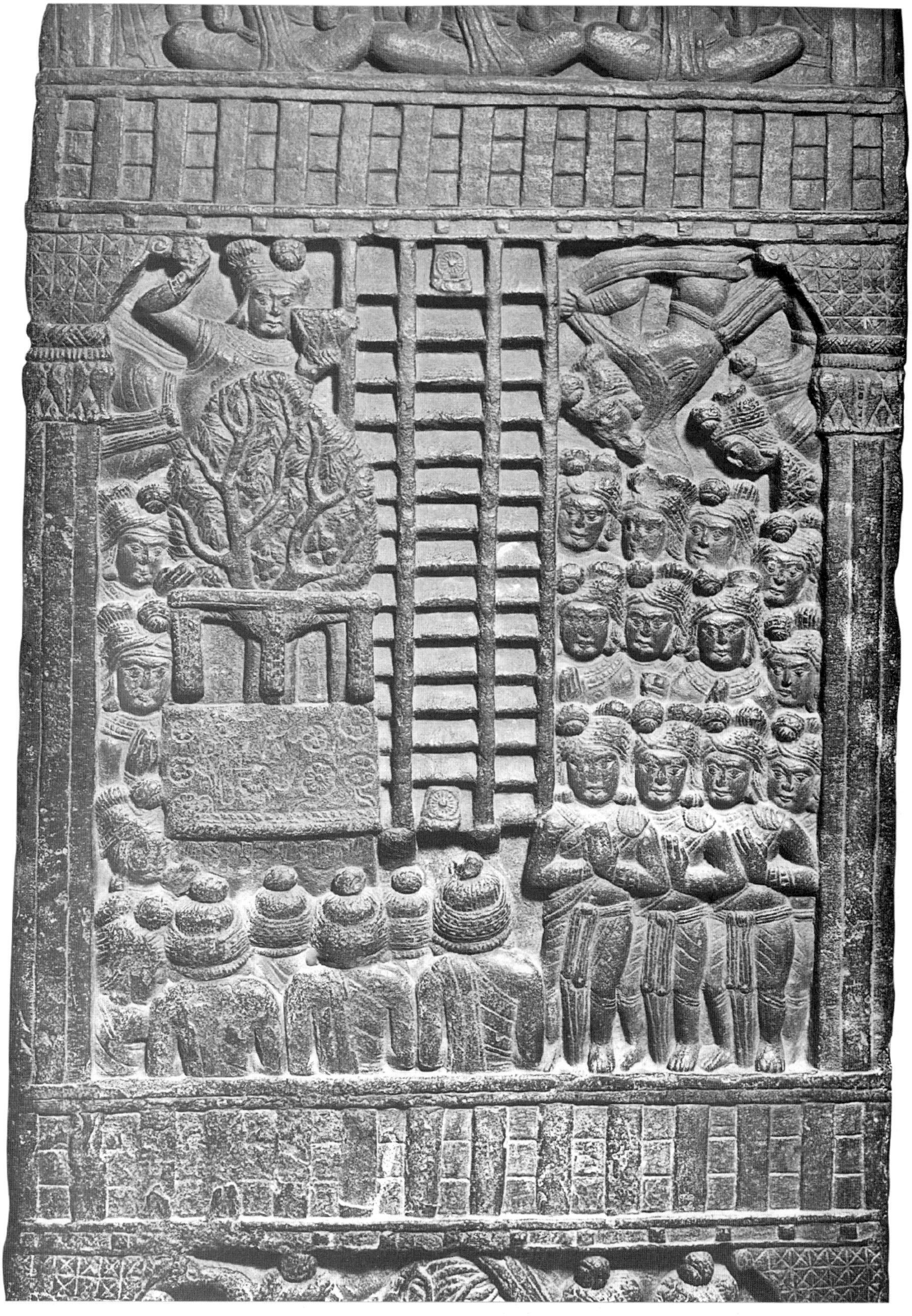

5.1 Panel showing Descent at Sankissa, great railing, western gate, corner pillar, first century BCE, Bharhut. IM 187.

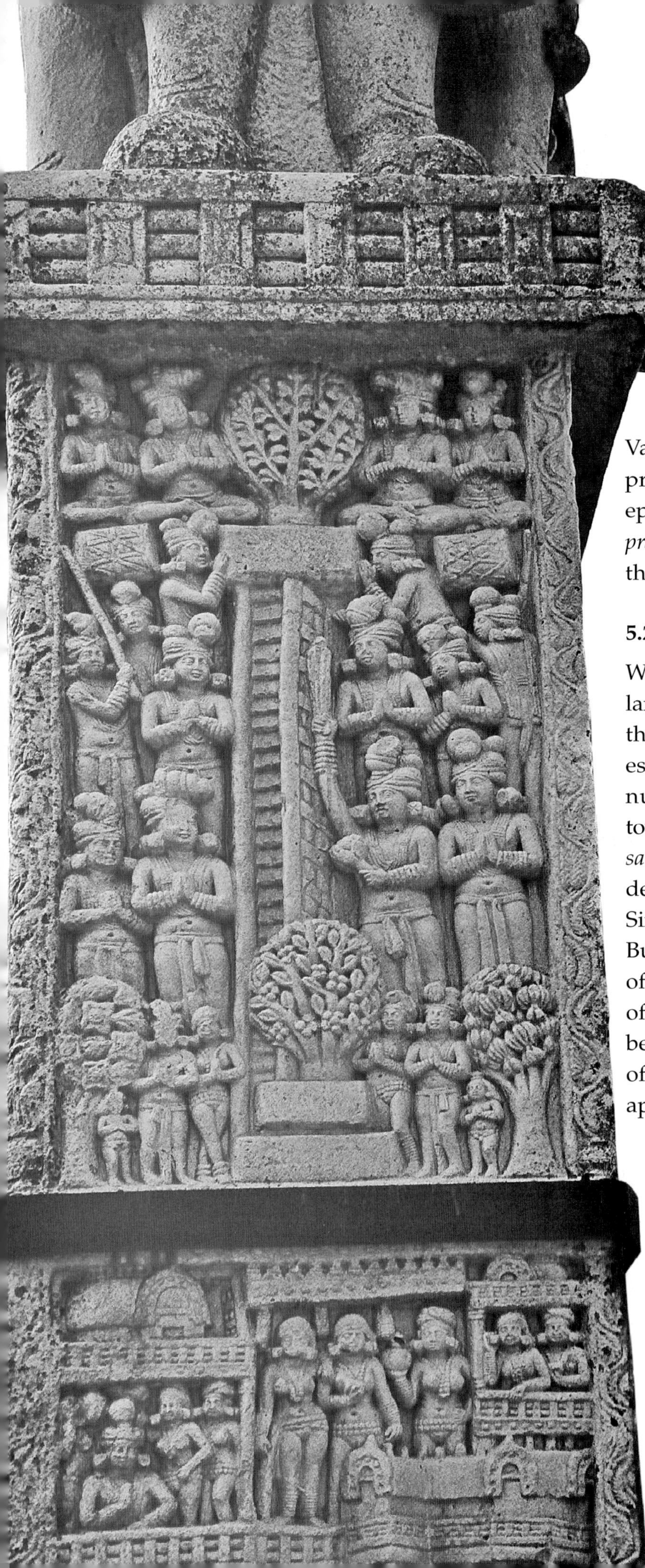

Vasantasenā is ineligible to enter due to her profession as a prostitute.[10] In fact, one of the epithets used for a prostitute in the play is *prakāśanārī*,[11] a woman who has been exposed (to the public gaze).

### 5.2 The Nun

While we assume that nuns were visible on the landscape of early society, they are noticeable by their absence in the visual world of art. This is especially perplexing given the evidence that nuns donated prolifically and generously towards the Jaina ascetic orders and the Buddhist *saṁgha* and their monuments. It has been demonstrated by Kumkum Roy and Upinder Singh, through a study of epigraphs from early Buddhist monuments, that almost three-fourths of the donative inscriptions at Bharhut, and half of those at Sāñcī, mention women, many of them belonging to the order of the nuns, as the patrons of these monuments. Some, like Buddhamitra, appear to have made multiple donations to the

5.2 Descent at Sankissa, *stūpa* 1, first century CE, Sāñcī, Madhya Pradesh.

*saṁgha* in more than one region, in this case at Śrāvastī and again at Sārnāth.[12]

Dominant ideologies shape artistic representation at any given point in time. In early art this representation almost makes nuns invisible. These *bhikkhuṇī*s are relatively outside the gender-boundaries being formulated or crystallised during the period. Does their invisibility in art have something to do with regulating fluid gender boundaries? How may the absence of an entire class of women be accounted? These are two of the questions being examined in this section.

The *Therīgāthā*, a collection of hymns attributed to senior nuns, offers a testimony to the fact that at least Buddhist nuns had a voice of their own that it was heard by many, including other nuns. *Therī*s such as Paṭācārā had a large following. Many nuns are also mentioned in inscriptions at Sāñcī, Bodh-Gayā and Bharhut. They are referred to as *bhikkhuṇī, bichhunī* or also as *samanikā* or *pavajitikā*,[13] though they are not accorded honorific epithets of the kind applied to monks, such as *bhadamita, aya (aryo)*, and *bhadamataya.* We find both nuns[14] and monks[15] having female disciples, but none of the nuns having a male disciple. Barua perceives these as indicating an inferior position being accorded to the nuns in the *saṁgha* hierarchy in comparison to the monks.[16]

However, the epigraphic and textual presence of nuns is not translated into visual terms. My investigation into the catalogues of various museums in India and Pakistan[17] has revealed only one nun, namely Utpalavarṇā, in sculptural depictions related to the life of the Buddha. Utpalavarṇā was a senior nun whose verses find a place in the *Saṁyutta Nikāya*, describing her encounter with Māra.[18] After preaching his doctrine to the gods and his mother, the Buddha descended at Śrāvastī from the heaven of thirty-three gods or *Tuṣita* Heaven. Here the nun Utpalavarṇā first welcomes him.

This episode is often depicted either separately, or as part of the eight miracles related to the life of the Buddha. Among the many examples is the Miracle of Śrāvastī scene found at Bharhut (*Pl.* 5.1), Sāñcī (*Pl.* 5.2), Kauśāmbī, Gandhāra and in other regions. I will be discussing only four representative depictions here. One is from Kauśāmbī, now in the Allahabad University Museum, two are in the Mathura Museum[19] and the fourth is from the Butkara region in the Swat region of Pakistan and now in the Saidu Sharif Museum, Peshawar.[20]

At Mathurā a panel (*Pl.* 5.3), datable to the Kuṣāṇa period, has bas-relief of five episodes from the life of Buddha:[21] From right to left these are: the Birth of Buddha, Meditation at Bodh-Gayā, Descent from the Heaven of the Thirty-three Gods, the First Sermon at Sārnāth, and the *parinirvāṇa* (death). It is in the descent from the *Tuṣita* Heaven that we see the nun Utpalavarṇā. This episode is depicted through the presence of three ladders. At the bottom of the central one there is a female figure kneeling in adoration. She is shown wrapped in monastic garments, the *ticivara,* including, one assumes, a *samakacchikā* (bodice) prescribed for *bhikkhuṇī*s. Her head is shaven. In a similar panel, from the same area (*Pl.* 5.4), only the portion showing Utpalavarṇā paying obeisance at the bottom of the central stairway survives of what must have been a larger relief panel.

In the Butkara panel, at the Peshawar Museum, there seems to be only one scene in the panel: The Descent of the Buddha and his reception by Utpalavarṇā whose shaven head and monastic attributes are clearly seen.

The name Utpalavarṇā is inscribed in early

Brāhmī script in Prākṛt as *Uppalavannā* on a *vedikā* found at Kauśāmbī.[22] Here, on the fifth pillar, though the motifs are badly eroded, one can make out a figure dressed in monastic robes, bending at the waist with folded hands towards a pillar or a pedestal. In the background, a staircase with banister railing is visible above her.

These seem to be the some surviving representations of the members of the *bhikkhuṇī saṁgha.* V.S. Agrawala has published a group of fragmentary terracottas from Ahicchatra, datable to CE 550-650, claiming these to be representations of nuns.[23] According to him these are dressed in monastic attire which consists of an upper scarf, an *uttarasaṅga,* which is wrapped diagonally upon the upper body, falling over the left shoulder. The portion below the waist is covered by a petticoat. However, the identification of these figures as nuns is problematic, given the fragmentary nature of the terracottas.

As against this, monks are given a place in a large number of visual representations. One of the most eloquent is that of the distribution of food to monks, found on a railing of a *stūpa* now housed in the Mathura Museum. There is evidence of depictions of Jaina monks in pre-Kuṣāṇa and Kuṣāṇa sculptures as well. Representations of monks are prolific in the Gandhāra region also.

One can only speculate as to why nuns are not allowed the same kind of visual projection as monks. One reason may be that the Buddha himself was reluctant to admit women into the order and had to be persuaded by Ānanda on behalf of Mahāprajāpati Gotamī, Buddha's foster mother.[24] In the Digambara Jaina tradition while they are indeed given epithets such as *āryikā* or

5.3 Scenes from the Life of Buddha, top centre — Descent at Sankissa welcome by nun Utpalavarṇā, second century CE, Mathurā, UP. GMM No. 00.H1.

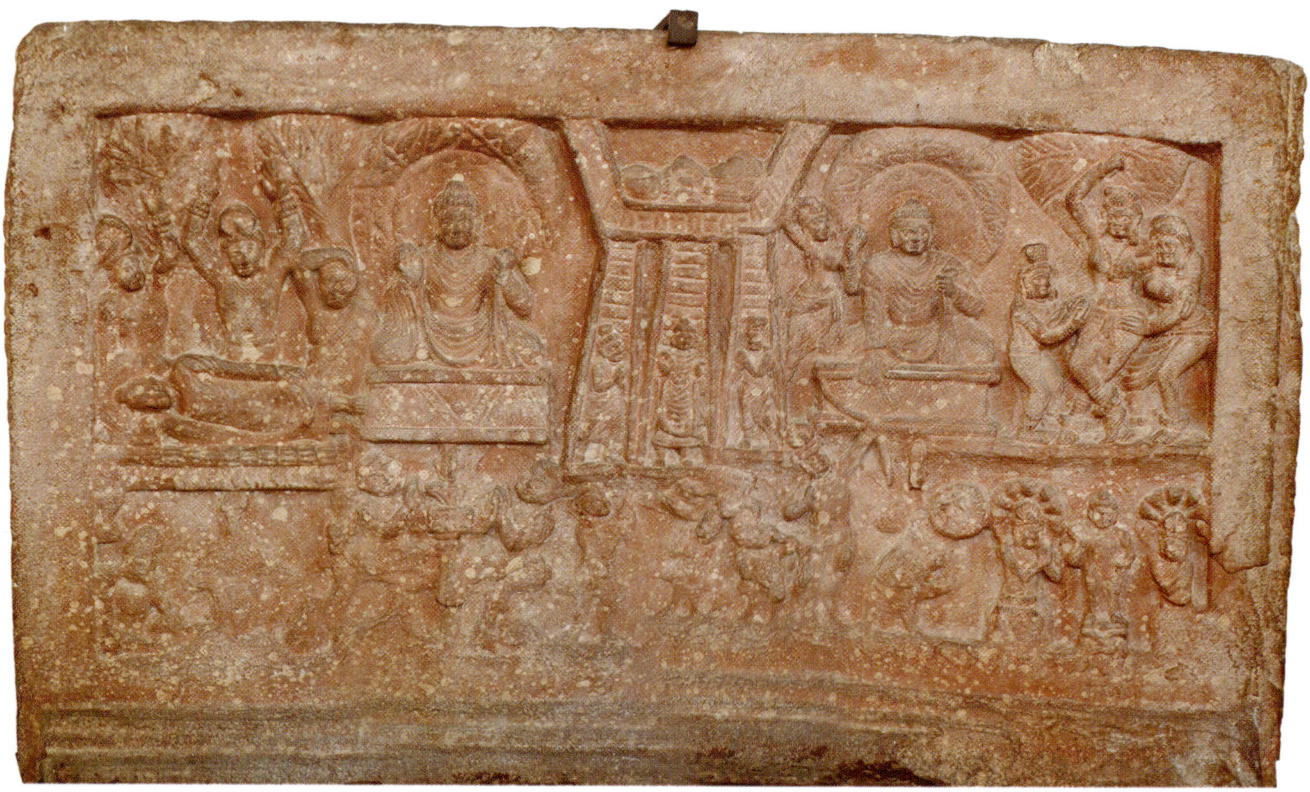

*sādhvī* (noble and venerable ladies), nuns are technically not considered mendicants. Rather they are thought of as celibate, spiritually advanced laywomen, *sukṛṣṭā-śrāvikā*.[25] The earliest example of women who renounced worldly commitment and retired to caves is found at Sittanavasal which can be dated to the second century BCE. It is only in the Śvetāmbara sect that women enjoy the full status of mendicancy and are less restricted.

In Buddhism, while both nuns and monks are denied sexuality, the restrictions on nuns seem stricter in their insistence of guarding it. In the Bhikkhuṇīpātimokkhapali section of the *Vinaya*, a *bhikkhuṇī* is forbidden to have sexual intercourse with any male[26] and she should not allow a male to touch her above the knees. "A *bhikkhuṇī*, overflowing with desire, were to consent to rubbing or rubbing up against or taking hold or touching or pressing against, below the collarbone of a male who is overflowing with desire, above the knees, she too becomes defeated, not in communion."[27] This helps us establish the portions of the female body which are viewed as the locus of sexuality.[28] There are further rules that prohibit any contact with male sexuality such as accepting food given by men overflowing with desire or while she herself is overflowing with desire.[29] There are also rules against displaying the body by bathing naked[30] or entering a village without a bodice. Even contact with the *bhikkhus* is restrained and regulated.[31] Any place where there is to be exposure to pleasure and temptation — such as occasions with dancing and music, a king's house, a picture gallery (*cittāgāraṁ*), a park (*ārāman*) or a pleasure grove (*uyyānaṁ*), etc.[32] — is prohibited.

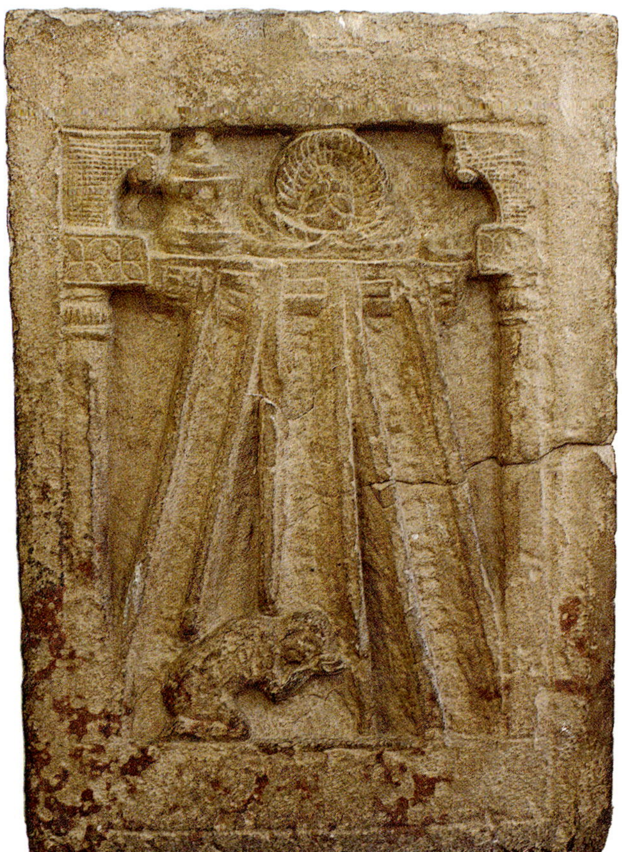

5.4 Utpalavarṇā, miracle at Śrāvastī, second century CE, Mathurā, UP. GMM.

Certain rules regarding sexuality, which are applicable to monks, are mentioned in the Bhikkhupātimokkhapali section. These rules exhort monks to guard against indulging in sexual intercourse, using lewd words that would normally be used by young men towards young women, and staying alone or lying down with a *bhikkhuṇī*. However, the difference between the Vinaya rules laid down for the *bhikkhu saṁgha* and the *bhikkhuṇī saṁgha* is that the rules for monks do not restrict their mobility or their contact with society, while in the case of the *bhikkhuṇīs* this is strictly supervised. The rules regarding sexuality for monks regulate their conduct; while those relating to the nuns do not just regulate their behaviour but also concern their body and physicality. This is emphasised through rules such as not allowing pubic hair to grow on their bodies, not rubbing the body above the knee, and having to wear an additional garment, the bodice. There is also regulation restricting their mobility. An analysis of places of origin of donees in the inscriptions at Sāñcī which indicates that the mobility of the women including nuns was relatively restricted in comparison to men,[33] seems to bear this out. This difference suggests that there was a greater fear of female sexuality, with a concomitant potential for transgressions and therefore the need for additional precautions. It is difficult to state whether stricter rules for the nuns were to ensure their safety from violation[34] or whether these sought to restrict access to men (especially monks) for whom the latter supposedly posed a sexual temptation. As pointed out before, it is stated in the Vinaya texts that the lay public ridiculed nuns as being objects of pleasure and for use of the monks.

Whatever may have been the reason behind these stricter Vinaya rules for nuns, the fact remains that they were relatively absent from art. I think that this absence of representation reflected their comparatively low status in the *saṁgha* and may have been one way of disprivileging them. The agency of women in the monastic sphere was permitted but this was not translated into visual terms. They were allowed to make donations, but this act was not valorised by giving them a place in the visual record of the world, in contrast to donor couples. Another reason may have been that while asceticism was established as a worthy goal for men in all patriarchal religious ideologies, renunciation and the right to attain *mokṣa* or *nirvāṇa* was by no means a universally acceptable goal for women, as demonstrated earlier.

Reading absences and silences is an accepted methodological tool for recovering the voices of the marginalised sections of society who have been made invisible by the dominant tradition. Thus the absence in art of one category of women, viz. nuns, who are otherwise present in textual sources, can be significant. This absence is also an example of how art can be used to marginalise a section of women who are considered problematic. The monks who supervised the construction and commissioning of Buddhist monuments, perhaps, did not include nuns in the representational scheme.

It reinforces the idea of the subservience expected of them *vis-à-vis* the male monk order, the *bhikkhu saṁgha.* A *bhikkhuṇī* was always subordinate to a *bhikkhu*; even a senior nun had to stand up before a novice monk.[35] This subservient status of the nun — when she does appear — is seen internally within the depiction itself. The nun is shown as a kneeling figure whose only role is that of paying homage to the Buddha. Utpalavarṇā, the nun, is considered quite dispensable in the scheme representing the Descent of the Buddha at Sankisa. This incident is depicted entirely without the presence of the nun at Bharhut and Sāñcī (*Pls*. 5.1, 5.2).[36] However, this need not be regarded as unusual or indicative in so far as religious depictions of the period were mainly didactic or devotional in nature, the agency of humans not being considered universally significant. The main aim was to focus attention, not on individual personalities in the story, but rather on the main persona of the Buddha or his connection to the lesson or episode carved in the panel. Thus both nuns and monks could be omitted.

5.5 Woman fleeing, *chatradhāriṇī* and two males, obverse of a double-sided panel depicting scenes from *Mṛcchakaṭika*, Kuṣāṇa, late second century CE, red sandstone, Maholi, Mathurā. NM Acc. No. 2806. (facing page)

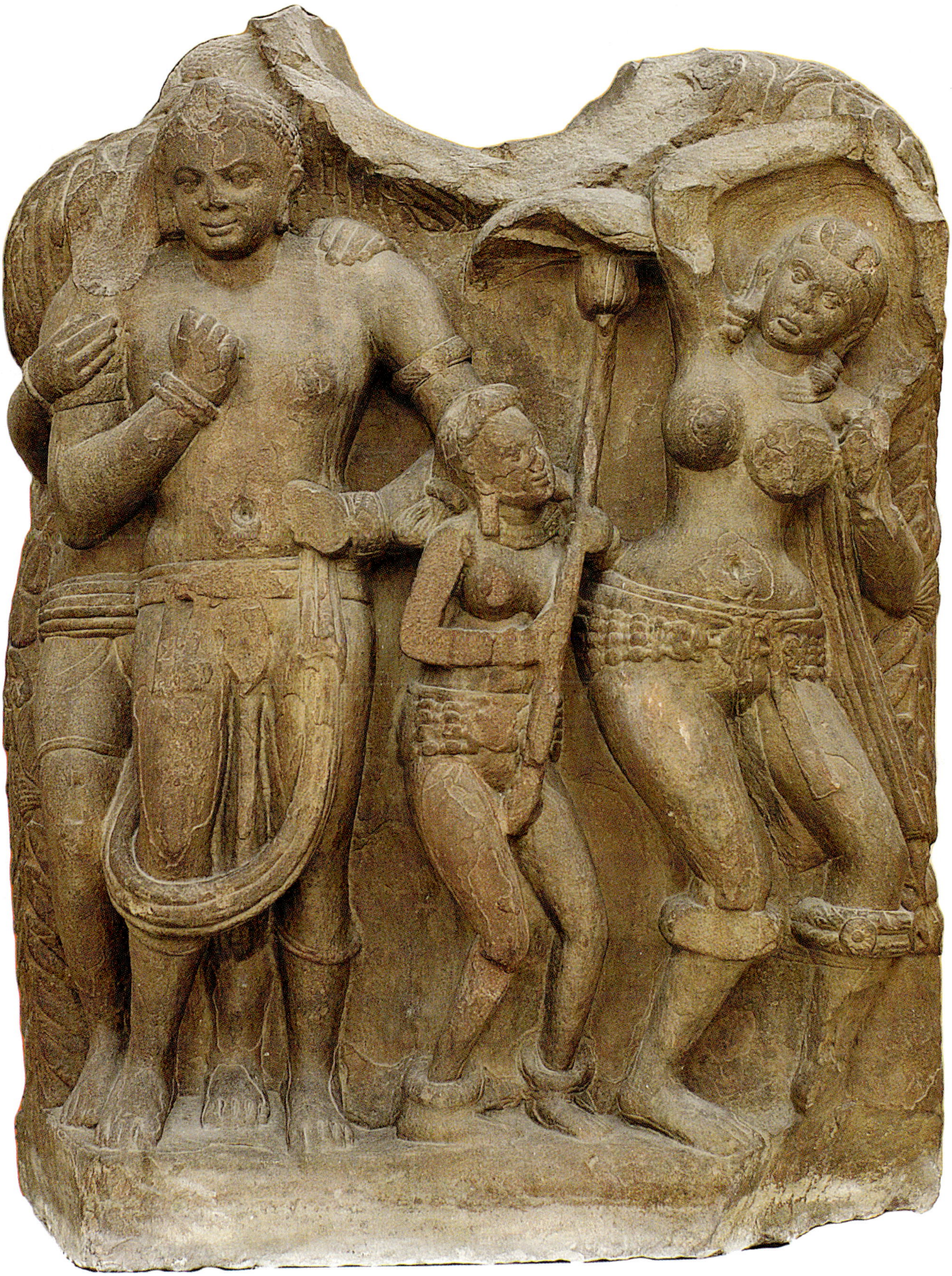

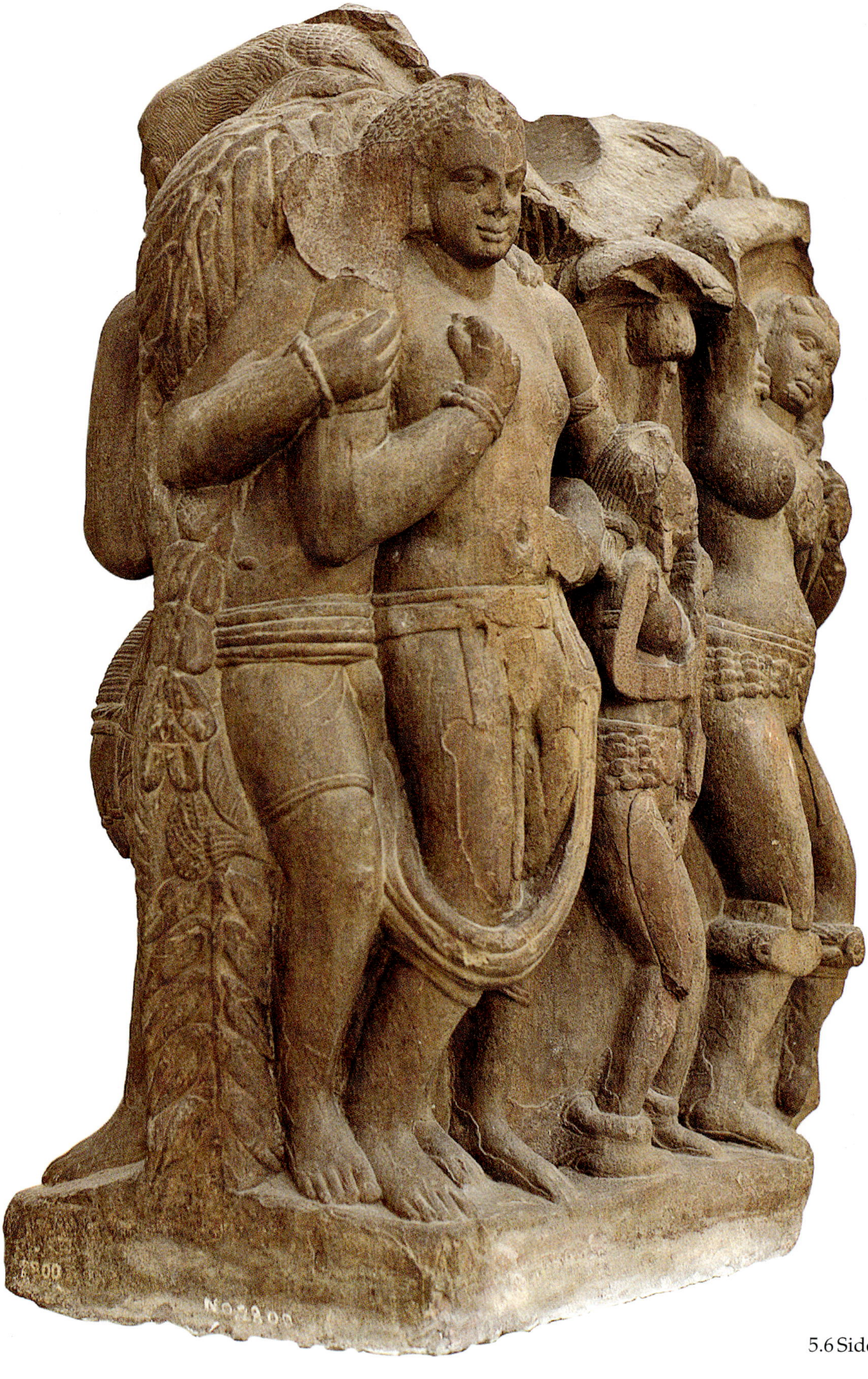

5.6 Side view of 5.5.

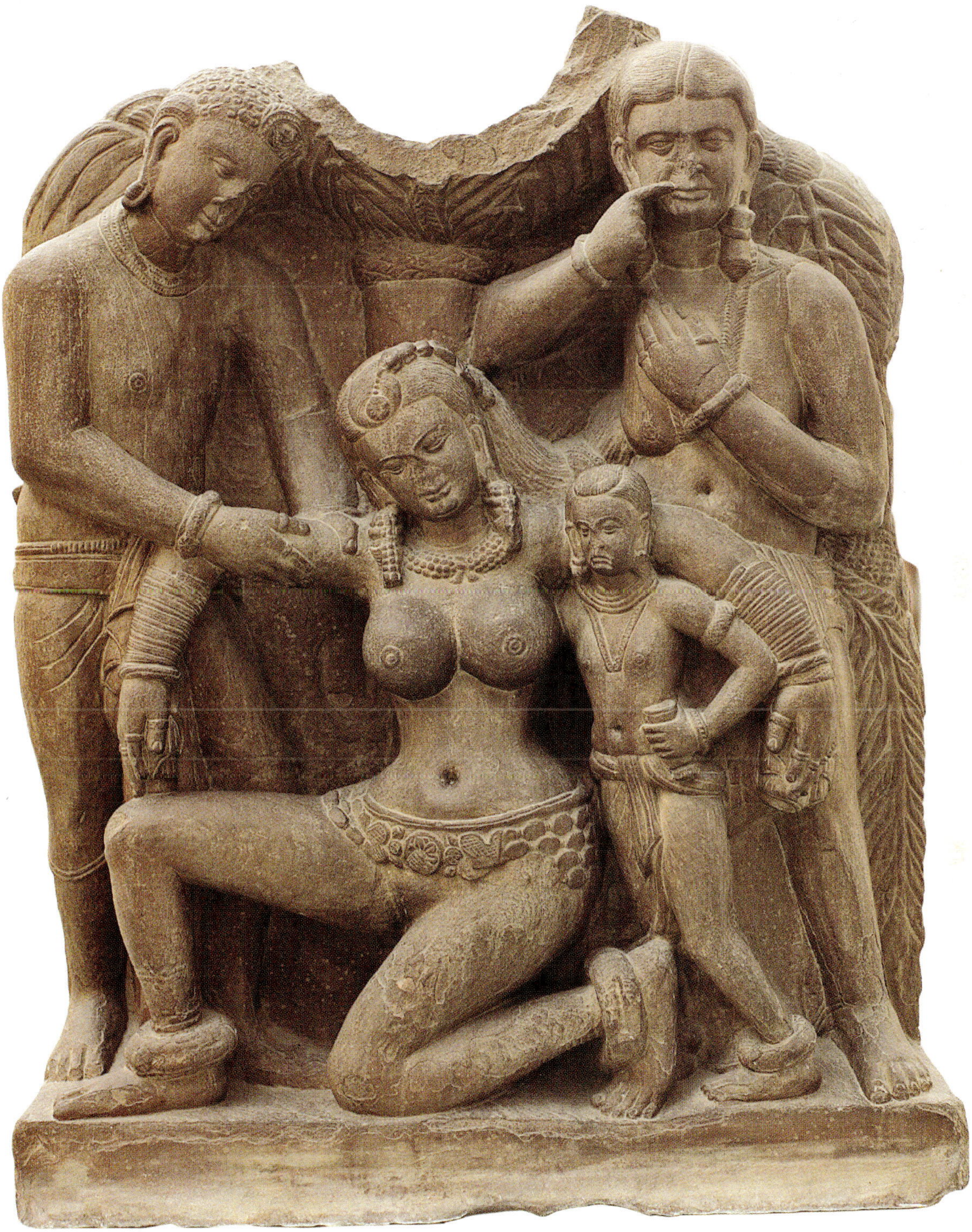

5.7 Kneeling woman supported by two male companions and a diminutive attendant, reverse of a double-sided panel depicting scenes from *Mṛcchakaṭika*, Kuṣāṇa, red sandstone, late second century CE, Maholi, Mathurā. NM Acc. No. 2806.

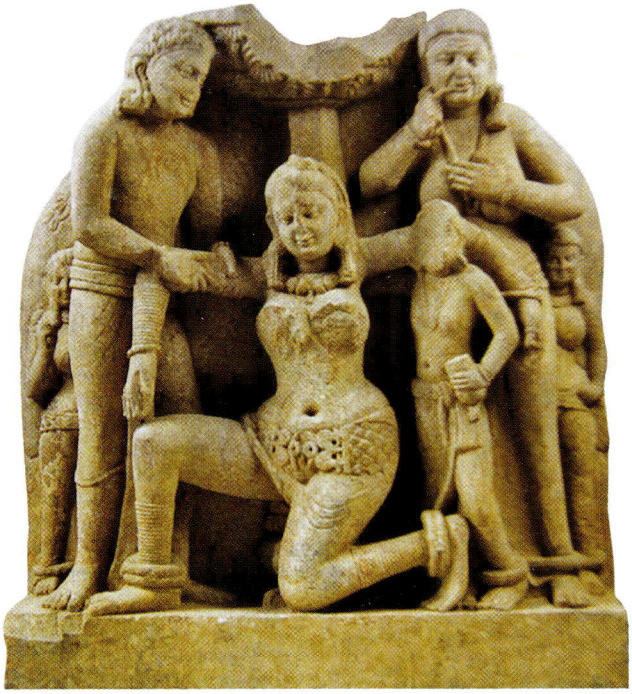

5.8 Kneeling woman supported by two male companions and a diminutive attendant, red Sikri stone, second century CE, Mathurā.

## 5.3 Courtesan Gaṇikā

There are depictions of many goddesses and maternal figures in the art of this period. But very few independent female figures that can be termed secular, or that come under the category of secular art, have been found so far. Two types belonging to this rare category are (a) the *mithuna-dampati*-spectator,[37] and (b) the drunken woman or courtesan.

In this section the focus will be on the latter type, since it refers to a category of women that occupy an ambivalent position in literature. Referred to variously as *veśyā* or *gaṇikā* in Buddhist and Brāhmanical textual tradition, these women were perceived as operating outside the control of, yet closely associated with, the patriarchal order. In the following analysis I will explore this dichotomy further, in both visual and literary texts.

### 5.3.1 THE SCULPTURAL EVIDENCE

There are two types that may represent *veśyā*s or *gaṇikā*s (prostitutes and courtesans). The first occurs in a series of reliefs identified with Vasantasenā, the heroine of the plays *Mr̥cchakaṭika* and *Daridra Cārudutta*[38] and the second in narrative friezes depicting the courtesan-turned-nun, Āmrapālī, making the donation of the mango grove to the Buddhist *saṁgha*.

It may be noted at the outset, that this exegesis on the representation of the *gaṇikā* in art and its gender implication is based on the acceptance of the view that the following pieces may be identified as featuring Vasantasenā, the protagonist of *Mr̥cchakaṭika* and *Daridra Cārudatta*. This identification has been widely accepted by scholars such as Sivaramamurti, Czuma, T.S. Maxwell, Stadtner and the National Museum in its label and catalogue, though alternative readings may be possible and valid, especially if new and substantive source material were to emerge.

We have so far found eleven depictions of a particular series that we may identify with Vasantasenā, all but one of which are from Mathurā; there are also some so-called bacchanalian scenes in terracotta, stucco and stone from associated areas such as Kauśāmbī and Taxila. These pieces are not all identical, but they do share similar representation and arrangement of figures. Eight of them are carved on both sides of stone panels, two are in relief on railing pillars, and one is an ivory piece. One is yet unpublished though it has been discussed in the text of the Sanghol catalogue as a bacchanalian scene.[39] The Begram ivories have been published[40] but the similarity of the series mentioned below with representations of Vasantasenā, a *gaṇikā* in the play *Mr̥cchakaṭika*, has not been established.

The most complete surviving representation of the Vasantasenā scene is on the Maholi panel from Mathurā.[41] It is made of red sandstone and is carved on both sides of a stone stele (*Pls.* 5.5 to 5.7). On one side is a scene of a woman kneeling (*Pl.* 5.7), apparently drunk or overwrought, being supported on the right by a dwarf and on the left by a man of natural proportions. On the far right is another woman, less voluptuous than the central figure, standing against a pilaster with a bowl at the top.

On the reverse (*Pl.* 5.5) we find, on the far right, the figure of a woman standing with a bend at the knees and the waist so that the figure is balanced. The sculpting of her body along with the clothing and jewellery approximates to the usual representation of *yakṣī* figures of the period. This includes voluptuous delineation of the body with round, full breasts, a narrow waist and wide hips. She is shown naked from above the waist, wearing a *mekhalā* and a profusion of necklaces, earrings and the like. The noteworthy feature is that her anklets are drawn up almost to her knees. This is an unusual feature compared to all other female figures of the time including the ones on the obverse. Her right arm is raised above her head, touching her headdress, scarf (*uttarīya*) above her head. On her immediate right, situated in the middle of the composition, is a diminutive female figure holding up a parasol (*chattra*). On the right of this female attendant are two men of whom only one is fully visible. One of them is apparently hiding behind the man in the front and can therefore be seen only in part. The man in the front appears to be well dressed but does not have a halo and it may therefore be said that he is an aristocratic though not a divine personage. The whole piece apparently is a stand for a bowl, which can be seen on the top of the pilaster, carved in the middle of the slab.

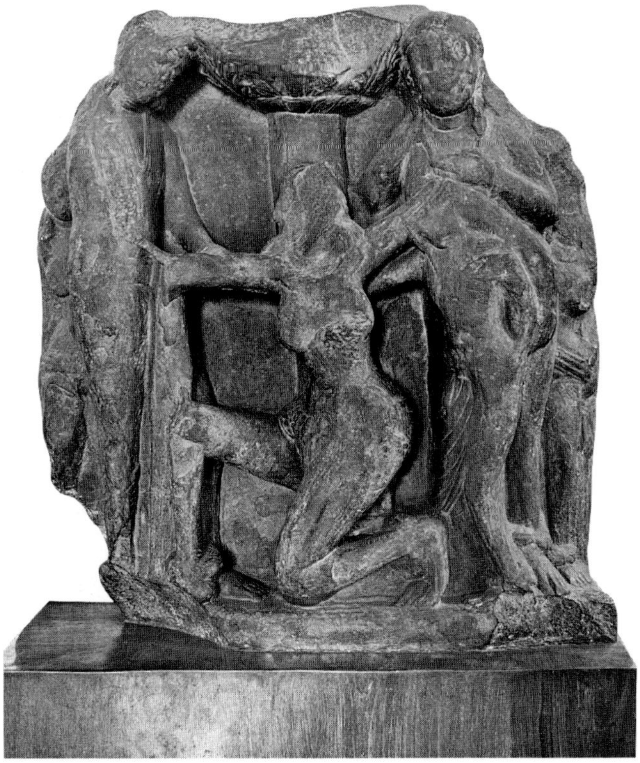

5.9 Kneeling woman supported by two male companions and a diminutive attendant, red Sikri stone, Mathurā, first-second century CE. Indian Museum, Calcutta.

The second image of the same variety belongs to a private collection and has been published by Donald Stadtner (*Pl.* 5.8).[42] Here again, the obverse features a kneeling female in the centre. Her features are more rounded than in the figures in the Maholi specimen and her face is downward looking rather than looking straight. Her left arm is resting on the shoulders of a diminutive man on her immediate left. The other arm forms a right-angle at the elbow, which is supported by a robust male figure on her right. The dwarf figure on the right holds a cup or goblet-like object in his left hand. Interestingly, he wears anklets while the other male figure in the composition do not [is he/she a eunuch or a bastard *bandhula*, mentioned in the play, *Mṛcchakaṭika*?]. Behind the dwarf is another feminine figure; there seem to be wrinkles or deep lines on her face and she has a finger raised

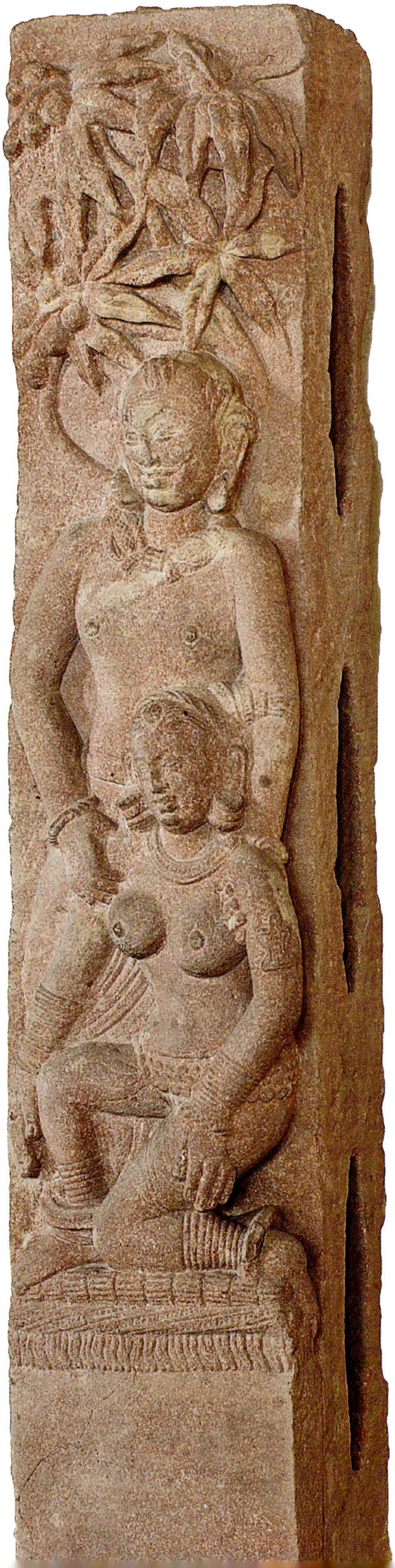

to her lips probably in dismay or wonder. Her left hand is placed in front of her (slightly drooping) breasts. The additional figures in this panel are the two attendant women, one on each side, both partially hidden.

On the reverse (not illustrated) is a row of three females of normal size, while a fourth is diminutive compared to the other figures in the composition. They all hold some objects in their hands, in the style of the *yakṣīs* of the *vedikā* pillars. In the hand of the one on the far left a laden tray is discernible, while on the third from the left one can see a *surāhī*-like vessel. Behind these figures is a profusely carved mango tree laden with fruits. In the middle is the pilaster, which ends at the top in a bowl.

The third panel (*Pl.* 5.14) also belongs to a private collection.[43] The composition on the obverse contains four female figures. The central one of these is seated on a tall stool that seems to be made of woven cane, judging from its cross-hatched pattern. She has her right foot planted on a slab while the left leg is slightly raised and held by a female attendant. The anklet is raised above the knee on this leg though it rests above the ankle in the other leg. The figure on the left is holding objects in both her hands; in the left hand there is a covered dish and in right a *surāhī*. The other figure on the right is holding a basket in her hand. In the centre of the panel, serving as a backdrop, is a richly carved *aśoka* tree, above which there are traces of a bowl. The entire composition seems to be set in a garden or orchard, which typically would have been situated outside a town for the pleasure of the *nāgarakas* (cultured folk).

On the reverse (*Pl.* 5.13), the composition of the Maholi panel is repeated with slight differences such as the placement of the diminutive figure, which is on the right here. The bowl is also somewhat differently delineated; here it is squarer and less integrated into the reverse side.

The fourth panel is in a fragmentary condition and is housed in a private collection.[44] On the obverse one can see

5.10 Kneeling woman being helped by male companion, second century CE, Kuṣāṇa, Sanghol, Punjab.

only one leg of a female figure, the torso of which is no longer extant. A kneeling attendant is removing the anklet from this leg. The position of the anklet, as usual in these depictions, is just below the knee. There are two more figures in the composition; one is a standing figure with a now unidentifiable object in the right hand. The other figure is not identifiable, due to erosion. There is an *aśoka* tree in the background. On the reverse the composition (*Pl.* 5.16) contains two males, one standing or hiding behind the other and holding the one in front. The face and body of the front male is very finely detailed, the drapery seems almost transparent so as to reveal the male genitalia. The face is rounded, adorned with a fillet-like wreath.

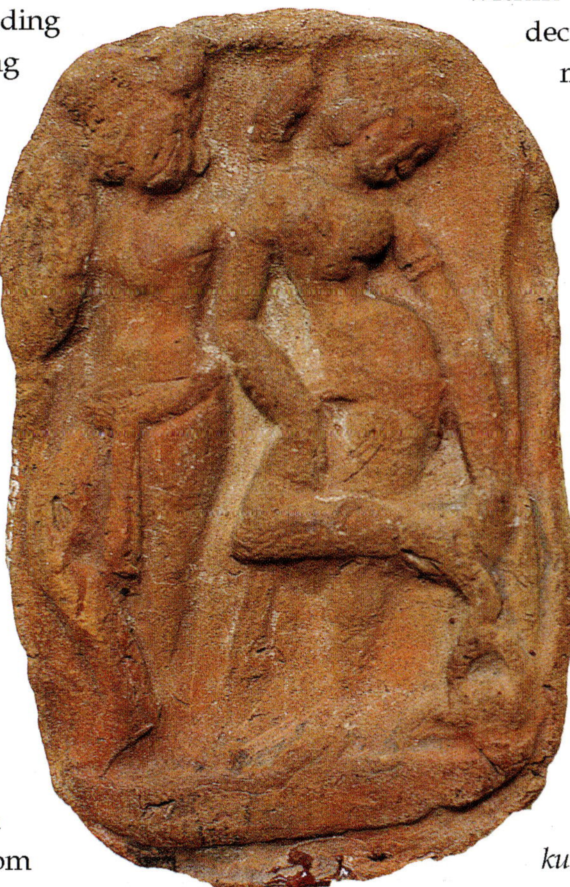

Fifth panel under discussion is from Naroli in Mathurā and now in Indian Museum (*Pl.* 5.9), Calcutta.[45] Though much defaced it can be identified as that of kneeling woman and associated figures. This too has a bowl on top with a pilaster supporting it from below.

The sixth piece is a fragment of a similar scene that has been culled out from the survey reports of Alexander Cunningham by Stadtner.[46]

Seventh is a panel in red Sīkrī stone on a pillar panel from Kaṅkālī Ṭīlā, Mathurā (*Pl.* 5.12) that is housed in the Mathura Museum.[47] It contains the scene of a woman with raised anklets, covering her head with a *dupaṭṭā*. The depiction of two men, one hiding behind the other, is repeated. An added element in this panel consists of torches, which these men hold, in their hands. In its detail, this composition has the essential elements of the "fleeing woman" representational type.

The eighth depiction under discussion here has been found on one of the panels of a *vedikā* pillar that must have encircled the *stūpa* at Sanghol (*Pl.* 5.10). This depiction may be placed within the *śālabhañjikā-yakṣī* decoration scheme, where the majority of other railing pillar reliefs depict female figures of the *yakṣī* type in various poses. Hitherto, it had been identified as bacchanalian scene in the manner of the Palikherā panel in the Mathura Museum (*Pls.* 5.17, 5.18), which depicts Kubera drinking in the company of his male and female companions/ attendants.[48] This Sanghol scene is an abbreviated version of the kneeling woman composition; bereft of male and female attendants or the so-called *kuṭṭanī* figure. Here a male figure is trying to raise a kneeling woman.

The ninth depiction, part of the Doris Wiener Inc. collection, New York (*Pls.* 5.15, 5.16), is a very interesting variation on the theme.[49] It may or may not have supported a bowl. In the centre of the obverse (*Pl.* 5.15) is a woman, who seems to be

5.11 A couple, with woman touching her ankle, terracotta, first century CE, Mathurā, GMM.

keeling over, with her left arm around the attendant female on the left. Unfortunately the legs below the knees are now damaged and one cannot make out the position of the anklets. The anklets of the attendant figure are however visible. On the far left of the main figure is another woman in a *tribhaṅga* posture, holding up an object in her left hand. On her right is a male figure whose upper portion is now defaced. He is dressed in an elaborate *dhotī* and has multi-stringed armlets and thick bracelets, giving him an opulent appearance. He is holding the breast of the central female figure. On the reverse (*Pl.* 5.16) is a man clad in similar attire to that of the male figure found on obverse, constraining the central female by holding both her arms from behind. On her left is a woman with right hand covering her mouth, holding a fan of a *pān*-like leaf in the other hand. On the far left of the panel is another man, perhaps an associate of the male figure. In the background, instead of the usual mango or *aśoka* tree, are two hanging tassels made of cloth, rope or flowers. They may even represent a curtain. This may suggest a hall, tent or similar setting. A similar device is seen in other panels from Mathurā (as in the so-called Saundarānanda railing pillar, now in the State Museum, Lucknow, discussed in the previous chapter). The lower end of the *dhotī* of the male figure, ending just below his knees, is like a thick roll of cloth, resembling an anklet. In other panels such as the Maholi panel, the lower edge of the *dhotī* is visible and the anklets are thicker and held together with a floral clasp carved on them.

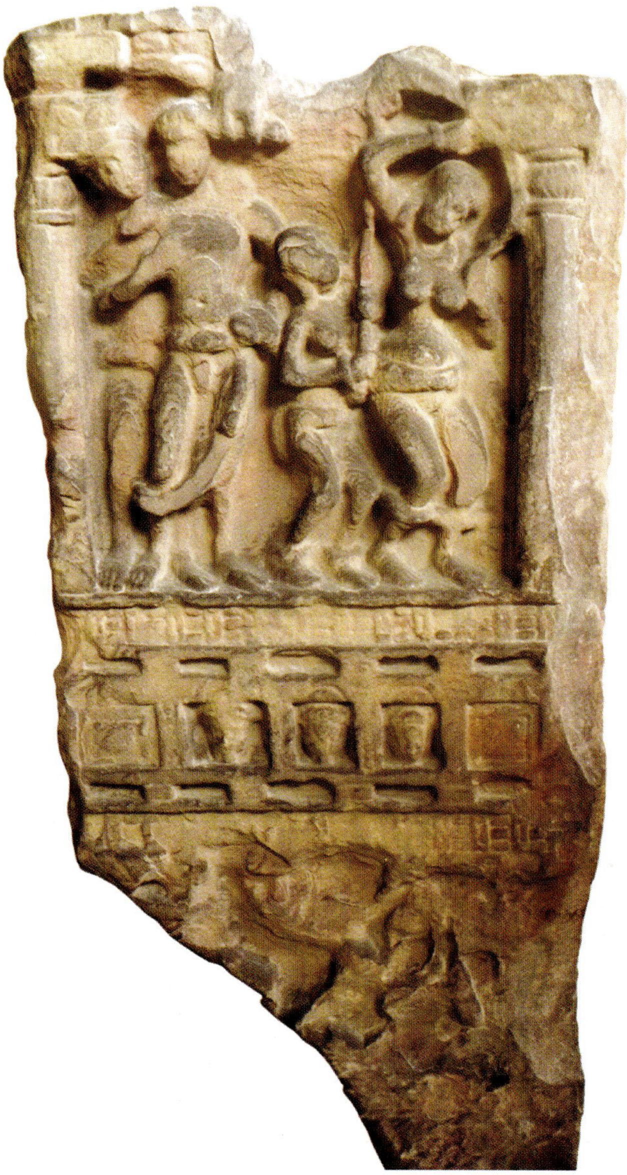

5.12 Woman covering her hair and with raised anklets, a *chatradhāriṇī* and two males, first-second century CE, Kaṅkālī Ṭīlā, Mathurā, GMM.

Similar panels are found carved on the ivories from Begram (*Pls.* 5.19, 5.20), now in the Musée Guimet and the Kabul Museum,[50] published in the excavation catalogue as series 200. [All the figures mentioned in connection with this series are from catalogue of Begram ivories published by J. Hackin et al., *Nouvelles Recherches Archeologiques A Begram (Ancienne Kapici) 1939-1940*, Paris, Imprimerie Nationale, 1954.] In two representations[51] a kneeling female figure is shown being supported on both sides by two standing female figures. In the usual fashion of the Begram ivories, the composition is framed within a doorway with pilasters on two sides

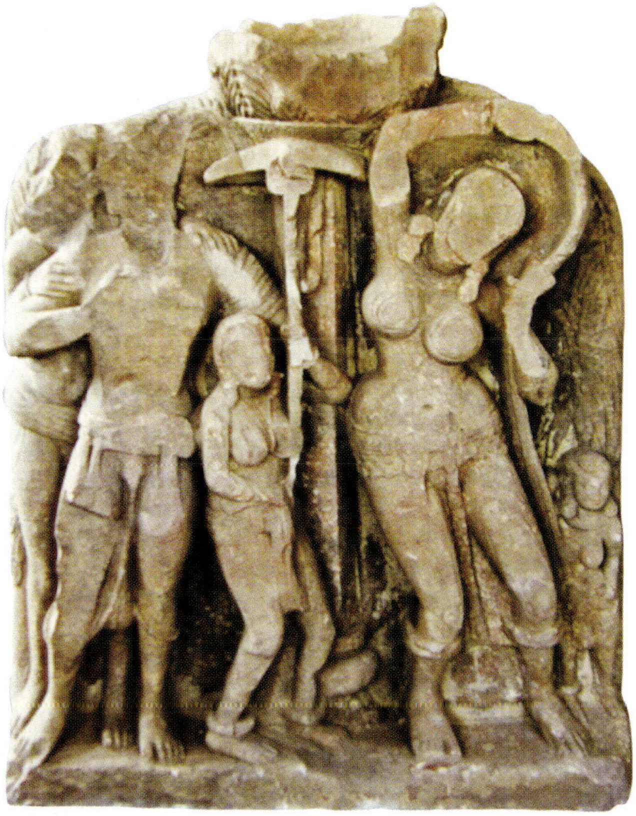

5.13 Women covering her head and wearing upraised anklets, a *chatradhāriṇī* and two males, red Sikri stone, second century CE, Kuṣāṇa.

topped by an architrave and an extended *gavākṣa*. The whole is surrounded by an *aśoka-latā*. The central kneeling female has her left leg extended outwards and the right leg folded under her. One arm is laid along the stretched-out leg while the other is held up by a female figure on the left. In the same series[52] a woman and a child are illustrated. The woman inclines laterally towards the child on the right who is shown touching the anklets on her right leg. The scene is framed within pilasters and topped by a *toraṇa* architrave. An *aśoka* tree behind the *toraṇa* suggests a courtyard or a garden setting. Carved next to this are three compositions[53] of female-female dyads standing in various *tribhaṅga* attitudes. Amongst these three one scene that is noteworthy (200q in the catalogue) depicts two women leaning towards a child standing between them in the middle. The figure on the left holds the child's hand in her right hand.

Another scene from the same site illustrates woman-with-child.[54] Here the woman places her left hand on the head of a child standing to her left. The child pulls at the end of the scarf or *uttarīya* of the female figure.

A "kneeling woman" representation has been discovered in the Deccan area, in Cave III at Nasik, which contains an inscription of Gautamīputra Śatakarṇī (CE 106-30).[55] The door has lintels or cross bars with voluted ends, similar to those on the *toraṇa*s of Sāñcī. The doorjambs are divided into five compartments. These *śākhā*s contain *mithuna*s, scenes of couples indulging in amorous activities. In one of the compartments, a man carries a woman. In another, there is a kneeling woman with a man supporting the female,[56] very much like the Sanghol panel. One panel illustrates a child next to a couple.

The scene showing a kneeling woman being assisted by a male companion has also been discovered in terracotta belonging to the Gupta period.[57]

We have some sculptures that may be related to the representational types described above. These are mainly the so-called bacchanalian panels found at Mathurā and in the Gandhāra region. The most significant among them is the Palikhera panel, which is carved on both sides and supports a bowl on top (*Pls.* 5.17, 5.18).[58] On one side is a corpulent figure identified by Vogel as Kubera seated on a stone platform, evidently drunk and supported on both sides by two attendants, one male and the other female. There are also two other dwarf figures on both sides. The obverse shows the same seated corpulent figure on the right. On the left are three standing

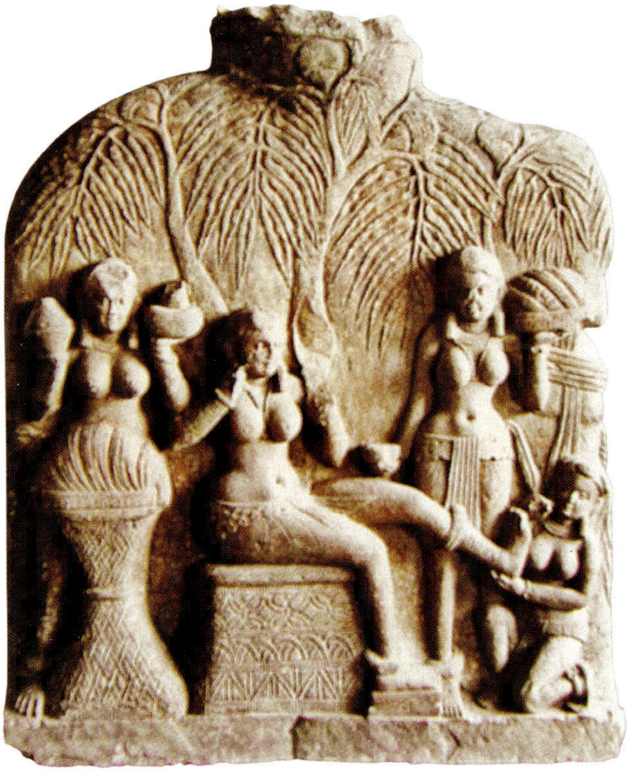

5.14 A group of four women, one seated in the middle with upraised anklets being removed, red Sikri stone, second century CE, Kuṣāṇa.

figures (two females and one male). The female figures are wearing knee-length pleated tunics and a long skirt. In the middle is a small figure that is so defaced that one cannot make out whether it is that of a child or a dwarf. There are also other bacchanalian scenes in terracotta and stone from both the Mathurā and Gandhāra regions.[59]

There was an attempt to investigate the portrayal of other *gaṇikā/veśyā* figures in the art of the post-Mauryan period in course of this study. The donation of the mango grove by Āmrapālī, a *gaṇikā* who became a nun, to the Buddha when he visited her is one of the significant events in the life of Buddha. She can be counted among the prominent early patrons of Buddhism along with Anāthapiṇḍika and Jīvaka.[60] While the contribution of the *seṭṭhi* (merchant householder) Anāthapiṇḍika is often valorised in sculpture (*Pl.* 5.22), along with the Jīvakarama donated by Jīvaka, the contribution of Āmrapālī was apparently not deemed worthy of being carved in stone. At the early Buddhist sites such as Sāñcī and Bharhut, narrative reliefs do not feature Āmrapālī. We have very few depictions of the courtesan's gift.[61] A rare example is the relief from the Sīkrī *stūpa* in Gandhāra, now in the Lahore Museum. Vidya Dehejia remarks that the female figure on the left, pouring water to signify the ratification of a gift, indicates that the donation of the mango grove is the subject of this relief.[62] The date is not mentioned and it appears to be a later depiction, probably after the heyday of Kuṣāṇa art at Mathurā. Two similar panels in the Gāndhāran tradition, datable to the third century CE are housed in the Chandigarh Museum. One panel (*Pl.* 5.21) clearly shows a female on the left of Buddha with a water vessel in her hand. The artist wants to emphasise both Āmrapālī's status as a Buddhist convert and the supremacy of the Buddha's doctrine.

### 5.3.2 IDENTIFICATION

There is some controversy regarding the identification of the figures in the 'bacchanalian' scenes discussed above since they do not fit into the usual *alasyakanyā/śālabhañjikā* model (*Pls.* 6.22, 6.23, etc.). Unlike the latter these are set in some kind of a narrative, and are a part of a composition with multiple figures and usually, though not always, support a bowl. In some contexts they may correspond to *mithuna* or *kāmaloka* (*Pls.* 1.12, 1.13) panels. Initially they were interpreted as bacchanalian scenes and grouped with others such as the Palikhera and Gandhāra reliefs. Stacy was the first to identify these as bacchanalian.[63] Vogel followed him.[64] Both these early colonial scholars labelled these types of

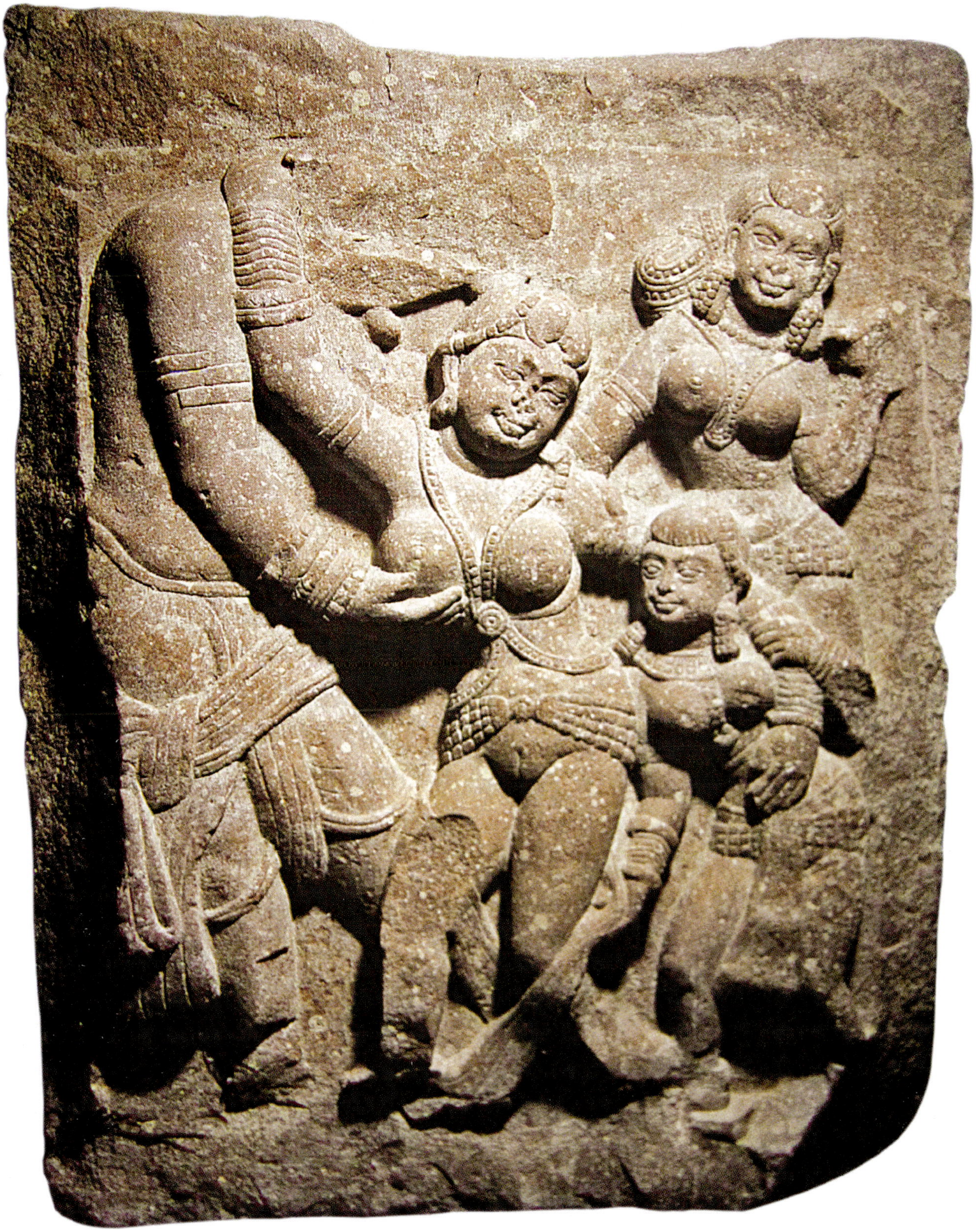

5.15 Male embracing the female figure intimately, with female companions, obverse of a double-sided panel, red Sikri stone, second century CE, Kuṣāṇa. Doris Wiener Collection.

scenes as representing either Silenus or bacchanalian activities, associating them with the Graeco-Roman examples found in the Gandhāra region. Most authors, including V.S. Agrawala[65] and Martha Carter,[66] followed this identification, labelling the Maholi and Naroli panels as bacchanalian scenes.

This attribution owed much to a cup held in the hand of the attendant figure. However, certain peculiarities in these reliefs cannot be explained simply by labelling them as women drinking wine, becoming intoxicated and thus losing control. The Maholi panel, for example, shows on the reverse a woman with her anklets either upraised or being taken off. Why should one particular combination of a kneeling woman accompanied by attendants (in a composition with or without one man hiding behind another) be interpreted as depiction of a woman becoming inebriated? There are other depictions, in stone and in terracotta, of women drinking either alone or in the company of a man. The answer to this may be sought in the Indian narrative/literary tradition, rather than in the suggestions of early European observers.

C. Sivaramamurti was the first to identify the Maholi relief as a scene from the Sanskrit play *Mṛcchakaṭikam* by Śūdraka.[67] According to him, the drunken lady on the obverse is located in a *veśāvāsa* (courtesan's house) where she is being offered wine by her maid in attendance even as she drops down drunk and is supported by a youth on the other side who in the Sivaramamurti's opinion represents "one of the many . . . lured by the charm of the *veśāvāsa*." Standing beside the principal female figure is the old *kuṭṭanī*, a picture of old age.

On the reverse, says Sivaramamurti, is the scene of a wealthy woman moving away from a couple of youths who are pursuing her. An umbrella held by her female attendant suggests her wealth and status. The anklets are pulled up tight to avoid jingling and she holds up her fluttering upper garment as if to cover her flower-bedecked coiffure.

According to him this scene tallies with the First Act of the play *Mṛcchakaṭikam*, which is based on the story of a poor, young merchant (*sārthavāhaho yuvā daridra*) Cārudatta, and a courtesan who is considered full of virtue (*guṇānurakta gaṇikā*) famous in Ujjayinī (Avantipur) as Vasantasenā.

As the story in the First Act unravels, the courtesan is pursued at night by Sakara, the worthless and foolish *rājaśalākā*, the king's brother-in-law. He is accompanied by the *viṭa*[68] and a *ceṭa*.

While in pursuit, the *viṭa* comes to know that Vasantasenā had fallen in love with the worthy Cārudutta whom she had seen in the temple of Kāmadeva, and decides to warn her. He warns her, saying, "True, Vasantasenā, that owing to this nocturnal darkness you cannot be seen, But, O timid one, this scent preceding from your chaplets (flower wreaths) in your hair, as well as (these your) jingling anklets will betray you" (tr. M.R. Kale).[69] Hearing this, Vasantasenā takes off her anklets and removes the scented flowers from her hair.

In the same Act, thinking in the darkness that he has caught Vasantasenā, Sakara first catches the *viṭa*, then the *ceṭa* and finally the maid servant (*dāsī*) of Cārudutta, Radanikā. He is otherwise a rather cowardly person, scared of the presence of another man. He keeps exclaiming, *bhava, bhava, manussaye, manussaye,* "Friend, friend, a man, a man" at the thought of being attacked or detected.[70]

It is very probable that the scene depicted on

the reverse of the Maholi relief (*Pl.* 5.5) illustrates this incident from the First Act of the play. The figure on the left, with anklets pulled up tight and covering her head, is Vasantasenā trying to suppress the sound of her anklets and the perfume of her floral chain. The two men standing one behind the other represent Saṁsthānaka/Sakara hiding behind either the *viṭa* or the *ceṭa* and clasping him, thinking he is Vasantasenā. The identification of the scene with an episode from *Mṛcchakaṭika* is supported by the presence of the diminutive female attendant in the middle who holds up an umbrella over the main female figure. In the play there is a mention of a female servant or *caṭi* who acts as a *chattradhāriṇī* (umbrella-bearer) who is to have a significant role in the Fourth Act of the play. In the First Act, however, Vasantasenā is alone, having lost her male and female servants, and is therefore an easy target for Sakara's uninvited advances.

The obverse of the sculpted scene from Maholi (*Pl.* 5.7), showing a kneeling figure with an attendant offering a cup, may well be a portrayal of a drunken woman who has lost control of her senses and is being helped to her feet by male and female attendants. However, another plausible explanation for this particular portrayal can be drawn from another scene from the play. This attribution is tentative, given that there is no direct and exact replication of the text in the image. The scenario one can suggest for the depiction is described below.

Vasantasenā is invited by Cārudatta to meet him in a garden, Puṣpakaraṇḍika *udyāna*, outside the city. Some confusion occurs with regard to carriages, due to which Vasantasenā goes off in Sakara's carriage. In the Puṣpakaraṇḍika *udyāna* Sakara strangles her, leaves her for dead and tries to pin the murder on Cārudatta. However, she is revived by a recently converted Buddhist monk, a *śākyabhikkhu*, and formerly a masseur-gambler whom Vasantasenā has helped. This *śākyabhikkhu* saves her from death and takes her to a *bhikkhuṇī saṁgha*, a community of nuns, where she seeks and receives temporary refuge. Thus, the obverse of the Maholi panel may illustrate an unconscious Vasantasenā being supported by the *śākyabhikkhu*. Perhaps a didactic message is being transmitted through this representation: that even a *gaṇikā* can be saved by faith and receive refuge in the faith, thus offering redemption to the wayward.

The sculpture in the Doris Wiener collection (*Pls.* 5.15, 5.16) is also probably related to this scene from the play, especially the reverse (*Pl.* 5.15), which can be interpreted as a man, probably Sakara, trying to constrain Vasantasenā while the *ceṭa* looks on. The woman on the left with her hand on her lips and holding a fan may be an attendant of Vasantasenā, added to the scene either to provide emphasis to the provocative nature of the moment, or as a witness. In the text, however, Vasantasenā is the only woman in the garden. On the obverse of this panel (*Pl.* 5.16) may be illustrated a scene from the Fourth Act, described above, where she is rendered unconscious by Sakara's brutality. Alternatively, as suggested by Stadtner,[71] it can be read as the last scene from the play, where Vasantasenā faints at the sight of preparations for Cārudatta's execution, he having been accused of killing Vasantasenā in order to steal her valuable jewellery. The tassels seen hanging in the background may suggest a stage, a *raṅgamaṇḍala*, complete with a curtain in the *nepathya*.[72]

It is possible to classify other panels from Naroli, Sanghol and other sites as matching either one or both the descriptions — the kneeling woman (*Pls.* 5.7 to 5.10) and the woman

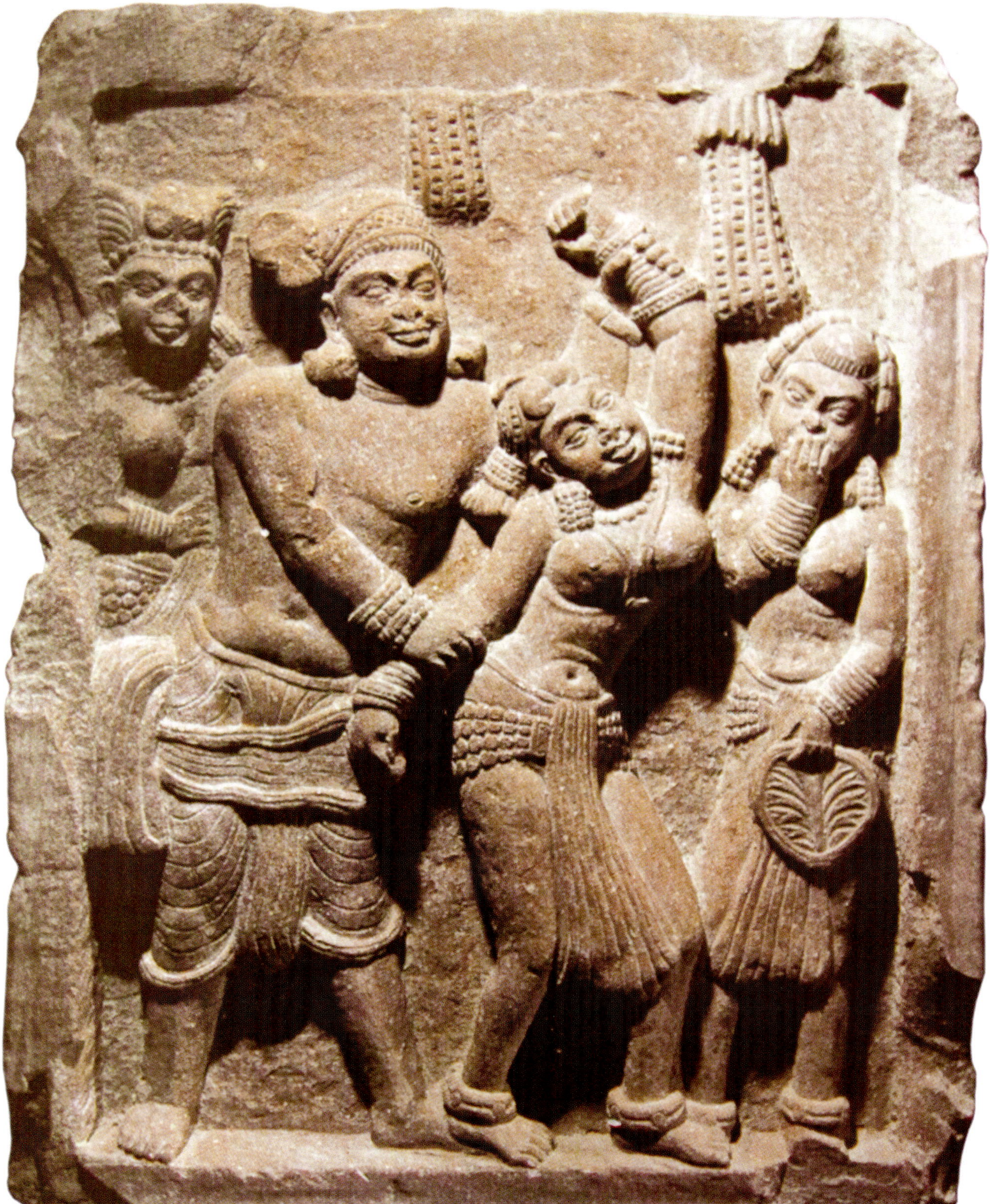

5.16 Male holding the arms of female in a constraining manner, with female attendants, tasseled curtain in background, reverse of a double-sided panel, red Sikri stone, second century CE, Kuṣāṇa. Doris Wiener Collection.

having her anklets below the knee (*Pls.* 5.6, 5.12, 5.13). An additional element seen in some of the reliefs is the depiction of one man hiding behind another man who probably illustrates the cowardly character of Saṁsthānaka hiding behind the *ceṭa* or the *viṭa* at the thought of being caught.

The identification of the sculptures is further strengthened by the no. 200 series from Begram (Excavations at Begram, DAFA catalogue) of which no. 78 has hitherto been identified as a dancing figure, though it is evidently akin to the compositions from Maholi, Naroli and Sanghol. Figure 76 No. 200b can be identified with the reverse of Maholi panel and is more like the private collection piece published by Stadtner, mentioned second in the list of reliefs given above. It is likely that this piece also suggests the removal of anklets (*nūpura*) by Vasantasenā.

The story of the play is visually elaborated further in the ivory panels from Begram. The depiction of two women with one child can be related to Act Six of the *Mṛcchakaṭika*. Radanikā, the maid, brings Rohasena, Cārudatta's son, who is crying, into Vasantasenā's presence. The latter consoles him by giving him her gold ornaments to cover his clay cart (thus justifying the name of the play, *Mṛcchakaṭika*, The Little Clay Cart). The other panels showing two women together may suggest one of the many discourses and dialogues that occur between Vasantasenā and Radanikā or Vasantasenā and other female attendants, *caṭṭīs*, in the course of the play.

An interesting gender portrayal may be posited on the basis of the identification of the above-described sculptural series with the story of the *Mṛcchakaṭika*. This suggests one of the choices that the sculptor/creator/designer made from his repertoire in order to depict a courtesan figure and a model through which a courtesan could be visually interpreted and depicted. In sheer physical terms, she is depicted as a typical youthful woman in Mathurā style of the Kuṣāṇa period: with ample hips, large globular breasts, and a slender waist she is a richly ornamented feminine figure standing in a *tribhaṅga* posture. The *gaṇikā*/*veśyā* is not depicted differently from the imagined and codified beings such as the *śālabhañjikās*, *yakṣīs* and performers of *aśoka dohada*.

The visual discourse seen in the portrayal of the main female figure in the *gaṇikā* reliefs and *yakṣī* figures, while constructed similarly in terms of physical elements, has some interesting points of departure. Unlike the *yakṣīs*/*śālabhañjikās*, who are usually sculpted as single figures, the courtesan/prostitute is seen within an ensemble of figures consisting of dependents and male admirers/pursuers, etc. which provides the relief with an internal context. This suggests that it was meant to depict some well-known story which may well have been that of the *Mṛcchakaṭika*. It is popularly believed that Śūdraka's play is based on an earlier version of the same plot, which is available in abbreviated form in a play composed by Bhāsa, the *Daridra Cārudatta*.[73] That two plays should both be based on the same story, and that the *Mṛcchakaṭika* is largely adapted from the latter, demonstrates that the story of Vasantasenā and Cārudatta was a popular theme.

Secondly, the figure is shown with a *chattra*, which in itself is an important part of the insignia signifying social and economic status. Thirdly, the central figure in the kneeling-woman-type relief is not looking at the viewer, and the gaze of all the other figures in the composition, except the old woman, is concentrated on the central figure. This firmly establishes the *gaṇikā* as the principal figure in the scheme. In fact, both the above points show that the kneeling woman and the woman with an umbrella over her are depicted as the key players, while some of the other figures, such as attendants, stand in a relationship of subordination and service to her.

Unlike the other narrative panels, where the main concern in depicting women is to illustrate an episode from the Jātaka or the *avadāna* stories, here the woman is the agency through which a message is sought to be communicated (see below). More light can be shed on this aspect if we analyse the context in which these panels were placed.

### 5.3.3. CONTEXT

The purpose of putting up sculptures depicting a courtesan is a vexed problem in so far as it shows a prostitute within religious edifices. Such a practice might normally be deemed inappropriate, especially in the context of Buddhism and Jainism which valorise celibacy and asceticism. (While there were different codes of behaviour for the monastic community and the laity, especially in relation to celibacy nevertheless asceticism was an ideal to be aspired for by all.) If we can establish the context in which these pieces are found, we may be able to determine the use to which they were put. We can also use this information to understand the manner in which men and women in contemporary society may have consumed art.

Unfortunately, the precise context of all the pieces cannot be determined since the original find spots have not always been recorded. The Maholi piece came from a monastery,[74] as did the one from the Kaṅkālī Ṭīlā. The former was probably a Buddhist establishment since a life-size statue of a *bodhisattva* was discovered in the vicinity; while the latter was a Jaina *stūpa* and monastery. The railing pillar from Sanghol constituted part of the *vedikā* scheme around the *stūpa*, one of the many with *yakṣī* figures. The Naroli piece too might come from a monastic context.

It is to be noted that none of the *gaṇikā* panels are found at the earlier pre-Kuṣāṇa sites such as Bharhut, Bodh-Gayā or Sāñcī, which were primarily Buddhist pilgrimage centres. They have all been found at sites of the Kuṣāṇa period that were associated with commercial centres such as Mathurā, Sanghol and Begram. As we have already noticed in other representational categories, such as Śrī-Lakṣmī/Dugdhadhāriṇī and *yakṣī* figures, there is an increased sexualisation of imagery over time in our period when art centres shift to more urban mercantile areas.[75]

Three of these Vasantasenā reliefs (the so-called bacchanalian scenes) have ornamented objects that functioned as stands for bowls. In the absence of textual collaboration from contemporary sources, various theories have been put forward by scholars regarding the possible use of the bowls set above these panels. Vogel suggested that they contained wine for some kind of bacchanalian ritual associated with Kubera or Pañcika. He makes this claim on the basis of the fact that similar Kuṣāṇa-period bowls have been discovered in the Mathurā region that show a single figure, a pot-bellied *yakṣa,* perhaps Kubera himself, carrying a bowl on his head (similar to example from Pītalkhorā – *Pl.* 6.9).[76] This cannot be substantiated, however, since no contemporary text is known to refer to a ritual or rituals in which bowls containing wine were placed on a sculptured stand.

According to J. van Lohuizen-de Leeuw, some of the *yakṣa* bowls may have been used for depositing flowers as offerings.[77] Alternatively, they may have functioned as bowls for the collection of offerings that were subsequently distributed to the monks and nuns belonging to the *saṁgha*. An architrave panel from Mathurā[78] depicts a monk pouring something into the bowl of another monk behind whom there is a line of monks, which seems to provide visual evidence of the practice of food distribution among the monastic community. It is also given in the Vinaya rules that alms in the form of food, robes and bowls be given to the monks.[79] However, the interpretation of the bowls crowning *yakṣa/gaṇikā* panels as representing the bowl of the Buddha has been contested by Ananda K. Coomaraswamy, who says that the stone vases are unlike the Buddha's alm bowl in shape, and also that the ornamentation of these was explicitly forbidden by the Vinaya.[80] He is convinced that they were part of some ablution ritual since the *yakṣa*s are connected with water. They may have been used for ritual purification before entering the precincts of the *vihāra/stūpa*.

While analysing the function of the *gaṇikā* panel we have to bear in mind that this representational type was used as a stand for bowls only at certain sites. At other places, such as Sanghol, Kaṅkālī Ṭīlā and Begram, it was used as a decorative motif, one among many others, on the *stūpa* railings. It may have been used in an entirely secular context as in case of Begram, where the ivories were used as furniture pieces, probably in a palace or a harem. Thus, we have multiple uses of the same representation. This suggests, on the one hand, the popularity of the motif based on the wide prevalence of the Vasantasenā story; on the other hand, it attests to the fact that the religious and the secular were not necessarily two hermetic categories but freely borrowed from each other and from a common cultural base.

### 5.3.4 EPIGRAPHIC EVIDENCE

We have quite a few references to prostitutes and courtesans in the literature of the post-Mauryan period, be it canonical Buddhist texts, the popular Jātaka stories, or secular literature. However, direct references to them are rare in epigraphic sources. Unfortunately, the relief panels we study here do not carry any inscriptions that could provide us with a clue to the meaning and function of these depictions.

An extensive study the *Epigraphia Indica* and *Corpus Inscriptionum Indicarum*, that record the names, occupations and lineages of the donors and donees, has revealed only three epigraphs that may refer to courtesans/prostitutes from this period. This scarcity is rather surprising given the frequent references to *veśyā*s in the Buddhist texts, both as temptresses and as donors. In fact, many famous *therī*s were formerly courtesans, *pūrṇa gaṇikā,* such as Āmrapālī and Ardhakāśī.

Chronologically perhaps the first epigraph that may mention a "prostitute" is the Jogīmaṛha cave inscription from Rāmgaṛh which has been dated to the second century BCE. According to Cunningham the inscription reads *sutanukā nāma devadāsīnyi taṁ kāmayi thā balanaseya devadinā nāma lūpadakhe*.[81] Lüders has interpreted this as "The temple servant (*devadāsī*) Sutanukā by name (the copyist) Devadinā by name the Balanaseya (native from Benares) loved her." Banerji-Sastri have translated the epigraph literally as "About the female servant of a monastery, Sutanukā by name, is a female servant of the monastery, Her, Varuṇaseva (perhaps a devotee of Varuṇa) caused to fall in love, Devadinā by name, officer-in-charge of offences against Vinaya."[82] Bloch however interprets Devadinā to be a sculptor rather than a scribe, a *rūpa-dakha* nor *lipi-dakha*. If we accept Bloch's interpretation, then this particular evidence of a *devadāsī* (a temple "prostitute") being connected to a sculptor is

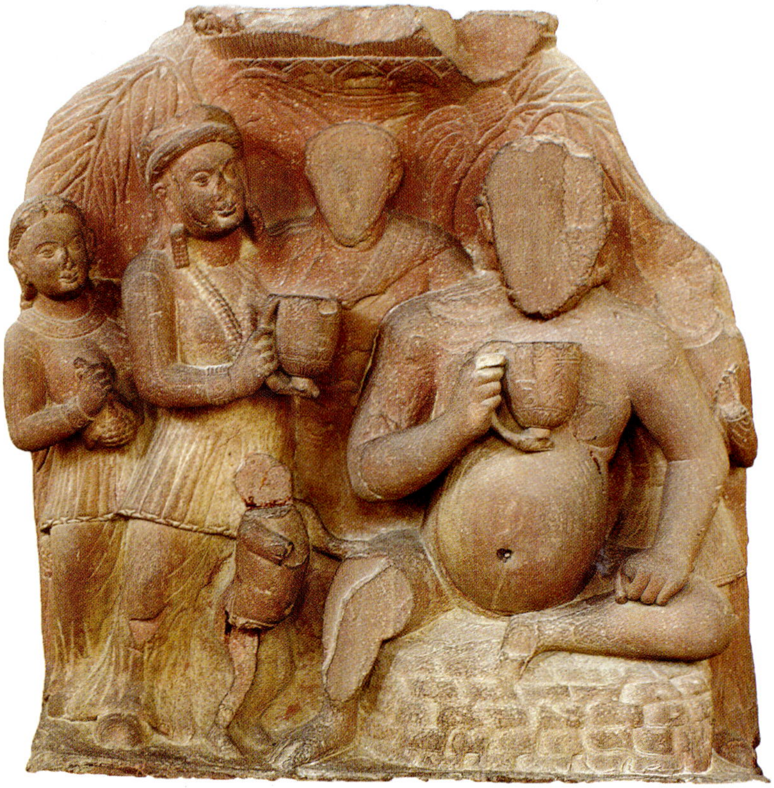

5.17 Corpulent man, perhaps Kubera, drinking from a cup with attendants, second century CE, Palikherā, Mathurā, GMM.

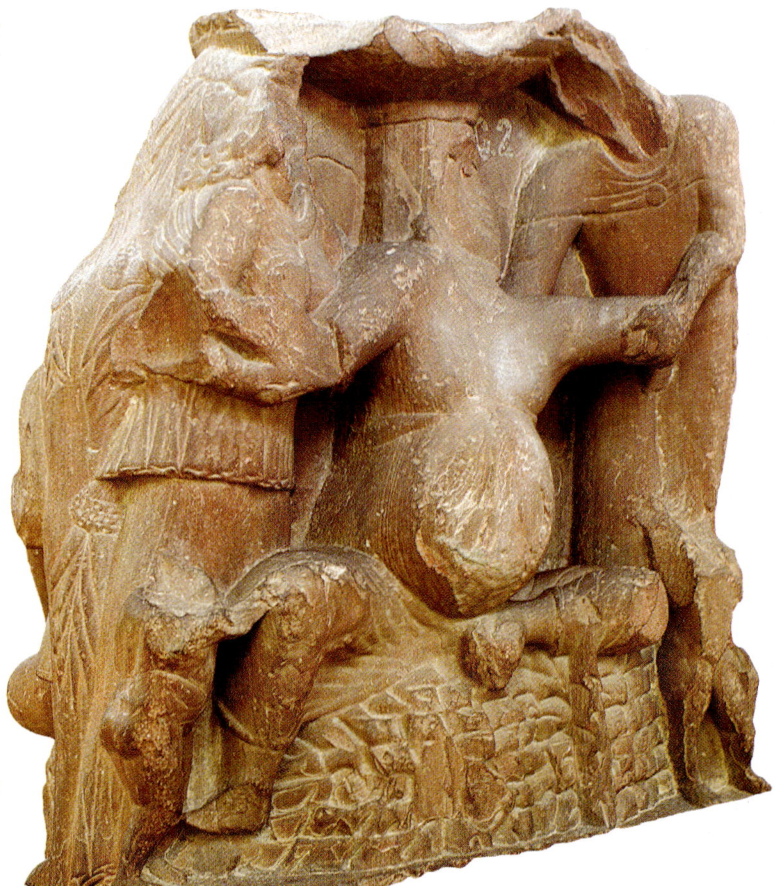

5.18 Reverse of *Pl.* 5.17, with drunken man(/) being assisted by companion.

significant.[83] This suggests that a prostitute enjoyed a certain socio-economic status in so far as a sculptor is not ashamed of admitting his love for a prostitute in an inscription. This lends certain respectability to the profession, which is also cautiously indicated in the texts such as the *Mṛcchakaṭika* where Cārudatta, once wealthy and a very respected merchant, falls in love with a courtesan, Vasantasenā. Secondly, a "prostitute" may well have served as a model for sculptures of various *yakṣīs*, *śālabhañjikās* and *alasakanyās* carved on the monuments of the period.

A related piece of epigraphic evidence on the role and position of the courtesans in contemporary society has been discovered in the vicinity of Jogīmaṛha, in an inscription in the Sitābeṅgā caves. The text reads — *adipayanti hṛdyaṁ. svabhāva guru kavayo ae ratayam . . . dūle vasantīya. hasavanabhūte. kadusphataṁ evaṁ alaṅg.* Bloch has read this as "poets venerable by nature kindle the heart at the spring festival of the full moon, when frolic and music abound, tie around their neck thick garlands of jasmine."[84] This epigraph is significant given the location and architecture of the Sitābeṅgā cave, which has a large semi-circular opening about 1.8m high with a vaulted roof. Its most important architectural aspect is the fashioning of the steps, some of them semi-circular in plan, to provide access to the rectangular chamber. According to S.P. Gupta it was probably a meeting place of the elite on festive occasions. Mirashi, while supporting this premise, elaborates that if one combines this with the evidence from the Jogīmaṛha cave, it is highly probable that the *nāgaraka*, urbanised young men, engaged in amorous sport in the company of courtesans-*gaṇikās*-*devadāṣī*[85] in caves and gardens just outside the town (such as the Puṣpakaraṇḍika *udyāna* mentioned in the *Mṛcchakaṭika*).

The second reference comes from Mathurā. It refers to an *āyāgapaṭṭa* discovered from Kaṅkālī Ṭīlā dedicated jointly by the *veśyā* Loṇaśobhikā, described as a senior *ajja*, and by her junior, Vasu. They dedicated this votive stone to the *arhat*s for the benefit of their spiritual adviser, parents and the community.[86]

The third reference is provided by a small terracotta plaque on which the only words apparently legible "*gaṇikā (?)dayasya*"[87] are engraved. On the left is a banana tree and in the centre is a woman clad in a *sāṛī*, which is supported by a girdle. She is seen turning her body towards the left. On the right can be seen a short woman with both hands raised above her head. There is a suggestion that the plaque was painted red. Given the fragmentary nature of the epigraph and the damage to the plaque itself, it is difficult to draw any conclusions from it except that *gaṇikās* were visible in the socio-religious sphere. Perhaps in this case the *gaṇikā* had the plaque made for some ritual linked to the banana tree and the red colour (traditionally associated with fertility rituals), or that she had donated it, or that she herself is depicted as part of some cultic ritual.

These references to *veśyā-gaṇikās* in inscriptions assume significance given the contradictory nature of the discourse regarding prostitutes that we find in literature. The *veśyā-gaṇikās* are reviled and respected at the same time. It is evident from the epigraphs that *veśyā-gaṇikās* were allowed access to the religious and social life of the period and were active in it. They participated as patrons (Loṇaśobhikā and Vasu); and the reference to Sutanukā suggests that they were also objects of love. They may have even posed as models for *yakṣī-śālabhañjikā* figures.

One can make an additional observation to the effect that none of the donations at the early

Buddhist sites (Bharhut, Bodh-Gayā, and Sāñcī) is made by courtesans. Nor do we find that there is any depiction of the kneeling-woman-type at these locations. Concomitantly, one notices a progressive decrease in the number of women donors from Bharhut to Mathurā. Though it would require further research to establish whether any connection exists between representation and patronage, the above two observations might suggest an increase in patriarchal dominance and commoditisation of women with a corresponding sexualisation of representation with depictions of *kāmaloka*, erotic *mithuna*s and *veśyā-gaṇikā*s.

### 5.3.5 GENDER DELINEATIONS

I do not contend that, by depicting Vasantasenā on the façade or elsewhere of a religious edifice, this figure of the courtesan is being privileged, either as an individual or as a representative of the class of *gaṇikā*s.

What is attempted is an explanation of the reason for using the particular theme and to retrieve and articulate the possible meanings informing this depiction, through an analysis of posture, ornamentation and the underlying context. The depiction of a courtesan in Buddhist and Jaina complexes is intriguing. The very setting in which it is found is an important indicator of how gender roles ascribed to non-wives were constructed.

The element of choice in selecting a story whose protagonist is a prostitute becomes significant in view of the existence of other representational possibilities that could be, and were, used to portray the danger posed by women to enlightenment or *nirvāṇa,* such as the episode of Sundarī and Nanda or of Māra's daughters.

This problem should be seen in relation to societal and religious structures. By the post-Mauryan period, prostitution was an established practice though its earliest evidence is found in the later Vedic period.[88] The fact that prostitutes are often mentioned and cautioned against, and that stories were built around them from seventh-eighth century BCE onwards, signifies that they existed in contemporary society and that rules therefore had to be made to deal with them. In the *Nāṭyaśāstra,* dealing with courtesans is called *bāhyopacāra,*[89] behaviour with outsiders, thus putting the *veśyā-gaṇikā*s beyond sanctioned societal space. In the *Mṛcchakaṭika* itself the courtesan is referred to as *prakāśanārī*, one who has been exposed[90] suggesting a public woman. Despite such disapproval by normative patriarchal tradition, *gaṇikās/veśyā*s were accepted, if not approved, by the socio-legal-political structure they inhabited.

The rules and attitudes relating to prostitutes and prostitution differ greatly in various textual traditions and the ideologies that the texts represent.[91] The *Manusmṛti,* which epitomises a highly stratified *varṇāśrama* patriarchal society, is unequivocal in its disapproval of prostitutes. It enjoins that one should not accept gifts from a king, those who run slaughterhouses, oil presses or taverns, nor from those who live off whorehouses; a priest should not accept food from a whore; the king should recognise whores, and others like them, as open thorns for people.[92] However, the attitude of Buddhist ideologues was not so severe and many prostitutes were accepted into its fold — as donors, and even into the *bhikkhuṇī saṁgha*.

Undoubtedly, the *gaṇikā*s commanded a certain status within the socio-economic order of the period. This is exemplified by the fact that contemporary texts cannot avoid mentioning the presence of prostitutes and the need to formulate rules on how an individual or a state should conduct himself/itself with a *veśyā* or *gaṇikā*. Women, especially high-caste women were not supposed to interact with them, as gleaned from only negative injunctions prohibiting contact with public women. The *Kāmasūtra* and *Nāṭyaśāstra* devote one section each to prostitutes, the former being commissioned at the request of the *veśyā*s of Pāṭaliputra. The *Arthaśāstra* also has a section on the economic affairs of *gaṇikā*s.

It is also significant to note that the *Arthaśāstra* mentions only one section of women under an economic category, namely the *gaṇikā*s, and advocates that a *gaṇikādhyakṣa* be appointed to oversee their income and expenditure along with their conduct with customers.[93] The *Arthaśāstra* mentions *rūpajīvā* (prostitute) as not only paying taxes but as an important instrument of the state in so far as they were to act as spies. It classes actors, buffoons, dancers, singers, players on instruments, mimics, rope dancers, jugglers, wandering bards, pimps and unchaste women in the same category as *gaṇikā*s, and says that the same rules will apply to all of them.

The economic importance of these prostitutes seems to have been matched by their social position. In the Buddhist texts many courtesans are mentioned as being initially famed for their beauty and later for their piety. *Gaṇikā*s like Ardhakāśī were responsible for the fame of their city as well as their community.[94]

One reason why *gaṇikā*s were accorded an important place in early Buddhist texts such as

5.19 Carved in high relief, the left woman appears to be in a *śālabhañjikā* posture while in the right are two servants attending the fainted woman who is seated below, highly ornamented in the style of Mathurā, ivory, late first to early third century CE, Begram. Kabul Museum No. 58.1.42.

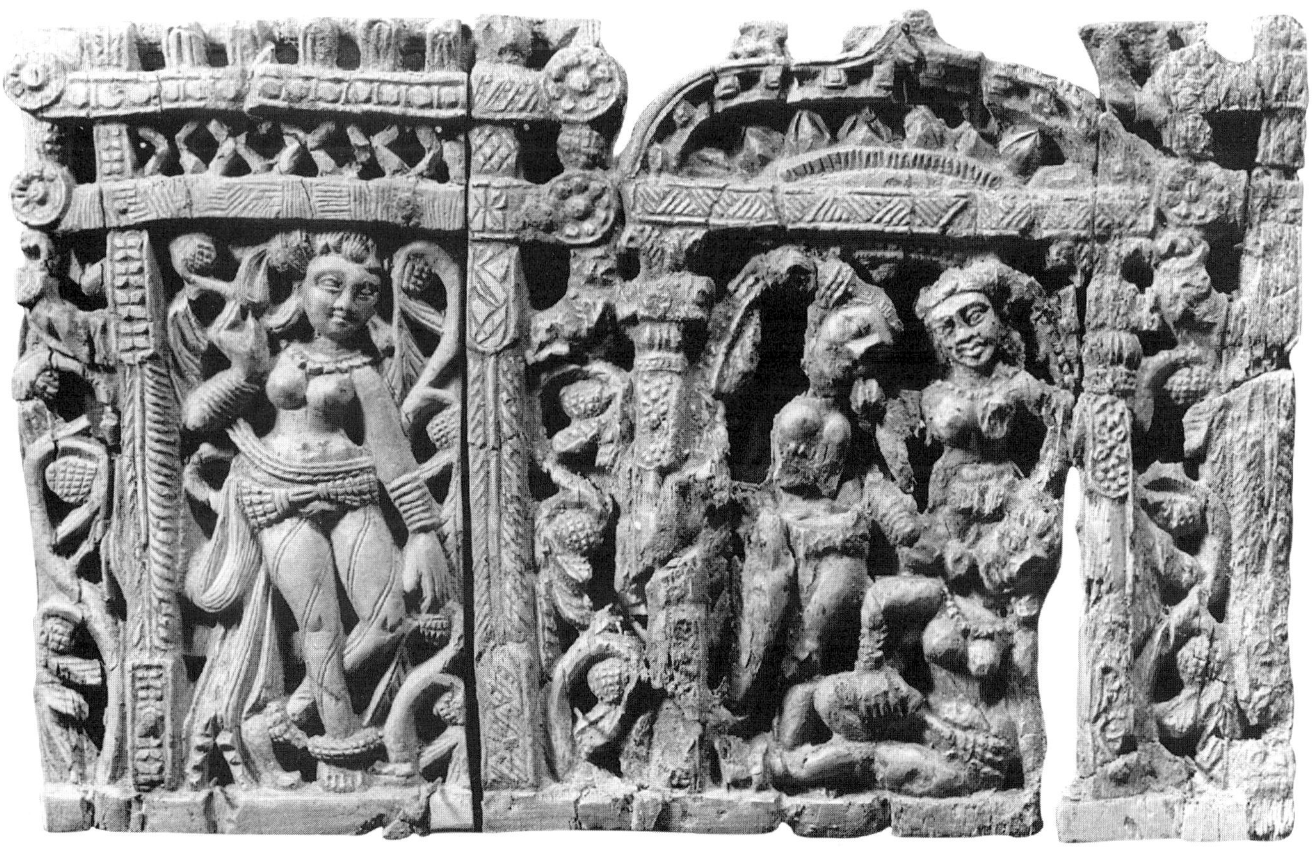

the *Therīgāthā* and the Jātakas was that many courtesans converted to the righteous path of Buddhism and joined the *bhikkhuṇī saṁgha.* Noteworthy examples of this are Vimalā, Ardhakāśī, Āmrapālī and Samā. The *Therīgāthā* commentary also suggests that these *gaṇikā*s were quite well connected to prosperous sections of society: for example, Sirimā was the daughter of a *seṭṭhi* of Varanasi.[95] In fact, if the Jātaka stories reflect even a fraction of contemporary reality then courtesans must have had considerable resources at their disposal.[96] Inscriptions from the period confirm that courtesans such as Loṇaśobhikā and Vasu made contributions to the Jaina order which must have considered them acceptable.

The *Theragāthā* (Psalms of the Monks) may provide us with an important clue as to why a *gaṇikā* was chosen to be portrayed on Buddhist structures. The text contains two significant verses attributed to *thera* Nāgasumala and *thera* Sundarasamudda. Nāgasumala is purported to have said, "Ornamented, well dressed, wearing a garland, anointed with sandal, a dancing girl dances to music in the middle of the road. I entered for alms. As I was going along I saw her ornamented . . . like a snare of death spread out. Then well reasoned thinking arose in me, the peril became clear, disgust with the world was established."[97] Sundarasamudda is even more explicit and says "ornamented, well dressed, carrying a garland, adorned, with her feet reddened with *lac*, having put on slippers, a courtesan. Taking off her slippers (standing before me with cupped hands spoke to me softly and sweetly with a smile) you are young to have gone forth. Abide in my teachings, enjoy human sensual pleasures. I shall give you wealth; I promise you truly; (if you do not believe me) I shall indeed bring fire. When we are both old, supported by sticks, we shall both go forth; both ways it will be a winning throw. . . . *And when I saw the courtesan beseeching me with cupped hands, ornamented, like a snare of death spread out,"*[98] making clear that a prostitute is like a snare that binds and tempts at the same time. Both the verses refer to temptation offered by the physical charms of a prostitute-woman, inviting the ascetic-man to leave the path of penance. The ever-present danger of the woman as epitomised by the prostitute is highlighted here. It is difficult to say whether the "feminine" *gaṇikā* figure in sculpture personifies Temptation in its totality or only female-induced enticement against which all followers of the faith, especially men, had to guard.

Courtesans also offered enticements to nuns: "What are you almswomen doing with the holy life? Why not now enjoy the pleasures of the senses, and join the holy life when you are old."[99]

The *Therīgāthā*, which consists of verses supposedly composed by senior nuns, sheds light on the state of mind of some of the *gaṇikā*s who left their profession to join the *bhikkhuṇī saṁgha*. *Therī* Ardhakāśī says "My wages (of prostitution) were as large as the (revenue of the) country of Kāśī; having fixed that price, the townspeople made me priceless in price. Then I became disinterested in my figure and being disgusted I was disinterested in it. . . . The Buddha's teaching has been done."[100] Vimalā, the former *gaṇikā* says "Intoxicated by my (good) complexion, my figure, my beauty and fame haughty because of my youth, I despised other women. *Having decorated this body, very variegated, deceiving fools, I stood at the brothel gate, like a hunter having spread out a snare.* Showing my ornamentation. *Many a secret place (referring to private body parts) was revealed* (emphasis mine). I did various sorts of conjuring, laughing at many people. Today (that same) I, having wandered for alms with shaven head, clad in the outer robe, am seated at the foot of a tree, having obtained the stage of non-reasoning."[101] The idea of standing at the brothel gate, luring unwary customers through ornamenting and embellishing of the female form seems similar to the role that majority of relief panels played. These were positioned as bowls at the entrance or were on the doorjambs of monastic establishments. The signal to the viewer, unlike that given by *gaṇikā* at the brothel gate, was not to entice but to warn. That they may have unintentionally also attracted male spectators[102] passing by the monument in an urban environment is a probability we should consider. Āmrapālī's verses[103] also repeat the idea of the impermanence of a beautiful female body as if to instruct the viewer about the transience of life. Āmrapālī repeatedly mentions her youthful beauty and its transformation into an ugly old frame with withered breasts, thinning hair, foul odour and wrinkled skin. In the Maholi panel described above, the impermanence of youth and beauty can be seen visually constructed through the contrast between the young beautiful central figure and the old figure standing next to her in the kneeling-women panels. She is shown with all the signs of old age. Disgust with superficial elements such as physicality and this-worldly aspect is sought to be created through the beauty of the body in the Buddhist ideology in text, oral tradition and art, especially of the prostitute.

The presence of the old woman with drooping breasts and wrinkled face next to Vasantasenā in the depictions discussed above, such as the Maholi panel, is also significant. As pointed out by Sivaramamurti, it highlights the attractiveness of the latter.[104] There existed alternatives to the voluptuous portrayal of women. Thus, we see that not all women are shown as young and beautiful. The body itself is a signifier that carries social meanings in representation by a process of repeated identification with the normative; and also a consistent objectification of deviations from these norms.[105] Thus, through the relentless process of materialising, a body acquires its signification, it comes to seem fixed and natural.[106]

In the light of this conceptualisation, it is significant that it is the "female" body of a *gaṇikā*, which was recreated through the repeated use of the same depiction. We have seen in the Introduction that the body of women in general, and prostitutes in particular, are of the greatest importance in deciding sexual availability as well as her place in social classification. In contemporary texts, synonyms used for *veśyā* or prostitute are *rūpajīvā* or *rūpajīvaṇī*, and her attendants are called *rūpadāsīs*.[107] Terms such as *rūpajīvā* imply a woman whose livelihood is dependent on her beauty (beautiful form). Thus, beauty and ornamentation are of primary importance in deciding the category to which an ordinary *veśyā* or an elite *gaṇikā* would belong. In such a case, alluring form is critical to the depiction of a prostitute in a relief sculpture.

In the *Arthaśāstra*, a prostitute is classified into first, middle and highest rank according to her beauty and splendid jewellery. If she were to lose beauty then she could become a nurse (*mātṛkā*), but if she were to lose her jewellery to a thief, then either she or the thief was to be fined.[108] In the *Kāmasūtra* also there is an attempt to combine economic and socio-sexual criteria as markers of status where women who earned their living through rendering sexual services are classified as *kumbhadāsī* (water carrier), *paricārikā* (female servant), *kulaṭā* (unchaste woman), *svairiṇī* (self-willed woman), *naṭī* (dancer),

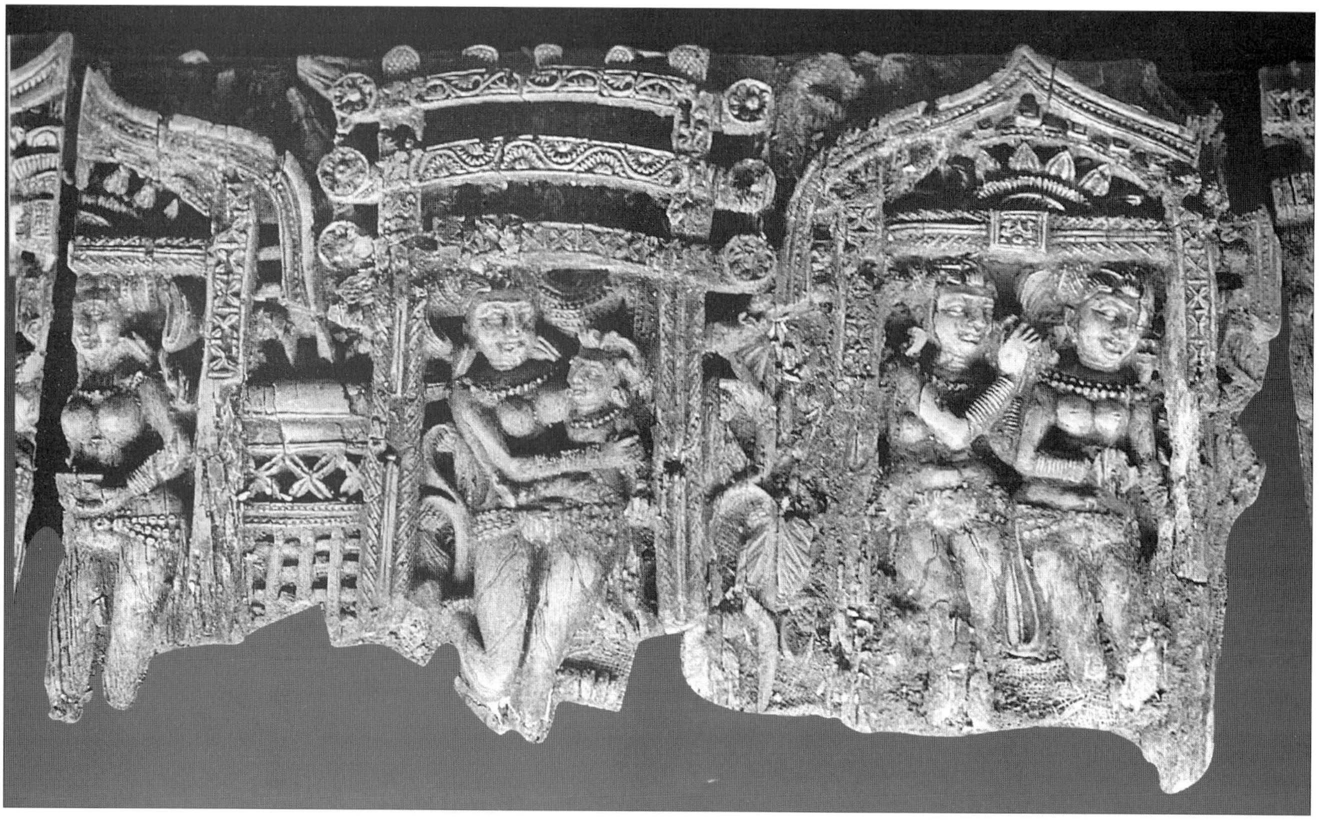

5.20 A *toraṇa* and *caitya* arched doorways, beneath which are seen mother and child in the central door and two standing women on either side, highly ornamented in the style of Mathurā, ivory, late first to early third century CE, Begram. Kabul Museum.

*rūpajīvā* (dependent on her physical charms) and *gaṇikā* (courtesan) who is at the top of the hierarchy.[109]

As mentioned before, the *Nāṭyaśāstra* is a very important text that devotes an entire chapter to *bāhyopacāra*, dealing with courtesans. Like the *Kāmasūtra*, it discusses the conduct of a *vaiśikaḥ* (specialist) who is especially adept at dealing with prostitutes, *veśyopacāra*. Women are classified on the basis of the stages of youth through dress, ornament and their limbs as well as [inner] qualities.[110] It is clear from the description of these four stages that the body and its ornamentation are of primary importance when it comes to imagining the female as a woman, especially as a public woman. According to the *Nāṭyaśāstra*, a woman in her primary youth has an enthusiasm for sexual acts and her assets are plump thighs, cheeks, hips and firm breasts conducive to (lit. charming in) love's pleasures.[111] Similarly, full and round limbs, full breasts and slender waist — or the lack of these — characterised secondary stages. It is said that a woman with reduced female charms because of slightly pale cheeks, hips, lips, breasts, as well as reduced enthusiasm for sexual acts, is considered an enemy of sexual intercourse.[112] While good clothes and jewellery are desirable for housewives also, their importance for women who earn their living by selling their allure, youth and body is more.

The symbolism of clothing and jewellery, whether employed to conceal, accent or expose the body beneath, carried clear and immediate messages for the viewer concerning not only the reproductive and erotic availability of the wearer, but also her or his position with the community, society and family. In this case at least we find that jewellery and clothes are of vital importance, and moot not only for the identification but also for all that they denote — wealth, youth and beauty. The plot of the play is built around the depositing of Vasantasenā's jewellery with Cārudatta, its subsequent theft and recovery, and Cārudatta's indictment for stealing it and murdering Vasantasenā. In the sculpture itself we see the female figure profusely bejewelled with rings on all her fingers, anklets, *mekhalā*, etc. which may have been an artistic convention of the time or may have carried special meaning related to the story.

For religious traditions, such as Jainism and Buddhism, that privilege asceticism and celibacy for the monastic orders and as an ideal for the laity, prostitutes posed a double threat — that their (sexual) availability posed a constant temptation, and that this sexuality was not productive. However, in the Buddhist Jātakas courtesans/sex workers are not represented as being sexually insatiable,[113] which is one of the characteristics of *strīsvabhāva*.[114] Sex work is considered their occupation and therefore the emphasis is more on the economic transactions involved than on condemnation of the *gaṇikā*s/*veśyā*s on moral grounds, perhaps because sexual conduct is their legitimate conduct and not the deviant behaviour of an errant wife. Thus their sexuality does not threaten the legitimate social order.

This sexuality of a prostitute is not considered "productive"; especially when she produces male children. Such children were known as *bandhula*s (bastards).[115] In the *Mṛcchakaṭika*, Maitreya asks them who they are and their reply is, "We are indeed *bandhula*s that sport about like cubs of elephants, being reared in other people's houses, fed on others' food, begotten by other men upon strange women, enjoying others' riches, possessing no (particular) merit to speak of."[116] In the early Buddhist tradition, instances of prostitutes like Salavatī, the courtesan of Rājgṛha and courtesan of Kauśāmbī ordering that their male children be put in a winnowing basket and cast away on a dust heap are recorded.[117] In the *Arthaśāstra* it is enjoined that teachers (*naṭuva*) shall train the sons of prostitutes to be actors (*raṅgopajīvī*).[118]

Significantly, a later text suggests that though sexual relation with one's own wife is necessary for the perpetuation of the family, sexual intercourse with courtesans is necessary for avoiding sickness.[119] The prostitute makes the wife possible.[120] The institution of prostitution is a channel for permitting and celebrating male sexuality on one hand. On the other prostitution by its inherent promiscuity provides a symbolic opposition to the chastity of the wife. Through the institution of female prostitution, male sexuality is allowed and legitimised and female sexuality controlled.

It is clear that in contemporary patriarchal society the wife was the norm. At the end of the play Vasantasenā is accorded the title of *vadhū*,

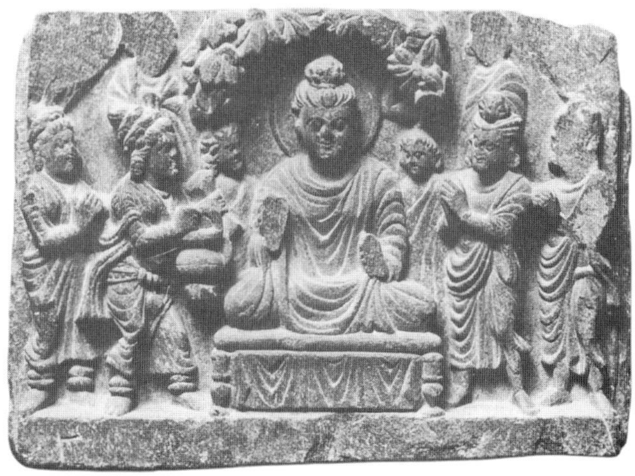

5.21 Gift of Āmbrapālī, Gandhāra, third century CE, blue schist. GMAG.

wife of Cārudatta, by the new king Āryaka.[121] Thus in the play we have a resolution that restrains and redirects the sexuality of the prostitute by according her marital status. In the *Therīgāthā* the solution is denial of sexuality by joining the *bhikkhuṇī saṁgha*. In the Jātakas, unconverted *gaṇikā*s may come to an uncomfortable end such as dishonour and death, yet there is a "relative absence of stereotyping and the creation, transmission and preservation of varied representations" of courtesans that allows us to move beyond the debate on *strīsvabhāva*, women's nature.[122] As pointed out earlier, unrestrained sexuality in the *gaṇikā/veśyā* is not seen in terms of misogynist *strīsvabhāva* or stereotyping, as it forms part of the role to be performed by her. This is, however, never visualised in the narrative tradition at Bharhut, Sāñcī or other early Buddhist sites, where some Jātaka tales dealing with errant wives and ogresses are often themes chosen for representation. In the case of the Jātaka tradition, through the figures of the errant wives and ogresses, there is a stereotyping and reliance on misogynist concepts such as *strīsvabhāva*.

We should also consider the bacchanalian element in the portrayal, in so far as depictions of women drinking intoxicating liquor. It strengthens the image of evils connected to the material world, especially corrupting attachment to loose women. This becomes clear when we examine various negative references to drinking in literature, both by men and women. It is women, however, who are warned against drinking and it is said in both Brāhmanical and Buddhist literature that one of the signs of an undesirable wife is a woman who drinks too much. It is also said that women have a proclivity towards inebriation and it is likely that a bad wife or mistress will squander wealth on drinking. Even if we are to read a bacchanalian aspect in the panels then the overwrought and uncontrolled lolling of the main female figure may be a reminder to the viewer of the negative consequences of transgressing the conventional female behavioural pattern.

The Vasantasenā series is vital for us because it highlights the ambiguous position of women in society and art. On one hand the very choice of the subject has significant gender indicators built into it that highlight ideal gender roles and the transgression of them. On the other hand, wealth and status associated with the *gaṇikā*s is reinforced in such a depiction through her entourage of dependents and admirers. Even if we do not concede that the reliefs depict an episode from the *Mṛcchakaṭika*, we have to admit that the woman is central to the composition and is accompanied by clearly subservient men who help and support her. This is in contrast to other so-called bacchanalian scenes such as the Palikhera piece in which the central figure is that of the pot-bellied male figure identified with Kubera.

There is also certain powerlessness built into some of the depictions. In one of those noticed by Stadtner, now in the Doris Wiener Inc. collection, the man is shown constraining a woman which carries a clear message of the superior physical male power (maybe that of Sakara overpowering Vasantasenā) though this is not necessarily morally justified in the text of the play itself. The sexual availability of the courtesan is also an issue. In the play itself the *viṭa* says to Vasantasenā that it is her duty as a courtesan to be available to all, without favour.[123] The *Arthaśāstra* also emphasises this injunction and prescribes

5.22 The gift of Anāthapiṇḍika, great railing, first century BCE, Bharhut. Indian Museum, Kolkata. (facing page)

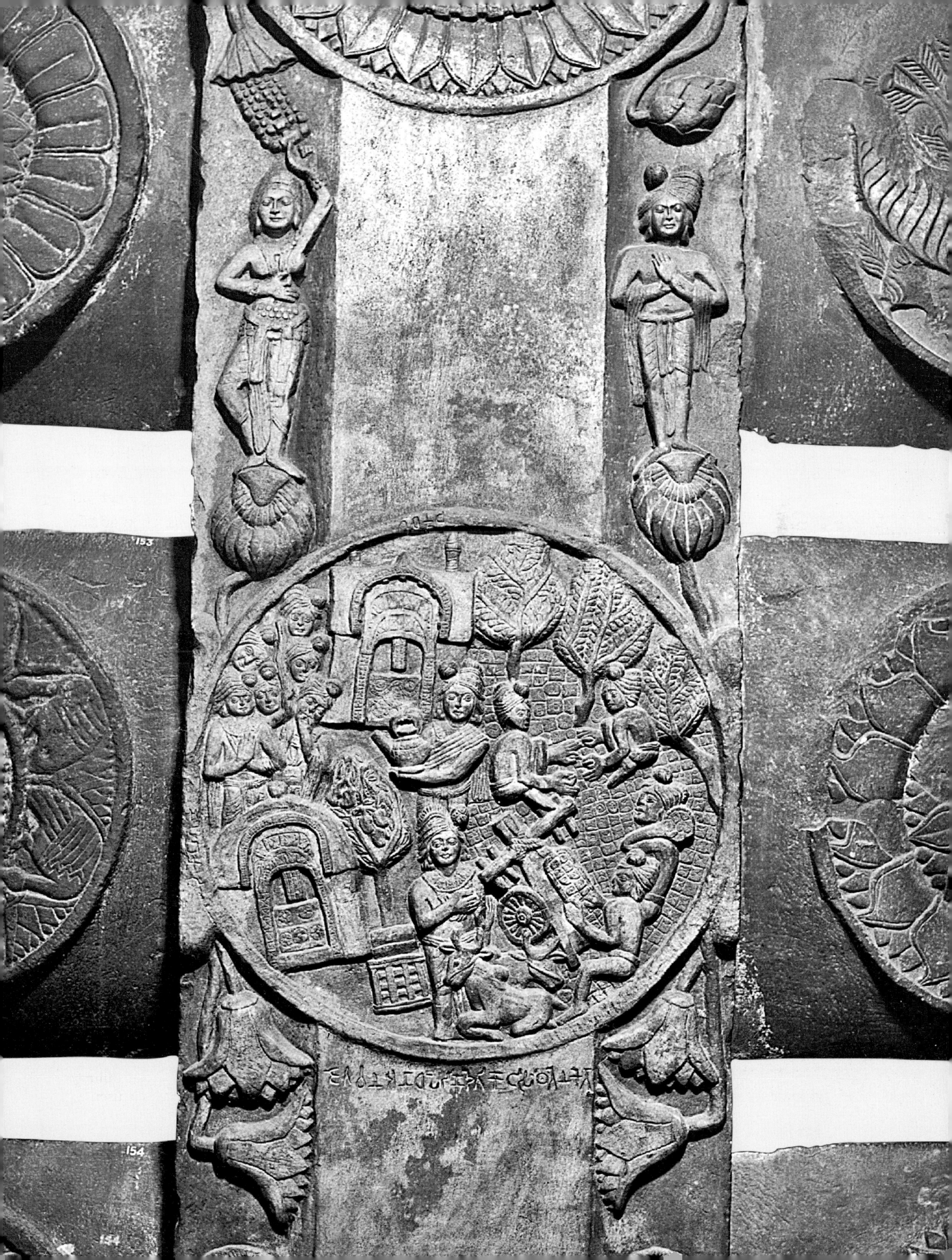

that if a *gaṇikā* accepted money from a customer and then refused to co-operate then this shall be dealt with as an offence. However, in the play itself Vasantasenā refuses to sell her body to the Saṁsthānaka or to anyone else.[124]

In the *gaṇikā* depictions in the relief panels, the sexual availability of a courtesan is indicated through the constituted body. Perhaps the message conveyed by such portrayals was the temptation personified by female figures, and the resistance to it by ideal ascetic males. Thus in this particular depiction we can see the interplay of beauty, sex, gender, power and asceticism. The danger of feminine beauty is epitomised by the *gaṇikā* of the period with her knowledge of the arts and culture. She is the ultimate lure that a monk/layman is offered to step away from his chosen path of renunciation/non-attachment. Given this context, is it probable that the visual representation of the Vasantasenā story functioned as a warning in more than one way? That is, did it not only convey the temptation offered by women, but also to women and warned of the dangers of transgressing social norms and stepping into the category of the unguarded women, becoming non-wives? A sub-text of the *gaṇikā* being put forth as warning or as an example of temptation may have informed the depiction which also indicated their obvious opulence, their attractiveness, their admirers and a seeming valorisation of their sexuality.

While both the nun and prostitute are problematic within the emerging engendered identities, the prostitute finds relatively more space in the art of the period. This may seem to suggest that unrestrained sexuality was seen to be better or at least less problematic than sexuality denied altogether? We have found many instances where women's sexuality seems to be valorised and celebrated, even if it is through the agency of *gaṇikās/veśyās*. The *gaṇikā* fits in more adequately within conceptual notions of the times. Her sexuality and mobility, although problematic, is more easily contained and even celebrated or valorised within an overarching patriarchal normative structure. The social reality of the relative autonomy and economic strength of the prostitute is undeniable and has to be noted and accepted by most commentators. Their socio-sexual status has an element of charm and celebration and relative autonomy that is regulated through the state which represents the emerging patriarchal structures.

### Notes and References

1. *Nāṭyaśāstra* XXV, 74-9; Cowell, *Jātaka*, no. 418, 425.
2. Prostitutes had considerable economic resources at their command and were under the supervision of a mother, *mātū* who may have been the manager of the *veśāvāsa* or the prostitute's house. *Mṛcch.* Act IV, pp. 133-35. The nuns had considerably less autonomy. They needed the consent of their parents, husbands or male relations before they could become nuns. As nuns they had to function under an elder nun and obey the Buddhist *bhikkhuṇī saṁgha* rules, which as a whole had to be subservient to the Buddhist *bhikkhu saṁgha*. See, I.B. Horner, *Women Under Early Buddhism*, New Delhi: Motilal Banarsidass Publishers Pvt. Ltd., 1999 (reprint), pp. 118-161.
3. *Mbh.* VI. 5766 a courtesan — *vara*, a harlot, courtesan; V.S. Apte, *The Practical Sanskrit- English Dictionary*, New Delhi: Motilal Banarsidass, 3rd edn. 1965 p. 805, *varakanyakā* — a girl taken in turn, a harlot, a courtesan. There are many words with *vara* like *varamukhyā* denoting the head or chief of a number of courtesan or *varasundarī*, *varaṇaseva*, practice of harlotry or a set of harlots.; ibid., 882, *gaṇikā* — a harlot, a courtesan, also a female elephant or a kind of jasmine flower. *Gaṇeru* is also a female elephant or a prostitute. *Rūpajīvā* — a harlot, a prostitute, a courtesan; *veśyā* — a harlot, a prostitute, a courtesan, a concubine. In *Pali English*

*Dictionary*, p. 241 *vesi* and *vesiyā* — a woman of low caste, a harlot, a prostitute; *gaṇikā*, courtesan.

4. *AŚ*, II.XXVII. 25.
5. Cf. I. B. Horner, op. cit., pp. 231-32.
6. *Vinaya Piṭaka*, IV, pp. 259-60, 278.
7. L. Sternbach, "First Supplement to Veśyā Synonyms and Aphorisms", in *Bharatiya Vidya*, Bombay, 1947, pp. 62-63 who quotes from *Kāmasūtra*, 8.103, *Śānti-Parva*, 4052.
8. Vijaya Ramaswamy, *Walking Naked, Women, Society and Spirituality in South India*, IIAS, Shimla, 1997, pp. 10-11.
9. *Mṛcchakaṭikam*, Act I, pp. 26-27.
10. Ibid., Act I, verse 67.
11. Ibid., Act III, verse 7: Kumkum Roy, "Representing the Courtesanal Tradition: An Exploration of Early Historical Texts", in *JRAS* of Mumbai, vols. 77-78 for 2003, *NŚ*, p. 124; *MWSE*, a public woman or a prostitute, p. 653.
12. *Epigraphia Indica*, vol. X, Lüders List (henceforth LL), nos. 573, 589. Also Upinder Singh, "Sanchi: The History of Patronage of ancient Buddhist establishment", *IESHR*, vol. XXXIII, no. 1, 1996, pp. 1-37.
13. LL Nos. 1240, 1242, 1315.
14. LL Nos. 573, 589.
15. LL No. 38.
16. Barua, *Bharhut*, vol. 1, Patna: Indological Book Corporation, 1979 (reprint), p. 45.
17. National Museum, *Treasures of the National Museum*, Delhi, 1985; J. Ph. Vogel, *Archaeological Museum at Mathura*, Delhi: Indological Books House, 1971; Pramod Chandra, *Stone Sculpture in the Allahabad Museum: A Descriptive Catalogue*, Poona: American Institute of Indian Studies, 1970; *Museum Für Indische Künst, Berlin, Catalogue*, Berlin: Staatliche Museen Preussischer Kulturbesitz, 1986 are some examples.
18. *Saṁyutta Nikāya*, 5. Māra finding her tries to frighten her with wiles of seducers. Knowing it to be Māra she replies, "Were there a hundred seducers, a thousand seducers, I fear not thee, for all my mind is wholly self-controlled."
19. GMM. No. H.1 and GMM No.39.2868, *c*. first century CE, near Mahavan, Mathurā.
20. Cf. Susan L. Huntington, "Aniconism and The Multivalence of Emblems: Another Look", *Ars Orientalis*, vol. 22, 1992, fig 5.
21. Ht 2'22", width 3'5 ½"
22. Fragment of a *stūpa* railing, buff sandstone, ht. 53 cm, 1.1m, 24 cm. Acc. No. KS.08, Kauśāmbī, Śuṅga, Kausambi Museum, Allahabad University; Aruna Tripathi, *The Buddhist Art of Kauśāmbī (From 300 BCE to CE 550)*, New Delhi: D.K. Printworld Pvt. Ltd., 2003, p. 66, fig. 28.
23. V.S. Agrawala, "The Terracotta Figurines from Ahichchhatra", in *Ancient India*, no. 4, pp. 150-51.
24. See *supra*, chapter 3, Section 1 for Mahāprajāpati. On the reluctance of Buddha to admit women into the Order see I.B. Horner, op. cit., pp. 104-06.
25. Padmanabhan Jaini, *Gender and Salvation: Jaina Debates on the Spiritual Liberation of Women*, New Delhi: Munshiram Manoharlal, 1991, p. 3.
26. *The Patimokkha*, ed. William Pruitt and tr. K.R. Norman, Oxford: Pali Text Society, 2001, p. 119.
27. Ibid.
28. I feel that we cannot view the naked or partially clothed body as a traditional practice without significant gender indices built into it. See Chapter, Gender and Art, Section on nakedness.
29. *The Patimokkha*, p. 127.
30. Ibid., p. 171.
31. Ibid., p. 181.
32. Ibid., p. 171.
33. Kumkum Roy, "Women and Men Donors At Sanchi: A Study of The Inscriptional Evidence", in K.D. Bajpai, ed., *Position and Status of Women in Ancient India*, vol. I, Varanasi, 1992, p. 214.
34. I.B. Horner, op. cit., p. 157.
35. For further details see, I.B. Horner op. cit., p. 119.; Vijaya Ramaswamy, op. cit., Introduction.
36. For example, at Bharhut, instead of the nun there is a crowd of kings, ministers and people at the bottom of the ladder. In the various versions of the story, he was greeted upon his descent by

Sāriputra the Elder or by vast congregation of men and gods. Bharhut, Western Gate, Corner, Ajātaśatru Pillar, Right Side, Middle bas relief; cf. B.M, Barua, *Bharhut*, pt. II, p. 38, pl. XVII.

37. Infra, Chapter 4.
38. The identification was first made by C. Sivaramamurti, *Indian Sculpture*, Delhi, 1961, pp. 36-37. It has since then been accepted by many authors. Stanislaw J. Czuma, *Kushana Sculpture: Images From Early India*, Cleveland: The Cleveland Museum of Art, 1985, pp. 109-10; D. Stadtner, "The Little Clay Cart in early Mathura" in *Orientations*, vol. 27, no. 1, 1996.
39. *Kuṣāṇa Art from Saṅghol*. p. 27.
40. Hackin, J. and Others, *Nouvelles Recherches Archeologiques A Begram (Ancienne Kapici)*, 1939-1940, Paris: Imprimerie Nationale, 1954.
41. It measures 104 cm in height and is 76 cm wide and has been dated to the Kuṣāṇa era, second century CE. It has often been published (fn. 38) and is housed in the National Museum (Acc. No. 2800).
42. Donald M. Stadtner, op. cit., figs. 2a and 2b, p. 40. It is comparable in size with the Maholi panel and measures 102 cm in height and is 88 cm wide. It is also of red Sīkrī sandstone.
43. Ibid., figs. 3a and 3b, p. 41. Height 113 cm, width 92 cm.
44. Ibid., figs. 4a and 4b. p. 42. It is 105 cm high and 40 cm wide.
45. Kneeling woman supported by two male companions and a diminutive attendant, red Sīkrī stone, Mathurā, Indian Museum, Calcutta, height 57 cm and width 54 cm. It is of red Sīkrī stone and was discovered from a village near Mathurā.
46. D. Stadtner, op. cit., fig 9, p. 46; *ASIAR*, Calcutta, 1880, vol. XI, Pl. XX.
47. Upper panel of a jamb, Kaṅkālī Ṭīlā, Mathurā, red sandstone. GMM No. 371. Its height is 85 cm.
48. *Kuṣāṇa Art from Sanghol*, p. 27.
49. D. Stadtner, op. cit., fig. 5a and 5b, p.43. It is 70 cm high, with a width of 54 cm and a depth of 21 cm.
50. J. Hackin and others, op. cit.
51. Ibid., figs. 78 and 200 r, q.
52. Ibid., fig. 76, No. 200 b.
53. Ibid., figs. 79, No. 200, d, c, q.
54. Ibid., fig. 75, No. 200.
55. J. Fergusson and J. Burgess, *The Cave Temples of India*, Oriental Books Reprint Corporation, 1969 (rpt.), Pl. XX.
56. Devangana Desai, *Erotic Sculptures of Early India: A Socio-Cultural Study*, New Delhi: Tata Mcgraw Hill, 1985, p. 23. She identifies it as a bacchanalian scene, portraying a drunken woman supported by her lover. This theme was popular in Mathurā and other places in the same period. Couples depicted here are of mildly amorous kind. This cave of Nasik was a *vihāra* where monks stayed after renouncing worldly pleasures. Apparently there is contradiction between the inscription on the entrance and the erotic depictions. The inscription states "Renunciation of pleasure (*bhoga*) of all kinds." By the second century CE *mithuna* was considered an auspicious motif, and therefore portrayed on the door of temple. This is not mentioned specifically in any *śilpaśāstra* but it is recommended in Jaina Sūtra literature that *yugalika*s be carved on religious edifices.
57. Now in Allahabad Museum.
58. J. Ph. Vogel, *Mathura Museum Catalogue*, C2, p. 83. This is 5' 5" high, the width at the base is 3' 5" and the thickness is 1' 6".
59. See Martha C. Carter, "Dionysian Aspects of Kushana Art", *Ars Orientalis*, vol. 7, 1968, pp. 121-46.
60. Baurua, *Bharhut*, pt. II, pp. 42-44, Pl. XVI and pp. 27-31, Pls. XXVIII and LVIII.
61. E.g. Gift of Āmrapālī, Gandhāra, blue schist. GMAG 1109.
62. Vidya Dehejia, *Discourse in Early Buddhist Art: Visual Narratives of India*, New Delhi: Munshiram Manoharlal, 1997, p. 15.
63. L.R. Stacy, "Note on the Discovery of relic of Grecian Sculpture in Upper India", in *JRASB*, vol. 5, 1836, pp. 567-70.
64. J. Ph. Vogel, op. cit., C2.
65. V.S. Agrawala, "A New Bodhisattva and A

Bacchanalian Group from Mathura", in *JISOA*, 1939, pp. 67-72.

66. Martha C. Carter, op. cit., pp. 121-46.

67. C. Sivaramamurti, *Indian Sculpture*, New Delhi: Allied Publishers, 1961, pp. 36-37.

68. *MWSE* p. 961, describes a *viṭa* as a voluptuary, sensualist, bon vivant, boon companion, rogue, knave. He resembles in some respects the *vidūṣaka*, being represented generally as a parasite on familiar terms with his associates but at the same time accomplished in the arts of poetry, music and singing. Incidentally, in the play he speaks in Sanskrit while Sakara speaks in Ardhamāgadhī. This seems to indicate that he was higher on the cultural scale than the king's brother-in-law.

69. *Mṛcch.*, Act I, p. 40 *kāmaṁ pradoṣatimireṇa na dṛśyase tvaṁ, saudāmanīva jaladodarasandhilīnā, tvaṁ sūcayiṣyati tu mālyasamudbhavoyaṁ, gandhaśca bhīru mukharāṇi ca nūparāṇi.*

70. Ibid., p. 47.

71. D. Stadtner, op. cit., pp. 43-44.

72. *Nāṭyaśāstra*, chapter II.

73. V.V. Mirashi, *Indological Research Papers*, Nagpur: Vidarbha Samsodhan Mandal, 1982, pp. 17-32 is of the opinion that the *Mṛcchakaṭika* is the original play from which Bhāsa adapted his abridged version, the *Daridra Cāruduttam.*

74. V.S. Agrawala, *Mathura Museum Handbook*, Allahabad 1939, p. 71.

75. See Chapter 1 Gender and Art.

76. J. Ph. Vogel, op. cit., chapter 5, p. 87, also see chapters 8, 9, 10, 11, 24, 25, 26, 27, 28 and 29. V.S. Agrawala, *Mathura Museum Catalogue: Architectural Pieces in Mathura Museum*, Varanasi: Prithvi Prakashan, 1963, Catalogue, nos. KT 55, 138, 240, 242, 346 and 499; also see K.D. Bajpai, "A New Inscribed Image of a Yaksa", in *India Antiqua*, Leiden, 1947, pp. 7-8 The inscription reads, "Mahārāja, Graha Yakṣa, called Dharmanitya, makes it known that in his hand is the *prasāda* of the god."

77. J. van Lohuizen-de Leeuw, *Indian Antiquary*, 1947, pp. 234-35.

78. V.S. Agrawala, *Mathura Museum Catalogue: Architectural Pieces in Mathura Museum,* Varanasi: Prithvi Prakashan, 1963, fig XXXV, b.

79. I. Horner, op. cit., pp. 218-29.

80. A.K. Coomaraswamy, *Yakṣas*, pt. II, New Delhi: Munshiram Manoharlal, 1998.

81. A. Cunningham, *Corpus Inscriptionum Indicarum*, vol. I, pp. 33, 105, 1877; Bloch, *ARASI*, 1903-4, pp. 124ff ; Fleet, *JRAS*, 1907, p. 511; Lüders List, No. 921.

82. A.P. Banerji-Sastri, *The Castaways of Indian Society*, Calcutta, 1989, pp. 278, 280.

83. We cannot be certain that a *devadāsī* did in fact mean a temple prostitute. The first reference to a *devadāsī* is found in the *Arthaśāstra* which recommends that old *devadāsī*s who have ceased to attend temples on service, mothers of prostitutes, mendicant or ascetic women should be employed to cut wool, fibres, cotton, hemp, panicle and flax AS, 2.XXIII.113, p. 125. *urṇāvalkakārpā satulaśaṇaksaumāṇi ca vidhāvanyangākanyāpravrajitāndaṇd apratikāriṇībhī rupajivanatṛkabhirvṛdhharajadā-sibhiv ryuparatopasthānadevadāsībhiś ca kartayet* — There is a mention of a *veśyā* dancing for Śiva in the temple in *Meghadūta* (vv. 34-35) but the first connection between prostitution and the temple is found in early medieval literature.

84. Cf. S.P. Gupta, *Roots of Indian Art*, New Delhi: B.R. Publishing Corp., 1980, pp. 197-98.

85. V.V. Mirashi, op. cit.

86. Now in GMM; LL. 102; In the *Indian Antiquary* 33, 1904.

87. S.C. Kala, *Terracotta Figurines From Kauśāmbī Mainly in The Collection of The Municipal Museum Allahabad*, Allahabad: Municipal Museum, 1950, Pls. III a and b, p. 44.

88. Nicole Namouchi, *Kaufliche Liebe: Prostitution im alten Indien*, Frankfurt am Main: Peter Lang Verlag, 1995, pp. 17-33.

89. *Nāṭyaśāstra*. Chapter XXV.

90. *Mṛcch.*, Act III, v. 7; Kumkum Roy, "Representing the Courtesanal Tradition", in *JRAS* of Mumbai, vol. 77-78, 2002-3, p. 124.

91. For a detailed exegesis on the differing perceptions of courtesans/*veśyās* in post-Mauryan textual tradition see Kumkum Roy, op. cit., pp. 115-35.

92. *Manusmṛti*, ed. Wendy Doniger, 4.219, pp. 259-60.

93. *Arthaśāstra*, 2.XXVII, p. 137.

94. Like Āmrapālī and Ardhakāśī; *Vinayamahāvagga*, viii, 1, 2 and *Vinaya-Cullavagga*, X, 22, 1.

95. I.B. Horner, op. cit., p. 44.

96. Kumkum Roy, op. cit., p. 125; Cowell, *Jātaka*, II, p.59, 435. See also *Vinaya Piṭaka*, viii, 1, 2; I, p. 268).

97. *Theragāthā*, PTS, 1969, 267-70, p. 32.

98. Ibid., p. 48: *Alaṁkatā suvāsanā māladhārī vibhūṣitā alaṭṭakatāpādā pādukaruyha vibhuṣitā veśikā; pādukā oruhitvana purato pañjalīkatā sā maṁ sanheṇa mudunā mhitapubbaṁ abhāsatha; yuvāsi tvam pabbajito tiṭṭāhi mama sāsane, bhuñja māṇusake kāme, aham vittaṃ dadāmi te। saccan te paṭijānāmi, aggiṁ vā te haram aham; yadā jiṇṇā bhavissāma ubho daṇḍaparāyanā, ubho pi pabbajissāma, ubhayattha kaṭaggaho; tañ ca disvana yācantiṁ vesikaṁ pañjalikataṁ alaṁkaṛtaṁ suvasanaṁ maccupāsam va oḍḍitaṁ; tato* — *Theragāthā*, ed. Oldenberg, PTS, 1966, 2[nd] cdn. 459-65.

99. Cf. I.B. Horner, op. cit., p. 231; *Vinaya*, iv., p. 278.

100. *Therīgāthā*, PTS, 1971, 25-27, p. 4.

101. Ibid., 72-76.

102. See infra, chapter Gender and Art, the section on the naked and provocative bodies.

103. *Therīgāthā*, 252-72.

104. C. Sivaramamurti, op. cit., p. 37.

105. Judith Butler, *Bodies that Matter*, New York, 1993, pp. 1-23.

106. While certain bodies are made possible, liveable and material through this constituting process, other bodies are practically disavowed, excluded from the realm of lived possibility.

107. *MWSE*, pp. 886, 396, *rūpajīvanā* — subsisting on beauty of form, a prostitute, *rūpajīvā* — making a living by beauty of form, living by prostitution, a harlot; *rūpiṇikā*, dimun. *Rūpiṇī*.

108. *AŚ*, 2.27. 123.

109. Kumkum Roy, op. cit., p. 120.

110. *NŚ*, 25.43: *sarvāsāṁ nāriṇāṁ yauvanalīlāścatasraḥ syuḥ। nepathya rūpa ceṣṭā guṇaistu śṛṅgāramāsādhya॥*

111. *NŚ*, XXV.44: *pīnorugaṇḍa jaghanādharastanaṁ karkaśaṁ ratimanojñyaṁ। surataṁ prati sotsāhaṁ prathamaṁ tadyovanaṁ gṭeyaṁ॥*

112. *NŚ*, XXV.45-48.

113. Kumkum Roy, op. cit., p. 121.

114. Supra, Chapter 1; also Uma Chakravarti, "Impulse control of Women", in *Women in Ancient India*, vol. II, Varanasi, 1992, pp. 127-44.

115. *MWSE*, p. 89, *bandhula* is inclined, bent, depressed, lovely, charming and a bastard.

116. *paragūhalalitāḥ parānnapuṣṭāḥ parapuruṣairjanitāḥ parāṅganāsu; paradhananiratā guṇeśvavācyā gajakalabhā iva bandhulā lalāmaḥ* — *Mṛcch.*, Act 4, pp 162-63.

117. I.B. Horner, op. cit., p. 89.

118. *AŚ*, II.XXVII.29.

119. Cf. L. Sternbach, op. cit., p. 9.

120. G. Lerner, *The Creation of Patriarchy*, New York: Oxford University Press, 1986, pp. 134-39.

121. *Mṛcch.*, Act X, p. 402: *ārye vasantasene parituṣṭo rājā bhavatīṁ vadhuśabdenānugṛhaṇāti.*

122. Kumkum Roy, op. cit., p. 119.

123. *Mṛcch.*, Act VI, p. 132; also see Kumkum Roy, op. cit., p. 127.

124. Ibid., Act I, pp. 40-41; p. 135.

# 6

# Yakṣī-Śālabhañjikā

## Cultic and Architectural Motif

The art of the post-Mauryan period is overwhelmed by the presence of voluptuous female figures carved on the railing posts of the *vedikā*s and *toraṇa*s of *stūpa*s and other religious edifices. These have been identified as *yakṣī*s and *śālabhañjikā*s.

In this chapter there is an attempt to mainstream the *yakṣī*, a representational type which in sheer quantitative terms overwhelms its male counterparts, the *yakṣa*s. Despite this overwhelming presence, in the art historical literature on the subject *yakṣī*s are discussed in a single chapter, usually at the end of the monograph or book. Here, I seek to give primacy to the image-type as well as to integrate it within the overall visual discourse. There is an attempt also to bring to the forefront the seminal role of *yakṣī* figures in the artistic development of the female form and the subsequent representation and perception of the ideal female body in Indian art.

The function and form of the *yakṣī-śālabhañjikā* evolved over the 500 years. Both the form and function were conditioned by the context in which the sculptures were placed, for example whether these were free standing or part of the architectural arrangement. There is also transformation, not only in the image, but also in the posture, gesture, gaze and movement of the figure, all indicating an increased sensualisation in the representation of the female form.

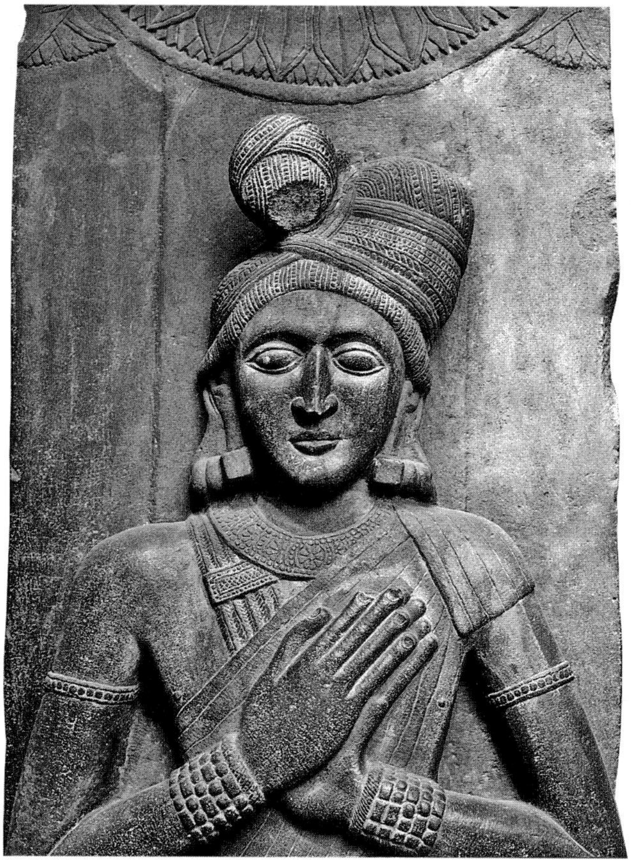

6.1 *Yakṣa* Supravāsa standing on an elephant, railing pillar, first century BCE, Bharhut. IM 76.

## 6.1 Yakṣa: Nature and Worship

*Yakṣas*[1] form an ambiguous and somewhat amphibian category in Indian art and mythology. They are intimately connected with waters, trees and cities.[2] In the metaphysical tradition, recorded mainly in early Brāhmanic texts, the *yakṣa*[3] is virtually synonymous, or rather coincident in reference, with Ātman, Puruṣa, Mr̥tyu, Agni, Prajāpati, Brahman, Manas, etc.[4] These are all designates of that single spiritual principle which assumes a diverse multiplicity of aspects through its immanence in all things, being at the same time both essentially invisible, and yet always manifesting itself and in this sense recognisable.[5]

In the Buddhist Jātaka texts datable to the post-Mauryan period, *yakṣas* are seen as the guardians of the cities, or they live in trees outside the cities, or are placed as guardians and votive deities of city gates, toll-gates or in the palace gardens. They were worshipped by city dwellers, belonging to all strata of society, from the king and his counsellors to the gardeners and merchants. The worship of the Rukkha Devatā or the Yakṣa of the trees was especially popular among women desiring children, as seen in the Jātaka stories.[6] In later representations of the

6.2 Nāga King Cakravāka, south gate, corner pillar, first century BCE, Bharhut. IM 195. Inscribed: Gift of Dharmarakṣita.

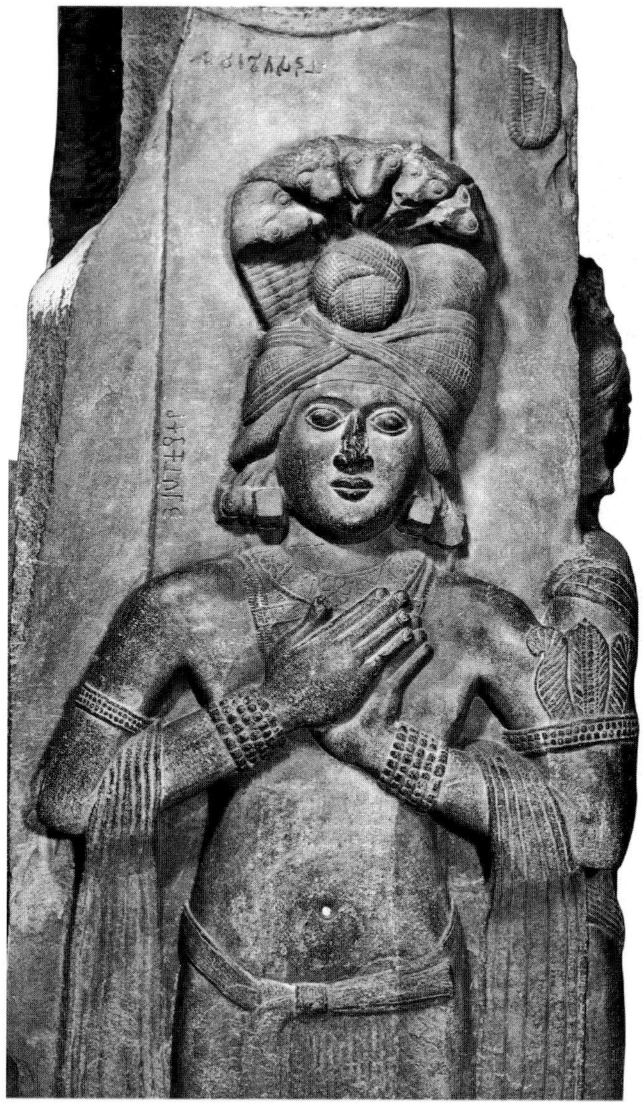

Birth of the Buddha at Amarāvatī and Nāgārjunakoṇḍa, the presentation of the infant Buddha to the Rukkha Yakṣa to seek his blessings is noticed (*Pls.* 3.1.8, 3.1.14, 6.4).

The origin of image worship in Jainism and Buddhism roughly dates to the second century BCE, the earliest images featuring the *tīrthaṁkara* and, a little later, the Buddha, and having for their model ancient *yakṣa* statues.[7] Coomaraswamy has shown that the term *yakṣa* was originally synonymous with *deva* (tree-spirit) and he emphasised their close connection with the waters. He thus regards *yakṣa*s as vegetation spirits, directly controlling and bestowing upon their devotees, *bhakta*s, fertility and wealth.[8] *Yakṣa* sculptures are also the earliest known Indian iconic representations. *Yakṣa*s were probably carved as cult images to be worshipped independently and also as subsidiary or attendant deities.

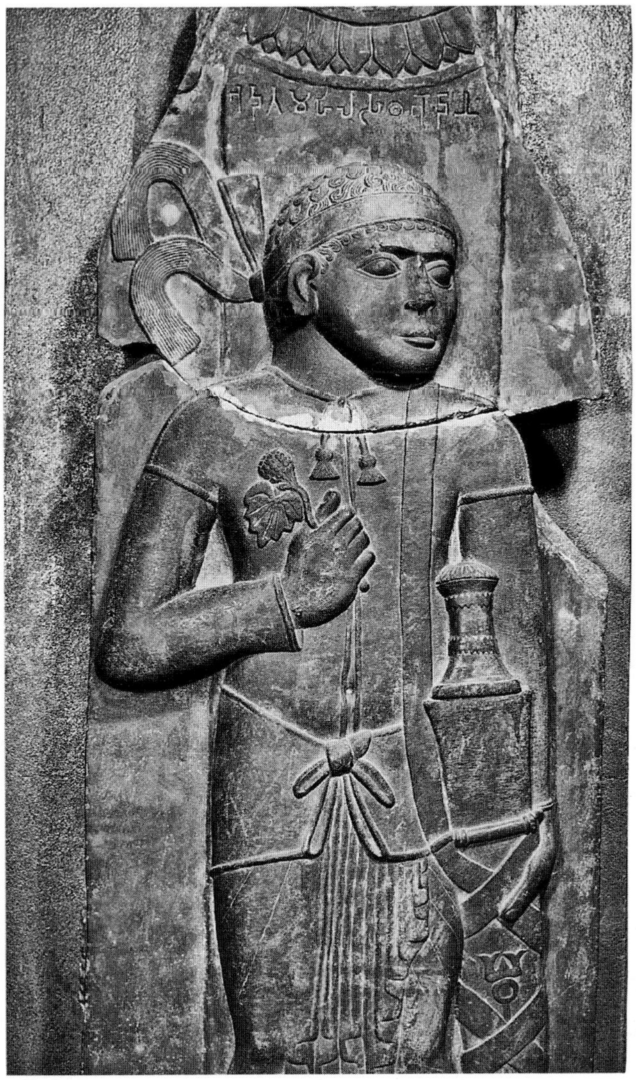

6.3 Foreign king, corner pillar, first century BCE, Bharhut.

It has been shown by R.N. Misra that the *yakṣa* cult is a relic of non-Aryan popular worship, and that concepts of primitive religions — including nature worship, animism, and ancestor worship, along with the borrowing of traits from *rākṣasas*, *kinnaras*, *guhyakas*, *piśācas*, *devas*, *gandharvas* and so forth — helped in its evolution.[9] The *yakṣa* cult was also closely connected with the worship of mother goddesses.

Later, by post-Śuṅga period, *yakṣa*s were absorbed into the *bhakti* cult and relegated to the lower ranks of its pantheon. Buddhism and Jainism could not remain oblivious to this element of popular worship. In fact, the Buddha is purported to have been presented to the tree *yakṣa* at Lumbinī immediately after his birth; a representation of this is found at Amarāvatī and Nāgārjunakoṇḍa as mentioned above. The depictions of earliest Buddhist shrines, showing the *bodhi*-tree, were fashioned after the tree-shrines of *yakṣa*s. The *yakṣa-caitya*s, in the form of a platform around a tree, represent one of the ancient forms of structural shrines.[10] Mahāvīra is always reported to have stayed in *yakṣa āyatana*s or *yakṣa caitya*s such as the Pūrṇabhadra *caitya*. Early texts like the *Bhagavatī-Sūtra*, *Tattvārthabhāṣya*, and the *Kalpasūtra* mention *yakṣa*s. The *Aupapatikasūtra* also mentions the place of Mahāvīra's first sermon made at the shrine of a tree spirit called Pūrṇabhadra outside the city of Campā. This suggests an early Jaina

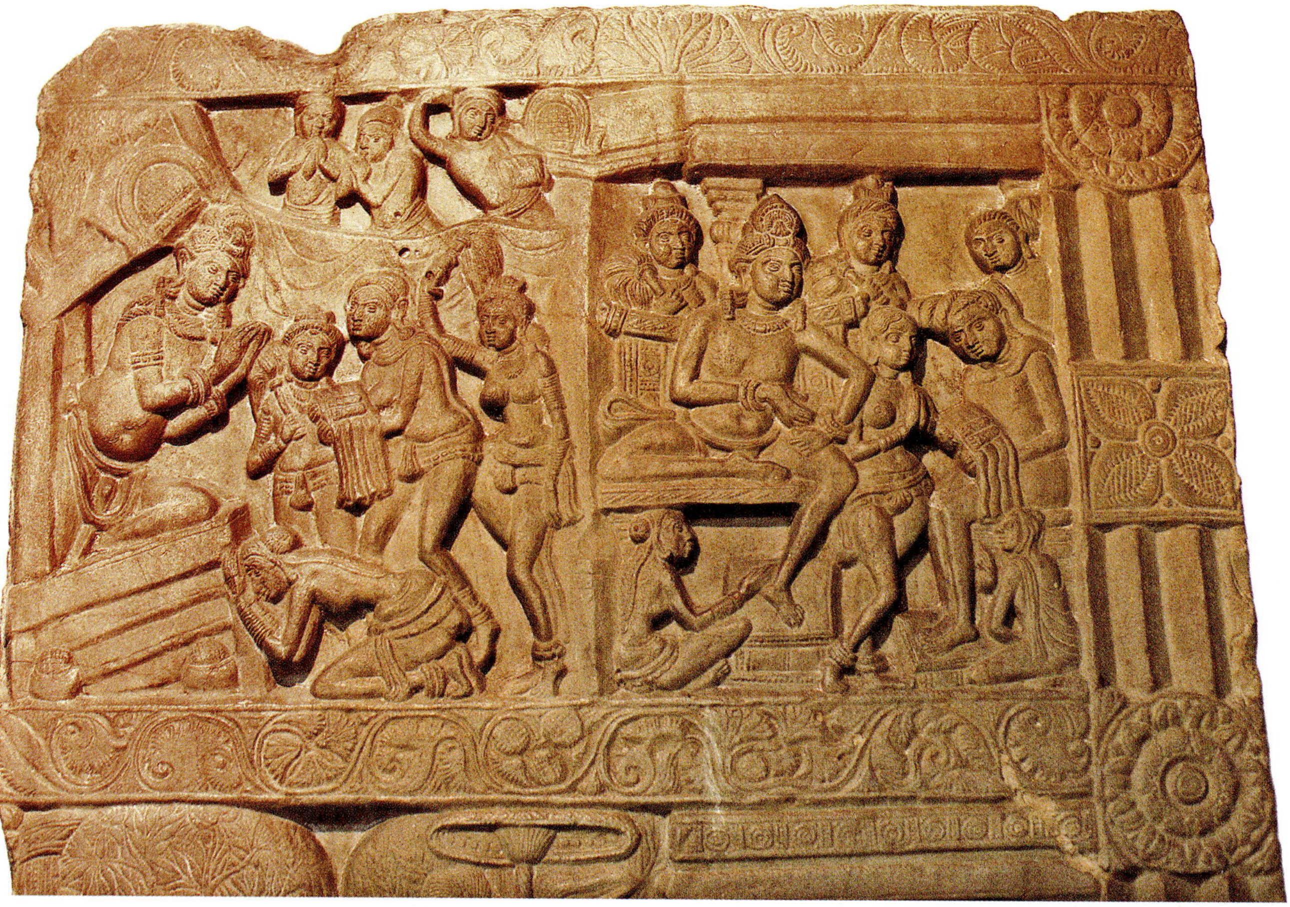

6.4 Presentation of the infant Buddha to the tree *yakṣa*, *c.* third century CE, Ikṣvāku, Nāgārajunakoṇḍa. National Museum.

strategy of incorporating local cults, and fits together with the perception that the earliest *jina* images were influenced by *yakṣa* cult.[11]

The earliest *yakṣa* sculptures, however, do not seem to belong to any particular sectarian stream. The sheer number and the size of these images strongly suggest that they had an autonomous and popular base. The sculptures are usually very large, life-size or bigger, richly attired and bejewelled, standing in the *samabhaṅga* posture, gazing straight from an imposing height, and radiating an aura of authority. One of the best examples of this would be the Parkham *yakṣa*, now in the Mathura Museum (*Pl.* 1.1). This sculpture is almost twice the life-size, as is the Besanagar *yakṣa*. An inscription accompanying the former image identifies it as Maṇibhadra *yakṣa*, one of the *yakṣa*s associated with Kubera, and a special protector of merchants.

Among the *yakṣa*s, the most prolific representations are those of Kubera, the deity of wealth, prosperity and fertility. He is also referred to as Jambhala, Dhanada and Vaiśrāvaṇa. He lives on Mount Kailāsa and his city is called Alakā. He is usually shown as a pot-bellied dwarf with moustaches (*Pl.* 6.10). He holds a purse in his hand and his consorts are Hāritī and Ṛddhi. He is supposed to ride a *naravāhana*. However, in his earlier portrayal as Kupiro Devatā at Bharhut (*Pl.* 3.2.15; for other illustrations of Bharhut *yakṣa*s see *Pls.* 6.1 to 6.4), he is shown in a realistic human form without a pot belly and is neither crouching nor dwarfish.

This kind of *yakṣa* with a cultic, divine significance does not appear at Sāñcī, either on the *stūpa* II and *stūpa* III (which are early) or *stūpa* I (which is later). Here we find instead two kinds of *yakṣa*s: as weight-bearing Atlantes supporting the *toraṇa* architrave, or as a protector of the gate[12] carved at the base of the *toraṇa-stambhas* at cardinal points (*Pl.* 6.7).

A similar function is attributed to the *yakṣa*s in the early Buddhist *caitya*s and *vihāra*s of the Deccan. At Pītalkhorā, larger than life-size, club-bearing *yakṣa*s guard the stairway of Cave 4 (*Pl.* 6.6 also see *Pl.* 6.8). The *yakṣa-dvārapāla*s are also seen at Bhaja. Although similar in form to the

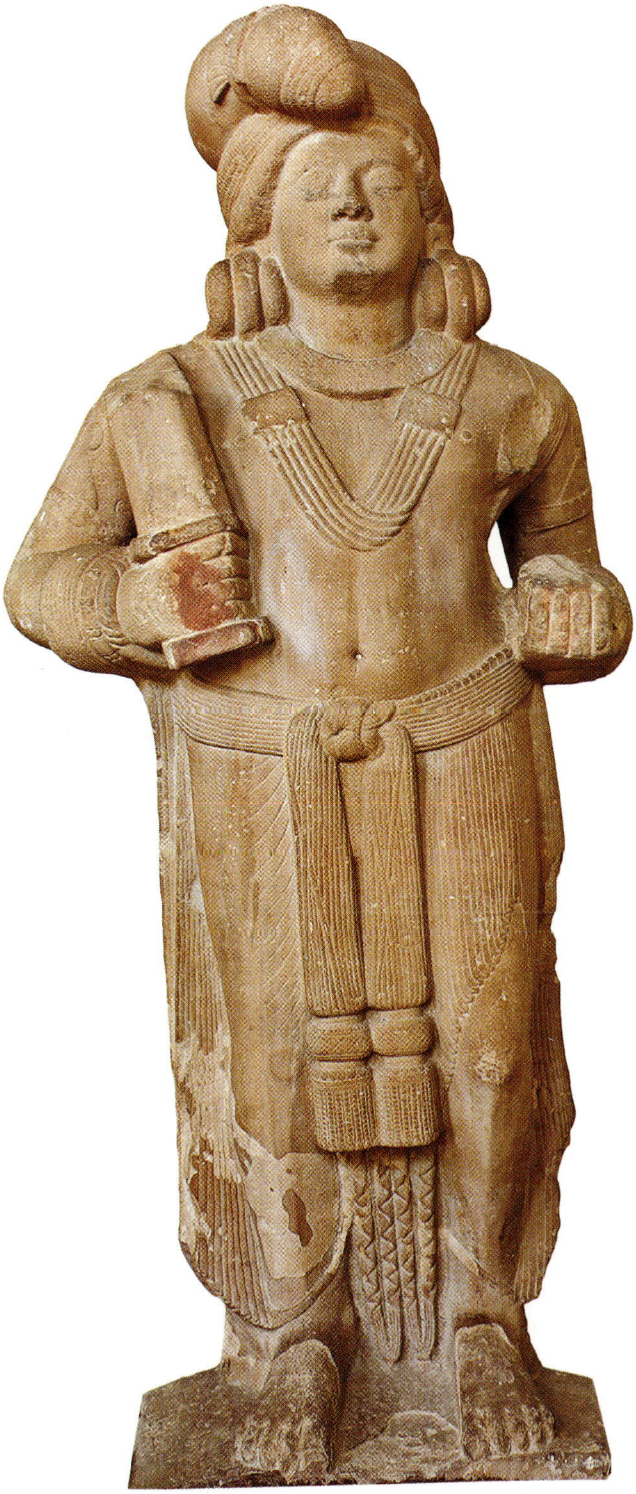

6.5 Massive *yakṣa* carved in the round, second century CE, Mathurā, GMM

6.6 *Yakṣa* as *dvārapāla*, first century BCE, Cave 4, Pītalkhorā, Maharashtra.

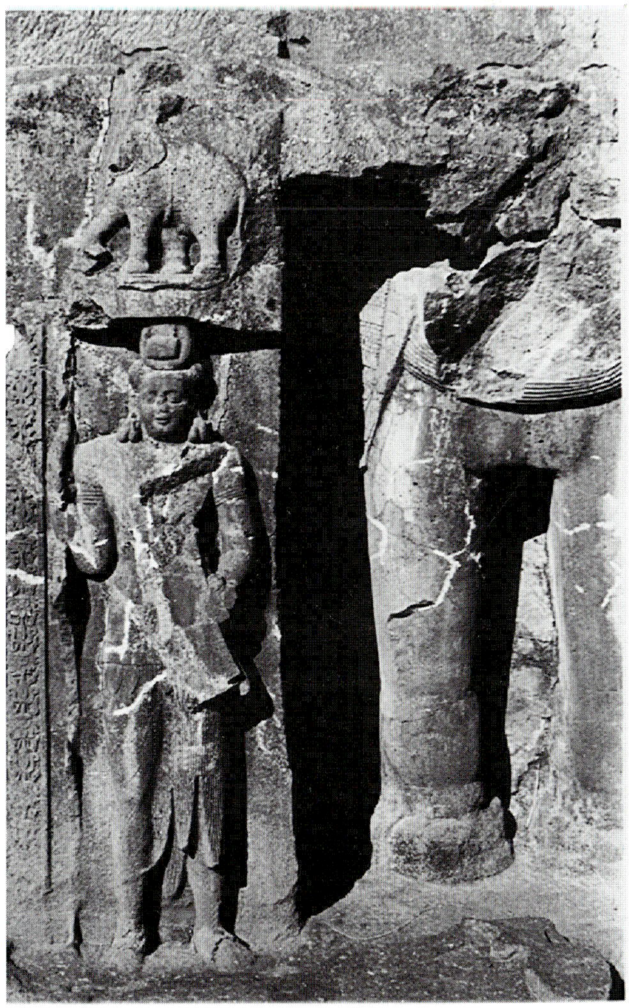

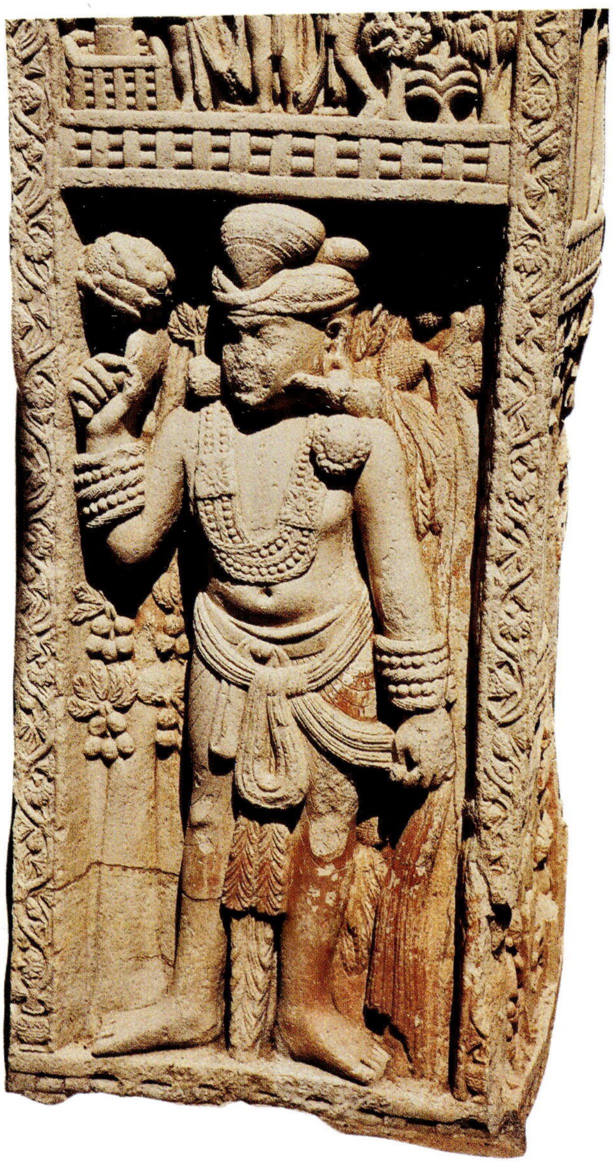

6.7 *Yakṣa* as Guardian of the Entrance, *stūpa* II, first century CE, Sāñcī.

earlier north and central Indian figures, these do not have the same aura of power about them. They are devoid of attributes such as a purse, and here entrusted with spears or swords to guard structures. A similar trend of de-divinisation of the *yakṣa*s is witnessed in the northern regions in Kuṣāṇa art at Mathurā. Here the solidity is retained but not the attributes of divinity that provided cult status to the Parkham or Besanagar *yakṣa*s. Not only are they made guardians of monuments, they are also made to serve as *vāhana*s, on which the *yakṣī* figures stand, indicating some kind of reversal in power relations in which the feminine steps on the *yakṣa* and thereby presumably reduces him to an inferior position. I have been unable to find any textual references to this role of *yakṣa*s in contemporary texts.

Thus we see that in depicting *yakṣa*s, their representation is neither uni-dimensional nor static, they appear either beautiful or awful in accordance with their nature,[13] and that they change both in form and style over a span of five centuries under study. From mammoth, statuesque divinities commanding respect, they are transformed into *yakṣārohas*, *bhāra-putraka*s or supports having the *kalpalatā* issuing from their navels and mouths. They are relegated to the

6.8 Dwarf *yakṣa* as supporter of the stair rise, second century BCE, Cave 3, Pītalkhorā.

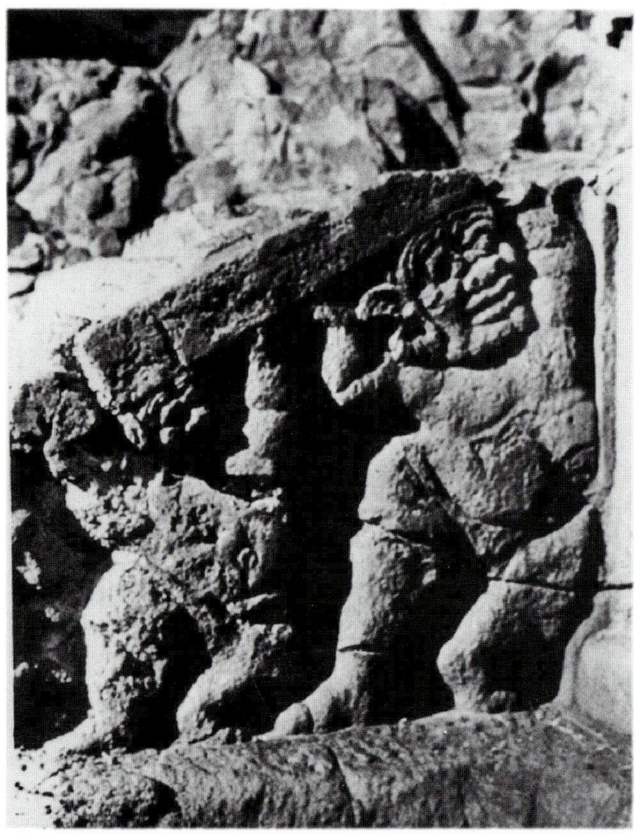

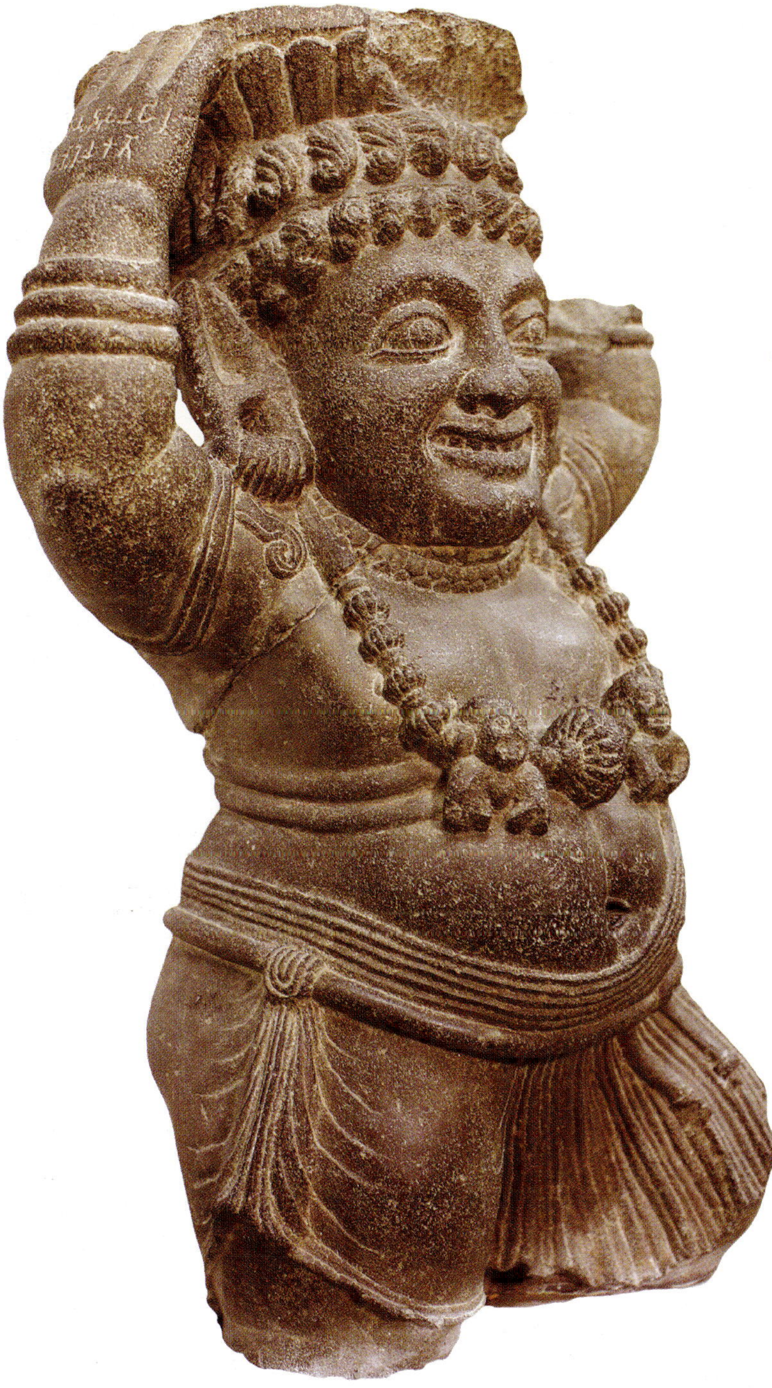

6.9 *Yakṣa*, gift of Kanhadāsa, Sātavāhana, 98 × 46 × 34 cm, first-second century CE, stone, Pītalkhorā. NM Acc. No, 67. 195.

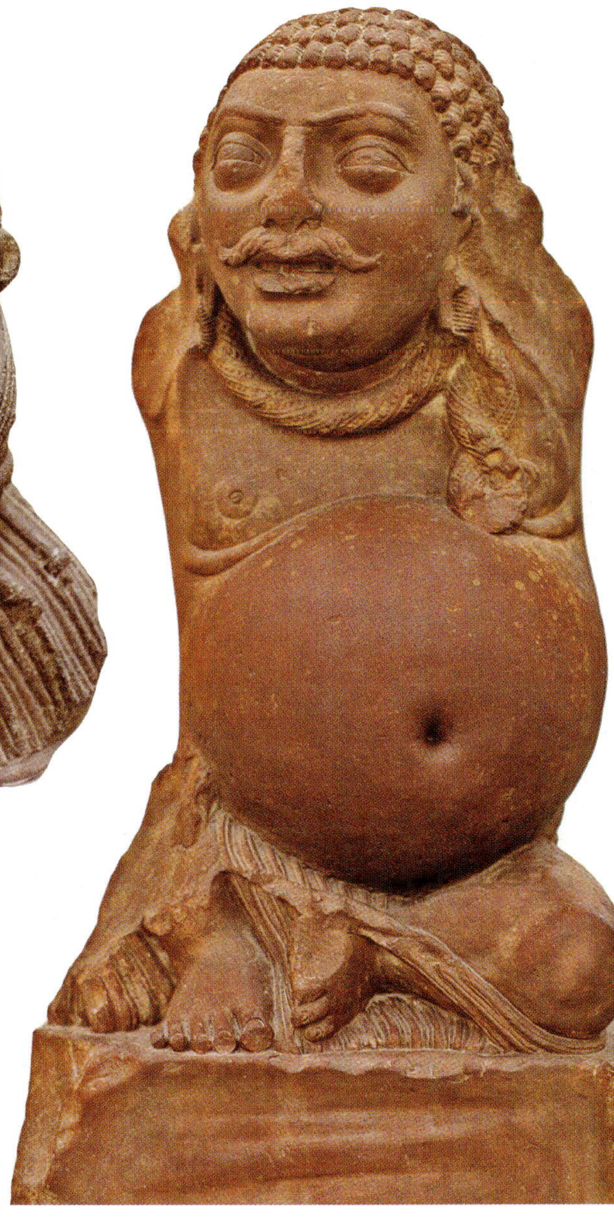

6.10 Kubera as pot-bellied *yakṣa*, 96 x 45.5 x 36 cm, red sandstone, second century CE, Ahicchatra, UP. NM Acc. No. 59.530/2.

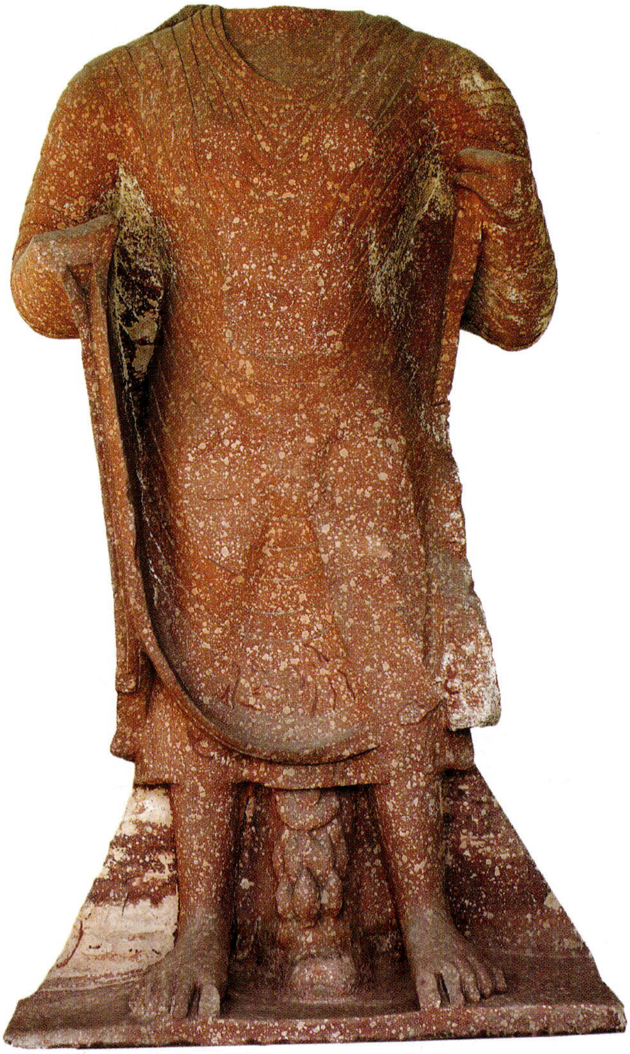

6.11 Buddha standing, red sandstone; ht. .820 m, second century CE, Mathurā, GMM.

*pedya*s of the temple doorways in keeping with their roles as guardian deities or become *vāhana*s for other divinities. In the Kuṣāṇa period, Brāhmanic and Buddhist images, such as those of Viṣṇu, the Buddha and *bodhisattva*, appropriate the statuesque and divine elements of *yakṣa* imagery (*Pls*. 6.11, 6.12).

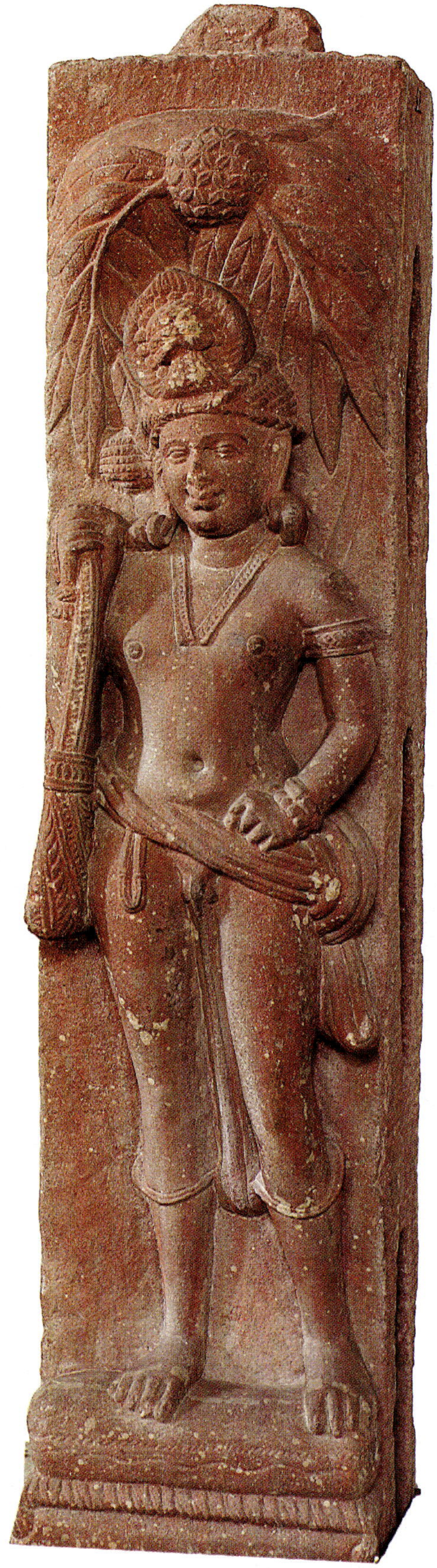

6.12 *Bodhisattva* figure derived from *yakṣa* iconography, second century CE, railing pillar, Kuṣāṇa, red sandstone, Mathurā.

## 6.2 Yakṣīs

*Yakṣīs* constitute one of the enigmatic types in early Indian art history. Despite the ubiquitous nature of their representation on monuments there is scant direct information provided in the textual or epigraphic sources. In such a situation, any inferences we draw on their identities are bound to be speculative.

In the early inscriptions at Bharhut, some female figures are deified as *yakṣīs* or *devatās* (*Pls.* 6.13, 6.14). However such appellations are not found in later epigraphs, though contemporary texts refer to sculptures of *śālabhañjikās* and *Apsarases* embellishing religious and secular buildings.

*Yakṣī* is but one of several semi-divine beings like the *devatās*, *gandharvīs*, and *Apsarases*. There is reason to suppose that the *vṛkṣakā* was conceived as a *yakkhinī*, though the *Mahābhārata* seems to identify it as a *devatā*, a *yakṣī*, a *dānavī*, an *apsaras*, a fair *daitya* girl, a lovely maiden of Nāga king, a *rākṣasī* in the woods or the spouse of Varuṇa or Soma or Kubera or Yama.[14]

The earliest appearance of *yakṣīs* at Bharhut, Bodh-Gayā, Patna, Moosanagar and Kauśāmbī, all of the post-Maurya period, indicates their close connection with the cult of fertility. (In the early period, *yakṣīs* are seminal to an understanding of the complex nature and worship of feminine fertility.) In the early Śuṅga period, larger than life-size images of *yakṣīs* were worshipped as independent, powerful deities. The presence of *yakṣīs* and *devatās* at Bharhut attest to the power wielded by the female principle in the religious and artistic discourse.

In the Sātavāhana and Kuṣāṇa monuments at Sāñcī, Amarāvatī, Nāgārjunakoṇḍa and Mathurā, the female divinities are associated with vegetation and water; they are scantily clothed and decorated but their sexual organs are emphasised. These *śālabhañjikā-yakṣīs* are shown with one leg either resting on a tree trunk or entwining it. They are sometimes accompanied by a child.[15]

In Jainism, *yakṣīs* were introduced as the female consorts of the *yakṣas* belonging to the *Vyāntara* class of gods, and appeared, later in the early medieval period, along with them as

6.13 *Yakṣī* Sudassanā, railing pillar, first century BCE, Bharhut. IM 43. Inscribed: (a) *Yakṣī* Sudassanā, (b) gift of pillar by lay brother Bhanaka of Chukulaniya.

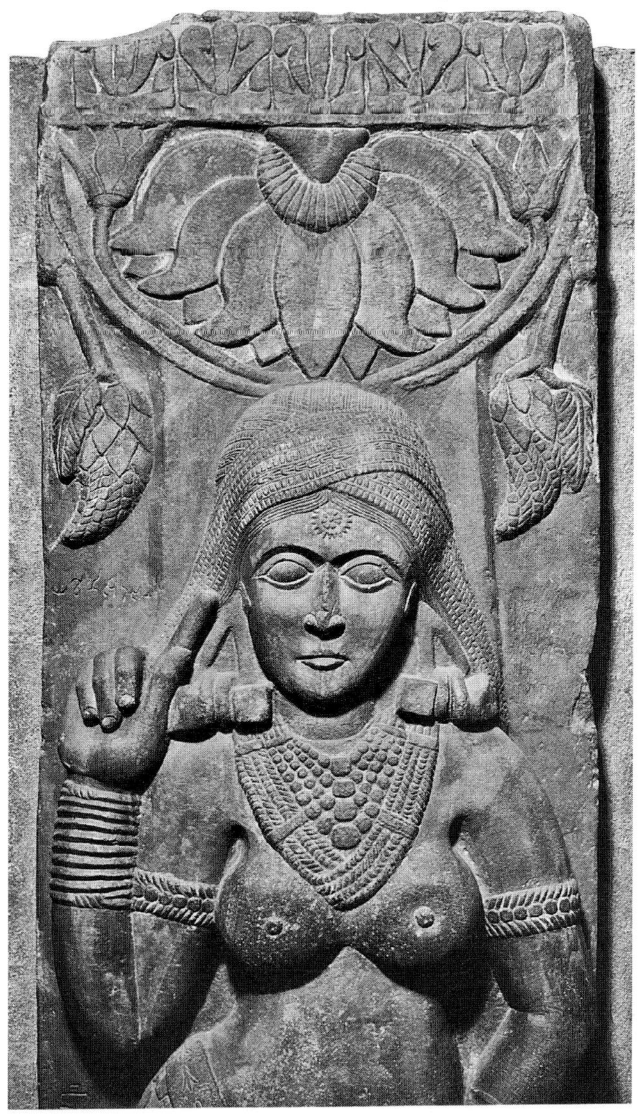

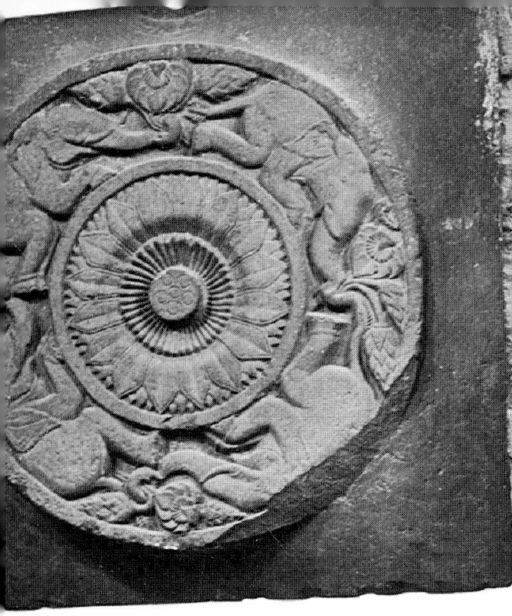

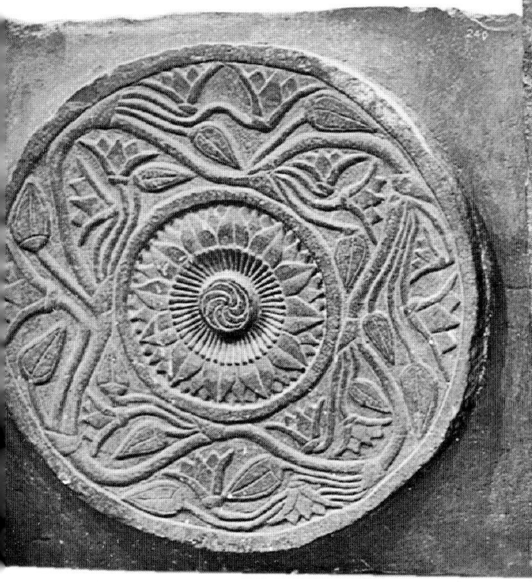

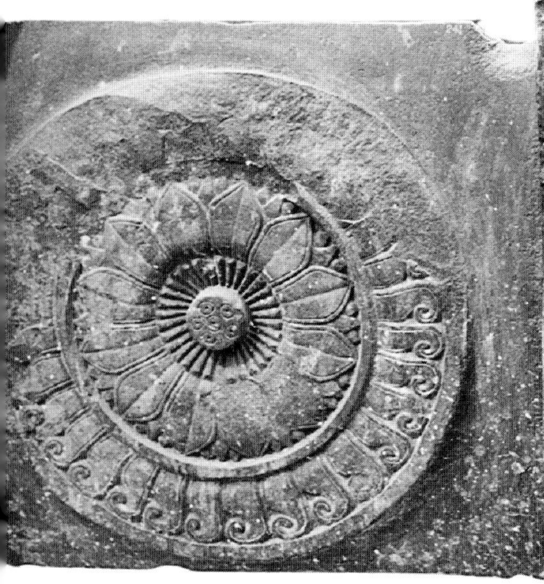

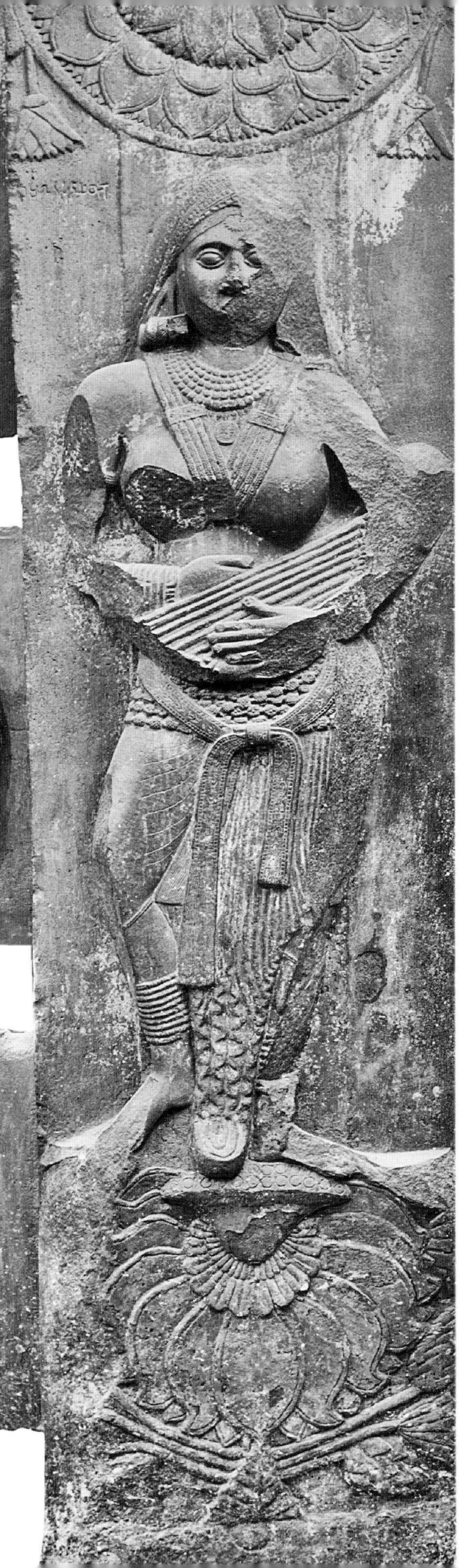

6.14 *Yakṣī* playing a stringed instrument, standing on lotus, first century BCE, Bharhut. IM 243. Inscribed: Pillar Gift of Dharmagupta.

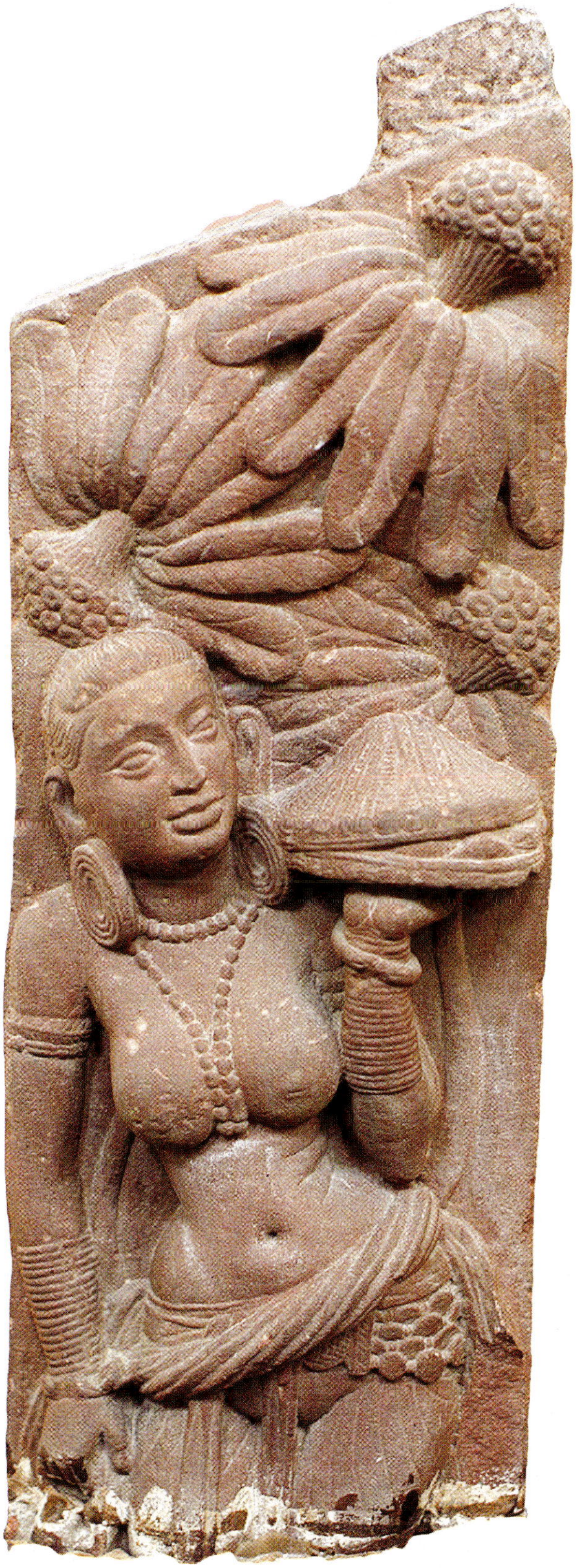

6.15 *Prasādikā*, red sandstone, second century CE, Kuṣāṇa, Mathurā. GMM.

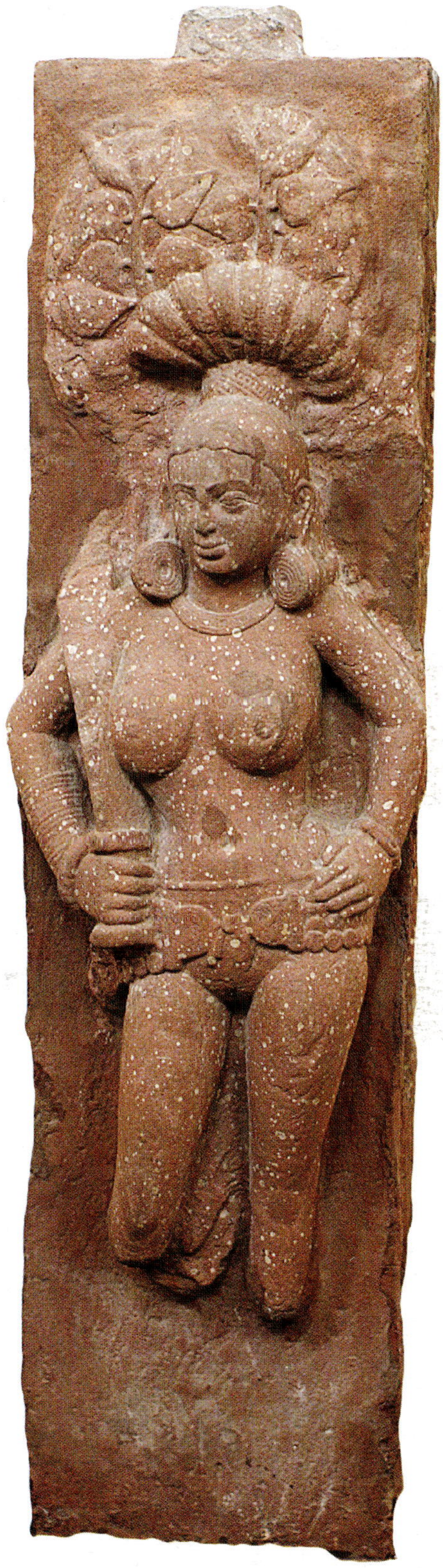

6.16 *Yakṣī* with a sword, railing post, red sandstone, first century CE, Lakṣmaṇgaṛh, Mathurā district, UP. GMM No. 00J.63.

tutelary deities or the *śāsana-devatā*s of *tīrthāṁkara*s (Śvetāmbara and Digambara traditions being different), each having her own *vāhana* and attributes. *Yakṣī*s were regarded as protectors of the *tīrtha*s of their respective *tīrthaṁkara*s and also helpers in the practice of *dharma*.[16] Gradually *yakṣī*s came to mean much more than mere consorts and some of them developed independent cults, not necessarily embodying purely Jaina traits. This is well indicated in the case of the Yakṣī Ambikā.

*Yakṣī*s may be classified as follows:

### 6.2.1 TYPE A

These are very solid, static figures standing in the *samabhaṅga* posture carved in the round, female counterparts of the *yakṣa*s, found at Mathurā, Besanagar and Bharatpur area. Their size and form suggest that they were female counterparts of *yakṣa*s such as the Parkham and Besanagar images, but they are proportionally smaller in size than the *yakṣa* figures (*Pl.* 1.2). It is likely that they were principal objects of worship (in cults centring on *yakṣa*s and *yakṣī*s).

### 6.2.2 TYPE B

These figures are incorporated into the decorative scheme of the architecture. This development is not confined only to female figures; *yakṣa*s are also deployed in a similar manner. The examples from the Bharhut, Kauśāmbī and Haryana regions reveal elements of sensuality but retain a certain amount of divine serenity too; they seem to have a certain cultic and symbolic significance.

Carved on the corner pillars of the *vedikā* of the Bharhut *stūpa*, we find three female figures

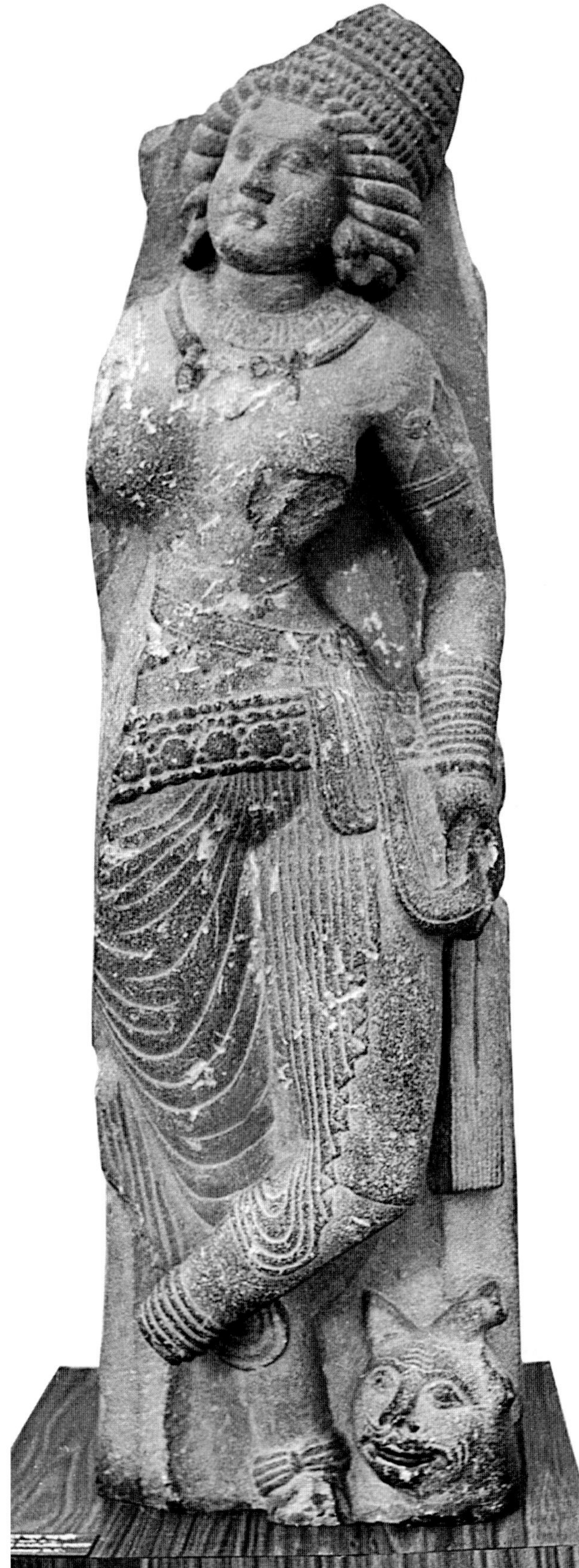

6.17 *Yakṣī* standing on an animal, railing post, first century BCE, Bodh-Gayā, Bihar.

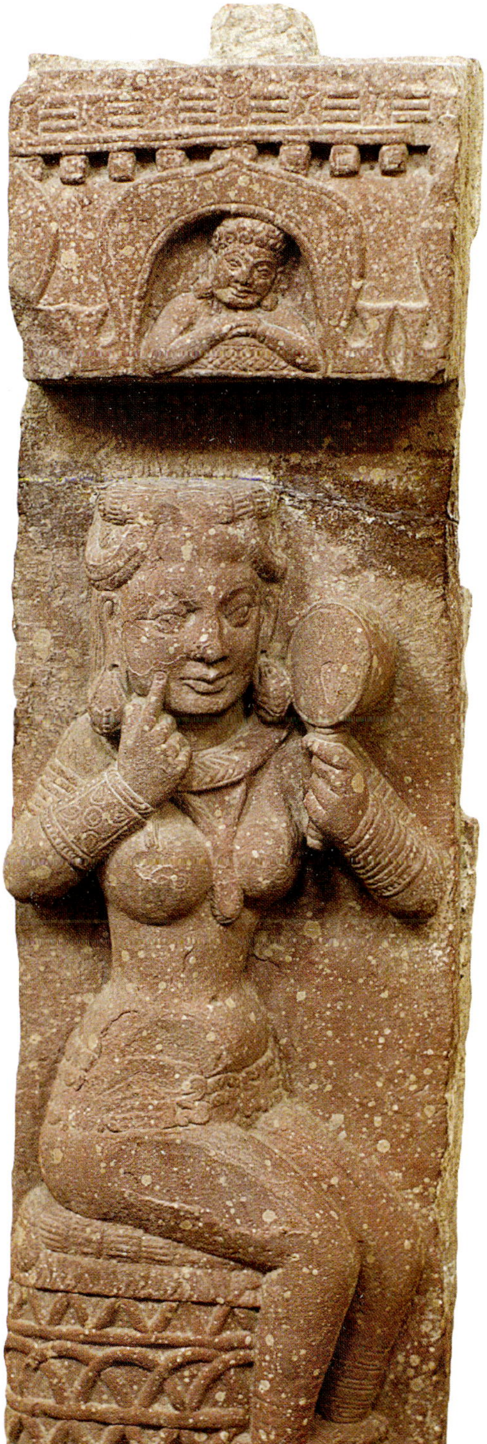

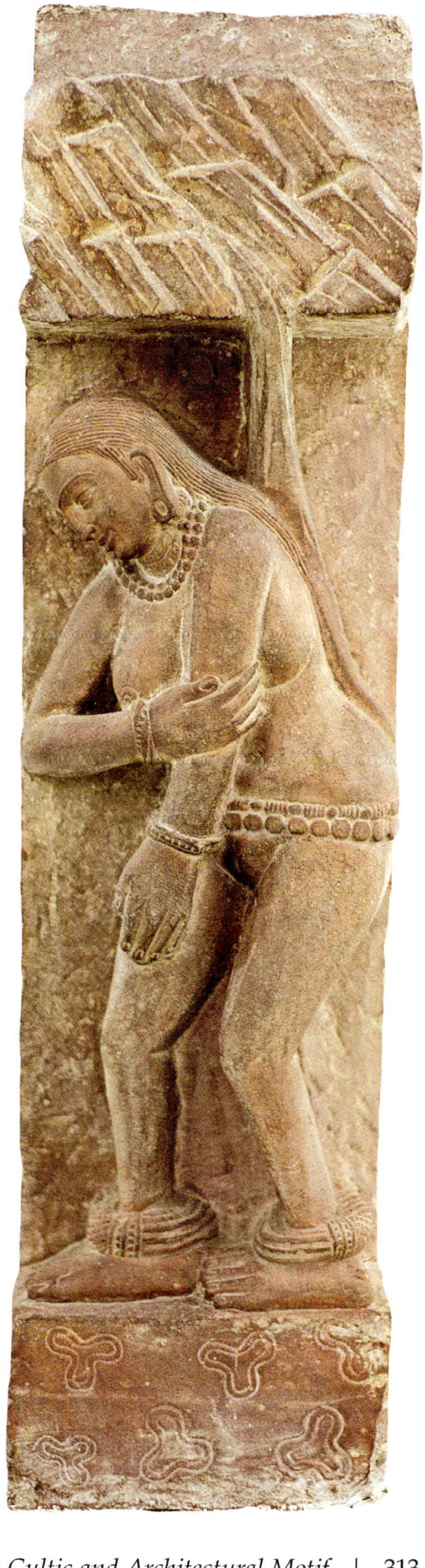

6.18 *Yakṣī* holding a mirror, railing post, first century CE, red sandstone, Mathurā district, UP. GMM.

6.19 Lady taking a bath, railing post, second century CE, Mathurā, Kuṣāṇa. NM Acc. No. J 278.

accompanied by three label inscriptions identifying them as the Yakkhinī Sudasanā (*Pl.* 6.13) (Yakṣīṇī Sudarśanā),[17] the Yakhī Chadā (*Pl.* 6.29) (Yakṣī Candrā)[18] and the gift of a *yakhī* by Koda (Kroda).[19] Of these *yakṣī*s, Candrā is discussed below as a *śālabhañjikā*, along with Culakoka Devatā (*Pl.* 6.28). A figure similar to that of Sudasanā *yakṣīnī* is that of Sirimā Devatā (*Pl.* 2.2.17), both of whom are standing, but the former is in a slight *dvibhaṅga* flexion, touching the sash at her waist, while the latter stands straight with one hand hanging by her side and the other is raised. In the visual discourse, it is difficult to distinguish between the *yakṣī* and the *devatā* figure in the early art at Bharhut. All these figures are shown wearing elaborate *dhotī*s falling in pleats in the middle and tied with a multi-stringed pearl *mekhalā* at the waist with a band or a sash over it. The figures are shown to be profusely bejewelled. Undoubtedly there is a degree of divinity attached to these figures. Can we say that the essential character of the *yakṣī*s and *devatā*s was largely similar and therefore the visual similarity? Some scholars seem to think that the terms were used interchangeably, but, given the high level of sophistication and attention to detail in the construction of the *stūpa*, would the people who built it or the pilgrims who came to visit the shrine not be aware of the difference? It is also interesting to note that, unlike their male counterparts such as Kupiro (*Pl.* 3.2.15), Supravāsa (*Pl.* 6.1) and Suciloma *yakṣa*s whose hands are folded in *namaskāra-mudrā*, symbolising either supplication or homage, the *yakṣī*s and *devatā*s are either in *śālabhañjikā* stance or holding some object such as a lotus bud in their hand. It seems that these figures did indeed have some cultic significance linked to vegetation/tree and fertility.

Later figures of type B are found at Mathurā, Sanghol and other sites in north India associated

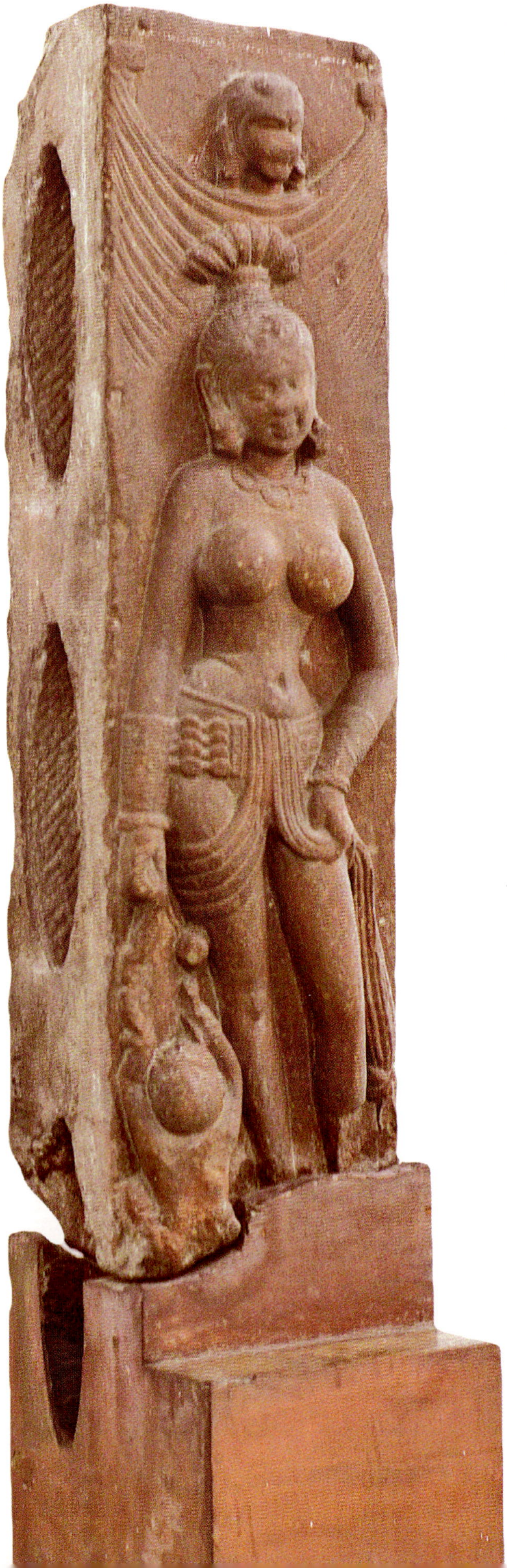

6.20 Woman and child, railing post, second century CE. Mathurā, Kuṣāṇa. NM Acc. No. J 16.

with Kuṣāṇa art. These figures are also found on the *vedikā*s and railposts, generally surrounding the *stūpa* or other religious edifices such as a Nāga temple. The *yakṣī* figure in Kuṣāṇa art is characterised by a voluptuous body: full round breasts, thin waist and wide hips. Draped from the waist down in a transparent *dhotī* the figures reveal their private parts (*Pls.* 6.16, 6.21, 6.22, 6.23, 6.25, 6.26). The figure is usually profusely ornamented with a prominent *mekhalā* or jewelled waistband, necklaces, bracelets, ankle bands and arm bands. The coiffure is elaborate. Great attention is paid by the sculptor to enhancing her physical beauty. This is also done through posture, which is usually *tribhaṅga*, and through the movement of the body in performing various playful (*Pl.* 6.16) and at times provocative actions (*Pls.* 6.19, 6.21). They are depicted engaged in various activities such as drinking wine (*Pls.* 6.25, 6.26), bathing under a waterfall (*Pl.* 6.19), tying the sash of the waistband (*Pl.* 6.22), playing with birds, with balls or swords (*Pl.* 6.16) in hand, in the company of children (*Pl.* 6.20) and in myriad other ways (*Pls.* 6.15, 6.18, 6.23, 6.24).[20] The *śālabhañjikā-dohada* is but one of the postures carved on the railing post. Often there are spectator figures on top of the rail post (*Pls.* 6.18, 6.20, 6.22, 6.25) that either gaze at or interact with the female figure below, for example reaching out for the pitcher held up by the *yakṣī* (*Pl.* 6.26).

It is important to assert here that it would be erroneous to designate all female figures on the *vedikā*s and *toraṇa*s of the Kuṣāṇa period as either *yakṣī*s or *śālabhañjikā*s. As will be seen below, the term *śālabhañjikā* refers to a specific imagery.

The *yakṣī* is also seen as a meta-category under which a number of other female figures are classified. Even attendant figures are classified as *yakṣī*s and as such may not have had any cultic significance. *Yakṣī* is

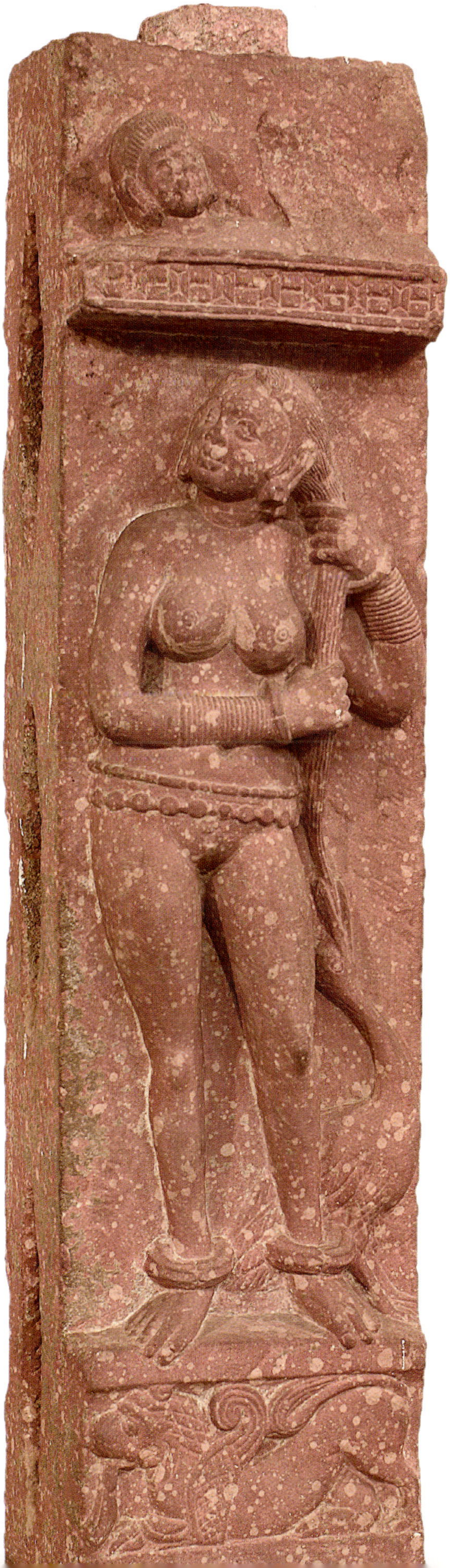

6.21 A swan drinking water from the woman's wet hair, railing post, second century CE, Kuṣāṇa, Sanghol.

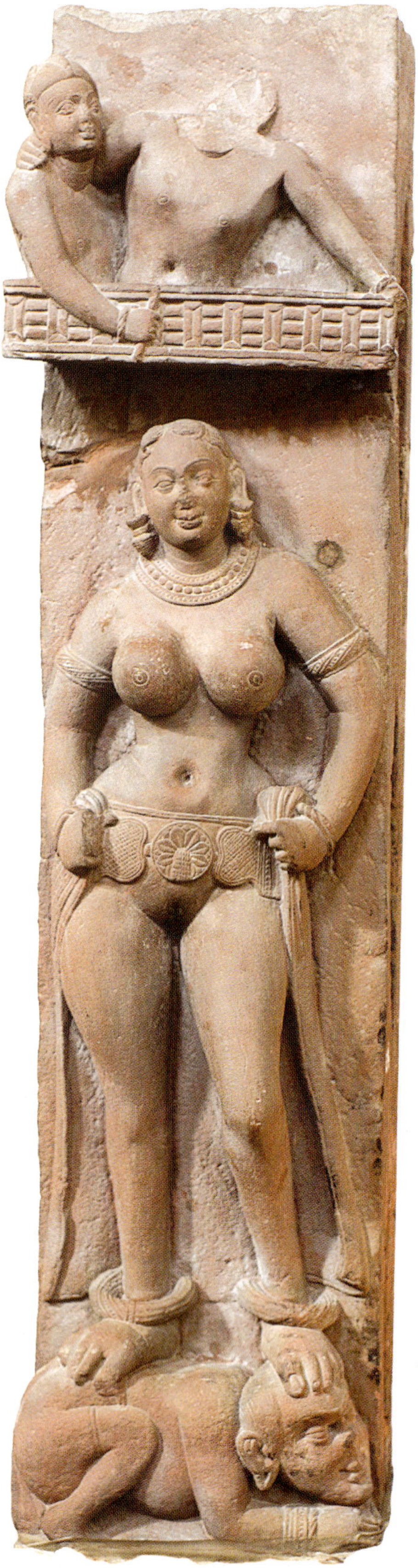
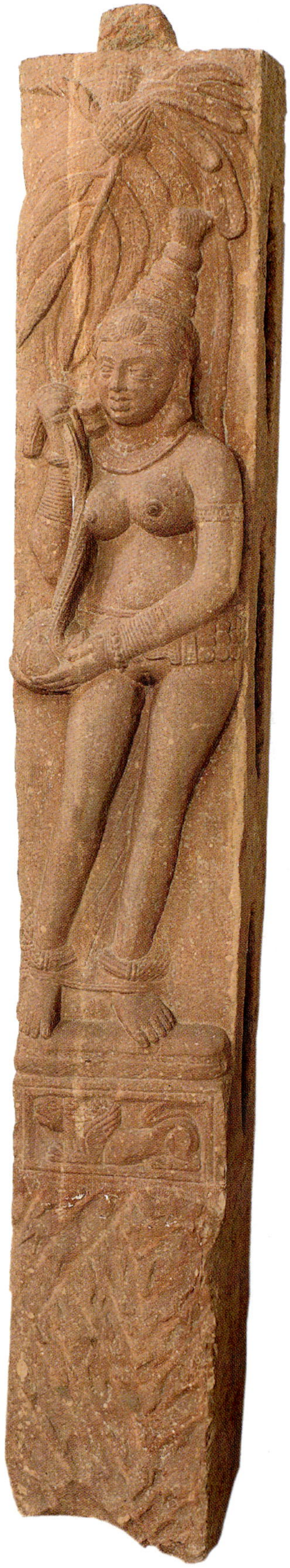
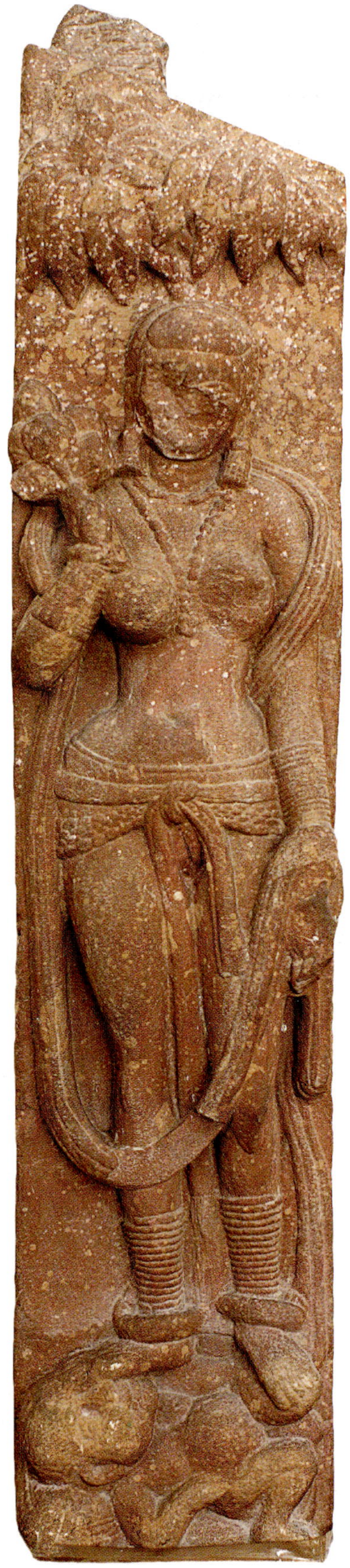

a term that we use for the sake of convenience to denote the depiction of female figures of the Type B kind. However, we cannot ascribe semi-divine status associated with *yakṣīs* or *śālabhañjikās* to all female figures carved on railings, some of whom may represent human women, perhaps donors or servants, such as the lamp-carrying figure. These are usually clothed, wearing an opaque *dhotī* or petticoat-like skirt (*Pl.* 6.27), and may even wear a breast band to cover the upper body. The ornaments are not so profuse and elaborate, nor are the postures voluptuous.

The *yakṣī* imagery seen in Kuṣāṇa art is also shared by other representational types. The representations of women on the furniture pieces from Begram in Afghanistan (*Pl.* 6.44) replicate the beautiful forms of the *yakṣīs* of Mathurā. Similar female imagery is also found on panels on *toraṇa* pillars and in railpost depictions of *mithuna* (*Pls.* 4.18, 4.19) and *kāmaloka* scenes (*Pls.* 1.12, 1.13) and also narrative panels such as Vasantasena scenes. In fact, with reference to the *yakṣī* figures on the Bharhut, Sāñcī and Mathurā railings, P.K. Agrawala is of the opinion that they represent incomplete *mithunas*[21] waiting to be united with a male partner and thus belonging to the discourse of pleasure and sexuality.

On the other hand, in the textual and visual tradition, the *yakṣī* identity is often ascribed to

6.22 (Left) *Yakṣī* holding waistband or *uttarīya*, railing post, red sandstone, second century CE, Jaisinghpura, Mathurā district. GMM No. 00J.10.

6.23 (Middle) Woman holding a garland, railing post, second century CE, Kuṣāṇa, Sanghol.

6.24 (Right) A woman holding a bunch of lotus buds, with a spectator looking over the curtain, railing post, second century CE, Kuṣāṇa, Sanghol.

6.25 A woman drinking from a goblet as a spectator looks on, railing post, second century CE, Kuṣāṇa, Sanghol.

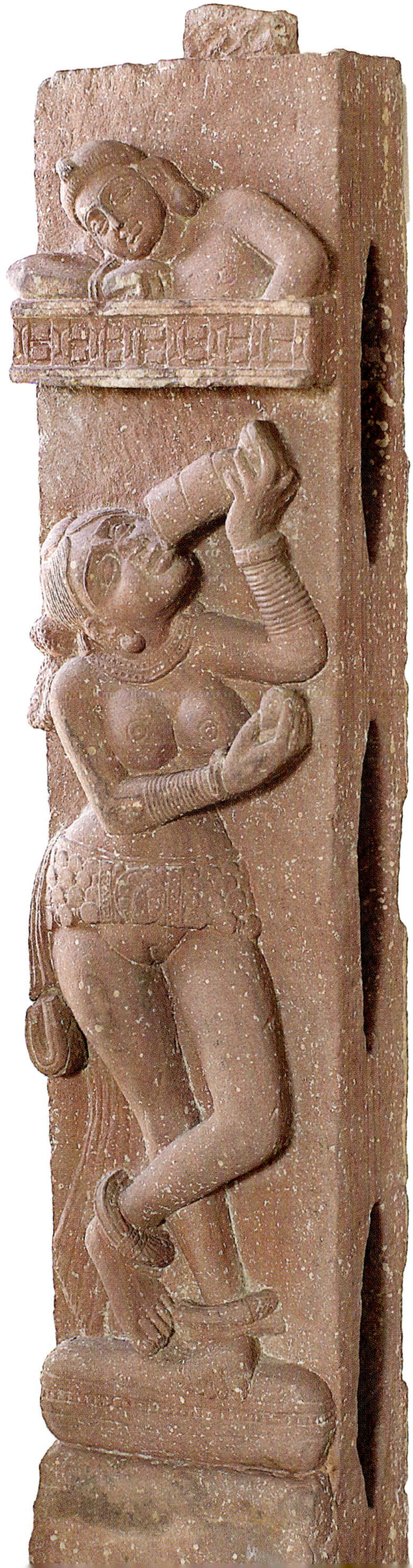

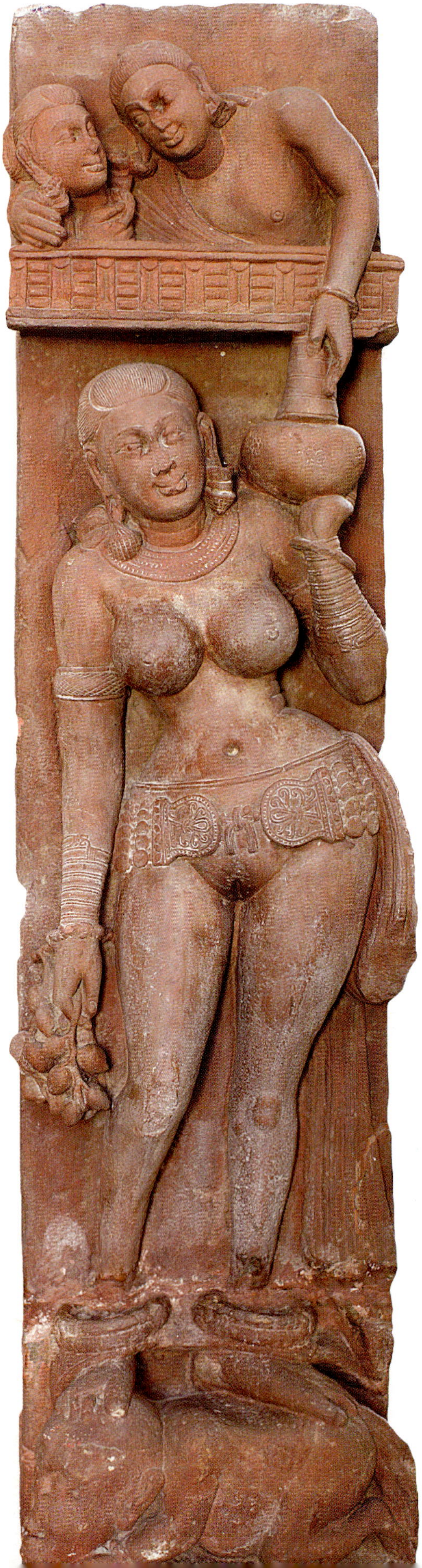

divine entities such as Hāritī. Hāritī becomes the consort of Kubera and as such plays an important part in the Kubera-and-Hāritī cult. Visually, Hāritī image shares more in terms of form and representation with other divine feminine figures such as Ṣaṣṭhī or certain Mātṛkā figures of Mathurā, rather than with the *śālabhañjikā*s. It is the Māyādevī figure that develops from the *śālabhañjikā* imagery.[22]

Hāritī (*Pls*. 3.2.1, 3.2.3, 3.2.4) is a *yakṣī* with a cult of her own and is part of the Kuber-Hāritī duo. In terms of imagery, she is depicted in a manner similar to other female divinities such as Ṣaṣṭhī (*Pl*. 3.4.1) rather than the *yakṣī-śālabhañjikā*s. Of the maternal figures it is Māyādevī (*Pls*. 3.1.13, 3.1.16 to 3.1.18) who is represented in the manner of a *śālabhañjikā*.

The Kuṣāṇa period marks a very important stage in the development of the *yakṣī* form. The voluptuousness of form and the transformation in posture suggest the increasing sensualisation of figure (a hallmark of Mathurā art). Besides posture, this is seen in the transparency of dress and movement of the body seen in activities of these females, which are often provocative. However, we have to keep in mind that *yakṣī*s were carved religious edifices which would suggest that she was an established motif symbolising *maṅgala* (auspiciousness).

One trajectory of the development of *yakṣī*s took them towards being perceived as ogresses in narrative art; this is discussed in the next chapter. The Jātakas see such figures as ogresses who are sometimes redeemed by their maternal instincts, reflecting dichotomy between the textual position and the actual representation.

6.26 Woman holding a *surāhī*-like vessel and a bunch of fruits, railing post, second century CE, Kuṣāṇa, Sanghol.

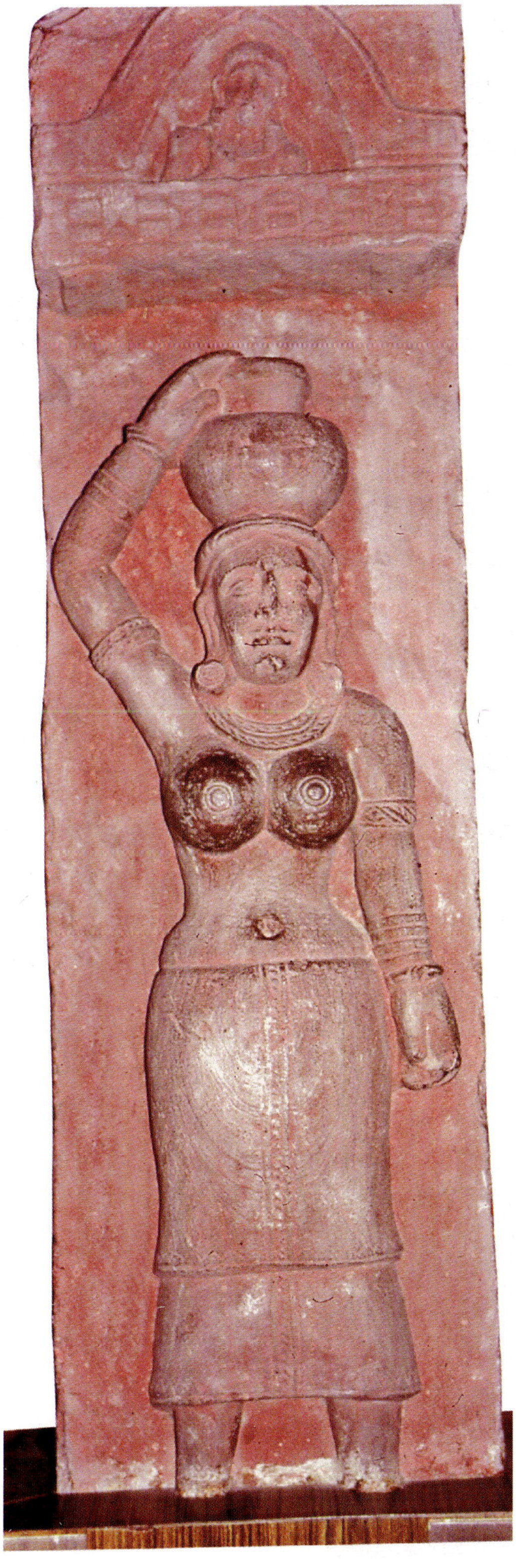

6.27 A woman wearing a petticoat holding a *surāhī*-like pot, perhaps a wine vessel, railing post, second century CE, Kuṣāṇa, Mathurā. SML.

Gail Sutherland says that while the sculptural representations of *yakṣī*s display images of benign female sexuality and rampant fertility, the literary examples, both Hindu and Buddhist, exhibit an aspect that is almost entirely frightening and demonic.[23] The benevolent *yakṣī* is frequently encountered as a dryad or aquatic nymph, the *Apsaras*es. The *yakṣī* and *yakṣa* pillar reliefs at Bharhut, Sāñcī and Mathurā depict similar primeval dryadic motifs. I feel that an analysis such as Sutherland's collapses two complementary but distinct categories of sexuality of the insatiable ogress and the fertility of the dryadic *yakṣī*s, which fails to take into account the changes in the imagery of *yakṣī-śālabhañjikā*s that took place over 500 years.

### 6.3 Śālabhañjikā and the Dohada Imagery

A specific kind of *yakṣī* imagery is that of *śālabhañjikā* and *dohada* depictions which combine women with trees, but which also symbolise other actions. There are many sculptural specimens of these; we will be selecting only a few which shed some light on the constitution of the *śālabhañjikā* representation or its changing shape. In terms of depiction, it shows a woman in *tribhaṅga* posture leaning against the trunk of a tree, holding its drooping branch with one upraised hand while the other hand is placed on the hip.

The earliest portrayal of women and trees, combining *śālabhañjikā*s with the *dohada*, may be seen on the railing pillars surrounding the *stūpa* at Bharhut. Here the female figure is shown standing in *tribhaṅga*, holding a branch arching above her head with her right hand, and embracing (with her left arm around the upper trunk) a young blossoming tree. Similarly, the left leg is entwined around the lower trunk of the tree while the other is placed on the *vāhana*, which may be an elephant, lion (*vyāḷa*) or horse. An intimate organic identity is established between the female and the tree through such an act.

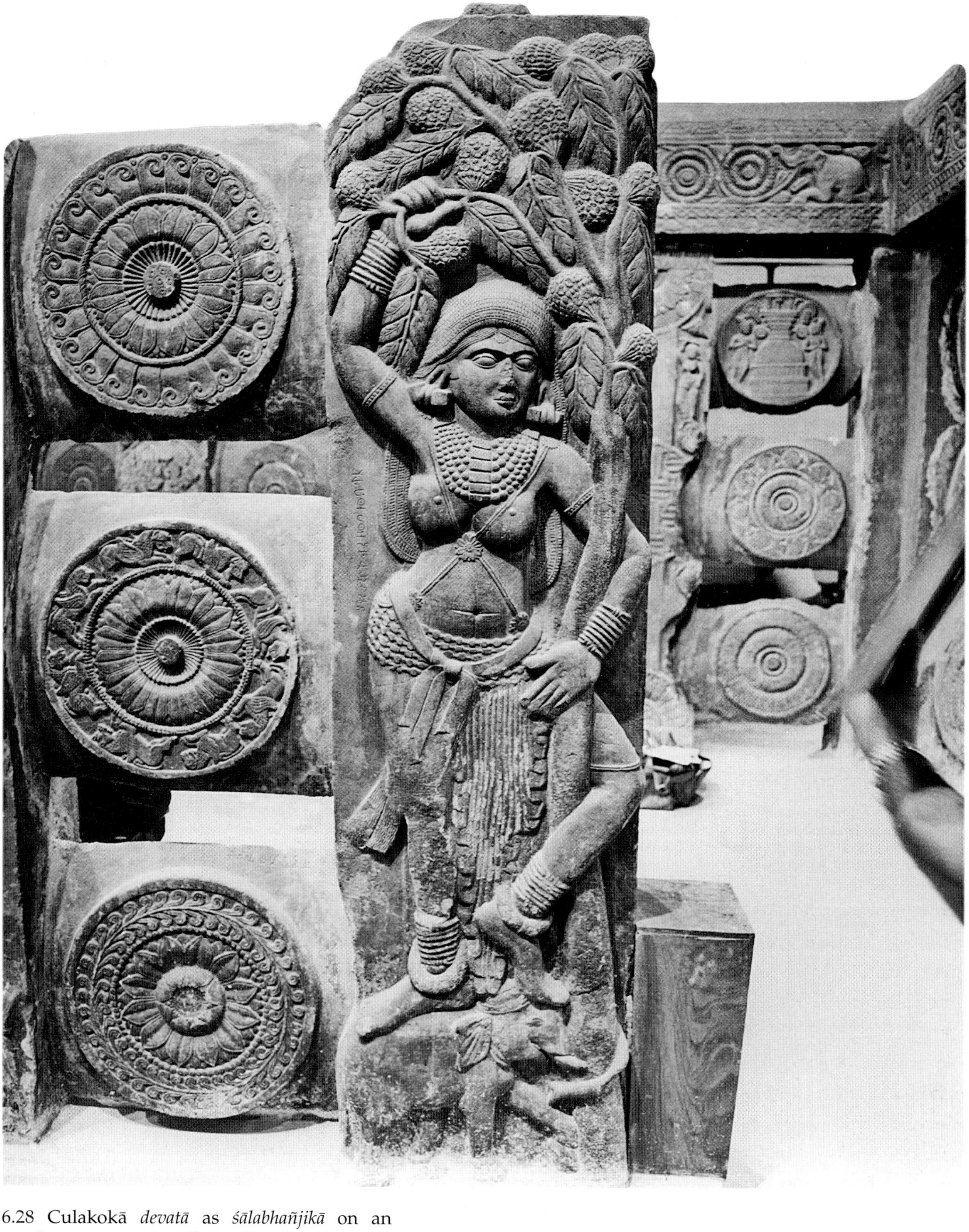

6.28 Culakokā *devatā* as *śālabhañjikā* on an elephant, great railing pillar, first century BCE, Bharhut. IM 62.

These figures have been labelled by their creators as Culakoka Devatā (*Pl.* 6.28), Candra Yakṣī (*Pl.* 6.29) and an unnamed female, perhaps Madhyakoka Devatā (*Pl.* 6.30).[24] Usually clad in an elaborately pleated *dhotī* that reaches the ankles, these figures are also profusely adorned with ornaments and bands of flowers or sun and moon marks decorating the face. The gaze is focused sideways, with eyes turned either to left or right. This kind of *śālabhañjikā* depiction continues to adorn railing pillars and panels until the first century CE, as is seen on *stūpa* II at Sāñcī (*Pl.* 6.33) and a fragment from Kauśāmbī (*Pl.* 6.32).[25]

At Bodh-Gayā, a novel element is added to the *śālabhañjikā* composition. Here she embraces and is shown actually climbing the tree (*vṛkṣārohaṇa);*[26] her male partner kneeling at the base of the tree supports her right foot (*Pl.* 6.31). The pair and the tree are bound together in a dynamic relationship in this composition, either having some cultic significance or simply following an earlier poetic convention.

A double-sided bracket with *śālabhañjikā*s carved on both sides, discovered in Patna, anticipates beautiful and sensuous *toraṇa śālabhañjikā*s of the gateways of *stūpa* I at Sāñcī. The Sāñcī figures have been carved in the round as brackets attached to the architrave of the *toraṇa* (*Pl.* 6.34). Standing in an exaggerated *tribhaṅga*, their feet balanced on the projection that functions as a base, the *śālabhañjikā*s hold the branch of *aśoka* or mango trees curving in an arch above them with one hand, while the other is curled around the trunk of the tree. They are adorned with elaborate ornaments including bands of anklets, multi-stringed *mekhalā, upavīta*-like pearl-string, a necklace dangling between the breasts, and *karṇakuṇḍalas*. The hair is braided into a thick plait that hangs down to the waist at the back, or is dressed in an elaborate coiffure. The gaze is focused outwards towards the distant landscape. The pudendum is clearly visible under the transparent *dhotī*.

From these early *śālabhañjikā*s evolved an immense variety of female figures represented with trees during the Kuṣāṇa period. At Kauśāmbī, Mathurā and Sanghol (*Pls.* 6.36 to 6.42), the *śālabhañjikā*s continued to be depicted standing in *tribhaṅga*, only rarely in *atibhaṅga*, on a *nara* (*Pl.* 6.38) or *yakṣa-vāhana* (*Pl.* 6.42). The female form is voluptuous here, with round full breasts, a thin waist and wide hips. The figures are nominally clothed in *dhotī*s which are indicated only by the folds at the bottom, leaving the body exposed to the gaze of the viewer. The female form is accentuated by the various ornaments, ranging from a multi-stringed pearl *mekhalā*, thick bands of *nūpura*s, *keyūra*s and the like. The hair is set in elaborate coiffures (*Pls.* 6.29, 6.36). The figures are shown either frontally (*Pl.* 6.39), or in three-quarter profile (*Pl.* 6.37) or with their backs to the viewer (*Pl.* 6.40), either kicking a tree, or holding its branch (*Pls.* 6.38, 6.41) or plucking its fruit (*Pl.* 6.40). In one of the earlier examples of this variety, from the Mehrauli area in Delhi (*Pl.* 6.36),[27] the female figure is shown adorned with a disc on her belly that is similar to the stone discs from Taxila, Ropar, Murtazinganj, etc. It may be that these small stone discs were used as ornaments as pendants strung on a long string, or that the devices on them — such as honeysuckle patterns, mother goddesses, rows of animals and the like — added symbolic value to the female figures. In later specimens, this disc-like ornament is missing.

*Śālabhañjikā*s were also used as a device to separate and demarcate panels in bas-reliefs illustrating the life of the Buddha. At Mathurā[28] *śālabhañjikā*s flank the meditating Buddha,

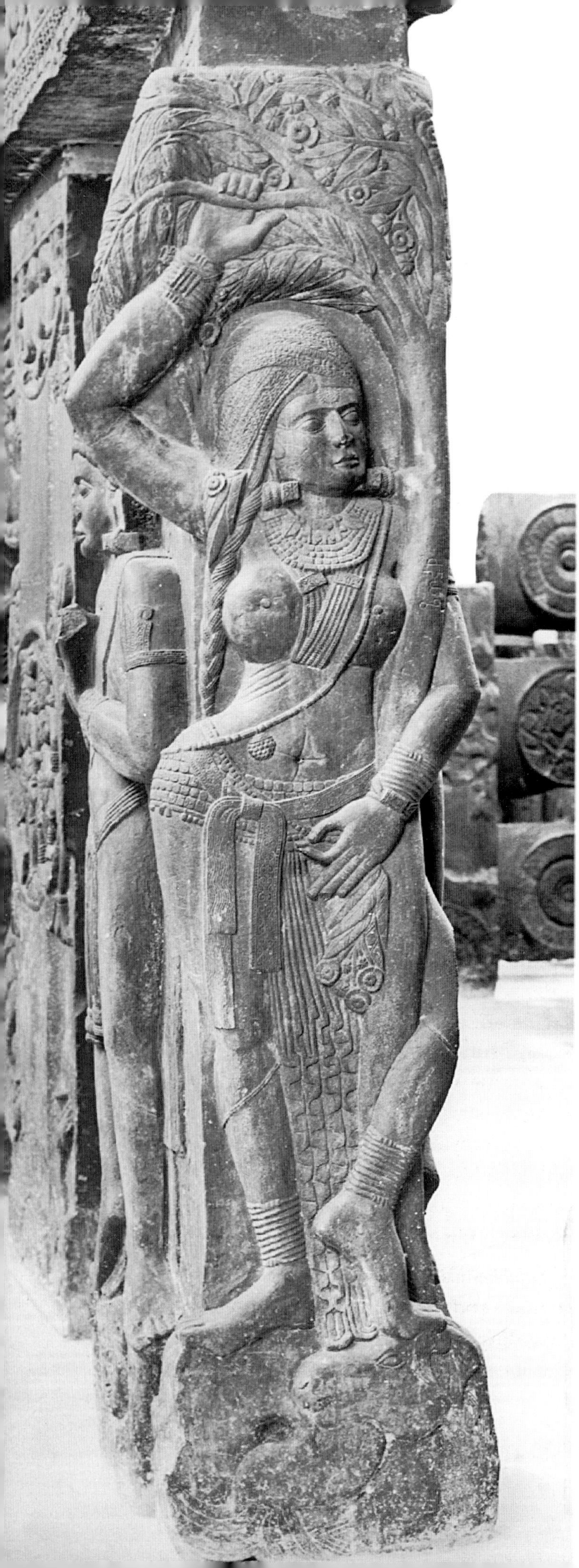

separating this episode from the next (*Pl.* 6.45); also at Nāgārjunakoṇḍa[29] a *śālabhañjikā* is positioned at the end of the *āyaka* panel simulating a *toraṇa śālabhañjikā*. Similar use of female figure is found on a mirror frame from Taxila (*Pl.* 6.43)[30] which may or may not have served a ritual purpose. At Begram too, *śālabhañjikā* figures have been found in a secular context (*Pl.* 6.44), decorating the backs of furniture pieces. The woman-and-tree motifs are among the myriad depictions of women engaged in various pleasure pursuits in the art of Begram.

### 6.3.1 DOHADA RITUAL

There is a familiar belief in India that the touch of a beautiful woman's foot would blossom the *aśoka* tree.[31] This survives in sculpture up to the eighteenth century.

The word *dohada*[32] means a pregnancy longing, and the tree is attributed to this feeling, like a woman; its petals cannot open until it is satiated. Thus the whole concept, even in its latest form as mere piece of rhetoric, preserves the old connection between trees and tree spirits and human life.[33]

The *dohada* imagery like the *śālabhañjikā* shows a woman and tree, but in this case, she has one foot placed against the trunk of the tree, as if kicking it. This is, however, one variety of *dohada* among many, since the term implies direct and indirect contact of a tree with a woman. From Kalidāsa's *Meghadūta*, Pisharoti has identified ten types of plants or vegetation that crave a certain kind of contact with a young woman: *Priyaṅgu*, a creeper, blossoms from the touch of a woman; *bakula* (*Mimusops elengi*) through the sprinkling of liquor gargled from women; *aśoka* (*Jonesia*

6.29 *Yakṣī* Candrā as *śālabhañjikā*, great railing, pillar, Bharhut. IM.

6.30 Unknown female figure, *śālabhañjikā*, great railing, first century BCE, Bharhut. IM.

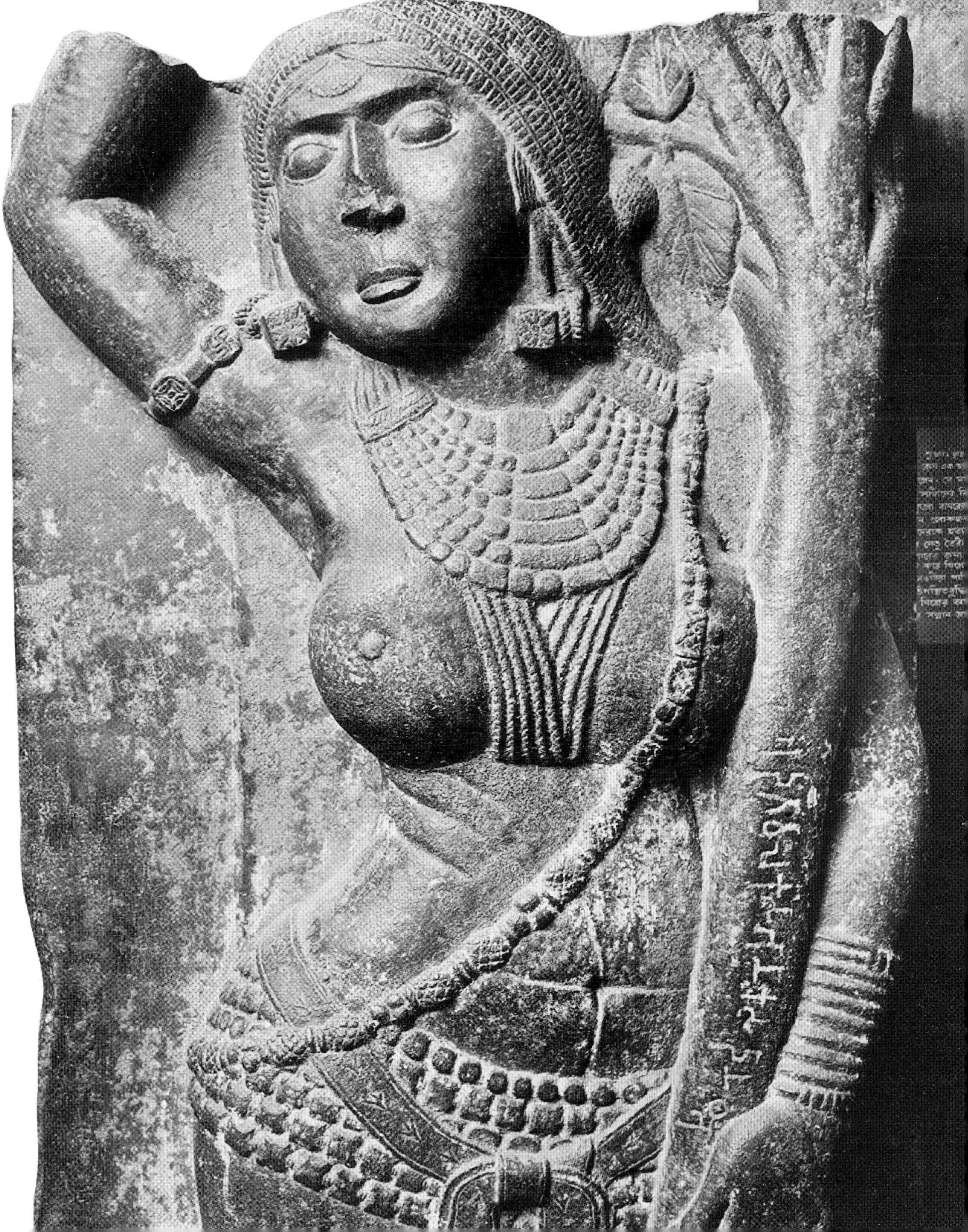

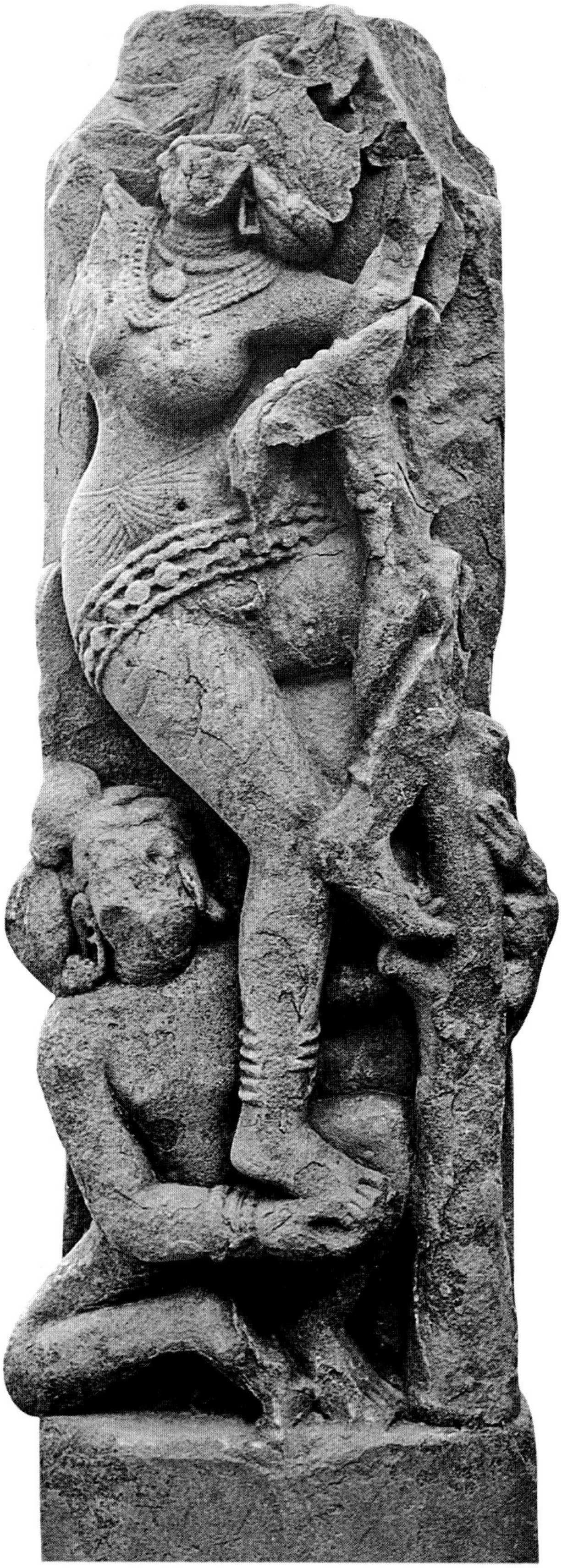

*asoka*) desires a kick from the foot of a woman; *tilaka* (*Clerodendrum phlomidis*) and *kurabaka* (red *amaranth*) blossom from their glance and embrace respectively; *mandāra* (*Erythrina indica*), from their sweet words; *cuta* (*mangifera indica*), by blowing with their mouth; *nameru* (*Elaeocarpus ganitrus*) from their music and *karṇika* (*Pterospermum acerifolium*) from the dancing of women in front of it.[34] He seems to have inadvertently left out *campaka* (*Michelia champaca*), which blooms on hearing her sweet laughter.

### 6.3.2 ŚĀLABHAÑJIKĀ

For Coomaraswamy[35] there is no motif more fundamentally characteristic of Indian art than that of Woman and Tree. Coomaraswamy cites a passage from the *Mahābhārata* where "goddesses born in trees (are) to be worshipped by those desiring children, such goddesses being designated as dryads, *vṛkṣakā* or *vṛddhikā*."[36]

He does not differentiate between the *śālabhañjikā*s found in early art at various sites such as Bharhut, Bodh-Gayā, Sāñcī, Mathurā and Amarāvatī, but remarks that the female figures associated with trees are voluptuous beauties, almost nude, but always provided with broad jewelled belts, *mekhalā*s, as they appear in pre-Mauryan terracottas of fertility goddesses and signify a long life (*āyuṣya*) charm.[37] Sometimes these dryads, in varied poses, stand on vehicles; a lotus support is exceptional.

In sheer numbers and in its traditional continuity, the *śālabhañjikā* image is a potent and powerful indicator of the importance it gained in the art of the period. However, it was not a frozen form, but a dynamic image that changed and

6.31 Woman being helped by male companion to climb a tree, first century CE, Bodh-Gayā, Bihar.

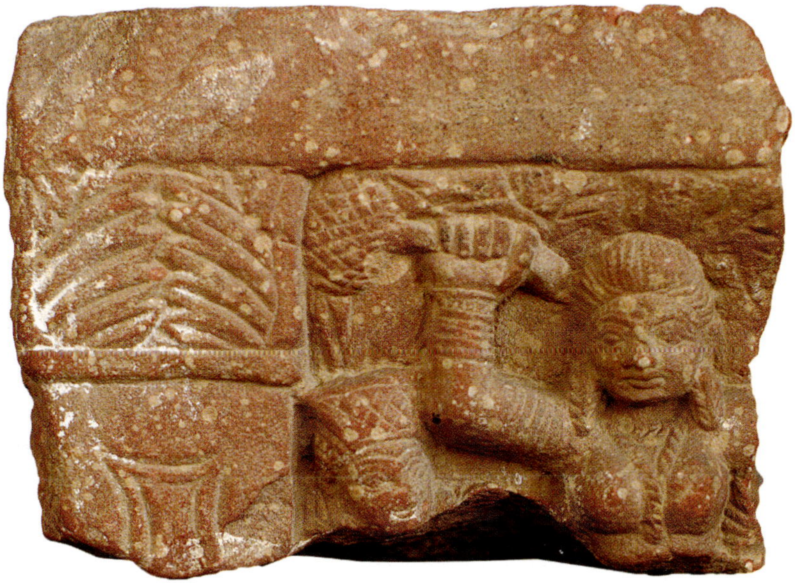

6.32 *Śālabhañjikā* and a female adorant, second-first century BCE, Kauśāmbī, Allahabad district, UP.

adapted itself. There is also a transformation of meanings attached to it. It was a kind of a meta-representation from which figures of Māyādevī, the *gaṇikā* figure, etc. derived their imagery as seen before.

The intentionality of this imagery cannot be read from epigraphs at Bharhut. The term *śālabhañjikā* is not mentioned. Very limited information may be gleaned from the texts datable to post-Mauryan period. Although in the immediately subsequent literature, the references to both *śālabhañjikā*s and *dohada* imagery are profuse.

A study of dedicatory inscriptions (by lay-men and lay-women, monks and nuns) accompanying *śālabhañjikā*s, reveals that there is no difference based on gender or status in the imagery.

We need to examine the imagery itself as also its placement to understand the form and function of *yakṣī*/*śālabhañjikā*. We see that the *śālabhañjikā* was not

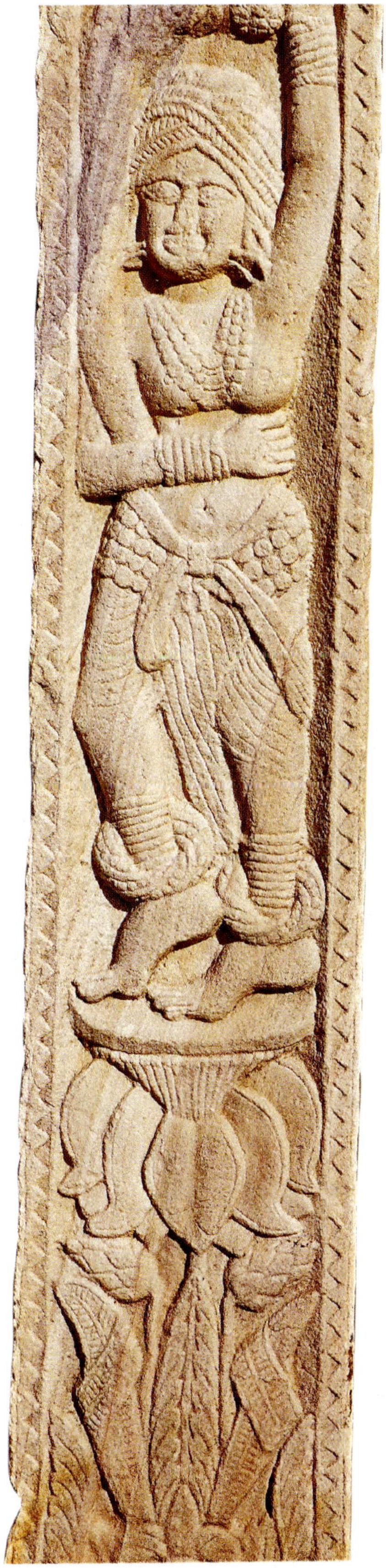

6.33 *Śālabhañjikā*, railing pillar, *stūpa* 2, first century BCE, Sāñcī.

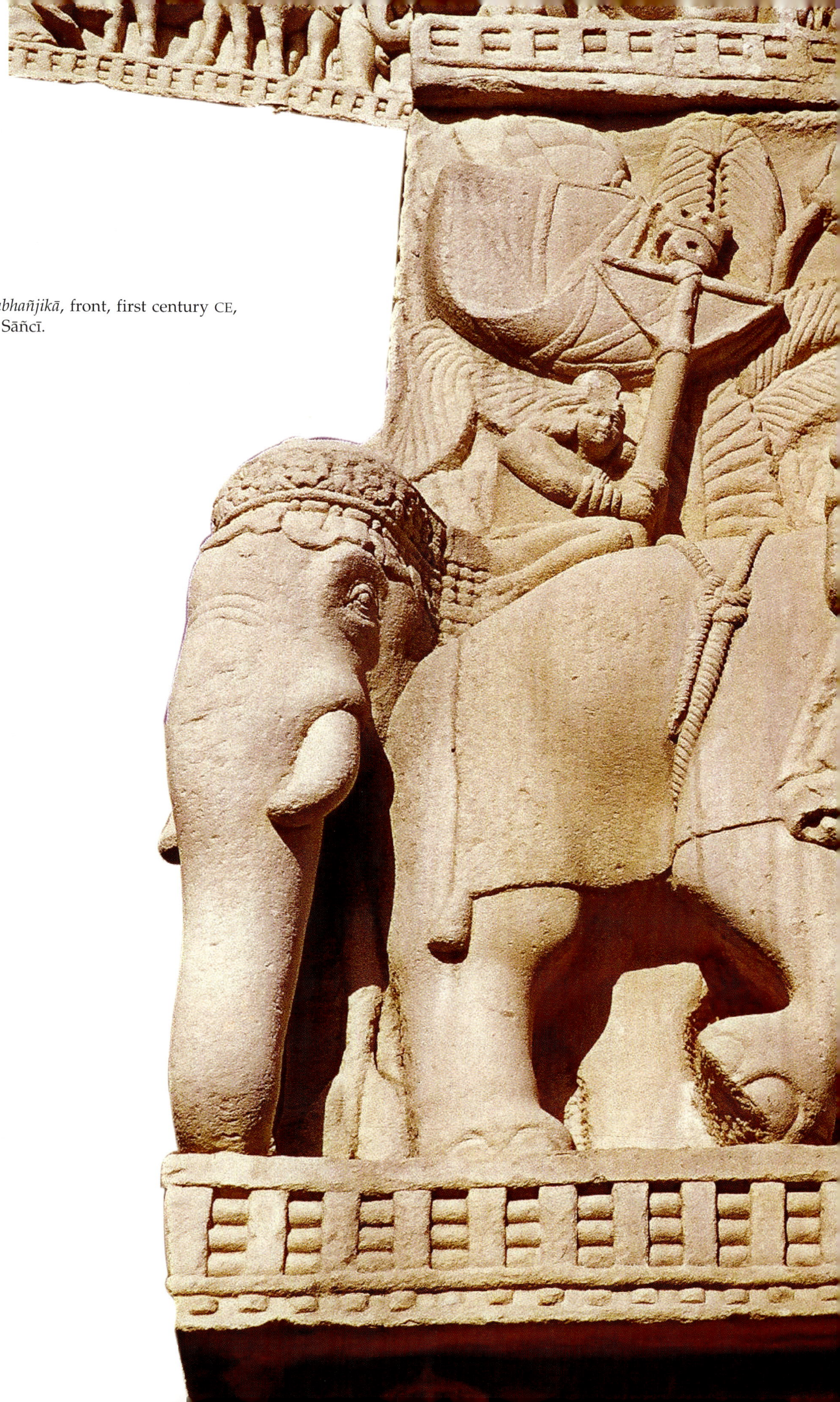

6.34 *Toraṇa Śālabhañjikā*, front, first century CE, from *stūpa* 1, Sāñcī.

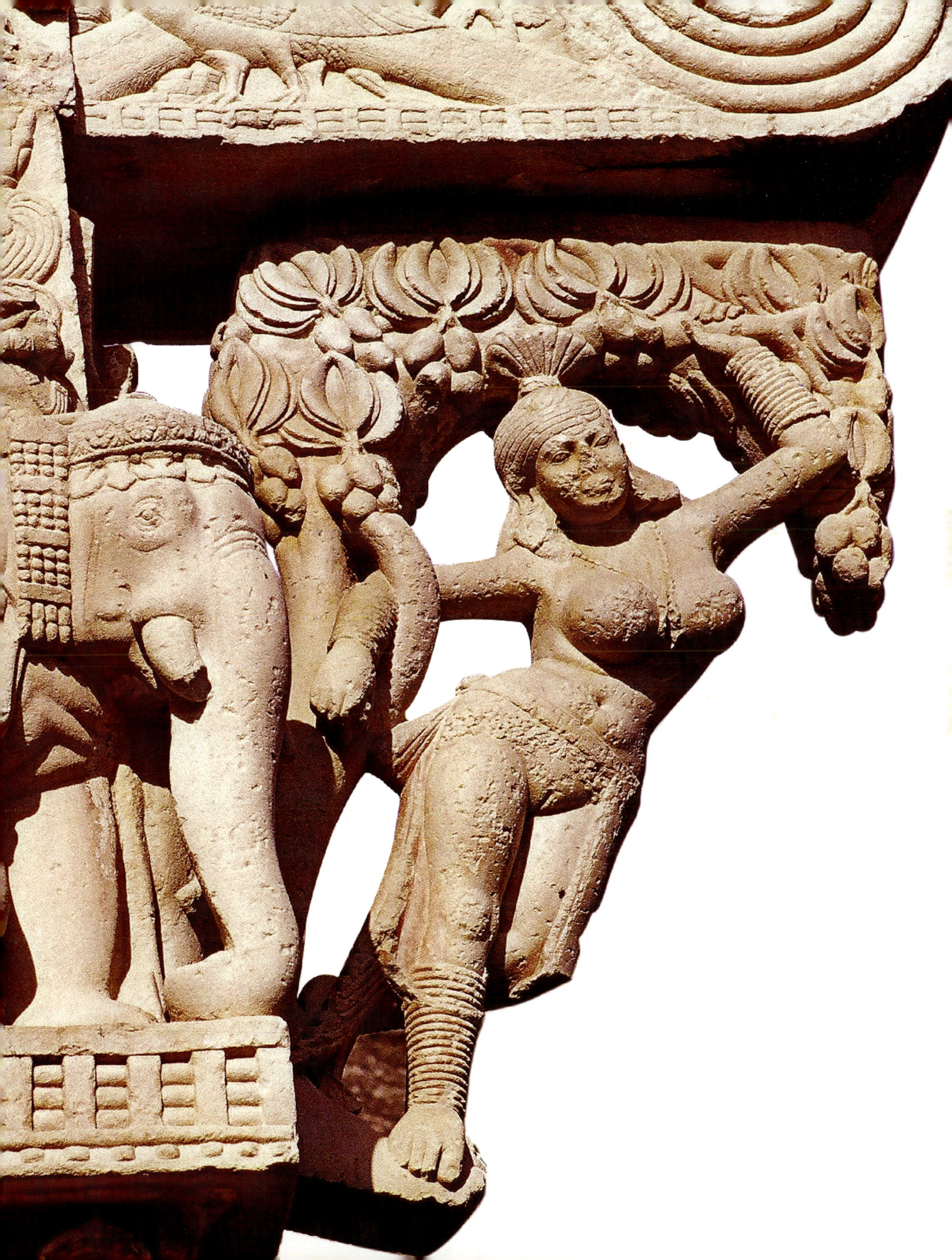

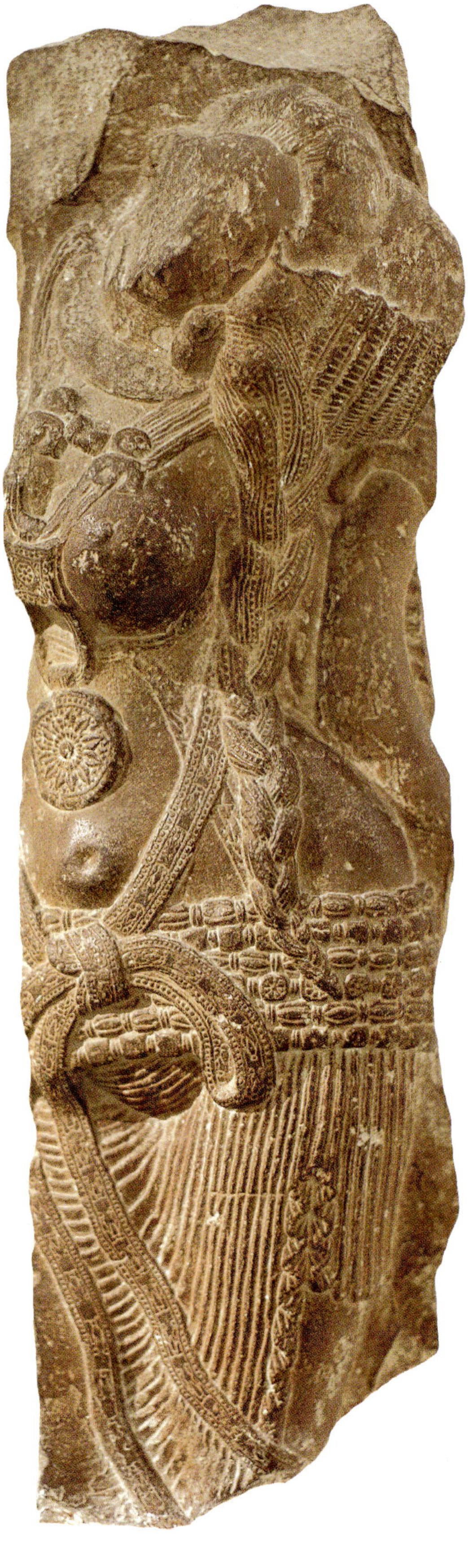

used as a cult object, unlike the *yakṣī*, though it was probably the prototype on which this image was based. It was definitely used for *alaṁkāra*. Unlike the cult images, it was not *guhya* or secret but placed in the open and in very prominent places. Its function was decorative, but the issue is as to whether this was their primary function. Scholars have suggested that *śālabhañjikā*s, because of their origins from the *dohada* belief, stood for fertility. The question is, fertilising what: the monument, the donor or the viewer? What is its position in the textual sources?

Bharhut has been reconstructed and so it is difficult to comment on its positioning, but their size seems to suggest the importance of their role, as they are found both on the great *vedikā* and the *toraṇa*.

The role of the *yakṣī/śālabhañjikā* may be indicated by the reliefs on votive stele from Mathurā (e.g. of Siyavasa), where dancing figures are shown on both sides of the miniature *stūpa*. This suggests that the presence of *śālabhañjikā* or similar figure was essential to religious edifices and secular structures such as *nepathya* — proscenium and other performance spaces — in order to make them auspicious, *maṅgala*.

The representation of a woman holding or standing under a tree occurs repeatedly in almost all layers of the Śuṅga and Kuṣāṇa arts. A question that needs to be asked is whether the *aśoka* tree was seen as inherently male, and if so, then was this symbolism representative of the *puruṣa/prakṛti* dichotomy? While in the earlier depictions at Bodh-Gayā and Bharhut, the woman is shown actually performing the *dohada*, in Sanghol and Mathurā, the maiden is only holding a branch or standing under a tree. The

6.35 *Śālabhañjikā*, Śuṅga, first century BCE, Mehrauli, New Delhi, Stone. NM Acc. No. 59.539.

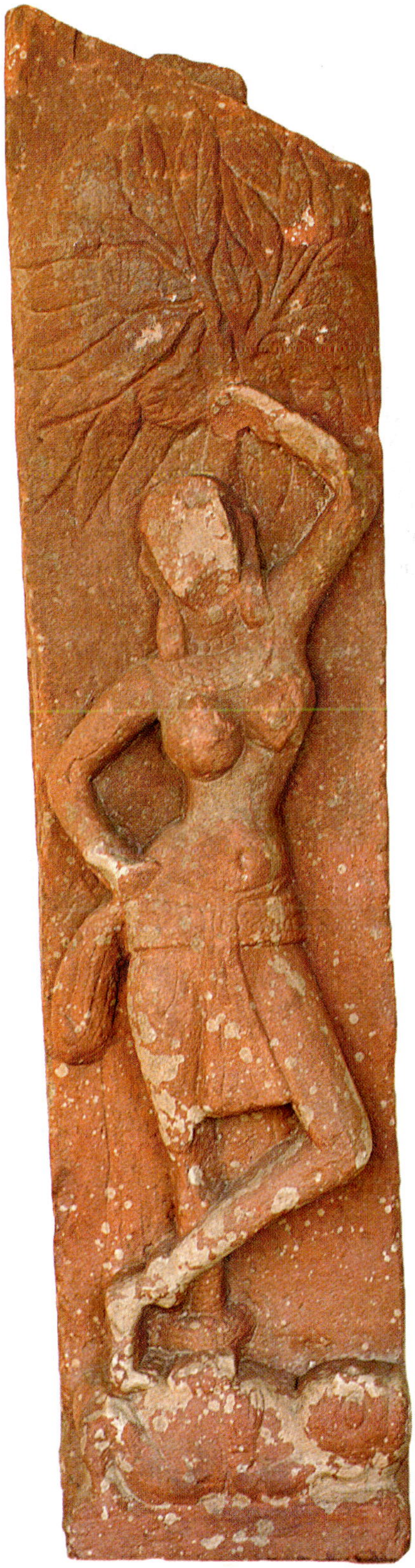

6.36 *Śālabhañjikā*, red sandstone, railing pillar, second century CE, Koṭā, Mathurā district, UP. GMM.

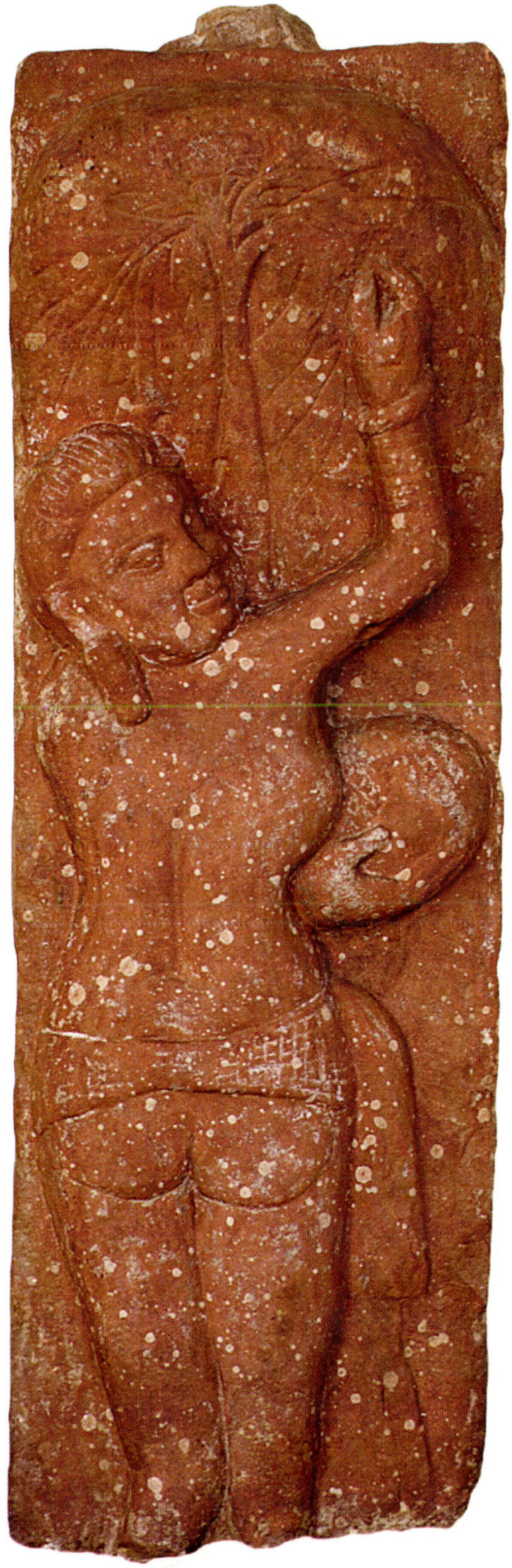

6.37 *Śālabhañjikā*, red sandstone, second century CE, railing pillar, Mathurā district, UP. GMM.

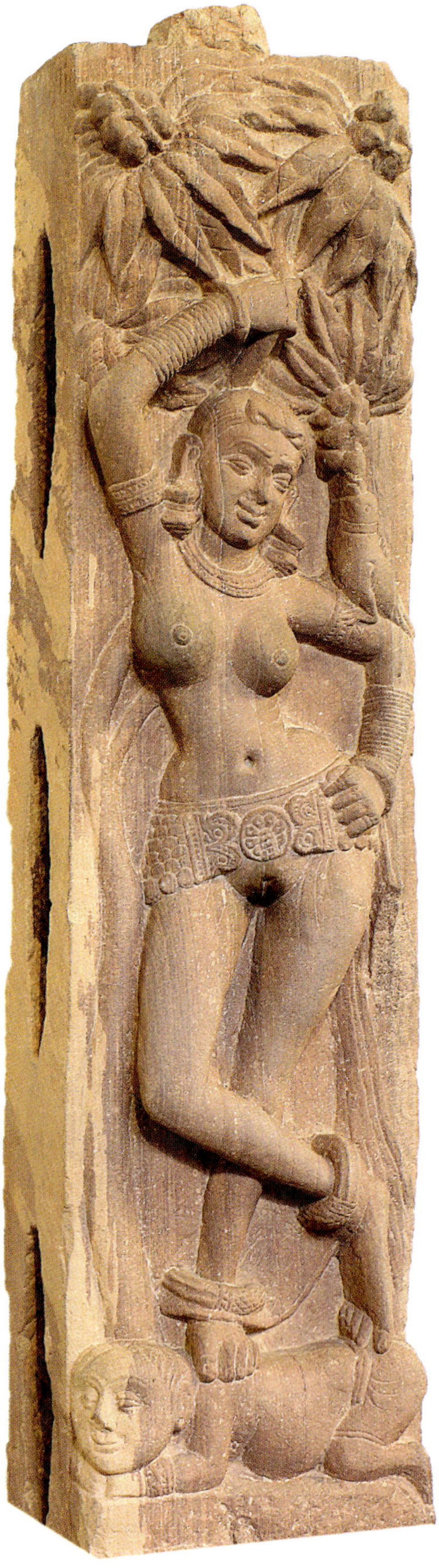

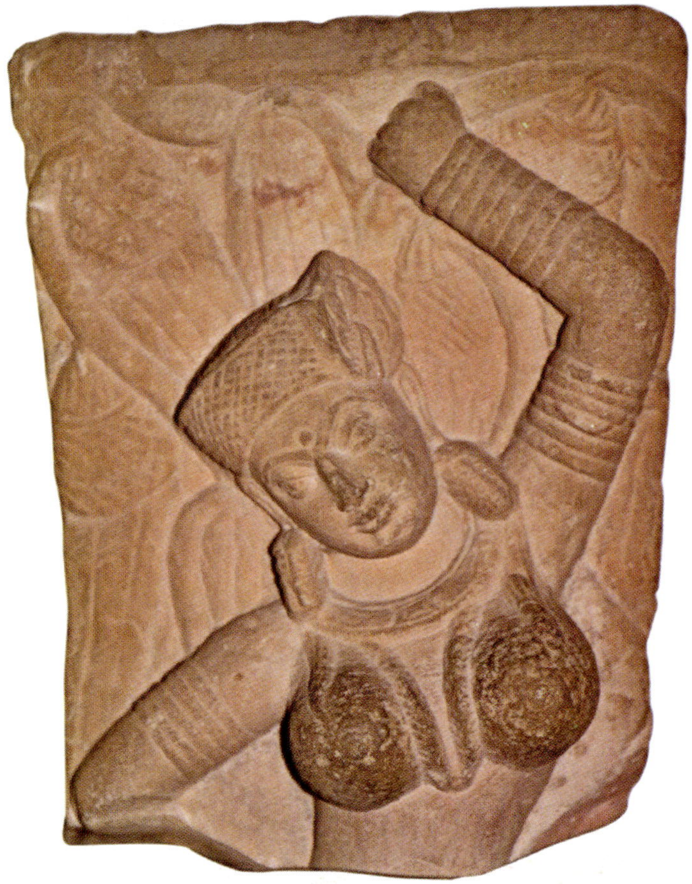

6.39 Torso of a *śālabhañjikā*, red sandstone, second-third century CE, Mathurā. SML.

6.38 *Śālabhañjikā* standing on dwarf *yakṣa*, railing pillar, red sandstone, second century CE, Sanghol.

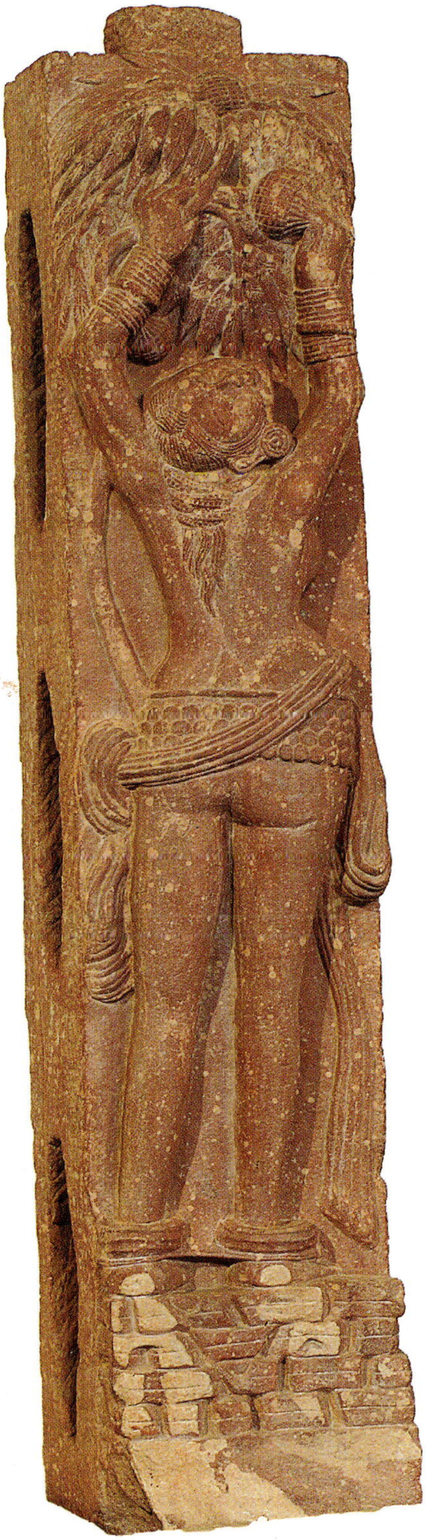

6.40 Back view of a woman holding fruit hanging from a tree, railing pillar, second century CE, Kuṣāṇa, Sanghol.

posture and apparel also become more sensual in the Kuṣāṇa period in comparison to the earlier period. It has been suggested by Devangana Desai that there is an increased sexualisation of the *śālabhañjikā* image.[38]

### 6.4 Context: Architectural Elements

*Śālabhañjikā* in the lexicons is given as an image or a figure made of *śāla* wood, or a kind of a game played in eastern India, also a harlot or a courtesan.[39] The term *śālabhañjikā* is also understood to be an architectural element/ ornament carved on the *vedikās*, *toraṇas* and *stambhas* of various buildings. However, it did not start off as a mere architectural ornament. This is borne out by the figures at Bharhut, where they are bending or touching a branch of a tree and with legs twined around the trunk and have been labelled as *yakṣī* or *devatā*. This would imply that some kind of divine or cultic status was ascribed to these figures. It is also significant that the *śālabhañjikā* imagery was shared by the venerated person of Māyādevī in the "Birth of The Buddha" series.

Two sources may reveal how *śālabhañjikās* were

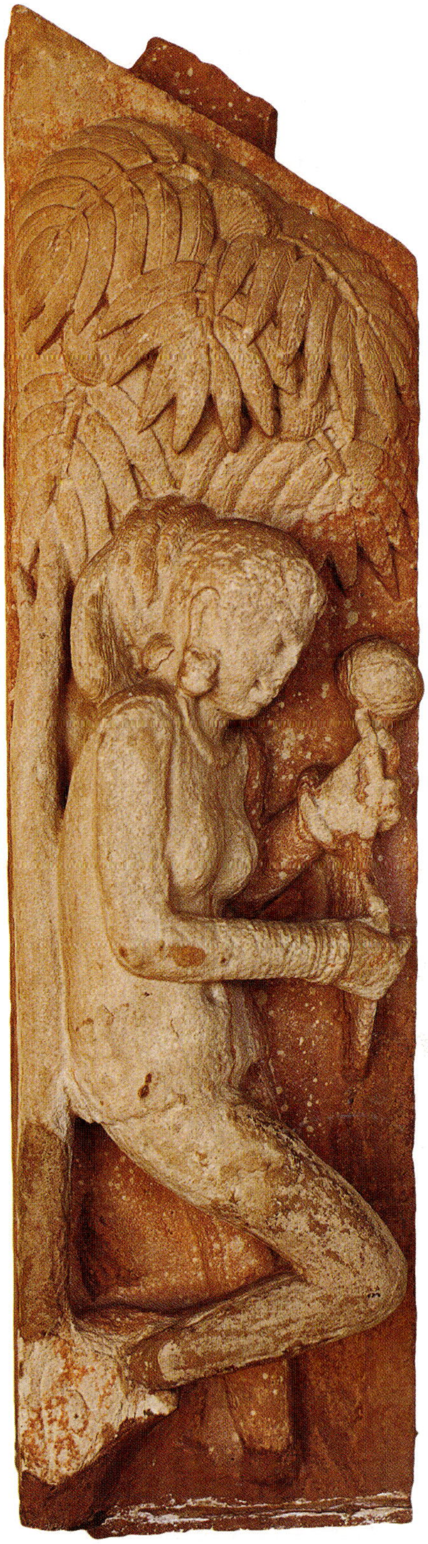

6.41 *Śālabhañjikā* kicking or touching tree with her foot, railing pillar, second century CE, Kuṣāṇa, Sanghol.

perceived in ancient society. One of them is a verse from the *Buddhacarita* by Aśvaghoṣa: "Another leaning on the side of a window, with her willow form bent like a bow, shone as she lay with her beautiful necklace hanging down, like a statue in an archway made by art, a *toraṇa śālabhañjikā*."[40] The context of this verse is that Śuddhodana, agitated by the prophecy that Prince Siddhārtha would renounce the world, set the harem girls to tempt him to stay. One of the women appeared as beautiful and attractive as a *toraṇa śālabhañjikā*. In the *Nāṭyaśāstra* there is a reference to *śālastrī* which was probably another

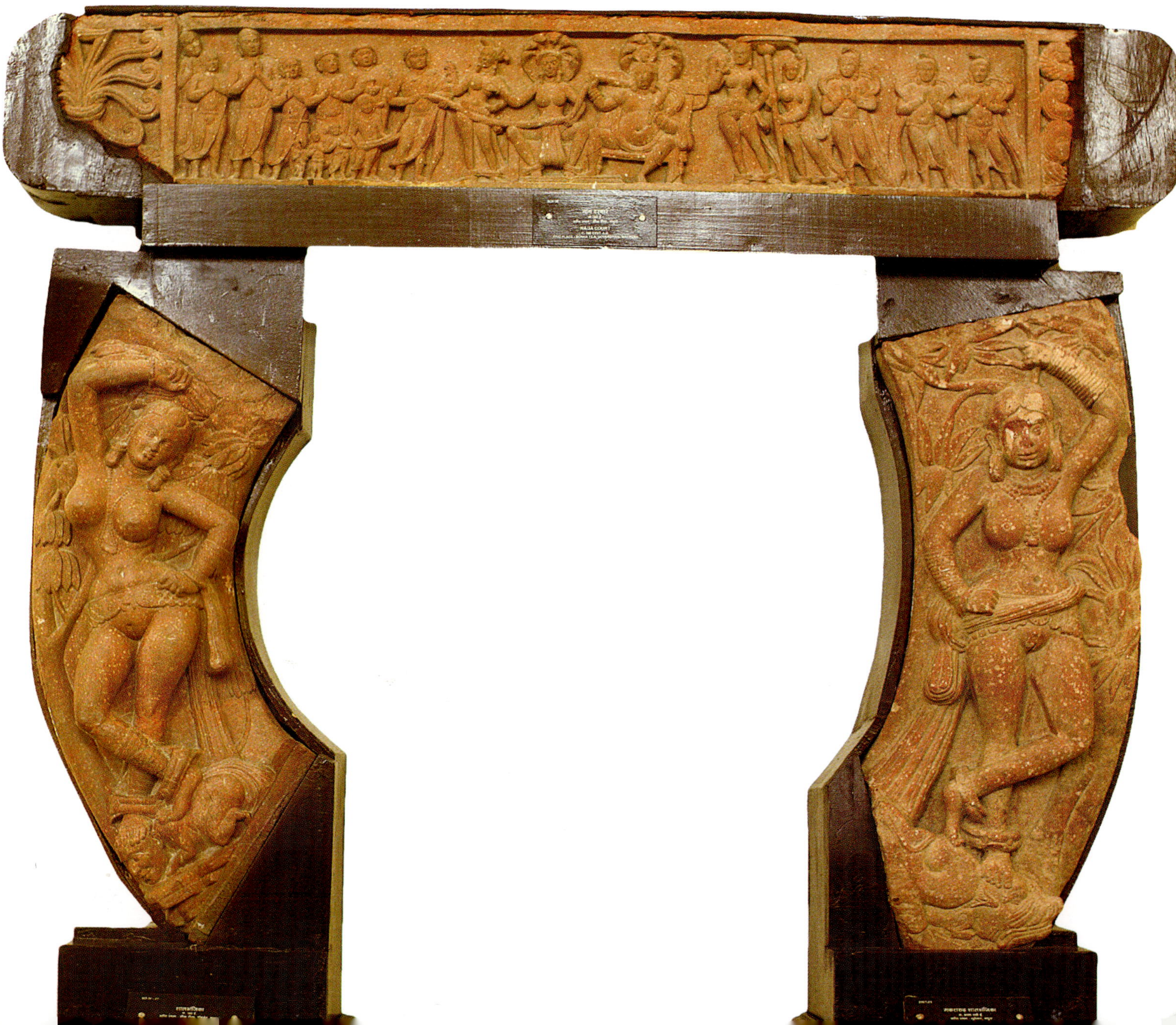

6.42 *Śālabhañjikā*s flanking doorway, with Nāgarāja in his court on upright, second century CE, red sandstone, Kuṣāṇa, Soṅkh.

term for *śālabhañjikā*: "In the interior of the playhouse . . . after raising (for the stage or *raṅgapīṭha*) a plinth eight cubit [square], pillars should be raised to support the roof of the playhouse. These pillars should be fixed to the roof with proper fasteners and be decorated with figures of women with tree."[41]

Some idea of where and how the *śālabhañjikā*s were placed *vis-à-vis* the *stūpa*s can be obtained from Śvetāmbara Jaina texts, *Rājapraśnīya Sūtra* and the *Jīvājīvābhigama Sūtra*, datable to the first century BCE.[42] In the *Rājapraśnīya Sūtra* references to *śālabhañjikā*s are found in relation to the construction of a *prekṣāgṛha* of a *vimāna*, on the orders of Sūryabhūdeva, by semi-divine beings known as *abhiyogika deva*s. Sūryabhūdeva ordered that a *yāna vimāna* be made which would have, among other elements, a number of *śālabhañjikā*s, full of *līlā* and expression (*hāva-bhāva*) and *vilāsa yukta*. Apparently his wishes were fulfilled and the *prekṣāgṛha* was built that was endowed with a number of pillars, high and well-constructed *vedikā*s and *toraṇa*s, decorated with *śālabhañjikā*s. While describing the *dvāra*s (doors) of this *vimāna* he says that these are ornamented by sporting *śālabhañjikā-krīḍa*, with *vyāḷarūpa*s and snakes made of various precious stones (*maṇi-ratna*).[43] Importantly, he says that on both sides of the doors are *niṣidhikon* (sitting rooms) with rows of *śālabhañjikā*s sixteen each.[44] These are in various forms of play-*līlā-krīḍa* and well established and appealing form (*supratiṣithat manojña rūpa*).[45] Also (in *khaṇḍika* 200)[46] there is a description on the conduct of a ritual at the *stūpa* or *vimāna* of the *arhant* — whereby a *cāmara* was passed/waved over the deities such as *śālabhañjikā*s/*vyāḷarūpa*s carved on the doorways and gateways. This would suggest that the *śālabhañjikā*s deserved worshipful respect. One might add that it is recommended that among other motifs such as *śālabhañjikā*s, the *aṣṭa maṅgala*s should be carved on the gateway. The *śālabhañjikā* through association may be considered to be part of the scheme of *maṅgala* (auspicious symbols).

In the post-Mauryan period, the *śālabhañjikā*s and the *dohada* sub-types have been found only in architectural contexts. Mostly they are seen on the *vedikā* pillars and gateways, coinciding with the *toraṇa śālabhañjikā*s and *stambha yoṣita*s (young women carved on pillars), mentioned in the textual traditions.

At Bharhut, we have three large *śālabhañjikā*s on the *vedikā*. At Sāñcī, they adorn the *toraṇa* as free flying bracket figures on the eastern and northern gates. At Soṅkh, a *toraṇa* fragment carved with a *śālabhañjikā* in high relief has been noticed in the precincts of a Nāga temple. In Mathurā, at Kaṅkālī Ṭīlā (which is a Jaina site) and at Kauśāmbī, these were probably found at *stūpa* sites. We know from Jaina texts that *śālabhañjikā*s adorned the *toraṇa*s of *stūpa*s. It is clear that by the Kuṣāṇa period *śālabhañjikā*s are not confined to Buddhist sites alone or carved in the context of structures belonging to what we know today as major religions, but also minor religious cults like the Nāga cult.

The architectural context of the *śālabhañjikā* imagery is apparent from their depictions at Begram, Nāgārjunakoṇḍa, Amarāvatī, and from *śilāpaṭṭa*s such as that of Sivayasa[47] from Mathurā. In the *Buddhacarita*, the human animate subject (the sleeping female attendant) is compared to an inanimate architectural object (the *toraṇa śālabhañjikā*) which clearly indicates the latter's primary function as an ornament within an architectural setting. We have to place the *śālabhañjikā* within the discourse of architecture, and take them out of the discourse of fertility to enable us to get a more accurate estimate of this imagery.

#### 6.4.1 ORIGIN AND IDENTIFICATION

The debate on the identification of *śālabhañjikā*s has been a prolonged one. At first all such figures were seen as Māyādevī giving birth to the Buddha. Coomaraswamy said that these represented *vṛkṣasa*s and *vūddhakā*s.[48] The image originated as a *yakṣī*. *Yakṣī* was considered a *vanadevī* in Kālidāsa's writings, and in his *Meghadūta*, the travails of a *yakṣa* separated from his *yakṣī* wife are described in a passage wherein he desires the touch of her left foot (*vāmapādābhilāṣin*) like a *dohada*.[49] Other poetic constructions as described in the *Padataditakam*,[50] part of the Caturbhānī, with a *vilāṣinī* and a kneeling dwarf, are also part of the *śālabhañjikā* lore. U.N. Roy takes the Sāñcī and Mathurā figures to be symbols of external allurement, presented to the viewer just as Śuddhodana presented lovely damsels to tempt the Buddha and dissuade him from leaving the palace and kingdom.[51] He cites from the *Buddhacarita*, Canto 4, to suggest that the *stambha yoṣitā* motifs which are chiselled on the brackets of the *toraṇa*s and the pillars of the *vedikā*s of Śuṅga-Kuṣāṇa art, and which are characterised by charming damsels with firm and close-set breasts and hips veiled by translucent robes and girdles with occasionally kneeling dwarfs under their feet, represent elements of external allurement and worldly attractions, whereas the water bubble-like dome of the *stūpa*, surrounded by railposts, is a symbol of momentary nature of life and the certainty of death.

We have not found any epigraph that labels these images as *śālabhañjikā*s. The only inscriptions are on the Bharhut *stūpa* where they are labelled as *yakṣī*s and *devatā*s as we have seen above. All information pertaining to *śālabhañjikā*s is found in texts. The *vṛkṣakā*s of the railing pillars are properly to be described as *yakṣī*s as proved by inscriptions accompanying similar figures at Bharhut.

One thing is clear, mainly from Jaina and Buddhist texts, that by the post-Mauryan era, *śālabhañjikā*s at least represented an artistic device used to embellish architectural pieces and were known as *toraṇa śālabhañjikā*s[52] and *stambha yoṣitā*s.[53]

Their origins may have been in some game or in the postures adopted during this game. Some useful surveys of texts that mention *śālabhañjikā*s have been attempted by Vogel, Pisharoti, Roth and Roy. Vogel was the first to point out that the origin of the *śālabhañjikā* motif may lie in a game played by women of the east who went to the *śāla* forest and plucked the flowers as described by Pāṇini in his *Aṣṭādhyāyī* datable to the fifth century BCE. This game was well known in both Buddhist and Jaina texts, where *uddulakapuṣpabhañjikā*s are mentioned. Roth has interpreted this game to represent the hopes and desires of young women to have children, "as pure, gay and beautiful as the blossoms of the *Śāla*-tree. From the point of view of her own fertility, it must have been very auspicious for a young woman to catch hold of the branch of a tree, which stands in full splendour of its blossoms."

### 6.5 Śālabhañjikā and Eroticism

One of the most debated issues in art is the apparent sensuality seen in artworks and the purported asceticism of most religious systems within which this art was produced. And the indicator of this is the eroticised provocative treatment of *yakṣī-śālabhañjikā* figures.

The *yakṣī-śālabhañjikā* imagery has been at the root of much debate in analysing ancient Indian art history. Given the profusion in which these pieces were discovered, along with the religious

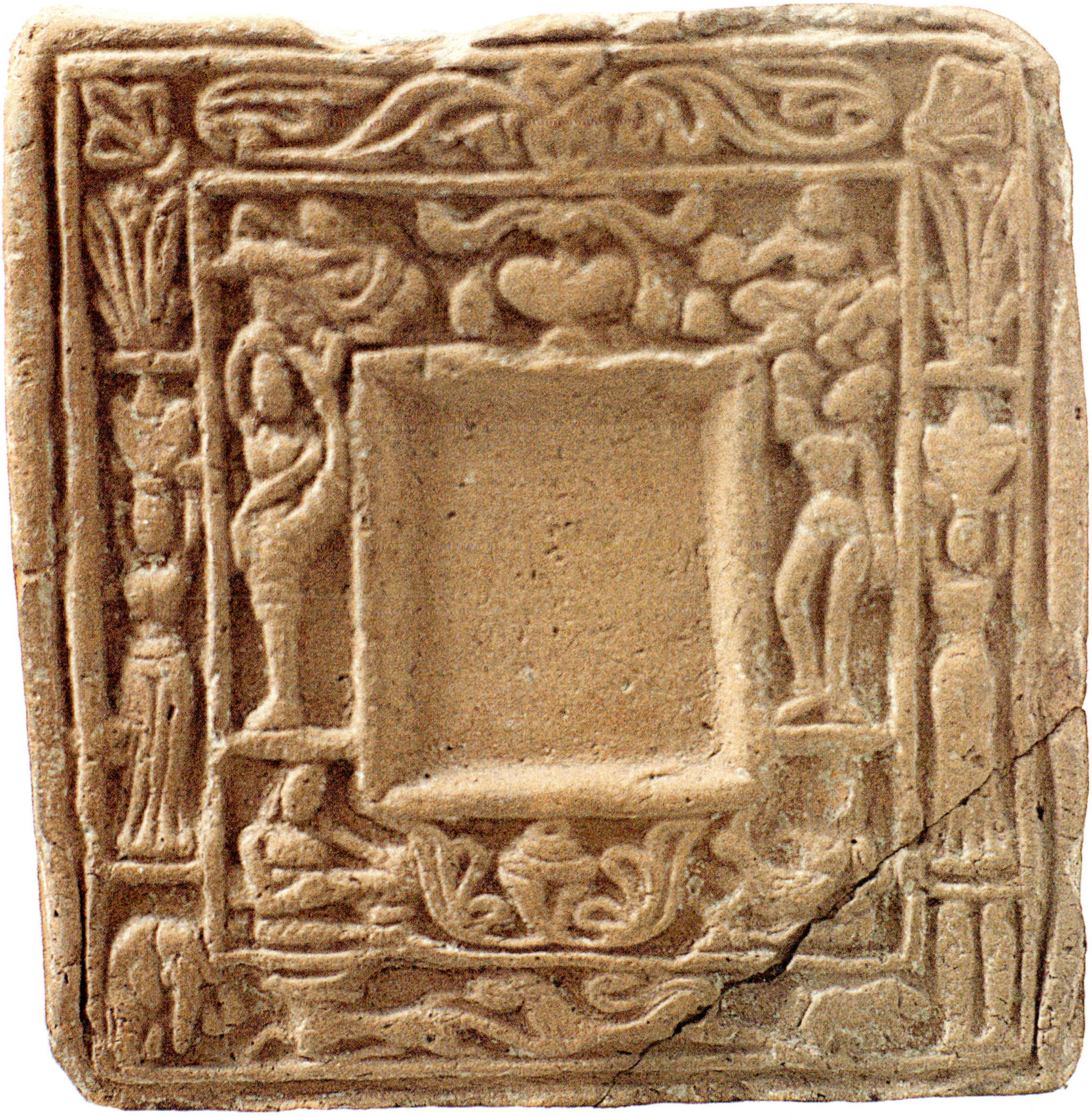

6.43 *Āyāgapaṭṭa* or mirror frame, terracotta, second-first centruy BCE, Taxila, Gandhāra. NM Acc. No. 85.B.M. 51/13

contexts in which they were set, *yakṣī-śālabhañjikā* images came to be reviled for their blatant sensuality. An epitome of Victorian Puritanism, Vincent Smith, wrote about the Mathurā *yakṣīs*, and I quote, "They exhibit lasciviousness combined with grossness. While Chanda and Culakoka and their sisters have the appearance of heavenly nymphs, their unworthy descendants are mere courtesans, exhibiting their opulent charms and gaudy jewellery."[54] J. Ph. Vogel comments that the Mathurā figures have a singular lack of distinction in their aggressive nudity. Gustav Roth disagrees, opining that the figures at Mathurā are nearer to the everyday secular world and display more human artfulness and worldly affinities than the earlier figures at Bharhut. However, he also observes "how much more the graceful pose of a woman raising her arm for any other purpose may have appealed to the aesthetic sentiments of the people of India,"[55] in the context of the artists of ancient India copying the graceful pose of young women plucking flowers during the *śālabhañjikā* festival, transforming it into a fixed artistic pose of a female seizing the branch of a tree. R.C. Sharma[56] says that "in the earlier styles of Bharhut and Sāñcī the womenfolk seem to have played a simple and innocent role. They are there as a part of society either to perform worship and rituals, to earn charity or are seen as supernatural beings, as objects of worship, i.e. as *yakṣīs* and *devatās*. But the artist of Mathurā served a different purpose through shaping their extra round breasts, heavy hips, graceful postures, suggestive movements, attractive looks and inviting gestures."[57] "Apparently the artist at Mathurā aims at revealing the secrets of female beauty through voluptuous forms, blending sensuous emotion with religious and spiritual fervour," according to Roth. A more philosophical view, given below, is taken by Coomaraswamy and Stella Kramrisch, who viewed the *śālabhañjikā* imagery in a spiritual context.[58]

Pisharoti has tried to prove that the *dohada* imagery is erotic both in content and intent. According to him, seen in the context of *alaṁkārika* (ornamentation) terminology, all the activities performed by lovely women to bring a tree to bloom in off-season are *uddīpanavibhāvas* which form a part of *śṛṅgāra rasa*, or the erotic sentiment. Within this they can be seen as representing *saṁbhoga śṛṅgāra*, love in togetherness, which can mean sexual union also.

Very often they hold with one hand a branch of a tree under which they stand, sometimes one leg is twined around the stem of the tree; this is an erotic conception, for *latā* is both "creeper" or "vine" and "women," "Tree after tree thou climbest, like a lustful girl" (*AV* V.5.3), "as the creeper embraces the tree on all sides, so do thou embrace me" (*AV* VI.8.1), and "when will Tarita's daughter cling to me, even as a forest creeper to some forest tree." (*Ummadanti Jātaka*, no. 527).

### 6.6 Fertility, Fertilisation and the Feminine

A commonly held view is that the *śālabhañjikā-yakṣī* motif became popular in the post-Mauryan architectural *alaṁkāra* scheme because it denoted fertility.

Stella Kramrisch observes that in the *śālabhañjikā* motif the vegetative and the feminine coalesce so organically as to transmit the creative generative energy from one to the other.[59]

Coomaraswamy says that the *śālabhañjikā* figures are placed on Buddhist and Jaina monuments because these are fertility figures; women, accustomed to invoking the blessings of a tree spirit would approach the railing pillar images with similar expectations. These images, like those of *nagas* and *yakṣas*, are often set up at

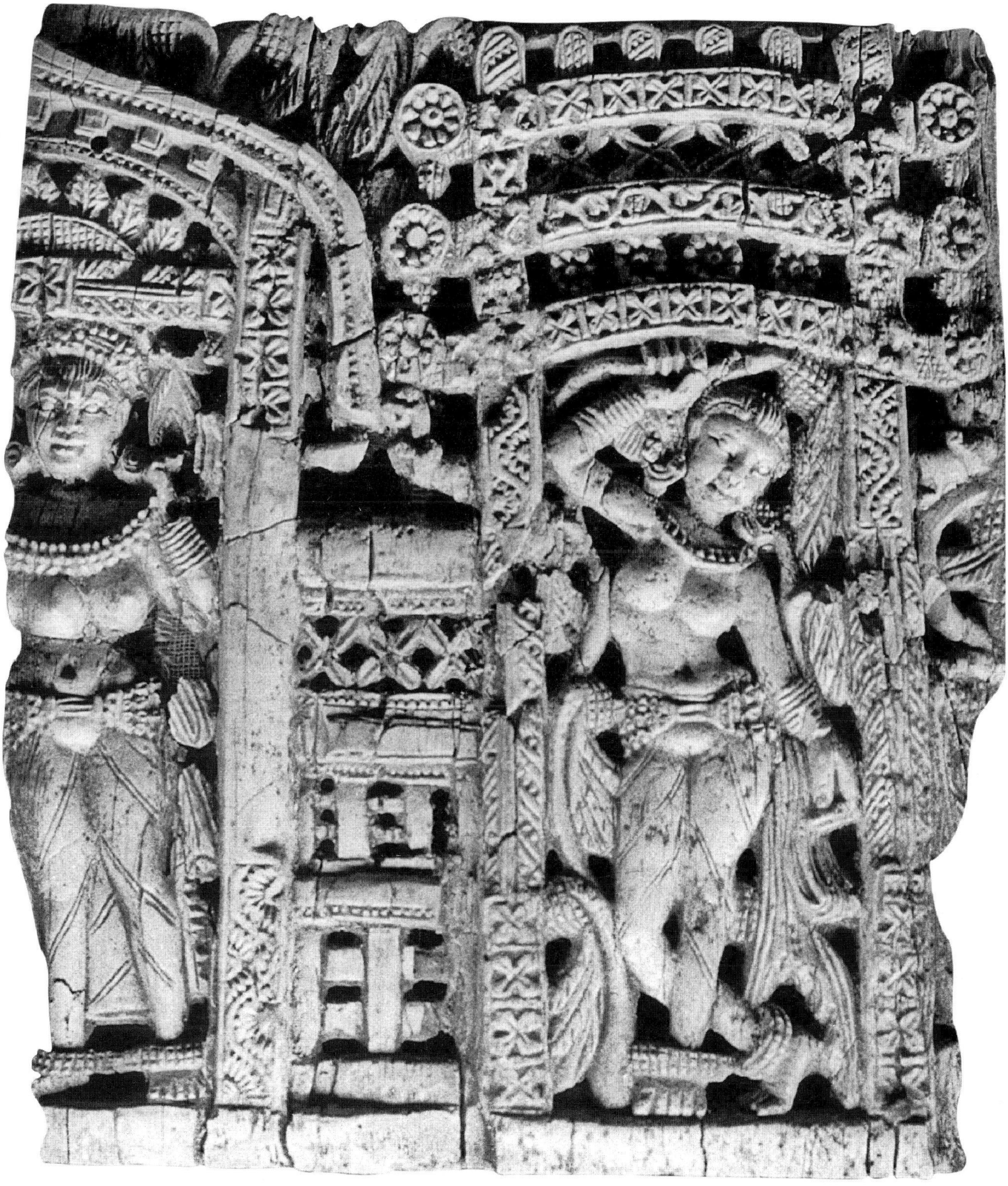

6.44 Two female figures carved in high relief, the left one stands in *samabhaṅga* and the right in *tribhaṅga* holding a branch of a tree in her right hand, ivory, late first to early third century CE, Begram, Kabul Museum.

Buddhist and Jaina sites. From these *yakṣī* types was derived the Nativity of The Buddha, the *aśoka* tree *dohada* motif in classical literature, and the river goddesses of medieval shrines.[60] As a part of the fertility motif, *yakṣa*s and *yakṣī*s were also linked to water cosmology.[61]

I feel that this reading is restricted. Firstly, there is an evolution in the imagery of the *śālabhañjikā* from the second century BCE through the third century CE. The origins of the image lie in a fertility deity and scholars have tried to link this to terracotta mother-goddess figures from the previous period. It is, however, significant that such terracotta figurines (*Pls*. 2.2.18, 2.2.19) are found in profuse numbers from the Śuṅga-Kuṣāṇa period, and continued to be made later along with the *śālabhañjikā* figure. This would suggest that the latter probably had a separate representational role.

Not many scholars seem to be concerned about the problematic nature of viewing *śālabhañjikā* / *dohada* images as fertility figures. We need to delve further into the treatment of as well as the textual references to the *śālabhañjikā* imagery in early literature to shed some light on this. The first question is, whose fertility? (1) If the fertility relates to the tree, then is the tree male or female? (2) If it pertains to the fertility of the woman, then the active agent should be the woman who should blossom, not the tree. In the Māyādevī incident and others it is the tree that blossoms at the touch of a woman. Also in the festival of *śāla* in spring, from which the imagery is posited to have originated, the flowers are already in blossom and the women enjoy plucking them. (3) If we are to assume that they conferred fertility on the viewer, then we will have to accept that this was an act of homoeopathic/sympathetic transfer of the tree's ability to bloom or grow or reproduce. There are no references to this anywhere.

There is also the issue of the analogous figures that are not performing the act of bending the branch or kicking the tree. In a later text, the *Śilpa Prakāśa*, there is a reference to *alasakanyā*s, the latter-day derivatives of the *śālabhañjikā*s, leading to fructification/fulfilment of a monument.[62] The text gives descriptions of sixteen kinds of *alasa-kanyās* which have been translated as indolent maidens. In local terminology, they are called *Nārībandha* and are considered an integral part of architecture. "As a house without a wife, as frolic without a woman. So without (the figure of) woman the monument will be of inferior quality and bear no fruit. . . . Woman is most beautiful, when adorned with all ornaments."[63]

It is unlikely that the trees associated with *yakṣī-śālabhañjikā*s were considered to be holy and were worshipped as mentioned by Coomaraswamy[64] and V.S. Agrawala[65] at the time though at some point of time they may have been considered holy and worshipped or adored.

In an important intervention on the functionality of the *dohada-śālabhañjikā* figures, Pisharoti has observed that at least in the case of the *dohada*, the perceived primary role of the female figures is that of fertilisation.[66] It is believed that the direct or indirect touch of beautiful young women will cause a tree to grow and bloom. Thus, the woman does not derive fertility from the tree, rather, she causes it. He has identified the tree as male who desires the female. The *aśoka*, the *śāla* and the ten varieties of tree that flower, bloom or grow at the touch of a woman, are all male.

Gustav Roth,[67] in his study of the woman-and-tree motif in Indian art, partly agrees with Pisharoti in attributing a fertilisation-significance to the *dohada* ritual. However, he differentiates between *dohada* and *śālabhañjikā*

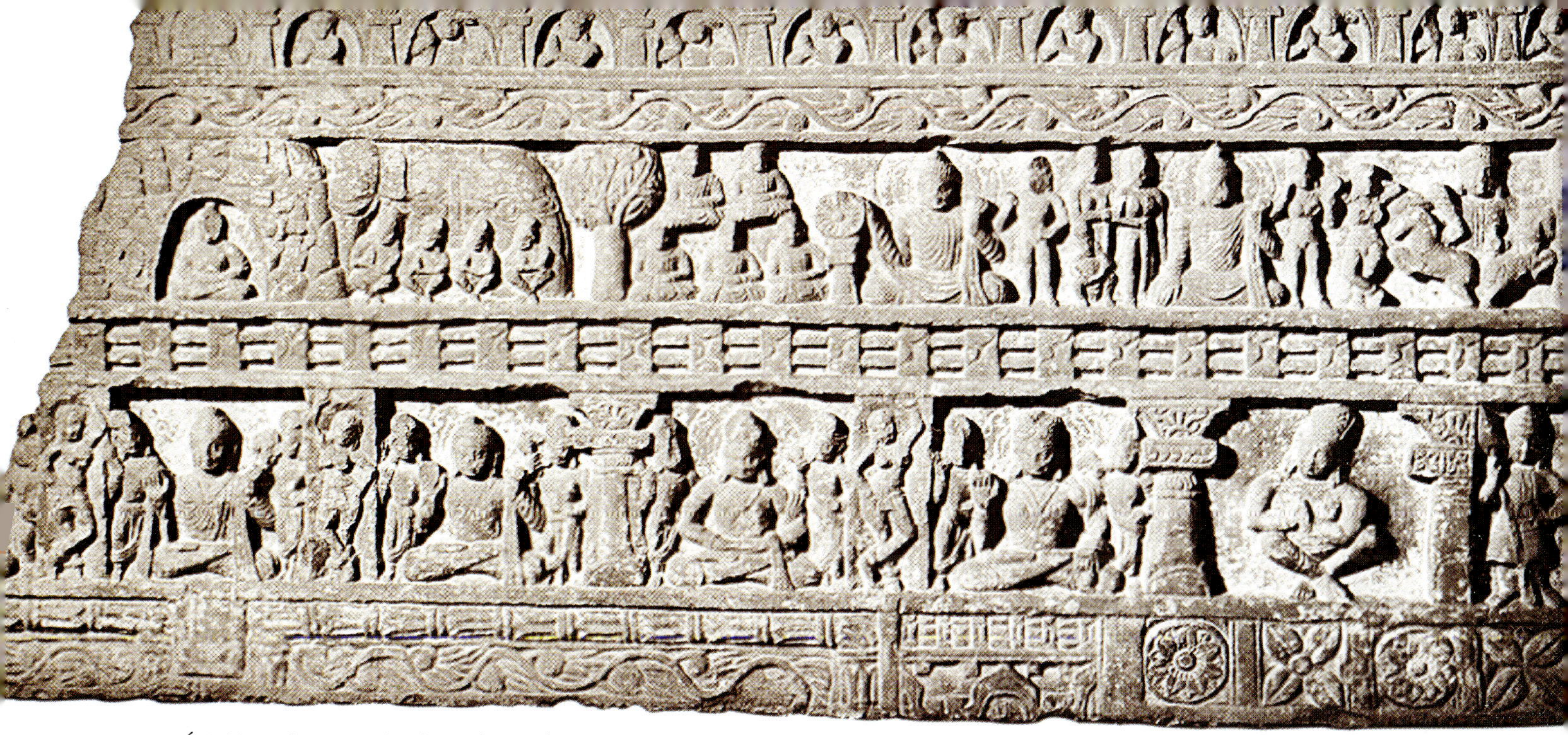

6.45 *Śālabhañjikā*s on both sides of meditating Buddha, red sandstone, second century CE, Jamalpur Mound, Mathurā. SML B. 208.

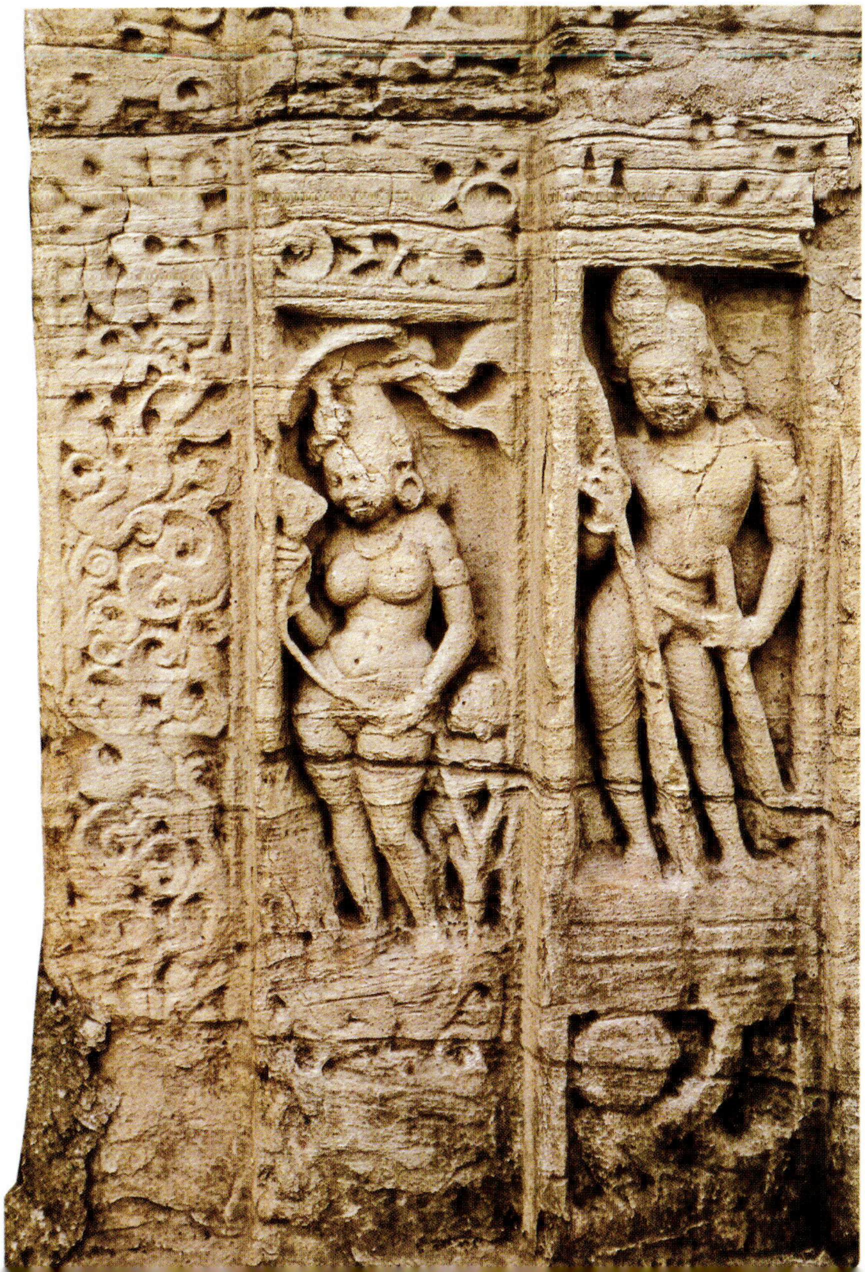

6.46 River goddess in a *śālabhañjikā-yakṣī* posture, doorjamb of a temple, early fifth century CE, Gupta period, Udaygiri, Madhya Pradesh.

figures as we have seen above. For him, the *śālabhañjikā*s derive fertility from the tree, so the fertilisation works in the opposite direction to that of the *dohada* figures. The tree also helps decorate the woman portrayed, making her more alluring. Pisharoti's view of equating *dohada* with fertilisation of the tree and representing amour has been refuted by B.M. Barua,[68] especially with regard to the Bharhut images of women-and-tree which, he says, represent *yakṣīṇī*s, *devatā*s, and *devakumārī*s, who are represented as female devotees or actresses. As the former, they gather flowers and fruits for offering, or they are ready with such offerings, or are performing the act of adoration. As actresses they are shown as taking part in musical or gymnastic performances.[69] This argument against the erotic nature of *yakṣī* figures is inherently flawed because even if we were to concede that the female figures represented actresses, their performance itself is gendered. Also, even at Bharhut there are other representations that depict deliberate performance such as acrobatic activity.

This dismissal of any association of the *śālabhañjikā* with active sexuality and eroticism stems from a desire to distance frankly and apparently provocative female imagery from "sexual" behaviour. The *śālabhañjikā*, as we demonstrated above, is not a representation of any human entity but an architectural motif or device. As such it was no doubt meant to depict voluptuous and beautiful female figures that added to the visual value of the building in the eyes of the audience of the art on these edifices. This does not preclude the possibility that these figures embodied notions of *maṅgala*, plentitude and fertility in their being.

## Notes and References

1. *MWSE*, p. 838: *yakṣa*, n. a living supernatural being, spiritual apparition, ghost, spirit; also a class of semi-divine beings [attendants of Kubera, exceptionally also Viṣṇu; described as sons of Pulastya, of Pulaha, of Kaśyapa, of Khasa or Krodha: also as produced from the feet of Brahmā; though generally benevolent, occasionally classed with *piśācas* and other malignant spirits; and sometimes said to cause demonical possessions].
2. A.K. Coomaraswamy, *Yakṣas: Essays in the Water Cosmology*, ed. Paul Shroeder, Delhi: IGNCA, Oxford University Press, 1993, pp. 54-59; Chapter 5, *Yakṣa*s as Tutelary Deities, Patron Saints and Guardian Angels.
3. Derived from *yakṣīn* which *MWSE* gives as having a life, living, really existing.
4. A.K. Coomaraswamy, op. cit., p. 15.
5. Ibid., p. 17; *yakṣa*, habitually invisible, *guhya*, *antarhita*, *adṛśya*, manifests himself.
6. Cowell, *Jātaka* no. 50, 509.
7. U.P. Shah, "Beginnings of Jaina Iconography", *Bulletin of Museums and Archaeology in Uttar Pradesh* (henceforth *BMAUP*), no. 9. 1972, pp. 1-3.
8. A.K. Coomaraswamy, op. cit. part II, p. 13.
9. R.N. Mishra, *Yakṣa Cult and Iconography*, New Delhi, 1981.
10. A.K. Coomaraswamy, op. cit., pp. 63-66.
11. Paul Dundas, *The Jainas*, London, 1992, p. 30.
12. A.K. Coomaraswamy, op. cit., pp. 54-58.
13. Ibid., p. 18.
14. Ibid., p. 84.
15. R.N. Mishra, op. cit., pp. 104-31.
16. Nathuram Premi, *Jaina Sahitya aur Itihasa*, Bombay, 2nd edn., 1956, pp. 469 and 473-74 describes instances in which Śāsanadevatās presiding over the *tīrthas* of *tīrthaṁkaras* were called upon to resolve whether the *tīrtha* belonged to Śvetāmbaras or Digambaras. James Burgess (ed.), Weber (tr.) "The Śatruñjaya Mahātmayam," *Indian Antiquary*, vol. 30, pp. 305-6 states that the *tīrtha* of Śatruñjaya was re-established by Javada Seth after

he worshipped Cakreśvarī to disclose to him the location of the image of Ṛṣabha initially established there by Bāhubali and later lost. Burgess assigns the date eleventh century CE to this event.

17. LL. 790.

18. LL. 793.

19. LL. 871.

20. U.N. Roy, *Śālabhañjikā in Art, Philosophy and Literature*, Allahabad: Lokbharati Publications, 1979 has classified these into many types.

21. P.K. Agrawala, *Mithuna*, pp. 42-54.

22. Supra, Chapter 3.

23. Gail Sutherland, *Yakṣas: Disguises of the Demon*, Albany: SUNY, 1991 p. 138.

24. B.M. Barua, *Bharhut*, pt. III, Patna: Indological Book Corporation, 1979 (reprint), figs. 76, 73 and 76.

25. A *Śālabhañjikā* and a female adorant, second-first cenury BCE, Kauśāmbī, UP, Allahabad district, AM 64.

26. *MWSE*, p. 1008.

27. *Śālabhañjikā*, Śuṅga, Mehrauli, New Delhi, Stone, NM Acc. No. 59.539.

28. *Śālabhañjikā*s on both sides of meditating Buddha, Jamalpur Mound, Mathurā, SML B. 208

29. E.R. Stone, *Buddhist Art of Nagarajunakonda*, fig. 176, New Delhi: Motilal Banarsidass 1994.

30. Āyāgapaṭṭa or Mirror frame, Taxila, Gandhāra terracotta, NM Acc. No. 85.B.M. 51/13.

31. A.K. Coomaraswamy, op. cit., p. 86.

32. For a detailed exegesis on the term *dohada* see Gustav Roth, "The Women and Tree Motif", *Journal of The Asiatic Society, Letters and Science*, vol. XXIII, no. 1, 195., pp. 108-9 fn.

33. Ibid., p. 87.

34. K. Rama Pisharoti, "Dohada or the Woman and Tree Motif", in *JISOA*, vol. III, 1985. pp. 110-11.

35. A.K. Coomaraswamy, op. cit., p. 83, chapter 9: Woman and Tree, pp. 83-89.

36. *Mbh.*, III.231.16.

37. *AV*, VI.133.5.

38. Devangana Desai, Erotic Sculptures in India: A Socio-Cultural Study, Delhi: Tata McGraw-Hill Publishing Co., 1975, p. 26.

39. *MWSE*, p. 1067.

40. *Buddhacarita*, V.52.

41. *Nāṭyaśāstra*, II.92-95.

42. Roth, Gustav, op. cit., pp. 91-116.

43. *Rājapraśnīya Sūtra*, ed. and Hindi tr. Shri Ratan Muni, Sri Agam Prakashan Samiti, Beawar, Rajasthan, 1982, 121, p. 63. *ṇāṇāmaṇirayanavālaru-vagalīlatdiaśālabhañjiyyāgā.*

44. Ibid., 126, pp. 66-67: *tesi ṇām dārāṇam ubhao pāse duho ṇisīhiyāe solasa solasa sālabhañjiyā parivādio paṇṇattāo, tao ṇam śālbhanjiyāo līlatḍiyāo, supaitdayāo-sualamkiyāo, ṇāṇāviharāgavasaṇāo, ṇāṇāmallapinadvāo, mutdigijjhsumajjhāo, āmela-jamalajuyala-vaṭṭīya abbhuṇṇaya pīṇarayasamdiya-pīvarapaoharāo rattavagāo, asiyakesīao miuvisayapasattha-lakkhaṇasamvelilayaggasirāyāo isim asogavarpāyavasamutdiyāo vāmahattha-yagghiyaggasālāo isim achdacchikaḍakkhcitdieṇam lusamānio viva cakkhulloyaṇalesehi ye annamannam khijjmāṇio viva puḍaviparināmāo, sāmayabhāvamugayāo, candāṇaṇāo, candavilasiṇīo, candādhdasamaṇiḍālāo, candāhiyasomadamsaṇāo, ukkā viva ujjovemāṇāo, vijjughaṇamiriyasūradip pamtateyaahiyayara-sannikāsāo singāragārācāruvesāo pāsāiyāo jāva (darasaṇijjāo abhiruvāo padiruvāo) citdimti.* Roth has translated this to mean, "on both sides of each of the doors, on the double flankers, rows of 16 branch bending females on each side are arranged well supported, these branch bending females stand sportively, well adorned, with dresses of different colours, covered with different garlands; they have beautiful waists, which can be grasped by the length of a hand's grip, and breasts which are plump, fashioned, swollen, raised and round like a couple of diadems worn on top of the head, who have impassioned sideglances and dark hair, their hair is covered at the top with tender, spotless, auspicious symbols. Their bodies are leisurely inclined against *aśoka* trees and they seize the prominent parts of the branches with the left

hand. They, who seem to captivate (the senses of gods and men) with the gestures of their side glances, having turned their eyes aside, and who seem to exhaust themselves on account of embraces with their looks, whose features resemble the maturity of earth, who have entered into eternal existence, who have faces like the moon, who have foreheads like a half moon with an appearance even more pleasing than that of the moon, they who are shining like a meteor, with a splendour even more than the shining flow of the sun and the light particles of the lightning clouds, whose dresses are beautiful, because they are like an abode of ornaments, they are gracious . . . till . . . stand."

45. The reference here to well established mental form alludes in all probability to their minds not wandering towards the material or the gross elements, but remaining fixed on the Jaina doctrine.

46. *Rājapraśnīya Sūtra*, khaṇḍika 200, pp. 119-25

47. *Sivayasa Āyāgapaṭṭa*, Kaṅkālī Ṭīlā, Mathurā, late first century CE, Buff sandstone, SML, J. 555. Also *Loṇaśobhika Āyāgapaṭṭa*, GMM Q.2.; Sonya Rhie Quintanilla, "Āyāgapaṭṭas: Characteristics, Symbolism and Chronology," in *Artibus Asiae*, vol. LX, no. 1, pp. 79-137, fig. 2 and 26.

48. A.K. Coomaraswamy, op. cit., p. 83.

49. Kālidāsa's *Meghadūta* II.18. *ekah sakhyāstava saha māyā vāmapādābhilāṣī*. Also *Kumarsambhavam* III.26 and *Malvikāgnimitram* III.12.

50. Padatilakam, cf. Pisharoti, op. cit., p. 112.

51. U.N. Roy, *Śālabhañjikā in Art, Philosophy and Literature*, Allahabad: Lokbharati Publications, 1979, pp. 63-65.

52. *Buddhacarita*, V.52.

53. U.N. Roy, op. cit., chapters 2 and 3.

54. Cited in Roth, op. cit., p. 100 fn.

55. J. Ph. Vogel, "Woman and Tree", *Acta Orietanla*, VII, p. 224, cited in Roth, op. cit, p. 100 fn.

56. R.C. Sharma, *The Mathura School of Art*, New Delhi: Agam Kala Prakashan, 1984, pp. 136-37.

57. N. Ray, AIU., p. 524.

58. Stella Kramrisch, *Indian Sculpture in Philadelphia Museum*, Philadelphia, 1960; p. 33, A.K. Coomaraswamy, op. cit., p. 85.

59. Stella Kramrisch, op. cit., p. 16.

60. A.K. Coomaraswamy, op. cit., p. 85.

61. Ibid., p. 169.

62. Supra, Chapter 1.

63. *Śilpa Prakāśa*, ed. and annotated by A. Boner and S.R. Sarma, Leiden: E.J. Brill, 1966, p. 46. While we are aware of the difficulty in using this work as a completely authentic text, the spirit of this passage reflects the sentiments expressed in a much earlier text, the Śvetāmbara Jain Prakrit *Rājapraśnīya Sūtra*.

64. A.K. Coomaraswamy, op. cit, p. 85.

65. V.S. Agrawala, *Ancient Indian Folk Cults*, Varanasi: Prithvi Prakashan, 1970, pp. 114-26.

66. Pisharoti, op. cit., pp. 114-15.

67. Gustav Roth, op. cit., 105 fn.

68. B.M. Barua, *Bharhut*, pt. III, p. 83.

69. Ibid. According to him, "a view indeed gathered ground in Indian literature, both ascetic and erotic, opining that woman is all sex or lust. All her gestures and postures, all her movements and playful activities are interpreted as a sign or expression in different ways of her lustful self. It is really in this very character that she has been represented in many of the bas-reliefs at Bharhut. But even this is no evidence in support of Pisharoti's interpretation of the tree and woman motif."

# 7

# Māra's Daughters, Apsarases and Ogresses

## Strategies of Evil, Seduction and Temptation

This chapter is an attempt to explore the manner in which "evil" was constructed and located, mainly in Buddhist ideology, and the role women played in this construction and location. In the textual tradition ranging from later Vedic times onwards, it is taken as a given that women are inherently uncontrolled. They represent disorder, disruption, inversion and anarchy, sexual or otherwise. The "truth" of this "axiom" becomes progressively more convincing for the authors of Buddhist canonical and Śāstric texts, in which sexual depravity is but one sign of the evilness of women. The intrinsic feminine nature or the *svabhāva* of women — their inability to behave in any other manner — is called into question. Before entering into this exploration of "evil," let us remind ourselves that the previous chapters explicate the dialectic, or it may be termed the conflict, between the prescriptive texts on the one hand and the visual discourse in representing women, on the other.

### 7.1 Māra's Daughters and the Temptation of Buddha

Māra and his daughters are metaphors for the attachments or attractions that are believed to delude one from the true path to renunciation, but their representation in visual art forms seems to imply that they have an objective reality standing for an autonomous omnipresent evil, as we shall explain.

In the art of the period, representations of evil propensities and the essential nature of Māra's noose (*pāśa*) are often attempted. This is largely done through two episodes related to Māra: *Māra-dharṣaṇa* (the defeat of Māra and his army), and *Māra-dhītaro* (the temptation embodied by Māra's daughters). These scenes visually depict personifications of evil as well as the strategies that they employ to delude, tempt and scare both the Buddha and the Buddhist faithful from the path of righteousness which leads to salvation.

It is important to assemble the manifestations of the power of Māra in art and thought, since Māra along with his sons and daughters personify negative powers, epitomising what is regarded as Male Evil and Female Evil. Māra is predominantly referred to as "the Evil One" (*pāpīm*).[1] In Buddhism, the figure of Māra is almost omnipotent. He appears almost as an evil alter ego of the Buddha, the good teacher capable of leading a devotee towards enlightenment and *nirvāṇa*.

Etymologically the term Māra is related to the Pāli *maccu* and Skt. *mṛtyu* and means the one who kills or causes death.[2] The epithet *antaka*, meaning "being at end or making an end,"[3] is applied to Māra, and he is further associated with the gods Yama (Death) and Kāma (Desire);[4] occasionally even the name Kāma is used to refer to Māra.

Yama is the god of death, the judge and ruler of the dead, while Kāma[5] is the god of sensual love and worldly enjoyment in the Vedic-Brāhmanic tradition. The use of both of these as synonyms for Māra or for concepts closely associated with him clearly rests on Buddhist views in which death and worldly desires are coordinates.[6] It may be relevant to state at this point that Kāmadeva as Agni provides *āyuṣ* (life) and the epithet *viśvāyuṣ* (universal life) is conferred upon him in the Vedas.[7]

Aśvaghoṣa in the *Buddhacarita* is unambiguous in identifying Kāmadeva as the desire-inducing aspect of Māra.[8] He says, "whom in the world they call the God of Love, him of the bright weapon and also the flower arrowed, that same one, as the monarch of the activities of passions and as the enemy of liberation, they style Māra." Māra attempts to shoot arrows of love at the Buddha in vain and retires dejected.[9]

Other names and terms associated with Māra include *Kānhā*, *Kali*, *yakkha*, *pamattabandhu* or *pramattabandhu*.[10] *Kānhā* is *Kṛṣṇa*, meaning black or dark, which is also associated with the concept *Kali*, which in the Buddhist texts means "wicked" or "evil." *Yakkha* or *yakṣa*, as seen in the previous chapter, is a semi-divine being, who may be either malignant or benevolent depending on the context. *Pamattabandhu* or *pramattabandhu* means friend or relative (*bandhu*) of the careless or the indolent (*pramatta*). It is apparent that although

7.1 Temptation of Buddha and Defeat of Māra, *toraṇa*, middle crossbar, north gateway, rear face, first century CE, *stūpa* 1, Sāñcī. (facing page)

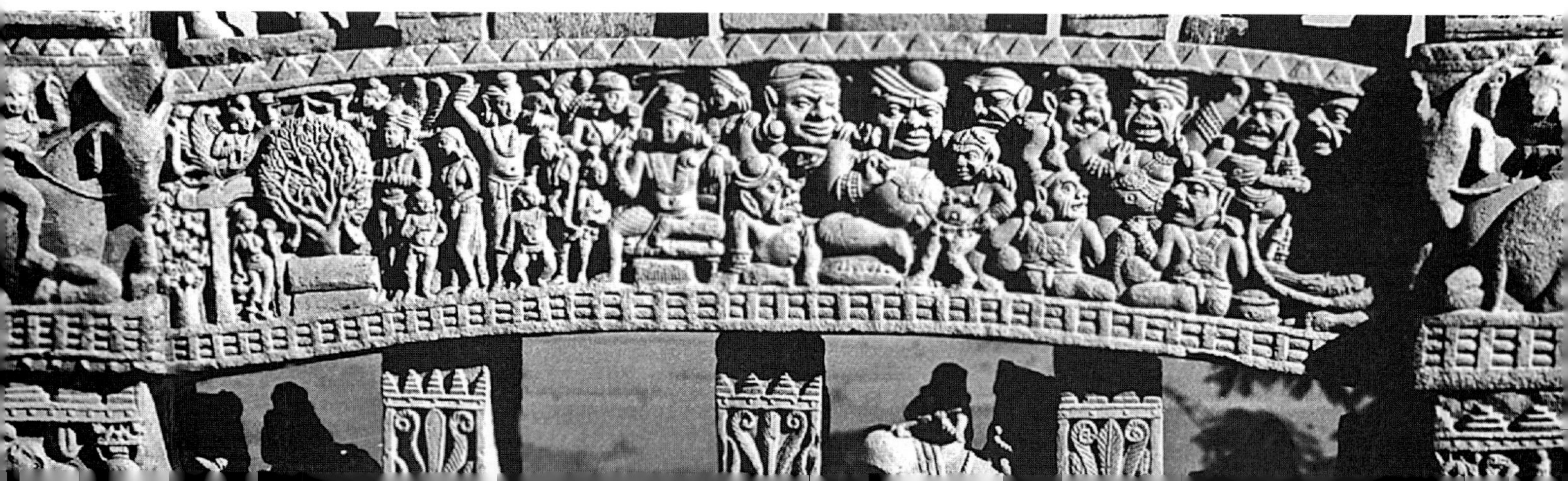

7.2 Detail of Māra's Army, Defeat of Māra, *toraṇa*, middle crossbar, north gateway, rear face, *stūpa* 1, first century CE, Sāñcī.

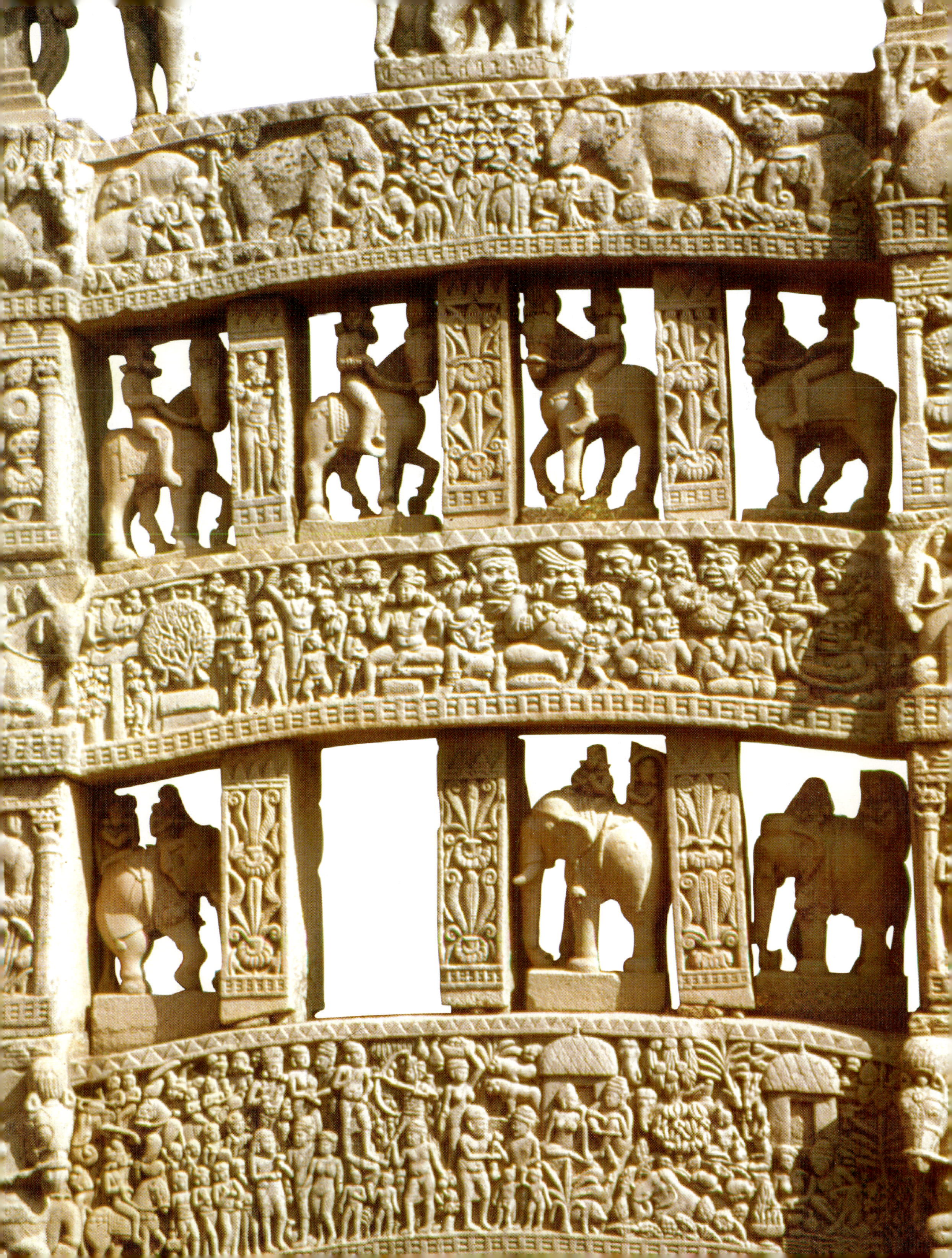

most of these terms — and indeed the concept of Māra itself — grew out of the context of Vedic, Brāhmanic and Upaniṣadic terminology, Māra is nevertheless principally a Buddhist symbol. The Buddhist Māra as a philosophical-mythical motif embodies all those alluring forces of sense-pleasure and bondage in and to the world that obstruct and challenge a person trying to achieve *mokṣa*.[11]

In order to achieve his "evil" agenda Māra employs many strategies. His deeds may be characterised as follows: Māra reviles, he inclines people towards sense desire, and is aggressive; he blinds and perplexes, obstructs and interrupts; he possesses and holds in bondage; and he kills and destroys. Specifically, he makes two attacks on the Buddha at the time of enlightenment at Bodh-Gayā in which he uses varied techniques. These attempts are unsuccessful and he retires vanquished and dejected, while the Buddha achieves *bodhi* (enlightenment), a victory that is represented iconically in the form of the Buddha touching the earth in the *bhūmisparśa-mudrā*, asking the earth to witness this event.

Māra's daughters make two principal assaults on the Buddha on the behest of Māra: the first immediately before illumination, to prevent his attaining Enlightenment, and the other four weeks later with the objective of persuading the Buddha to enter *nirvāṇa* without preaching his doctrine. The daughters display their bodies and use all sorts of feminine wiles in order to entice the *bodhisattva*, and then the Buddha, from the True Path. Māra's daughters — the *Māra-kanyā*s — are named *Āratī* (Discontent), *Pṛti* (Delight), and *Tṛṣṇā* (Thirst); his three sons are *Vibhra* (Caprice), *Harṣa* (Gaiety) and *Darpā* (Wantonness).[12] The daughters have also been called *Tanhā* (Craving), *Āratī* (Discontent) and *Rāga* (Passion).[13] They are known elsewhere as *Āratī* and *Rati* (Erotic Passion; also the name of Kāmadeva's wife).[14] The names of the sons and daughters are self-explanatory, indicating the masculine and feminine traits believed to operate in the realm of evil, conceived of as offspring or incarnations of the unified Evil One. As embodied in his daughters, these traits emphasise Māra's role as essentially one of encouraging people's innate inclinations towards sense desires, rather operating as an external agent actively enticing them away from the Buddhist path.

When Māra does not succeed with his enticements, he attacks with objects of fear in order to make the Buddha and his followers "feel dread and horror and creeping of the flesh."[15] He tries to do this in the guise of a mighty snake and by causing an earthquake.

At the time of the enlightenment he also attempts to prevent this auspicious event from taking place by loosening his army on the meditating *bodhisattva*. This moment is described in the *Buddhacarita* as follows: Māra "sent forth his army of horses, elephants, *rākṣasa*s with features of elephants, asses, horses and camels, or countenances of tigers, bears, lions and elephants, one eyed, many mouthed, three-headed, with pendulous bellies and speckled bellies. Without knees or thighs or with knees vast as pots or armed with tusks or talons, or with skulls for face or with many bodies or with half their faces broken off or with large visages. Ashy grey in colour, tricked out with red spots, carrying ascetics' stave . . . tall as toddy palm . . . or the stature of children."[16] In this description of the *Māra-dharṣaṇa* or *Māra-vijaya* episode, "evil" is represented as scary and grotesque and is associated with abnormalities based on size and appearance such as those of giants and dwarfs and spotted beings.

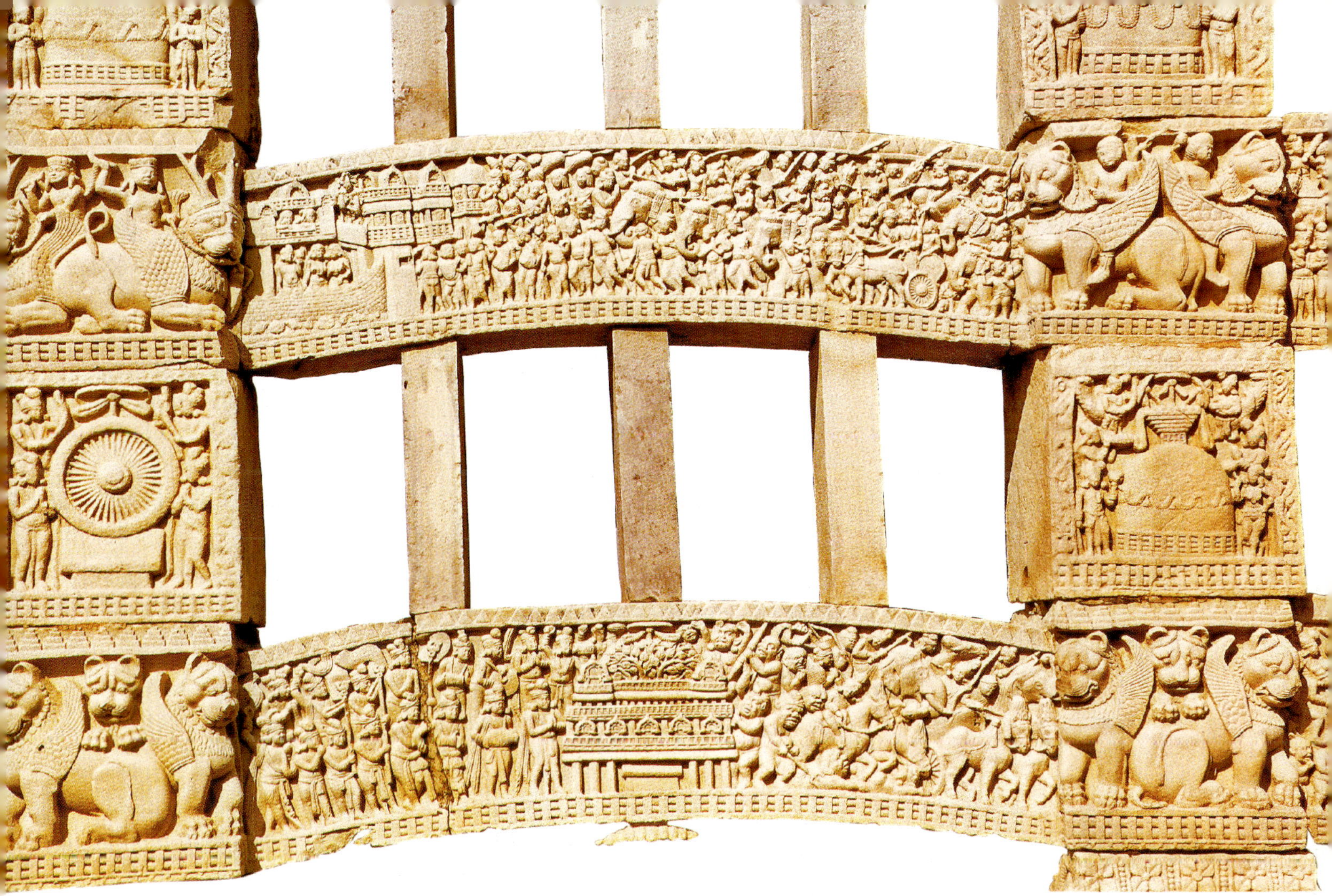

7.3 Defeat of Māra, bottom crossbar, western gateway, rear face, *stūpa* 1, first century CE, Sāñcī.

7.4 The assault of Māra, coping, second century CE, Amarāvatī.

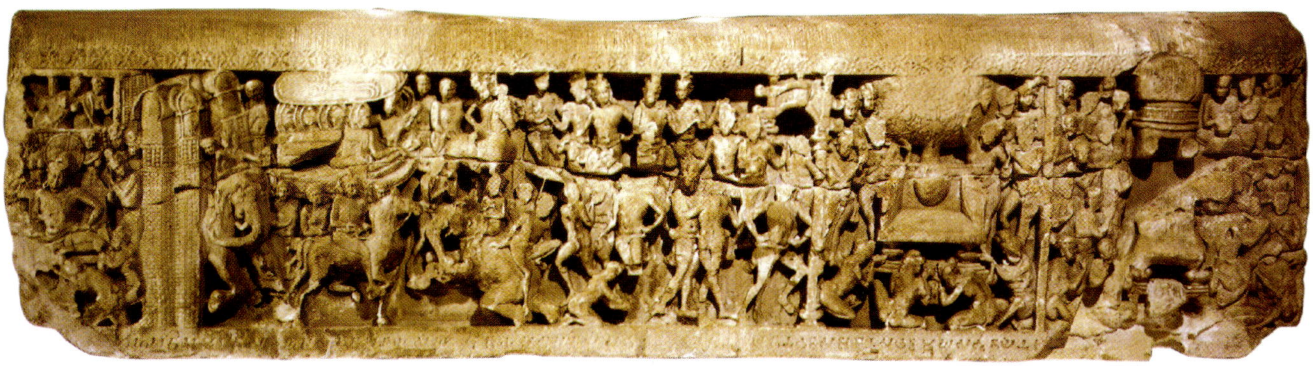

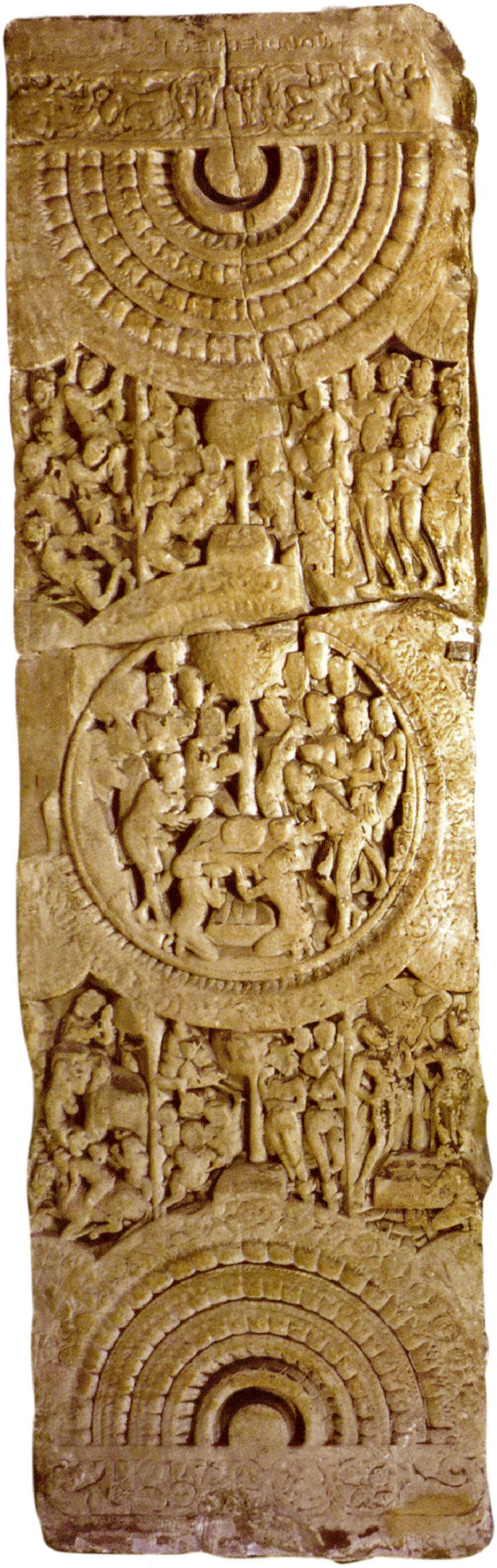

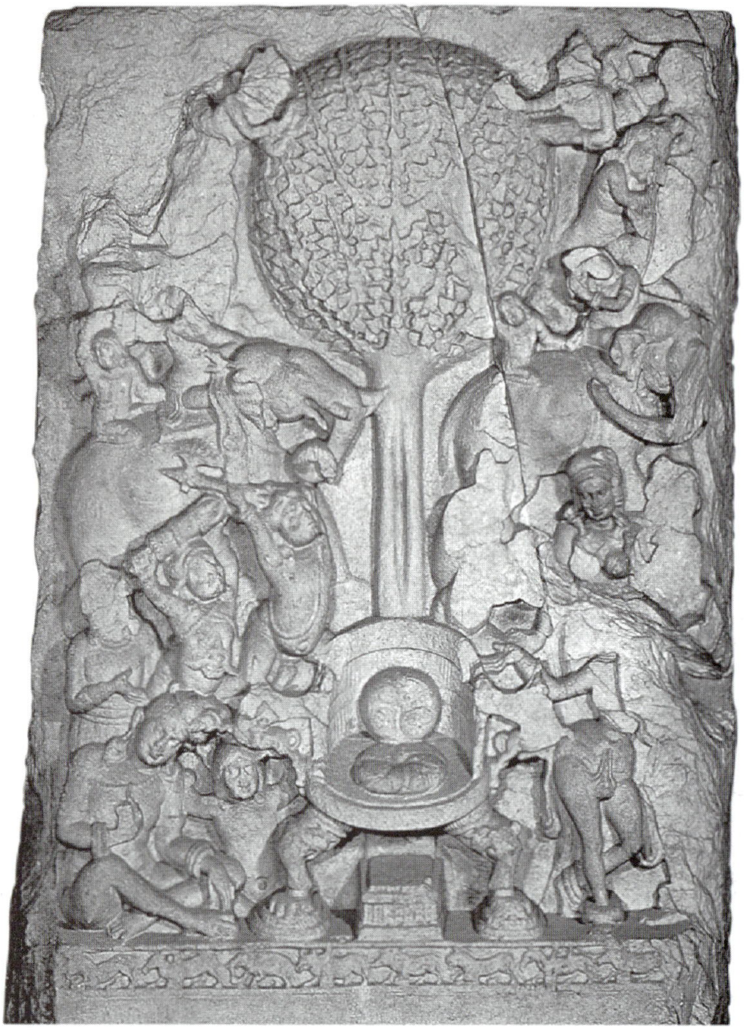

7.6 Attack on Buddha by Māra's army and temptation offered by his daughters, second century CE, Amarāvatī. Musee Guimet, Paris.

7.5 The temptation of Buddha by Māra's daughters and assault of Māra's army, second century CE, Amarāvatī.

The *Buddhacarita* adds that Māra commanded his excited army of demons to terrify the *bodhisattva*. The demons obey by mounting various scorching assaults on his body and mind. "There was wind of intense violence, the stars did not shine and the moon gave no light and a deeper darkness of light spread around, as the attack continued."[17] But the *bodhisattva* is neither frightened nor moved from his concentration, and the army flees in disarray.

Perhaps the best examples illustrating such Māra episodes are found at Ajantā, dating from the Gupta–Vākāṭaka age. But the tradition of depicting Māra's attacks can be traced back to the first century CE. Although these are contemporary with the earliest mention of the episodes in the textual tradition, it is difficult to establish a direct parallel between text and image.[18] The *Māra Sutta* is the first text to mention the three daughters of Māra (*Tanhā, Āratī* and *Rāga*) tempting the Buddha,[19] and the *Buddhacarita* is datable to the late first or early second century; otherwise these two episodes

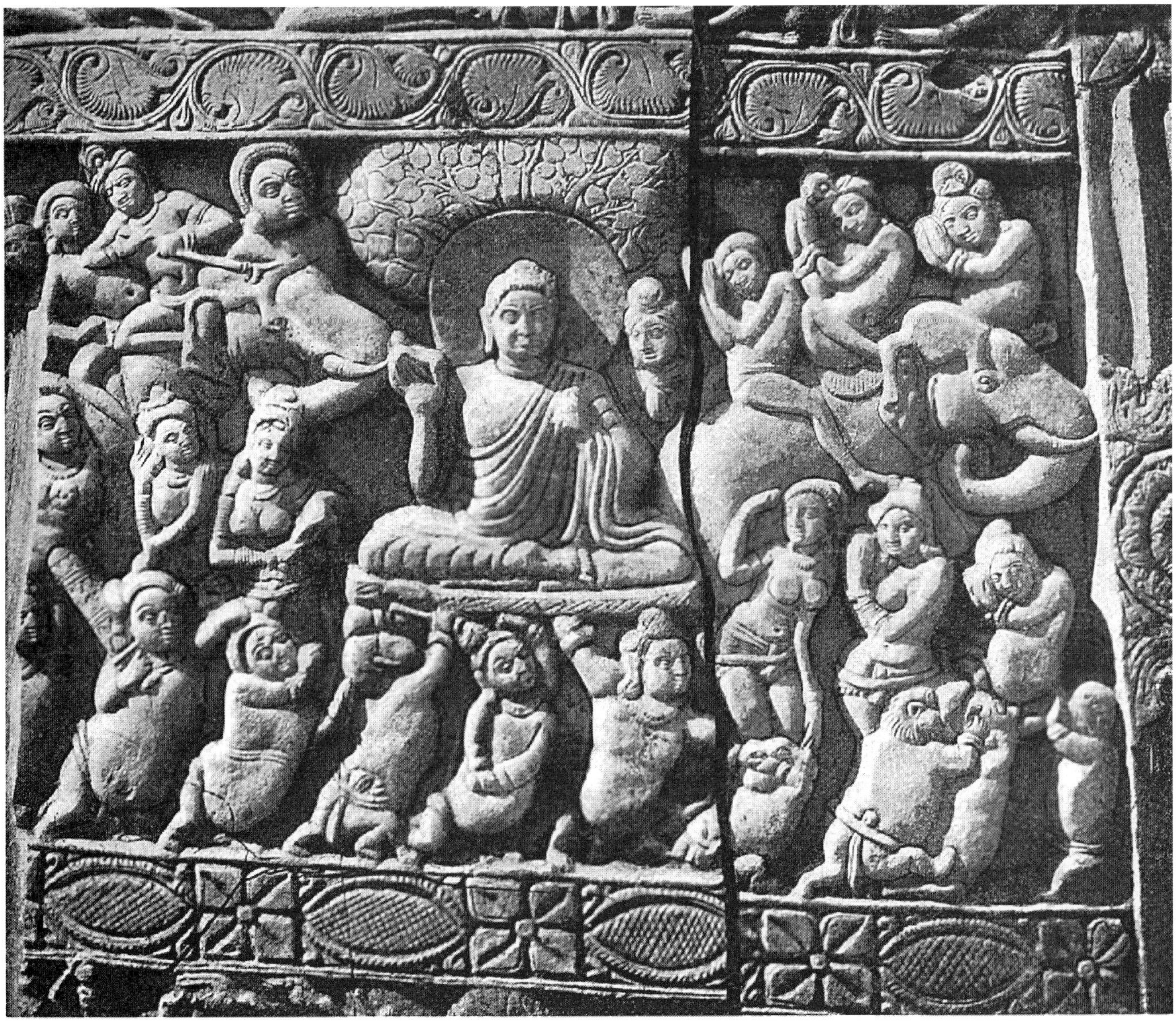

7.7 Attack on the Buddha by Māra's daughters and army, dome slab, third century CE, Nāgārjunakoṇḍa.

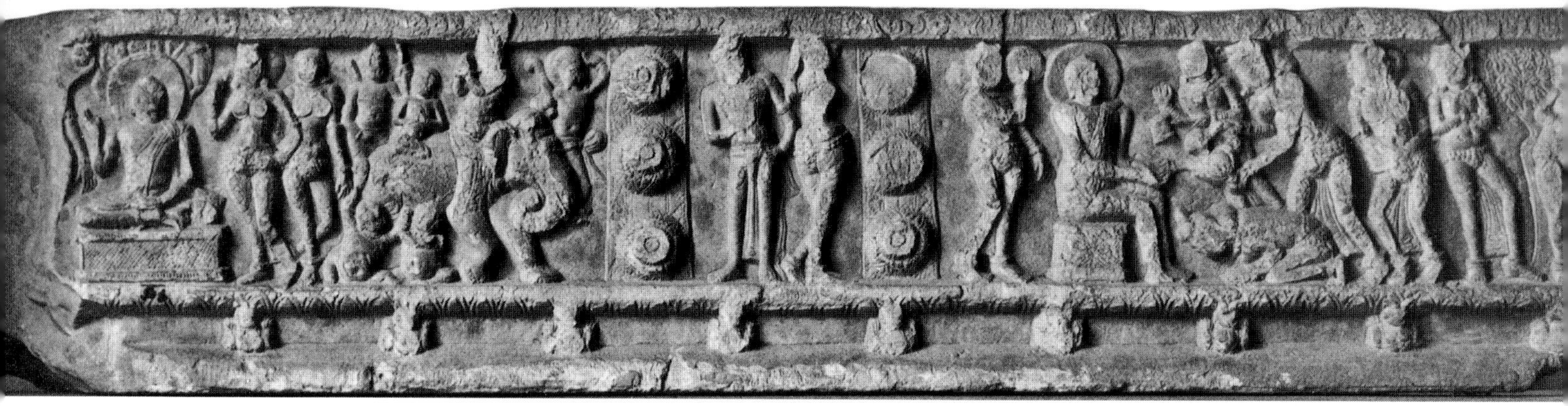

7.8 Māradhitaro and Māra *dharṣaṇa*, second-third century CE, Goli. Madras Museum.

illustrating Māra's attempts to lure and frighten Buddha at Bodh-Gayā are not known in the earliest layers of Theravāda canon.[20] In the later versions of Māra's attempts at making ensure that Buddha did not destroy his Kingdom of Evil, just before Enlightenment Māra with his army launches an attack on the Buddha. He fails in this attempt and the Buddha attains Enlightenment and Māra again tries to prevent the Buddha from spreading his message and he then sends his daughters to seduce *tathāgata*. And finally, he again tries to persuade the Buddha to attain *nirvāṇa* without having taught his doctrine. Here again his daughters try to distract and tempt Buddha at Sārnāth.[21] In the *Nidānakathā*, redacted in Sri Lanka in the fifth century CE, the incident of Māra's daughters trying to seduce the Buddha is narrated as occurring after the enlightenment at Bodh-Gayā when his daughters found Māra dejectedly drawing lines on the ground after failing to defeat the Buddha.[22] The *Lalitavistāra* presents a more complete version of the story, combining *Māra-dharṣaṇa* (Defeat of Māra) or *Māra-vijaya* (Victory over Māra) and the temptation by the *Māra-kanyās*.[23]

Neither the *Māra-dharṣaṇa* nor the *Māra-dhītaro* episode is depicted in the early Buddhist narrative art at Bharhut. The first example of Māra's attack on the meditating Buddha is seen on the reverse of the middle crossbar of the northern *toraṇa* of *stūpa* I at Sāñcī (*Pls.* 7.1, 7.2).[24] In the upper left corner is the *bodhi-druma*, one of the aniconic forms of the Buddha. Further to the left, a female figure holding a tray and ewer in her hands (probably Sujātā offering food) is worshipping the tree. Near the centre of the crossbar one can see a royal personage seated on a *caukī*-like seat,[25] surrounded by small children and female figures carrying a *chatra* and a *cāmara*. Marshall has read this as Māra with his daughters and sons, desperately seeking to save the paramountcy of evil, which is threatened by the Buddha's imminent Enlightenment. Between this scene and the *bodhi* tree a group of male and female worshippers are depicted, in whom Marshall recognises the vanquished daughter and son of Māra and indeed Māra himself paying homage to the Master who withstood all temptation. On the right is a group of figures with large grotesque faces and disproportionate pot-bellied bodies in whom may be recognised Māra's army of *rākṣasas* and *piśācas*.

Another version of the attack mounted by Māra's army on the Buddha is illustrated on the reverse of the lowest lintel of the western gateway (*Pl.* 7.3).[26] A *bodhi* tree set on a *vajrāsana* surrounded by a shrine-like structure (symbolising the Buddha meditating under the *bodhi* tree at Gayā) is set in the middle of the composition. On the right one can see a group of grotesque figures fleeing in disarray, some leaning over the head of an elephant, others being thrown off their horses, still others stumbling and falling, even running a trident into the body of one of their own party. Marshall identifies the demon with a bow in his hand as Māra,[27] since he is synonymous with Kāma, the god of love, whose weapon is the bow.[28] On the left, a group of male figures with folded hands are seen bearing garlands and banners and playing musical instruments, portraying the delight of the *deva*s at the great victory over Māra by the Enlightened One. The solid *bodhi* tree standing between the forces of Evil and Good, protecting the latter by defeating the former, is very effectively delineated here and creates a considerable visual impact.

7.9 A panel showing scenes from the life of Buddha including Māra's assault, second century CE, Mathurā, GMM.

The Assault of Māra must have been a popular theme at Amarāvatī, given that it was carved repeatedly, not only on the pillars and railing of the *stūpa*, but also on the miniature *stūpa*s adorning the drum. One of the earliest representations from Amarāvatī is found on a stone stele datable to the second century CE.[29] Māra is shown as an old man, wearing a knobbed headdress and a *dhotī*, kneeling with hands folded in front of a raised area with two *buddhapāda*s. The stele bears an inscription which reads *cāpāla cetiya mārā yācate osaṭh-ita* [*ti*] — "In the Cāpāla *caitya*, Māra seeks renunciation (of life)."[30] This refers to the incident when the Buddha was residing at the Cāpāla *caitya*, perhaps the residence of a *yakṣa* named Cāpāla. Here Māra begged Buddha to renounce his life and the Buddha informs Māra that he would die within three months.

The most comprehensive depiction of *Māra-dharṣaṇa* scene (first noticed by Coomaraswamy), however, comes from a coping of the Amarāvatī

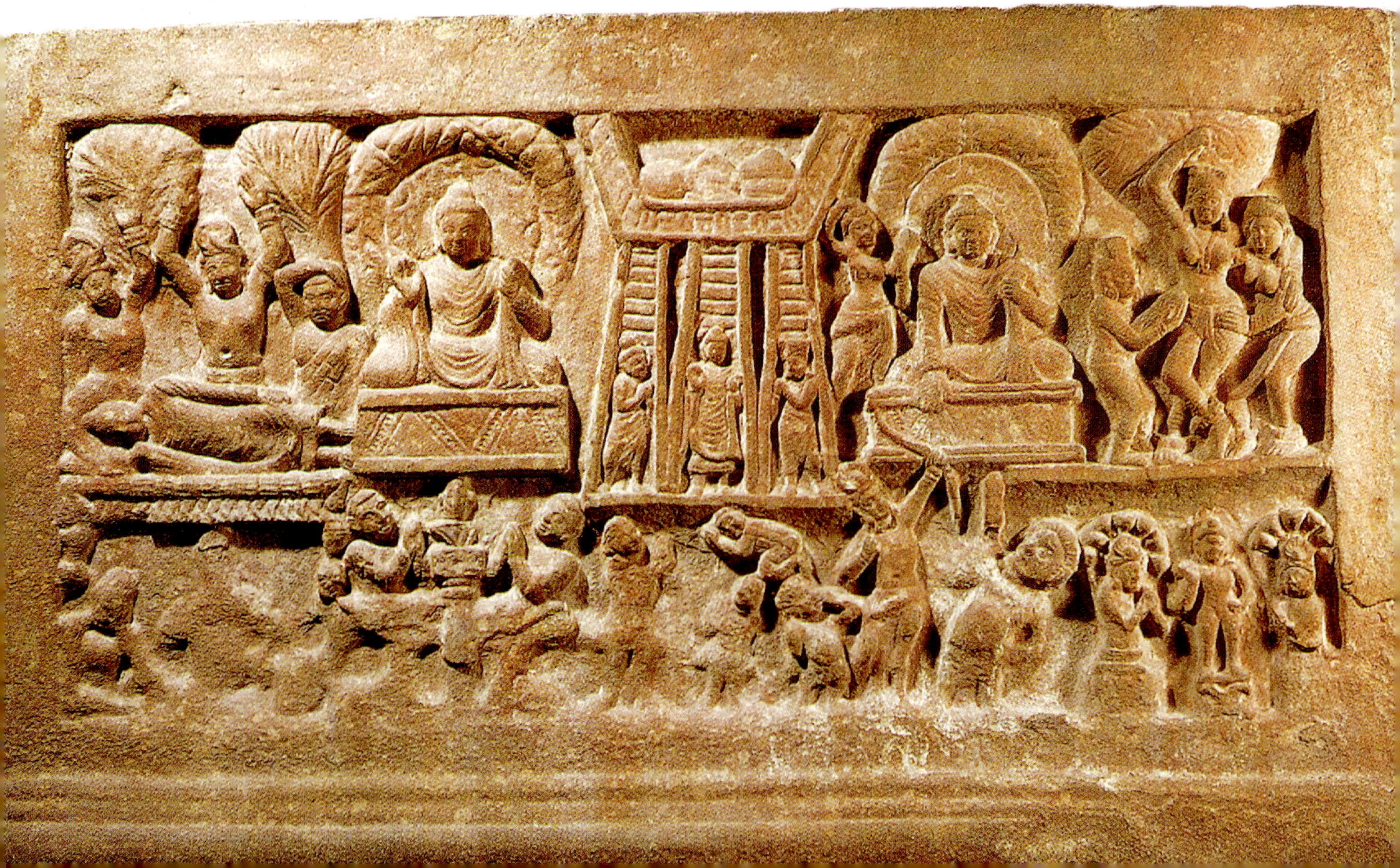

*stūpa*,[31] now in the Madras Museum,[32] followed by Sivaramamurti.[33] It shows Māra with his demon army, consisting of dwarf, grotesque men mounted on lion-faced flying horses, surrounding a roofed pavilion, with an empty throne placed in front of a *bodhi* tree. A similar scene can be found on the inner face of a railing coping (*Pl.* 7.4).[34] It is sculpted in four registers, with the Assault of Māra occupying the major register, and an empty throne surrounded by devotees occupying the third register to the right. This scene is crowded with mounted men and elephants; however, there are no grotesque figures or composite animals. The central figure is mounted on a horse. Behind him is an elephant passing through the elaborate gateway of a palace or a city. In front of this is another or the same elephant bending down to allow a male person to descend. Behind both the elephant and the horse is a palanquin carried by male attendants with five male figures seated inside. Though it lacks the energy and movement of the previously described piece now in the Madras Museum, the scene may be identified with Māra's Assault as Māra is known to have ridden an elephant during the assault.

The *Māra-dharṣaṇa* episode is also depicted on the railing pillars (*Pl.* 7.5)[35] and on friezes carved on drum slabs[36] along with drum pilasters. On one such drum pilaster[37] the temptation of the Buddha by the *Māra-kanyā*s is depicted. The Buddha is shown seated on a throne with his right hand raised in *abhaya-hasta,* instead of being lowered in the *bhūmisparśa-mudrā*. To the right and left of the throne stand female figures, one of whom has her hands raised in worship, perhaps representing Pṛthvī or the Earth Goddess; while the other female may be Māra's daughter (perhaps signifying all the three daughters) who is seen standing with her hand raised above her head provocatively. Below the throne are four dwarfs who are shown

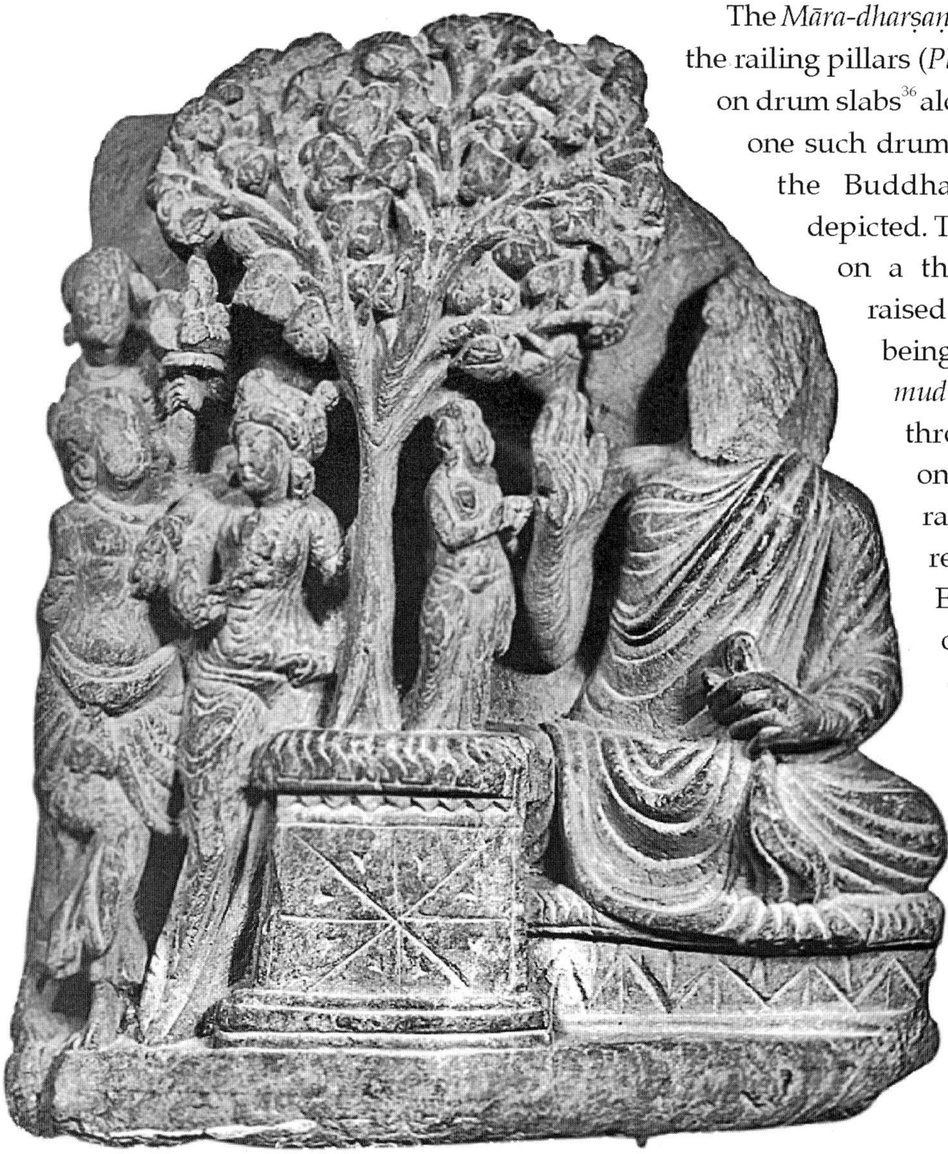

7.10 Māra's daughters, schist, third century CE, Gandhāra. Prince of Wales Museum, Mumbai

touching it with their raised hands; these figures may be part of Māra's army.

In a relief panel, also from Amarāvatī, which is now housed in the Musée Guimet, Paris, both episodes, *Māra-dharṣaṇa* and *Māra-dhītaro*, are carved together, perhaps due to the proximity of the incidents as described in the texts (*Pl.* 7.6). In the centre of the composition is a tall *bodhi* tree with a raised seat and a cushion below it. On the left hand side one can see a male figure seated on an elephant, perhaps representing Māra, attacking the tree. Below this are a number of dwarf figures with somewhat distorted bodies and round-eyed faces who carry weapons such as axes and clubs, moving towards the tree. Seated cross-legged in the corner at the bottom is a male figure making a *vitarka* gesture with his right hand. This may indicate Māra arguing with the Buddha. The right side is much abraded and it is difficult to make out the details. A standing female figure standing in a *tribhaṅga* posture and a portion of another female are visible, in all probability indicating Māra's daughters displaying their charm to tempt the meditating Buddha.

At Nāgārjunakoṇḍa also the *Māra-dharṣaṇa* and *Māra-kanyā* episodes have been compressed into one representation (*Pl.* 7.7).[38] Seated under the *bodhi* tree, in the middle of the composition, is the Buddha with a large halo behind him and his right hand raised, perhaps in the *vitarka-mudrā*. His throne is being lifted by three dwarfish grotesque demons. In front of these are more weapon-carrying dwarf demon figures, some of which have bird and animal faces. On the top right and left are elephant and *deva*s on the right. To the left behind the elephant is visible a large

7.11 Māra army attempting to frightened the meditating Buddha at moment of enlightenment, second-third century CE, Gandhāra.

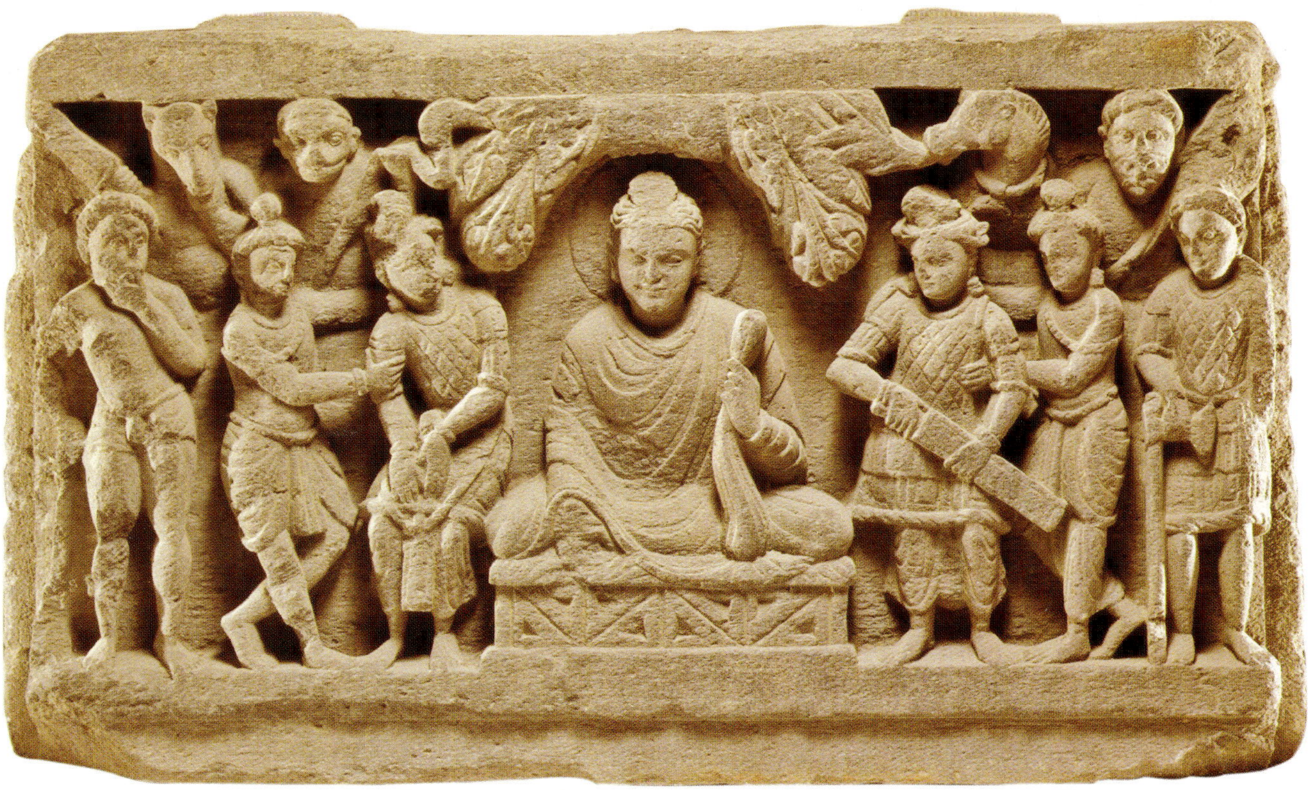

demonic face which may belong to Māra. The middle part of the panel is occupied by four female figures, two on each side of the Buddha. The figure to his immediate right, standing in a provocative *tribhaṅga* posture with her left hand raised above her head, represents either one of Māra's daughters or stands for all of them. Of the other three females, two have their hands folded in *añjali-mudrā* and one carries a *cāmara* in her right hand. The same conflation of the Assault and Temptation is also found on a fragment, now in the Madras Museum, where Māra, his daughters and dwarf army surround an empty throne.

The theme is also carved on the dome slab of *stūpa* 2 at Nāgārjunakoṇḍa[3], where the narrative starts with the central register revolving around the enlightenment sequence. The attack of Māra's demon armies and the temptation of his daughters occupy the central register.

In the Gāndhāran tradition, the *Māra-dharṣaṇa* episode is sometimes represented in the form of the figure of Buddha seated under the *bodhi* tree, touching the earth in *bhūmisparśa-mudrā* and surrounded by threatening male figures (*Pl.* 7.11).[40] One Gandhāra fragment depicts a group of soldiers wearing Graeco-Roman uniforms and brandishing weapons who may represent Māra's host since the faces of some of them resemble monkeys and other snouted animals with long hair, baring their teeth.[41] In a similar fragmentary stele now in the Chandigarh Museum (*Pl.* 7.12), the male figures are shown drawing their swords and threatening an unknown figure to the right. One can make out the presence of a goat-headed figure and perhaps a bear-faced one also.[42] In another relief from the Gāndhāran school, now in the Rijkmuseum voor Volkenkunde, Leiden,

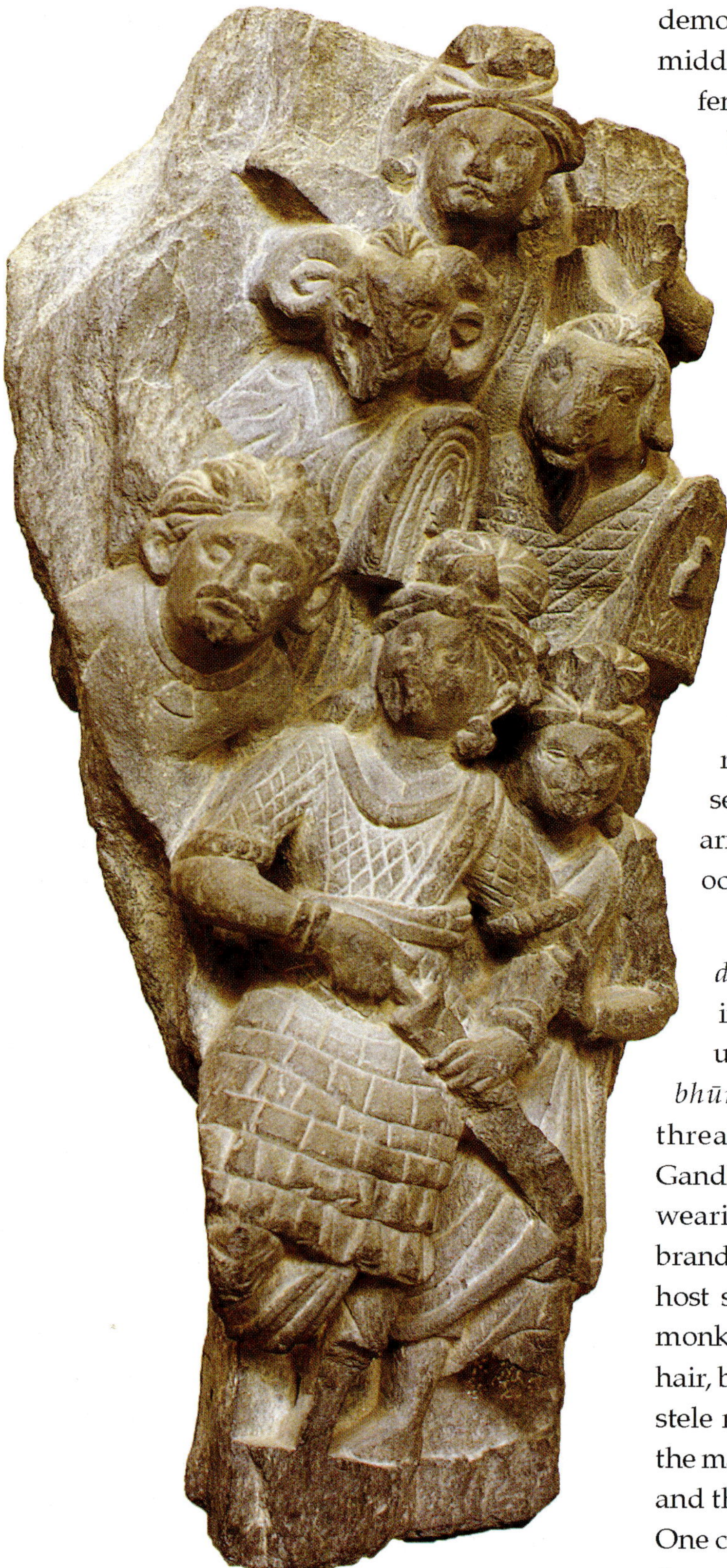

7.12 Māra's army, some with animal faces, schist, third century CE, Gandhāra. GMAG. 543.

these attacking hordes range on both sides of Buddha.[43] Māra himself is sometimes shown with a bow.[44] The *Māra-kanyā* scenes in this tradition are represented in the form of dancing figures in a *tribhaṅga* posture (*Pl.* 7.10), with or without male companions.[45]

Māra's omnipresence is also suggested in some other sculptures, where he and his companion appear as spade-carrying farmers who interrupt the Buddha's discourse with silly questions like, "Do you know where I could find my lost oxen?"[46]

The panoramic scenes dealing with Māra's attempts to vanquish the Buddha have not been found at Kuṣāṇa-period Mathurā. What we have is a fragmentary carving that shows the Buddha seated under the *bodhi* tree, flanked by three females on each side.[47] Perhaps these represent Māra's daughters. In scenes from the life of the Buddha (GMM.00.H1) (*Pl.* 7.9), the second episode of the Buddha's enlightenment has him seated with *bhūmisparśa-mudrā* on the left, while a female figure standing to his right probably represents all three daughters of Māra rolled into one. This is confirmed by the presence, immediately below, of a male figure, probably Māra as Kāmadeva, shooting off an arrow from a bow towards the Buddha. Standing on the left of this figure is a dwarf with a large face, who may represent Māra's army symbolised by this single figure. Similarly, in part of a sequence of eight episodes from the Buddha's life, he is shown with two instead of three female figures in seductive poses (arms raised and standing in *tribhaṅga*). Also seen here is a crouching figure that may represent Māra himself.

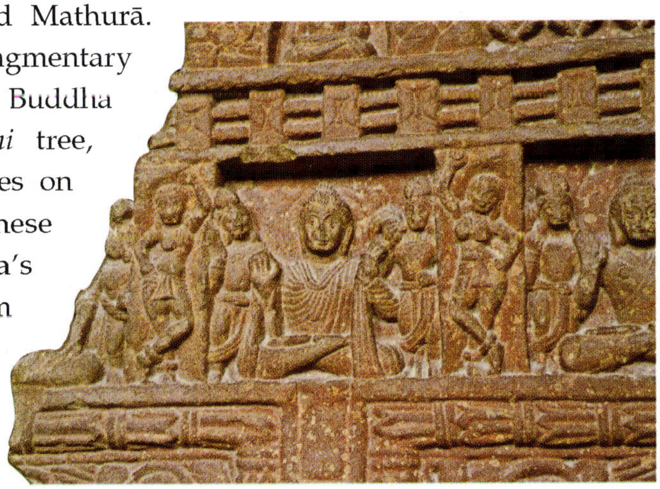

7.13 Part of panel showing Māra's daughters tempting Buddha, second century CE, Jamalpur Mound, Mathurā, SML No. B.208

On a slab carved with scenes from the life of the Buddha[48] dating to about the second century CE, the enlightenment scene is depicted with a dwarf carrying a *makara-dhvaja*, the emblem of Kāmadeva, symbolically representing the presence of Māra. On a Mathurā doorjamb carved in Kuṣāṇa style[49] showing scenes from the Buddha's life, the topmost panel depicts the Buddha receiving an offering of grass and the lower panel the offering of bowls by the *lokapāla*s. On the middle panel only a male figure is carved, to the left of an elephant. This may be a synoptic version of Māra's attack on the Buddha at Bodh-Gayā. It is given in the *Lalitavistara* that Māra attacked Buddha seated on an elephant with his army of dwarves milling around him.[50]

Perhaps the most detailed treatment of Māra's temptation is shown on a relatively large carved architectural fragment excavated from the Jamalpur mound at Mathurā (*Pl.* 7.13).[51] This is divided into three levels; the uppermost narrow band contains eleven male and female busts in niches. The middle level, beginning from the left, shows (1) the Buddha in the Indraśaila, (2) the Buddha turning the *dharmacakra* at Sārnāth, (3) the enlightenment at Bodh-Gayā, (4) the *Māra-kanyā* scene, and (5) the sun-god at the extreme end of the relief. In the fourth scene, the Buddha appears seated in *bhūmisparśa-mudrā* and surrounded by three feminine figures and one male figure. Of these only one female, on the far left, is in *tribhaṅga*. On the lower register are further depictions of the Buddha and *bodhisattva*s flanked by devotees. Reliefs of *stambha-śālabhañjikā*s separate three of the panels.

An interesting horizontal frieze from Ramnagar near Ahicchatra (now in the Lucknow Museum) depicts four scenes from the Buddha's life including the First Sermon, *parinirvāṇa*, and the two attacks by Māra.[52] The piece has been dated by P.K. Agrawala to the second century CE?[53] In the *Māra-dhītaro* episode, Māra himself is shown to the left of the Buddha with a bow and arrow in his hands, identifying him with Kāmadeva. *Māra-kanyā*s are shown on the Buddha's right, holding up a crocodile-topped banner, a *makara-dhvaja*, which is the emblem of Kāmadeva.[54] The *kanyā*s are also seen in dancing and provocative attitudes to the right. Such a depiction of *Māra-dhītaro* or *kanyā*s may refer to the question put to Buddha by Arati, one of the daughters of Māra, as to whether or not it was possible to escape lustful thoughts (*kāma-sanna*).[55] Also seen in the panel is a horse-headed figure seated in a posture indicating despair. This may be Māra since in later texts such as the *Matsya Purāṇa*, Kāma is described as horse headed.[56]

Kāmadeva as Māra[57] is quite prominent in the Kuṣāṇa art of Mathurā, particularly in the terracotta tradition. I would suggest that Kāmadeva, the god of love and earthly passion, in a less hegemonic art tradition represented by terracotta, was venerated and even celebrated at a popular level. Perhaps it was to combat such popular earthly enjoyment of the senses that Māra (as Evil) together with his daughters (epitomising sense desires) were configured and displayed on the walls and gateways of Buddhist monuments.[58] This would have been a corollary, of course, to the main intention, which was to highlight the greatness of the Buddha in withstanding great temptations with courage and determination. The representations may embody the hope that the pilgrim-audience would emulate this restraint.

As we have seen in all the portrayals, be these from Sāñcī, Amarāvatī, Gandhāra or Mathurā, Māra's daughters are physically attractive in appearance given that they attempt erotic seduction. The qualities they embody are not attractive. They deploy this beauty through the instrument of their bodies (however unsuccessfully) to arouse the commission of evil on the part of the man they seek to tempt inspired by Māra-Kāmadeva. In constituting Female Evil that is Māra's daughters, the conventional stereotyping of feminine beauty as dangerous is reiterated. They are set apart from other beautiful temptresses such as prostitutes (*gaṇikā*s) only in so far as they personify evil in the absolute or metaphysical sense.

On the other hand, male Evil, personified by Māra's army, is imagined and portrayed in both texts and visuals as distorted, ugly, grotesque and bestial, since their instruments of evil are brute force and their purpose is to frighten and to inspire the fear of death [the negative counterpart of the joy of sexuality]. Here one can recover engendering both in terms of physical appearance and in qualities that masculine and female evil embody on one hand, and of the strategies of achieving evil goals on the other. Women use their bodies to entice and men use force to subdue. In the visual discourse, sensual temptation is feminine. It may also be noted that iconographically *Māra-kanyā*s share many elements with *śālabhañjikā-yakṣī*s. Both are beautiful figures that are usually shown standing in a *tribhaṅga* posture with one arm upraised. Since Māyādevī is also shown in similar posture in the scene of the Buddha's miraculous birth, however, one cannot conclude that all female figures having this iconography connote deliberate temptation; yet even in the case of the mother of the Buddha, it was undoubtedly used to emphasise her female reproductivity.[59]

Māra himself adds confusion of the intellect to distract the Buddha and the *bhikkhu*s and *bhikkhuṇī*s of the *saṁgha*, to attract them to his side, into the world of sense desires, and away from the path of Enlightenment. Sometimes he tempts the Buddha to become a universal monarch and sometimes to use his powers to win riches to achieve *nirvāṇa* immediately without preaching to others. Māra's role is to encourage man's internal inclination towards sense desires. An evocative word picture of Māra's powers is drawn by the parable of the herd of deer: the man who does not desire the good of the deer "might place a decoy and might tether a female decoy as a lure" to decoy the deer on to a "treacherous road" leading to a "low lying marshy ground." The great herd of deer means *satta*, or beings, and the male and female are emblematic of the passion of delight, *nandi-rāga*, and ignorance, *avijjā* (Skt. *avidyā*). And the man desiring not to do good is Māra *pāpima*.[60] There are many instances of Māra trying to distract *therī*s, nuns such as Alavikā[61] and Kisā Gotamī[62] from the path of Enlightenment and meditation. He even challenged *therī* Somā to her right and ability to reach *nirvāṇa* since she was a woman.[63]

### 7.2 Apsarases

*Apsarases* are not construed as universally evil, unlike Māra's daughters. They occupy a somewhat ambivalent position in early Indian art and thought. *Apsarases* as celestial nymphs belong to the court of Indra,[64] entertaining him with dance and dalliance. They obey the commands of Indra which often take the form of orders to seduce virtuous ascetics and kings whose overwhelming virtue threatens his paramountcy. *Apsarases* also often descend to earth to take human male partners, cohabit with them, and produce children, but on certain conditions generally disadvantageous to the males. As such, the *apsarases* often deploy their charms as per their own independent will and are not bound to any man, divine or human, even though they are often believed to be the consorts of *gandharvas*. Neither are they generally condemned for such behaviour, nor are relations with *apsarases* looked down upon *per se*, unlike the case of their mundane counterparts, the *gaṇikās* (courtesans). This is acknowledged even within the comparatively misogynist Buddhist tradition recorded in Aśvaghoṣa's *Saundarānanda* where *apsarases* are described as, "ever young, ever busied in love alone and enjoyed jointly by those who have earned merit; celestial being, union with them is no sin. In them is centred the reward of austerities of the divine world."[65]

*Apsarases* are, on the one hand, often depicted on votive *stūpas* (*Pl.* 7.14) as one of the auspicious symbols along with *yakṣī-śālabhañjikās*, and on the other they indicate and demarcate the celestial realm of Indra or the Tuṣita Heaven that becomes even more charming and heavenly due to their presence. *Apsarases* along with other demi-gods are carved on Hindu temples also

7.14 *Apsarases* dancing around the *stūpa*, Lonaśobhikā's *āyāgapaṭṭa*, red sandstone, second century CE, Kaṅkālī Ṭīlā, Mathurā district, UP. GMM No. Q 2. (next page)

7.15 Misakesi, Sudassanā, Alambuṣā, Subhadā and Padmāvatī *accharās* (*apsarases*), Prasenjit Pillar, first century BCE, Bharhut. IM 273. (facing next page)

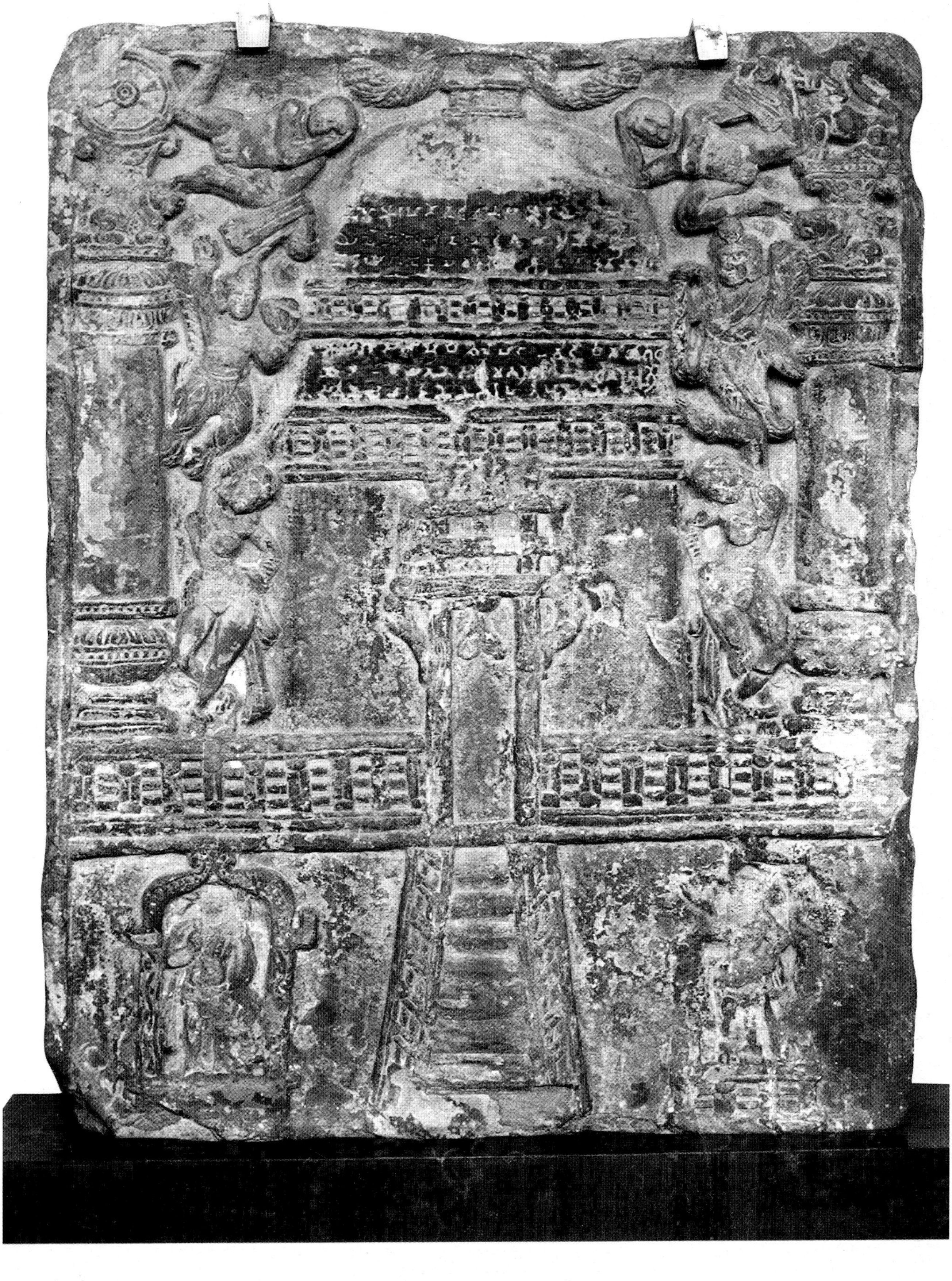

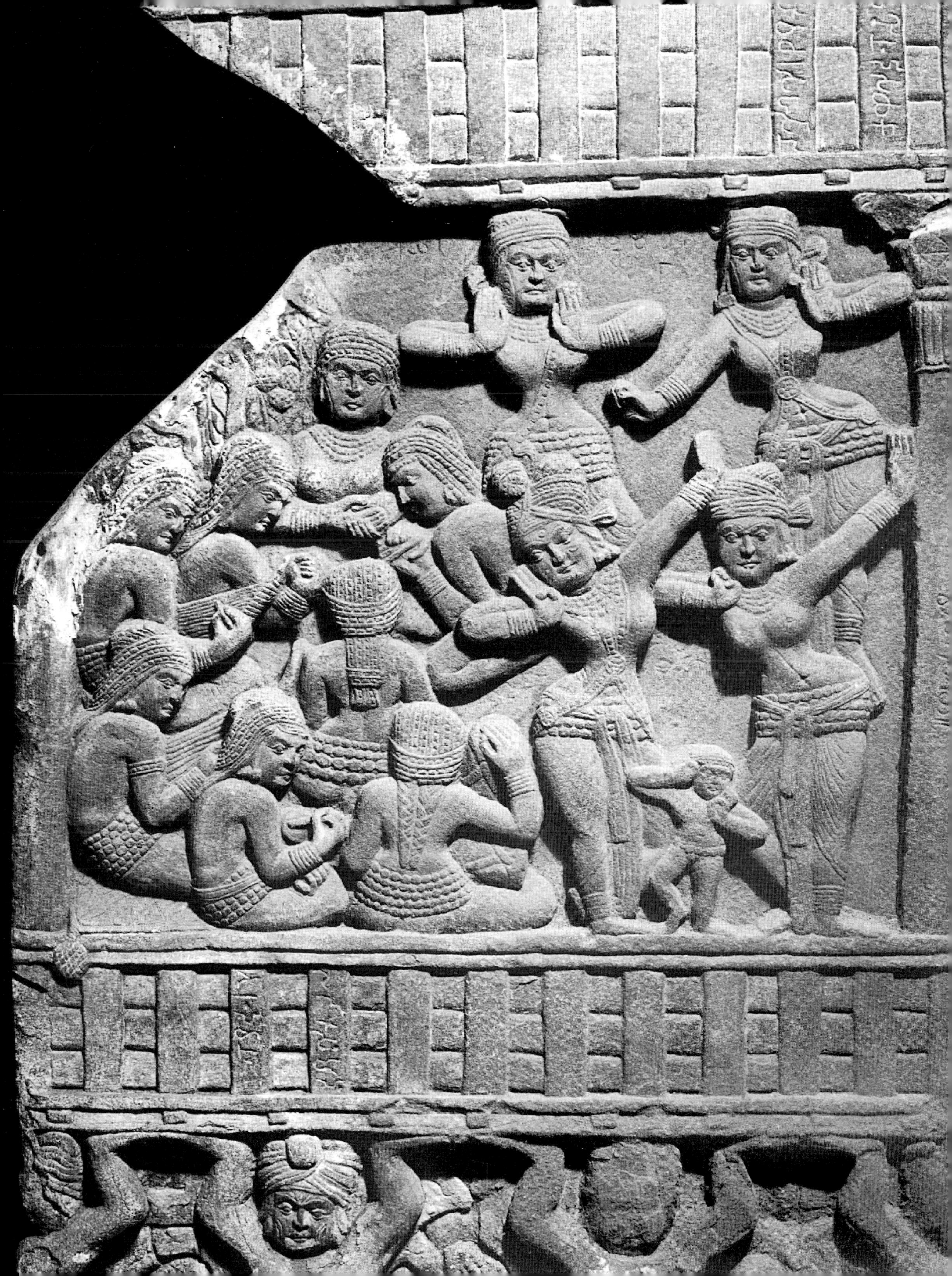

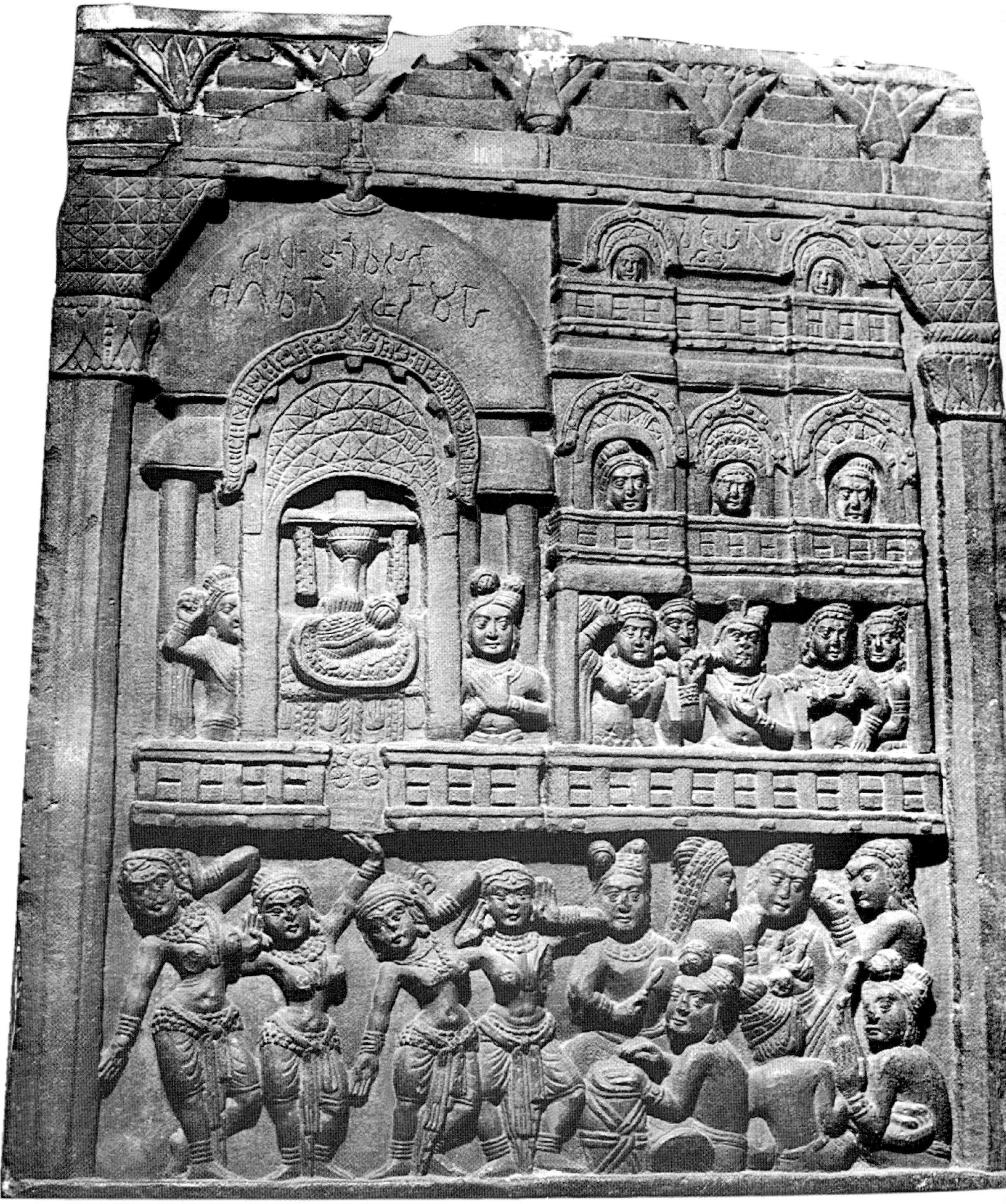

where they belong to the category of *āvaraṇa devatā*s or surrounding *devatā*s. Stella Kramrisch has explained that in the Paurāṇic tradition, the form of Celestial Beauties is embodied intellect. And *apsarase*s, *naṭikā*s (dancers), *yakṣīṇī*s and *dig-devī*s (goddesses of directions) were all forms and images of Śakti.[66]

Some feminine figures in the post-Mauryan terracotta tradition have been identified with *apsarase*s.[67] As has been mentioned before, the *pañcacūḍa* type of figure may have been one such figure. *Apsarase*s such as Rambhā are embodiments of wish fulfilling[68] and wear five symbols of auspiciousness.[69]

*Apsarase*s are not construed as universally evil; their presence was in fact considered beneficial and auspicious for the monuments. The depictions of *apsarase*s that have been selected from early Buddhist art for study reveal contradictory tendencies. At Bharhut *apsarase*s are shown rejoicing in the Vaijayanta Palace and the Sudharma Hall in the heaven of 33 gods (*Pl.* 7.16) as part of the worship of the Hair Lock[70] and dancing on the occasion of the Buddha's Enlightenment on the Prasenjit Pillar. The dancing *apsarase*s carved on these railing pillars at Bharhut present them as a motif symbolising joy and religious fervour. As part of the narrative visual discourse, however, an *apsarās* is not necessarily perceived as benevolent and beautiful.

At Bharhut there is a group of dancing figures carved on the Prasenjit Pillar (*Pl.* 7.15)[71] that are labelled as Miśrakeśī, Sudassanā, Alambuṣā, Subhadrā and Padmāvatī *apsarase*s.[72] They form a part of a group of 12 female figures arranged in three groups each. The first one with dancers occupies the right half. The second comprising singers is arranged in the middle and the third with ladies playing instruments takes up the lower and left periphery of the panel. The dancing figures are in two rows, Alambuṣā and Miśrakeśī, in the front and Padmāvatī and Subhadrā at the back, all of whom are delineated frontally. A small boy, also seen dancing, is placed in the front between two dancers. The names mentioned in the label inscriptions correspond to some of the names given in the list of *apsarase*s found in the *Nāṭyaśāstra* which enumerates the following: Mañjukeśī, Sukeśī, Miśrakeśī, Sulocanā, Saudāminī, Devadattā, Devasenā, Manoramā, Sudatī, Sundarī, Vidagdhā, Sumalā, Santati, Sunandā, Sumukhī, Magadhī, Arjunī, Saralā, Keralā, Dhṛti, Nandā, Supuṣkalā and Kalabhā.[73]

7.16 *Apsarase*s dancing in the Vaijayanta Palace and Sudharma Hall of the Gods, railing pillar, first century BCE, Bharhut. IM 182. (facing page)

The dancing celestial women are supposed to epitomise beauty, and are seen to possess well-ornamented, charmingly tall forms, slim waists, and graceful poses. Yet they are not carved in voluptuous proportions. The attitude and the treatment of the body of the celestial dancers suggest that they were not meant to signify temptation to the viewer. Rather, it is likely that they are dancing in elation, celebrating the historic moment of the Buddha's achievement of *bodhi*.

At Amarāvatī, Nāgārjunakoṇḍa and on some steles from Mathurā, miniature *stūpa*s (*Pl.* 7.14) are carved at three levels. Often in the middle, dancing female figures flank the *stūpa-toraṇa*, perhaps notionally indicating the celestial realm through the imagery of *apsarase*s paying homage to the *stūpa*.

This does not hold true of all *apsarase*s, as is evident in the depiction of the Ṛṣyaśṛṅga story[74] from Mathurā, where the *apsarase*s do not seem to

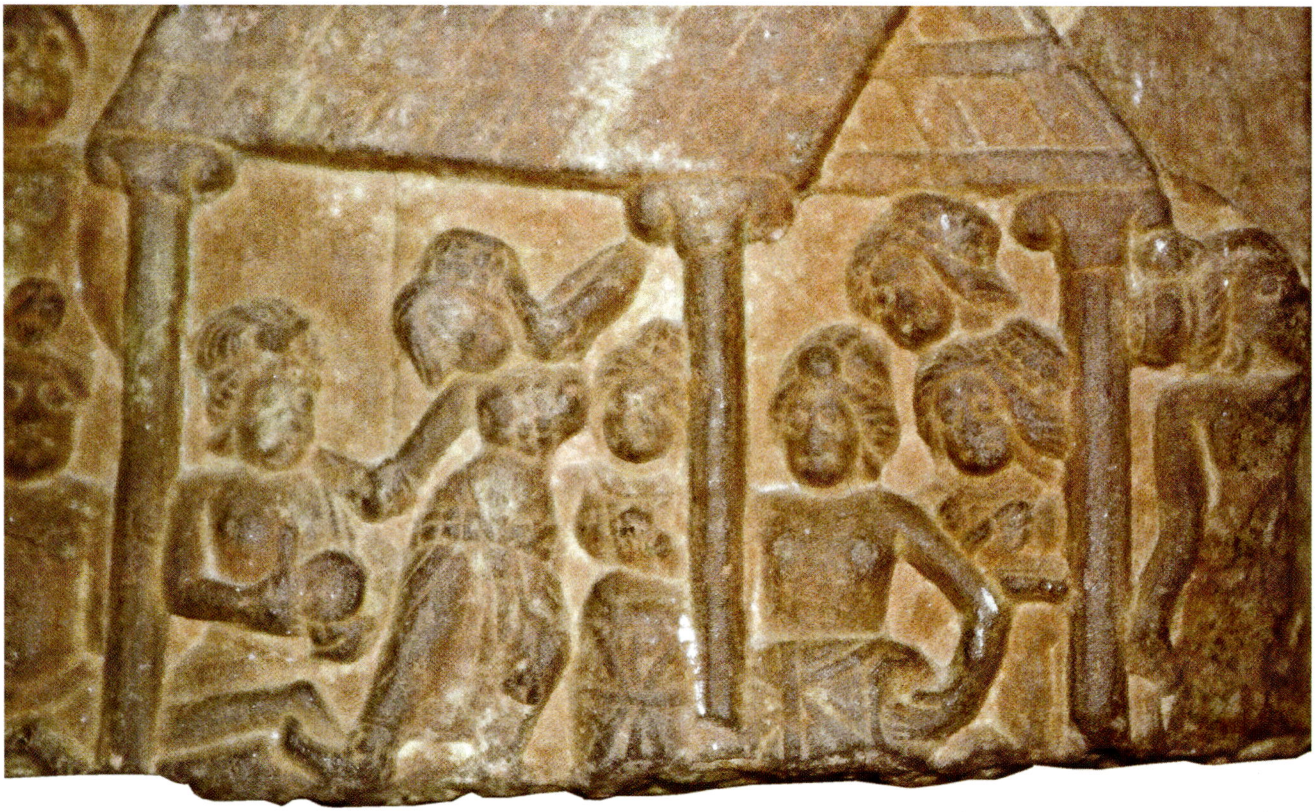

7.17 *Apsarases* dancing in the celestial court, second century CE, Mathurā. SML.

be perceived as either benign or auspicious. A similar representation is found on a railing pillar from the Bhūteśvara mound in Mathurā (*Pls.* 7.18, 7.19).[75] This pillar is divided into three panels of which the lowermost contains the depiction of a young male figure being forced into the embrace of a larger female figure. Above the frame of railing and pilasters, instead of the usual *caitya* windows, we have three thatched roofs of huts depicted here. In the middle panel, a couple is seated on what look like two high seats made of bricks or stones. Under this seat one can see two deer facing each other. Above the pillar-and-architrave frame, one can see banners or garlands festooned between three towers; the two corner-towers seem bigger than the one in the middle which is more in the nature of either a pillar (*stambha*) or an emblem (*dhvaja*). The composition and treatment suggest an urban site. Above this are a group of women, two of whom are in front and seem to be leaning forward against either a parapet made of diagonally-placed thin stones or a draped curtain. The finial is a *kapota* with one full and two half-*caitya* windows. Three moments are depicted here, one set in the forest hermitage, another in the city, and the last may be indicative of an observation tower/window/theatre. Another antiquity showing the Ṛṣyaśṛṅga episode carved on the lower three panels of a railing post has been unearthed at Govindgaṛh,[76] with cult of worship of the *uṣṇīṣa* in the uppermost register. It is datable to perhaps the first century BCE, marking the beginning of Kuṣāṇa art.

One version is carved in low relief on a fragment of a pillar from the Jaina *stūpa* at Kaṅkālī Ṭīlā in Mathurā (*Pl.* 7.20).[77] In a square panel, a seated couple is carved in the centre,

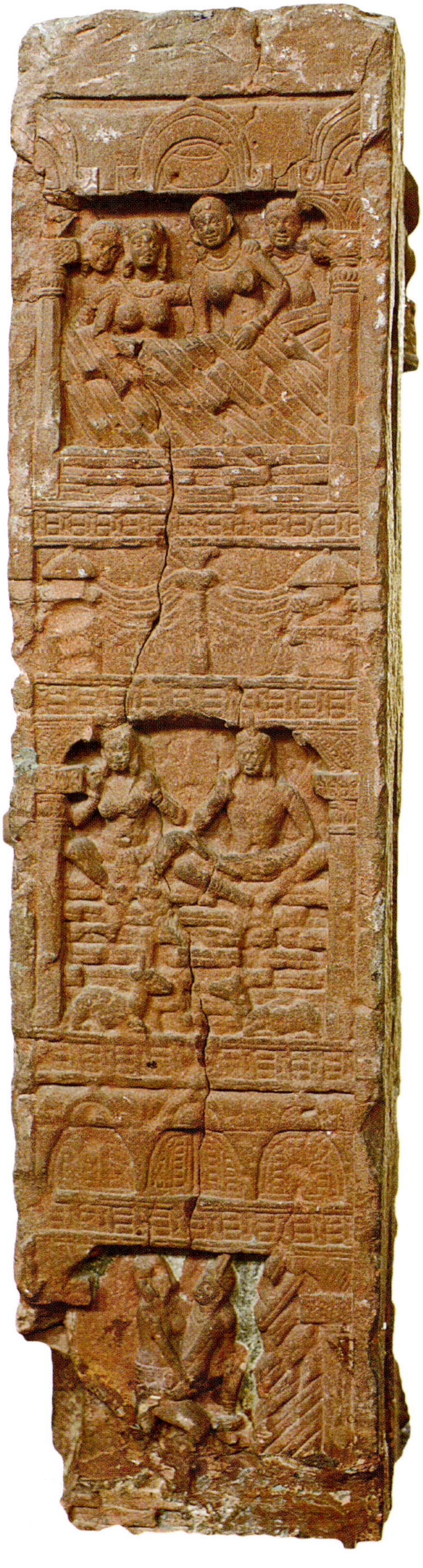

7.18 Rail post with Ṛṣyaśṛṅga scene in bottom panel, red sandstone, second century CE, Bhuteśvara Mound, Mathurā district, UP. GMM No. 151.

7.19 Detail of lower panel of *Pl.* 7.18.

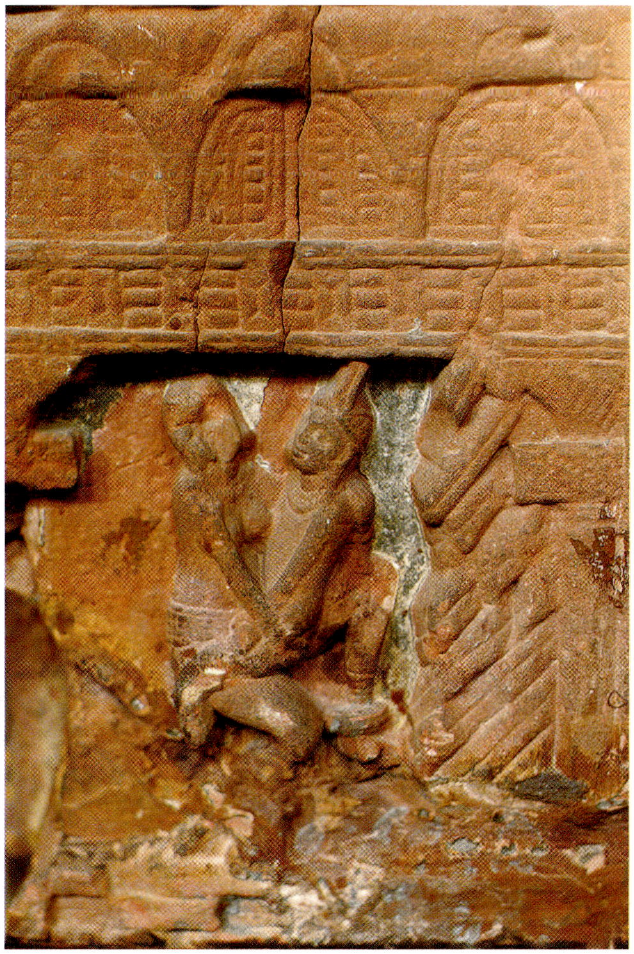

seemingly suspended in the middle. The woman holds a man in her lap. She is shown in three-quarter profile behind the man who is in profile. She is young-looking, displaying abundant breasts with incisions made to indicate nipples. Her *dhotī* is transparent, and she also wears earrings, bracelets, and ankle-rings. Her hair is dressed in bun-plait arrangement. She holds the man in her lap with her right hand under his hip and is seen leaning into his body and face, her face touching his. The man is enclosed within the embrace of the woman. He is portrayed wearing a *dhotī* and is ornamented with earrings. A single horn emerges from the turban, proving his identity as Ṛṣyaśṛṅga, the sage with a deer horn (*Pl.* 7.23). In the background an *aśoka* tree and banana trees are visible on both sides, probably depicting a forest dwelling. The panel seems to be the uppermost panel of a railing since it is topped by a *kapota* containing one full *caitya* window and two half *caitya* windows. Pilasters on both sides with a lotus and winged-lion capital enclose the scene underneath this panel.

The inscription accompanying the scene is donative in character and states: "Adoration to the *arhats*. A *toraṇa* has been erected by order of *lahastinī* (*Bālahastinī*), a lay pupil of the ascetics with her parents, together with mother-in-law and father-in-law."[78] Thus, from the inscription we know that the donor who patronised this scene was a married woman, well integrated into the family structure. This reinforces the view that patronage was not gendered in the same terms as the choice of misogynist themes represented. Imagery such as that of Ṛṣyaśṛṅga *being* forced and seduced by divine/human women may have played a significant role in the process of socialisation of norms regarding appropriate gender behaviour. The internalisation of these norms, by men and women, was both generated and further perpetuated by the patriarchal social order.

The identification with sage Ṛṣyaśṛṅga can be based on the horn sticking out of the turban of the male figure.[79] References to Ṛṣyaśṛṅga are found in both Buddhist and Brāhmanic literary traditions. In the Buddhist Jātaka collection two versions of the story of the sage Ṛṣyaśṛṅga's (Iśiśiṅga's) seduction by a female are narrated: the *Alambuṣā Jātaka*[80] and the *Nalinikā Jātaka*.[81] The scene depicted on the Kaṅkālī Ṭīlā *toraṇa stambha* and Bhūteśvara railing pillar described above probably refers to the *Alambuṣā Jātaka*. According to this story, once a doe conceived a male child after consuming grass and water mingled with the semen of a *bodhisattva*-ascetic. (It is this moment from the legend that has been illustrated at the early site of Bharhut and is labelled as *Isimigiya Jātaka* (*Pl.* 7.22, for Mathurā see *Pl.* 7.21).[82] The child thus born is named Iśiśiṅga (Ṛṣyaśṛṅga of the *Rāmāyaṇa*) because of the horn on his head. His father warns him of the temptations offered by the beautiful women of the Himalayan country, temptations that result in utter destruction to all who fall under their sway. Iśiśiṅga continues to practise penance for a long time and in the process threatens the realm of Sakka (Śakra, Indra). Indra sends Alambuṣā, the most beautiful *apsaras* of his court, to seduce the ascetic and thus destroy his virtue. On seeing the *apsaras*, Iśiśiṅga, struck by her beauty, exclaims:

> . . . Fragrant as golden sandalwood, in brightness like the sun
> A slim and winsome maid art thou, right fair to look upon.
> So soft and pure, with slender waist and firmly springing gait,
> Thy movements so full of grace, my heart they captivate.
> Thy thighs like trunk of elephant are finely tapering,

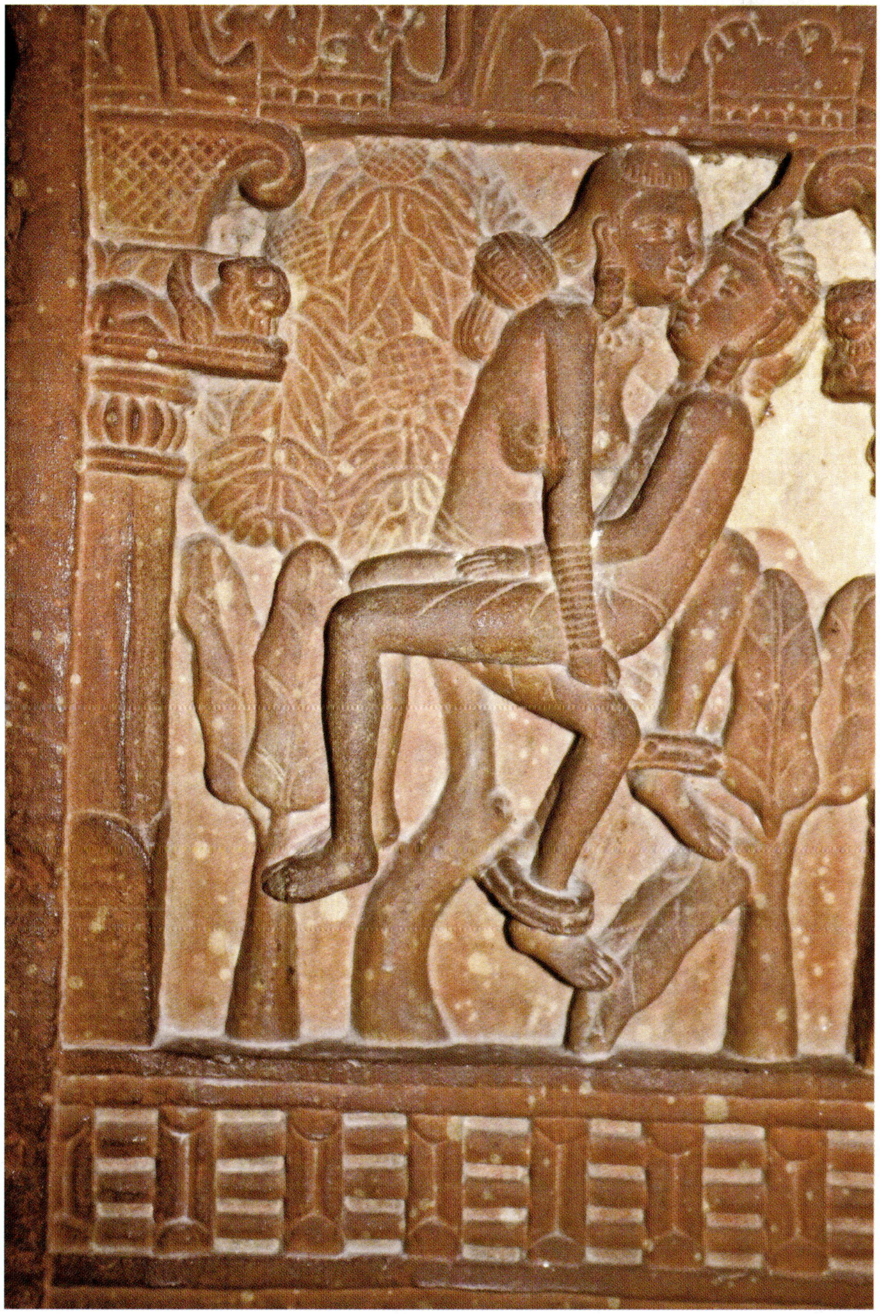

7.20 *The Alambuṣā Jātaka*, with the *apsaras* Alambuṣā embracing Ṛṣyaśṛṅga, second century CE, Kaṅkālī Ṭīlā, Mathurā. SML.

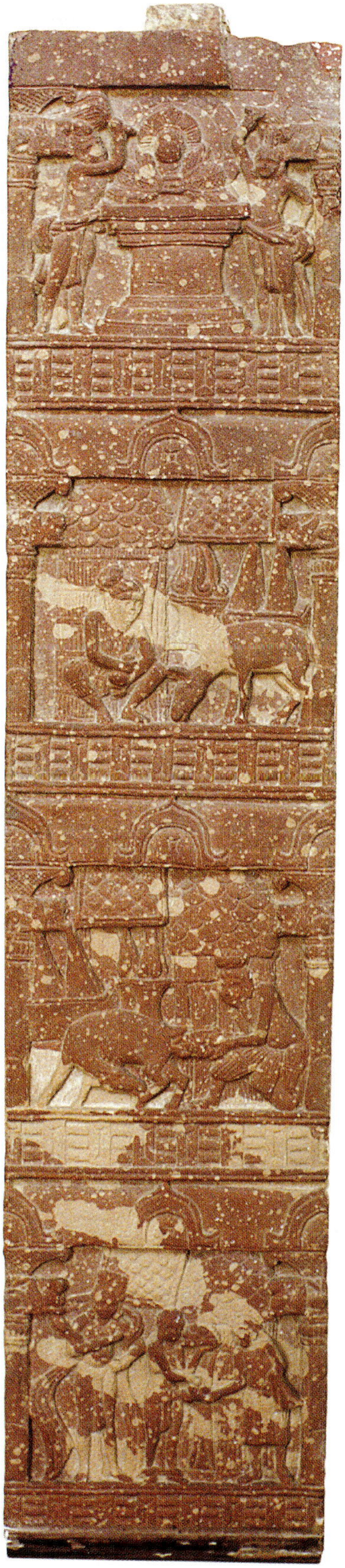

7.21 *Ṛṣyaśṛṅga Jātaka*, railing post, red sandstone, second century CE, Mathurā, GMM.

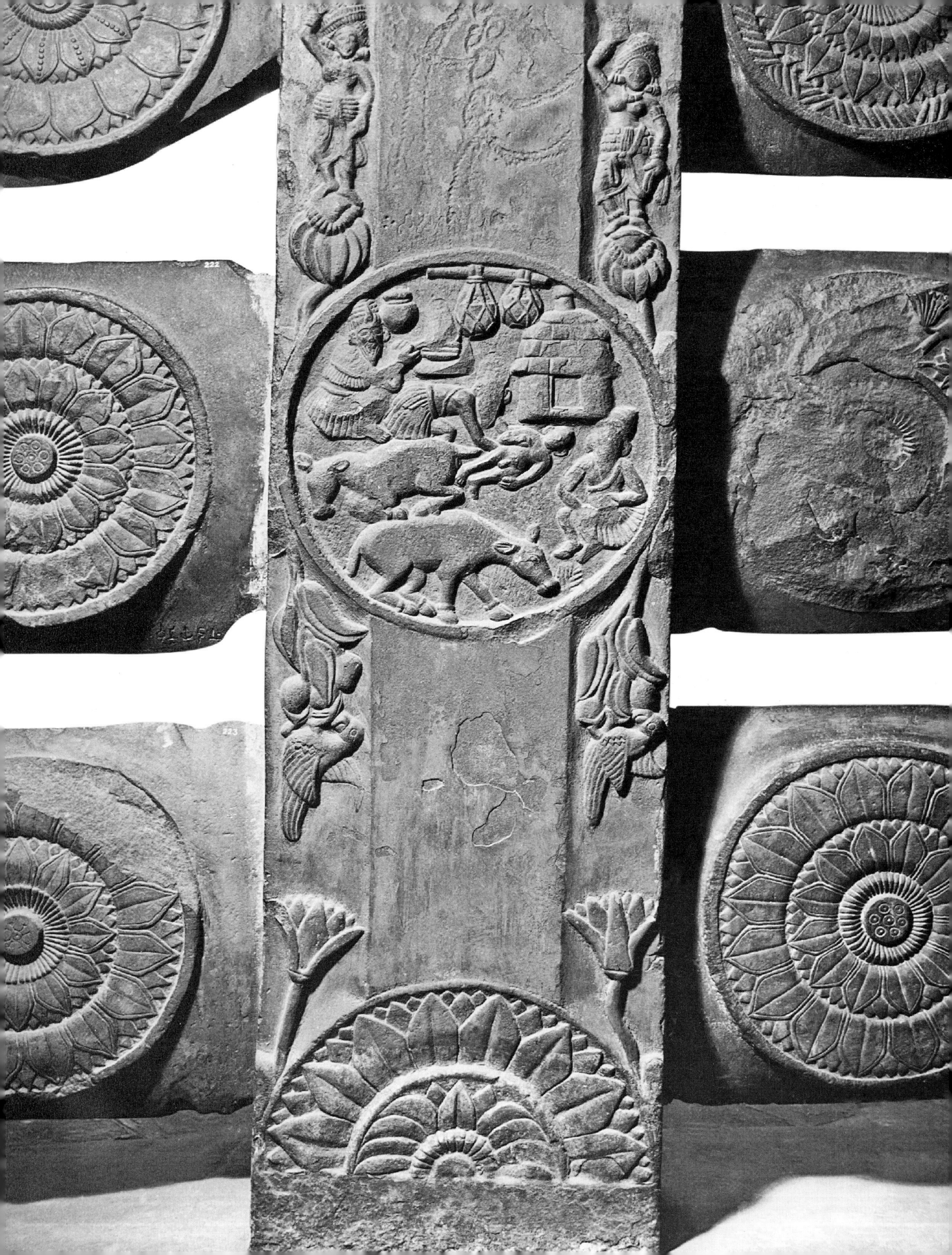
222
223

Thy buttocks soft to touch and like to any dice board.
With down like lotus filaments thy navel marked, I ween,
As though with black collyrium 'were charged, from far is seen.
Twin milky breasts like pumpkins halved, their swelling globes display,
Firm set, although without a stalk all unsupported. . . .[83]

Using her charm, Alambuṣā succeeds in seducing Ṛṣyaśṛṅga and destroying his virtue, but after three years he "came to his senses" and forsook sensual desire and re-entered meditation. Alambuṣā, terrified of his ascetic prowess, begs for forgiveness, which is granted by the ascetic. Sakka, too, pleased with her, grants her a boon of her choice. She requests, ". . . let me never tempt a saint to violate his vow."

In the *Nalinikā Jātaka*, the protagonist Nalinikā is the daughter of the king of Benares. She is sent to seduce Iśiśiṅga and bring him to the capital in order to induce rain. She obeys the command and on reaching the hermitage plays with balls to attract his attention.[84] She also poses naked, exposing her lovely limbs to his gaze. He is charmed but, not knowing the difference between men and women, assumes her to be another male sage; he thus disports with her. His father returns and brings young Iśiśiṅga to his senses. The latter realises that Nalinikā is like a female *yakkha* and resumes his ascetic life.[85]

A similar tale is found in the *Rāmāyaṇa* in which it is the *apsarās* Rambhā who is sent by Indra to distract Ṛṣyaśṛṅga.[86] In Aśvaghoṣa's *Saundarānanda*, Ṛṣyaśṛṅga is mentioned as one of the great beings that are seduced, in this case by a

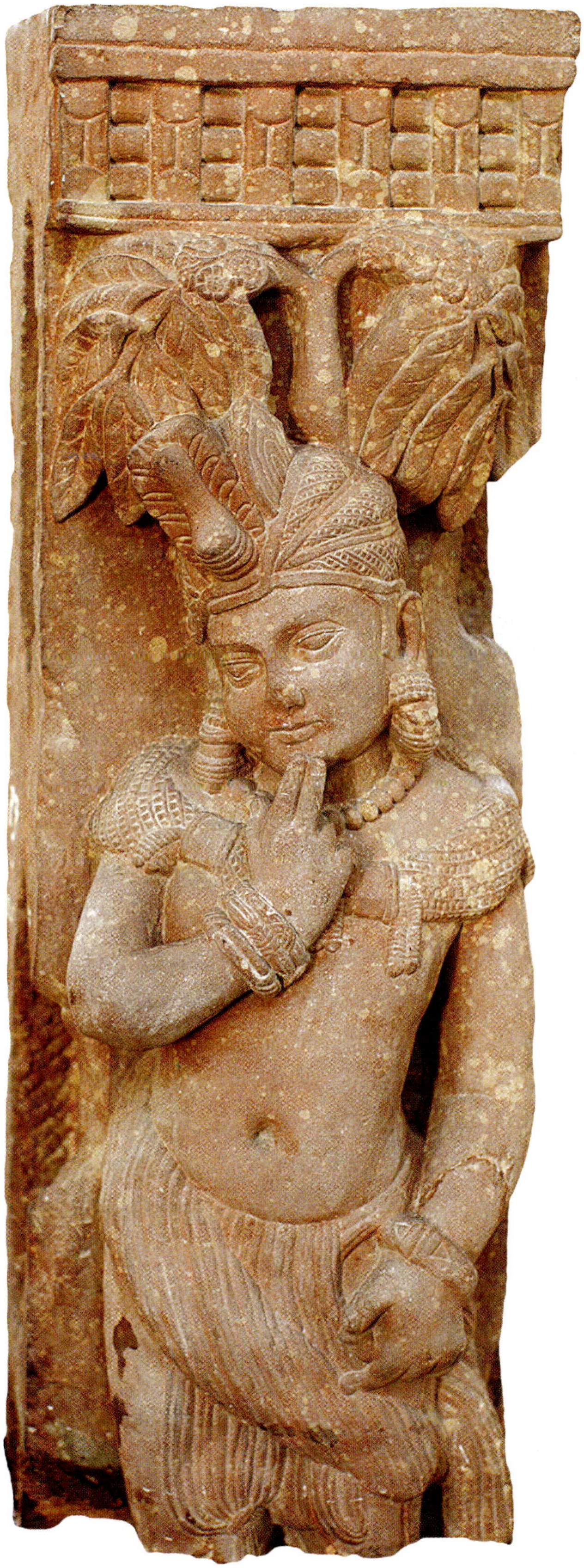

7.22 *Isimiga (Alambuṣā) Jātaka*, railing medallion, first century BCE, Bharhut. IM 225-26. (facing page)

7.23 Ṛṣyaśṛṅga, rail post fragment, standing, red sandstone, third century CE, Chaubārā Ṭīlā, Mathurā district, UP. GMM No. J 7.

female named Śāntā.[87] According to the belief current in western Himachal, it is King Daśaratha who causes Ṛṣyaśṛṅga to be brought to the capital of his kingdom in order to relieve a drought that had been prevailing there.[88]

The predisposition to view women as sexually insatiable is reinforced through the physical constraining of the man on her lap by the *apsaras*es, like the ogresses/*yakṣī*s discussed below. Such an act also signifies the sexual dominance of Alambuṣā/Nalinikā. It also points towards the perceived moral degradation of women in general. There is an implication of an inversion of power relations, seen in the role reversal of a woman as constrainer[89] exerting control and thus suggestive of anarchy, both social and familial.

The issue of redemption of women through male agency is also addressed in the depiction of this popular tale. Under the influence of "steadfast power and courage"[90] of male virtue personified by the sage, Alambuṣā is reformed and promises never to tempt and lead saints astray. Thus, unrestrained and potentially dangerous female sexuality is contained, tamed and brought under control by the male social and moral code.

In the stories above, human and semi-divine women are used to perform the function of the seductress of the virtuous and innocent male. This is in itself a significant representation. It highlights the notion of universal and destructive female sexuality, be it the case of Māra's daughters, *gaṇikā*s, attractive wives of the Jātakas and *Theragāthā* or *yakṣīṇī*s as discussed in previous chapters.

Another idea that pervades the textual and visual narrative discourse is that feminine beauty, an essential attribute of femininity, even that of an *apsaras* like Alambuṣā destroys virtue. *Apsaras*es are the epitome of beauty to whom all other females, be they human or divine, are compared. Such a notion does run contrary to the perception, echoed in most textual traditions, that *apsaras*es, as celestial beings, are free to establish sexual or even temporary marital relations with men without incurring the wrath and condemnation of the ideologues. The contradiction between the narrative tradition of the Jātakas (both in text and image) on one hand, and the canonical literature on the other, reveals the porous nature of the patriarchal ideology in the period. Depending on the context in which they are placed, *apsaras*es may be auspicious, *maṅgala,* or they may epitomise dangerous and eternal temptation. Thus in the *apsaras* figure, the contradictions and fissures in the dominant patriarchal discourse are visible, even if only partially.

### 7.3 Ogresses/Yakṣīs

*Apsaras*es, *nāginī*s, *rākṣasī*s and *yakṣī*s share many similar characteristics, being situated socially outside prescribed patriarchal norms, and physically visualised as beautiful. *Yakṣī*s, given their ambivalent disposition, can change form and can employ illusion to fulfil their desires upon hapless humans.[91] However, they often take the shape of ogresses with malevolent natures. The element of shifting indefinite form lends itself well to the need or desire to project and locate evil on to an amorphous female presence that defies containment or location in any fixed categories.[92]

In the *Jātaka-kathā* collection there are prolific references to such ogresses,[93] though their portrayal in art is not so frequently encountered. I discuss here the visual rendering of two narratives featuring ogresses: the *Pādukuśala-mānava Jātaka* and the *Valāhassa Jātaka*, and one

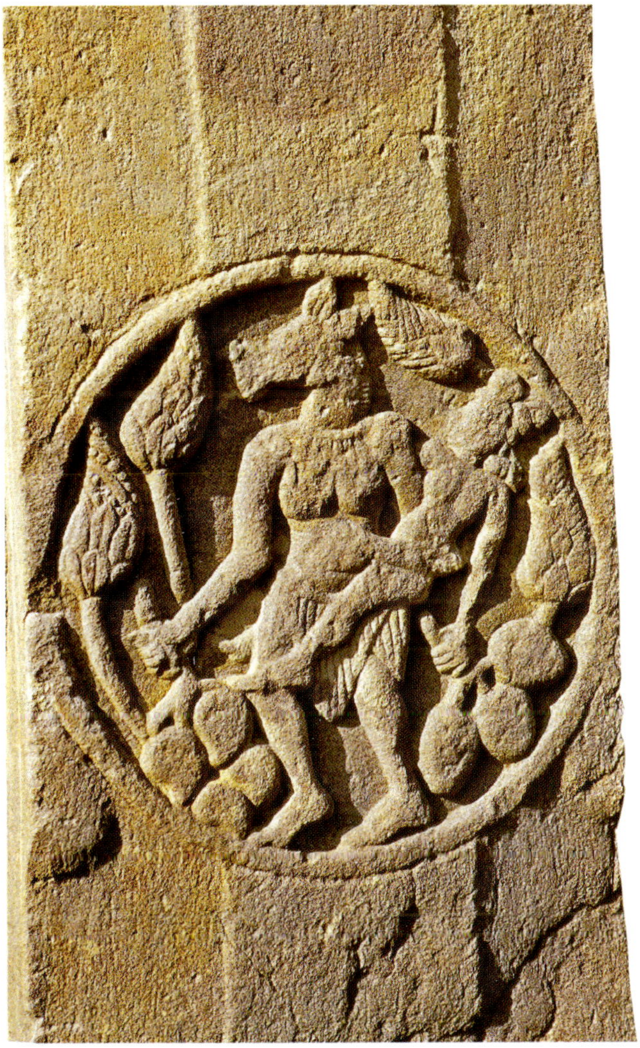

7.24 *Pādukuśalamānava Jātaka*, railing medallion, *stūpa* 2, first century BCE, Sāñcī.

Jātaka describing the activities of an ogre, the *Samugga Jātaka*.

At Sāñcī, on a medallion on a railing pillar of *stūpa* II we have the illustration of the *Pādukuśalamānava Jātaka* (*Pl.* 7.24). This portrays a horse-headed *yakṣī* carrying a young male straddled on her hip.[94] Her horse-face is turned to her right. She has a large body with flattened breasts, seemingly tied by a piece of cloth, and she wears a short knee-length garment made of bark. In her right hand she seems to be clutching a bunch of coconuts and the youth on her hip holds a bunch of

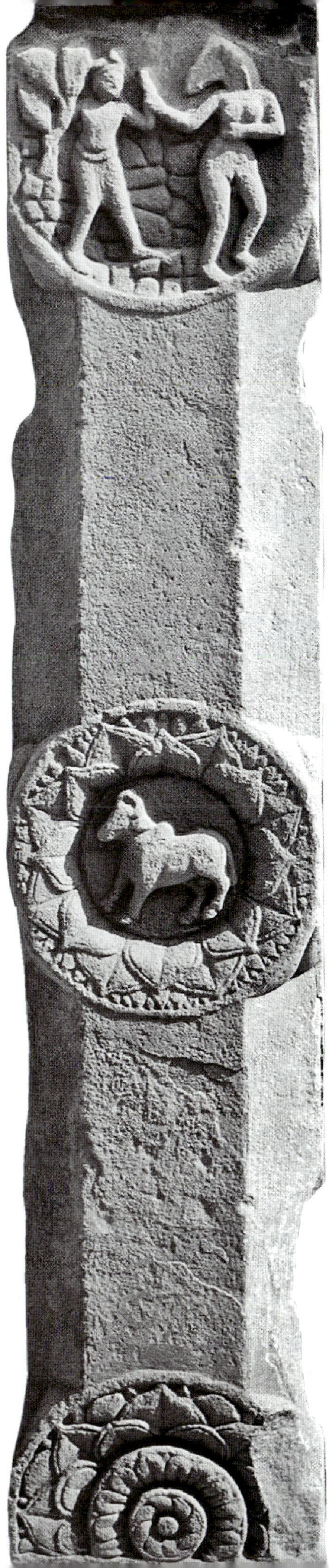

7.25 *Pādukuśalamānava Jātaka*, railing pillar, upper medallion, first century BCE, Bodh-Gayā.

breadfruit or jackfruit in his left hand. The background is made up of three lotus buds rising from their stems.

Commentators have identified the youth in the Sāñcī example with the son of the *yakṣī*[95] on account of his smaller size in comparison to the female. I feel that this figure represents the brāhmaṇa whom the *yakṣī* has hoisted on to her back to carry away. It is difficult to comment on the symbolism of the fruits; it could simply be food looted from the caravan of merchants or it might stand for fertility in general. Gail Sutherland has observed that there is an important link between morality and food, where impure food of the *yakṣī*s leads to corruption.[96] This brings forth another motif of inversion of natural order as evinced through unrestrained femininity.

*Pādukuśalamānava Jātaka* is illustrated on a railing pillar at Bodh-Gayā (*Pl.* 7.25).[97] Here an earlier episode from the story is shown in which the *yakṣī* captures the handsome Brāhmaṇa who later becomes the father of her child. The horse-head of the *yakṣī* is much abraded now, but still one can make out that it was turned towards her right, looking at the male figure standing clasping a tree with one hand, as if resisting the pull exerted by the female. His raised left hand is grasped in the right hand of the *yakṣī*. The background seems to be made of rocks or bricks.[98] A similar depiction was found at Gurgaon in Haryana (*Pl.* 7.26) and is now in the Mathura Museum.[99] The horse-headed *yakṣī*, standing to the right of the male, touches his right shoulder with her left hand. He seems to hold a rounded fruit in one of his hands. She is shown with pendant breasts and exposed pudendum. It is apparent that the man is being abducted by the

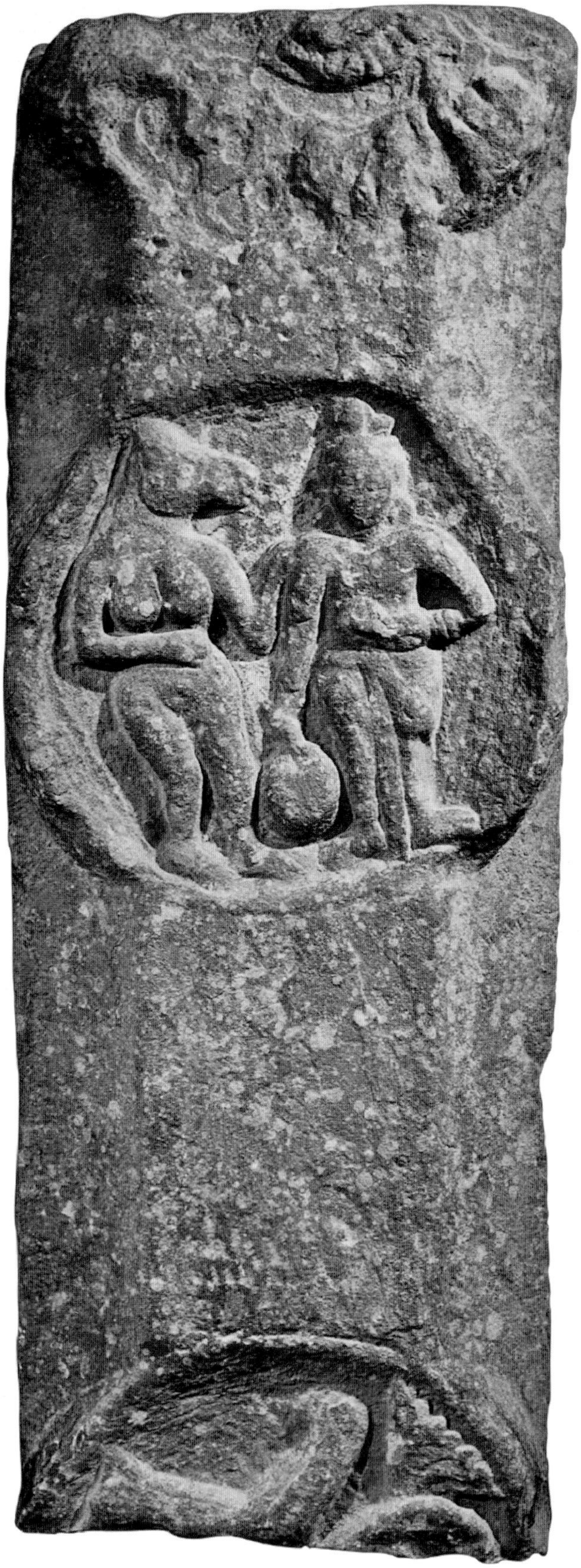

7.26 *Pādukuśalamānava Jātaka*, rail post, first century CE, Gurgaon, Haryana. GMM.12.191

*yakṣī* against his will. Representations of the *Pādukuśalamānava Jātaka* featuring this *assamukhī yakṣī* or horse-headed ogress have also been found at Mathurā[100] and Pāṭaliputra.[101] At Bhaja, a horse-headed *yakṣī* is seen with a male figure (*Pl.* 7.27), perhaps the brāhmaṇa youth.[102]

The *Pādukuśalamānava Jātaka* is a long story, the first part of which relates to the episode of a female *yakkhī* and a brāhmaṇa, as seen in sculptures.[103] According to this tale, because a queen is unfaithful to her husband, she is born as a horse-headed female[104] *yakkhī* in her next birth, and in this form she serves Vaiśrāvaṇa for three years who grants her the privilege of devouring merchants passing through her territory. Then she comes upon a rich and handsome brāhmaṇa and carries him on her back to her cave, *lenaguha*, in order to eat him. Instead, conceiving a passion for him, she takes him as her husband. From him she conceives a child who is actually a *bodhisattva*, and after 10 months of pregnancy she delivers the baby. This *bodhisattva*, on reaching adolescence, rescues his father, and father and son together escape the control of the cannibal mother who dies of grief at the loss of her family. Thus in the text the ogress-*yakṣī* is deprived even of her half-human child, who as per the then current social mores belongs to the father.[105]

It seems significant that from the story of the brāhmaṇa-*yakṣī* son who is endowed with the gift of reading signs, it is the horse-headed, bark-clad *yakṣī*'s abduction of the fair brāhmaṇa that is chosen to be carved in a synoptic manner at Sāñcī, Bodh-Gayā, Gurgaon and Mathurā. For a viewer familiar with the *Jātaka* tradition, the moment frozen in stone may recall the complete tale visually, as it is only the episode regarding a *yakṣī* transgressing the sexual, social and moral code set for all women that has been chosen for depiction.

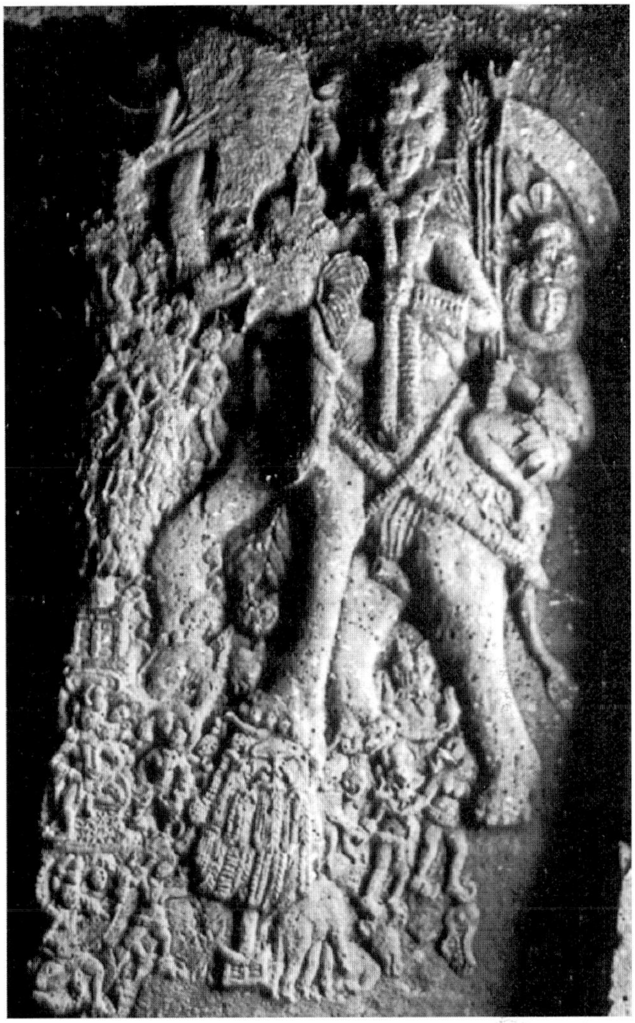

7.27 Assamukhī *yakṣī* and youth, *Pādukuśalamānava Jātaka*, in lower right corner, first century BCE, Bhaj Caves, Maharashtra.

Another story featuring cannibalistic and sexually active female *yakṣīs*, whose victims are freed by a *bodhisattva*, is narrated in the *Valāhassa Jātaka*, which is illustrated on a pillar from Mathurā (*Pl.* 7.28). The pillar is divided into three panels, each showing an episode from the *Valāhassa Jātaka*.[106]

The lowest panel (*Pl.* 7.29) is divided into two sections of which the lower part is filled by two female faces, which are large in size and round in shape, a feature emphasised by hair parted in the

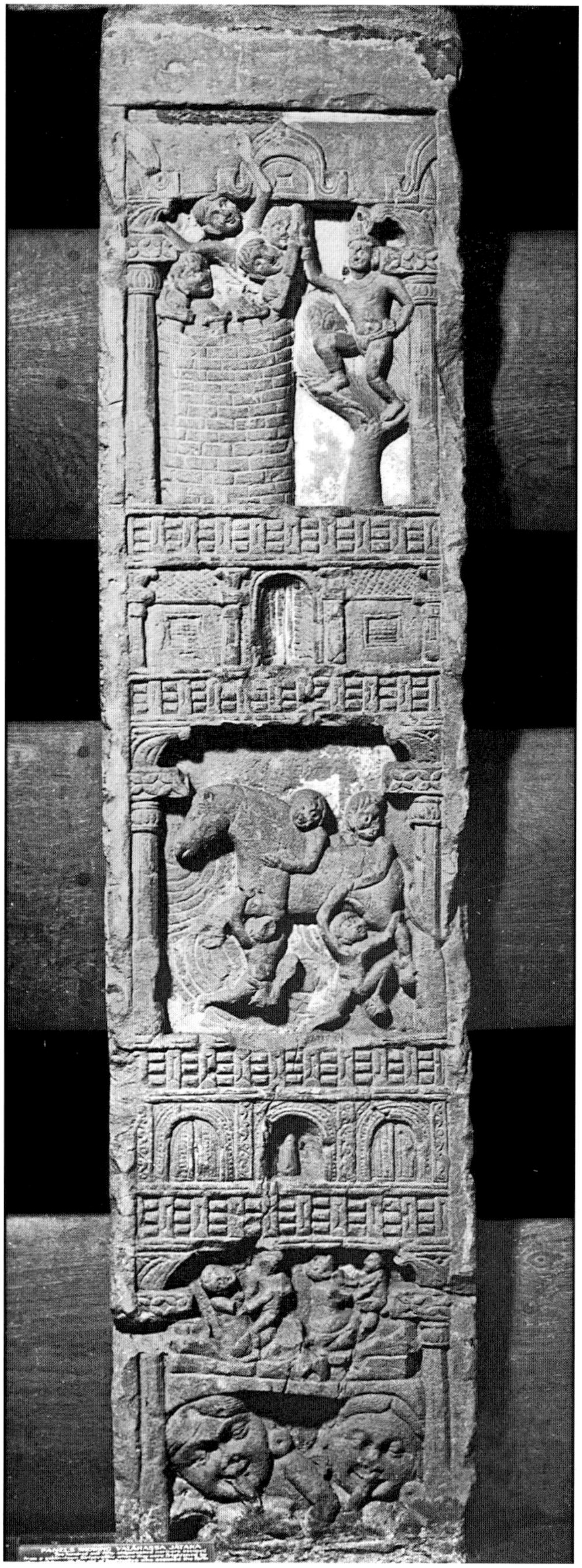

middle. Their visages are tilted towards the right and left edges of the panel, with their gaze directed towards the viewer. Their tongues are shown hanging out, which may be an indicator of lasciviousness/licentiousness or merely a device to frighten. Above this sub-panel, another composition with two half-reclining couples is set. On the left is a large female figure lying against a diagonally-placed headboard. She is shown to be pulling a smaller, punier male figure towards her half-reclining body. Her face is turned towards the man who seems to be seated on her lap. On the right hand side of this panel is another couple in which the male is shown seated on the knees of the larger kneeling female figure. The man is perhaps trying to apply force against the shoulder of the female with his hand as if to stave off her advances. Two pilasters topped by two curved half-arches enclose this whole panel. Above this is a *vedikā* topped by three windows of which two on each side are shut while the one in the middle seems to be open.

The middle panel (*Pl.* 7.30) shows four figures clinging to a high-stepping horse; in the foreground one man is clutching the foreleg of the horse while the other man holds the hind leg with one hand and with the other hand grasps the hand of the man on the other side the horse. Visible above the horse are the faces of two men also clinging to the other side of the horse. In the foreground and behind the horse and figures, one can see a number of lines that may denote water, probably the sea. Pilasters similar to the one seen in the lowest panel enclose this scene also, topped by a similar *vedikā* and *caitya*-window pattern in the middle. On both sides of this window is a windowpane-like aperture.

7.28 *Valāhassa Jātaka*, rail posts, red sandstone, second century CE, Bhūteśvara Mound, Mathurā. IM. 24845/M.15a,b.

The space in the uppermost panel is divided vertically into two sections. On the left is a turret-like structure (signifying a city or a mansion made of bricks or rectangular stones, often seen in Mathurā relief sculptures depicting cities). Four male figures can be seen emerging from this structure. Of the four, the faces of only three can be seen, while the torso of the fourth figure is visible. All the faces seem to wear smiles and the one is seen as waving his arms (in joy or thanksgiving). On the right is a tree; in the cleft of this tree is a male figure that seems to be half-crouching and half-standing in three-quarter profile. With one arm he is waving at the figures on the left while his right hand is resting on his waist. He wears a *dhotī*, a necklace and *karṇa-kuṇḍala*. A conical turban crowns his oval-shaped face. The finial of this panel is a *kapotāli* carved with two half *caitya* windows on the sides and a full *caitya* window in the middle.

This is a visual narration of the *Valāhassa Jātaka*. The Buddha recounted this story to a backsliding *bhikṣu* who had become distracted by a finely dressed woman. In order to illustrate how "women tempt men by their figure and voice, scent, perfumes and touch, and by their wiles and dalliance . . . get men in their power . . . ruin them, their character, and wealth," the Buddha compares all women as a category to the *yakṣīs* of the story.[107] The tale itself is set in Sri Lanka, where a *yakṣa* town called Sirisavatthu is inhabited by she-goblins, *yakṣīs*. The *yakṣīs* lure shipwrecked merchants to their city where they make some of these men their husbands and devour the rest. The *yakṣīs* create the illusion of a normal domestic scene with agrarian activities, grazing cattle and so forth, and use it along with their personal charm to tempt the merchants. Once they enraptured 500 such merchants and made them their husbands. The chief merchant, realising the man-eating propensity of the *yakṣīs*, entreats his fellow merchants to escape before it is too late. However, only 250 heed him. They are later rescued by a *bodhisattva* in the form of a flying horse which is white all over and is beaked like a crow, with hair like *muñja* grass, possessed of supernatural power and the ability to fly through the air. This *bodhisattva*-horse allows the merchants to climb on to his back and hold on to his tail as he flies them home. Those who stay behind are eaten by the *yakṣīs*.

An earlier rendition of the same *Jātaka* may also be found at Bharhut (*Pl.* 7.31), albeit in an abbreviated form, on the upper half-medallion of a railing pillar. The inscription says that this was the gift of (a scene of) a horse by *Sulabdha* of

7.29 Detail of *yakṣīs*, *Valāhassa Jātaka*. IM. M.15a,b.

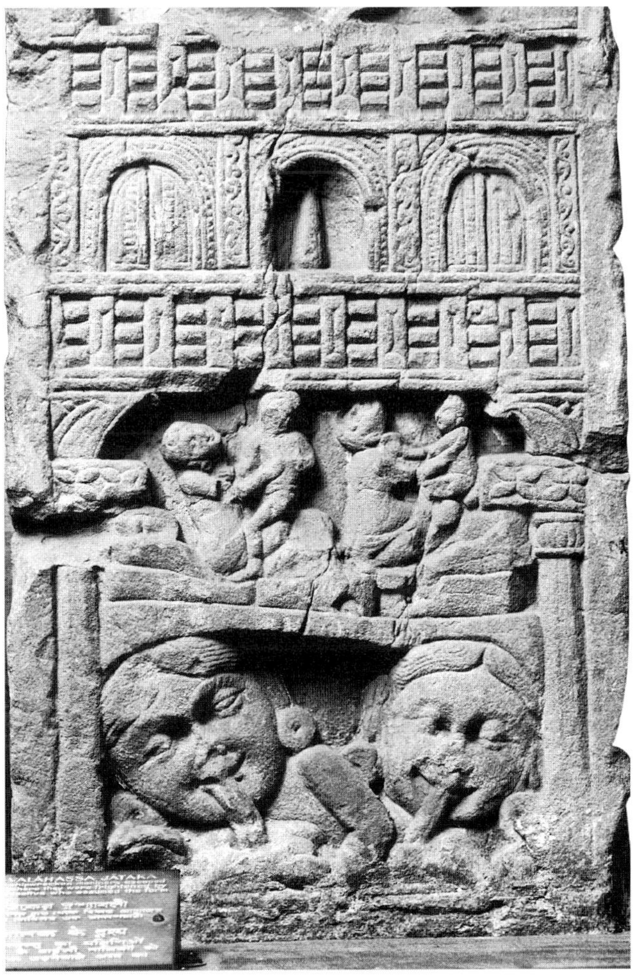

*Bimbikanadikata*. It depicts a horse, beautifully caparisoned and harnessed, in the centre. A man stands on one side of the horse holding on to its tail with one hand and with an arrow-shaped object pointed towards the sky on the other. This figure seems to be flying through air. On the left-hand side, a man is seen on the other side of the horse, holding its reins in his hands. This can be read either as the *Valāhassa* or *Mahājanaka Jātaka*.[108] The female *yakkhī*s are not represented in this version.

The Mathurā illustration of the *Valāhassa* tale conveys similar messages as *Pādukuśalamānava Jātaka* to the viewer. Both feature cannibalistic females with strong uncontrolled sexuality.[109] In both the Jātakas illustrated above, we have *yakṣī*s who give in to the evil nature of their selves, *strīsvabhāva*, using their beauty to lure men[110] who are rescued by a *bodhisattva*, who is not only male but also internalises within himself the qualities of self-control and asceticism. The *bodhisattva* rescues the pious believers from the clutches of such *yakṣī*s while the greedy non-believing merchants who refuse his help are eaten by the *yakṣī*s.

The ogresses shown to have strange round faces in the *Valāhassa* story at Mathurā, are comparable to an extent with Māra's army depicted at Sāñcī, and are in contrast to the beautifully rendered *śālabhañjikā-yakṣī* figures. They are also depicted as constraining men by pulling them into an embrace as in the Ṛṣyaśṛṅga representations from Mathurā. The physical control through use of force is also seen in the *Pādukuśalamānava Jātaka* episode with the ogress holding the male brāhmaṇa on her hip or pulling him towards her. In this case also she is neither rendered as beautiful nor is she adorned with gorgeous jewellery and garments, rather she is dressed in tree-bark, suggesting a lower cultural status. In size, the evil *yakṣī*s of both tales are shown as being bigger than the males, again suggesting an inversion of the natural, physical order and therefore of the right and accepted moral norms. Misogyny as well as fear of female sexuality are both implied here.

In the *Valāhassa* episode, the male merchants who as a group succumb to temptation and share in the pleasures offered are not censured (the censure and punishment are reserved for not accompanying the *bodhisattva*); the moral pressure of being good is on the *yakṣī*s who because of their inherent female nature, cannot maintain standards set for women.

If we were to reverse the situation and look at stories of seduction of the lonely wives of merchants by other men, the latter do not come in for censure or even notice, while the unfaithful wife is reviled. These men therefore are neither textualised nor visualised. On the contrary in the Jātaka text itself we do have some tales of cannibalistic male *yakṣa*s who are converted to the faith by *bodhisattva*s in many guises.[111]

A rather complex and interesting rendering of a tale can be seen carved on a panel of a railing pillar at Bharhut (*Pl.* 7.32) in which a tricky Vidyādhara outwits a *dānava-rākṣasa*.[112] The inscription accompanying it reads *vijapi vijādharo*, "the spell-muttering Vidyādhara." This square composition contains a couple, of whom the female is seated on a big rectangular box and holding a bunch of three ball-like flowers in her raised right hand. To her right stands a male figure in the process of either putting on or unwinding his turban as is evident from a length of rolled cloth held in his left hand that continues from the half-tied turban he holds with his right hand. His armour, bound up with his dagger

7.30 Detail of rescue by *boddhisattva*, *Valāhassa Jātaka*. IM. M.15a,b. (facing page)

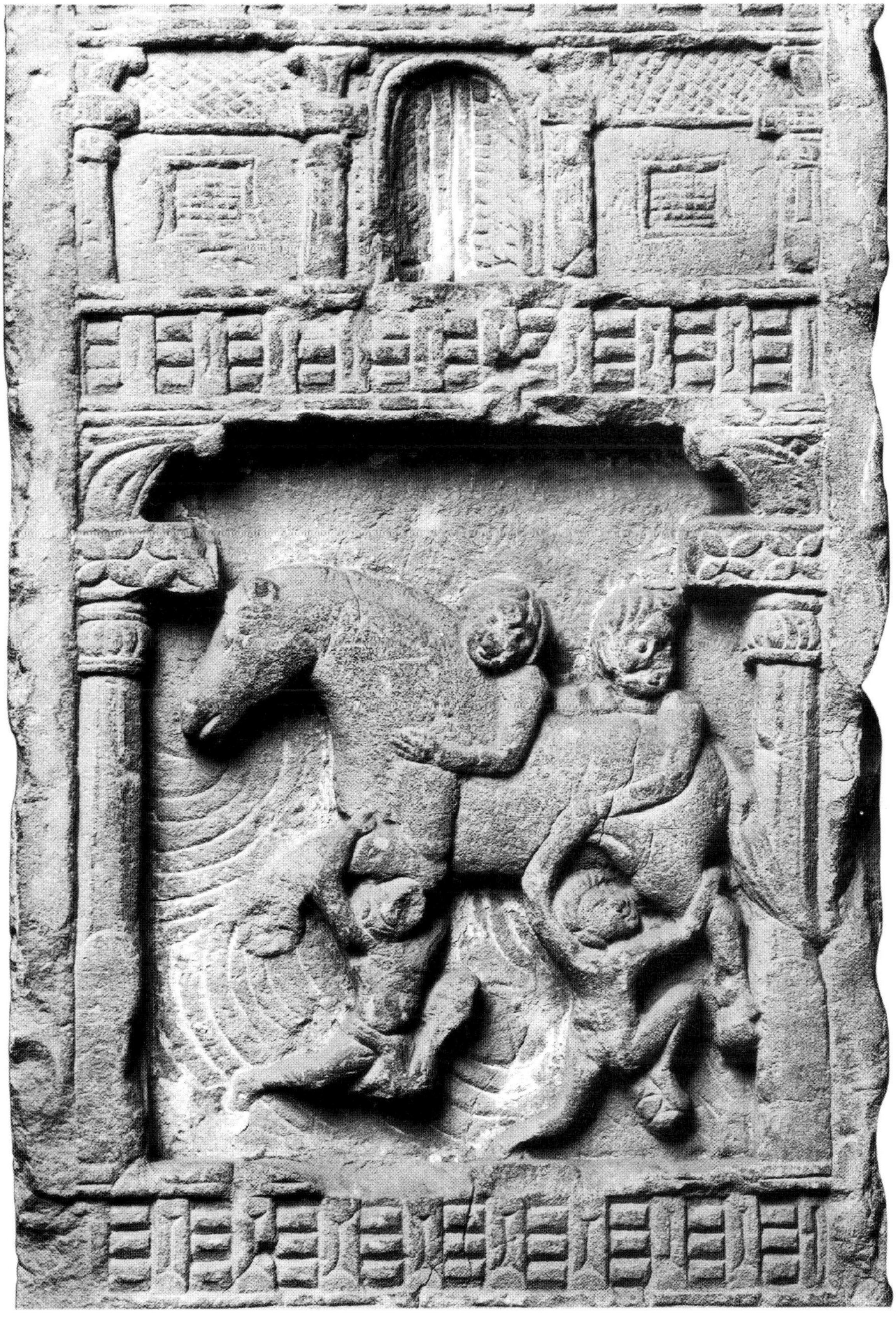

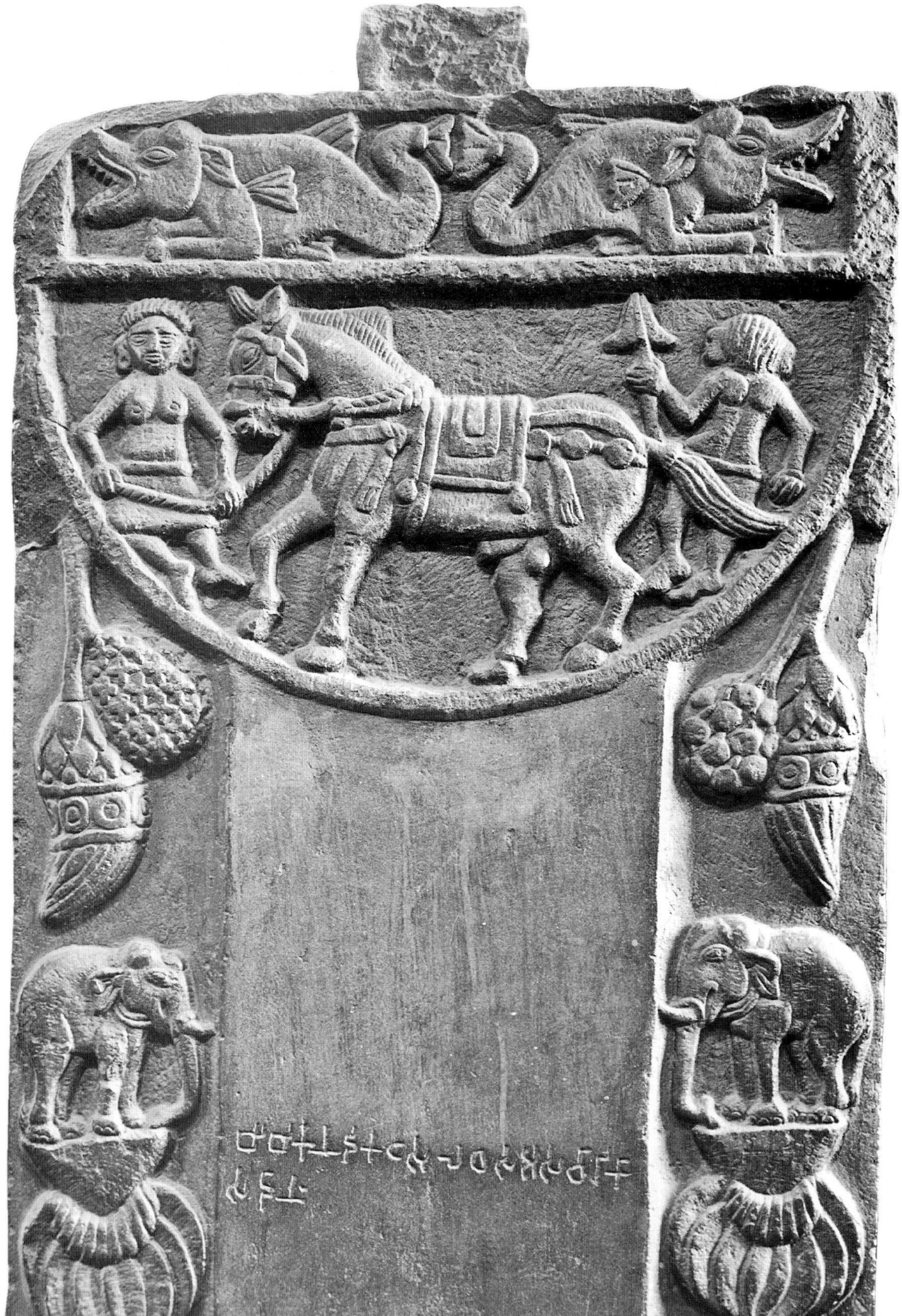

7.31 Woman leading a caparisoned horse, with a male in the rear, perhaps *Valāhassa Jātaka*, half medallion, railing pillar, first century BCE, Bharhut. IM 244. (facing page)

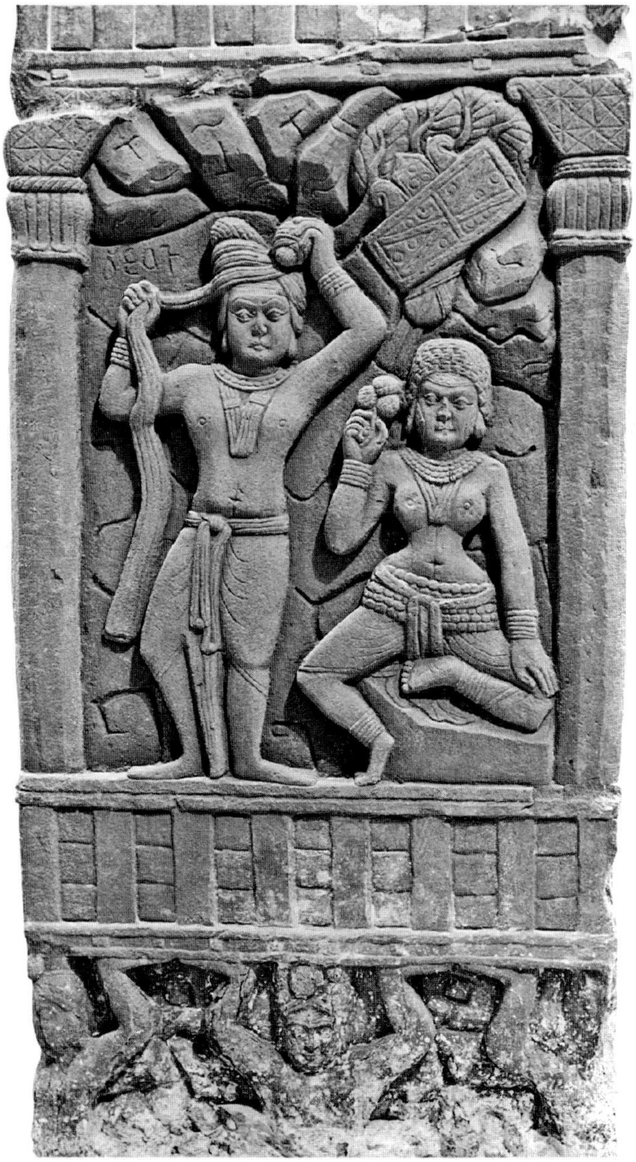

7.32 *Vijapi Vidyādhara Jātaka*, south gate, corner pillar, panel, first century BCE, Bharhut. IM 269.

resting in its sheath, is hanging from a tree carved in the left corner of the composition. According to Barua,[113] this is an illustration of the *Samugga Jātaka*.[114] The *Jātaka* tells the story of the kidnapping of a beautiful and noble woman by a cannibalistic *dānava rākṣasa* who forces her to become his wife. He carries her everywhere in a box, which he swallows so that it lies secure in his belly. One day, as he lays the box aside to take a bath, the woman is allowed to come out into the open. She looks up and sees Vāyu's son, perhaps Vidyādhara, walking in the sky, carrying a dagger. She makes a sign of affection towards him and invites him down. She then makes him lie down in the box and covers him with her body, and thus the demon carries both back towards his cave. Inside the box, the lady and the flying being develop a sexual relationship. On the way the demon meets a *bodhisattva*-ascetic who is his friend. This sentient being, perceiving Vāyu's son, warns him of the magical powers of this being. The *dānava-yakṣa*, who now becomes disgusted at the infidelity and ingrate behaviour of his wife, frees her from marital bonds.

Certain impressions regarding gender relations emerge from the textual version. First, the apparent use of feminine wiles by the woman to free herself from the demon; to survive she seeks the help of the Vidyādhara, attracting him with her beautiful body. Secondly, the woman is supposed to have disported herself with the Vidyādhara-magician, even as they were inside the box — such is the nature of women. Thirdly, the *yakṣa-dānava* comes in for no censure for either carrying her off or for cannibalism. At the end of the tale, it is he who is saved from the magical flying being and he is converted to the faith; the woman is set free, not because it was the right thing to do but because of her infidelity and ingrate behaviour. Visually, however, all that we

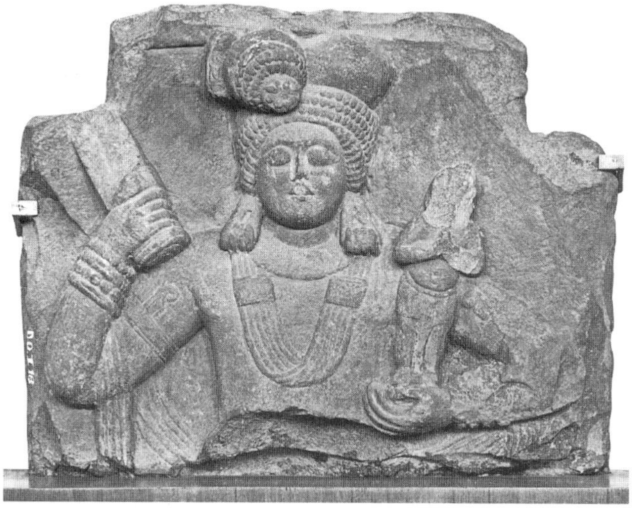

7.33 Threatening male figure, *yakṣa* bearing a club and small male figure, red sandstone, third century BCE, Mathurā district. UP. GMM No. I.18.

see is the Vidyādhara-magician and the woman in a particular setting. Is it possible that the folk tradition as redacted by the monk-editors of the Jātakas was more misogynist in content than the original? This certainly appears to be the case as the visual representation does lend itself to multiple interpretations.

It may be noted that in all the text-images described above, a *bodhisattva* as *yakṣa* can be a benign person, who also has magical and transforming abilities whereby he can transform himself into a horse. However, despite sharing such traits with her male counterpart, *yakṣī*s are never *bodhisattva*s.

Gail Sutherland points out that the evil *yakṣī*s in the textual tradition usually inhabit forests and wild places and thus are seen as undomesticated and unrestrained. Their solitary wanderings divorce them from a safe image of the bound and the maternal and immediately evoke for a chance male beholder the embodiment of sexual licence.[115] This is reflected in the artistic tradition of rendering these tales, where the environment inhabited by the ogresses is rocky and wild. In a manner of speaking, the ogress-*yakṣī* is the semi-divine counterpart of the human "non-wife" who is the "other" of the conventional wife who conforms to the dominant patriarchal discourse.

The representation of women as ogresses seeks to deny them their humanity, locating them nearer the realm of the beasts. They are the embodiment of evil masquerading in the female form, their duplicity is characteristic of dissembling feminine wiliness. Her largeness may be a signifier of her promiscuous sexuality, something which cannot be controlled or harnessed. The same largeness is seen in the *yakṣī* as well.

Obversely, there is a potentially subversive quality in this sort of "grotesque" body in which the *yakṣī*s and ogresses are represented. It may be noted how this transgressive aspect of largeness was largely transferred only to the female body of the *yakṣī* and is rarely attached to the *yakṣa* in either the textual or visual representations.

### Notes and References

1. J.W. Boyd, *Satan and Māra: Christian and Buddhist Symbols of Evil*, Leiden: E.J. Brill, 1975, p. 73.
2. *MWSE*, p. 811, comes from the root *mṛ*, killing, destroying, etc. *PSD* says Māra, p. 530, means killing, destroying, bringing death, pestilence, etc.
3. *MWSE*, p. 43.
4. J.W. Boyd, op. cit., pp. 74ff.
5. For a discussion on the connection between Māra, Kāmadeva and Buddha in Vedic and Buddhist religious texts, see Ananda K. Coomaraswamy, *Yakṣas*, 1993, pp. 25-34.
6. J.W. Boyd, op. cit., pp. 74-75.
7. A.K. Coomaraswamy, op. cit., p. 25.
8. *Buddhacarita*, Canto XIII.2: *yaṁ kāmadevaṁ pravadanti loke citrāyudhaṁ puṣpaśaraṁ tathāeva, kāmapracārādhipatiṁ tameva mokṣadviṣaṁ māramudālharanti.*

9. *Buddhacarita*, Canto XIII.16: "when Śambhu, god as he was, was pierced with this arrow, he became agitated with love towards the mountain king's daughter. That very arrow causes this man (Buddha) no feeling. Is it that he has no heart or that his is not that arrow."

10. J.W. Boyd, op. cit., p. 75.

11. P.K. Agrawala, "The Depiction of Māra in early Buddhist Art", in K. R. Kooij and H. van der Veer ed., *Function and Meaning in Buddhist Art*, Groningen: Egbert Forsten, 1995, p. 125.

12. *Buddhacarita*, XIII.3.

13. *Saṁyutta Nikāya*, I, 124.

14. *BA*, XV, 128; *BAC*, XV, 160.

15 *Saṁyutta Nikāya* I, 104, 128, 129, 130, 160-4; *bhayam chamabitattam lomahamsam*.

16. *Buddhacarita*, XIII.19-24 for description of Māra's army.

17. Ibid., XIII.25-29.

18. Geri Hockfield Malandra, "Māra's Army: Text and Image in Early Indian Art" in *East And West*, New Series, 31, 1981, pp. 121-30, has attempted to link some texts with specific representations.

19. *The Book of Kindred Sayings: Saṁyutta Nikāya*, Rhys Davids, PTS, pp. 128-59; *The Saṁyutta Nikāya of Sutta Piṭaka*, ed. Leon Feer, 124-27. The *sutta* is part of its Book IV entitled Māra Saṁyutta; Cited in Vidya Dehejia, *Discourse in Early Buddhist Art*, New Delhi: Munshiram Manoharlal, 1997, p. 56.

20. Soon after the composition of the early canon, the Padhana Sutta of *Sutta Nipāta* speaks of Māra visiting Gotama on the bank of the river Nirañjana and of Māra's tenfold army which was classified by Buddha as Lust, Aversion, Hunger, Thirst, Craving, Sloth, Cowardice, Doubt, Hypocrisy, False Glory and Lauding oneself while condemning others: *The Sutta Nipāta*, ed. Dines Andersen and Helmer Smith, 425-29; 74-78. Cited in Vidya Dehejia, op. cit., pp. 56 and 302ff.

21. Edward Conze, *The Life of Buddha: As Legend and History*, New Delhi: Motilal Banarsidass, 1993, pp. 73-79, 85.

22. *Nidāna Kathā*, tr. T.W. Rhys Davids, 190-98: Cited in Vidya Dehejia, op. cit., p. 56.

23. *The Lalitavistara Sūtra: The Voice of Buddha*, vol. 2, ch. 21-22, 246-535. *The Beauty of Compassion*, Gwendlyn Bays. Trans. from French. Cited in Vidya Dehejia, op. cit., p. 57.

24. J. Marshall and A. Foucher, *The Monuments of Sanci*, pt. II, Pl. 29.2.

25. A Nāgaraja is seated in a similar posture in a lintel from Soṅkh, kept in Government Museum, Mathura.

26. J. Marshall and A. Foucher, op. cit., Pls. 61.3 and 62.3; Ludwig Bachofer, *Early Indian Sculpture*, New Delhi: Munshiram Manoharlal, 1973, Pl. 49, xxxiii.

27. Ibid.

28. P.K. Agrawala, "Early Images of God Kāma", in *JISOA*, New Series, vol. XVI-XVII, Calcutta, pp. 5-14.

29. P.K. Agrawala, op. cit., p. 125.

30. A. Ghosh and H. Sarkar, "Beginnings of Sculptural Art in South-East India: A Stele from Amaravati", *Ancient India*, nos. 20-21, 1967, pp. 170-71.

31. J. Burgess, *The Buddhist Stupa of Amaravati and Jaggayapeta*, Tribner and Co., 1887, Pl. XXI,2.

32. A.K. Coomaraswamy, "Buddhist Reliefs from Nāgārjunakoṇḍa and Amarāvatī", *Rupam* 38-39, April-July 1929, pp. 72-73.

33. C. Sivaramamurti, "Amarāvatī Sculptures in the Madras Government Museum", *Bulletin of the Madras Government Museum*, New Series-General Section, IV, Madras: Government Press, 1942, pp. 179-81.

34. Robert Knox, *Amaravati: Buddhist Sculpture from the Great Stupa*, London: British Museum Press, 1992, Pl. 37, p. 96.

35. Ibid., pp. 53-54, fig. 8; Bachofer, op. cit., Pl. 128, p. xl, two inner jambs of the inner railing, ht. 1.10m, Madras Museum.

36. Robert Knox, op. cit., pp. 131 and 149, figs. 69 and 77.

37. Ibid., p. 158, fig. 83.

38. Elisabeth Rosen Stone, *The Buddhist Art of Nāgārjunakoṇḍa*, New Delhi: Motilal Banarsidass,

1994, p. 71, fig. 193.

39. Vidya Dehejia, op. cit., p. 176. fig 153, now in Nagarjunakonda Museum; also Elisabeth Rosen Stone, op. cit., p. 73, fig. 211.

40. *Gāndhāran Sculpture in the Government Museum and Art Gallery, Chandigarh*, ed. D.C. Bhattacharya, Chandigarh: Government Museum and Art Gallery, 2002, fig. 37, p. 87. (henceforth *Gāndhāran Sculpture*).

41. R. Parimoo, *Life of Buddha in Indian Art (Aṣṭa-Mahā-Pratihāra): An Iconological Analysis*, New Delhi: Kanak Publications, 1982, p. 19, fig. 22.

42. *Gāndhāran Sculpture*, Chandigarh, fig 96, p. 146; also figs. 144, 558.

43. Ibid., p. 19, fig. 22; also see M. Hallade, *Gandharan Art of North India and the Graeco-Buddhist Tradition in India, Persia, and Central Asia*, New York: H.N Abrams, 1968, Pl.72.

44. *Gāndhāran Sculpture*, Chandigarh, fig. 416, p. 118.

45. Ibid., fig. 286, p. 108.

46. Ibid., fig. 96, p. 92.

47. GMM No. H.6, 00.H1, 00.N2, 44.3119.

48. GMM no. 6117; P.K. Agrawala, op. cit., p. 129, fig. 10.

49. R.C. Sharma, *Buddhist Art of Mathurā*, New Delhi: Agam Kala Prakashan, 1984, fig. 174.

50. Edward Conze, op. cit., p. 75.

51. Buddha's Life Scenes, Jamalpur Mound, Mathurā, spotted red sand stone, 1.26 × .57m, SML No. B. 208, Lucknow.

52. P.K. Agrawala, op. cit., pp. 129-30, fig. 9, State Museum Lucknow No. 46.13, Cf. R.C. Sharma, op. cit., p. 246, R. Parimoo, op. cit., p. 21, figs. 25, 25A.

53. P.K. Agrawala, op. cit., p. 131.

54. P.K. Agrawala, "Early images of God Kāma", in *JISOA*, New Series, vol. XVI-XVII, Calcutta, pp. 5-14; A male figure with *makara-dhvaja* is seen in AM No. 2434.

55. T.O. Ling, *Buddhism and Mythology of Evil*, London, 1962, p. 127, Cf. Parimoo, pp. 99f; P.K. Agrawala, "The Depiction of Māra in early Indian Art", p. 131.

56. P.K. Agarwala, "Early Images of God Kāma," pp. 5-14.

57. *Buddhacarita*, XIII.3.

58. *Dhammapada*, vv. 103-105, says that "One's own self conquered is better than all other people; not even a *deva*, a *gandharva*, not Māra with *Brahman* could change into defeat the victory of a man who has conquered himself and always remains under restraint."

59. This may be compared to breast-offering figures, perhaps, in the sense that they also do not deliberately seek to represent seductiveness. But the Indian (male) tradition of depicting women has always included the representation of them "caught unawares" in an innocent posture that a man nevertheless finds seductive. This is an ancient convention. To what extent this convention represents a deliberate male devaluation of women is highly debatable [especially as women do play the "innocent seduction" game in reality, and no one suggests that they thereby devalue men]. The Sanskritic tradition delights in puns and double meanings, and such female figures are certainly an example of this, transferred from the literary sphere to the visual arts. The sexual nature of this particular double meaning can be debated in gender terms, but not the importance of the double meaning in itself, which is an embedded part of the Sanskrit intellectual heritage, accurately reflecting the complexity of perceived reality and having, no gender content whatever.

60. J.W. Boyd, op. cit. pp. 81-4; *MN*, I, 118; *DN*, II, 262.

61. *Therīgāthā*, PTS (1964), App. 1, p. 180.

62. I.B. Horner, *Women Under Primitive Buddhism*, New Delhi: Motilal Banarsidass, 1999, p. 307; Also *Saṁyutta Nikāya*, PTS, pp. 160-61.

63. *Therīgāthā*, xxxvi, PTS (1964); Another version of this episode is found in the *Saṁyutta Nikāya*, V.2. This is a very important hymn in which a nun asserts her ability to reach *nirvāṇa*, irrespective of her gender. Soma challenges the notion that there is something inherent in a woman's nature that would preclude her from achieving religious beatitude. Supra, Chapter One, Section on *Strīsvabhāva*.

64. Stella Kramrisch, *The Hindu Temple*, pt. II, pp. 140ff. She adds that the term *apsarās* signifies "moving in water," i.e. in celestial vapour. They are also known as *Surāṅganā*s or *Surasundarī*s.

65. *Saundarānanda*, X.36. in the same text, X.33, reiterates that *apsaras*es are the reward that ascetics gain for austerities practised.

66. Stella Kramrisch, op. cit., p. 340. She adds that as active power and causal stress, her image is embodiment of movement: as *apsaras*, she is movement in the atmosphere, as *yakṣiṇī*, she is movement in the vegetation, as *naṭikā* she is movement in the body of man.

67. Stella Kramrisch, "Indian Terracotta", *JISOA*, 1939, pp. 99-100; However, not all scholars agree with this identification, for example Joachim K. Bautze in *Early Indian Terracottas*, E.J. Brill, Leiden, 1995 p. 14 would simply like to call such a figure a goddess rather than ascribe any specific celestial identity.

68. *Mbh.*, 13.3.11, =191: 38, 2, =2203, Cf. Stella Kramrisch, op. cit., p. 99.

69. *Kālivilāsa Tantra*, ch. 33, sl. 13, Cf. Stella Kramrisch, op. cit., pp. 99-100.

70. Barua, *Bharhut*, pt. III, Patna: Indological Book Corporation, 1979 (reprint), Pl. XLII, scene 39.

71. Ibid., pt II, pp. 9-11, scene 34. Southern Gate, Prasenjit Pillar, Lower Bas Relief, Outer Face. Also see A.K. Coomaraswamy, *La Sculpture de Bharhut*, Vanoest, Editions d'art et d'histoire, Paris, 1956, planche VIII, fig. 23.

72. Barua and Sinha, nos. 146-150. The complete inscription along with the labels reads: *sadikā sammadam turam devanām alambusā accharā, misakesi acchara, padmuvati accharā, subhadā accharā*.

73. *Nāṭyaśāstra*, I.47-50. The text says that Brahmā created the *apsaras*es from his mind in order to skilfully embellish the performance of a divine drama that entailed the projection of *śṛṅgāra rasa bhāva*. *Śṛṅgāra* cannot be performed by men alone and so *apsaras*es were introduced. *NŚ*, I.43-47.

74. The tale must have had a considerable didactic value for the Buddhist ideologues, given that it continued to be carved on *stūpa* railings and facades from Śuṅga period onwards.

75. GMM. No. 151.

76. Govindgaṛh, Railpost showing the cult of *uṣṇīṣa* and episode of Ṛṣyaśṛṅga, first century BCE, spotted red sandstone, Mathurā, GMM, no, 76.40; *Cf.* R.C. Sharma, *Buddhist Art [:] Mathura School*, Wiley Eastern Ltd. Delhi, 1995.

77. V. Smith, *Jain Stupa and Other Antiquities*, Allahabad: Govt. Press, 190, p. 29, Pl. XXVIII.

78. *nama aham tanam srāmana sravikaye lahastinīye toraṇam prati(sthāpi) sha māta pithi, saha sasru sasurena*. V. Smith, op. cit., p. 29, pl. XXVIII. He does not identify the scene as illustrating the Ṛṣyaśṛṅga legend; he does describe it as representing what he calls an "indelicate attitude." Presumably, he meant the blatantly sexual position being assumed by the female in forcibly holding the male atop her. The author's Victorian bias against exhibition of sexuality in general and female sexuality in particular is obvious in this statement.

79. A large portrayal of the sage Ṛṣyaśṛṅga has been found from Bhūteśvara *stūpa* in Mathurā, GMM J.7, Ht: 2'7½".

80. Cowell, *Jātaka*, no. 523.

81. Ibid., no. 526.

82. Barua, *Bharhut*, pt. II, scene 131, pp. 145-46; A.K. Coomaraswamy, op. cit., planche XXXI, fig. 85. The inscription reads, *Iśiśimgiya Jātakam*, *Ṛṣyaśṛṅga Jātaka*. In the upper half of the medallion we see an aged hermit with *jaṭā*s piled on his head and wearing two short garments of leaves, seated on his legs in the right while his hut can be seen on the left. A sacred fire is burning between the hut and the hermit. Above this one can see an earthen pot covered with an earthen lid. Above these are two earthen pots hanging from a horizontally fixed bamboo or wooden bar. The second part of this story is seen in the middle where the same ascetic is stooping as if to pick up or help a child lying on the ground with his feet touching the back of a doe — representing the birth of the child Ṛṣyaśṛṅga. The lower half of the panel shows the doe drinking water in the centre and the *ṛṣi* seated on the haunches in the right hand corner — obviously the moment of conception.

83. Cowell, *Jātaka*, 523, vol. V, p. 81.

84. The description matches one of the ball-playing *yakṣīs* carved on the railing pillar of the Bhūteśvara *yakṣī*, also seen at Saṅghol. It may be possible that depictions such as these on Buddhist monuments became symbols of seductive behaviour.

85. Cowell, *Jātaka*, vol. V, p. 106.

86 *Rāmāyaṇa*, I.65.16, cited in S. Bhattacharji, *The Indian Theogony: A Comparative Study of Indian Mythology From The Vedas to The Puranas*, Cambridge: Cambridge University Press, 1970, p. 273.

87. *Saundarānanda*, VII.34.

88. In the Banjārā region of Western Himalayas, Ṛṣyaśṛṅga is worshipped in many shrines as Śṛṅga Ṛṣi, and the whole valley is believed to be part of his or his father's hermitage.

89. The opposite view of a man forcing a woman by pulling her towards him is found at Bharhut and also at Bodh-Gayā.

90. Cowell, *Jātaka*, V, p. 83.

91. Gail Sutherland, *Yaksas: Disguises of the Demon*, New York: SUNY, 1991, p. 138.

92. Ibid.

93. Cowell, *Jātakas*, no. 96 (the *Telapatta Jātaka*); no. 513 (*Jayadissa Jātaka*); No. 432 *Padukuśala mānava Jātaka*, No. 196 *valāhassa Jātaka*.

94. Vidya Dehejia, op. cit., p. 77, fig. 48 identifies this as monoscenic portrayal.

95 J. Marshall, *Monuments of Sanchi*, vol. III, Pl. 90.86(b).

96. Gail Sutherland, op. cit., p. 143.

97. R.L. Mitra, *Buddha Gaya*, pl. XXXIV.

98. Vidya Dehejia, op. cit., p. 77, fig. 48 identifies this as monoscenic portrayal.

99. GMM 12.191.

100. GMM 191, fragment, Ht. 2', the central medallion of a railing pillar datable to the first century BCE; SML No. B. 208.

101. Pāṭaliputra, Indian Museum. Also A.K. Coomaraswamy, *Yakṣas*, pt. I Pl. XII, fig. 1.

102. A.K. Coomaraswamy, *History of Indian and Indonesian Art*, New York: Dover Publications Inc., rpt., 1965, Pl. 27.

103. Cowell, *Jātaka*, No. 432.

104. In the *Viṣṇudharmottara Purāṇa*, III.42.13-14 the horse-headed female is called a Kinnarā, "the Kinnaras are said to be of two types; one having human face with horse's body and the other, human body with horse's face."

105. Gail Sutherland, op. cit., p. 140.

106. Railing Pillar, Bhūteśvara, Mathurā, U.P. second century CE, red sandstone. Size: 126 ×29.5 cms., Indian Museum, Calcutta No. M.15b. The reverse shows a *yakṣī* standing on a dwarf *yakṣa*, holding her thick necklace on the shoulders with one hand, while the other hands holds the looped end of the cloth tied around her waist.

107. Cowell, *Jātaka*, no. 196.

108. Cowell, *Jātaka*, no. 539 : the Jātaka also features a flying horse.

109. Gail Sutherland, op. cit., p. 138. notes that in Buddhist Jātaka tales the devouring tendencies of the *yakkhinī* are, unlike the *yakkha*'s, strongly sexual as well as alimentary.

110. Ibid., p. 139 has noted the connection between the beauty of women in general to the demonic in Buddhist literature and imagery. Asceticism is male and must defend itself rigorously against the seductive demands of, and attachment to, the world of the senses, which is conceived of as female.

111. Cowell, *Jātaka*, no. 398: *Sutano Jātaka*.

112 Bharhut, Southern Gate, Prasenjit Pillar, Lower Bas-relief, side. Barua, *Bharhut*, II, pp. 132-33, Pl. XXII.17c.

113. Ibid.

114. Cowell, *Jātaka*, No. 436.

115. Gail Sutherland, op. cit., p. 138.

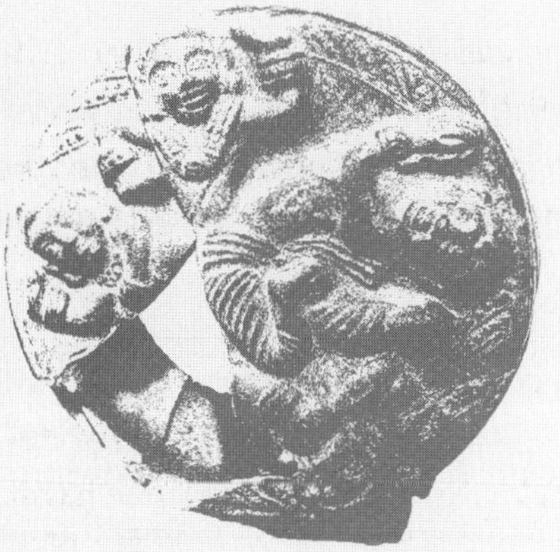

# Conclusion

The early Indian period that has been elucidated in this work is that of development of engendered representation in art, with the creation of both aesthetic and sexual archetypes and stereotypes. The engendering process is not a linear, monolithic development. Certain representations, both cultic and artistic, are representative only in this period and offer insights into the creation of gender roles both in art and society. The degree of patriarchal dominance is neither uniform over time, nor evenly spread over all religious ideologies. A multiplicity of voices has been discovered within rampant misogynisms that fracture, challenge or even invert this discourse.

In social terms the dominant misogynism is encompassed in the *strīsvabhāva-strīdharma* dichotomy. In visual terms, in the narrative friezes, this is translated into stereotypes of sexually voracious and dangerous temptresses having the form of ogresses, *apsaras*es or bad wives who lead the good-ascetic-male astray.

Stereotypes and archetypes were constructed on the basis of gender roles, rather than on sex. The feminine is essentialised as beautiful and graceful but also as physically uncontrolled or uncontrollable, while the masculine is seen as mentally restrained, competent and physically brave, and this perception is mirrored in artistic production. While there is an effort at creating aesthetically pleasing male and female forms, masculinity is projected through strong, solid, straight-standing and frontally-gazing figures taking the forms of semi-divine beings such as *yakṣa*s or human men like Nanda. In contrast, except for the divine feminine, femininity is imaged in voluptuous figures displayed in attractively flexed postures and gazing at their own bodies, both in positive figures such as *yakṣī-śālabhañjikā*s or negative ones like Māra's daughters.

Generic stereotypes of the female body and form are established in the earlier terracotta tradition, datable to the Mauryan and early Śuṅga period, through the so-called *pañcacūḍa apsaras*es or the mother goddesses. Elements of the imagery of these figures are taken over by the *yakṣī-śālabhañjika* figures at Bharhut and Kauśāmbī. There is a gradual sexualisation of imagery, especially in the case of the *śālabhañjikā*s. The earlier depictions on *stūpa* railings eschew overt sensualisation. Later images, both narrative and apotropaic, are more sensualised, and their reproductive sexuality is increasingly obvious.

The female body is essential in engendering the art of early India, especially given that the female and feminine were defined by their physical attributes. The majority of female figures in the art of the post-Mauryan period display prominently marked genitalia (explicitly or through transparent drapery) and prominent, round, full breasts, especially in the Kuṣāṇa artistic tradition. Ideologically women as sexual-reproductive beings are defined by their reproductive body. This is effectively elucidated through aesthetic representations.

The Lajjā-Gaurī and the breast-offering figures privilege primary and secondary female sexual organs, thus essentialising the female form and functions. Both these figural types emphasise biological reproductive potential, on the one hand, and female sexuality with its inherent erotic possibilities on the other. The depiction of the *yoni*, with or without anatomical appendages such as breasts and limbs, can be located within the discourse of reproduction considered as an exclusively feminine domain.

The worship and stark depiction of female sexual organs does not necessarily valorise the woman, nor indicate a symbolic valorisation of women. Her right of reproduction and her reproductive potential becomes her principal identity to the extent that the goddess is "reduced" to a vulva and related symbols such as the *pūrṇa-kumbha* pot-like womb, water being a universal indicator of life-giving force. The rounded, bloated form may also suggest actual pregnancy.

Representations of the breast, especially of a woman offering her own breast to the viewer/devotee, become important in the feminist discourse since bio-deterministic theories privileging the notion of woman-as-nurturer are based on the biological fact that only a woman-mother can breastfeed an infant baby. In the popular conception, the breast is considered an object of both desire and nurturing. Visually, a woman offering her breast emphasises women as source of universal giving and prosperity, embodying notions of physical fertility and universal prosperity. A visual analysis aimed at reaching a gender perspective lays emphasis on the fact that breasts are objects of the male gaze, a gaze that sexually commodifies the female body for male voyeuristic gratification.

Thus, dominant patriarchal art produces and consumes images of women in provocative postures and apparel. The changing imagery of the breast-touching female also suggests that female figures were increasingly sexualised with the crystallisation of urban patriarchal society, and separated from their original divine status that was based on an approximation to Śrī-Lakṣmī and Aditi.

A majority of images of the period are those of mother/mothering models or others related to the discourse of reproductive sexuality. The conception of woman as mother is central to the institutionalisation of patriarchy. That women's potential for motherhood is central to creating a gendered female identity is reflected in the fact that almost all divine feminine figures in the post-Mauryan period are hailed as mothers. What we see in the early period of the era is the manner in which the reproductive (a biological function) and nurturing (a gendered function) roles of women are emphasised. The anxiety over maternity in post-Mauryan society exhibits itself in the production of myriad mother-goddess figures concerned with fertility, pregnancy, childbirth and child protection. The anxiety, however, does not seem excessive when one considers the transitional and turbulent milieu, marked by invasions, expanding economy, and changing socio-religious structures, within which these images were produced and consumed.

Interesting sociological underpinnings related to the iconography of depictions of the Buddha's birth are revealed by an analysis of both the conception and delivery. In the former, the "taint" of sexuality is removed by symbolically representing an "immaculate conception" (through the white elephant seen in Māyā's dream) without compromising on the celibate and ascetic goals of the Buddhist faith. The delivery of the Buddha from the side of his mother, Māyādevī, who is shown to be standing — not in a normal birth-giving position — distances his birth from the normal woes related to womanhood such as the pain at childbirth.

The solidity and massive immobility associated with the mother figures strengthens their perceived engendered roles. This impression is partly projected by the sitting and standing posture with the gaze focused outward, and partly by the hand raised in *abhaya* or protection. Unlike the *yakṣī-śālabhañjikā* images, the divine mothers are always depicted clothed with a *dhotī* and/or a blouse, perhaps to indicate their supra-mundane status, and also as a mark of respect and reverence. There are 'human' women also who are shown clothed, in contrast to semi-divine *yakṣīs* who are found in the same architectural contexts. Cultic female figures are nude. Thus, it is difficult to posit any direct relationship between divinity and clothing.

Despite these common characteristics, the mothering figures in post-Mauryan art are visualised in a variety of ways. Dangerous, mysterious and powerful feminine forces associated with reproductive sexuality are demonised and divinised. Ṣaṣṭhī is seen as the deity of childbirth and also as a dangerous deity, part of the mytho-religious complex of *bālagraha*-Mātṛkās who combine maternal elements with the ability to destroy or be dangerous towards children. The latter role is epitomised by the anti-mother figure of Jātahāriṇī who holds children by their throat and arms in a threatening grasp. Hāritī, a cannibalistic ogress, is domesticated and controlled through conversion by the Buddha into a protector of children. Her depiction in art as a protective goddess is represented with generally more than one child clambering over her person. Her mate Pañcika, on the other hand, sits by her side with no children to intervene between the gaze of the spectator on his person. Perhaps an ideal social familial model is projected and reinforced by such compositions. It might also be one of the ways in which the sex role of woman as child producer was being socialised into the gender role of woman as child rearer and protector. When Hāritī is depicted in conjunction with Kubera-Pañcikā, the two deities symbolise different but complementary elements, the male being located within the discourse of material prosperity and the female within the discourse of maternality.

Hariṇaigameṣin as a *bālagraha* and as a god ensuring safe childbirth is a rare example of a male deity who is associated with the function of childcare and protection. I think that the presence of a male in a mothering role indicates a certain resistance to patriarchy-imposed gender roles that ascribe maternality only to women. Other male deities seen in representations of mother goddess figures are not the principal divine entities in the composition. Most of the goddesses, with the exception of Hāritī, are not spousified in this period; this occurs in the subsequent Gupta Era, when these divine feminine figures either disappear or transform into spouses or attendant deities in the process of absorption into patriarchal pantheons of Śiva and Viṣṇu.

The relative silence of the mainstream patriarchal religious discourse with regard to the identity and characteristics of certain female deities such as Lajjā-Gaurī, Ṣaṣṭhī, and goat-headed goddess is also significant. It reveals an attempt to make invisible and marginalise powerful and revered feminine images which were not, or could not be, assimilated into major pantheons as wives and consorts. The ignoring of the presence of such goddesses does not stop the production of mother-goddess figures. In an economy based on expanding agriculture, women play an important role both because their work is valuable in the fields and also because they have a control over nature's ritual and reproductivity. It is not surprising that they are ritually enshrined and celebrated in all religious systems in early India. The explanation for such a phenomenon may lie in various local cultic beliefs based on the relationship of women with life-giving sexuality, and on feminine socio-ritual practices related to pregnancy and childbirth.

There also exist alternative models of adoptive motherhood, for example, or social mothering, that are associated in myths and in art with divine motherhood, as is the case with the Mātṛkās, Naigameṣa/Naigameṣī and Buddhist and later Jaina traditions. Representations of Ṣaṣṭhī in association with Skanda and Viśākha, and of Ekānaṁśā with Balarāma and Vāsudeva, reveal alternative familial models to the husband-wife dyad.

In the visual discourse the wife is socialised into a pair, as part of a *mithuna* or *yugalika*. Though mothering figures dominate in art, in texts wifehood is valorised. The male-female couple as the *mithuna-dampati* representation has an almost ubiquitous presence in post-Mauryan art. The *mithuna* as a symbol of *maṅgala* is essential to the continuation of the created world, including monuments and other buildings. In an architectural context the motif thus acquires apotropaic functions. *Mithuna* is not however a passive category and is envisaged and depicted in various ways, probably carrying different symbolic values. The activities range from active sexual intercourse (*maithuna*) to hieratically delineated couples, standing straight or with the male paying obeisance to the goddess.

In narrative art within the Buddhist discourse specific cases are illustrated, such as Sundarī and Nanda, where we see royal, domestic and amorous scenes on the one hand and the renunciation of this pleasurable life on the other. In the textual discourse corresponding to these, the female form and nature are reviled, while renunciation and asceticism along with their rewards (in the form of *apsaras*es in heaven), are valorised. In other narrative episodes illustrating the Jātakas, the examples taken up for visualisation on the railings adhere to the misogynist *strīsvabhāva* and *strīdharma* discourse where the former is reviled through bad wives who follow their inherent evil, sexually uncontrolled nature, while good and dutiful wives who follow their *pativratā dharma* are praised. In visual representations, however, one has to make allowances for the precise moment chosen for depiction.

Alternatives to motherhood and wifehood are envisaged in the form of nuns and prostitutes who together constitute the non-wives. These are women who are outside the patriarchal family and yet still part of patriarchal society with its norms regarding sexuality and moral conduct. The relative misogynist disapproval of renunciation as an alternative life-choice for women, as voiced in the Buddhist patriarchal texts, is echoed in the omission of the nun from the depictions. The absence itself is a significant indicator of art being used to devalorise certain categories of women. In illustrating the story of Vasantasenā, the figure of the prostitute is set up as a warning for men not to give in to temptation and for women not to fall into the category of non-wives. The transient nature of physical beauty and youth may also be indicated here for the audience. The story itself, of a prostitute seeking refuge in the *saṁgha* and being saved, is also significant in projecting the strength of the Buddhist faith.

The third category of representation, which is quantitatively overwhelming, especially in the Kuṣāṇa period, is that of the *yakṣī-śālabhañjikā*s. These figures start in the early period as representations of divine creatures symbolising fertility, and are later co-opted into the *alaṁkāra* scheme as architectural motifs. The viewer thus did not view these as principal objects of worship, but only as subsidiary ornaments that added value to the principal object of adoration, the *stūpa* itself. Undoubtedly, these beautiful and bountiful maidens added to the attractiveness of the edifice, for the visual gratification of the pilgrims of both genders from all over the country and almost all classes. They also illustrate the theme of the progressive sensualisation especially of female imagery which is noticeable up to the Kuṣāṇa period.

Evil and its male and female agencies are visualised in the narrative art of the period. The *yakṣī* as ogress, such as the *assamukhī* (horse-headed) *yakṣī* is one such image who is projected as inhabiting the wild spaces and belonging to a tribal ethos and thus does not follow the socio-sexual norms prescribed by organised religion.

Here her cannibalistic proclivities and sexual insatiability are emphasised as her essential *strīsvabhāva* and posed as a warning to the viewer. The strategies that are employed by women to lure men are also revealing in terms of perceived gendered behaviour on part of evil. Women use their beauty and bodies but this sexual allurement is transient; their real form and nature underneath is grotesque and ugly, as declared in the *Valāhassa Jātaka* and similar stories.

The process of engendering is reflected by various attributes of the representations: nudity or its absence, ornamentation, gesture, direction of gaze, or context. For example, it may be concluded that nudity, especially with regard to female figures, is not universal in post-Mauryan art, and its depiction is predicated on the sex/gender representation sought to be projected through the art. Nudity is used to construct various female bodies: of *yakṣī-*

*śālabhañjikās*, mothers, prostitutes and wives; and the degree to which nudity is significant in constituting each category has been established. Such nakedness does not find much commentary in the textual tradition. Similarly it has been suggested that certain embellishments of the body through ornamentation carry embedded and differential meanings. The *mekhalā* has been shown tied around the waist of the *yakṣī-śālabhañjikās*, *gaṇikā* and females in the *mithuna* compositions from the earliest time till the Kuṣāṇa period. It may have been a symbol of long life, fertility and auspiciousness.

There is an essentially contradictory attitude in heterodox religions towards women; this is seen in the conflict between the ascetic ideal and the sensuous beauty.

The overall discourse of patriarchy which informs the art of the period is contextualised by a heightened urban sensibility as evidenced especially in narrative art. The *nāgaraka* (the cultivated urbanite) desired and patronised art that was sensuous, beautiful and reflected the urban ethos.

On the other hand, art was religious in context and we witness tensions between normative Brāhmanical patriarchy and actual representations. In the latter we see resistance, inversion and autonomy of the feminine domain from dominant misogynist discourse. The increased patriarchalisation of the organised religions leads to the disappearance of some female dominated cults and figures, and of the *bhikkhuṇī saṁgha*. This is predicated upon the decreasing agency of women in the patronage of artistic production. This attempt to recover the crystallisation of gender and the setting forth of gender archetypes in the pre-Gupta period has thus given interesting insights into the intention, agency and patronage patterns in early Indian art.

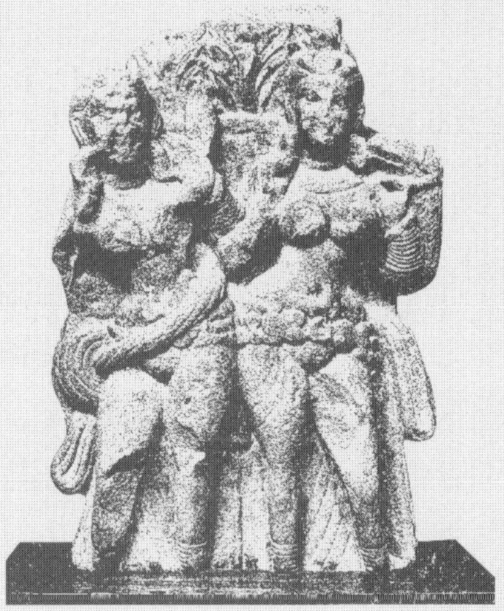

# Appendix

The post-Mauryan era saw a rapid expansion not only of the agrarian economy but also of urban centres, especially beyond the Gangetic basin. Simultaneously, there was a rise of new dynasties and ruling houses in areas that have been referred to as core areas or regional centres of the erstwhile Mauryan Empire. Khāravela in Orissa, the Indo-Greeks, the Śakas and the Kuṣāṇas in the north-west and Rajasthan, "tribal" monarchies and *gaṇarājya*s in Punjab, Rajasthan and Uttar Pradesh, the Sātavāhanas and Ikṣvākus in the Deccan, and the Saṅgam chiefdoms in the far south, all rose to prominence during this period. All these factors combined to make for a period of immense dynamism and cultural ferment. This process accelerated with the influx of foreigners and tribal communities into the social system. Mahāyāna Buddhism evolved into a powerful religious force that impelled the creation of sculptures of the Buddha and *boddhisattva*s. Brāhamanical religion saw the rise of the two powerful sects of Viṣṇu and Śiva together with an attendant pantheon, and this was reflected in both mythology and art. Ideological developments, such as the rise of the *bhakti* concept, were no less important.

As such urban centres naturally become the centres of artistic development. McAdam states, "cities became focal point not only of safe storage of surplus prior to its deployment but also for conspicuous expenditures for public building programmes and for maintenance of elite in luxurious surroundings. The historic role of cities has been as prime creative centres, of learning, artistic and philosophic ferment, fashioners of symbols."[1] Nenandru explicates this further, "art, literature and music, as well as most types of decorative objects are produced in the cities because it is here that one finds the concentration of those wealthy individuals and institutions that provide patronage or commercial markets for such cultural productions.[2]

It is fruitful to view the art of this period as "urban art," in so far as it was produced and consumed in geopolitical locales that have been termed as urban. The patronage of monumental building activity and for sculptures also came largely from non-agrarian communities such as merchants, guilds, monks and nuns. That this art was produced in an urban context cannot be overstated, a context that was different from that of the countryside. Niharranjan Ray has referred to art that is "rural" and "folk" in *Mauryan and Post Mauryan Art*, while S.P. Gupta too has alluded to this difference in his *Roots of Indian Art*. Terracottas have been considered as art objects that were produced and used by the non-elite for artistic and ritual purposes. These terracottas could have rural-urban connotations as well.

### City in Art and Art in the City

The relationship between art and city can be viewed at two levels: first being art that was produced and consumed within the city and second, art that reflected the city, its life, symbols and motifs. The sculptural tradition of the post-Mauryan period thematically alludes to an urban culture. In physical terms there are numerous representations of multi-storeyed buildings, palace interiors in contrast with forests, orchards, villages (*grāmas*). Religious edifices are also visible on these sculptures from the Śuṅga and Kuṣāṇa period. The subjects, especially secular subjects, seem to suggest a world that is urban — a world of courtesans, entertainers, *nāgaraka*s, wine drinkers, and spectators. In fact, the activities depicted on sculptural antiquities have a distinctly urban sensibility. In the more intimate and personal atmosphere of a small settlement such as a village, such representations would seem inappropriate, a view reinforced by the texts of the period.

In artistic production of this period, an urbanised space is deliberately and self-consciously depicted. This is inhabited by men and women who are simultaneously witnesses to and participate in the urbanised milieu. This is done through setting art in city architecture suggested by fortified walls, gates, banners multi-storeyed buildings with balconies and alcoves. This is contrasted to rural and forest spaces as in the *Ṛṣyaśṛṅga* and *Padukuśalamānava* Jātakas.

The representation of the city and urban architecture in art has been studied and commented upon. The two monographs by Amita Ray and Ananda K. Coomaraswamy make contributions of significance.

One of the most visible features of urban art is the fortifications, which are also the distinguishing structure that sets off the city from the village. It is an ideal category in the sense that it sets up a mental image of the city as a separate entity, distinguishable from the mass of the countryside around it, standing out with its ramparts and buttresses. It is of course also an important physical entity in that it offers protection to the inhabitants. The artists did not miss this significance of the fortification for the urban centre. One of the oft-repeated motifs in the art of the period is the city wall. The *prākāra* of the city, or the dry ditch that surrounds the moat, is the site where we see (in the narrative friezes) a lot of activity in the form of women coming down to fetch water from the moat and soldiers guarding the towers. The city-gate, too, is the site of varying activity as can be gleaned from the *Mṛcchakaṭika* and other works.

The city serves as a safe centre for the deployment of surplus collected from the surrounding countryside. Kauṭilya has also commented on this, as have the Jātakas. Cities are also the centre and foci for the production of craft and art which go on to create an urban environment. These range from monumental structures to small luxury items like ivory furniture that serve the elite. The sharpened class differentiation in cities is reflected through the production and consumption of such art objects.

Towns and cities are marked by an urban sensibility, reflected in an urban culture — a culture that contains a strain of the discourse of pleasure, marked by sophistication of the arts, leisure, luxury and sensuality. This urbanity is mirrored in contemporary texts such as the *Mṛcchakaṭika*, *Kāmasūtra*, *Saundarānanda*, where there are references to the *nāgaraka*, the sophisticated elite who is a connoisseur of and is well versed in the arts. The terracottas perhaps due to their urban origins have sophisticated *nāgaraka* aspects in their technique and presentation. Some of them exemplify the tastes of *nāgaraka*s and their *nāyikā*s who made use of toys of clay, ivory, horn, etc. Many city sites have been the source of terracottas with secular themes, for example a terracotta from Rājghāṭ depicts wrestling and elephant circus, which were the pastimes of the *nāgaraka*s. Here, wine jars and wine drinkers, pleasure gardens, and similar themes are also depicted.[3]

In the end of the first century CE or the beginning of the second century, if a commercial traveller, a *sārthavāha* or a student travelled from Taxila to Benares after having completed his business or studies, he would probably travel with a caravan of traders for security along a well-travelled trade route. En route he passes through numerous cities, vastly different in terms of their size as well as function. Taxila would be a medium-sized emporium and imperial centre, Mathurā larger and he would of course go through bigger settlements such as Kauśāmbī, Vidiśā and Rājgīr. The largest of them all would be Pāṭaliputra, which is 241 ha in diameter. As he approaches the city, he would be met by a monastery or a *vihāra* probably set in a garden called an *arāma* adjacent to a *stūpa*. He would probably see saffron-clad monks returning from their daily round of begging from the city. And then he would come to the city-gates, imposing on one hand and the hub of activity on the other.

### Sacred and Profane Space

The connection between space that can be considered sacred be it the *stūpa* or *devālaya* and the city seems a complex one in the post-Maurya era. Though demarcated and often located physically outside the city, these sacred complexes were an integral part of the urban landscape. Meister has also called these suburban complexes albeit in connection with the cave sites of the Deccan.

R.S. Sharma has also commented on the essential socio-cultural connection between Buddhism and urbanisation, in which he has pointed out that Buddhism encouraged or accepted many urban practices, such as prostitution, usury and eating-houses, which had hitherto been frowned upon by Brāhmanism.[4] It is therefore not surprising that the Buddhist *saṁgha* was patronised by urban communities such as guilds, merchants and artisans. We have numerous inscriptions that give us information about the patrons. From Sāñcī itself, we can see the majority is from urban centres, many from nearby Vidiśā. Further in Bharhut, near Satnā, donors from Vidiśā and Ujjain abound.

If one is to look at the inscriptions as revealing patronage patterns of art and architecture in the Buddhist realm, we can see that there is a large degree of equality in terms of what is donated by whom. Patronage is relatively gender and class neutral. A *bhikkhu*, a *bhikkhuṇī*, a guild, a king, all have donated pillars with the same device, the lotus, carved on them irrespective of their status and gender.

There is also a rather integral relationship between secular and religious art as seen in the city. Meister has commented on the composition of the monastic complex with its multiple cells and the multiple stories in the Deccan replicating a palace structure. Further, architectural elements such as the *gavākṣa* and the pavilions are shared both by sacred and profane architecture.

Urban culture merits an analysis of house plans and town plans to see how far the ideal of leisure and pleasure reflected in the texts was translated into reality. Some excavations of towns as in Śiśupālgaṛh, can be identified with the ideal town plan idealised in the *Arthaśāstra*. The architecture of the *stūpa*s, *vihāra*s, the *caitya*s as well as secular buildings, and the decorative elements on the same would also make for a useful research on how art and architecture were used to represent power and gender relationships and how space was organised. However, there are questions such as how religious and profane spaces or private and public spaces can be examined through their appearance only in textual sources as the excavation reports are forthcoming on these issues. This is however, not the focus of this work.

### Material Background

The post-Mauryan era saw a rapid expansion not only of the agrarian economy but also of urban centres, especially beyond the Gangetic basin; this expanding economy in turn provided a boost to commerce and craft production. The agrarian sphere sees not only a physical expansion but also witnesses a change in agrarian relationships with the beginnings of land grants. Trade and commerce both internal and external, boost urbanisation and monetisation. This period is undoubtedly the richest in finds of multi-metallic currency — an indicator of an economic fabric of considerable complexity. This leads to a growing importance in the influence of merchants and guilds in societal spheres including patronage patterns. There was a thrust into areas that were hitherto at a lower cultural level, which initiated a process of acculturation. Simultaneously there was a rise of new dynasties and ruling houses in areas that have been referred to as core areas or regional centres of the erstwhile Mauryan Empire. All these factors combined to make a period of immense dynamism and cultural ferment.

With the influx of foreigners and tribes into the Brāhmanical system, major social and cultural changes take place. Socially this is the beginning of crystallisation of *jāti* identities and there is also a tumult due to *jāti* mobility. These socio-economic changes impel changes towards the reinforcement of private property relations, while in the matter of socio-legal jurisprudence, patri-locality and patri-linearity become increasingly established as the norm. These institutions obviously lead to a progressive devolution in the economic status of women. A progressive result of the entrenching patriarchy is the desire to control or circumscribe female sexuality in marriage and family to ensure legitimate inheritance.

Mahāyāna Buddhism evolves into a powerful religious force that impelled the creation of sculptures of Buddha and *bodhisattvas*. Brāhmanical religion sees the rise of two powerful sects of Viṣṇu and Śiva with attendant pantheon that were reflected in both mythology and art. Ideological developments were no less important as the concept of *bhakti* became important.

### Temporal and Spatial Scope

**Period**: Post-Mauryan centuries have been a time of transformation and acculturation and intermingling of cultures, while also expanding urbanisation, a relevant period to study urban art is from second century BCE through the fourth century CE.

**Geographical Limits**: Urban centres were coming up almost all over India, with an efflorescence of dynasties enumerated above.[5]

The *raison d'être* of these cities was based on religion, trade and political power. The functions of a town were not defined and exclusive; these could and did overlap as in Taxila, which was a political, economic and cultural centre. Any typological study of urban centres takes into account differences based on polity, regions and ethnicity. Thus, Taxila evolved very differently from Vaiśālī and thus the art and architecture of these areas were also different. The brief exposition on ten towns given below taken as sample explicates on their significance and variations.

**Charsada**:[6] known in ancient Indian texts as Puṣkalavatī, was presided over by a city goddess. It was important during the Indo-Greek and Kuṣāṇa period. Two of its mounds have shown evidence of planning — Bala Hisar and Shaikhan. It was excavated by Marshall, Wheeler, Spooner and Dani. It was probably a great economic centre as well as a Buddhist site. Charsada was one of the most important sites in north-western India.

**Taxila**:[7] was extensively excavated by Marshall, though some of his conclusions are being challenged. Inhabited from the sixth century BCE to the third century CE, all three mounds Bhir, Sirkap and Sirsukh reveal information about the post-Mauryan era. Of these Sirkap and Sirsukh belong to the post-Mauryan era. It was a religious and commercial site and we find rich art and artifactual material from here.

**Suṅet**:[8] situated near modern Ludhiana, this site is significant for its link not only with the imperial dynasties of the Indo-Greeks and the Kuṣāṇas but also the "tribes" of north India like the Yaudheyas. It lay on the trade route that connected Taxila with middle Gangetic valley and received influences from north, west and east. It was successively the capital of an independent state, came under the overlordship of Indo-Greeks and later the Kuṣāṇas.

**Sanghol**:[9] situated between Sirhind and Ludhiana, this site has the potential of providing extensive information on post-Mauryan urbanisation, however the whole mound has not yet been exposed. It shows signs of planning around the monastery (personal communication with R.S. Bisht, the excavator). It is also important for the 117 antiquities found near the *stūpa*. This important site was noticed by Hieun Tsang and reported as Saṁghapura. It also lay on the main east-west trade route. It could provide important evidence of alternative political and art tradition to the overarching imperial schools of art, though the influence of Mathurā art is more pronounced here. Ropar,[10] ancient Rūpanagar, is a site in its proximity that mirrors some of the developments at Sanghol.

**Mathurā**:[11] was and remains a significant religious centre. It was also a seat of political power and lay on a major trade route. It was the eastern capital of the Kuṣāṇa kings and an important centre of art. In terms of style, the Mathurā school of art marks a significant moment in art history and it can be viewed as a foundational period in terms of thematic and iconographical evolution of classical art. The post-Mauryan layers have been extensively explored by A. Cunningham, S. Piggot, M.C. Joshi and Herbert Hartel.

**Kauśāmbī**:[12] in UP has been identified with Kosam. It has been extensively excavated by G.R. Sharma, though many of his conclusions, specially regarding dating, are disputed (by G. Erdosy and others). The excavations have revealed a palace, fortifications, a monastery called Ghoṣitārāma, and residential quarters. There was a Buddhist site of significance. It should be studied in conjunction with the nearby site of Bhītā.[13]

**Besanagar**:[14] near Vidiśā. It was probably an important capital of the Śuṅgas. It was an important commercial city linking the north with south. The pillar of Herodotus reveals its importance for the early Bhāgavata cult while its proximity to Sāñcī, Andher, Śatadhārā, Sunārī and Bhojpur *stūpa*s suggests its links with Buddhism during the post-Mauryan period.

**Ujjain**:[15] was an important politico-ecomonic centre, as it marked the middle of the north-south trade route, the *dakṣiṇāpatha*. Its significance can be judged from frequent references to it in literature. It has revealed a coherent town plan and a dependable archaeological sequence.

**Śrāvastī**:[16] modern Sahet-Mahet. It was an important Buddhist site and is also associated with the Śuṅgas.

**Pāṭaliputra**:[17] modern Patna. Though it is associated mainly with the Nanda-Mauryas, it remained an important seat of power in ancient India. Excavations have revealed a continuous cultural sequence. It is important to study the site as it can be linked to other important sites of the middle Gangetic valley such as Vaiśālī[18] and Bodh-Gayā.

**Cave Sites**: While early cave monuments such as Kārle, Pītalkhorā, Ghaṭotkacha, Kānheri, Bhaja, Bhedsā are not precisely linked with a specific urban centre, they were linked to the urban process as most of them lay on major trade routes and derived their patronage from urban classes.

## Notes and References

1. Robert McAdams, in G. Possehl ed., *Ancient Cities of the Indus*, New Delhi: Vikas Publishing House, 1979.

2. S. Nenandru, "Introduction, Art and the City", in *Journal of Urban History*, vol. 21, April 1994.

3. Devangana Desai, *Erotic Sculptures of India: A Socio-Religious Study*, Delhi, 1986, pp. 17-18.

4. R.S. Sharma, *Perspectives on Social and Economic History of Ancient India*, New Delhi: Munshiram Manoharlal, 1983.

5. Similarly, the art of the multimetallic coins found in such profusion during the time can be used to reconstruct the style, symbols and postures used to exalt royal power. Power that was reflected in the urban context can be seen in the legends found on coins that provide the name of the town where these were minted. Coins are also principal source of information when it comes to "tribal" monarchies and *gaṇarājyas* of north India. Places like Sunet have revealed rich post-Mauryan layers and the art of such centres provides a counter-view to the largely urban art of large and powerful dynasties such as the Indo-Greeks, Kuṣāṇas and Śakas.

6. R.E.M. Wheeler, *Charsada*, London, 1962.

7. Suthankar, *Annual Report of the Archaeological Survey of India* (henceforth *ARASI*), 1914-15, pp. 36-41; B.C. Law, *Historical Gleanings*, Calcutta, 1922; Ibid., *Historical Geography of Ancient India*, Paris, 1954; R.C Majumdar, *The Classical Accounts of India*, Calcutta, 1960; J. Marshall, *Taxila*, 3 vols., Cambridge, 1913/1951; M. Sharif, "Excavation at Bhir Mound", Taxila, *Pakistan Archaeology*, no. 6, 1969, pp. 7-99; A.Ghosh, "Taxila (Sirkap), 1944-45", *Ancient India*, 4, 1948, pp. 41-84.

8. *ARASI*, 1983-84, pp. 67-70.

9. *ARASI*, 1968-69, pp. 25-26; *ARASI*, 1969-70, pp. 30-31; *ARASI*, 1970-71, pp. 30-31; *ARASI*, 1971-72, pp. 39-41; *ARASI*, 1977-78, pp. 43-44; *ARASI*, 1980-81, p. 46; *ARASI*, 1984-85, pp. 62-64.

10. Y.D. Sharma, *Protohistoric Remains*, Archeological Remains, Monuments and Museums, part 1, Delhi, 1964; Ibid., "Patterns of Living as Unfolded by Excavations at Rupar", *Lalit Kala*, pts. 1-2, 1955-56, pp. 121-129.

11. B.C. Law, *Historical Geography of Ancient India*, Paris, 1954, pp. 106-10; N.L. Dey, *A Geographical Dictionary of Ancient India*, Delhi, pp. 127-28; H.P. Chakraborti, op. cit., pp. 169-73; D.M. Srinivasan, ed., *Mathura: A Cultural Heritage*, AIIS and Manohar Books, Delhi, 1989; M.C. Joshi, "Mathura as an Ancient Settlement", in D.M. Srinivasan, op. cit., pp. 269-74; A. Cunningham (rep.), *ASI Report for the Year 1871-72*, Varanasi, 1966, pp. 13-46; S. Piggott, *Some Ancient Cities of India*, Bombay, 1945; *ARASI*, 1954-55; *ARASI*, 1973-74, pp. 31-32; *ARASI*, 1974-75, pp. 48-50; *ARASI*, 1975-76, pp. 53-55; *ARASI*, 1976-77, pp. 54-56.

12. N.N. Ghosh, *Early History of Kauśāmbī*, Allahabad 1935; B.C. Law, *Kauśāmbī in Ancient Literature*, Delhi 1939; G.R. Sharma, *Excavations at Kauśāmbī*, Allahabad, 1958; Ibid., *Excavations at Kauśāmbī (1957-59)*, Allahabad 1960; A. Cunningham, *The Ancient Geography of India*, 1963 pp. 30-35; *ARASI*, 1953-54; *ARASI*, 1966-67, *ARASI*, 1960-61, pp. 33-35; K.K. Sinha, 1973, Stratigraphy and Chronology of Early Kauśāmbī, in D. P. Agarwal and A. Ghosh, eds., *Radiocarbon and Indian Archeology*, Bombay, 1973; B.B. Rai, Paper on Syena Chiti, Paper on Udayana Palace, *Purattava*, 1985; G. Erdosy, 1988, *Urbanisation in Early Historic India*, Oxford, 1988; Makkan Lal, *Summary of Four Seasons' Work in Kanpur Distt.*, ME, pp. 181-99.

13. A. Cunningham, *The Ancient Geography of India*, vol. 3; John Marshall, *ARASI*, 1911-12; Excavations at Bhita, 1915, pp. 29-94.

14. N.L. Dey, *A Geographical Dictionary of Ancient India*, Delhi 1971, rpt.; B.C. Law, *Historical Geography of Ancient India*, Paris, 1954, pp. 336-40; H. Chakraborti, *Trade and Commerce in Ancient India*, Calcutta, pp. 192-95; D.R. Bhandarkar, "Excavations at Besanagar 1913-14", *ARASI*, 1917, pp. 186-226; M. Hamid, "Excavations at Sanchi", *ARASI*, 1936-37, pp. 84-87; M.D. Khare, *ARASI* 1963-64, pp. 16-17; *ARASI*, 1964-66, pp. 19-20; *ARASI*, 1965-66, pp. 23-24; *ARASI*, 1975-76, pp. 30-31; *ARASI*, 1976-77, pp. 33-34.

15 B.C. Law, *Ujjayini in Ancient Literature*, Delhi 1944; H. Chakraborti, *Trade and Commerce in Ancient*

*India*, Calcutta, 1966; *ARASI,* 1955-56, p. 19; *ARASI*, 1956-57, pp. 20-28; *ARASI*, 1957-58, pp. 33-36; Banerjee, *ARASI*, 1965, pp. 14-15.

16. K. Sinha, *Excavations at Sravasti*, 1958-62, Varanasi, 1967.

17. Patil, *The Antiquarian Remains in Bihar*, Patna, 1963, pp. 373-78; H. Chakraborti, op. cit., 1966, p. 182; R.C. Majumdar, *The Classical Accounts of India*, Calcutta, 1960; S. Spooner, *ARASI,* 1913-15; Altekar, Misra, "Report on the Kumrahar Excavations", *ARASI*, 1951-55, 1959. S. Spooner, *ARASI,* 1915-17; B.P. Sinha, and Lala Aditya Narain, *Pataliputra Excavations*, 1955-56, Patna, 1970.

18. K. Deva, and Mishra, *Vaisali Excavations*, Vaisali, 1985; B.P. Sinha, and Sita Ram Ray, *Excavations at Vaisali*, Patna, 1968.

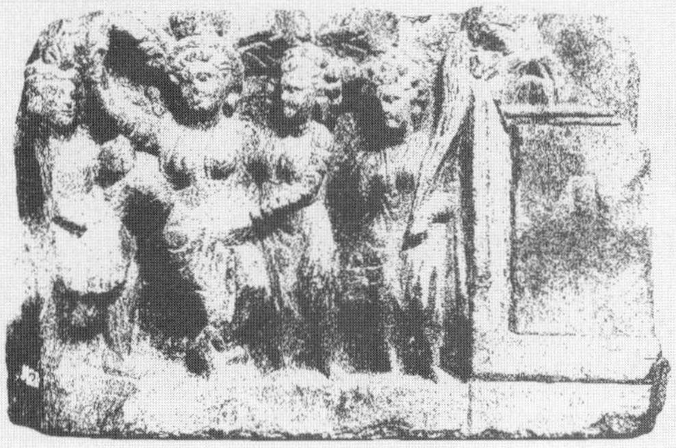

# Bibliography


## Primary Sources

Kausalyayan, Anand, *Anguttara Nikaya*, vol. III, Kolkata: Mahabodhi Sabha (n.d.).

Kangle, R.P., *Arthasastra*, parts I, II and III, New Delhi: Motilal Banarsidass, 1992 (repr.).

Shastri, Ganesh, *Asvalayana Grihyasutram*, Pune: Anandashram, 1978.

Satavalekar, Damodar, *Atharvaveda*, 4 vols., Paradi: Swadhyaya Mandal, 1983-85.

*Bhoja's Samarangana-Sutradhara*: Vastushastra, 2 vols., Pushpendra Kumar (ed.), Delhi: New Bharatiya Book Corporation, 1998.

*Brahmanda Purana*, Bombay: Venkatesvara Press (n.d.).

*Brihat Devata*, Harvard Oriental Series, vols. 5 and 6, A.A. Macdonell (ed. and tr.), Cambridge: Harvard University Press, 1904.

*Dharmasutras: The Law Codes of Apastamba, Gautama, Baudhayana and Vasishtha*, Patrick Olivelle (ed. and tr.), Delhi: Motilal Banarsidass, 2003.

*Gilgit Manuscripts*, 4 vols., Nalinaksha Dutt (ed.), Delhi: Sri Satguru Publications, 1984.

*I-Tsing: A Record of the Buddhist Religion As Practiced in India and the Malay Archipelago A.D. 671-695*, J. Takakusu (tr.), New Delhi: Munshiram Manoharlal, 1966 (repr.).

*Jivajivabhigam Sutra*, 2 vols., Rajendra Muni (ed.), Beawar: Sri Agam Prakashan Samiti, 1989-91.

*Kamasutra of Vatsyayana*, Mulk Raj Anand and Lance Dane, New Delhi: Arnold Heinemann, 1982.

*Lalitavistara*, 2 vols., S. Lefmann (ed.), Tokyo: Meicho-Foky-Kai, 1977.

*Mahabharata*, 19 vols., Poona, Bhandarkar Oriental Research Institute, 1933-59.

*Manava Gryhasutra of the Maitrayanika Sakha with the Commentary of Astavakara*, Ramakrishana Harshaji Sastri (ed.), New Delhi: Panini, 1982.

*Natyasastra Ascribed to Bharata Muni*, 2 vols., Manmohan Ghosh (ed. and tr.), Calcutta: Granthalaya Pvt. Ltd., 1967.

*Prakrit Gatha Saptasati*, Radhagovinda Basak (ed.), Calcutta: Asiatic Society, 1971.

*Rajaprashniya Sutram*, Ratan Muni (tr.), Beawar: Sri Agam Prakashan Samiti, 1982.

*Rajatarangini of Kalhana*, 2 vols., Vishva Bandhu (ed.), Hoshiarpur: V. V. Research Institute, 1963-65.

*Ṛgveda Saṁhitā*, 6 vols., H.H. Wilso (tr.), Delhi: Nag Publishers, 1977.

*Sankhayana Grhyasutram Belonging to the Rigveda*, S.R. Sehgal (ed.), Delhi: Sri Satguru Publications, 1987.

*Satapatha Brahmana*, 5 vols, Julius Eggeling (tr.), Delhi: Motilal Banarsidass, 1966.

*Saundarananda of Asvaghosa*, E.H. Johnson (ed.), Delhi: Motilal Banarsidass, 1975.

*Śilpa Prakāśa by Kaulacara*, Ramachandra, Alice Boner and Sadasiva Rath Sarma (tr.), Leiden: E.J. Brill, 1966.

Si-Yu-Ki, *Buddhist Records of the Western World*, Samuel Beal (tr.), Delhi: Oriental Books Reprint Corporation, 1969 (repr.).

*Suśruta Saṁhitā Edited with Ayurveda Tattva-Sandīpikā*, Ambikadutta Shastri (ed.), 2 vols., Varanasi: Chaukhamba Sanskrit Sansthan, 1979.

*Taittirīyasaṁhitā of the Black Yajuraveda with the Commentary of Bhaṭṭa Bhāskara Miśra*, Mahadeva Shastri (ed.), Delhi: Motilal Banarsidass, 1986.

*The Books of Discipline (Vinaya Piṭaka)*, 6 vols., I.B. Horner (tr.), London: Pali Text Society, 1949-66.

*The Book of Kindred Sayings (Samyutta Nikaya)* vol. 1, C.A.F. Rhys Davids (tr.), London: Pali Text Society, 1917.

*The Buddhacarita or Acts of the Buddha*, E.H. Johnston (tr.), Delhi: Motilal Banarsidass, 1972.

*The Dhammapada: A Collection of Verses Being One of the Canonical Books of the Buddhist*, F. Max Müller (tr.), Delhi: Motilal Banarsidass, 1965.

*The First Buddhist Women Translations and Commentary on the Therigatha*, Susan Murcott, Berkeley: Parallex Press, 1998.

*The Jataka or Stories of the Buddha's Former Births*, tr. from the Pali by various hands, 6 vols., E.D. Cowell (ed.), Delhi: Motilal Banarsidass, 1990.

*The Laws of Manu*, tr. Wendy Doniger with Brian K. Smith, Delhi: Penguin Books, 1992 (repr.).

*The Laws of Manu*, tr. Georg Bühler, SBE, vol. 25, Oxford: Clarendon Press, 1886; New Delhi: Low Price Publications (repr.), 2002.

*The Manorathapurani: Anguttaranikaya Atthakatha*, Nalanda, Nand Kishore Prasad (ed.), Nava Nalanda Mahavihara, 1976.

*The Mrchchha-Katika of Sudraka*, M.R. Kale (ed.), Delhi: Motilal Banarsidass, 1972.

*The Patimokkha*, William Pruitt (ed.) and K.R. Norman (tr.), Oxford: Pali Text Society, 2001.

*The Samyutta Nikayapali*, 4 vols., J. Kashyap (ed.), Nalanda: Pali Publication Board, 1959.

*The Thirteen Principal Upanishads*, Robert Ernest Hume (tr.), London: Oxford University Press, 1965.

*Theragatha*, K.R. Norman (tr.), London: Pali Text Society, 1969.

*Therigatha*, Mrs. Rhys Davids (ed.), London: Oxford University Press, 1909.

*Therigatha: The Elders' Verses*, II, K.R. Norman (tr.), London: Pali Text Society, 1971.

*Tryambakayajnavan's The Perfect Wife: Stridharma-paddhati*, E. Julia Leslie (ed. and tr.), New Delhi: Penguin Books, 1995.

*Śilpa Prakāśa*, A. Boner and S.R. Sarma (ed. and annot.), Leiden: E.J. Brill, 1966.

*Visnudharmottara Purana (Third Khand)*, 2 vols., Priyabala Shah (ed.), Baroda: Oriental Institute, 1958-61.

*Woven Cadences of Early Buddhists (Sutta Nipata)*, F.M. Hare (tr.), London: Geoffrey Cumberlege, 1947.

*Yajnavalkya Smriti*, Narayan Ram Acharya (ed.), Bombay: Nirnaya Sagar Press, 1949.

*Yajurveda Saṁhitā*, Damodar Satavalekar (ed.), Pardi: Swadhyaya Mandal (n.d.).

**Epigraphic Sources**

*Epigraphia Indica*, vol. II, James Burgess (ed.), Calcutta: Supdt. of Govt. Printing, 1894.

*Epigraphia Indica*, vol. X, 1909-10; vol. XXIX, 1951-52.

*Inscriptions of Asoka: Corpus Inscriptionum Indicarum*, vol. I, E. Hultzsch (ed.), Delhi: Indological Book House, 1969 (repr.).

*Kharosthi Inscriptions with the Exception of those of Asoka*, Sten Konow (ed.), Calcutta: Central Publication Branch, 1929.

Lüders, Heinrich, *Mathura Inscriptions*, Klaus L. Janert (ed.), Göttingen: Vandenhoeck and Ruprecht, 1961.

––– (ed.), *Bharhut Inscriptions*, New Delhi: Archaeological Survey of India, 1963.

**Secondary Sources**

Agrawala, P. K., "Early Images of God Kama", *Journal of the Indian Society of Oriental Art*, New Series, vol. XVI-XVII, 1987-89, pp. 5-14.

——, "Identification of the So-Called Nagi Figures As Goddess Sasthi", *East and West*, vol. 21, 1971, pp. 325-29.

–––, *Skanda-Karttikeya*, Varanasi: Prithivi Prakashan, 1967.

——, "The Depiction of Mara in Early Buddhist Art", in K.R. van Kooij and H. van der Veere (eds.) *Function and Meaning in Buddhist Art*, Groningen: Egbert Forsten, 1995, pp. 125-34.

——, "The Headless Nude Goddess and Her Identification", in T.S. Maxwell (ed.) *Eastern Approaches: Essays on Asian Art and Archaeology*, New Delhi: Oxford University Press, 1992, pp. 63-73.

——, *Mithuna: The Male-Female Symbol in Indian Art and Thought*, Varanasi: Prithivi Prakashan, 1983.

Agrawala, R.C., "Kṛṣṇa and Baladeva as Attendant Figures in Early Indian Sculpture", *Indian Historical Quarterly*, vol. XXXVIII, no. 1, 1962, pp. 86-88.

——, "Matrika Reliefs in Early Indian Art", *East and West*, vol. 21, nos. 1-2, March -June, 1971, pp. 79-89.

Agrawala, V.S., *A Catalogue of the Brahmanical Images in Mathura Art*, Lucknow: Historical Society, 1951.

——, *Ancient Indian Folks Cults*, Varanasi: Prithivi Prakashan, 1970.

——, "Goddess Shashthi on the Yaudheya Coins", *Journal of the Numismatic Society of India*, vol. V, 1943, pp. 29-32.

——, *Indian Art*, Varanasi: Prithivi Prakashan, 1965.

——, *Masterpieces of Mathura Sculpture*, Varanasi: Prithivi Prakashan, 1965.

——, *Mathura Museum Catalogue: Architectural Pieces in Mathura Museum*, Varanasi: Prithivi Prakashan, 1963.

——, *Mathura Museum Handbook*, Allahabad, 1939.

——, "Miscellaneous Fragmentary Figures", *Journal of the U.P. Historical Society*, vol. XXIII, 1950, pp. 102-18.

——, "Presiding Deity of Childbirth amongst the Ancient Jainas with Special Reference to Figures in the Mathura Museum", *Jaina Antiquary*, vol. II, no. IV, March 1937, pp. 75-79.

——, "Terracotta Figurines of Ahichchhatra, District Bareilly, Uttar Pradesh", *Ancient India*, no. 4, 1947-48, pp. 104-79.

——, "A New Bodhisattva and a Bacchanalian Group from Mathura", *JISOA*, 1938, pp. 67-72.

Altekar, A.S., *The Position of Women in Hindu Civilization from Prehistoric Times to the Present Day*, Delhi: Motilal Banarsidass, repr., 1978.

Ali, Daud, *Courtly Culture and the Political Life in Early Medieval India*, Cambridge: Cambridge University Press, 2006.

Apte, V.S., *The Practical Sanskrit-English Dictionary*, Delhi: Motilal Banarsidass, 1965.

Asher, Catherine B. and Thomas R. Metcalf (eds.), *Perceptions of South Asia's Visual Past*, New Delhi: AIIS and Oxford University Press, 1994.

Atre, Shubhangana, *The Archetypal Mother: A Systematic Approach to Harappon Religion*, Pune: Ravish Publishers, 1987.

Auboyer, Jeanine, *Daily Life in Ancient India: From Approximately 200 BC to AD 700*, Bombay: Asia Publishing House, 1965.

Bachhofer, Ludwig, "Die Hariti Von Skarah Dheri", *Ostasiatische Zeitschrift*, 1936, pp. 100-07.

——, *Early Indian Sculpture*, New Delhi: Munshiram Manoharlal, 1973 (repr.).

Bajpai, K.D. "A New Inscribed Image of a Yaksa", in *India Antiqua : A Volume of Oriental Studies.* Presented by his friends and pupils to Jean Phillippe Vogel, Leiden: E.J. Brill, 1947, pp. 8-9.

Banerjea, J.N., *The Development of Hindu Iconography*, Calcutta: University of Calcutta, 1956.

Banerji Sastri, A.P., "The Jogimarha Cave Inscription" *Journal of Bhandarkar Oriental Research Society*, no. 3-4, 1923, pp. 273-93.

——, *The Castaways of Indian Society*, Calcutta, 1989.

Barua, B.M., *Bharhut*, 3 pts., Patna: Indological Books Corporation, 1979 (repr.).

Bautze, Joachim Karl, *Early Indian Terracottas*, Leiden: E.J. Brill, 1995.

Bawa, Seema, *Religion and Art of the Chamba Valley (AD 700-1300)*, Delhi: Agam Kala Prakashan, 1998.

Behrendt, Kurt, "An Unnoticed Relief from the Bhilsa Topes and Its Relationship to the Sculpture of Sanchi", *South Asian Studies*, vol. 16, 2000, pp. 1-9.

Berger, John, *Ways of Seeing*, New Delhi: Penguin Press, 1975.

Bhattacharji, Sukumari, *The Indian Theogony: A Comparative Study of Indian Mythology from The Vedas to The Puranas*, Cambridge: University Press, 1970.

Bhattacharyya, N.N., *The Indian Mother Goddess*, New Delhi: Manohar, 1977.

Biswas, S.S., *Terracotta Art of Bengal*, New Delhi: Agam Kala Prakashan, 1981.

Bolen, Kathleen M., "Prehistoric Construction of Mothering", in Cheryl Classen (ed.) *Exploring Gender through Archaeology*, Wisconsin: Prehistory Press, 1992.

Bolon, Carol Radcliffe, *Forms of the Goddess Lajja Gauri in Indian Art*, Pennsylvania: Pennsylvania State University Press, 1992.

Boyd, James W., *Satan and Mara: Christian and Buddhist Symbols of Evil*, Leiden: E.J. Brill, 1975.

Burgess, James (ed.), *Epigraphia Indica*, vol. II, Calcutta: Supdt. of Govt. Printing, 1894.

——, *Report on the Buddhist Cave Temples and their Inscriptions*, Varanasi: Indological Book House, 1964 (repr.).

---, *The Buddhist Stupas of Amaravati and Jaggayyapeta in The Krishna District: Madras Presidency, Surveyed in 1882* by James Burgess, with Translations of the Aśoka Inscriptions at Jaugada and Dhauli by Georg Bühler, Varanasi: Indological Book House, 1970 (repr.).

Butler, Judith, *Bodies that Matter: On the Discursive Limits of "Sex"*, New York: Routledge, 1993.

——, *Gender Trouble: Feminism and the Subversion of Identity*, New York: Routledge, 1990.

Carlleyle, A.C.L., *Report of a Tour in Eastern*

*Rajputana in 1871-72 and 1872-73*, A.S.I. Report, vol. VI, Calcutta: Supdt. of Govt. Printing, 1878.

Carter, Martha L., "Dionysian Aspects of Kushana Art", *Ars Orientalis*, vol. 7, 1968, pp. 121-46.

Chakravarti, Uma, "Beyond The Alterkarian Paradigm: Towards a New Understanding of Gender Relations in Early Indian History", in Kumkum Roy (ed.) *Women in Early Indian Societies*, New Delhi: Manohar, 1999, pp. 49-71.

——, "Conceptualising Brahmanical Patriarchy in Early India: Gender, Caste, Class and State", *EPW*, April 1993.

——, "Development of the Sita Myth: A Case Study of Women in Myth and Literature", in Lalitha Gopalan (ed.) *Women and Culture*, Delhi, 1985.

——, *Men Women and Beasts: The Interface between High Tradition and Popular Tradition in Cultural Production*, New Delhi: Nehru Memorial Museum and Library, 1992.

——, "Preliminary Observations on the Impulse Control of Women in Early India: Ideology, Kinship and the State As Mechanisms of Control", in K.D. Bajpai (ed.) *Position and Status of Women in Ancient India*, Varanasi, 1992, pp. 127-44.

Chakravarti, Uma and Kumkum Roy, "Breaking Out of Invisibility: Rewriting the History of Women in Ancient India", in S. Jay Kleinberg (ed.) *Retrieving Women's History Changing Perspectives of the Role of Women in Politics and Society*, Berg, Unesco, 1988.

Chandra, Moti, "Recent Sculpture in the Prince of Wales Museum", *Prince of Wales Museum Bulletin*, no. 9, 1964-66.

——, "Nidhisringa (Cornucopia): A Study in Symbolism", *Prince of Wales Museum Bulletin*, no. 9, 1964-66, pp. 1-33.

——, "Studies in the Cult of the Mother Goddess in Ancient India", *Prince of Wales Museum Bulletin*, no. 12, 1973, pp. 1-47.

Chandra, Pramod, *Stone Sculptures in Allahabad Museum: A Descriptive Catalogue,* vol. I, Poona: American Institute of Indian Studies, 1970, p. 37.

—— "The Cult of Sri Lakshmi and Four Carved Discs in Bharat Kala Bhawan", in Anand Krishna (ed.) *Chhavi : Golden Jubilee, Volume Bharat Kala Bhavan, Banaras*, 1971, pp. 139-48.

Chapeker, B.N., *Report on the Excavations at Ter*, Poona, 1958.

Chattopadhyay, Bhaskar, *The Age of the Kushanas: A Numismatic Study*, Calcutta: Punthi Pustak, 1967.

Classen, Cheryl (ed.), *Exploring Gender through Archaeology: Monographs in World Archeology*, no. 11, Wisconsin: Prehistory Press, 1992.

Chodorow, Nancy, *The Reproduction of Mothering: Psychoannalysis and the Sociology of Gender*, Berkeley: University of California Press, 1978.

Cobezon, Jose (ed.), *Buddhism, Sexuality and Gender*, Albany: State University of New York Press, 1985.

Codrington, "Iconography: Classical and Indian", *Man*, vol. XXXV, 1935, no. 70.

Coomaraswamy, Ananda K., "Buddhist Reliefs From Nagajunakonda and Amaravati", *Rupam*, nos. 38-39, April-July 1929, pp. 70-76.

——, "Early Indian Iconography, II: Sri Laksmi", *Eastern Art*, vol. I, no. 3, 1929, pp. 175-89.

——, "Early Indian Terracottas", *Museum of Fine Arts Bulletin*, vol. XXV, Boston, 1927.

——, *History of Indian and Indonesian Art*, New York: Dover Publications, 1965.

——, *La Sculpture De Bharhut*, Paris, Vanoest, 1956.

——, "La Sculpture De Bodhgaya", *Ars Asiatica*, vol. XVIII, 1935.

——, *Yaksas: Essays in the Water Cosmology*, New Delhi: Indira Gandhi National Center For the Arts, 1993.

——, *History of Indian And Indonesian Art*, New York: Dover Publications, repr., 1965.

Chattopadhyaya, B., *Kushana State and Indian Society*, Calcutta: Punthi Pustak, 1975.

Conze, Edward, *The Life of Buddha: As Legend and History*, Delhi: Motilal Banarsidass, 1993.

Czuma, Stanislaw J., *Kushana Sculpture: Images from Early India*, Cleveland: The Cleveland Museum of Art, 1985.

Dallapiccola, Anna Libera and Lallemant, Stephanie Zingel Ave (eds.), *The Stupa: Its Religious, Historical and Architectural Significance*, Wiesbaden: Franz Steiner Verlag, 1980.

Dasgupta, K.K., *Tribal History of Ancient India: A Numismatic Approach*, Calcutta: Navabharat Publishers, 1974.

Dasgupta, Shashi Bhushan, *Aspects of Indian Religious Thought*, Calcutta: Firma KLM, 1977.

De Beauvoir, Simone, *The Second Sex*, Middlesex: Penguin Books, 1987 (repr.).

Dehejia, Vidya, "Aniconism and Multivalence of Emblems", *Ars Orientalis*, vol. 21, 1991, pp. 45-66.

—, *Discourse in Early Buddhist Art: Visual Narratives of India*, New Delhi: Munshiram Manoharlal, 1997.

— (ed.), *Representing the Body: Gender Issues in Indian Art*, New Delhi: Kali For Women, 1997.

Desai, Devangana, *Erotic Sculpture of India: A Socio-Cultural Study*, New Delhi: Tata McGraw Hill, 1985.

---,"Social Background of Ancient Indian Terracottas", in D. Chattopahyaya (ed.) *History and Society: Essays in Honour of Prof. Niharranjan Ray*, Calcutta, 1978, pp. 143-68.

—, "Terracottas and Urban Culture in Ancient India", in *National Museum Bulletin*, nos. 1-6, 1983, pp. 59-65.

Desai, Vishakha, "Reflections on the History and Historiography of Male Sexuality in Early Indian Art", in Vidya Dehejia (ed.) *Representing the Body: Gender Issues in Indian Art*, New Delhi: Kali For Women, 1997, pp. 42-55.

Deshpande, M.N., "The Rock Cut Caves of Pitalkhora in the Deccan", *Ancient India*, no. 15, 1959, pp. 66-93.

Dhavalikar, M.K., *Masterpices of Indian Terracottas*, Bombay: D. B. Taraporevala, 1977.

Dobbins, K. Walton, "A Note on The Hariti Image from Skarah Dheri, Year 399", *East and West*, vol. 17, nos. 3-4, 1967, pp. 268-72.

Donaldson, Thomas, "Propitious-Apotropaic Eroticism in the Art of Orissa", *Artibus Asiae*, vol. 37, no. 1-2, 1975, pp. 75-100.

Dundas, Paul, *The Jains*, London: Routledge, 1992.

Ferguson, James, *Tree and Serpent Worship*, London: India Museum, 1873.

Ferguson, James and James Burgess, *The Cave Temples of India*, Delhi: Oriental Books Reprint Corporation, 1969 (repr.).

Fleet, J.F., "The Tradition about the Corporal Relics of Buddha", *Journal of the Royal Asiatic Society of Great Britain and Ireland*, 1907, pp. 341-63.

Foucher, A., *On The Iconography of the Buddha's Nativity*, MASI No. 46, Delhi: Manager of Publications, ASI, 1934.

—, "Sur l'Interpretation de quatre bas reliefs de Bharhut", *Revue Des Arts Asiatiques*, vol. XIII, no. 1, 1939-42, pp. 1-9.

Gangoly, O.C., "The Mithuna in Indian Art", in *Rupam*, nos. 22-23, April-July, 1925, pp. 54-61.

Getty, Alice, *The Gods of Northern Buddhism*, New Delhi: Munshiram Manoharlal, 1978.

Ghosh, A. and H. Sarkar, "Beginnings of Sculptural Art in South-East Asia: A Stele From Amaravati", *Ancient India*, nos. 20-21, 1964-65, pp. 168-77.

Gonda, J., *Aspects of Early Visnuism*, Delhi: Motilal Banarsidass repr., 1993 (first edn., Leiden, 1954).

—, "The Simantonnayana as Described in the Grhyasutras", *East and West*, vol. VII, 1956, pp. 12-31.

Gopinath Rao, T.A., *Elements of Hindu Iconography*, 2 vols., Delhi: Motilal Banarsidass, 1968.

Gross, Rita M., *Buddhism after Patriarchy*, Albany: State University of New York Press, 1993.

Guha-Thakurta, Tapti, "What Makes for the 'Authentic' Female Nude in Indian Art", in Shivaji K. Panikkar et al. (eds.) *Towards A New Art History: Studies in Indian Art*, New Delhi: D.K. Printworld, 2003, pp. 358-84.

Gupta, Chandrashekhar, "Some Interesting Plaques of Lajja From Paunar", in A.V. Narasimhamurthy and K.V. Ramesh (eds.) *Giridhara Siri: Essays in Indology; Dr. G.S. Dikshit Felicitation Volume,* Delhi: Agam Kala Prakashan, 1987, pp. 45-50.

Gupta, Parmeshwari Lal, ed., *Patna Museum Catalogue of Antiquities*, Patna: Patna Museum, 1965.

Gupta, S.P., *Roots of Indian Art*, Delhi: B.R. Publications Corporation, 1980.

—— (ed.), Kushana Sculptures from Sanghol 1st-2nd Century AD; *A Recent Discovery*, vol. I, New Delhi: National Museum, 1985.

Hackin, J. et al., *Nouvelles Recherches Archeologiques A Begram (Ancienne Kapici)* 1939-40, Paris: Imprimerie Nationale, 1954.

Hackin, J. and J.R. Hacking, *Recherches Archeologiques A Begram: Chantier no. 2 (1937)*, Paris: Les Editions D'Art Et D' Histoire, 1939.

Haldar, J.R., *Early Buddhist Mythology*, New Delhi: Manohar, 1977.

Hallade, Madeleine, *The Gandhara Style and the Evolution of Buddhist Art*, London: Thames and Hudson, 1968.

Harper, Katherine Anne, *Seven Hindu Goddesses of Spiritual Transformation: The Iconography of the Saptamatrikas*, New York: The Edwin Mellen Press, 1989.

Hartel, Herbert, *Excavations at Sonkh*, Berlin: Dietrich Reimer Verlag, 1993.

Horner, I.B., *Women under Primitive Buddhism*, Delhi: Motilal Banarsidass, 1999 (repr.).

Huntington, Susan, "Aniconism and The Multivalence of Emblems; Another Look", *Ars Orientalis*, vol. 22, 1992, pp. 111-56.

Jaini, Padmanabhan, *Gender and Salvation: Jaina Debates on the Spiritual Liberation of Women*, New Delhi: Munshiram Manoharlal, 1992.

Jaiswal, Suvira, *Origin and Development of Vaisnavism*, New Delhi: Munshiram Manoharlal, 1985.

Johnston, E.H., "A Terracotta Figure at Oxford", *Journal of Indian Society of Oriental Art*, vol. X, 1942, pp. 94-102.

——, tr. and ed., *The Buddhacarita or Acts of the Buddha*, Delhi: Motilal Banarsidass, 1972.

——, tr. and ed., *Saundarananda of Asvaghosa*, Delhi: Motilal Banarsidasss, 1975.

Joshi, N.P., *Catalogue of Brahmanical Sculptures in the State Museum Lucknow*, 2 pts., Lucknow: State Museum, 1972-89.

——, "Devi Ekanamsa ki Kusana Kalina Murtiyam", *Bulletin of Museums & Archaeology in U.P.*, no. 1, March 1968, pp. 24-29.

——, "Devi Sannmukhi Ya Sasthi", *Bulletin of Museums & Archaeology in U.P.*, no. 3, June 1969, pp. 38-41.

——, *Mathura Sculptures*, Mathura, Archaeological Museum, 1966.

——, *Matrikas: Mothers in Kusana Art*, New Delhi: Kanak Publications, 1986.

——, "Two Mātr̥ka Plaques in the State Museum Lucknow", *Bulletin of Museums & Archaeology in U.P.*, no. 1, March 1968, pp. 18-23.

Kala, S.C., *Teracottas Figurines From Kausambi, Mainly in the Collection of the Municipal Museum Allahabad*, Allahabad: Municipal Museum, 1950.

——, *Terracottas in the Allahabad Museum*, New Delhi: Abhinav Publications, 1980.

Kane, P.V., *History of Dharmasastra*, 5 vols., Poona: Bhandakar Oriental Research Institute, 1962-75.

Kleinberg, S. Jay, ed., *Retrieving Women's History: Changing Perspectives of the Role of Women in Politics and Society*, Berg: Unesco, 1988.

Knox, Robert, *Amaravati: Buddhist Sculpture from the Great Stupa*, London: British Museum, 1992.

Kooij, K.R. van and Veere, H. van der, eds., *Function and Meaning in Buddhist Art*, Groningen: Egbert Forsten, 1995.

Kosambi, D.D., *Myth and Reality: Studies in the*

*Formation of Indian Culture*, Bombay: Popular Prakashan, 1962.

Kramrisch, Stella, "An Image of Aditi-Uttanapad", *Artibus Asiae*, vol. XIX, 1956, pp. 259-70.

——, *Grundzuge Der Indischen Kunst*, Hellarau bei Dresden, Avalun-Verlag, 1924.

——, "Indian Terracottas", *Journal of Indian Society of Oriental Art*, vol. VII, 1939, pp. 89-110.

——, *The Hindu Temple*, 2 vols., Calcutta: University of Calcutta, 1946.

Krishna Murthy, K., "Vestiges of Hariti Worship in Andhra", in Anita Ray and Others (eds.) *Indian Studies: Essays Presented in Memory of Prof. Niharranjan Ray*, Delhi: Caxton Publications, 1984, pp. 57-58.

Lerner, Gerda, *Creation of Patriarchy*, New York: Oxford University Press, 1986.

——, *The Majority Finds Its Past: Placing Women in History*, New York: Oxford University Press, 1979.

Leslie, E. Julia, "Strisvabhava: The Inherent Nature of Women", in N.J. Allen et al. (eds.) *Oxford University Papers on India*, vol. I, part I, Delhi: Oxford University Press, 1986, pp. 28-58.

Ling, T.O., *Buddhism and Mythology of Evil: A Study in Theravada Buddhism*, London: George Allen and Unwin, 1962.

Lüders, H., *Mathura Inscriptions: Unpublished Papers*, K.L. Janert (ed.), Göttingen: Vandenoeck and Ruprecht, 1961.

Lyons, C.L. and Ann Olga Koloski-Ostrow, *Naked Truths about Classical Arts:An Introduction*, http:/www.stoa.org/diotima/essays/naked truths.html.

Macdonell, A.A., *The Vedic Mythology*, Varanasi: Indological Books House, 1963.

——, *Vedic Index of Names and Subjects*, 2 vols., Varanasi: Motilal Banarsidass, 1958.

Majumdar, N.G., *A Guide to the Sculpture in the Indian Museum*, 2 vols., Delhi: Manager of Publications, 1937.

Malandra, Geri Hockfield, "Mara's Army: Text and Image in Early Indian Art", *East and West*, vol. 31, 1981, pp. 121-30.

Marshall, J., *The Monuments of Sanchi*, 3 vols., New Delhi: Archaeology Survey of India (n.d.).

Maxwell, T.S., *Visvarupa*, Delhi: Oxford University Press, 1988.

Meister, Michael W. et al. (eds.), *Encyclopaedia of Indian Temple Architecture: North India, Foundations of North Indian Style*, New Delhi: American Institute of Indian Studies, 1988.

Meyers, D.T., S. Mater, and J. Kristeva (eds.), *Feminist Thought: A Reader*, NY: Routledge, 1997.

Michalowski, Kazimierz, *Art of Ancient Egypt*, New York: Harry N. Abrams (n.d.).

Miller, Barbara Stoler (ed.), *The Powers of Art: Patronage in Indian Culture*, Oxford University Press, Delhi: 1992.

Meyers, D. et al. (eds.), *Feminist Thought: A Reader*, New York: Routledge, 1997.

Mirashi, V.V., *Studies in Indian Indology*, 4 vols., Nagpur: Vidarbha Samshodhan Mandal, 1960-66.

Misra, Ram Nath, *Yaksha Cult and Iconography*, New Delhi: Munshiram Manoharlal, 1981.

Mitra, Rajendralal, *Buddha Gaya: The Hermitage of Sakya Muni*, Calcutta: Bengal Secretariat Press, 1878.

Monier-Williams, M., *A Sanskrit-English Dictionary*, Delhi: Motilal Banarsidass, 2002.

Murcott Susan, *The First Buddhist Women: Translation and Commentary on the Therigatha*, Berkeley: Parallex Press, 1998, pp. 74-91.

*Museum für Indische Kunst, Berlin, Catalogue*, Berlin: Staaliche Museen Preussishcer Kulturebesitz, 1986.

Nagaswamy, R., "From Aditi to Kundalini (From Prehistoric Visirkal to the Historic Sricakra)", in Lokesh Chandra and Jyotindra Jain (eds.) *Dimensions of Indian Art: Pupul Jayakar Seventy*, vol. I, Delhi: Agam Kala Prakashan, pp. 323-33.

Namouchi, Nicole, *Kaufliche Liebe: Prostitution in*

*Alten Indien*, Franfurt Am Main, Peter Lang Verlag, 1995.

Wendy Doniger, *The Origins of Evil in Hindu Mythology*, Delhi: Motilal Banarsidass, 1988.

Pal, Pratapaditya, *Indian Sculpture*, vol. I, Los Angeles: Los Angeles County Museum of Art, 1986.

Panikkar, Shivaji K., *Saptamātṛkā Worship and Sculptures*, New Delhi: D.K. Printworld , 1997.

Panikkar, Shivaji K., Parul Dave Mukherjee and Deeptha Achar, eds., *Towards A New Art History: Studies in Indian Art*, New Delhi: D.K. Printworld, 2003.

Parimoo, Ratan, *Life of Buddha in Indian Sculpture (Aṣṭa-Mahā-Pratihāra)*, New Delhi: D.K. Printworld, 2010.

Paul, Diana, *Women in Buddhism: Images of the Feminine in the Mahayana Tradition*, Berkeley: University of California Press, 1979.

Pisharoti, K. Rama, "Dohada or the Women and Tree Motif", *Journal of the Indian Society of Oriental Art*, vol. III, 1935, pp. 110-24.

Poster, Amy G., *From Indian Earth: 4000 Years of Terracotta Art*, New York: The Brooklyn Museum, 1986.

Premi, Nathuram, *Jaina Sahitya aur Itihasa*, Bombay, 2[nd] edn., 1956, pp. 469 and 473-74.

Punia, D.S., "New Evidence of Pre-Kushana Sculpture from Gurgaon District (Haryana)", *East and West*, New Series, vol. 31, 1981, pp. 133-34.

Quagliotti, Anna Maria, "An Inscribed Image of Hariti in the Chandigarh Museum and Art Gallery", *Silk Road Art and Archeology*, vol. 6, 1999-2000, pp. 51-60.

Ramaswamy, Vijaya, *Walking Naked: Women Society and Spirituality in South India*, Shimla: Indian Institute of Advanced Studies, 1997.

Rao, Manjushree, *Sanchi Sculptures*, New Delhi: Akay Book Corporations, 1994.

Ray, Himanshu Parbha, *Monastery and Guild, Commerce under the Satavahanas*, Delhi: Oxford University Press, 1986.

Ray, Niharranjan, *Maurya and Post-Maurya Art*, New Delhi: ICHR, 1975.

Rhys Davis, T.W. (ed.), *Pali-English Dictionary*, New Delhi: Oriental Books Reprint Corporation, 1975 (repr.).

Roth, Gustav, "The Women and Tree Motif", Journal of the Asiatic Society, *Letters and Science*, vol. XXIII, no. 1, 1957, pp. 91-116.

Rowland, Benjamin, *Art in East and West*, Cambridge: Harvard University Press, 1965.

Roy, Kumkum, "Of Theras and Theris: Visions of Liberation in The Early Buddhist Tradition", in Vijaya Ramaswamy (ed.) *Researching Indian Women*, New Delhi: Manohar, 2003. pp. 75-96.

—, "Representing the Courtesanal Tradition: An Exploration of Early Historical Texts", *Journal of the Asiatic Society of Mumbai*, vol. 77-78, 2002-03, pp. 115-35.

— (ed.), *Women in Early Indian Society*, Delhi: Manohar, 1999.

—, "Women and Men Donors at Sanchi: A Study of the Inscriptional Evidence", in L.K. Bajpai, (ed.) *Position and Status of Women in Ancient India*, vol. I, Varanasi, 1988, pp. 209-23.

Roy, U.N., *Salabhanjika in Art Philosophy and Literature*, Allahabad: Lokbharati Publications, 1979.

Sahai, Bhagwant, *Iconography of Minor Hindu and Buddhist Deities*, New Delhi: Abhinav Publications, 1975.

Sankalia, H.D., "The Nude Goddess or Shameless Women in Western Asia, India and South Eastern Asia", *Artibus Asiae*, vol. XXIII, 1960, pp.11-123.

Shah, U.P. "Harinegamesin", *Journal of the Indian Society of Oriental Art*, vol. XIX, 1952-53, pp. 19-41.

—, "Beginnings of Jaina Iconography", *Bulletin of Museum and Archaeology in Uttar Pradesh*, no. 9. 1972, pp. 1-14.

Sharma, R.C., *Buddhist Art: Mathura School*, Delhi: Wiley Eastern, 1995.

——, *Buddhist Art of Mathura*, Delhi: Agam Kala Prakashan, 1984.

Sharma, R.S., *Indian Feudalism: c. 300-1200*, Calcutta: University of Calcutta, 1965.

——, *Perspectives in Social and Economic History of Early India*, New Delhi: Munshiram Manoharlal, 1983.

Sharma, Y.D., "Past Patterns in Living as Unfolded by Excavations at Rupar", *Lalit Kala*, nos. 1-2, 1955-56, pp. 121-29.

Shukla, S.P., "Some Interesting Kusana Terracottas in The State Museum, Lucknow", *Bulletin of Museums & Archaeology in U. P.*, no. 4, December. 1969, pp. 31-35.

Singh, Upinder, "Sanchi: The History of Patronage of Ancient Buddhist Establishment", *IESHR*, vol. XXXIII, no. 1, 1996, pp. 1-37.

Sivaramamurti, C., "Amaravati Sculptures in the Madras Government Museum", *Bulletin of the Madras Government Museum*, New Series — General Section, vol. IV, Madras Government Press, 1942.

——, *Indian Sculpture*, New Delhi: Allied Publishers, 1961.

——, *Sri Lakshmi in Indian Art and Thought*, New Delhi: Kanak Publications, 1981.

Smith, Vincent A., *The Jain Stupa and Other Antiquities of Mathura*, Allahabad: Government Press, 1901.

Sponberg, Alan, "Attitudes towards Women and the Feminine in Early Buddhism", in Jose I Cabezon (ed.) *Buddhism Sexuality and Gender*, 1985, pp. 3-35.

Stacy, L.R., "Note on the Discovery of Relic of Grecian Sculpture in Upper India", *Journal of the Asiatic Society of Bengal*, vol. 5, 1836, pp. 567-70.

Stadtner, Donald M., "The Little Clay Cart in Early Mathura", *Orientations*, vol. 27, no. 1, 1996.

Sternbach, Ludwig, "First Supplement to Vesya Synonyms and Aphorisms", *Bharatiya Vidya*, 1947.

Stone, Elizabeth Rosen, *The Buddhist Art of Nagarjunakonda*, Delhi: Motilal Banarsidass, 1994.

Sutherland, Gail, *Yaksas: Disguises of the Demon*, New York: SUNY, 1991.

Thakur, Vijay Kumar, *Historiography of Indian Feudalism towards A Model of Early Medieval Indian Economy c. AD 600-1000*, Patna: Janaki Prakashan, 1989.

Thapar, Romila, *Asoka and the Decline of Mauryas*, Delhi: Oxford University Press, 1985.

Tiwari, J.N., *Goddess Cults in Ancient India with Special Reference to the First Seven Centuries AD*, Delhi: Sundeep Prakashan, 1985.

Tripathi, Aruna, *The Buddhist Art of Kausambi: 300 BC to AD 550*, New Delhi: D.K. Printworld, 2003.

Vatsyayana, Kapila, *Classical Indian Dance in Literature and the Arts*, New Delhi: Sangeet Research Academy, 1968.

Varadpande, M.L., *History of Indian Theatre*, New Delhi: Publications Divisions, 1987.

Vogel, J. Ph., *Archaeological Museum at Mathura*, Delhi: Indological Books House, 1971 (repr.).

Waddell, L.A., *Report on the Excavations at Pataliputra (Patna), The Palibothra of the Greeks*, Delhi: Sanskaran Prakashak, 1975.

Wilson, Liz, *Charming Cadavers: Horrific Figurations of the Feminine in Indian Buddhist hagiographic Literature*, Chicago: The University of Chicago Press, 1996.

Zimmer, Heinrich, *The Art of Indian Asia: Its Mythology and Transformations*, 2 vols., New York: Bollingen Foundation, 1960.

——, *Maya Der Indische Mythos*, Zurich: Rascher Verlag, 1952.

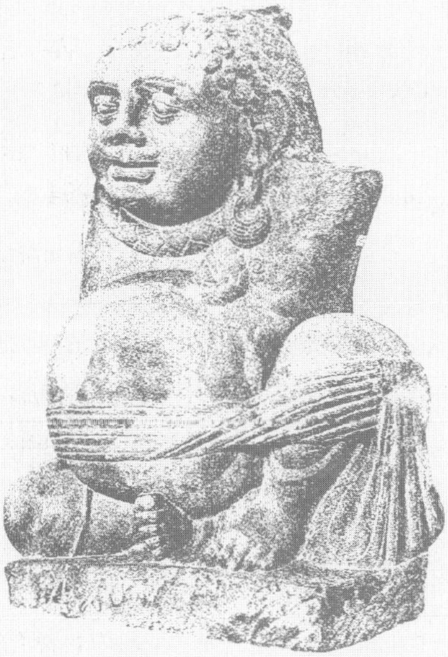

# Index

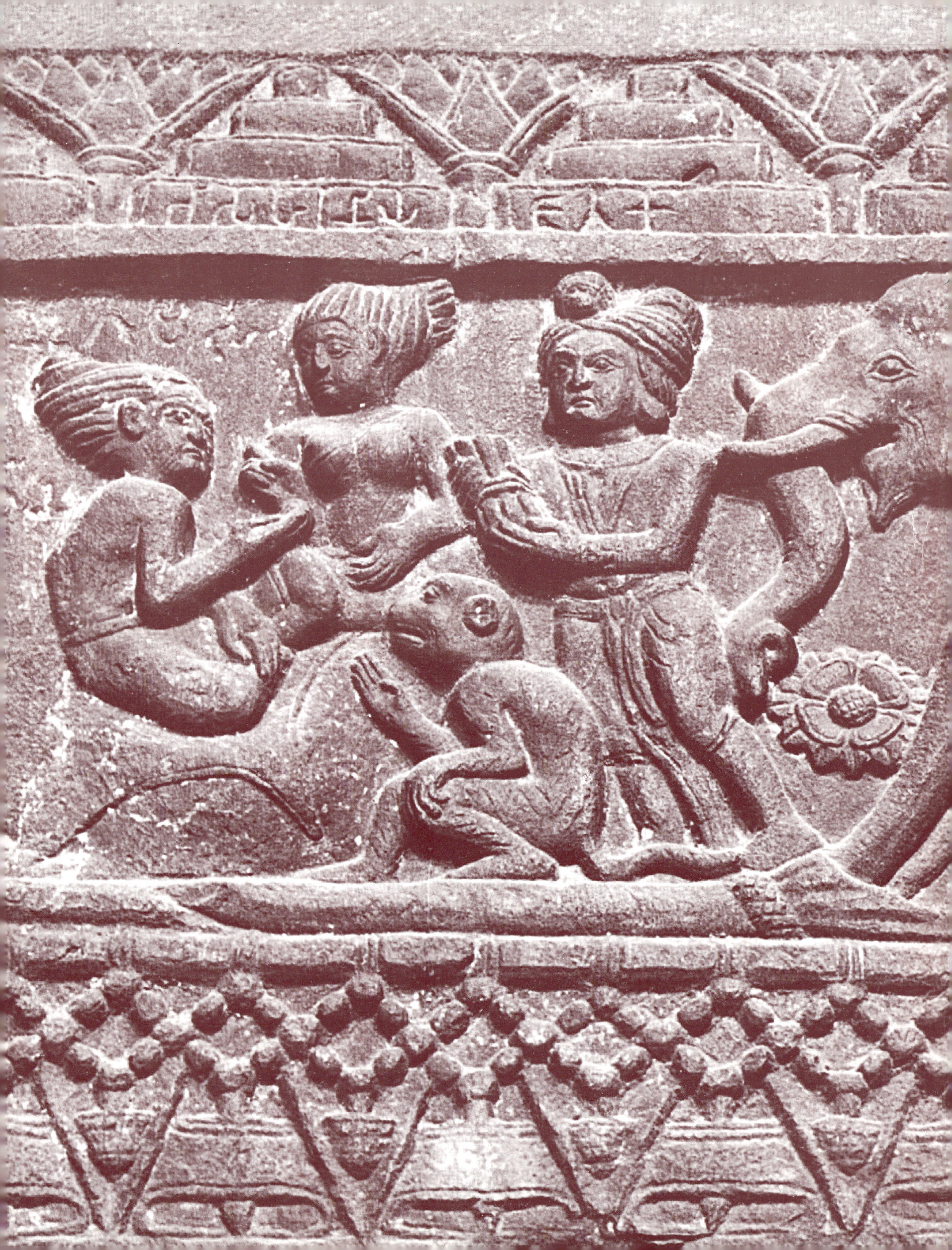